The Contemplative Skeptic:

Spirituality for the
Non-Religious and the Unorthodox

BARRETT A. EVANS

Apocryphile Press
1700 Shattuck Ave #81
Berkeley, CA 94709
www.apocryphilepress.com

Copyright © 2020 by Barrett A. Evans
Printed in the United States of America
ISBN 978-1-949643-49-7 | paperback
ISBN 978-1-949643-50-3 | epub

All rights reserved. No part of this book may be reproduced, stored in a retrieval system, or transmitted in any form or by any means—electronic, mechanical, photocopy, recording, or other-wise—without written permission of the author and publisher, except for brief quotations in printed reviews.

Please join our mailing list at
www.apocryphilepress.com/free
We'll keep you up-to-date on all our new releases,
and we'll also send you a FREE BOOK. Visit us today!

To Katie and Sam

Now abide these three: doubt, humility, and love ...

> What has never been put in question has not been demonstrated. ... Scepticism is thus the first step towards truth. It must be applied generally, for it is the touchstone.
>
> —**Denis Diderot** (1713-1784)[1]

She who knows that she does not know is the best off.
He who pretends to know but doesn't is ill.
Only someone who realizes he is ill can become whole.

> —*Tao Te Ching* (6th c. BCE?)[2]

Love, and do what you will: whether you hold your peace, through love hold your peace; whether you cry out, through love cry out; whether you correct, through love correct; whether you spare, through love do you spare: let the root of love be within, of this root can nothing spring but what is good.

> —**St. Augustine of Hippo** (354-430)[3]

Table of Contents

Introduction 1
A merging of skepticism and the contemplative path

PART I DOGMA DECONSTRUCTION

[1] **It Is Proper to Doubt** 7
Doubt as a form of honesty

[2] **Breaking Hell's Spell** 9
Why threats of hell should not be cause for anxiety

[3] **The Whole Counsel of God** 15
Contradictions in God's character in Scripture

[4] **Old Testaments and Apocryphas** 20
Diversity in "Old Testament" and Hebrew Bible collections

[5] **Did God Really Say?** 26
Diversity in New Testament and Post-New Testament canons

[6] **The Scripture Must Be Broken** 34
Bible versions, variances, and textual problems

[7] **Errors, Probably** 47
Why the Bible probably contains mistakes

[8] **What Does the Scripture Say?** 52
The ambiguous nature of biblical teachings

[9] **Sleeping or on a Journey?** 66
The biblical god's apparent absence

[10] **Ancient Skeptics** 69
Critiques of Christianity from its early centuries

[11]	**Supernatural Scrupulosity** 73
	Dogmatic speculative belief as spiritual malady
[12]	**The Last Days Daze** 77
	A historical survey of the Second Coming
[13]	**Another Wise Lord** 87
	Zoroastrianism and its links to the Abrahamic faiths
[14]	**Unfulfilling Prophecies** 92
	The dubiousness of predictive biblical prophecy
[15]	**Pondering Parallels** 101
	Parallels between Christianity and other Mediterranean religions
[16]	**No Law at All** 105
	The deep flaws of the Old Testament Law
[17]	**Musings on Miracles** 111
	Why the fantastic stories in the Bible are likely ahistorical
[18]	**The Odd God** 117
	Strange and surprising Bible verses
[19]	**An Unknown Sin** 121
	Slavery in Christian history and Scripture
[20]	**All Things Are Permissible** 132
	Torture and persecution in Christian history
[21]	**Resurrection Reflections** 143
	Why a literal Resurrection is improbable
[22]	**The Great Grab Bag (pt.1): Led by the Spirit** 151
	The unreliability of subjective Christian leadings
[23]	**The Great Grab Bag (pt.2): Reasons of the Heart** 165
	Worldwide religious diversity and human error
[24]	**The Great Grab Bag (pt. 3): By the Numbers** 174
	Quantified religious diversity and doubt's universality

Table of Contents

PART II THE CONTEMPLATIVE SKEPTIC'S PATH

[25] The Prayer of St. Spurious 185
The Peace Prayer of St. Francis and the unimportance of origins

[26] Light in the Dark Night 187
Finding solace while leaving dogmatic religion

[27] True Believers Anonymous 190
A 12-step program for faith addicts

[28] Reflections on a Buddhist Atheist 195
Insights from secular Buddhist Stephen Batchelor

[29] Einstein's Creed, Spinoza's God 199
Skeptical and subtle divinity in Einstein and Spinoza

[30] There Is Yet Something in It 204
Leo Tolstoy's mildly supernatural and non-traditional theism

[31] A Euthanasia of Fanaticism 208
Thomas Jefferson and the freedom of religious thought

[32] Crying Out in the Wilderness 212
The Desert Fathers and the good and bad in dogmatic religion

[33] The New Apatheism 217
Giving up strident views on religion or a-religion

[34] Hearsayings of the Prophet 221
Selective value in the hadith of Islam

[35] A Partial Imitation of Christ 224
Insights from Thomas à Kempis

[36] Invincible Ignorance 227
The relative ignorance of everyone

[37] Experiments with Truth 229
A selection of Gandhi's religious reflections

[38] The Noble Fundamentalist 234
Remembering exemplary traditional Christians

[39]	**The Most Excellent Way** 240
	Love and 1 Corinthians 13
[40]	**Inordinate Attachment and the Ordered Life** 242
	The poisonous and practical in St. Ignatius of Loyola
[41]	**A More Balanced Way** 247
	Light from the Tao Te Ching; Darkness in The Divine Panorama
[42]	**Sinners of Light, Saints of Darkness** 251
	Virtues and flaws of Mother Teresa and Christopher Hitchens
[43]	**Praising Jesus, Reforming Christ** 257
	Following a greater Jesus
[44]	**Wonder with Me** 261
	Cultivating wonder through the lorica form
[45]	**The Compass of Compassion** 264
	Gandhi's guiding principle
[46]	**Children of the Moment** 266
	Insights from the Sufis
[47]	**A Litany on Humility** 269
	Adaptation of a Roman Catholic litany
[48]	**Wonders of the Worlds** 271
	Awe of the universe as spiritual discipline
[49]	**Undesirable Desire** 276
	The danger of desire in the Bhagavad-Gita
[50]	**Memento Mori** 278
	Remembrance of death as spiritual discipline
[51]	**The Noble Psycho-Ethical Path** 281
	A (non-supernatural) Buddhist strategy to lessen suffering
[52]	**Wisdom Cries Out** 285
	Biblical proverbs and enlightened self-interest
[53]	**Sayings of the Master** 288
	Counsel from Confucius

Table of Contents ix

[54]	No Body but Yours 291
	The Stations of the Cross re-imagined
[55]	Anima Foci 296
	The importance of focus and a re-working of the Anima Christi
[56]	Taoist Training 298
	Insights from the Seven Taoist Masters
[57]	Make Your Own Meditation 301
	Developing a reflective meditation practice
[58]	A Page from the Love Doctor 304
	Pragmatic advice from St. Francis de Sales
[59]	The Love of the Beautiful 307
	An adaptation from the Eastern Orthodox Philokalia
[60]	A Look on the Bright Side 312
	Focusing on the positive as spiritual discipline
[61]	Living in a Cloud of Unknowing 315
	Accepting a theology of ignorance
[62]	Spiritual Exercises for Contemplative Skeptics 318
	Spiritual disciplines without supernaturalism

An Afterword 322
Doubt, humility, and love

Acknowledgments 324

Endnotes 325

Select Bibliography 513

Introduction

... *A merging of skepticism and the contemplative path*

While studying to be a pastoral counselor in seminary, I came to the realization that the dogmatic underpinnings of my conservative Protestant faith were probably not tenable. After sincerely exploring the early church fathers, Eastern Orthodoxy, Anglicanism, and especially Roman Catholicism, I gave up spirituality for good.

Or so I thought. It turned out that while I benefitted in significant ways from rejecting dogmatic faith, I also suffered from the absence of certain aspects of the spiritual experience—especially a sense of focus and purpose, an encouragement to live for others, and the solace of certain contemplative disciplines. My sense of loss became even more noticeable to me as I furthered my studies on other religions of the world. This process has led me to conclude that a richer life comes from a combination of both a hearty skepticism and what has traditionally been called the spiritual path.

St. Augustine of Hippo (354-430) believed that love should be the central guidance for behavior: "Love, and do what you will."[4] Although I wholeheartedly share this sentiment, I depart from Augustine significantly on the issue of dogma. Too often people have felt constrained by religions—frequently under threat of pain in this life or especially the next—to believe things that are unverifiable and improbable. Perhaps ironically, dogmatic religious claims now seem to me to critically undercut two of the most valuable spiritual ideals for fallible people—humility in the face of complexity and honesty in the light of human limitations. And so, to Augustine's dictum I would add another: Be honest, and believe what you want.

In essence, this book is meant to be a skeptical "devotional" or a compendium of contemplative freethought.[5] For this general idea of a skeptical devotional I am indebted to certain strains of the Christian tradition which, in the words of the editors of one series of religious classics, have held contemplative reading to be "essential to any deliberate spiritual life."[6]

The Contemplative Skeptic is broadly divided in two parts. The first section, entitled "Dogma Deconstruction," is centered around a skeptical analysis of traditional and "fundamentalist" religious beliefs. While attempting to highlight the damaging nature of religious manipulation and indoctrination, I explore such issues as the inherent problems with denigrating doubt, ethical and rational difficulties with the doctrine of hell, ethical shortcomings of both biblical teachings and the beliefs of prominent Christian saints, canonical diversity (i.e., the different collections of holy books among believers), textual difficulties in the Bible, challenges of biblical interpretation, the implausibility of miracle stories, and problems associated with the vast diversity of competing supernatural ideas. Although primarily meant to help underscore the improbable and even harmful nature of certain traditional religious doctrines, I also make efforts in this section to avoid the distorting effects of judgmentalism and hypercriticism—and so also remark at times on the triumphs of the faithful as well as the failures of those with more skeptical inclinations. Dogmatism, credulity, prejudice, and contempt are of course common human pitfalls, and the failures of religious orthodoxies are perhaps best seen as just particular manifestations of the frailties that afflict us all in various ways and in varying degrees.

The second section, entitled "The Contemplative Skeptic's Path," focuses more on the selective appropriation of spirituality. While retaining and even building upon the skeptical base established in Part I, here I attempt to redeem and refine the best insights in some prominent spiritual traditions of the world. Drawing from a variety of religious and skeptical sources, topics for contemplation include the present moment, the passing of time, mortality, compassion, authenticity, nondogmatic thinking, honesty, simplicity, non-attachment, humility, ignorance, contentment, stillness, positive thinking, and wonder. In order to assist with constructing a skeptical spirituality, I suggest psychological-ethical exercises as well as apps, audio downloads, and internet resources. A search for a nexus of ethics, wisdom, and healthy contemplative practice is thus the overall focus of this section. And while personally subscribing to an agnostic approach, I present here a full range of nondogmatic skeptical options from agnostic atheism, to deism, to pantheism, to more subtle and rational forms of theism. This broader presentation of skepticism is meant to not only give the book a wider appeal, but also to encourage freedom of thought and exploration.

While each meditation is meant to stand on its own, I have loosely grouped them in the above two categories to give the book more coherence and structure. While it is of course appropriate to read the book straight through, too much emphasis on the "dogma deconstruction" section could skew a reader's perception of my understanding of the potential value of certain spiritual ideas and practices. Therefore, I would encourage the reading of meditations out-of-order and based on what seems most needful at the moment. Alternating between Parts I and II is also appropriate.

This book is not for everyone. Although I think the world becomes a better place as dogmatism and supernaturalism wane, life is often difficult and traditional religions seem to work for many people. But for those of us who find certain aspects of them to be both untrue and oppressive—agnostics, deists, pantheists, atheists interested in spirituality, and other non-traditional thinkers—I hope this book will be both a boon and a "blessing." Furthermore, while I am doing my best to be both accurate and fair, this is of course just one fallible person's crack at a very complex topic. Reject what you find wrong or unhelpful, retain what appears to be true and beneficial. In the words of Christian Scripture: "test everything; hold fast to what is good" (1 Thess. 5:21).[7]

A note on quotations: Although I very intentionally am trying not to misrepresent anyone's work, it is also true that I often take individual thoughts or "quips" of various saints and religious thinkers out of their theological frameworks. Of course, I make no claims that their systems of thought would support my general approach. Sometimes (especially in the introductory quotations for each meditation), such quotations are placed in an ironic sense to highlight an inconsistency in a dogmatic religious system. Other times, I regard the quotation as a valuable insight in a flawed worldview. Of course, the use of religious concepts to critique religion has a long pedigree:

> Excuse the wrangling sects, which number seventy-two:
> They knock at Fable's portal, for Truth eludes their view.
>
> —**Hafiz of Shiraz** (14th c.), Sufi poet[8]

PART I
Dogma Deconstruction

[1] It Is Proper to Doubt
... *Doubt as a form of honesty*

> Indeed, it is proper to doubt, Kālāmas, and to be perplexed. When there is a doubtful situation, perplexity arises. In such cases, do not accept a thing by recollection, by tradition, by mere report, because it is based on the authority of scriptures, by mere logic or inference, by reflection on conditions, because of reflection on or fondness of a certain theory, because it merely seems suitable, nor thinking: "This religious wanderer is respected by us." But when you know for yourselves: "These things are unwholesome, blameworthy, reproached by the wise, when undertaken and performed lead to harm and suffering"—these things you should reject.
>
> —**The Buddha** (563-483 BCE?)[9]

In this famous passage from the *Discourse to the Kālāmas*, the Buddha makes a simple statement that can seem completely radical for the mind held in dogmatic religious thinking. Namely, that it is proper to doubt the doubtful.[10] In almost any other area of inquiry, this proposition is entirely uncontroversial. In many religious systems, however, doubting the dubious is seen as a grievous moral failure. It is even considered scandalous by many to question whether traditional religious beliefs are true. In the words of Sikh scholar Hew McLeod, "Every religion includes a host of followers for whom the academic analysis of the faith is treated as a heinous crime or something approaching one."[11]

A major part of letting go of the dogmatic life is to release the rather extraordinary notion that having doubts about complex, unverifiable, and speculative metaphysical ideas and fantastic miracle stories is worthy of the worst sorts of condemnation. It would seem that the confidence of any belief, no matter what the area of inquiry, should be commensurate only with its likelihood, the quality of the evidence behind it, and its capacity to bring good to the world. Doubting the dubious may be best understood not as sin but as an ethical act—and an indispensable and foundational step in seeking what is true. As medieval philosopher and theologian Peter Abelard (1079-1142) wrote in his controversial *Sic Et Non*: "Indeed, the first key of wisdom is defined as constant or frequent questioning .... [T]hrough doubting, we arrive at questioning; in questioning we perceive the truth."[12]

In extolling the virtues of doubt, I do not have in mind the harsh, unyielding doubt of the dogmatic or uniformly anti-religious contrarian. Rather, it is the doubt that strives to remain teachable, is deeply interested in new questions and perspectives, and is fully cognizant of the finite and fallible nature of human judgments.[13]

I would further posit that acknowledging reasonable doubts is not only ethically sound, but psychologically healthy as well. Modern cognitive theory in fact views defective thought patterns as a primary cause of mental suffering. As one psychology text explains: "Cognitive therapy perceives psychological problems as stemming from commonplace processes such as faulty thinking, making incorrect inferences on the basis of inadequate or incorrect information, and failing to distinguish between fantasy and reality."[14] Within this framework, doubting unrealistic religious ideas may be seen as a path to better mental health through a more thorough personal honesty.[15]

[2] Breaking Hell's Spell[16]

...Why threats of hell should not be cause for anxiety

> The souls of impious Zoroastrians and of all nonbelievers go to hell.
>
> —*How Different Religions View Death and Afterlife,*
> Zoroastrian perspective[17]

> You should first of all know ... that the diversity of men in religions and creeds, plus the disagreement of the Community of Islam about doctrines, given the multiplicity of sects and the divergency of methods, is a deep sea in which most men founder and from which only a few are saved. Each group believes that it is the one saved, and "each faction is happy about its own beliefs."
>
> —**Al-Ghazali** (c.1058-1111), classic Islamic scholar[18]

Blaise Pascal (1623-1662) is often cited in traditional Christian apologetics for the formulation of his "Wager." In short, the Pascal's Wager insists that a choice must be made about whether God exists: "Let us assess the two cases: if you win you win everything, if you lose you lose nothing. Do not hesitate then; wager that he does exist."[19] A traditional doctrine of hell is inextricably connected with Pascal's logic. While Pascal maintained that there was no negative consequence for believing in a non-existent God, he clearly held that failing to believe in his existent God would bring the worst conceivable consequences of a literal damnation.

In the context of both the Wager section itself and his *Pensées* as a whole, it is clear that Pascal's choice for God's existence was synonymous with the choice for Roman Catholicism. As scholar A. J. Krailsheimer has noted, Pascal's Wager is properly viewed in its setting: "For it must be recognized that Pascal is trying to persuade his interlocutor not merely to believe, but in so doing to become a full member of the Catholic Church, the body of Christ outside of which he saw no salvation."[20] Belief in a divinity alone was clearly not enough for Pascal—Jews, Roman and Egyptian pagans, Calvinists, deists, Arians, Muslims, and other "heretics" are condemned in his thought system.[21]

Consequently, the traditional Protestant apologists who cite the Wager not only fail to recognize that they are on the losing side of Pascal's bet, but also highlight one of the core problems of the Wager itself. Namely, even if one accepts the unprovable idea that there is such a thing as a literal hell (which would seemingly have no evidence outside the speculations and declarations of traditional religious people), there is an exceedingly long and varied list of opinions about what might get one there. To accept the terms of the Wager without recognizing the numerous other alternatives is to engage in the grossest simplification of options. With its lack of logical force, cowing to the threat of the Wager seems nothing more than capitulation to irrational anxieties.

Both cognitive and cognitive-behavioral therapies encourage the challenging of unfounded fears as a key to psychological health. The concept of hell would thus appear to be the most drastic possible form of what Albert Ellis (1913-2007) called "awfulizing"—an excessive fear of an extreme outcome even when evidence would suggest such thinking to be unreasonable.[22] Psychologists of religion have in fact proposed that beliefs in literal hells survive not due to their plausibility, but rather because they act as a powerful negative reinforcement for behavioral control—not to mention a dark source of pleasure for those wishing for the punishment of their enemies.[23]

There is no doubt that the threat of literal damnation presents one of the more difficult emotional challenges for those leaving traditional forms of religion. As Pascal himself noted, "Custom is our nature. Anyone who grows accustomed to faith believes it, and can no longer help fearing hell, and believes nothing else."[24] As it is also clear that anxiety often encourages self-interest, supports irrational thinking, and encourages timidity, fearing a literal hell seems to erode the ground of both compassion and courage. It is no wonder that some liberal theologians have suggested that hell should be viewed only as a psychological state in this life—suggesting that salvation in part means release from the literal concept of hell itself.[25] Supporting this general sentiment, American orator and freethinker Robert Ingersoll (1833-1899) believed that compassion compelled him to save people not from hell, but rather from the belief that it existed:

> Think of the lives it has blighted – of the tears it has caused – of the agony it has produced. Think of the millions who have been driven to insanity by this most terrible of dogmas. ... It is a great pleasure to drive the fiend of fear out of the hearts of men, women and children. It is a positive joy to put out the fires of hell.[26]

For those troubled by the notion of hell, the innumerable different opinions on what causes damnation oddly seem to provide considerable relief. For the myriad condemnations are not only highly speculative, but also often mutually exclusive as well. They also expose the blunt reality that multitudes of people have spent their lives being fearful of being damned for reasons that are entirely unknown, considered to be patently false, or believed to be utterly insignificant to immense swaths of humanity. Ironically perhaps, the concept of hell also seems be the divine enactment of the most vividly and completely opposite impulse to the golden rule—a precept which is commonly held by believers to be the pinnacle of religious ethical teaching. For those not familiar with the immense variety of beliefs on damnation, some examples of the curious, exclusivist, and mutually opposing ideas on the subject should help illustrate the utterly tenuous position of those who claim knowledge about the fate of the undetectable souls of dead people.

There are many unexpected or even quirky threats of damnation in the pages of religious history. In centuries past, some Jews believed that Jesus of Nazareth was a Savior to no one—but was instead spending the afterlife boiling in hot excrement.[27] Italian poet Dante Alighieri (1265-1321) placed a mutilated Prophet Muhammad deep in the eighth circle of hades.[28] Many Taoists and Buddhists, though not believing in an eternal hell, have held that denying the law of karma leads to lengthy stays in hellish realms.[29] Jains have believed that those who kill any living being—even bugs—will be damned for long periods.[30] The 4th-century Catholic bishop Eustathius held that anyone who got married would go to hell.[31] The Emperor Justinian (c.482-565) curiously anathematized any who believed that resurrected bodies would be spherical.[32] Perhaps surprising to Protestant Christians, the Council of Chalcedon in 451 condemned all who denied that Mary was the Mother of God,[33] while the Second Council of Constantinople in 553 cursed all who denied that Mary was a virgin until her death.[34] The 7th-century Pope Honorius was specifically condemned by the Third Council of Constantinople in 681 for believing that Christ only had one will—and interestingly, the prominent Protestant apologist William Lane Craig (b.1949) also would appear doomed by this declaration.[35] St. Jerome (347-419) thought that the rich were bound for the underworld, warning wealthy believers that "hell will welcome you in your golden clothes."[36] The Eastern Orthodox Council of Constantinople oddly declared in 1583 that everyone who used the Gregorian calendar was under the curse of anathema.[37] Some Hindus, who have traditionally believed in non-eternal hells, have claimed that those who do not worship gods like Shiva and the elephant-headed god Ganesha "will certainly go to hell."[38] Zoroastrians, who hold that hell lasts for thousands of years, have believed that those who wash in springs or streams are doomed.[39] Aztecs believed that all were damned except warriors killed in battle, women who die in childbirth, those struck by lightning, and those who are drowned.[40] The Jewish Talmud notes that men who engage in frequent gossip with women will go to hell.[41] While traditional Muslims are often criticized for requiring women to wear the hijab, a 3rd-century Christian work called the Acts of Thomas declared that women who did not cover their heads would be strung up in hell by their hair.[42] Fiery Calvinist Reformer John Knox (1514-1572) claimed that women who rule over men and their supporters were bound for damnation.[43] The monk Nichiren (1222-1282) consigned to hell any Buddhist who relied on the *nembutsu* prayer and believed that salvation was by grace through faith in the Amida Buddha.[44]

While fundamentalist Protestant Christians are well known in the West for believing that they have the only path to heaven, many other groups have held exclusivist views as well. For instance, Zoroastrians have believed that only devout followers of their "Good Religion" would be saved from damnation.[45] Early Mormons espoused their new faith as the only way to heaven.[46] Ancient Palestinian Jews held that only the circumcised of their number would avoid hell.[47] Sunni[48] and Shi'a[49] Muslims often argue that only their particular groups are on the path to Paradise. Defunct since antiquity, the Qumran Jewish sect thought that those outside their group were condemned.[50] Long-extinct Ebionite Christians believed that salvation was only for Christians who obeyed the Mosaic Law.[51] Early Anabaptist Christians, fueled by the intense persecution they often suffered at the hands of Roman Catholics and other Protestants, commonly believed that only their number was destined for heaven.[52] Although there are now no Donatist Christians, the once-thriving North African sect believed that it was the sole ark of salvation.[53] Believing that they are following the teachings of Church Fathers like St. Augustine (354-430) and St. Cyprian (c.250-258),[54] many of the Eastern Orthodox faithful have held that no one is saved outside their ecclesiastical body.[55]

Likewise, there have been many believers of various types who have held mutually exclusive or opposing views of what beliefs bring damnation. For instance, Christians have anathematized each other for believing that the Holy Spirit proceeded from the Father and the Son[56] and for holding that He proceeded from the Father only.[57] Christians holding that Christ had two natures[58] or only one nature have also condemned each other.[59] Both those Christians denying[60] and believing in justification by faith alone have damned each other.[61] In the Arian controversy, those who believed that Jesus was fully God and those who believed that he was divine in a lesser sense issued mutual anathemas.[62] Christians who are not baptized by immersion as adults,[63] those who get baptized again as adults,[64] and unbaptized infants[65] have all been thought to be destined for damnation. While Roman Catholics traditionally considered those choosing cremation instead of burial as dying in mortal sin,[66] Zoroastrians have traditionally condemned all who buried corpses instead of exposing them on a "Tower of Silence" (*dakhma*).[67] Meat-eaters have been dispatched to hell,[68] as have been those who condemn meat-eaters.[69] In Calvinist controversies, those who believed in strict predestination[70] and those who believed in the freedom of the will could be threatened with damnation.[71] Christians have also anathematized those who do not venerate holy images[72] as well as those who do.[73] While many Protestant and Eastern Orthodox Christians have condemned those following the Roman Catholic pope,[74] Roman Catholics once believed that only those subject to the Roman Pontiff could be saved[75] —and that neither the repentant, the extremely pious, nor even martyrs could be saved unless they died in full communion with the Roman Catholic Church.[76]

Finally, there have been many other versions of hell that are either far less severe or have a very different sense of the fate of the "damned." Believers from Greco-Roman and Mesopotamian faiths held that the afterlife was typically a gloomy or shady place of existence.[77] Norse mythology posits a cold and dark underworld for most, ruled over by the goddess Hel.[78] Jehovah's Witnesses, though quite conservative Christians in many respects, understand the Bible to teach that the unbelieving dead simply pass out of existence.[79] Excommunicated Amish Joseph Joder (1797-1887), like other universalist Christians, wrote that traditionalist teachings about an eternal hell were not found in the Bible and were simply a distortion of its teachings.[80] Likewise, church father Origen (c.185-c.254) also entertained the idea of universal salvation, suggesting that perhaps even Satan himself would eventually be saved.[81] Anglican C.S. Lewis (1898-1963) described hell in terms of a bleak and dismal realm instead of a torturous inferno.[82] Modern Eastern Orthodox believer Alexandre Kalomiros has explained that most Christians have gravely misunderstood the afterlife and that hell is simply the pain of receiving God's pure love by those who hate him. He even noted that God "never returns evil for evil, He never takes vengeance. His punishments are loving means of correction …. They never extend to eternity."[83]

The Greek philosopher Socrates (469-399 BCE) provides a wonderful window from which to view the morass of conflicting threats, condemnations, and opinions that have issued from religious leaders, thinkers, sages, and prophets throughout the millennia. Often referred to as the principle of Socratic or "simple" ignorance, Socrates held that he was wiser than others only because of his capacity to admit his own ignorance.[84] While this principle can have broad application, Socrates specifically applied it to human fears about the afterlife:

> Surely this is the objectionable kind of ignorance, to think one knows what one does not know? But in this, gentlemen, here also perhaps I am different from the general run of mankind, and if I should claim to be wiser than someone in something it would be in this, that as I do not know well enough about what happens in the house of Hades, so I do not think I know ….[85]

[3] The Whole Counsel of God
...Contradictions in God's character in Scripture

> It is most difficult to understand the disposition of this Bible God, it is such a confusion of contradictions; of watery instabilities and iron firmnesses; of goody-goody abstract morals made out of words, and concrete hell-born ones made out of acts; of fleeting kindnesses repented of in permanent malignities.
>
> —**Mark Twain** (1835-1910), American novelist and satirist[86]

> If gods do evil then they are not gods.
>
> —**Euripides** (c.480-406 BCE), Greek playwright[87]

While it can be fruitful to investigate more trivial discrepancies in the Bible, it is perhaps more instructive to focus on biblical material that shows the profound contradictions in the character of God. According to the Scriptures themselves, is God a perfectly good and ethical Being? Or do literal[88] and straightforward readings of the texts suggest that He, if real, would have the most profound of moral flaws and failings? Inspired by St. Paul's sermon in Acts then, here is a look at "the whole counsel" of the Bible (cf. Acts 20:27, ASV[89]) on its God's character:

> God says his kingdom belongs to little children (Matt. 19:14), but also orders multitudes of babies to be brutally slain (1 Sam. 15:1-3, Deut. 2:31-34),[90] slaughters children himself (Exod. 11:4-5, 2 Sam. 12:13-14, Hosea 9:12, 16), and inflicts them with diseases and starvation (Deut. 32:24-25, Lam. 2:11-12, Ezek. 5:9-12). He uses bears to maul youths (2

Kings 2:23-24) and ordains miscarriages and the cruel deaths of pregnant women and their fetuses (Hosea 9:9-17, Hosea 13:16).[91]

God says we should not punish the innocent (Deut. 24:16, Ezek. 18:20, James 5:5-6), but also curses all people before they are born because a man ate a piece of fruit (Gen. 3:14-19, Rom. 5:18-19) and punishes children for their parents' misdeeds (Exod. 20:5, Exod. 34:7, Jer. 32:18). God says that peacemakers are his blessed children (Matt. 5:9), but also causes war and violence (Josh. 11:20, Isa. 13:3-5).[92] God further says he will damn those who do not feed the hungry and visit the sick (Matt. 25:41-43), but himself causes famine and brings illness to thousands upon thousands (1 Chron. 21:14, Num. 25:4-9, Num. 16:43-49).[93]

God says he hates human sacrifice (Deut. 12:31, Jer. 7:31), but calls the murder of two people an "atonement" which satisfied his anger (Num. 25:7-13), asks that certain people be "devoted to destruction" for his sake (Lev. 27:28-29, Josh. 6:15-21), and sacrificed himself as a human to somehow appease his own wrath (Rom. 3:24-25, Heb. 10:10). God likewise says do not murder (Exod. 20:13), but also kills innumerable people—often for trivialities or the sins of others (Exod. 11:5, 1 Chron. 13:9-10, 2 Sam. 24:15-17, Rev. 9:15). God's prophet orders the deaths of hundreds of rival seers (1 Kings 18:40),[94] and he himself destroys families (Num. 16:32), wipes out cities (Gen. 19:24-25, Josh. 8:24-27), and even drowns the entire population of the earth (Gen. 7:23). While Satan is described as a "murderer from the beginning" in Scripture (John 8:44), God slaughters millions in the Bible while the devil kills just a handful.[95]

God says that those who get angry will be judged (Matt. 5:21-22), but his own anger burns deeply until it is sated by human blood (Josh. 7:22-26) and he creates many only to be "objects of wrath" (Rom. 9:22). God also says he is patient and slow to anger (Num. 14:18, Ps. 145:8, Exod. 34:6), but also becomes angry quickly, immediately striking people dead (2 Sam. 6:6-7, Acts 5:1-10, Acts 12:21-23).[96] God further says that his anger lasts for a moment and not forever (Ps. 30:5; cf. Mic. 7:18), but also that it is everlasting (Jer. 17:4, Mal. 1:4; cf. Rev. 20:10, Matt. 25:46).

God says we should plainly speak the truth (Matt. 5:37) and not lie (Col. 3:9) and that Satan is the "father of lies" (John 8:44), but he also deceives prophets (Ezek. 14:9), sends lying spirits to ensure disaster (1 Kings 22:22-23), and provides powerful delusions to ensure condemnation (2 Thess. 2:11). God also says that he does not tempt anyone or cause them to do evil (James 1:13-14) and that Satan is a tempter (Matt. 4:3), but he himself sends evil spirits into people to influence and corrupt their behavior (1 Sam. 18:10-11, Judg. 9:23), hardens people's hearts so that they will act without prudence and justice (Josh. 11:20, Exod. 11:9-10), and commands a man to murder his own son (Gen. 22:2; Heb. 11:17-19). God further claims he wants all to be saved (1 Tim. 2:4), but also hardens hearts so that some cannot believe (Rom. 9:18, Mark 4:11-12).

God says that his blessings are for the merciful (Matt. 5:7), that it's a sin to withhold forgiveness (James 2:13), and that we should be merciful like he is (Luke 6:36), but he also refuses to pardon iniquities, sending those who don't forgive others to be tormented in the afterlife (Matt. 6:14-15, Matt. 18:32-35, Luke 12:10).[97] God likewise says that love keeps no record of wrongs (1 Cor. 13:4-5) and that he is love (1 John 4:8), but then keeps track of every careless word uttered (Matt. 12:36-37), keeps records of every deed of humanity for the Last Judgment (Rev. 20:12-15), and visits punishment double (Isa. 40:2, Jer. 16:18, Rev. 18:6) or even sevenfold for sins (Lev. 26:21). With complete foreknowledge of all events, he has set up a system wherein most people end up in hell (Matt. 7:13-14, Acts 4:12, John 3:18).

God says that we should love our enemies (Matt. 5:43-48) and that those who know him cannot hate (1 John 4:8). But he also hates those who honor idols (Ps. 31:6), disobedient Israelites (Lev. 26:23-30, Lev. 27:30), those who despise him (1 Sam. 2:30), the bloodthirsty and deceitful (Ps. 5:6), lovers of violence (Ps. 11:5), those who cause discord in a family (Prov. 6:19), Esau and the Edomite people (Mal. 1:2-4), and the non-elect (Rom. 9:11-18). He threatens pestilence, cannibalism, and brutal foreign armies for his own people, noting that he "will abhor" them if they disobey (Lev. 26:23-30); he further claims he will show many "everlasting contempt" (Dan. 12:2). He also says to bless and not curse (Rom. 12:14, Luke 6:27-28), but himself curses many times—often through his messengers (Gen. 12:3, Deut. 28:15-20, 1 Cor. 16:22, Gal. 1:8).[98]

God says that we should treat others as we wish to be treated (Matt. 7:12) and be kind (1 Cor. 13:4-5), but he also threatens to curse his people, rebuke their children, and even "spread dung" on their faces (Mal. 2: 1-3). He directs thousands of virgins to be given as spoils after battle (Num. 31:17-35; cf. Deut. 21:10-14), kills people with poisonous snakes (Num. 21:6), sets lions upon them (1 Kings 20:35-36, 2 Kings 17:25), slays them with hailstones (Exod. 9:25, Josh. 10:11), and sends plagues of frogs, gnats, flies, boils, and locusts (Exod. 8-9). He likewise infects people with tumors (1 Sam. 5:6), burns people to death (2 Kings 1:10-12, Num. 16:35), is pleased when worshippers of other gods are slain (2 Kings 10:25-30, 2 Chron. 15:13), torments people but won't allow them to die (Rev. 9:5-6), and exterminates people, expressly noting: "I will not pity or spare or have compassion when I destroy them" (Jer. 13:14). In perhaps the most sadistic passage in the Bible, he threatens a horrific litany of curses and torments, including disaster, panic, fiery heat, drought, blight, mildew, boils, ulcers, scurvy, itches, madness, blindness, mental confusion, locusts, worms, hunger, thirst, nakedness, exile, various diseases, fear, anxiety, despondency, and even the reduction to cannibalism of one's own children (Deut. 27-28). Not only does he threaten such things, but he said he would "take delight" in inflicting such "ruin and destruction" (Deut. 28:63).

Reading certain parts of Scripture, we can readily see our own moral shortcomings and failures, knowing we lack the fullness of what St. Paul called the "fruit of the Spirit"—"love, joy, peace, patience, kindness, generosity, faithfulness, gentleness, and self-control" (Gal. 5:19-24). While our own failings are often more than apparent, we also see that God seems many times agonizingly bereft of his own Spirit, being hateful, angry, jealous, murderous, vindictive, cruel, unmerciful, sadistic, and lacking in self-restraint. While God at times appears merciful and caring in the Bible, Scripture also presents him as an Omnipotent Pharisee,[99] laying heavy moral burdens on the shoulders of humanity but being unwilling to behave with the decency that has marked the lives of so many traditional Christians that I have known (cf. Matt. 23:1-4).

If those who say they know God but don't keep his commands are dishonest (1 John 2:4), would not a god who many times grossly violates his own moral laws be either hopelessly inconsistent or himself a fraud? As Mark Twain remarked, "Surely the Source of law cannot violate law and stand unsmirched; surely the judge upon the bench cannot forbid crime and then revel in it himself unreproached."[100] Ironically, a method of discernment provided by Jesus himself appears to show the God of the Christian Scriptures as a false prophet at times, who comes in a guise of goodness but whose deeds often demonstrate that he is unworthy of his worshippers:

> Beware of false prophets, who come to you in sheep's clothing but inwardly are ravenous wolves. You will know them by their fruits. Are grapes gathered from thorns, or figs from thistles? In the same way, every good tree bears good fruit, but the bad tree bears bad fruit. A good tree cannot bear bad fruit, nor can a bad tree bear good fruit. ... Thus you will know them by their fruits (Matt. 7:15-20).

While "God's Word" is often presented as a source of faith, frank observations on its whole counsel can instead cultivate great doubt about both the ethical character and the potential existence of the God it purports to describe. This is in fact the burden of many traditional forms of Christian faith—to extol the necessity of belief in certain things that the Bible itself suggests are not true. In the revealing words of the prominent Protestant Reformer Martin Luther (1483-1546), "If, therefore, I could by any means comprehend how that same God can be merciful and just, who carries the appearance of so much wrath and iniquity, there would be no need of faith."[101]

[4] Old Testaments and Apocryphas
...Diversity in "Old Testament" and Hebrew Bible collections

> But also those books should not be omitted which are agreed to have been written before the advent of the Savior, because even though they are not accepted by the Jews, yet the Church of that same Savior has accepted them.
>
> —**St. Augustine of Hippo** (354-430) on the "Apocrypha"[102]

> There are further distinctions among the Orthodox Churches: the Armenian, Syriac, Coptic, Georgian, Slavonic, and Ethiopian churches all have different canons, and only the Ethiopian Orthodox have canonized other books like 1 Enoch and Jubilees. This lack of agreement among the churches should be borne in mind when one speaks of the Bible as "the" Christian Bible.
>
> —**Timothy Law,** modern historian of Christianity[103]

The Hebrew Bible or "Old Testament" has had a tremendous diversity of content in various times and places. Some dissenting Christians have in fact claimed that there is no "Old Testament" at all: Marcion (c.100-c.160) thought that the books of Judaism were too divergent in doctrine from the message of Jesus of Nazareth and so excluded them entirely.[104] The Paulicians, dating from the 7th or 8th century, also rejected the whole Old Testament, as did medieval Cathar and Bogomil sects.[105] Canonical differences among modern believers range from the five books of the now tiny Samaritan sect[106] to the massive and fluid 50-plus canon of Ethiopia's Beta Israel community.[107] In short, there is a large collection of Jewish religious works that have been considered to be inspired by God by some believers while thought to be apocryphal or dubious by others. One Muslim apologetical website sums up this general problem well: "one man's scripture is another man's apocrypha."[108]

Although not always known by modern Christians, Jewish believers have had numerous disputes and diverging opinions on the canonicity of books. The long-extinct sect known as the Sadducees, who denied the doctrine of the resurrection of the dead (Acts 23:8), rejected Daniel as non-authoritative and may have just held to a five-book canon like the Samaritans. The Song of Songs (Song of Solomon) and Esther were extensively debated among Jews before acceptance, as were Ezekiel, Ecclesiastes, and Proverbs. Sirach (Ecclesiasticus) was also considered for a time before it was excluded by mainstream Judaism—and Sirach itself does not mention Esther, Ruth, or the Song of Songs in its review of the Jewish Scriptures.[109]

In another interesting example of divergent opinion, the Jewish community at Qumran appears to have rejected the book of Esther[110] while accepting Enoch and the Book of Jubilees.[111] While Jews typically have the opposite view on the canonicity of these three books today, Ethiopian Jews in fact *accept* Enoch and Jubilees. It is also worth mentioning that diaspora Judaism for some time was not uniform in its reception and rejection of books; its collections sometimes differed from those of their Palestinian Jewish brethren.[112] As modern critical scholar Bart Ehrman notes, "It is not completely clear which books which later came to be the Old Testament were accepted as Scripture in Jesus' day …. Jews were in the process of formulating their canon at the same time as the Christians."[113]

Supported by sessions of both the Council of Florence (1442) and especially the Council of Trent (1546),[114] Roman Catholics definitively accept certain books that are typically excluded by Protestants and most modern Jews. Commonly referred to as the "Apocrypha" or the "Deuterocanon," these seven books are Tobit, Judith, 1 & 2 Maccabees, Wisdom, Sirach, and Baruch. While the African councils at Hippo (393) and Carthage (397) that helped define the common 27-book New Testament generally affirmed these books as Scripture,[115] there was considerable variation in opinion about them among early Catholics. Origen (c. 185-c.254) apparently utilized all the books of the Roman Catholic Apocrypha as Scripture at points—although his official list as recounted by Eusebius of Caesarea (c.263-c.340) suggests he just accepted the Letter of Jeremiah (Baruch 6).[116] Eusebius himself noted that Wisdom and Sirach were debated and places them among "the disputed Scriptures."[117] Pope St. Gregory the Great's (c.540-604) Bible did not accept the modern Roman Catholic Deuterocanon[118] and St. Jerome (347-419) is well known for questioning these books as well.[119] St. Augustine, highly praised among Protestant Reformers, appears to have held to the modern Roman Catholic canon. While Baruch is less clear, he definitely regarded Tobit, Judith, 1 & 2 Maccabees, Wisdom, and Sirach as Scripture.[120] While discussing the books of the Maccabees, St. Augustine distinctly noted that the Church and the Jews had different conceptions of the confines of the Old Testament:

> These are held as canonical, not by the Jews, but by the Church, on account of the extreme and wonderful sufferings of certain martyrs, who, before Christ had come in the flesh, contended for the law of God even unto death, and endured most grievous and horrible evils.[121]

Showing further diversity, Catholic bishop Theodore of Mopsuestia (350-428) rejected not only the Roman Catholic Deuterocanon but also Job, the Song of Songs, Ezra, and Nehemiah.[122] In his Easter letter of 367, Athanasius included Baruch in his Bible but relegates Esther to a list of profitable but non-canonical books.[123] Melito of Sardis (2nd c.) excluded Esther as well.[124] The *Apostolic Canons* included not only 1 & 2 Maccabees but 3 Maccabees too.[125] The Code of the Canons of the African Church (419) included Tobit, Judith, 1 & 2 Maccabees, Wisdom, and Sirach.[126] The 2nd c. (?) Muratorian Canon, though otherwise a New Testament list, affirmed the book of Wisdom.[127] A late 13th-century canon defined by the Nestorian Metropolitan Mar Abd Yeshua contains not only Wisdom, Sirach, Baruch, Tobit, and "the Maccabees," but also includes the Traditions of the Elders, a book by the Jewish historian Josephus, the Narrative of the Sons of Solomona, a book allegedly written by King Herod, an account of Jerusalem's destruction attributed to Titus, and "the book of Asenath the wife of Joseph the son of Jacob the righteous."[128] Martin Luther also apparently had some misgivings about the book of Esther, once noting: "I am so great an enemy to the second book of the Maccabees, and to Esther, that I wish they had not come to us at all, for they have too many heathen unnaturalities."[129] As another interesting exception to general Protestant sensibilities, early Anabaptists exhibited some disagreement about the authority of the Roman Catholic Apocrypha—some scholars have concluded that most regarded the books as Scripture.[130] The most common Apocrypha prooftext for Anabaptists was apparently Sirach 15:14-17—which was used to defend the doctrine of free will.[131] Of further note, Protestant Reformer Andreas Karlstadt (1480?-1541) wanted to keep the Roman Catholic Apocrypha as Scripture but give the books a lower degree of authority.[132]

As mentioned, the five-book canon of the Samaritans is the smallest collection of Old Testament books among modern believers and includes only Genesis, Exodus, Leviticus, and Deuteronomy. Mainstream Judaism has traditionally named 24 books in its canon while also insisting that the "Oral Law" of the Talmud was a necessary part of God's revelation as well.[133] Karaite Jews, however, rejected the Talmud and relied on the 24 books alone.[134] Modern scholar Timothy Lim notes that the standard Protestant Bible has 39 Old Testament books (the re-ordered 24 Jewish books), the Roman Catholic Bible has 46 plus three additions, and the Eastern Orthodox Bible has 49 books plus 11 additions.[135] Furthermore, the Eastern Orthodox canon has some fluidity that the Roman Catholic canon now lacks. For instance, the Slavonic Orthodox include 2 Esdras while the Greek Orthodox do not.[136] And while 3 Maccabees is a standard book in Eastern Orthodoxy, some have even considered 4 Maccabees to be potentially canonical as well.[137] Further showing the difficulty in speaking in absolute terms, St. Philaret of Moscow (1782-1867), in opposition to the majority of his Eastern Orthodox brethren, deemed his Church's Deuterocanon to be useful for catechumens but nonetheless noncanonical.[138] As Metropolitan Timothy "Kallistos" Ware also illustrates, the Eastern Orthodox Church, despite its precise clarity on many doctrinal matters, still has some residual divergence of opinion about the exact status of its deuterocanonical books:

> The Septuagint [Greek Old Testament] contains in addition ten further books, not present in the Hebrew, which are known to the Orthodox Church as the "Deutero-Canonical Books." These were declared by the Councils of Jassy (1642) and Jerusalem (1672) to be "genuine parts of Scripture"; most Orthodox scholars at the pres-

ent day ... consider that the Deuterocanonical Books, although part of the Bible, stand on a lower footing that the rest of the Old Testament.[139]

Other communions add still further diversity—and sometimes lack precision in their lists as well. As explained by *The Catholic Encyclopedia*, "The Monophysites, Nestorians, Jacobites, Armenians, and Copts, while concerning themselves little with the Canon, admit the complete catalogue [of the Roman Catholic Deuterocanon] and several apocrypha besides."[140] For example, modern Armenian (Oriental Orthodox) priest Vazken Movsesian accepts the Roman Catholic Deuterocanon, 1 & 2 Esdras, and 3 Maccabees—but also notes that all these books are "considered by some as apocryphal."[141] The Ethiopian Orthodox Church, also part of the Oriental Orthodox or "Monophysite" communion, traditionally claims 46 Old Testament books—although this enumeration could be larger as it combines some books that are often separated in other canons (e.g., 1 & 2 Samuel, 1 & 2 Kings, and Ezra & Nehemiah).[142] Furthermore, the Ethiopian Orthodox accept books not found in other Christian communions—like Tegsats (Reproof), Josephas the Son of Bengorion, and 1, 2 & 3 Meqabyan (i.e., "Ethiopian Maccabees").[143] Ethiopia's Jewish community Beta Israel has the large Old Testament of the Ethiopian Orthodox Church plus multiple additional books that are regarded as sacred and often used in liturgical rites and rituals—these include the Commandments of the Sabbath, the Book of Abba Elijah, the Book of Angels, the Apocalypse of Gorgorios, the Testament of Abraham, the Death of Moses, the Apocalypse of Ezra, the Book of Disciples, and other works.[144] Lastly, the aforementioned book of 2 Esdras, usually rejected by Christian communions but accepted by the Slavonic Orthodox and Ethiopian Orthodox, references a total of 94 books. The language is perhaps symbolic—and describes how 24 of these books were for all to read while 74 were meant for only "the wise among your people" (2 Esdras 14:45-46).[145] Unlike many biblical books, 2 Esdras interestingly seems to directly claim to be canonical: "This is the word of the Lord; receive it and do not disbelieve what the Lord says" (2 Esdras 16:36).

Although many traditional Protestants will argue that the Old Testament canon was decided by the "Old Testament Church," this argument is encumbered by the disagreements within Judaism which survived after the advent of the Christian era—and which continue even to this day in pockets as shown by the Samaritan and Beta Israel communities.[146] Traditional Protestants who rely on the "council" at Jamnia (or Javneh, c. 75-117 CE) to support their position also have the awkward position of relying on the spiritual authority of Jewish believers who rejected Jesus as the "Word of God" in the flesh[147] —while at the same time discarding the opinion of St. Augustine, who has commonly been regarded as one of the most astute and Spirit-filled leaders in early Christianity. Furthermore, there are Old Testament books that the Jesus of the four Gospels did not reference—and a smaller group of Old Testament books that is not cited in the New Testament at all. Interestingly, these unmentioned books include some that were heavily disputed in Judaism—like Ecclesiastes, Esther, and the Song of Songs. Roman Catholics claim that certain books of their Deuterocanon are referred to in the New Testament—and 2 Maccabees 7 may well be cited in Hebrews 11:35-27. Furthermore, Wisdom 2:12-20 bears a striking resemblance to a passage in the gospels; many Christians have considered it a "direct prophecy" (cf. Mt 27:39-44).[148] The book of Enoch, which as mentioned is canonical in the Ethiopian Orthodox Church and was most likely in the Qumran community as well, is referenced in Jude 14-15 as containing a valid prophecy.

The words of one liberal Bible scholar, while applicable to many areas of religious controversy, seem to apply well to this issue of which believers should be trusted to have identified the correct Jewish or Old Testament canonical books:

> There is no prophetic solution for this prophetic quandary: to whom can one appeal—for who is higher than God? — to adjudicate between His own conflicting spokesmen?[149]

[5] Did God Really Say?
...Diversity in New Testament and Post-New Testament canons

> Among the disputed books, although they are known and approved by many, is reputed, that called the Epistle of James and Jude. Also the Second Epistle of Peter and those called Second and Third of John .... Moreover, as I said before, if it should appear right, the Revelation of John .... There are also some who number among [the spurious books] the gospel according to the Hebrews, with which those of the Hebrews who have received Christ are particularly delighted.
>
> —**Eusebius of Caesarea** (c.263-c.340), early Catholic historian[150]

> The apocryphal Gospels certainly deserve to be apocryphal; but one may suspect that a little more critical discrimination would have enlarged the Apocrypha not inconsiderably.
>
> —**Thomas Huxley** (1825-1895), British agnostic[151]

Protestant Reformer John Calvin (1509-1564) once remarked that determining the correct books of the Bible was straightforward since "Scripture bears upon the face of it as clear evidence of its truth, as white and black things do of their colour, sweet and bitter do of their taste."[152] While such claims to personal infallibility with canonical selection (implicit or otherwise) are fairly common in traditional Protestant circles, historic disputes about the contents of the New Testament affirm that Christians have often found the proper contents of Scripture to be anything but obvious.

There were a great number of different Gospels and other scriptures that were written and read by early Christians. As many scholars have noted, Gnostic[153] and Jewish Christian groups were prominent in the early centuries of the common era. These groups regarded themselves as orthodox and as the true carriers of writings with God's message. Early Gnostics, who claimed the direct inspiration of the Holy Spirit,[154] wrote gospels and scriptures which included the Gospel of Thomas, the Gospel of Mary, the Gospel of Truth,[155] the Gospel of Philip, the Wisdom of Jesus Christ, the Book of Thomas the Contender, the Apocalypse of Peter, Dialogue of the Savior, and the Secret Book of John.[156] Some Jewish-Christian groups used the Gospel According to the Ebionites or Gospel of the Nazareans.[157] Church historian Eusebius of Caesarea noted that some Jewish followers of Jesus, in addition to excluding all St. Paul's letters, also rejected all gospels except the Gospel of the Hebrews.[158] Some Jewish and Gnostic Christians used the gospels of Matthew, Mark, Luke, and John but interpreted them quite differently. The followers of Marcion (c.100-c.160), who had an 11-book canon, used only what is usually thought to be a redacted version of Luke's Gospel.[159]

However, it was not just among non-catholic or "heretical" Christians where textual diversity existed.[160] While it would seem that Matthew, Mark, Luke, and John are the earliest surviving gospels,[161] it is unclear how many other such early gospels have been lost to history. The Gospel of Luke itself attests to this textual variety, noting that "many" authors had already "set down an orderly account" about Jesus of Nazareth by the time Luke was penned (Luke 1:1-4). One New Testament scholar appears to correctly identify the implications here:

> Looking back at the vantage point of two thousand years of history, it is ironic that the only Gospel preface that gives any information at all about matters of composition and authorial intention begins by revealing the potentially ominous existence of "many" other narratives already in circulation.[162]

There was also for a time a significant amount of regional differences in early catholic[163] circles regarding gospel texts in general—and often churches would recognize and use just one of the eventual four standard canonical texts. As New Testament scholar and moderate believer Bruce Metzger (1914-2007) explained:

> There is reason to believe that only one Gospel was in use in some churches long before the canon was finally settled. It appears that only the Gospel according to Matthew was at all widely read in Palestine, that there were churches in Asia Minor which used only the Gospel according to John at the outset, and so with Mark and Luke in their special areas.[164]

Perhaps the most prominent of these differences concerns the Gospel of John, which was rejected by some both in Rome and the so-called "Alogoi" in Asia Minor.[165] The Alogoi, though largely orthodox according to early Catholic Epiphanius (c.315-403),[166] contended that the Gospel of John had false theological beliefs and confused the order of events—and therefore could not be Scripture.[167]

Some of the eventually excluded writings that enjoyed the most Catholic approval were the Shepherd of Hermas, 1 & 2 Clement, Tatian's Diatessaron (a Gospel harmony), the Didache, the Epistle of Barnabas, the Epistle to the Laodiceans, the Apocalypse of Peter, and 3 Corinthians.[168] The Muratorian Canon, possibly a 2nd-century document, has a 23-book New Testament which included the Apocalypse of Peter and makes no mention of Hebrews, James, 1 & 2 Peter, and 3 John. Such luminaries as Clement of Alexandria and Origen regarded the Didache as Scripture. Irenaeus, Tertullian, Clement of Alexandria, Origen, and others regarded the Shepherd of Hermas as Scripture.[169] Books that were disputed but eventually accepted by Catholics included 1 John and 1 Peter—but most especially 2 Peter, 2 John, 3 John, Jude, Revelation, Hebrews, James, and Philemon.[170] While an interesting (but unfortunately spurious) letter from Jesus of Nazareth to King Abgar of Edessa was thought to be authentic by some for a time,[171] the historical Jesus apparently chose not to write anything down for posterity nor pick an authorized biographer or theologian before his death. Such confusion, it would seem, was inevitable.

Although it is clear that there was a growing sense of the bounds of the New Testament canon in the early Catholic Church, it is also important to realize that disagreement among early Catholics was not confined to obscure individuals, fringe theologians, or believers before the famous Council of Nicaea in 325. St. Cyril of Jerusalem (c.313-386) excluded Revelation from his Bible[172] as did both St. Gregory of Nazianzus (c.330-c.390)[173] and St. Amphilochius (c.340-c.395)—who even noted that "by far the majority say it is spurious."[174] The *Apostolic Canons* (late 4th c.) also omitted Revelation, but included 1 & 2 Clement.[175] As with many Christians in Syria, it appears that St. John Chrysostom (c.347-407) excluded 2 Peter, 2 & 3 John, Jude, and Revelation from the Bible, never citing them in any of his many works.[176] It was in fact not until 367—over 250 years after the last New Testament writing was likely penned—that the staunchly pro-Nicaean bishop Athanasius became the first individual to actually list the New Testament writings in their precise and eventual 27-book Catholic form. After his pronouncement, a synod at Rome in 382 with Pope Damasus and St. Jerome gave their support for Athanasius' New Testament list. Soon afterwards, a council at Hippo with St. Augustine (393) and then a council at Carthage (397) further added to a gathering consensus.[177]

While for some these councils were thought to be authoritative, closer inspection reveals that disagreements among believers about the proper contents of the New Testament have continued since the fourth century and persist even to the present day. The traditional 5th-century Syriac Bible known as the Peshitta, still used by the Assyrian Church of the East or "Nestorian" Church, has a 22-book New Testament that excludes 2 Peter, 2 & 3 John, Jude, and Revelation.[178] Bishop Theodore of Mopsuestia (350-428) rejected 2 Peter, 2 & 3 John, Jude, and Revelation, as apparently did bishop Theodoret (c.393-c.466), who never referenced these works in his many writings.[179] A movement arose in France during St. Augustine of Hippo's lifetime that sought to canonize his writings; it apparently lasted for almost 100 years.[180] The Paulicians, a dissenting group dating from the 7th or 8th century, rejected Peter's epistles and seem to have most valued Paul's letters and the Gospel of Luke.[181] Prominent Orthodox Syrian theologian St. John of Damascus (d. 749) accepted 1 & 2 Clement.[182] The Georgian (Eastern) Orthodox apparently did not even have a translation of Revelation until the 10th century—according to one scholar, the book is still not officially part of their New Testament.[183] The Armenian (Oriental) Orthodox Church apparently did not accept the book of Revelation until the late 12th century;[184] furthermore, the Armenian monk Mechitar of Airivank (c.1290) expressed a desire to include the Advice of the Mother of God to the Apostles, the Books of Criapos, and the aforementioned Epistle of Barnabas in the Bible.[185] A late 13th-century canonical list compiled by Assyrian Church of the East Metropolitan Mar Abd Yeshua contains the 22-book Peshitta New Testament but adds the Diatessaron.[186] In the upheavals of the Protestant Reformation, Roman Catholic scholar Erasmus (1466?-1536) doubted the authenticity of James, 2 Peter, 2 & 3 John, and Jude.[187] Although it is not entirely clear based on my research, *The Catholic Encyclopedia* notes that in the early 20th century the Armenian Orthodox Church still accepted 3 Corinthians—and that the Coptic Church still retained 1 & 2 Clement.[188] The modern Ethiopian Orthodox Church's 35-book broader New Testament includes the Didascalia, the book of Clement (a different work than either 1 or 2 Clement), the Book of the Covenant, and other works.[189]

Some Protestants have also voiced doubts about the confines of the New Testament. Martin Luther himself is well known for considering the exclusion of Revelation, James, Jude, and Hebrews—and some in the later Lutheran tradition actually did so.[190] Interestingly, Reformer Andreas Karlstadt (1480?-1541) advocated a three-fold division of Scripture based on differing degrees of authority—the Roman Catholic Apocrypha, Hebrews, James, 2 & 3 John, Jude, and Revelation all merited the lowest rung.[191] The lines of the New Testament are further obscured by modern moderate or liberal Protestant scholars who have denied the authenticity of traditionally canonical books or have fundamentally reinterpreted how the concept of canon should be understood. Renewing the doubts of many earlier Christians, 2 Peter is perhaps the most widely disputed book among modern Christian scholars.[192] Other New Testament books commonly considered to be spurious include 1 Timothy, 2 Timothy, Titus, 2 Thessalonians, Colossians, Ephesians, 1 Peter, and Jude.[193] Of course, there has also been much discussion about the reliability of the traditional four Gospels—owing to both their anonymous nature and their apparently diverging accounts. Additionally, some modern believers have also given the Gospel of Thomas a quasi-canonical status.[194] Some followers of Martin Luther King, Jr. (1929-1968) even advocated for adding his "Letter from a Birmingham Jail" to the New Testament![195]

Widening the net a bit more, there is an array of writings that believers of varying stripes have claimed to be inspired by God (while not always necessarily "canonical") and congruent with the message of Jesus. Eastern Orthodox believers hold that the doctrinal definitions of Seven Ecumenical Councils (325-787) infallibly present Christ's teachings.[196] According to Roman Catholic piety, St. Catherine of Siena's 14th-century mystical work the *Dialogue of St. Catherine* was "dictated under the inspiration of the Holy Ghost."[197] Likewise, Julian of Norwich (1342-1416) is credited by many in the Roman Catholic Church as having received revelations from God.[198] Anabaptist radical David Joris (c.1501-1556) claimed that the Scriptures were insufficient and would need to be supplemented by his own writings.[199] Spiritualist Jakob Boehme (1575-1624) claimed that his book *Brilliant Dawn* was given to him by God "word for word."[200] The Swedenborgian Church, based on the "New Revelation" of Emmanuel Swedenborg (1688-1772), holds that Swedenborg's writings are divinely authoritative, find their source "in the Lord alone,"[201] and are the predicted Second Coming of Christ.[202] Roman Catholic popes are said to have made infallible *ex cathedra* pronouncements regarding the Marian doctrines of the Immaculate Conception (1854) and the Assumption (1950). The Mariavite Old Catholic Church, a splinter group from the Roman Catholic Church, holds that Mother Maria Franciszka received a direct revelation from God—although in 1906 Pope Pius X claimed her revelations were in fact "delusions."[203] While there have apparently been over 2,000 documented sightings of St. Mary since 40 CE,[204] many Roman Catholics specifically believe that the Virgin appeared near Mexico City (1531), Lourdes (1858), Fatima (1917), and Medjugorje (1981) to bring special messages from God.

There are other groups which claim to be followers of Jesus—and which have additional Scriptures. The Book of Mormon, whose supernatural origins were allegedly attested to by numerous witnesses,[205] is held by the Church of Jesus Christ of Latter-Day Saints to be "a volume of holy scripture comparable to the Bible" that was "written by many ancient prophets by the spirit of prophecy and revelation."[206] As one historian notes, early Mormons believed that "their new religion was to Christianity what Christianity was to Judaism: its culmination."[207] This "culmination" produced yet more Scriptures—and along with the Book of Mormon, The Doctrine and Covenants and The Pearl of Great Price became part of the Mormon canon.[208] Mormon denominations are not in total agreement on their Scriptures, however—the Church of Christ (Temple Lot), for example, uses The Book of Commandments instead of The Doctrine and Covenants. Relatedly, this smaller Mormon sect has never held to such controversial beliefs as polygamy, baptism for the dead, celestial marriage, and the existence of many gods.[209]

The prophet Mani (216-c.276), founder of the Manichaean religion, declared himself to be the completion of the work of the Buddha, Zoroaster, and Jesus of Nazareth—even claiming that he was the "Apostle of Jesus Christ" as well as the "Paraclete" that Christ had promised. According to one historian, Mani claimed to have received supernatural revelations and believed himself to be "the last of the prophets of God, bearing the whole and final truth, of which previous religions had been but partial manifestations."[210] In addition to Mani's letters and other writings such as the Shabuhrgan, the Living Gospel, the Treasure of Life, the Epistle of the Foundation, the Book of Mysteries, and the Book of the Giants, the Manichaeans accepted the aforementioned Gospel of Thomas and the Shepherd of Hermas—but excluded the Acts of the Apostles.[211]

Muslims, who regard Jesus as a prophet and believe themselves to be the authentic carriers of his teachings, generally hold that the Qur'an is the infallible word of God and is the extension of both Torah and Gospel (Sura 3:3-4). The Qur'an itself states, "This Book is beyond doubt revealed by the Lord of the Creation" (Sura 32:2).[212] Although rejected by some Muslims, collected traditions about Muhammad and his early followers, commonly referred to as hadith, are also standardly held to be a divinely-ordained part of the Islamic canon.[213] The Hindu *Bhagavad-Gita* holds that all worship to other gods goes to Krishna; in fact, some Hindu devotional practices are focused on Jesus.[214] Baha'i believers, who accept Jesus as one of God's "Manifestations" or prophets, hold that the more than one hundred volumes written by Baha'u'llah (1817-1892) are divine in origin and validated by the prophecies of all the world's major religions—including Judaism, Christianity, and Islam.[215] As Baha'u'llah himself remarked in one of his own works, "This is the luminous Tablet, whose verses have streamed from the moving Pen of Him Who is the Lord of all worlds."[216]

While Christians of various types (with differing beliefs and canonical lists) have generally rejected these claimed revelations of purported Christ-followers as false and discordant with the will of God, it must be remembered that Jews rejected the various Christian Scriptures as false and unorthodox as well. In other words, traditional Jews would lump

Muslim, Mormon, Manichaean, and Baha'i Scriptures in the same general category as both "orthodox" and "heretical" Christian ones.

Ultimately, the "clear evidence" of what constitutes a divinely inspired writing thus seems to be dependent on subjective individual perceptions about the intentions of God,[217] and is thus a far more precarious endeavor than the "white and black" issue that John Calvin claimed it to be. While uncertainty would appear especially unavoidable if one adheres to Calvinistic notions of total depravity and the damaging effects of sin on human judgment,[218] the selection and rejection of scriptural books requires even believers to repeatedly answer in the negative that ancient question of the serpent— "Did God really say?" (Gen. 3:1, NIV).

[6] The Scripture Must Be Broken[219]
...Bible versions, variances, and textual problems

> Orthodox believe that the changes in the Septuagint [a Greek translation of the Hebrew Bible] were made under the inspiration of the Holy Spirit, and are to be accepted as part of God's continuing revelation.
>
> —**Timothy "Kallistos" Ware** (b.1934), Eastern Orthodox historian[220]

> Although in very many cases the textual critic is able to ascertain without residual doubt which reading must have been original, there are not a few other cases where he can come only to a tentative decision based on an equivocal balancing of probabilities. ... In textual criticism, as in other areas of historical research, one must seek not only to learn what can be known, but also to become aware of what, because of conflicting witnesses, cannot be known.
>
> — **Bruce Metzger** (1914-2007), New Testament scholar and moderate believer[221]

Although there are some holdouts from different traditions, it is acknowledged by most believers that the modern texts and translations of the Bible are based on flawed manuscripts. There is a significant degree of differing opinions about how significant these flaws are—nonetheless, it seems indisputable that different editions of the Christian Scriptures have had variants and errors.[222] The history of textual transmission further shows that different readings or even different stages of textual development have been considered canonical by different churches and communions.[223] It is clear that, even with the supposed guidance of the Holy Spirit, multitudes of sincere and "orthodox" believers over the course of many centuries have been reading—and continue to read—interpolations and variants unawares.

Different modern translators not only disagree on the best way to render the text in modern languages, but also on what variants should be translated or otherwise marked in the text. Sometimes translations will make a textual note about a problem in the text while others will not. Some versions of the Bible regard passages as canonical where others not only remove the text in question—but fail even to mention that there is a dispute. While there are surely at times better and worse reasons for choosing different variants, the vagaries of textual evidence (as best seen in the chance finding of the Qumran scrolls) and the limits of human knowledge and judgment will always render the process imperfect. Fair-minded and well-trained experts sometimes disagree.[224] While the sophistication of textual criticism has developed considerably in modern times, these general issues have been known about for centuries. For example, despite all his confidence in canonical and doctrinal matters, Protestant Reformer John Calvin (1509-1564) confessed some confusion about whether the story of the woman caught in adultery in John 7:53-8:11 was scriptural:

> It is plain enough that this passage was unknown anciently to the Greek Churches; and some conjecture that it has been brought from some other place and inserted here. But as it has always been received by the Latin Churches, and is found in many old Greek manuscripts, and contains nothing unworthy of an Apostolic Spirit, there is no reason why we should refuse to apply it to our advantage.[225]

Believers in different cultures and ages have often become attached to different translations and editions of the Scriptures. For instance, some Lutherans have argued that the vowel points inserted into the Hebrew biblical text by medieval Jewish scholars were inspired;[226] conversely, medieval Kabbalist Bahya ben Asher felt that the Hebrew text was intentionally crafted without vowels so that it could be understood in "countless, wondrous ways."[227] Another interesting example is the Peshitta Bible, an Aramaic version deemed authoritative in the Assyrian Church of the East

(Nestorians) and the Syrian Orthodox Church. Although not validated by modern scholarship, Syrian Christians have traditionally argued that Aramaic was the original language of the New Testament. (Interestingly, the Peshitta lacks the aforementioned story of the woman caught in adultery in John 7:53-8:11.) As one Nestorian Patriarch shows, the loyalty to the Peshitta among Syrian Christians can be quite strong:

> With reference to … the originality of the Peshitta text, as the Patriarch and Head of the Holy Apostolic and Catholic Church of the East, we wish to state, that the Church of the East received the scriptures from the hands of the blessed Apostles themselves in the Aramaic original, the language spoken by our Lord Jesus Christ Himself, and that the Peshitta is the text of the Church of the East which has come down from the Biblical times without any change or revision.[228]

St. Augustine (354-430) encouraged knowledge of Greek and Hebrew in case the "endless diversity of the Latin translators" brought the meaning of passages into doubt.[229] Even still, many Catholic believers were deeply suspicious of St. Jerome (347-419) when he made his Vulgate translation due to changes in customary Latin readings.[230] By the time of the Protestant Reformation, these reservations had disappeared and Roman Catholic theologians argued that the Vulgate itself was unquestionably authoritative.[231] Although scholarship at the time showed that some readings in the Vulgate were very likely unoriginal, the Vatican I Council still proclaimed definitively in 1870:

> The complete books of the old and the new Testament with all their parts, as they are listed in the decree of the said council and as they are found in the old Latin Vulgate edition, are to be received as sacred and canonical.[232]

Famously in the English-speaking world, adherents to the King James Version (KJV) have mightily resisted findings that certain of its readings were very probably not original. An elaborate theological response was developed in some circles where the King James translation is actually deemed to be inspired itself. Sometimes proponents of this view suggest that salvific issues are at stake:

> Then those that are not in the KJV don't have every word of God, and so how can they live? In order to get to be saved we must follow Christ. ... So, if a person uses the false "versions" they don't have Jesus' Word. If they don't have his Word, they can't continue in his Word. Therefore, they are not his disciples, and don't know the truth, nor are they set free.[233]

It is often forgotten that the Greek Septuagint was the favored text of the Old Testament among many in the early Catholic Church. St. Augustine (354-430), like the Eastern Orthodox Church today, held that the Septuagint translation itself was divinely inspired:

> For the Septuagint translators are justly believed to have received the Spirit of prophecy; so that, if they made any alterations under His authority, and did not adhere to a strict translation, we could not doubt that this was divinely dictated.[234]

The authors of the various books of the Greek New Testament many times quote from the Septuagint instead of the Masoretic Hebrew text.[235] Furthermore, in some cases it appears that the Septuagint has a more original version of the text—and it is actually the Masoretic text that has suffered more corruption with the advance of time.[236] Some Old Testament books—like Esther and Daniel[237]—have sizeable additions in the Septuagint that have long been regarded as unoriginal (but which non-Protestant Christian communions generally regard as canonical anyway). Conversely, the Book of Jeremiah provides the most intriguing example of a book that is significantly *shorter* in the Septuagint—many scholars hold that it is shorter than the Masoretic text because it represents an earlier stage in development.[238] Lastly, it should be noted that the Septuagint tradition itself, like the Masoretic text, has its own varying versions and variant readings.[239]

An example of a changing text could be applied to the New Testament gospel tradition itself. It has long been observed that the gospels of Luke and Matthew have material that is word-for-word the same as the gospel of Mark—and that Mark may well be a source material for both other gospels. If this is indeed the case,[240] the following conclusion of two Anglican scholars would appear to follow: "Neither Matthew nor Luke treats Mark as we would treat 'inspired Scripture.' Each takes the utmost liberty to edit, to rewrite, and to alter material that is before him."[241]

The reasons for the errors and variants in the Scriptures are manifold but are often due to the persistent human characteristic to make oversights and lapses in memory and judgment, even when the utmost care is used to faithfully copy an original. Copying errors and scribal corruptions have included the following:

- A copyist accidentally omits a word, sentence, or phrase (and possibly adds the omitted text back in elsewhere).
- A copyist makes a note in the margin which becomes part of the text in the hands of a later copyist.
- A scribe miscopies familiar words in the place of unfamiliar ones.
- A copyist transposes a word or group of words.
- Poor penmanship results in the inability of later copyists to accurately read the text. Later copyists incorrectly "guess" at what the original word was.
- A copyist sees—or thinks he sees—an error in the text and seeks to correct it.
- A copyist adds oral[242] or written material not found in the original document.
- A scribe dislikes a detail or description in the text and then alters it to fit his own theological understanding.[243]

At times, opponents of conservative Christianity have overstated the degree of corruption to the New Testament, implying that the texts are so radically corrupt that we have little idea what their original form was. Even though there are many thousands of variants, the large majority of true New Testament difficulties seem to be fairly small. Although it is challenging to estimate such things, some more moderate Christian scholars contend today that perhaps 95% of the reconstructed New Testament text is in its original form now. Even those apologists and dogmatic Christians who overstate the case cannot bring themselves to assert that the modern critical text is error-free—although as much as "99.9% free from real concern" has been claimed.[244] (Arguments concerning the purity of the Old Testament, with its composition and transmission over a much longer period of time, are more problematic. There was likely some considerable oral tradition involved in some books, and at times early developments in the textual tradition seem somewhat conjectural.)[245]

Even if the "100% pure" original compositions[246] were possessed, however, that would of course have no necessary bearing on who authored any particular text, if there was a forgery or an accidental misattribution of a text, if the content of a text is truly the teaching of Jesus or an apostle or prophet, if (in the case of the New Testament) the sayings of Jesus were accurately translated from the Aramaic that Jesus spoke to koine Greek, if all of the events or teachings described in texts are a unified harmony historically or theologically, or, most importantly, if the text was ever the "Word of God" in any specific sense in the first place. The issue regarding variants and interpolations, though perhaps not the most significant problem for traditional types of Christianity, is just one of the many issues that exposes the speculative metaphysics inherent in dogmatic Christian formulations.

And I think that is more to the heart of the issue. It seems fair to hold that the great majority of the content of the reconstructed New Testament texts[247] is reliably representative of the original Greek. As even critical New Testament scholar Bart Ehrman has noted, although there are some New Testament variants that are in his opinion "quite significant," the "vast majority of these changes are insignificant, immaterial, and of no importance for the meaning of the passages in which they are found."[248] The fact that there are errors in the text, to whatever degree, is but a part of the wider uncertainties that surround the whole dogmatic Christian endeavor.

For those wanting specific instances of textual problems as expressed in different English translations, what follows is a sample of some intriguing variants in the New Testament. Note abbreviations as follows: King James Version (KJV), New International Version Study Bible (NIV), Revised Standard Version (RSV), New American Standard (NAS), New American Bible (NAB), and New Revised Standard Version (NRSV).[249]

Issue Verse(s) with Variant reading *in bold italics*	Variant included in text without notation	Variant included in text but with brackets or footnote	Variant excluded from text but with footnote	Variant excluded from text without comment	Potential Implication
Does human anger always bring God's judgment? "You have heard that it was said to those of ancient times, 'You shall not murder;' and 'whoever murders shall be liable to judgement.'²² But I say to you that if you are angry with a brother or sister ***without cause***, you will be liable to judgement" Matt. 5:21-22a	KJV		NRSV, NIV, RSV	NAS, NAB	A believer may be in God's graces if he is angry with someone with cause—or he may bring God's judgment for anger regardless of the reason.

The Scripture Must Be Broken 41

How did Jesus teach people to pray? "Pray in this way .... And do not bring us to the time of trial, but rescue us from the evil one. *For the kingdom and the power and the glory are yours forever. Amen.*" Matt. 6:9-13	KJV	NAS	NRSV, NIV, RSV	NAB	Christians may not be saying the "Lord's prayer" properly. Praying differently than Jesus commanded could affect a prayer's efficacy.
Is fasting needed for successful exorcisms? *"But this kind does not come out but by prayer and fasting."* Matt. 17:21 "He said to them, "This kind can only come out through prayer *and fasting."* Mark 9:29	KJV	NAS (Mt 17:21 in brackets)	NRSV, NIV, RSV, NAB	NAS (Mk 9:29)	A Christian may be unsuccessful against demonic forces if he or she doesn't fast.

How does the Gospel of Mark end? Options for the ending of the Gospel of Mark include: -Ending at verse 8. -The "longer ending" of Mark 16:9-20. -The "shorter ending." -The "Freer Logion" ending.[250]	KJV (longer ending)	NRSV (longer and shorter endings); NIV (longer ending); RSV (longer and shorter ending); NAS (longer and shorter ending), NAB (longer and shorter endings but longer ending noted as canonical).	NRSV (Freer Logion); NAB (Freer Logion).	NIV (shorter ending and Freer Logion); KJV (shorter ending and Freer Logion); RSV (Freer Logion); NAS (Freer Logion).	There are twelve verses in the "longer ending" in question. (These verses are frequently deemed non-original.) Furthermore, there are about five sentences of text in the "shorter ending" and the "Freer Logion" combined that are generally rejected. The longer ending famously notes that believers can heal the sick as well as handle snakes and drink poison without being harmed. God may judge those who reject part of his Word or believers may die from drinking poison or picking up snakes—as in the case of Kentucky preachers Jamie Coots and John David Brock.[251]

Did angels attend Jesus? Did he drop sweat like blood? *"Then an angel from heaven appeared to him and gave him strength. In his anguish he prayed more earnestly, and his sweat became like great drops of blood falling on the ground."* Luke 22:43-44	KJV, NAS	NRSV, NAB	RSV		Did Jesus need an angel's help during his temptation? (Would he have failed without it?) If he did need the help, this could have implications for how his humanity and/or divinity are regarded.
Did Jesus ask God to forgive those who crucified him? *"Then Jesus said, 'Father forgive them; for they know not what they are doing.'"* Luke 23:34	KJV, NAS	NRSV, NIV, RSV, NAB			If Jesus did not forgive those who crucified him, perhaps he will be less forgiving towards those who have offended him in general. Perhaps his general approach is the harshness of Matt. 25 or Revelation.[252]

Is the story of the woman caught in adultery legendary? John 7:53-8:11	KJV	NRSV, NIV, RSV, NAS, NAB (but noted as canonical).[253]			Twelve verses are in question. Many believers look to this passage for solace, but Jesus may have supported the death penalty in an instance like this—like he appears to have in Matt. 15:3-4 when he affirms the OT commandment: "Whoever speaks evil of father or mother must surely die."
Did Jesus say something that was untrue? "Go to the festival yourselves. I am not **yet** going to this festival, for my time has not yet fully come." John 7:8 (Jesus then goes up to the festival "in secret" in v.10.)	KJV	NIV	NRSV, RSV, NAB	NAS	If the "yet" is not original, was Jesus mistaken, or dishonest, or did he change his mind? Does this verse support the Alogoi's position that John should not be canonical? If Jesus had a moral lapse, was his sacrifice then not efficacious? This passage, which was critiqued by critics like Porphyry in the early centuries CE,[254] is an example of how even one word could cause significant problems.

Should women be silent in church? *"... [W]omen should be silent in the churches. For they are not permitted to speak, but should be subordinate, as the law also says. If there is anything they desire to know, let them ask their husbands at home. For it is shameful for a woman to speak in church."* 1 Cor. 14:34-35	KJV, RSV, NIV, NAS		NRSV ("Other ancient authorities put verses 34-35 after verse 40"); NAB ("often considered an inter-polation").[255]		Whether women should "be silent" in church has obvious implications for worship and leadership roles. The general issue of women in the church involves other textual issues, as many scholars regard the "Pastoral Letters" (1 & 2 Tim. and Titus) as non-Pauline—and thus potentially non-authoritative.[256]

Additions to Daniel		NRSV		NIV,	Involving a
		(removes		NAS,	dispute over 174
These sections		all addi-		RSV	verses, these
of text are part		tions to			"additions" bring
of the Roman		Apoc-			up interesting
Catholic, Eastern		rypha			questions. Can
Orthodox, and		section);			later supple-
Oriental Ortho-		NAB			ments to a text
dox canons:[257]		(includes			still be author-
(1) The Prayer		all in text			itative? Does
of Azariah and		and notes			a canonical
the Song of the		as canoni-			work have to be
Three Jews (68		cal).[258]			written all by
verses between					the same person
3:23 and 3:24)					at the same
(2) Susanna (Ch.					time? Why can't
13 in Vulgate; 64					authentic believ-
verses)					ers filled with
(3) Bel and the					the Holy Spirit
Dragon (Ch. 14					make assess-
in Vulgate; 42					ments about the
verses)					inspiration of
					variants without
					recourse to tex-
					tual evidence?

Additional material in Jeremiah: Although this textual issue is widely known, of the six English translations noted here only the NAB describes the problem. Unlike with the Additions to Daniel and Esther, here it is the Septuagint that is approximately 1/6th *shorter* than the Hebrew Masoretic text.[259] What does such a large discrepancy suggest for the reliability or inspiration of the book in general? The NAB notes that Jer. 33:14-26 "appears to be the post-exilic composition of an inspired writer who used parts of the prophecies of Jeremiah—often, however, in a sense different from the prophet's."[260]

[7] Errors, Probably

...Why the Bible probably contains mistakes

> If one account in Holy Writ is at variance with another, and it is impossible to resolve the difficulty, just dismiss it from your mind. ... In their accounts of Christ's deeds and miracles they do not observe a uniform order and often ignore the proper chronological sequence.
>
> —**Martin Luther** (1483-1546), *Sermons on the Gospel of St. John*[261]

> The age when ecclesiastical censures were sufficient in such cases has passed away. ... For philosophy and history alike have taught them not to seek what is "safe," but what is true.
>
> —**Henry Sidgwick** (1838-1900), regarding the findings of biblical criticism[262]

The Bible probably contains scientific, historical, logical, and theological discrepancies and errors. This has been admitted to varying degrees by many prominent Christians over the centuries and, except to those who have accepted inerrancy as a dogma of faith, seems to be an almost irresistible conclusion to those who have looked carefully into the many problems in the biblical texts.

While often couched in terms of humility before God, it rather appears to be a form of bias or prejudice that upholds a strident belief in inerrant Scriptures. Protestant apologists Norman Geisler and Thomas Howe rather flatly state the dynamic of an extreme inerrantist position in a fairly classic formulation of circular reasoning:

> This is not to say that there are not *difficulties* in our Bibles. ... It is only to point out that there are not actual *errors* in the Scriptures. Why? Because the Bible is the Word of God, and God cannot err.[263]

With such an approach, "difficulties" in the Bible *by definition* cannot result in a conclusion of error. They are simply excluded from consideration no matter what the evidence suggests. While St. Augustine of Hippo (354-430) also used allegorical and not just literal and grammatical-historical interpretations,[264] he also forwarded the idea that biblical errors are not "allowable":

> If we are perplexed by an apparent contradiction in Scripture, it is not allowable to say, the author of this book is mistaken; but either the manuscript is faulty, or the translation is wrong, or you have not understood. ... Otherwise, not a single page will be left for the guidance of human fallibility, if contempt for the wholesome authority of the canonical books either puts an end to that authority altogether, or involves it in hopeless confusion.[265]

While Augustine was of course right in noting that humans are very prone to error, there is no reason to think that this reality of human fallibility would not apply to theological opinions about the nature and purity of religious texts. As progressive evangelical Peter Enns notes, if a conclusion about the Bible can only be reached when we "dismiss, mishandle, or vilify compelling information unfriendly to our doctrine"[266] —when in essence holding to the "Truth" requires believing things that evidence suggests are not true—a much more profound and "hopeless" confusion seems to arise. The virtue of loyalty or faithfulness, while having genuine merit in many circumstances, should not degenerate into a stubborn and unassailable conflation of one's own spiritual opinions with the Mind of God.

While the existence of errors in the Scriptures is supported by strong and substantial evidence, it would still appear wrong-headed to claim certainty about a particular perspective on any individual textual difficulty. Nondogmatic approaches deal in probabilities, in evidence, in the acknowledgment that knowledge is incomplete and reasonings could be flawed. Certainty and stridency about metaphysical and theological positions—or their negation—is probably best regarded as unnecessary, unhelpful, and discordant with the limitations of the human mind. As one neurosurgeon explains, feelings of certainty themselves should perhaps be best understood as vivid and potentially deceptive emotional states rather than indicators of rectitude anyway:

> But modern biology ... is telling us that despite how certainty feels, it is neither a conscious choice nor even a thought process. Certainty and similar states of "knowing what we know" arise out of primary brain mechanisms that, like love or anger, function independently of rationality or reason. Feeling correct or certain isn't a deliberate conclusion or conscious choice. It is a mental sensation that happens to us.[267]

What follows are not some of the more "major" problems in the Bible that are addressed in other meditations. Rather, these are smaller matters—the type of sometimes minor or even trivial discrepancies and errors that do little other than to expose that the Scriptures are most probably not the perfect "dictation of the Holy Spirit"[268] that many traditionalist or fundamentalist Christians have claimed them to be.[269]

- **Has God been seen?** God has been seen by over 70 people (Exod. 24:9-11), or by just Moses when face-to-face (Num. 12:6-8) or just his back (Exod. 33:20-23). God has never been seen by anyone (John 1:18, 1 Tim. 6:16) except Jesus (John 6:46).[270]

- **Does God change his mind?** God changes his mind about bringing disaster on Israel or other nations (Exod. 32:14, Jonah 3:10, Jer. 26:19, Jer. 42:10), about making Saul king (1 Sam. 15:35), about destroying Jerusalem (1 Chron. 21:15) and about sending locusts and fire (Amos 7:1-6). God never changes his mind (Num. 23:19).[271]

- **Do people praise God after death?** No one remembers or praises God after death (Ps. 6:4-5, Ps. 115:17-18, cf. Eccles. 9:10).[272] Those in heaven will worship him forever (Rev. 5:11-13, Rev. 7:9-12).[273]

- **Can animal sacrifices atone for sin?** Animal sacrifices atone for sin (Lev. 5:16, Lev. 6:6-7, Lev. 10:17). Animal sacrifices cannot atone for sin (Heb. 10:4; cf. Isa. 1:11-12, Hos. 6:6).[274]

- **Who incited King David to take a census?** God incited David to take a census (2 Sam. 24:1). Satan incited David to take a census (1 Chron. 21:1).[275]

- **Who was the high priest that gave bread to David?** Jesus states that Abiathar was the high priest that gave the Bread of the Presence to King David (Mark 2:26). 1 Sam. 21:1-6 relates that Ahimelech, the father of Abiathar, was the priest in the story.[276]

- **How many generations are in Jesus' genealogy?** There are 42 generations from Abraham to Jesus, suggesting a significance behind three 14-generation periods (Matt. 1:17). There are 58 generations from Abraham to Jesus (Luke 3:23-34).[277]

- **Did the devil show Jesus all the kingdoms of the world in the beginning or the end of the temptation?** It was early during the temptation (Luke 4:1-13). It was the last attempt at temptation before the devil left him (Matt. 4:1-11).[278]

- **Did Jesus carry his own cross or did Simon of Cyrene carry it?** Jesus carried his cross by himself (John 19:16-17). Simon of Cyrene carried the cross (Matt. 27:31-32, Mark 15:20-21; Luke 23:26).[279]

- **Was Jesus crucified before or after the Passover?** He was crucified before the Passover (John 19:14). He was crucified after the Passover (Mark 14:12).[280]

- **Did those crucified with Jesus malign him?** Both men maligned him (Mark 15:32; Matt. 27:44). One man maligned him and the other defended him (Luke 23:39-43).

- **When was the stone in front of the tomb rolled back/removed?** It was rolled back in the presence of Mary Magdalene and another woman (Matt. 28:1-2).[281] The stone was removed before Mary Magdalene arrived (John 20:1), or before Mary Magdalene and three other women arrived (Mark 16:3-4; Luke 24:1-2).

- **Did the visitor(s) to the tomb tell the apostles about the Resurrection right away?** They did not say anything to anyone (Mark 16:8). They quickly ran to tell the apostles (Matt. 28:8, cf.

Luke 24:9). Just Mary Magdalene ran to tell Peter and John (John 20:2).[282]

- **Did anyone go to heaven before Jesus?** No one went to heaven before Jesus (John 3:13). Enoch (Gen. 5:24, Heb. 11:5) and Elijah went to heaven before Jesus (2 Kings 2:11).
- **Is Jesus coming back soon or in thousands of years?** Jesus is said to be "coming soon" (Rev. 22:20) as the time was "near" (Rev. 22:10), it was the "last hour" (1 John 2:18)—so short in fact that he was "at the doors" (James 5:8-9). Jesus is coming back in an indiscriminate amount of time that could be thousands of years (2 Pet. 3:3-10).

In the final analysis, perhaps examining and admitting the likelihood of biblical errors is just another healthy exercise in the admission of human fallibility. While errors can be an occasion for existential angst or religious crisis, they are perhaps better utilized as an opportunity for the frank and cathartic realization that our bedrock human frailties will probably never be wholly avoided or circumvented. Even our most treasured "gospel truths" seem inevitably prone to mistake, inaccuracy, and distortion. And while it does indeed appear to be the case that those who advocate biblical inerrancy are mistaken, this does not mean that those who hold to traditional views of the Bible are less moral, less intelligent,[283] or (of course) less human than those of a more skeptical inclination. As journalist Kathryn Schulz notes in her *Being Wrong: Adventures on the Margin of Error*, finding error in others is perhaps most valuable when it becomes an exercise in human solidarity and empathy—and a warning against the corrosive effects of mockery or judgmentalism:

> Being right may be fun but, as we've seen, it has a tendency to bring out the worst in us. ... To be judgmental, we must feel sure that we know right from wrong, and that we ourselves would never confuse the two. But the experience of erring shows us otherwise. It reminds us that, having been wrong in the past, we could easily be wrong again .... [I]t reminds us to treat other people with compassion, to honor their possible rightness as well as their inevitable, occasional wrongness. Instead of taking errors as a sign that they are ignorant or

idiotic or evil, we can look to our own lives and reach the opposite conclusion: that they are, like us, just human.²⁸⁴

[8] What Does the Scripture Say?[285]
...*The ambiguous nature of biblical teachings*

> One day some old men came to see Abba Anthony. ... Wanting to test them, the old man suggested a text from the Scriptures, and, beginning with the youngest, he asked them what it meant. Each gave his opinion as he was able. But to each one the old man said, "You have not understood it." Last of all he said to Abba Joseph, "How would you explain this saying?" and he replied, "I do not know." Then Abba Anthony said, "Indeed, Abba Joseph has found the way, for he has said: 'I do not know.'"
>
> —**Sayings of the Desert Fathers**[286]

> Besides, arguments about Scripture achieve nothing but a stomach-ache or a headache.
>
> —**Tertullian** (c.155-c.220), early Catholic church father[287]

The *American Heritage Dictionary* defines "ambiguous" as "1. Susceptible of multiple interpretation. 2. Doubtful or uncertain."[288] Perhaps more than any other work, the Bible has embodied the fullness of this definition, taking on wide interpretive variances that have grown exponentially as the Judeo-Christian Scriptures have been translated into hundreds of languages[289] and studied all over the globe by numerous generations of academics, missionaries, mystics, and believers of all different types. While the sheer variety of interpretive diversity is far too extensive to catalogue in a short essay, the somewhat loose sampling of examples below suggests how interpretations that have been evident, clear, or central to some believers have been considered to be plainly false by many others. It is also fair to say that some interpretations that have been the cause of great controversies in one age and place have been thought wholly trivial by others—if they have even been thought of at all.

Allegorical and hidden interpretations. While some Jews and Christians have been suspicious of allegorical interpretations or even thought they were "the trick of Satan,"[290] other believers like Philo (c.20 BCE-42 CE) have found hidden meanings and claimed to uncover profound senses of the text beyond more straightforward readings.[291] Likewise, medieval Jewish scholar Maimonides (1135-1204) thought it necessary to use allegorical interpretations when literal readings were "contradicted by evidential proof."[292] The medieval Jewish Kabbalists held that the Hebrew Bible was best and most fully understood through an esoteric and mystical approach that focused on ten aspects of or emanations from God known as *sefirot*.[293] Although many Christians have rejected allegorical methods, the New Testament itself utilizes the approach on occasion (Gal. 4:21-31, 1 Cor. 9:8-10, 1 Cor 10:1-11).[294] The early Catholic Church had an ongoing tension between the Antiochene approach to scripture, which favored literal and historical readings of the texts, and the Alexandrian approach, which favored mystical and allegorical approaches.[295] By the Middle Ages, a four-fold interpretation of Scripture was generally espoused by the Roman Catholic Church: literal, allegorical, moral, and anagogic (heavenly).[296] St. Bernard of Clairvaux (1090-1153) famously read the Song of Solomon as an allegory, asking Jesus to spiritually kiss him "with the kiss of his mouth" (cf. Song of Sol. 1:2).[297] Sometimes called "bibliomancy," some Christians have thought that the Bible could speak to them individually by selecting verses at random—a practice condemned by St. Augustine (354-430).[298] Likewise, others claim to have found hidden "codes" in the Bible which, when deciphered, can reveal the timing and character of future events.[299] In contrast to many traditional Protestants that prize literal readings, one rabbi noted in the Talmud that a person who "translates a verse in the Bible literally has perpetuated a fraud."[300]

Atonement of Christ. Outreach Judaism, a modern Jewish group that seeks to halt the influence of fundamentalist Protestant evangelists, holds that the Christian doctrine of the Atonement of Christ is inherently unbiblical. Referencing Ezek. 18:19-20 and its assertions that no person's righteousness or wickedness can be transferred to another, Rabbi Tovia Singer argues that "Ezekiel forever condemned Christendom's central doctrine of vicarious atonement, and slammed the notion that an innocent human being can die for the sins of the wicked."[301] Interestingly, the Eastern Orthodox have also been known to assert that the idea of a vicarious or substitutionary atonement is unscriptural or even a "heresy," claiming that it was unknown for the first 1,000 years of Christianity until it was developed by St. Anselm of Canterbury (c.1033-1109).[302]

Asceticism. Although Reformers often viewed the desert fathers as misguided souls who were trying to earn their salvation by the path of "works righteousness,"[303] St. Athanasius (c.296-373) once wrote of the desert monk Antony of Egypt (c.251-c.356) that his extreme ascetical life was in fact none other than "the discipline that he had learned from the Scriptures."[304] Augustine of Hippo (354-430) had a similar view of Antony, even linking his own conversion in part to hearing about the life of the saint.[305] John the Baptist was considered as a model Christian ascetic to the desert fathers, living in the wilderness on a meager diet without physical comforts (Matt. 3:4);[306] Elijah was sometimes cited as an Old Testament example.[307] Some early Christians like Origen (c.185-c.254) apparently took Matt. 19:12 literally, castrating themselves so that they might live as eunuchs for the kingdom of God.[308] Conversely, the Talmud notes that marriage and marital relations are a biblical duty based on Gen. 2:18 and Gen. 9:7.[309] Interestingly, some rabbis have considered the independent fasting of individuals to be sinful, an inhibitor of good deeds, and a kind of self-harm (Prov. 11:17).[310]

Baha'i interpretations. Baha'is teach that the Christian Scriptures, when rightly understood, predicted the coming of Baha'u'llah (1817-1892) as the true "Second Coming" of Christ.[311] They understand passages in Matt. 24, Mark 13, Luke 17, Luke 21, and John 16 to be generally supportive of this view.[312] While Jews understand the covenant promises of Abraham (Gen. 17:6-7) to come through Sarah and Muslims through Hagar, the Baha'is understand that the prophecy was also fulfilled through Keturah (Gen. 25:1-2), from whom they believe Baha'u'llah to be descended.[313] Baha'is also believe that the "healing of the nations" described in Rev. 22:2 will only come in a "Most Great Peace" when the peoples of the world all recognize the truth claims of Baha'u'llah.[314]

Birth control and abortion. Along with Catholic Church fathers, Martin Luther, and virtually all confessional Christians before the Anglican Church broke ranks in 1930,³¹⁵ Reformer John Calvin (1509-1564) believed that the Bible denounced the use of birth control. He believed that to "pour out seed" outside of intercourse was "horrible" and that coitus interruptus was "double horrible." In his explication of the story of Onan in Gen. 38:8-10, Calvin further explained: "When a woman in some way drives away the seed out the womb, through aids, then this is rightly seen as an unforgivable crime. Onan was guilty of a similar crime, by defiling the earth with his seed, so that Tamar would not receive a future inheritor."³¹⁶ Other prooftexts employed against birth control include a divine command to "be fruitful and multiply" (Gen. 9:1) along with verses that tout the blessings of children (Ps. 127:4-5) and even the act of childbearing itself (1 Tim. 2:15).³¹⁷ Many conservative Protestants today, however, reject the widespread, traditional Christian views on contraception and hold that the Bible takes no position on the issue.³¹⁸ While opposition to abortion is likewise early and commonplace in the Christian tradition, more moderate and progressive believers have pointed out that the New Testament has no specific reference to abortion either—and so are more inclined to put the issue under the same general umbrella of Christian liberty (John 16:13, Rom. 14:4-5).³¹⁹ Traditionalists often cite verses like Job 31:15, Ps. 139:13-16, Jer. 1:5, and Luke 1:44—which they believe imply an anti-abortion ethic.³²⁰ In one noteworthy example of a more moderate approach, the 1971 Southern Baptist Convention resolution affirmed the "high view of the sanctity of human life, including fetal life" while still permitting "the possibility of abortion under such conditions as rape, incest, clear evidence of fetal deformity, and carefully ascertained evidence of the likelihood of damage to the emotional, mental, and physical health of the mother."³²¹ As evidenced by the Talmud, Jewish rabbis have often found that the Bible did not prohibit birth control for minors, pregnant women, or nursing mothers; furthermore, abortion was deemed permissible to save a woman's life.³²²

Clarity of Scripture. The Calvinist *Westminster Confession of Faith* (1646) asserted that the clarity of Scripture was such that "those things which are necessary to be known, believed and observed for salvation, are so clearly propounded" that both the "learned" and the "unlearned" can readily understand them.³²³ However, the Eastern Orthodox Council of Jerusalem (1672)—which regarded Calvinists as exceedingly poor interpreters of Scripture and heretics who were under "anathema"[324]—declared that the Bible itself indicates that it is not clear:

> If the Divine Scriptures were plain to all Christians that read them, the Lord would not have commanded such as desired to obtain salvation to search the same [John 5:39]; and Paul would have said without reason that God had placed the gift of teaching in the Church [1 Cor. 12:28][325] and Peter would not have said of the Epistles of Paul that they contained some things hard to be understood [2 Pet. 3:16]. It is evident, therefore, that the Scriptures are very profound, and their sense lofty; and that they need learned and divine men to search out their true meaning, and a sense that is right, and agreeable to all Scripture, and to its author the Holy Spirit.[326]

Anabaptist Menno Simons (1496-1561) also condemned Reformed Christians, strikingly asserting that their biblical interpretations were "the falsehood of the serpent," "spiritual dung," and the "horrible, abominable draught of the golden cup of the Babylonian harlot."[327] John Calvin likewise thought that Anabaptists were foolish and ignorant biblical exegetes, calling their readings of Scripture "a mortal error as deadly as the plague" and a "fantasy of their brain."[328] In his *Exegetical Fallacies,* modern evangelical D. A. Carson lamented that even when interacting with fellow evangelical Protestants with a similarly "high view" of the same 66-book Bible, it was still "very distressing to contemplate how many differences there are among us as to what Scripture actually says."[329] Carson goes on to warn of fifty-six interpretive errors—including sixteen word-study fallacies, eight grammatical fallacies, eighteen logical fallacies, seven presuppositional and historical fallacies, and seven other fallacies. On top of all these, Carson cautions that even after a text is properly understood, there are still "new dangers" that are lurking—and a believer may well interpret a passage correctly but then misapply it in the present day.[330]

Divinity of Christ. Traditional Jewish belief asserts that the Trinity is both completely incorrect and "absolutely forbidden" by the Hebrew Bible since the Oneness of God is emphasized in verses like Deut. 6:4 (NIV): "Hear, O Israel: The Lord our God, the Lord is one."[331] Many modern scholars believe that Christological views developed over time and note that certain parts of John have a higher Christology not found in the other canonical gospels and Acts.³³² Arians and other non-Trinitarians (like Christadelphians, Church of God General Conference, Oneness Pentecostals, and Jehovah's Witnesses)³³³ have denied that the Bible teaches the Trinitarian notion that there are three divine Persons that are all co-eternal, co-equal, and fully the same God.³³⁴ There are a number of different verses used by various Christians to "prove" Jesus was not fully God—but divine in a lesser sense.³³⁵ They have claimed that the Scripture shows Jesus' lesser status by communicating that he can have different desires than God (Matt. 26:39), is not omniscient like God (Mark 13:31-32), increased in divine favor as he grew (Luke 2:52), is lesser than the Father (John 14:28), was sent forth from "the only true God" (John 17:3), was made Lord by God (Acts 2:36), will be subject to God (1 Cor. 15:27-28), is the image of God and the firstborn of creation (Col. 1:15), or is the "beginning" or "origin" of God's creation (Rev. 3:14).³³⁶ Equating Jesus with divine wisdom, Arius (d.336) himself apparently used Prov. 8:22 as a crucial text in his theology in which he equated Divine Wisdom with the created Christ: "The Lord created me at the beginning of his work, the first of his acts of long ago."³³⁷

Gnostic interpretations. Gnostic Christians of numerous types had many interesting interpretations of Jewish and Catholic Scriptures. For instance, the author of the Testimony of Truth thought that Genesis 3 exposed the Lord as a false and "malicious envier" while showing the snake to be a benevolent friend of humanity. To do this, the author pointed out that it was the Lord who intended to keep Adam and Eve from the knowledge of good and evil—and that God was in fact wrong that the first couple would die the day they ate the forbidden fruit (Gen. 2:17). Further, the author explained that the snake was correct that Adam and Eve would not perish if they ate, but rather would know how to distinguish good from evil (Gen. 3:4-5; Gen. 3:22).³³⁸ Gnostic Christians (of various and sometimes competing types) regarded themselves as the holders of Truth, asserting that early Catholic Christians were overly literal in their interpretations and often missed central ideas about the divine.³³⁹

Head coverings. Although fairly standard in even the recent past, it is common for the Pauline directive for women to cover their heads to be seen as irrelevant today (1 Cor. 11:6-16). However, women in conservative groups today like the Amish and Mennonites, the Eastern Orthodox, and Middle Eastern Christians still preserve the practice. Furthermore, the modern "head covering movement" in American evangelicalism believes that women should once again follow St. Paul's injunction.[340]

Interpretive guides and principles. Rabbinic Judaism has traditionally relied heavily on the "Oral Law" of the Talmud when interpreting the Scriptures.[341] The Qumran community held that their Teacher of Righteousness was the only legitimate interpreter of the Jewish Law.[342] Mystical Kabbalist Jews have often given the *Zohar* a canonical-like status, believing it to be a wholly reliable explication of the Hebrew Scripture.[343] Jewish scholar Maimonides (1135-1204) interpreted all miracle stories in the Bible with angels as visions or dreams (and not physical manifestations); many other miracles he considered to be natural events.[344] Though he eventually joined the Montanist sect,[345] church father Tertullian at one time asserted that non-Catholics had no right to even interpret the Scriptures since they were Catholic documents.[346] Early Catholics like Tertullian, Hippolytus (c.170-c.235), and St. Irenaeus (fl. c. 175-195) held that there was a "Rule of Faith" or early creed that was a necessary interpretive key for the understanding of Scripture.[347] Markedly different interpretations of the greatly influential St. Augustine's understandings of Scripture have been extremely influential on both Protestants and Roman Catholics.[348] Reflecting on thirteen individuals deemed "arch-heretics" in the early Catholic tradition, St. Vincent of Lérins (d. c. 445) complained that Scripture seemed to be "capable of as many interpretations as there are interpreters"—and therefore counseled that the most widely-held and standard Catholic interpretations should be considered to be the most reliable.[349] John Wesley (1703-1791) held that the understanding of Scripture must be informed by not just tradition, but reason and experience as well.[350] Reformed Christians often assert that clearer passages of Scripture should guide the interpretation of less clear passages (but can still deeply disagree among themselves and with other believers about which passages are clear and what they mean).[351] Some Eastern Orthodox have held that the spiritual compendium called the *Philokalia* is indispensable in understanding the Bible.[352] Mary Baker Eddy (1821-1910) and her Christian Scientist followers claimed that her non-traditional book entitled *Science and Health with Key to the Scriptures* was necessary to comprehend Scripture—and that her book was in fact the promised Second Coming of Christ.[353]

Neo-orthodox theologian Karl Barth (1886-1968) thought that there was a great danger in fundamentalist approaches that made the Bible into a "paper pope" and "no longer a free and spiritual force, but an instrument of human power."[354] 20th-century liberation theology interpreted Scripture through a lens of concern for the poor and the need to confront unjust social and political structures.[355] Modern feminist theology seeks to view Scripture in ways that support women's liberation, equal rights for women, and exploring feminine qualities in the divine.[356] Ps. 22:9-10, Deut. 32:18 and Prov. 8:1-11 have been understood as showing God as midwife, mother, and divine wisdom (Sophia).[357] In opposition to the apparent thrust of verses like Lev. 20:13 and Rom. 1:26-27, some progressive Christians hold that the New Testament not only does not condemn loving same-sex partnerships, but that an unqualified criticism of gay marriage calls one's most basic spiritual sensibilities into question.[358] A common prooftext in a gay hermeneutic is 2 Sam. 1:26, which describes Jonathan's love for David as "passing the love of women."[359] Other modern interpretive approaches include the Afrocentric, Mujerista, Postcolonial, and Womanist perspectives.[360]

Islamic interpretations. Islam claims to be the true heir of both Judaism and Christianity and has distinctive biblical interpretations. In Ibn Ishaq's early biography of Muhammad, the Prophet himself proclaims that he "confirms the revelation which Moses brought" and that "you will find it in your scripture—'Muhammad is the apostle of Allah!'"[361] More specifically, Muslims have held that the future prophet referred to in Deut.18:18 is Muhammad.[362] Likewise, many Muslims maintain that the "Advocate" mentioned in John 14:16 is their Prophet. Other passages which Muslims have claimed to predict Muhammad include Isa. 21:7 and Hab. 3:3.[363] Interestingly, one hadith explains that the Qur'an is "the most recent information" from God and that the Bible is not fully reliable because texts have been altered.[364]

Justification.[365] While traditional Protestants often regard the doctrine of "justification by faith alone" as a major and essential part of the Christian message,[366] I was quite surprised as a seminary student to discover that this understanding of Scripture seems to be absent from the history of biblical interpretation before the 16th century.[367] The earliest church fathers;[368] creeds and ancient "Rules of Faith";[369] fourth-century giants like St. Augustine,[370] St. John Chrysostom,[371] and St. Basil;[372] Church Councils;[373] medieval figures like the church historian and biblical commentator Bede,[374] St. Francis of Assisi,[375] St. Bernard of Clairvaux,[376] and St. Thomas Aquinas;[377] "proto-Reformers" like Peter Waldo,[378] Jan Huss,[379] and John Wycliffe;[380] old communions like the Assyrian Church of the East, the Oriental Orthodox,[381] and the Eastern Orthodox;[382] many Anabaptists;[383] and even some Anglicans (including apparently C. S. Lewis)[384] have all read the Bible to teach that "discipleship," obedience, or good works are also necessary for salvation. Traditional Protestants often cite verses like Rom. 3:21-26, Gal. 2:15-16, and Eph. 2:8-9—the last of which specifically notes that salvation is "through faith," and "not the result of works." Often noting that James 2:24 expressly states that salvation is "not by faith alone," Roman Catholics[385] and others cite verses that suggest that salvation requires believers to act on Christ's words (Matt. 7:21), obey and suffer ([25]...27Matt. 16:24-27, Rev. 20:12, John 2:8-9),[386] be baptized (Acts 2:38, John 3:5),[387] forgive others (Matt. 6:14-15),[388] not judge others (Matt. 7:1-2), not sin in particular ways[10] (1 Cor. 6:9-10), do acts of mercy[4546] (Matt. 25:44-46),[389] unite faith to love (1 Cor. 13:1; cf. Gal. 5:6b),[390] eat and drink Jesus in the eucharist (John 6:54),[391] not fall away (Matt. 24:13, Heb. 6:4-12), not speak against the Holy Spirit (Matt. 12:32), and confess Christ before others[33] (Matt. 10:32-33, cf. Rom. 10:9-10).[392]

Lending money with interest. In great contrast to the essentially universal opinion today, Christians in the early and medieval periods commonly believed that the Bible taught it was a grave sin to lend money with any interest. Verses such as Ps. 15:5, Exod. 22:25, Deut. 23:19, and Luke 6:34 were classic prooftexts.[393]

Marriage and divorce. While modern American Protestantism typically defines marriage as "between one man and one woman," radical Anabaptists and other Christians have at times claimed that the Old Testament model of polygamy was acceptable, using passages like 2 Sam. 12:7-8 as prooftexts.[394] Radical Anabaptist Jan van Batenburg (1495-1538) not only adopted an Old Testament polygamy model, but also held that divorce was mandatory for anyone having an "unbelieving" spouse based on the commands in Ezra 10:3.[395] In a famous 1539 incident involving Philip Hesse, Martin Luther sanctioned a bigamous marriage on what he believed were biblical grounds; Luther was also known to allow divorce and remarriage for women with impotent husbands.[396] Some Christians have read the Bible to teach that divorce and remarriage is a damnable sin (Mark 10:11-12, Luke 16:18, 1 Cor. 6:9-10);[397] others have held that divorce can be forgiven like any transgression and that re-marriage is not adultery.[398] Basing its reasoning in part on the living authority of the Church (1 Tim. 3:15),[399] one modern Greek Orthodox catechism places the valid reasons for divorce as approximately thirteen—among them are apostasy from Eastern Orthodoxy (1 Cor. 7:15), adultery (Matt. 19:9), attempted murder, voluntary abortion, ordination as monk or bishop, desertion, insanity, leprosy, and lengthy imprisonment.[400] Roman Catholicism has likewise allowed divorce for aspiring monastics; for example, St. Bernard of Clairvaux (1090-1153) persuaded his sister to leave her husband for a convent (cf. Luke 18:29-30).[401] While the Mosaic Law allows divorce for a husband if he generally "finds something objectionable" about his wife (Deut. 24:1), the Talmud, thought to be an authoritative and even divinely inspired guide to biblical interpretation, gives five specific reasons for a wife to sue for divorce. These include impotence, repulsive disease, and objectionable occupation.[402]

Perpetual Virginity of Mary. St. Jerome, who translated the entire Bible from the Greek and Hebrew into Latin, wrote a book in 383 called *The Perpetual Virginity of the Blessed Mary* where he argued from "the actual words of Scripture" for a position that many Protestants assume to be a heretical late Catholic accretion.[403] Although Tertullian (c.155-c.220) denied the perpetual virginity of Mary,[404] such prominent patristic figures as St. Augustine of Hippo (354-430),[405] St. John Chrysostom (c.347-407),[406] St. Athanasius (c.296-373)[407] and Origen (c.185-c.254)[408] appear to have supported it. Perhaps surprisingly due to the general opposition to this viewpoint among modern Protestants, Martin Luther, John Calvin, Ulrich Zwingli, John Wesley, and Anabaptist Balthasar Hubmaier also seem to have generally agreed with Jerome on this point.[409]

Property and possessions. Some modern American pastors like Kenneth Copeland and Creflo Dollar believe that the Scriptures teach a "prosperity gospel" wherein God rewards faithfulness with material blessings (Deut. 8:18, Mark 10:30, James 4:2).[410] In stark contrast to this view, St. Antony of Egypt, upon hearing the reading of Matt. 19:21-22 and then Matt. 6:34, understood that Scripture was enjoining him to literally give up all his possessions.[411] Many Roman Catholics, Eastern Orthodox, Oriental

Orthodox, and Protestants of different types have likewise believed that the Bible taught either "holy poverty" or the call to material simplicity. St. Clare of Assisi (1193/4-1253) even believed that "the kingdom of heaven is promised only to the poor" (cf. Luke 6:20),[412] holding straightforwardly that it is "easier for a camel pass through the eye of a needle than for a rich man to enter the kingdom of heaven" (Matt. 19:24).[413] Believing that he was to "conform in every way to the rule of right living given to the apostles," St. Francis of Assisi thought he should literally not carry any money, wear shoes, or carry a staff (Matt. 10:9-10).[414] In a reference to Matt. 19:21, St. Bernard of Clairvaux (1090-1153) called the selling of all possessions to give to the poor part of a "shortcut to salvation."[415] The Anabaptist Hutterites of the 16th century held that private property was "the greatest enemy of love, and the true Christian must render up his will and become free from property if he would be a disciple" (see Acts 2:44-45, 4:32).[416]

Purgatory and Praying for the Dead. In contrast to standard Protestant beliefs, Roman Catholics have argued that purgatory is a biblical doctrine. Perhaps the most common prooftext used for purgatory is 1 Cor. 3:11-15, wherein the believer with inferior works "will suffer loss," but then "will be saved, but only as through fire."[417] Breaking with his Protestant co-religionists, C. S. Lewis (1898-1963) argued: "Our souls demand Purgatory, don't they? ... I assume the process of purification will normally involve suffering. Partly from tradition; partly because most real good that has been done me in this life has involved it."[418] Conversely, the Eastern Orthodox Council of Constantinople in 1583 called the idea a "Greek myth."[419] In addition to being practiced by Jews since before the time of Jesus, Catholic Old Testament Scripture explicitly recommends the practice of praying for the dead (2 Macc. 12:44-46).[420] Commenting on these verses, St. Augustine explained that "even if it were read nowhere in the Old Testament, the authority of the universal Church which clearly favors this practice is of great weight, where in the prayers of the priest which are poured forth to the Lord God at His altar the commemoration of the dead has its place."[421]

Rapture. The pre-tribulation premillennial Rapture, in which Christ "raptures" up all true believers into heaven before a period of intense persecution (and which is the basis of the popular *Left Behind* fiction series), is based on a reading of Scripture (esp. 1 Thess. 4:16-17) that did not exist as the teaching of any denomination until the 19th century. Despite differences in details, historically Christians did not separate a "rapture"-type event with the Second Coming of Christ.[422] Roman Catholics, Eastern Orthodox, Anglicans, Lutherans, and Presbyterians generally reject the pre-tribulation Rapture as an incorrect or even heretical reading of Scripture.[423]

Sacraments and ordinances. Based on their readings of Scripture, Roman Catholic, Eastern Orthodox, and Ethiopian Orthodox[424] believers hold the Scriptures teach that there are seven sacraments. Early Catholics had significant variation on this issue. As one Greek Orthodox theologian has aptly noted: "The number and kinds of the sacraments were not the same in the early centuries, because Scripture does not formulate dogmata systematically."[425] As a modern example of this reality, the Assyrian Church of the East also has seven sacraments but is the only communion that believes that the Sign of the Cross and Holy Leaven (Malka) are among them.[426] Presbyterians usually hold to two sacraments and Lutherans three.[427] St. Francis of Assisi (1181-1226), who St. Bonaventure thought "received from God an understanding of the Scriptures" in a unique and powerful way,[428] cited the words from John 6:54-55 and Mark 14:22-24 to show that those who don't believe the eucharist is literally "the most holy Body and Blood of our Lord Jesus Christ, are condemned" and that "no one can be saved unless he receive the Body and Blood of the Lord" from Roman Catholic priests.[429] Many types of Protestants believe that there are no sacraments—but rather only "ordinances." For example, the Separate Baptists in Christ, most United Baptist churches, the Church of God (Cleveland, TN), and the United Zion Church hold to the three ordinances of baptism by immersion, the Lord's Supper, and foot washing.[430] The Original Church of God, Inc. holds to five ordinances—baptism, tithing, free-will offerings, foot washing, and the Lord's Supper.[431] The Amish cite John 13:4-17 and 1 Tim. 5:10 as evidence that foot washing is mandatory for Christians.[432] The United Church of Christ has two "sacraments" (baptism and the Lord's Supper) and five "rites" (ordination, confirmation, consecration, marriage, and liturgical burial).[433] Though rejected by Protestants as a sacrament, the Roman Catholic Council of Trent (1545-1563) taught that the sacrament of Extreme Unction was enjoined by a "manifest and clear statement of the Apostle James" (James 5:14).[434] As shown in 1

Cor. 11:20-21 and Jude 12, the early church appears to have participated in an "agape meal" or "love feast" in connection with the eucharist. This appears to have largely died out as time progressed—although a few Protestant groups have attempted to revive it and in the 20th century it was used as "a means of reconciling Christians of different traditions in a liturgical rite distinct from the Eucharist."[435]

Tithing. While the giving of 10% of one's income to the church is emphasized as a necessary practice for the faithful in many Protestant communions (Luke 11:42, Lev. 27:30, Mal. 3:10), it was apparently not suggested by the clergy as a Christian duty until the sixth century in Gaul.[436] Christians today have various opinions about whether the Bible teaches that Christians must tithe—with many Christians believing that Scriptures like 2 Cor. 8:1-7 show that generosity is the only expectation.[437]

Unwritten Tradition. In opposition to the doctrine of "Scripture alone" prized by traditional Protestants (2 Tim. 3:16, Matt. 15:6, and Acts 17:11 are common prooftexts), St. Basil the Great (330-379) taught that it was not only "apostolic to abide also by the unwritten traditions," but that failure to heed unwritten tradition would "injure the Gospel in its very vitals."[438] Tertullian, St. Irenaeus, Hippolytus, and St. Augustine held similar views.[439] 2 Thess. 2:15 has often been read to justify this belief: "stand firm and hold fast to the traditions that you were taught by us, either by word of mouth or by our letter" (cf. 1 Cor. 11:2).

"Worldly" behavior. Citing a collection of New Testament verses like 2 Cor. 6:14, 2 Cor. 6:17, Rom. 12:2, James 4:4, 1 Pet. 4:2-4, 1 Cor. 5:11-13, and 2 Cor. 6:14-18, many traditional and fundamentalist Christian groups have sought to avoid a wide array of differing "worldly" behaviors. Playing cards, watching secular movies, gambling, smoking, dancing, watching television, listening to the radio, going to college, voting, joining any organization other than the church, going to carnivals, using telephones, and driving automobiles have all been condemned as the kinds of immoral or dangerous behavior that the Bible implicitly forbids.[440] Other fundamentalists have objected to slang, jesting, and silly talk (Eph. 5:4).[441] Others have fully rejected the drinking of alcohol, even claiming that the "wine" referred to in Scripture is actually unfermented grape juice.[442] Braiding hair, wearing wigs, wearing jewelry, and dressing in fine clothes have also been rejected as unbiblical (1 Pet. 3:3, 1 Tim. 2:9).[443] In contrast to stricter views, many Christians, citing passages like 1 Sam. 18:6, 2 Sam. 6:14, and Ps. 149:3, believe that dancing is permissible.[444]

Like their conservative counterparts, liberal scholars have had a tremendous range of opinion about who Jesus of Nazareth was and what he taught. As New Testament Bart Ehrman explains, the quest for the historical Jesus provides "an enormous range of opinion about how Jesus is best understood—as a rabbi, a social revolutionary, a political insurgent, an apocalyptic prophet: the options go on and on."[445] Likewise, the options for biblical interpretation on a host of other topics goes "on and on," as do the number of believers and scholars who hold that their particular understandings of the Bible are clear, important, and correct. It seems, however, that such differences of opinion often have no necessary correlation to sincerity, intelligence, piety, or ethical character. Although some interpretations and positions would surely seem to be more reasonable readings than others, much of the diversity in opinion appears to come from the lack of clarity and cohesion of the texts themselves—surely amplified by a thorny variety of human limitations, foibles, and biases.[446] While the history of biblical interpretation provides many different insights, perhaps the clearest lesson is that humanity has had a persistently bad habit of interpreting ambiguous holy texts in a fog of confidence.

[9] Sleeping or on a Journey?
...*The biblical god's apparent absence*

Then Elijah said to the prophets of Baal, "Choose for yourselves one bull and prepare it first, for you are many; then call on the name of your god, but put no fire to it."[26] So they took the bull that was given them, prepared it, and called on the name of Baal from morning until noon, crying, "O Baal, answer us!" But there was no voice, and no answer. They limped about the altar that they had made.[27] At noon Elijah mocked them, saying, "Cry aloud! Surely he is a god; either he is meditating, or he has wandered away, or he is on a journey, or perhaps he is asleep and must be awakened."[28]

—1 Kings 18:25-28

Rouse yourself! Why do you sleep, O Lord? Awake, do not cast us off forever!

—Ps. 44:23

In the story of Elijah's confrontation with the prophets of Baal, the Hebrew prophet mocks Baal's lack of response. Perhaps Baal is meditating, or has wandered off, or is on a journey, or is asleep. Despite the desperate efforts of Baal's prophets, there is no response from the heavens.

This lack of response also seems to be the experience of traditional Christians, who appear to be in the same position today as the prophets of Baal were in the book of 1 Kings. For if even the most devout and holy group of Christians were to ask God to rain fire down from the sky—or call for some other miraculous manifestation of divine power—would there not also be no voice and no answer?[447] It is here we see that Yahweh is just as open to the same sorts of criticism and disbelief as the prophet Isaiah is said to have levied against the other gods of antiquity:

> No, they are all a delusion;
> > their works are nothing;
> > their images are empty wind (Isa. 41:29).

The problem takes on further weight when both the goodness and omnipotence of God are asserted. Why does God not prevent debilitating disease, severe mental illness, and catastrophic injury? Where is He during the child's wasting illness, or famine, or rape, or miscarriage, or child abuse, or genocide? To put the enormity of the problem in scope, one merely needs to consider the incessant natural disasters, famines, wars, plagues, and other human tragedies that have plagued civilization both before and after the advent of Christianity. Consider the horrific example that there were nearly 12 million children under the age of five who died worldwide in 1990. That's an unimaginable 32,876 combined babies, toddlers, and preschoolers per day. There is a positive trend in that, due to the toil of organizations like UNICEF, "only" 6.9 million children under the age of five died in 2011. (That's down to 18,904 per day.) The majority of these deaths were from preventable causes like starvation and certain treatable diseases.[448] As historian Nicholas Shrady has noted, although natural disasters "grip us in a particularly sentient way," it is actually these mundane and routine tragedies of disease and starvation that cause the greatest human misery and death.[449]

People are often horrified by the bloody American Civil War—and rightly so. For perspective, consider that the bloodiest day in American history was the battle of Antietam in 1862, where there were 23,000 combined deaths and injuries.[450] Consider further that all American deaths in theatres of war between 1775 and 1991 were approximately 924,000.[451] The world has thus seen multitudes of daily Antietams of little children; it has seen the deaths of babies and preschoolers year after year which dwarf the national tragedies of great nations. Do Christians not pray for the cessation of such horrors? Why would a good and all-powerful God not help these children?

Perhaps there is some god that is meditating or sleeping or on a journey—or perhaps he has gone insane, died, been imprisoned by some other cosmic being, or become senile and forgotten humanity. Or perhaps he (or she) dwells completely outside the known universe and cannot interact with it. Perhaps he is even unaware that the earth exists—it being so small a planet circling just one star among countless stars in billions of galaxies. Perhaps the search for God is a literal quest of "Finding *Nemo*" (Lat. "No one"). Or perhaps some future cosmological discovery will bring new insights into the nature of the universe and the concept of divinity. Such metaphysical speculations are limitless and do very little to help us learn how to live well or to lessen human suffering and tragedy.

While the implausibility of certain religious beliefs has at times been a cause for mockery, it seems a more constructive and compassionate response to use such observations as a reminder of the real and often overwhelming pain in the world. While it is true that traditional religious dogmas have many times increased human suffering, they are also a reminder of the desperation and fear that often are at the heart of unwarranted beliefs. Showing the grander and more practical side of traditional faith, the early 20th-century preacher John Watson provides a reminder that no matter what a person believes, our fellow beings are always in need of both encouragement and compassion:

> This man beside us also has a hard fight with an unfavouring world, with strong temptations, with doubts and fears, with wounds of the past which have skinned over, but which smart when they are touched. It is a fact, however surprising. And when this occurs to us we are moved to deal kindly with him, to bid him be of good cheer, to let him understand that we are also fighting a battle; we are bound not to irritate him, nor press hardly upon him nor help his lower self.[452]

[10] Ancient Skeptics

...Critiques of Christianity from its early centuries

> Already in the second century, however, Celsus devoted part of his *True Doctrine* to a critical examination of the accounts of Jesus' life, and Porphyry paid even greater attention to the literary and historical analysis of the Scriptures. His dating of the Book of Daniel is still accepted by critical scholarship. The primary issue in the debate over the Bible was whether the Scriptures could be considered a reliable source for what they record.
>
> —**Robert Wilken**, *The Christians as the Romans Saw Them*[453]

> This work of Porphyry is perhaps the most ample and thoroughgoing treatise which has ever been written against Christianity. ... Even at this time of day Porphyry remains unanswered.
>
> —**Adolf von Harnack**, German theologian (1851-1930)[454]

It is often thought that the modern world has been unduly influenced by skepticism. Although it may be that rational thought is more prevalent in human affairs than it was in times past, it is a mistake to think that all people in the ancient world were unanalytical and unquestioningly accepted supernatural claims.

Many critiques of Christian dogmatic beliefs are documented as early as the second century. In fact, critics such as Celsus (2nd c.), Porphyry (232-305), and Julian the Apostate (c.331-363) developed arguments against Christianity that often sound quite familiar to modern ears. While these men did not always apply an equally rigorous approach to their own supernatural or metaphysical beliefs, their criticisms show that many of the strongest objections to common Christian dogmas were being articulated from the earliest stages of their development.[455] Here are some summaries of the criticisms offered by these specific ancient critics:

Celsus, pagan philosopher

Christians are too dogmatic and too reliant on faith without sufficient evidence;[456] they often retreat to fideism when asked difficult questions.[457] Christians can be also overly confident or even arrogant in their approach to ethics and religious doctrines.[458] Stories of the Resurrection could be better explained as hallucinations or dreams.[459] Evangelization's success is often grounded in ignorance and fear.[460] The Gospels have many accounts that parallel the deeds of magicians in the ancient world—including the calming of storms, the miraculous provision of food, healing, and the ability to know another's thoughts.[461] Jesus' return from the dead is not unique—other heroes and charismatic leaders are believed to have come back from the grave.[462] The good in Christianity has parallels in other traditions; for example, Plato taught a version of the golden rule.[463] The Gospels have many discrepancies and are not reliable histories of the life of Jesus; the accounts of the Crucifixion, the infancy narratives, and the genealogies of Jesus provide examples of this fact.[464] It is very difficult to offer a comprehensive critique of Christianity because there are so many different sects that believe such different things.[465]

Porphyry, Neo-Platonist philosopher

God killing his own creation in the Flood is morally problematic.[466] The story of Jonah is clearly a myth and should not be taken literally.[467] The Book of Daniel did not foretell future events but rather recorded historical ones.[468] If the Old Testament were a unique revelation from the only God then it would show greater learning. Other ancient peoples surpassed the Hebrews in law, art, philosophy, military tactics, astronomy, geometry, medicine, and general erudition.[469] People incurring horrific punishments for not believing poorly attested, fantastic stories is not sensible;[470] punishing a person eternally for finite sins is both cruel and discordant with justice.[471] Paul was wrong in believing that Christ would return soon;[472] his theology is sometimes inconsistent and irrational.[473] The apostles did not all agree in doctrine and had disputes with each other.[474] The claim in Mark 16:18 that believers can safely drink poison is not credible; Christians drinking poison suffer the consequences just like anyone else does.[475] The textual variants in the Gospels show that scribes and copyists committed errors in transcription and even made deliberate changes to the texts.[476]

Julian the Apostate, Roman emperor

God's character in the Old Testament is often unworthy of a man, let alone a deity. He is jealous, brutal, capricious, resentful, and cannot control his emotions.[477] The story of the Fall is nonsensical if taken literally. Why would God not create Adam to be able to distinguish between good and evil? How could a serpent talk to Eve?[478] The story of the Tower of Babel appears to be a fable; it is a poor explanation for the differing languages among peoples.[479] Avenging a father's sins on his children is unjust (Exod. 20:5).[480] The Immanuel passage in Isaiah 7:14 is a dubious reference to Jesus (cf. Matt. 1:22-25) and appears to say nothing about a god being born of a virgin.[481] Much in the Gospel accounts is likely mythological or legendary; their content is of questionable historical value.[482] Jesus taught people to obey the Law and Moses did not suggest that his Law was open for revision or subject to revocation; yet, Christians typically reject the Law.[483] Christians should recognize their religious stories as myths like other cultures do.[484]

Despite these weighty criticisms, even the most ardent opponents of Christianity like Julian the Apostate found that they were not able to condemn Christianity entirely. As the emperor Julian attempted to reassert pagan dominance in the Roman Empire, he recognized (albeit reluctantly) that Christians did a markedly better job of caring for the needy than had Roman polytheists.[485] As Christian historian Justo González explains, "While rejecting Christianity, Julian actually learned a great deal from it."[486] In one example, the church in Rome provided aid for as many as 1,500 widows in the year 250.[487] In another, Christians not only rejected the common practice of exposing infants, but even saved and cared for those left out to die by others.[488] As the church father Tertullian (c.155-c.220) famously explained in his *Apology*, outsiders often felt obligated to praise early Christians when they have lived up to their highest and best ideals: "The practice of such a special love brands us in the eyes of some. 'See,' they say, 'how they love one another.'"[489] Although Christian philanthropy has of course not been universally practiced, its ideal has endured throughout the centuries and has inspired great numbers of people to show more compassion for the less fortunate.

[11] Supernatural Scrupulosity
...Dogmatic speculative belief as spiritual malady

> I verily believe that the great good which has been effected in the world by Christianity has been largely counteracted by the pestilent doctrine on which all the Churches have insisted, that honest disbelief in their more or less astonishing creeds is a moral offence, indeed a sin of the deepest dye, deserving and involving the same future retribution as murder and robbery.
>
> —**Thomas Huxley** (1825-1895), British agnostic[490]

> Let them be fierce with you who have no experience of the difficulty with which error is discriminated from truth, and the way of life is found amid the illusions of the world.
>
> —**John Henry Newman** (1801-1890), Roman Catholic cardinal[491]

One of the traditional problems of the Catholic confessional, "scrupulosity" is usually characterized as intense feelings of anxiety wherein someone either exaggerates the degree of personal sinfulness or posits the existence of moral failure where there was none. *The Catholic Encyclopedia* defines scrupulosity as an indication of a conscience that is "seriously warped," swayed by "trifling reasons," "without any solid foundation," and often subject to a persistent "obstinacy" in outlook. In short, it is the "unfounded apprehension and consequently unwarranted fear that something is a sin which, as a matter of fact, is not."[492]

The history of Christian dogmatic controversies seems in large part to have been a lengthy struggle with this very malady. Although thousands upon thousands of religions, sects, and denominations have existed, it is commonplace for individual believers to have an amazing degree of confidence in declaring the most abstract and complex formulations of doctrine. Perhaps not surprisingly, some psychologists of religion have deemed this type of behavior to be thoroughly neurotic in nature.[493] Roman Catholic monk Thomas Merton (1915-1968) seems to accurately (and perhaps somewhat ironically) describe the problem: "We have become marvelous at self-delusion; all the more so, because we have gone to such trouble to convince ourselves of our own absolute infallibility."[494]

A survey below of some of the Trinitarian "heresies" of the first millennium of Christianity provides an intriguing example of "supernatural scrupulosity" in just one area of doctrine. Incredibly, those who have considered such opinions to be either unimportant or dubious were often shunned, judged to be wicked, excommunicated, anathematized, or even persecuted. In the face of so many complex and unverifiable doctrines, humility would seem to urge doubt—or at least a healthy degree of agnosticism. Claimants to such esoteric knowledge thus seem to be, in the words of a Sufi saying, "Those who do not know but play at knowing."[495]

- Adoptionism—The belief that Jesus was a man like any other but was "adopted" by God in a unique way.[496]

- Apollinarianism—The belief that the divine Word of God replaced the natural mind of Jesus.[497]

- Aphthartodocetism—The belief that Christ's human body was "incorruptible" before his Resurrection. The Byzantine emperor Justinian the Great (c.482-565) tried to impose this view as the official orthodoxy of his empire.[498]

- Docetism—The belief held that Christ gave the appearance of a man but was actually a pure spirit.[499]

- Eutychianism—The belief that before the Incarnation Christ had two natures, but that after the Incarnation had only one. This general view was approved by a council of bishops in Ephesus in 449—and then rejected by another council of bishops in Chalcedon in 451.[500]

- Gnosticism—A collection of early Christian groups with a variety of beliefs. Some believed that Jesus was one of 2, 12, 30, or even 365 gods.[501] Some Gnostics prayed to the divine as both Father and

Mother, said the divine Mother could be described as the Holy Spirit, or believed that the Trinity was Father, Mother, and Son.[502]

- Marcionism—The belief that the god of the Old Testament was a different being than the Father of Jesus Christ.[503]
- Melkitism—The belief that the two natures of Christ formed a "hypostatic union" of the Person of Christ.[504] "Melkite" was a pejorative term used by Monophysite Christians against the eventually successful Catholic view—a fact that highlights the reality that "orthodoxy" is a label claimed by every party in controversy.[505]
- Nestorianism—The belief that Christ is two persons (divine and human). The Patriarch Nestorius (c.386-c.450) incurred outrage by his assertion that "God is not a baby two or three months old" and for his criticism of the term "God-bearer" for St. Mary. While usually known as an arch-heretic, Nestorius is a saint in the Assyrian Church of the East.[506]
- Origen's view—The church father Origen (c.185-c.254) posited that the Son was less powerful than the Father and the Holy Spirit was less powerful than both the Father and the Son.[507]
- Patripassianism—Literally, the belief that the Father suffered. This was a pejorative term for those who thought that the Father, Son, and Holy Spirit were different "modes" of the same God.[508]
- Pneumatomachianism—The belief that the Holy Spirit was not formally God, but rather the supreme angel.[509]
- Melchisedechianism—The belief that the Old Testament figure Melchizedek was superior to Jesus because he was without parents and his beginning and end were shrouded in mystery.[510]

Instead of affirming or denying such speculative positions—which could be similarly gathered on a wide array of topics from many different religious faiths—a redirection of focus appears to be in order. There seems to be a much more productive strain of the Christian tradition that insists that spirituality is confirmed only by its results on the human heart. In the words of St. Mark the Ascetic (5th c.), "Each man's knowledge is genuine to the extent it is confirmed by gentleness, humility and love."[511] As some psychological studies have suggested that there is no necessary correlation between metaphysical or religious beliefs and humanitarianism,[512] it would seem worth investigating the common teachings of those from different traditions who were known for being full of "gentleness, humility, and love"—while still having a healthy degree of skepticism about whether their specific metaphysical beliefs were connected to their transformed characters.

[12] The Last Days Daze
...*A historical survey of the Second Coming*

> As the twentieth century ends and the portentous year 2000 looms, all evidence suggests that fundamentalist apocalyptic interpretations, endlessly refashioned, infinitely adaptable, and seemingly impervious to intellectual challenge, will retain their grip on the popular imagination, as they have for centuries.
>
> —**Paul Boyer** (1935-2012), historian correctly predicting future apocalypticism[513]

> Just as it was in the days of Noah, so too it will be in the days of the Son of Man. They were eating and drinking, and marrying and being given in marriage, until the day Noah entered the ark, and the flood came and destroyed all of them.
>
> —Luke 17:26-27

On the authority of Luke's Gospel, we are told that the Second Coming of Jesus will visit a sudden destruction like in the days of Noah's ark. There appears to be an ironic truth about this passage from a skeptical perspective. Namely, that the Second Coming will be the same type of event as Noah's Flood– non-historical and the unfortunate product of a vengeful religious imagination. 2 Peter further supports this general observation— that the Second Coming is just as sure a "fact" as both the formation of the earth "out of water and by means of water" and the destruction of the world through the Noahic Flood (2 Pet. 3:3-7).[514] Thus by an ironic "analogy of faith,"[515] the eschatological or "end times" myths of the early church are best understood to be just as unreliable as its creation and flood stories.

For those who harbor lingering fears of the Last Days, the historical "sense of the faithful" about eschatological events provides a further source of comfort. With some predictable regularity, the Second Coming of Christ has been believed to be an imminent event throughout Christian history. While some Christians have been bold enough to even name specific dates, many others have somehow "known" that the event would be coming in the near future or in their lifetimes.[516] Perhaps not surprisingly, such apocalyptic thinkers are not just confined to the United States or Western Europe, but have been present in various countries in the Middle East, Eastern Europe, Africa, South America, and Asia as well. The intensity of such senses of impending doom has often peaked in times of persecution, social instability, or a heightened sense of marginalization.[517] While relatively more sober religious minds have urged caution with predicting even approximate dates and times, a literal Second Coming itself has standardly been a fundamental doctrine of traditional Christians—being affirmed in the Apostle's Creed, the Nicene Creed, ancient liturgies, and many Protestant confessions and statements of faith. As will be shown below, not only fringe elements but also very prominent figures have been strong believers in an imminent End.

It is perhaps not surprising that devout Christians often become apocalyptic in outlook. Urgency and the imminence of Christ's return are the tenor of many passages in the New Testament letters. James notes that "the coming of the Lord is near" and that "the Judge is standing at the doors!" (James 5:8-9). Paul notes in 1 Corinthians that he is living at "the ends of the ages" (1 Cor. 10:11). 1 Peter also suggests to readers that the Christian community is living "at the end of the ages" (1 Pet. 1:20) and that "the end of all things is near" (1 Pet. 4:7). 1 John declares that it is in fact the "last hour" (1 John 2:18). The Book of Revelation has Jesus stating simply: "Surely I am coming soon" (Rev. 22:20; cf. Rev. 3:11). The events of Revelation are further said to describe "what must soon take place" and that "the time is near" (Rev. 1:1-3). Naturally, Christians have frequently interpreted such verses to mean that Christ was coming back *soon*. Somewhat incredibly perhaps, the unreliability of biblical sensibilities on this point has rarely tarnished general perceptions of the faithful about either the Scriptures or the Second Coming itself.[518]

Interestingly enough, the Coming of a Savior at the "end times" is not just a Christian preoccupation. Jesus and a Rightly Guided Leader ("Mahdi") play a role in the diverse ideas and movements surrounding the Islamic Eschaton and Final Judgment.[519] Baha'i believers hold that Baha'u'llah (1817-1892), who ushered in a new era in the spiritual life of humanity, was in fact a Second Coming of Christ.[520] In Mormon eschatology, Jesus will return and reign from both Jerusalem and Independence, Missouri.[521] Zoroastrians also believe that a Savior will come at the end of the world—and some scholars hold that the apocalypticism of the Abrahamic faiths actually has its genesis in Zoroastrianism.[522] Of course, many traditional Jews still await the initial coming of their Messiah, holding that Jesus of Nazareth was but one of many false Messiahs that have appeared throughout the centuries.

For those interested in examining some of the many historical manifestations of apocalypticism and messianic hopes, what follows is a sampling from the last 21 or so centuries:

In the 2nd c. BCE to the 1st c. CE, the Jewish Qumran community thought it was living in the last days.[523] As noted above, New Testament authors also appear to have believed that the end was at hand.

In the 2nd century, St. Ignatius of Antioch (c.35-c.107) thought he was living in the end times[524] and St. Justin Martyr (c.100-c.165)[525] thought the end would come quickly. The authors of 2 Clement[526] and the Shepherd of Hermas,[527] both considered canonical by many early Catholics, also believed that the end was imminent. The Montanist Christian sect thought the Second Coming would be in 172 in Phrygia in Asia Minor.[528]

In the 3rd century, church father Tertullian (c.155-c.220) thought that the end was "fast approaching"[529] —as did St. Cyprian (c.200-258).[530] Hippolytus (c.170-c.235) expected Christ's return in about 500—a year that would become popular for predictors in both East and West.[531] Hippolytus also wrote that several bishops in Syria and Pontus thought the world was about to end—and that a contemporary Syrian Christian was so certain that he had taken his followers out into the desert to await Christ's return![532] Followers of the Persian prophet Mani (216-c.276), who declared himself the "Apostle of Jesus Christ," believed that when the doctrines of Mani were accepted that the end would come. The Last Days in Manichaeism were predicted to include a Great War, the ultimate victory of the "Church of the Holy Spirit," the Last Judgment of Christ, and the reign of Christ and his Elect after which the world would burn in an immense conflagration lasting 1,468 years.[533]

In the 4th and 5th centuries: Lactantius (c.250-c.318) reiterated the belief that the year 500 was a good bet for Christ's Second Coming.[534] According to St. Athanasius (c.296-373), miracle worker St. Antony of Egypt held in the fourth century that Arianism was the "final heresy that would herald the arrival of the Antichrist."[535] St. Martin of Tours (316-397) thought the "beast" of Revelation was alive during his lifetime[536] and himself declared that repentance was especially urgent, "particularly at this time when the Day of Judgment is close at hand."[537] The fall of Rome in 410 was often thought to be a sign of the end times.[538] The fifth century in general was thought by many Christians to be a time of impending doom.[539]

In the 6th and 7th centuries: Pope St. Gregory the Great (c.540-604) thought the end was coming soon—although he thought that not all the signs would happen in his lifetime.[540] He remarked: "I don't know what is happening in other parts of the world, but in this country where we live the world no longer announces its end but demonstrates it."[541] Some Christian contemporaries of Muhammad (c.570-632) thought that he was the Antichrist.[542] There is some indication that Muhammad himself thought that the world was ending soon.[543] According to one hadith, Jesus' wrath will actually be against Christians when he comes again: "Allah's Messenger said, 'By Him in Whose Hands my soul is, son of Mary (Jesus) will shortly descend amongst you people (Muslims) as a just ruler and will break the Cross and kill the pig and abolish the Jizya (a tax taken from the non-Muslims, who are in the protection, of the Muslim government)."[544]

In the 8th through 10th centuries: Spanish monk Beatus of Liebana (d.798) predicted that the thousand-year reign of Christ would likely begin in 800.[545] Invading Muslims in the 8th century were seen by some Europeans as signs of the Apocalypse.[546] St. Alcuin of York (c.735-804) saw the raids of the Vikings as a sign that the end times were upon him.[547] The Blickling Homilies of the 9th century urged that the end was "very nigh."[548] The end of the second Islamic century brought a large wave of Muslim apocalypticism. Some felt that the apocalyptic figure known as the Mahdi, or Rightly Guided Leader, would appear in 815.[549] Though not convinced himself, the Abbo of Fleury (945-1004) remarked on the fears of the apocalypse sweeping the region of Lorraine at the end of the first millennium.[550] Invading Hungarians in the early 10th century were seen by some as signs of the Last Days.[551]

In the 11th and 12th centuries: The Turks' capture of Jerusalem in 1010 was thought by some Christians to be a sign of the end times.[552] Many participants in the First Crusade believed that their actions were helping to bring about the Apocalypse.[553] Many Muslim faithful believed that Jesus would come back around the 500th year of the Muslim era (early 12th c.) and call the world to submit to Islam.[554] Some Christians in the West thought that the Muslim sultan and conqueror Saladin (1138-1193) was the Antichrist.[555] Monk and abbot Joachim of Fiore (d.1202) claimed that the final battle between Satan and God would occur during his lifetime.[556] St. Norbert of Xanten (d.1134) thought that the Antichrist had already been born and was alive on earth.[557]

In the 13th century, Pope Innocent III thought that "the world was in its last days" and expected the end to come in 1236.[558] The Mongol invasions of Europe in the 13th century were seen by both Jews and Christians as a sign of the end times; anti-Jewish riots were fueled by the Jewish hope that the Mongols were the "lost tribes" of Israel who would rescue Jews from their Christian oppressors.[559] Some Jews also saw the loss of Crusader control in the Holy Land as a sign of the coming Messiah.[560] Some calculated 1260 as the date of their redemption; others reckoned it was 1280 or 1290.[561] Jewish scholar Nahmanides (d.1270) predicted that the Messiah would come in 1358.[562] Holy Roman Emperor Frederick II and his papal contemporaries called each other the Antichrist.[563] Some Franciscans saw St. Francis of Assisi as "the Angel of the Sixth Seal" from the book of Revelation and the sign of the final age of history.[564] In the 13th-century flagellant movement, thousands of lay Christians drew blood in self-flagellations to show repentance, being convinced that the end times were upon them.[565]

In the 14th century, John of Rupescissa (c.1310-1366) taught in his *Handbook in Tribulation* that a pair of Antichrists would come in 1365 and 1370.[566] Wat Tyler's Peasant Revolt in England (1381) was seen as a sign of the last days.[567] Arnold of Villanova (c.1240-1311) thought that the Antichrist would come in 1332 or 1368.[568] Visionary Na Prous Boneta (1296-1328) and several groups of Franciscan "dissidents" thought that Pope John XXII was the Antichrist.[569] Franciscan Frederick of Braunschweig made it known in 1392 that the Antichrist would come in four and a half years.[570]

In the 15th century, many radical Bohemian Taborites and "Wycliffites" believed in the imminent return of Christ.[571] St. Vincent Ferrer (1350-1419) thought that the Great Western Schism (1378-1417) and the resulting multiple popes were indicators that the Antichrist had already been born and the last times were upon his generation.[572] Girolamo Savonarola (1452-1498) preached the imminent end in Florence in the 1480's and 1490's, teaching that the Italian city would be the "New Jerusalem" and that Pope Alexander VI was the Antichrist.[573] Famed explorer Christopher Columbus (c.1451-1506) believed that the world would end in 1656.[574] Several Eastern Christians thought the end of the world would come in the seventh millennium after the creation of the world on September 1, 5508 BC. Many further reckoned that August 31, 1492 would be a pivotal date in the end times.[575] Some Jews thought the Fall of Constantinople in 1453 to be imbued with Messianic importance;[576] some Christians viewed the Sultan of the Ottoman Empire as the Antichrist for his sack of the great city.[577]

In the 16th century, Martin Luther (1483-1546) thought the Last Days were fast approaching.[578] He regarded the Catholic pope as the Antichrist; the pope returned the favor.[579] As Anabaptist historian William Estep further explains, "In common with other evangelicals, apparently all Anabaptists of the sixteenth century believed that the Lord's return was imminent."[580] Some Jews were fixated on the year 1575 as crucial in messianic history—"the year of the return of the scepter to Judah."[581] The prophetic figure Nostradamus (1503-1566) thought the end might come during a planetary alignment in 1565.[582] Many Franciscans in the Spanish American colonies thought the end of time was near since the gospel had now reached all the peoples of the earth (Matt. 24:14).[583] Many Ukrainian Eastern Orthodox Christians regarded the reunion of some Orthodox Churches with the Roman Catholic Church at the Union of Brest-Litovsk (1596) to be an apostasy—and a sign that the end of the world was nigh.[584] Some Muslims in India had a rising feeling about the coming end as the first Islamic millennium was beginning; some believed that Muhammad himself would rise from his grave.[585]

In the 17th century, Archbishop James Ussher (1581-1656), famous for believing that the world was created in 4004 BC, predicted the Second Coming would happen in 1996.[586] Some Puritan followers of Oliver Cromwell believed that the defeat of the English monarchy was a sign of the Second Coming.[587] Many late 17th-century Huguenots in France thought the persecutions they endured at the hands of Louis XIV were a sign of the Last Days.[588] The Great London Fire of 1666, with its destructive imagery and perceived demonic numerology ("666"), was thought by some to be a sign of the end times.[589] Sabbatai Sevi (1626-1676) had many thousands of Jews convinced that he was the long-awaited Messiah. To hasten the end, the faithful performed penitential acts and sold their possessions to pay for the journey to Palestine.[590] In the aftermath of the Patriarch Nikon of Moscow's liturgical reforms in the 1650's, the dissenting "Old Believers" regarded the change to the Latin cross from the traditional 8-cornered cross to be the "abomination of desolation" (Matt. 24:15-28) of the last days.[591] Calling his teachings the Faith of Christ, Russian peasant Danilo Filippov (fl. 1660-1700) declared himself to be the second Incarnation of Christ.[592]

In the 18th century, John Wesley (1703-1791), one of the founders of the Methodist movement, was impressed by Lutheran scholar Johann Bengel's opinions and came to believe that 1836 was the likely date for the millennium.[593] Great Awakening preacher Jonathan Edwards (1703-1758) speculated that the end of the reign of the Antichrist might be in 1866;[594] Edwards also reckoned that Christ's Kingdom might come in the year 2000.[595] The Russian sect known as the Dukhobors or "Spirit-Wrestlers" declared in the 1760's that Christ's return was at hand—and the idolatrous worship of icons should cease immediately.[596] Severe weather of the 1780's brought claims that the world was ending.[597] Claimed miracle-worker Ann Lee (1736-1784) was founder of the Society of Believers in Christ's Second Appearing—more commonly known as the Shakers. Although this time in a feminine incarnation, her followers believed that Mother Ann was the Second Coming.[598]

In the 19th century, the so-called "Prophet Hen of Leeds" created a stir in 1806 by laying eggs that were marked with the words "Christ is coming." Crowds gathered and showed visible signs of repentance—until it was discovered that the eggs had been previously laid and, after inscription, forced back into the hen![599] Luk'ian Petrov Sokolov of Moldova (d.1858) thought that the Second Coming would be in 1836 on Mt. Ararat; miracles supposedly attended his teachings.[600] William Miller (1782-1849), founder of the Millerite sect that was a precursor to Seventh Day Adventists, thought that Christ would return in 1843 and then 1844; his failed predictions were known by his many followers as "The Great Disappointment."[601] Also in 1844, the Báb (1819-1850), declared that he was in fact the Mahdi foretold in Muslim eschatology; Baha'is consider the Báb to be the forerunner of Baha'u'llah (1817-1892), the foretold Second Coming of Christ.[602] An apocalyptic group led by Silvestre Jose dos Santos in Brazil believed that they would peacefully march on Jerusalem and usher in the Kingdom of God; most were killed by government troops in 1820.[603] The early Mormons, or Latter-Day Saints, held that their sect was a restoration of the gospel and a sign of the return of Christ was imminent.[604] Prominent 19th-century American preacher D.L. Moody (1837-1899) was a fervent believer in the imminent end.[605] Amish settler Jonas Stutzmann (1788-1871) believed that the Second Coming would come in 1853; he even built a large chair for an expected over-sized Jesus to sit in![606]

In the early 20th century, Pentecostal believers in the "Topeka Pentecost" and the Holy Spirit's presence at the Asuza Street revival thought Jesus' return was imminent.[607] Charles Taze Russell (1852-1916), founder of the Jehovah's Witnesses, believed that Christ would be coming back in 1914.[608] Some American fundamentalists during World War I saw the times as fulfilling the prophecies of Daniel and Revelation.[609] The Korean-based Hyoo-go group, Mission for the Coming Days, believed that Christ was coming back on October 28, 1992 at 10:00 AM.[610] Billy Graham (1918-2018), renowned American evangelist and spiritual advisor to multiple U.S. Presidents, stated in 1950 that the apocalypse would come in one to two years.[611] African-American religious leader Father Divine (c.1876-1965), founder of the International Peace Mission Movement, claimed to be God incarnate and the Second Coming of Christ.[612] Hal Lindsey (b. 1929), author of the best-selling book *The Late Great Planet Earth*, taught that Jesus would likely return in 1988.[613] Canadian biblical prophecy enthusiast Grant R. Jeffrey (1948-2012) predicted the end of the world in 2000.[614] Fascist dictators Adolf Hitler and especially Benito Mussolini were frequently regarded as the Antichrist after their ascent to power—some creative expositors noted that Hitler's name could be numerically rendered as "666."[615] Preachers in the 20th century used the threat of nuclear war,

Islamic fundamentalism, ozone layer depletion, global warming, pollution, AIDS, illegal drugs, and abortion as signs of the end times.[616]

In the 21st century, radio preacher Harold Camping (1921-2013) predicted that the end of the world would come on September 6, 1994—and then on May 21, 2011 and then again on October 21, 2011.[617] Ann Graham Lotz (b.1948), likely repeating the error of her father Billy Graham, is convinced that Jesus will return in her generation.[618] Patriarch Kirill of the Russian Orthodox Church declared in 2013 that gay marriage was a sign of the Apocalypse and then in 2019 that the Antichrist may gain world control through the Internet.[619] A 2009 Pew Research article claimed that 20% of American Christians believe that Christ will return in their lifetime; a full 79% believed he would return someday.[620] A 2010 Pew Research article noted that 41% of Americans believe that the Second Coming will likely occur before 2050.[621] According to a 2012 Pew Research Center poll, more than 50% of Muslims in 9 out of 23 Muslim nations polled believe that the coming of the Mahdi will take place during their lifetimes; ISIS also holds that the Mahdi and Jesus are coming soon.[622] Current claimants to be the Second Coming of Jesus include Moses Hlongwane from South Africa, INRI from Brazil, Jesus of Kitwe from Zambia, Jesus Matayoahi from Japan, and Vissarion from Russia—who has 5,000 followers and has written a 16-volume *Last Testament*.[623]

The diverse and often intense beliefs about fantastic end times events are a particularly poignant example of the human susceptibility to delusional thinking. Apocalypticism also seems to be among the most powerful examples of the human proclivity to increase anxiety and suffering through fruitless endeavors and distractions. A Zen verse from the 13th-century appears to present a better perspective. Instead of focusing on an unknown and imagined future, monk Mumon Ekai taught that peace of mind came through awareness of beauty in the present moment:

> In spring, hundreds of flowers; in autumn,
>   a harvest moon;
> In summer, a refreshing breeze; in winter,
>   snow will accompany you.
> If useless things do not hang in your mind,
> Any season is a good season for you.[624]

[13] Another Wise Lord

...Zoroastrianism and its links to the Abrahamic faiths

Evidence of the similarities between Zoroastrianism and Judaism, Christianity, and Islam are diverse and range from theological to ethical to eschatological matters. Of particular interest in this respect are the following shared concepts and beliefs:

- God and Satan (or the devil)
- Angels and demons
- Heaven and hell (and Purgatory in Christianity)
- Resurrection of the body and life everlasting
- Individual judgment at death and cosmic last judgment
- Arrival of the Messiah
- Cosmic events during the end of the world
- The Armageddon battle followed by a millennium period. ...

[I]t is hardly conceivable that some of the characteristic ideas and practices in Judaism, Christianity, and Islam came into being without Zoroastrian influence.

—**S.A. Nigosian**, modern Zoroastrian scholar[625]

While traditional understandings in the "Abrahamic" faiths[626] posit that their religious tenets came in unadulterated form directly from God, critical scholars standardly hold that the beliefs of Zoroastrianism significantly influenced the doctrinal content of Judaism, Christianity, and Islam. As opposed to the rather vague ideas of the afterlife in the Torah and the other pre-exilic Jewish Scriptures, for example,[627] Judaism after Cyrus the

Great—the Zoroastrian who ended the traumatic Babylonian Captivity of the Jews in 538 BCE[628] —seems to have adopted new perspectives on Satan, hell, heaven, bodily resurrection, and the Final Judgment.[629] In a manner thoroughly common to Zoroastrian research, one scholar describes this general dynamic:

> It is widely accepted by biblical scholars that the later Jewish concepts of the devil, hell, the afterlife, the resurrection, the end of the world and savior imagery were all coloured by Zoroastrianism beliefs which, of course, have affected the very foundations of Christianity. Theologically as well as geographically, Iran, the bridge between East and West, has contributed immensely in the field of religion.[630]

Zoroastrians, who are known as "Parsis" in India due to their Persian origin, worship the god Ahura Mazda—a name meaning "Wise Lord."[631] Ahura Mazda is believed to be eternal, omniscient, omnibenevolent, uncreated, holy, the font of all truth, and the source of all good divine and earthly beings. Zoroastrians hold that Ahura Mazda's revelation to humanity was disclosed to the prophet Zarathustra, often known in the West by the Greek name Zoroaster. The Zoroastrian religion, though perhaps the smallest of the world religions today,[632] was once the official religion of the great empires of Persia. The Achaemenian Empire (c.550-330 BC), the Parthian Empire (c.141BC-224 CE), and the Sasanian Empire (c.224-651 CE) were all Zoroastrian realms.[633] The long run of the political might of the worshippers of Ahura Mazda ended with the Muslim conquests of the 7th century CE.[634]

While obscure to most moderns, Zoroastrians were influential in the ancient world and references to them are found within the pages of all the Abrahamic Scriptures. Due to his role in ending the Babylonian Captivity, the Jewish Scriptures hold Cyrus in highest esteem; the Zoroastrian Persian is in fact the only gentile in Holy Writ referred to as the Lord's "messiah" or "anointed" (Isa. 45:1).[635] The Gospel of Matthew has Zoroastrian priests or "magi" bow to the Christ child (Matt. 2:1-12).[636] The Qur'an demonstrates a familiarity with the magi or "Magians" as rival believers as well. Sura 22:17 states: "As for the true believers, the Jews, the Sabaeans, the Christians, *the Magians*, and the pagans, Allah will judge them on the Day of Resurrection."[637]

Like many world religions, Zoroastrianism has commonly presented itself as the only path to salvation. This sentiment persists among many of the faithful even into modern, more ecumenical times. In *How Different Religions View Death and Afterlife*, the question "What happens after death to people who are not of your faith?" is posed to the adherents from several different faiths. The Zoroastrian response is simply, "Their souls are consigned to hell until the final resurrection, at which time they are purified of their error and then saved." The vast majority of people go to the torments of hell—immediate salvation is thus only for the "good Zoroastrian."[638] While such exclusivity in such a small group may seem offensive or even preposterous to many, such notions of a pure and small remnant among the world's wicked majority is relatively commonplace in Judaism, Christianity, and Islam as well.[639] Jesus of Nazareth himself is said to have declared: "¹⁴ For the gate is narrow and the road is hard that leads to life, and there are few who find it" (Matt. 7:13-14). And in the words of 2 Esdras from the Bible of the Slavonic Orthodox, Armenian Orthodox, and Ethiopian Orthodox Churches, "there are more who perish than those who will be saved, as a wave is greater than a drop of water" (2 Esdras 9:15b-16).

Fostered in part due to a complex relationship of mutual exchange,[640] there are many other parallels between "the Good Religion" and the Abrahamic faiths. Like Christians, Muslims, and Jews, Zoroastrians believe that their faith originated from a divine message given to humanity. The Avesta—and especially the Gathas—are deemed to be sacred books that were revealed by Ahura Mazda himself.[641] Zoroastrianism also has a doctrine of free will[642] and holds that God will judge the thoughts, words, and deeds of everyone.[643] The ancient Persian faith has also denigrated the value of doubt and romanticized martyrdom. As one 9th-century CE Zoroastrian dogmatic text explains,

> And it should be said: "I am without doubt concerning the Good Religion which the Mazda-worshippers have accepted. Not for the love of body or soul, not for better or longer life, not for threatened death, will I renounce the good religion of the Mazda-worshippers. I am without doubt concerning it. I do not praise other religions, nor honour them, nor believe in them …."[644]

Like the Abrahamic faiths, Zoroastrians have been the persecutors of heretics, apostates, and members of other religions.[645] They have also been the object of intense persecution and systematic discrimination. It is traditionally held that the Parsis who fled to India in the 10th century largely did so for the sake of religious freedom;[646] it is well known that Zoroastrians have been persecuted by the Islamic State of Iran.[647] Despite such oppression, Zoroastrians have continued to maintain a high confidence in the rectitude of their own religion over others. As one 20th-century Zoroastrian catechist remarked, "The Zoroastrian religion overshadows all other religions with its superiority in the same way ... [that] a great tree overshadows small plants."[648] Likewise, other religions have often been considered by Ahura-Mazda's followers to be not only false, but demonic in origin.[649]

Zoroastrianism has also had its sects, theological controversies, schisms, orthodoxies and heresies, textual controversies, historical developments, and progressive movements. Two major historical heresies of Zoroastrianism were Zurvanism, which regarded "Time" as the first cause, and Mazdakism, which appears to have adopted elements of Gnosticism and Manichaeism.[650] Like Christianity, Zoroastrianism has a strong doctrine of the restoration of creation; a "healer of existence" is one term for a Zoroastrian believer.[651] The ancient faith also has a "Holy Spirit," Spenta Mainyu, who is considered both part of Ahura Mazda and distinct from him.[652]

Of course, Zoroastrianism is very different from the Abrahamic religions as well. For example, Zoroastrians have traditionally exposed their dead to vultures on *dakhmas* or "Towers of Silence."[653] Both burial and cremation have been traditionally viewed as morally reprehensible.[654] Old taboos also required the proper disposal of fingernail clippings, lost teeth, and hair due to their polluting qualities.[655] Traditionally, Zoroastrians washed with cow or bull urine to restore purity.[656] The satanic being in Zoroastrianism, Ahriman, is thought to have made all noxious animals and diseases. Among other creatures, he is said to have created water rats, frogs, and cats.[657] After sneezing or yawning, Parsis say "Broken be Ahriman," believing that sneezing is caused by the work of evil spiritual forces.[658] Perhaps surprisingly, Zoroastrianism rejects asceticism and regards fasting as a sin.[659]

Zoroastrians have traditionally worshipped at fire-temples. They have had such a high regard for the holiness of fire that many have mistakenly thought that they actually worshipped fire itself.[660] Interestingly, it is debated whether Zoroastrianism should be considered more monotheistic or polytheistic in nature.[661] Traditional Zoroastrianism encourages the worship of *yazatas* ("beings worthy of worship") and greater divine beings called *amesha spentas*.[662] The ancient faith appears to have become more monotheistic in emphasis through its contact with the Abrahamic religions.[663] Hell is not eternal in Zoroastrianism—although it is said to last for thousands of years. Mazda-worshippers in fact believe that the concept of an eternal hell is both immoral and incongruent with Ahura-Mazda's goodness.[664] The faithful are also known for their care for the elderly and commonly endow and build hospitals and hospices (*dharamsalas*) to provide for them.[665]

Textual issues pertaining to Zoroastrian scriptures are generally even more troubled and difficult than those of the Abrahamic faiths. The destruction wrought by Alexander the Great,[666] the Muslim conquests and occupation, and the general ravages of time have meant the loss of many holy texts. Additionally, Zoroastrian teachings generally had a much longer period of oral transmission than either Christianity or Islam.[667] As one scholar notes about the section of the Zoroastrian canon generally thought to be most authentic and reliable: "The Gathas were transmitted orally by the magi for centuries, with some variations and additions, before they were finally written down."[668] Zoroaster's dates, traditionally given as 628-551 BCE,[669] are widely disputed and generally regarded as uncertain. He may have lived sometime in the 13th through 12th centuries BCE[670] or the 17th to 15th centuries BCE[671] —though some scholars give different ranges and others doubt that he existed at all.[672]

Zoroastrianism provides an intriguing example of not only the diversity of human religious experience, but also the varied factors that give rise to modern religious expressions. Although the relative obscurity of Zoroastrianism today may suggest that it is unimportant or even trivial to modern life, its largely hidden influence on Judaism, Christianity, and Islam highlights the reality that humanity is often oblivious to the sources of its current religious consciousness. In the words of scholar Mary Boyce, Zoroastrianism's tiny size today may hide the surprising reality that it might have "exerted more influence on the religious history of mankind than any other single faith."[673]

[14] Unfulfilling Prophecies
...The dubiousness of predictive biblical prophecy

If by a prophet we are to suppose a man to whom the Almighty communicated some event that would take place in future, either there were such men, or there were not. If there were, it is consistent to believe that the event so communicated would be told in terms that could be understood, and not related in such a loose and obscure manner as to be out of the comprehension of those that heard it, and so equivocal as to fit almost any circumstance that might happen afterwards. It is conceiving very irreverently of the Almighty, to suppose he would deal in this jesting manner with mankind ….

—**Thomas Paine** (1737-1809), deist and American patriot[674]

The Bible … does not contain a single sentence that could not have been written by a man or woman living in the first century.

—**Sam Harris** (b.1967), *Letter to a Christian Nation*[675]

Predictive prophecy[676] has often been touted as one of the weightiest proofs for the divine origin of the Bible.[677] This has been a long-standing and often confident claim among traditional Christians. Early church father Justin Martyr (c.100-c.165), for instance, called the predictive prophecy of Scripture "the strongest and truest evidence" of the truth of his Christian faith.[678] Likewise, the Roman Catholic Baltimore Catechism of 1891 boldly states that "The prophets, taken together, foretold so accurately all the circumstances of the birth, life, death, resurrection and glory of the Redeemer that no one who carefully studied their writings could fail to recognize Him when He came."[679] Reformed and evangelical intellectual R.C. Sproul (1939-2017) had similarly confident assertions:

> One of the most astounding things, of course, is that the Bible literally has thousands of testable historical prophecies, cases in which events were clearly foretold, and that both the foretelling and the fulfillment are the matter of the historical record. The very dimension of the sheer fulfillment of prophecy of the Old Testament Scriptures should be enough to convince anyone that we are dealing with a supernatural piece of literature.[680]

While traditionalists frequently assert that denying the reality of the prophetic dimension of the Bible is based on a "theological bias that assumes true prophecy cannot take place,"[681] an analysis of the texts themselves rather suggests the greater likelihood of more naturalistic explanations. Since a prediction of a series of future events in a precise and comprehensive way would of course be an utterly amazing occurrence, other more mundane explanations would always seem to be more probable unless there was quite compelling evidence to the contrary.

Hence, while it is not at all surprising that traditional Christians have made claims about predictive prophecy, these lofty sorts of assertions regarding prophetic clarity and the confidence with which they are held are a bit bewildering.[682] For out of all the supposedly prophetic statements in the Scriptures, there appear to be none that give any persuasive evidence of an ability to tell the future. As has often been noted by skeptics,[683] fulfilled biblical prophecies seem to generally rely on: (1) taking language out of context, (2) utilizing scriptural material that does not appear to be predictive in nature, (3) relying on vaguely-worded and non-specific predictions, (4) creating typological or symbolic "fulfillments" that have questionable links to authorial intent, (5) rejecting the possibility that New Testament events could have been fabricated or distorted to match prophetic passages, and/or (6) referencing predictions that do not appear in the record until *after* the supposed fulfillments have already occurred.[684]

A review of a few "fulfilled" prophecies about Jesus in the New Testament may help illustrate the point. While the Gospel of Matthew claims that Isaiah has a prophecy of the Virgin Birth, serious difficulties arise as the young woman in Isaiah was to name the child Immanuel (and not

"Jesus"—cf. Matt. 1:21),[685] there is no mention that Immanuel's mother conceived without sexual relations first,[686] and the historical period described in Isaiah appears tied to more immediate events:[687]

Matthew 1:20b-25

[A]n angel of the Lord appeared to him in a dream and said, "Joseph, son of David, do not be afraid to take Mary as your wife, for the child conceived in her is from the Holy Spirit. She will bear a son, and you are to name him Jesus, for he will save his people from their sins." All this took place to fulfil what had been spoken by the Lord through the prophet: ***"Look, the virgin shall conceive and bear a son, and they shall name him Emmanuel",*** which means, "God is with us." When Joseph awoke from sleep, he did as the angel of the Lord commanded him; he took her as his wife, but had no marital relations with her until she had borne a son; and he named him Jesus.

Isaiah 7:14-17

"Therefore the Lord himself will give you a sign. ***Look, the young woman is with child and shall bear a son, and shall name him Immanuel.*** He shall eat curds and honey by the time he knows how to refuse the evil and choose the good. For before the child knows how to refuse the evil and choose the good, the land before whose two kings you are in dread will be deserted. The Lord will bring on you and on your people and on your ancestral house such days as have not come since the day that Ephraim departed from Judah—the king of Assyria."

The NIV Study Bible tries to salvage the traditional doctrine of the Virgin Birth by noting, "Mt 1:23 apparently understood the woman mentioned here to be a type (a foreshadowing) of the Virgin Mary. ... Jesus was the final fulfillment of this prophecy, for he was 'God with us' in the fullest sense."[688] While such a conjectural implication of course cannot be disproven, it does not seem at all what was being communicated in context—and would appear to fly in the face of claims that alleged prophetical fulfillments "should be enough to convince anyone that we are dealing with a supernatural piece of literature."

Likewise, though history remembers Jesus as "Jesus of Nazareth," there is no discernable prediction in the Hebrew Bible of Christ's hometown. Due to the late founding of Nazareth, the Old Testament in fact does not ever even mention the town or its inhabitants. Despite this fact, the Gospel of Matthew nonetheless seems to claim that Old Testament predicted what it did not mention: "There he made his home in a town called Nazareth, so that what had been spoken through the prophets might be fulfilled, 'He will be called a Nazorean'" (Matt. 2:23).[689] *The New Oxford Annotated Bible* offers this common, speculative resolution: "There is a similarity in sound and possibly meaning between the Aramaic word for *Nazareth* and the Hebrew word translated *branch* (Isa 11.1)."[690] This "fulfillment" thus seems not only unconnected to an actual prediction, but also quite a tenuous parallel in general. *The NIV Study Bible*'s general statements regarding Matthew's "fulfilled" prophecies seem to again underscore the overstated nature of claims regarding alleged biblical foretelling: "Matthew speaks of the OT being fulfilled, i.e., events in NT times that were prophesied in the OT—a powerful testimony to the divine origin of Scripture and its accuracy even in small details."[691] From a more skeptical perspective, the "small details" suggest that it is rather imaginative and speculative thinking at work here—and that we likely have not a heavenly but a very human process on display.

As another example, a prophetic fulfilment claimed for the flight of the infant Jesus out of Egypt seems also to be not only non-predictive, but also not referring to the Messiah. The fact that Hosea tells us that God's "son" is Israel—and further notes that this son is a sinful idolater—would suggest that Matthew again is ignoring context:

Matthew 2:13-15	Hosea 11:1-2
Now after they had left, an angel of the Lord appeared to Joseph in a dream and Said, "Get up, take the child and his mother, and flee to Egypt, and remain there until I tell you; for Herod is about to search for the child, to destroy him." Then Joseph got up, took the child and his mother by night, and went to Egypt, and remained there until the death of Herod. This was to fulfil what had been spoken by the Lord through the prophet, **"Out of Egypt I have called my son."**	When Israel was a child, I loved him, and **out of Egypt I called my son.** The more I called them, the more they went from me; they kept sacrificing to the Baals, and offering incense to idols.

Likewise, Matthew's claim that Isaiah was speaking of Jesus' forerunner John the Baptist appears both conjectural and indiscernible from context (Matt. 3:1-3 vs. Isa. 39:5-40:5). Further, the "fulfilled" prophecy in Matthew about the Massacre of the Innocents looks unrelated to (what's probably) the recording of a past event in Jeremiah (Matt. 2:16-18 vs. Jer. 31:15-17).[692] While retreat can always be made to a "type" or symbolic parallel, these are again not the kinds of specific and impressive predictions about Jesus' life that are so frequently promised.

Perhaps the most utilized prophetic passage in the Hebrew Bible, the famous "Suffering Servant" passage of Isaiah 52:13-53:12 has similar problems. Both Jewish believers and skeptical biblical scholars frequently interpret the passage as referring to the nation of Israel (cf. Isa. 49:3)[693]—and thus not foretelling a coming Messiah at all. Even if we grant that this passage is in fact an attempt at a predictive messianic prophecy, the vagueness of the text provides significant reasons to doubt the presence of a supernatural hand. Some of the content describes life events that are altogether common in human experience, and the claims that the servant would grow up (v. 2), have an average or unimpressive appearance (v. 2), and be familiar with suffering and infirmity (v. 3) could be applied to a wide swath of humanity. Likewise, it seems somewhat unremarkable that the servant would be "numbered with the transgressors" at death (v. 12; Luke 22:37), particularly since Isaiah already asserted that all people without exception are in fact transgressors (v. 6; cf. Rom. 3:23). Further, it is altogether common for religious leaders to be scorned by some (v. 3, etc.), revered by others (52:13), and thought to be highly regarded by a god (53:11-12). A parallel with other ancient Mediterranean soothsaying also seems noteworthy here. Apollo's oracle at Delphi in ancient Greece, for instance, famously used vague and cryptic statements as to make it "impossible for the oracle to be categorically wrong in its response."[694]

Again assuming that this passage is messianic, the repeated claim that the servant would not "open his mouth" (v. 7) would find an interesting parallel to Jesus being (mostly) silent before his accusers (Matt. 27:11-14; Mark 15:5, Luke 23:8-9; cf. Acts 8:32). However, the Gospel of John has Christ "opening his mouth" two times before the high priest and four times before Pilate—bringing the parallel into question after all (John 18-19). Since all humans of course die (and many have died brutally), even the supposed predictions regarding the violent nature of the servant's death (see v. 8, etc.) would seem to be more likely an educated guess than a supernatural prediction—especially when the common nature of religiously-related martyrdoms is considered (e.g., Socrates, Jewish martyrs under the Seleucids, many early Christian bishops, Mani, Ali, various heretics during the Middle Ages, martyrs of Jewish pogroms, Sufis like Al-Hallāj, various Protestant and Roman Catholics during the Reformation, the Báb, Eastern Orthodox leaders under communist dictatorships, Gandhi, Martin Luther King, Jr., etc.). More to the point, there is no mention in Isaiah of how exactly the servant will be descended from King David, or that he will be born to Mary and Joseph, or arrive during the reign of Augustus Caesar, or be raised in Nazareth, or be followed by twelve apostles, or institute a eucharistic meal, or cleanse the temple in Jerusalem, or be sentenced by Pontius Pilate, or wear a crown of thorns, or be killed by Roman-style crucifixion,[695] or be bodily raised from the dead on the third day, or ascend into heaven. And while the typical modern historian appears markedly more reliable than any biblical author, it nevertheless seems telling, despite an alleged connection with the same Spirit, that Gospel-writers looking backward so commonly have far more details than prophets do looking forward.

It also should be emphasized that events written in the New Testament could of course have been distorted or fabricated to fit supposed prophecies in the Old. For instance, John is the only gospel that has John the Baptist calling out to Jesus as "the Lamb of God who takes away the sin of the world" (John 1:29)—perhaps the words are meant to invoke the "lamb that is led to the slaughter" in Isa. 53:7.[696] Likewise, the character Joseph of Arimathea could be introduced or given wealth in the Gospels (see Matt. 27:57 vs. John 19:38-42)[697] as a hearkening back to the servant having "his tomb with the rich" (Isa. 53:9).[698] While the term "fabrication" may sound somewhat sinister at first consideration, it does not necessarily imply any sort of ill-intentioned deceit. Within a certain religious framework, devout believers could have trusted a pious but mistaken source—or even reasoned that certain events "must have happened" because of either an alleged Old Testament prophecy or other perceptions about what an incarnate god would necessarily do (or not do).[699] As St. Paul supposedly knew what had historically happened at the Last Supper "from the Lord" directly (1 Cor. 11:23-25), perhaps authors of the Gospels even felt that God was actually telling them—either in prayer or otherwise—what had once transpired in the life of their living Lord.[700] And finally, while the sacrificial nature of the servant's death in Isa. 53:10-12 may provide a remarkable parallel to Jesus for traditional believers, such unverifiable theological claims about the meaning of someone's demise (along with the problematic ethics about the efficacy of substitutionary human suffering), could seemingly be applied to any suffering and death at will.[701]

These sorts of investigations and analyses of biblical prophecy are always fairly complicated (not to mention somewhat conjectural), but fortunately infallible skill in the art of biblical interpretation seems unnecessary to reach a solid conclusion anyway. While the aforementioned six guidelines would appear sufficient to discount the likelihood of predictive biblical prophecy, perhaps a more comprehensive and convincing reason for doubt can be found in the fact that the level of knowledge in biblical prophecies seems to be fully constrained to the known realities of the ancient world.[702] Revealingly, no prophecies in the Bible envision future technological, geographical, or scientific discoveries or findings. In short, it would seem that the mind of the biblical god was completely ignorant of the discoveries of the modern world:

> Written before the Age of Exploration, there is no awareness of Australia, Antarctica, or the Americas. Written before the invention of telescopes, there is no description of nebulae, asteroids, solar flares, ringed planets, or red giant stars. Likewise, there is no understanding of the speed of light, the vast distances of space, the immense number of galaxies, nor even the heliocentric solar system. Written before the invention of the microscope, there is no knowledge of protozoa, bacteria, the cell, or other microscopic structures or beings. Written before the advent of modern transportation, there is no knowledge of the future rise of the locomotive, the automobile, the steamship, the diesel engine, or the airplane. Written before the dawn of the computer age, there are no predictions for the coming of electronic devices and the internet. Likewise, the telephone, telegraph, typewriter, and even printing press are beyond its vision. Written before the rise of modern medicine, there is no concept of vaccination, no understanding of DNA, no knowledge of how to develop modern pharmaceuticals, and no directions on how to perform life-saving surgical techniques. Written before the invention of modern weaponry, there is no awareness of the possibility of the manufacture of guns, modern artillery, grenades, submarines, battleships, missiles, tanks, or nuclear warheads. Written before the 19th century, there is no knowledge of the earth's prehistory, of dinosaurs, of evolution, or of the process of fossilization.[703] Written before the 20th century, there is no concept of plate tectonics or the possibility of space travel and visiting other planets.[704]

Simply put, the general character of the prophetic material provided in the Scriptures appears insufficient to justify belief that it was inspired by a Being that could predict the future. What we seem to be seeing more than "the strongest and truest evidence" of supernatural foretelling is rather a view into the complex and sometimes tenacious beliefs that arise in the human religious imagination.

While such conclusions seem reasonable, a further challenge remains. For after letting go of a faulty or fallacious belief, it can be altogether too easy to slip into a spirit of condescension or even antagonism toward those who are either unable or unwilling to follow. Yet as Zen master Thich Nhat Hanh (b. 1926) explains, discarding false beliefs is most liberating when it is not merely intellectual—but also part of a means to further transformation:

> When your mind is liberated your heart floods with compassion: compassion for yourself, for having undergone countless sufferings because you were not yet able to relieve yourself of false views, hatred, ignorance, and anger; and compassion for others because they do not yet see and are still imprisoned by false views, hatred, and ignorance and continue to create suffering for themselves and others.[705]

[15] Pondering Parallels

...Parallels between Christianity and other Mediterranean religions

And when we say also that the Word, who is the first-birth of God, was produced without sexual union, and that He, Jesus Christ, our Teacher, was crucified and died, and rose again, and ascended into heaven, we propound nothing different from what you believe regarding those whom you esteem sons of Jupiter.

—**St. Justin Martyr** (c.100-c.165), early church father[706]

Christians could not fail to note certain parallels between the sacred meals of the mystery cults and the sacraments of the Christians; the closer the parallels, the more convinced were Christians that these pagan sacraments were a diabolical parody of the Christian rites, directly inspired by evil spirits in order to lead the faithful astray.

—**Stephen Neill and Tom Wright**, modern New Testament scholars[707]

In his *First Apology*, early church father Justin Martyr explained that similarities between his form of Christianity and Roman paganism were in fact the result of the trickery of demonic powers. He argues that devils knew the writings of the Old Testament prophets and produced false wonders and stories to confuse humanity about the True Religion.[708] Alternatively, when he thought that Judaism predated pagan beliefs, he ascribed the similarities to pagan plagiarism.[709] Justin further argued that, because of these similarities, the Roman authorities should not persecute Christians—suggesting that it would be hypocritical to condemn people whose ideas were so similar to one's own.[710]

Justin includes the following among his doctrinal parallels between Christianity and paganism:

- Mystery rites involving wine[711]
- Baptismal rites[712]
- The suffering, death, and rising of gods and heroes[713]
- The ascension of gods and heroes into the heavens[714]
- Rewards and punishments in the afterlife[715]
- Virgin births[716]
- The future renewal of the world through fire[717]
- Miracles involving the healing of the lame, the sick, and the blind[718]

Although drawing parallels between religions can be the cause of oversimplification and inaccurate generalizations, the value of considering such comparisons is nonetheless clear to see. Studying the characteristics of Mediterranean religions that predated Christianity can inform about the cultural milieu in which the new faith arose; they can also provide potential explanations for the development of many early Christian beliefs and practices. The parallels appear to suggest that Christianity followed (or further developed) many patterns of other pre-existing Mediterranean religious traditions[719] —and perhaps even that people's religious imaginations tend to work in similar ways. Furthermore, while it is clear that Christianity borrowed heavily from Judaism, it also seems highly likely that Judaism itself was influenced by Zoroastrianism and religions of ancient Mesopotamia.[720] While Judaism and Christianity have distinctive elements and have of course influenced other religions in turn, the similarities in themes, concepts, and practices make the notion of Judeo-Christian religious purity a tough pill to swallow.

Often called the "Father of Ancient History," Herodotus was a 5th-century BCE Greek who sought to record historical and cultural information about societies in the ancient world. Although Herodotus is not a modern historian, he nonetheless displays a lively curiosity and significant investigative skills. He also demonstrates a clear intent to follow what is now considered a primary goal of careful historiography: "I am obliged to record the things I am told, but I am certainly not required to believe them."[721] His remarks and observations often transport the reader to a far different time and place, providing vivid accounts of the cultural groups that existed in the fifth century before the birth of Christ and of the ways that ancient peoples often wove miracles into their renderings of history. Herodotus' *Histories* thus provide a fitting platform to further investigate the types of parallels that Justin addressed in his *First Apology*.

In addition to confirming some of the parallels that Justin mentions, Herodotus demonstrates the existence of many more. While Samson (as well as David) are said to have killed myriads in the Old Testament, Herodotus shows that Hercules was believed to have done so as well.[722] While Jews are well known for their dietary restrictions, other cultures likewise had religious reasons for avoiding certain foods.[723] While the Hebrew Scriptures explain circumcision as the mark of a special divine covenant with the Israelites, Herodotus notes that Colchians, Egyptians, Ethiopians, Phoenicians, and Macrones also engaged in the practice.[724] God is said to have come down and inhabited the Israelite temple in the Bible, but other Mediterranean gods were thought to have entered temples as well.[725] Often just assumed to be standard fare in religions, other Mediterranean faiths held the speculative beliefs that petitionary prayer,[726] predictive prophecy,[727] and dreams[728] were means of (or manifestations of) communication with gods. There are also stories of divine voices, confirmed by witnesses or even coming from a cloud.[729] Likewise, Herodotus shows that animal sacrifice is commonly thought to be effective to propitiate gods or expiate sin—as is human sacrifice at times.[730] Sacred genealogies, found in the Old and New Testaments, also reflect a common Mediterranean practice of linking important figures to gods or heroes of the past.[731] While Christians and Hebrews alike claimed divine providence in their lives, the pagan gods were also known to orchestrate events and even "call" people to fulfill specific roles.[732] Gods likewise levy curses, control the weather, bestow miraculous powers, cause spiritual possession,[733] and are even called "Saviors."[734] While the Holy Spirit caused men to speak in different languages in Acts, an oracle of Apollo also miraculously spoke in a foreign tongue.[735] While King Herod is eaten by worms and then killed by God after blaspheming, the queen Pheretime suffered an almost identical fate due to "retribution from the gods."[736]

German theologian Adolf von Harnack (1851-1930) urged the acknowledgment of human fallibility and finitude when making historical assessments: "In history absolute judgments are impossible. ... Such judgments are the creation only of feeling and will; they are a subjective act."[737] Likewise when considering religious parallels, each enquirer should cast certainty aside and rather make a determination about probabilities. Which is more likely, that parallels arose through a cultural appropriation that came through interactions in trade, warfare, and the migration of people groups combined with a common human psychology? Or that an actual struggle between divine powers and demons brought forth similar miracle stories, theological beliefs, and religious practices? Perhaps we can do no better than to heed Justin Martyr's own advice, who pleads with his readers to assess traditional beliefs "after an accurate and searching investigation," making it our goal to attempt "to honour and love only what is true."[738]

[16] No Law at All

...The deep flaws of the Old Testament Law

As to the Old Testament, I insist that all the bad passages were written by men; that those passages were not inspired. I insist that a being of infinite goodness never commanded man to enslave his fellow-man, … never ordered one nation to exterminate another, and never told a husband to kill his wife because she suggested the worshipping of some other God.

—**Robert Ingersoll** (1833-1899), the "Great Agnostic"[739]

This is a judgment of hatred, "We have a law, and according to the law he ought to die (Jn 19:7)."

—**St. Bernard of Clairvaux** (1090-1153)[740]

In his classic apologetic work *Mere Christianity*, C.S. Lewis (1898-1963) argued that every person had an innate sense of the divine moral law that governed the universe. For examples, he described how people generally get upset when others take someone's seat, or cut in line, or fail to engage in some reciprocal sharing with some pieces of orange.[741] Assuming such arguments proved the existence of a divine moral law, they would also seem to far more conclusively disprove the divine authorization for literal readings[742] of the statutes and commands of the Old Testament—many of which appear to reinforce injustice and cruelty on a scale exponentially more weighty than the rather mundane examples that Lewis references to prove his point.[743]

Although sometimes overlooked in skeptical critiques of biblical ethics, it is indeed true that some of the laws and ordinances in the Pentateuch or Torah[744] do show a sense of justice and care for the needy (Lev. 19:10; Deut. 10:18-19, Deut. 14:29, Deut. 15:7-11, Deut. 24:10-22, etc.).[745] A form of the golden rule is found in the Law as well: "You shall not take vengeance or bear a grudge against any of your people, but you shall love your neighbor as yourself ..." (Lev. 19:18). Other passages, however, appear to be a foundation for persecution, stark injustice, abject cruelty, and religious inquisition—and seem to eviscerate literalist notions that the Old Testament could have been dictated by a morally perfect Being.

And tragically, such literal readings have been fairly commonplace throughout the history of Christian orthodoxy. For instance, fourth-century bishop St. Optatus of Milevis appealed to the story of the Golden Calf in Exodus as justification for killing dissenters (Exod. 32:27-28).[746] Protestants and Roman Catholics alike thought themselves on a centuries-long holy errand when killing witches, citing Exod. 22:18.[747] Crusaders used the brutal commands of Deut. 20 as a "blueprint" for siege warfare.[748] Also relying on Deut. 20, medieval Jewish scholar Maimonides (1135-1204) reasoned that a just ruler "may give orders to burn a man alive without being annoyed or angry or ill-disposed towards him" based on the brutal commands to annihilate towns in vv. 16-18.[749] The Spanish Inquisitors felt their stern punishments were justified by God's "holy" example, explicitly citing Old Testament passages like Deut. 13 and 17 when they handed down their merciless judgments.[750] John Calvin (1509-1564) appealed to the Old Testament Law (Deut. 13:5) as justification for the persecution and murder of "false prophets."[751] Horribly, in one instance in Calvin's Geneva, a girl was executed for striking her parents (Deut. 21:18-21).[752]

The Psalmist waxes eloquently on the flawless nature of the Old Testament Law in Psalm 19:7-10. While the author of Hebrews interestingly calls the Law "weak and ineffectual" (Heb. 7:18) and asserts that it has faults (Heb. 8:7), these rather strong criticisms would still seem much too lenient considering how far the Old Testament Law seems from perfection. What follows then is a questioning of the Law, based on the words of Psalm 19:

Can the law of the Lord be perfect (Ps. 19:7a), if it orders rapists and their victims to marry?

"If a man meets a virgin who is not engaged, and seizes her and lies with her, ... she shall become his wife. Because he violated her he shall not be permitted to divorce her as long as he lives" (Deut. 22:28-29).

Are the decrees of the Lord sure (Ps. 19:7b), when they counsel the extermination of polytheists?

"If you hear it said about one of the towns that the LORD your God is giving you to live in, that scoundrels from among you have gone out and led the inhabitants of the town astray, saying, 'Let us go and worship other gods' .... [Y]ou shall put the inhabitants of that town to the sword, utterly destroying it and everything in it" (Deut. 13:12-15, cf. Exod. 22:20).

Are the precepts of the Lord right (Ps. 19:8a), when they command the murder of friends and family?

"If anyone secretly entices you—even if it is your brother, your father's son or your mother's son, or your own son or daughter, or the wife you embrace, or your most intimate friend—saying, 'Let us go and worship other gods' .... [Y]ou shall surely kill them; your own hand shall be first against them to execute them, and afterwards the hand of all the people[10]" (Deut. 13:6-10, cf. Exod. 32:27).

Is the commandment of the Lord clear (Ps. 19:8b), when it gives towns a choice between slavery and wholesale massacre?

"When you draw near to a town to fight against it, offer it terms of peace. If it accepts your terms of peace and surrenders to you, then all the people in it shall serve you in forced labor. If it does not submit to you peacefully, ... you shall put all its males to the sword. You may, however, take as your booty the women, the children, livestock, and everything else in the town, all its spoil. ... But as for the towns of these peoples that the LORD your God is giving you as an inheritance, you must not let anything that breathes remain alive" (Deut. 20:10-16).

Is the fear of the Lord pure (Ps. 19:9a), when disobedient children are slaughtered?

"If someone has a stubborn and rebellious son who will not obey his father and mother, … then his father and mother shall take hold of him and bring him to the elders of his town …. They shall say to the elders of his town, 'This son of ours is stubborn and rebellious. …' Then all the men of the town shall stone him to death. So you shall purge the evil from your midst; and all Israel will hear, and be afraid" (Deut. 21:18-21).

Are the ordinances of the Lord true (Ps. 19:9b), when they counsel prostitutes to be burned alive?

"When the daughter of a priest profanes herself through prostitution, she profanes her father; she shall be burned to death" (Lev. 21:9).

Are they more to be desired than gold (Ps. 19:10a), when they permit slavery and slave beatings?

"As for the male and female slaves whom you may have, it is from the nations around you that you may acquire male and female slaves. … [T]hey may be your property. You may keep them as a possession for your children after you, for them to inherit as property" (Lev. 25:44-46).

"When a slave-owner strikes a male or female slave with a rod and the slave dies immediately, the owner shall be punished. But if the slave survives for a day or two, there is no punishment; for the slave is the owner's property" (Ex. 21:20-21).

Are they sweeter also than honey (Ps. 19:10b), when they command murder for minor or questionable misdeeds?

- "Whoever sacrifices to any god, other than the Lord alone, shall be devoted to destruction" (Ex. 22:20).
- "All who curse father or mother shall be put to death" (Lev. 20:9a).
- "If a man lies with a male as with a woman, both of them have committed an abomination; they shall be put to death; their blood is upon them" (Lev. 20:13).
- "A man or a woman who is a medium or a wizard shall be put to death" (Lev. 20:27).
- "Those who found him gathering sticks brought him to Moses .... Then the Lord said to Moses, 'The man shall be put to death'" (Num. 15:33-35).
- "Take the blasphemer outside the camp; and let all who were within hearing lay their hands on his head, and let the whole congregation stone him" (Lev. 24:14).
- "If ... evidence of the young woman's virginity was not found, ... the men of her town shall stone her to death" (Deut. 22:20-22).

A dilemma for the Christian faithful of different communions throughout the centuries, a sharp struggle of conscience has often emerged when believers have been confronted with the difficulty of following divine laws and commands that so deeply flout the dictates of both justice and the golden rule. While the profound ethical difficulties of the Law are often sidestepped by theologians who explain Old Testament barbarity as a product of a unique period of redemptive history,[753] such stances seem inadequate in the light of God's supposedly perfect foreknowledge, wisdom, justice, and love. The great American orator Robert Ingersoll (1833-1899) described the cognitive dissonance of Christian traditionalism on this general point succinctly: "the Devil entertains the same opinion to-day that Jehovah held four thousand years ago, but in the meantime Jehovah has remained exactly the same—changeless and incapable of change"[754] (cf. Mal. 3:6, Heb. 13:8).

When critiquing the cruelties of the Jim Crow legal system of the American South, the civil rights leader Martin Luther King, Jr. (1929-1968) provided a simple lens in which many laws and commandments of the Old Testament can be exposed for what they really are:

One may well ask: "How can you advocate breaking some laws and obeying others?" The answer lies in the fact that there are two types of laws: just and unjust. I would be the first to advocate obeying just laws. One has not only a legal but a moral obligation to obey just laws. Conversely, one has a moral responsibility to disobey unjust laws. I would agree with St. Augustine that "an unjust law is no law at all."[755]

It is further helpful (and even comforting) to note that many Christians and Jews have been very insistent on softening or even opposing direct commands in the Law. For instance, the Talmud, the "Oral Law" and interpretive lens for the Bible in rabbinic Judaism, somewhat surprisingly frowns upon even infrequent use of the death penalty.[756] In a sentiment cherished by existentialist psychologist and concentration camp survivor Viktor Frankl (1905-1997),[757] the Talmud even refreshingly proclaims that "whoever takes a single life it is as though he destroyed a whole world, and whoever sustains a single life it is as though he sustained a whole world."[758]

[17] Musings on Miracles

...Why the fantastic stories in the Bible are likely ahistorical

The facts upon which religions are based are ancient and marvelous, that is to say, as suspect as is possible in proving that which is the most incredible.[759]

— **Denis Diderot** (1713-1784), Enlightenment philosopher

Early biographers are preoccupied, not with historical fact, but with glorifying in every way the memory of one they believe to have been a Messenger of God or God Himself. Consequently, there is a rich accretion of myth and miracle, mysterious portents and heavenly signs, of residues from other religious beliefs and traditions, the propaganda, in fact, of an expanding faith.

— **Michael Edwardes**, Introduction to *The Life of Muhammad*[760]

While some faith traditions have viewed the rejection of sacred miracle stories as sign of inward pride and arrogance, astrophysicist Carl Sagan (1934-1996) reasoned rather that a sober view of the flaws of human judgments in fact favors skepticism of the miraculous: "Precisely because of human fallibility, extraordinary claims require extraordinary evidence."[761] Evidence for the truth of biblical miracles does not seem to meet this criterion due to their typical characteristics:

- Amazing stories that defy the laws of nature
- from pre-modern societies
- that may have been intended as didactic tales

- with apparently contradictory elements and details
- frequently in anonymous works or from unknown sources
- that in many instances may have been passed along in oral form for decades or, in the case of the Old Testament, even centuries[762]
- in disputed canons
- frequently accompanied by threats and inducements to believe by passionately religious individuals

American patriot Thomas Paine described miracle stories as "hearsay upon hearsay."[763] Commenting on the Virgin Birth of Christ, Paine noted how the doctrine is problematic not only because of its fantastic nature, but also because its source is unknown. Mary and perhaps Joseph, the only persons that could even attempt to give such testimony, have not written anything for us. We do not know how the writers of the gospels of Luke and Matthew, the only two authors who relate the story, came upon such information. It is at best hearsay and more likely hearsay multiplied. Even if we had the unquestionable testimony of Mary herself, however, a relentless question of probability would hound us still. For which is more likely—that a virgin should conceive or that a pregnant, unwed teenager in a traditional society would tell a tale?[764]

Furthermore, belief in only the Bible's miracles while rejecting miracles from other sources seems to be a form of bias. It is suggestive of special pleading, a type of argumentation that accepts an exception to a rule (skepticism towards miracle stories) without adequately justifying the exception.[765] In order to avoid the biases of culture and creed, it is helpful to consider the value of a consistent general approach to the miraculous.[766] Are the miracles of other religious traditions, paranormal claims, modern-day miracles, and urban legends all judged on the same criteria?

Taoism, Buddhism, Hinduism, Zoroastrianism, Islam, and other world religions describe many supernatural events which are often quite similar to biblical miracles. Walking on water, rising from the dead, ascending into heaven, flying, walking through walls, mind-reading, predicting the future, healing the sick, speaking in foreign tongues (glossolalia), spirit possession, living to extreme old age, predictive prophecies, drinking poison without harm, divine visions and dreams,[767] the hearing of heavenly voices, guidance through supernatural providence, controlling the weather or animals, divinely-caused calamities, appeasement of a god through animal or human sacrifice, prayers answered by a god, warriors granted supernatural strength, virgin births, and the like have a widespread popularity in human cultural and religious traditions.[768]

Even among Christians, there is often a bias towards the miraculous claims of one's own sect or time period. Medieval miracles are often scoffed at by moderns.[769] Marian apparitions and modern tales of Catholic saints enacting "biblical"-type miracles are frequently dismissed by Protestants.[770] The claimed glossolalia and faith healings of charismatics and Pentecostals are often rejected by other Christians. Tellingly, no sect or religion seems to have any greater prayer success rate than others—despite their claims of a closer connection with and a greater knowledge of the divine.

Modern miracles are frequently dubious in character and appear explicable by psychosomatic explanations, the placebo effect,[771] the laws of probability, or inaccurate or fanciful storytelling. Medical miracles often tend to be on the underwhelming side—cancer is claimed to be cured, but amputees do not regrow their limbs.[772] In the words of author Anatole France (1844-1924) after visiting the famed site of healings in Lourdes, France:

> Happening to be at Lourdes, in August, I paid a visit to the grotto where innumerable crutches were hung up in token of a cure. My companion pointed to these trophies of the sick-room and hospital ward, and whispered in my ear: "One wooden leg would be more to the point."[773]

Sathya Sai Baba (1926-2011), one of India's most famous modern gurus, had as many as 30 million followers in 165 countries and is viewed by many as a divine avatar or god-man. Many eyewitnesses claim he performed many miracles, including materializing holy ash and small precious objects, healing the sick, raising the dead, controlling the weather, reading minds, predicting the future, projecting his "astral body" anywhere in the world, and taking the form of other humans and animals. There have also been claims that his mother conceived while she was a virgin.[774] Prominent atheist and neuroscientist Sam Harris (b.1967) appears to cut through the special pleading when explaining why New Testament miracles should seem even more unlikely than similar, modern ones:

> So, consider as though for the first time the foundational claim of Christianity. ... [T]hat miracle stories of the sort that today surround a person like Sathya Sai Baba become especially compelling when you set them in the pre-scientific religious context of the first-century Roman Empire, decades after their supposed occurrence.[775]

As former conservative Protestant John Loftus asserts, the nature of ancient miracle stories seems so questionable that "there isn't any way to show that a miracle occurred in the ancient past at all, even if one did."[776] It may be possible that various historical (or quasi-historical) figures were born of virgins, or walked on water, or levitated, or healed people—but we seem to have no way to establish that any such claims are likely to be true. Furthermore, in a superstitious age there may have been pressure on early Christians to claim that Jesus had performed extraordinary miracles so that he would not appear inferior to other religious leaders, gods, and heroes. As Loftus further explains:

> If miraculous stories were being told about other great men during the day, then wouldn't early Christians be tempted to tell similar kinds of stories—and even greater stories—about Jesus, to prove he was greater than the others? In an environment where a great man is known by his great and even miraculous deeds, early Christians would have been faced with the choice of either telling tales of even bigger deeds done by Jesus or not gaining the attention of those who didn't believe Jesus was that great of a man.[777]

Among many other things, the Bible tells us that a snake talked (Gen. 3:1), men lived to be as old as 969 years (Gen. 5), a 600-year-old man put two of all the earth's animals on a single wooden boat (Gen. 7:6-24), a sea is parted after a man raises his hand (Exod. 14:21-22), a donkey talks after seeing an angel (Num. 22:27-28), people who look at a bronze serpent are healed from the effects of snake venom (Num. 21:6-9), walls of a city fall when people shout (Josh. 6:20), the sun and moon stop in the sky (Josh. 10:13), a man pulls down a temple with his bare hands (Judg. 16:20-30), a witch summons a dead man to speak to a king (1 Sam. 28:7-19), a flaming chariot with fiery horses appears and a man is taken to "heaven" in a whirlwind (2 Kings 2:11), an angel kills 185,000 soldiers (2 Kings 19:35), a dead man comes back to life after his body touches human bones (2

Kings 13:21), a metal axe head floats in the water (2 Kings 6:5-6), a disembodied hand writes on a wall (Dan. 5:5-7), a man spends three days in the belly of a big fish and lives (Jon. 1:17), three men are not harmed after being thrown into a blazing hot furnace (Dan. 3:26), a man feeds over 5,000 people with a few loaves of bread and fish (Matt. 14:13-21), a fish is caught with a tax payment in its mouth (Matt. 17:24-27), men walk on water (Matt. 14:22-31), a previously deceased man floats into the sky and disappears in a cloud (Acts 1:9), and handkerchiefs and aprons heal the sick and expel demons (Acts 19:11-12). Is it a sign of immorality to doubt the literal occurrence of such things? Does not honesty—a common core value of religious ethics—suggest that biblical miracles can be doubted in good faith? As famous "agnostic" Thomas Huxley (1825-1895) explained, it is difficult to reject the straightforward premise that it is ethical to doubt questionable ideas and occurrences:

> That which Agnostics deny, and repudiate as immoral, is ... that there are propositions which men ought to believe, without logically satisfactory evidence and that reprobation ought to attach to the profession of disbelief in such inadequately supported propositions.[778]

As a final thought, skepticism about supernaturalism is quite different from denying the reality of wonder. The natural world and scientific discovery present themselves in many ways as perhaps even more amazing than biblical miracle stories. Modern spaceflight, aeronautics, computers, robotics, electronics, pharmaceuticals, machinery, engineering, genetics, and the like often rival or even surpass the accounts of miraculous happenings of the Bible. A nuclear reactor may be more amazing than a burning bush (Exod. 3:1-6); a 4.5 million-lb. space shuttle[779] more astounding than a flaming chariot; a permanent undersea tunnel more ingenious than a brief parting of a sea; a floating battleship more impressive than a floating axe head; walking on the moon more spectacular than walking on water;[780] the saving of untold millions through vaccinations and medicines more impressive than healing a small number of disabled people; the communication of a satellite more awe-inspiring than the giving of the Ten Commandments. It seems arguable that the natural universe itself is so amazing that the term "miracle" could in a certain way apply to all events and all things: stars, cells, molecules, skyscrapers, rivers, galaxies, rockets, viruses, comets, telescopes, snowstorms, insects, human societies—and even human religions. Perhaps Thomas Paine had the right perspective here: "Every thing, therefore, is a miracle, in one sense; whilst, in the other sense, there is no such thing as a miracle."[781]

[18] The Odd God
...Strange and surprising Bible verses

There shall no strange god be in thee; neither shalt thou worship any strange god.

—Ps. 81:9, KJV

But Andrew answered and said to the brethren, "... I at least do not believe that the Savior said this. For certainly these teachings are strange ideas."

—**Andrew the Apostle** in the *Gospel of Mary*[782]

The Bible contains a wealth of cultural information about ancient peoples of the Middle East. Its more unusual commandments and stories suggest that it most probably does not originate from an omniscient mind—while also serving as a reminder that humanity has lived with a variety of bizarre cultural and religious practices. While Yahweh commanded against worshipping "strange" (i.e., foreign) gods in the Old Testament, it is also the case that he is a rather odd god himself, often displaying a preoccupation with gratuitous violence as well as peculiar sexual, scatological, and other matters. While such verses are not frequently the focus of Sunday sermons, they yet remain in the Bible—and seem to present unusual challenges for traditional theories of biblical inerrancy.

The Lord apparently hated looking at Israelite defecation and at one point ordered all feces to be buried. He warns that if he sees any fecal matter, he may even turn away from his chosen people (Deut. 23:12-14). Later, however, Yahweh seems more comfortable with excrement and in fact tells the prophet Ezekiel to lie on his side for 390 days and bake bread on human dung (Ezek. 4:9-12). In an odd story in the book of Tobit in the Roman Catholic and Eastern Orthodox Bibles, Tobit becomes blind after a sparrow defecates in his eyes (Tob. 2:10). The innards of a fish turn out to be both a cure for the blindness and the means to drive away demons (Tob. 6:8-9)!

While Jesus is often known to be a friend of the crippled and lepers, Yahweh did not allow people to offer food to him who had a blemish, were blind or lame, were a hunchback or dwarf, or who had scabs, a mutilated face, or a limb that was too long (Lev. 21:18-21). The Lord also comes across as hyper-sensitive about illegitimate children, commanding that they are not only not allowed in his assembly, but also that their descendants to the tenth generation should be banned (Deut. 23:2).

Yahweh sometimes seems profoundly indifferent to great suffering on the part of his creatures. He drowns almost all the animals of the world in a catastrophic flood (Gen. 7:23), calls for the wholesale slaughter of all livestock in conquered cities (1 Sam. 15:1-3, Josh. 6:20-21), and commands all the horses of a great army to be hamstrung (Josh. 11:6). Although at points God is represented as not desiring sacrifices (Ps. 40:6, Hosea 6:6), he also commands sacrifices (Exod. 20:24, Lev. 4-5) that can result in the deaths of thousands of animals. Some of the more drastic bloodletting is found in 2 Chron. 29-30 (25,000 animals), 2 Chron. 35 (33,000 animals), and 2 Chron. 7:5 (142,000 animals), and 2 Chron. 5:6—where there are so many slaughtered that "they could not be numbered or counted." On a smaller scale, Jesus cast demons into pigs which resulted in their deaths (Mark 5:11-13), and commanded that a healed leper make an animal sacrifice (Luke 5:14, cf. Lev. 14:1-7).

In one story in the book of Exodus, Yahweh starts to kill Moses because his son isn't circumcised. Interestingly, he then relents when the child's bloody foreskin is quickly removed by his mother and touched to Moses' feet (Exod. 4:24-26). While God may disdain foreskins, too much damage to the genitals is also apparently problematic—and so Yahweh commanded that those who have their testicles crushed or penis cut off to be barred from his assembly (Deut. 23:10). Furthermore, grabbing genitals can bring swift punishment—and under certain circumstances God wants a female perpetrator's hand to be cut off with "no pity" (Deut. 25:11-12). In another story, David, the anointed of the Lord, agrees to kill 100 Philistines to get their foreskins for King Saul (1 Sam. 18:27)—evidently without sinning (1 Kings 15:5). Utilizing a somewhat disconcerting simile, Yahweh says he wishes his relationship to Israel could be like a loincloth clinging to loins (Jer. 13:11). In a seeming affront to the golden rule, St. Paul remarks that he wishes his theological opponents would castrate themselves (Gal. 5:12).

While Judeo-Christian ethics typically encourage modesty, God caused King Saul to go into a naked prophetic frenzy (1 Sam. 19:20-24) and commanded the prophet Isaiah to walk around in the nude (Isa. 20:2-4). In describing the idolatrous practices of Jerusalem, Holy Writ curiously speaks of men "whose members were like those of donkeys, and whose emission was like that of stallions" (Ezek. 23:19-20). In contrast to traditional representations of Jesus, St. Paul taught that long hair on men was degrading (1 Cor. 11:14). In terms that most modern Westerners would deem misogynistic, 1 Timothy counsels that women "should learn in silence with full submission," should not "teach or to have authority over a man," and even that they "will be saved through childbearing" (1 Tim 2:11-15).

Interestingly, God commanded priests to wear special undergarments to avoid guilt and death (Exod. 28:42-44) and Jesus reportedly healed blind men by wiping saliva on them (Mark 8:22-25, John 9:6-7). Yahweh is rather inexplicably angered about the consuming of sacrificed animals at the wrong time (Lev. 19:7) and the eating of ostriches or shellfish (Lev. 11:12-16)—both of which are considered "abominations" or otherwise detestable acts. While pediatricians today standardly discourage spanking,[783] the Book of Proverbs counsels parents to beat their children with rods (Prov. 13:24, Prov. 22:15, Prov. 23:13-14).[784] If God is believed to have chosen all the content of the Scriptures, he unfortunately included many Psalms that have "imprecations" or curses in them. Among the most brutal are claims that those who dash infants on rocks will be blessed (Ps. 137: 8-9), that the righteous will be joyous when they "bathe their feet in the blood of the wicked" (Ps. 58:8-10), and that enemies should be hit with hot coals,[785] cast into pits (Ps. 140:10), blinded, or have "their loins tremble continually" (Ps. 69:23-28). In contrast to the ethics of the New Testament, enemies are openly declared to be despised with a "perfect hatred" (Ps. 139:19-22).

At certain points in the Bible, the will of God is supposedly discerned through the seemingly random practice of the casting of lots. This is the case both in the Old Testament, with the curious use of the Urim and

Thummim (1 Sam. 14:41, 1 Sam. 28:6, Num. 27:21), and even more surprisingly in the New Testament, where the apostolic replacement for Judas Iscariot is decided not by prayer or divine revelation but instead by lot (Acts 1:21-26).[786]

Renowned biologist Charles Darwin (1809-1882) famously quipped that he felt like he was "confessing a murder" when admitting that his theory of evolution was a better explanation for the development of life on earth than the stories in the book of Genesis.[787] Likewise, it can be emotionally uncomfortable for those steeped in traditional Christian dogmas to acknowledge that many passages in the Bible seem cruel, absurd, or even just plain odd. Directly confronting this cognitive dissonance, "Great Agnostic" Robert Ingersoll (1833-1899) describes how he came to the point where he felt compelled to abandon the biblical literalism of his youth. In his own words, his frank look at Scripture revealed it not as divine perfection, but rather "a mingling of truth and mistake, of wisdom and foolishness, of cruelty and kindness, of philosophy and absurdity—that it contained some elevated thoughts, some poetry, … —some hysterical, some tender, some wicked prayers, some insane predictions, some delusions, and some chaotic dreams." In terms that will resonate with many former fundamentalists, Ingersoll described his final break from inerrancy as a moment of reluctant but unavoidable honesty: "And yet in spite of all I heard—of all I read, I could not quite believe. My brain and heart said No."[788]

[19] An Unknown Sin

...Slavery in Christian history and Scripture

What God sanctioned in the Old Testament, and permitted in the New, cannot be a sin.

> —**Rev. Richard Fuller** (1804-1876), American pro-slavery advocate and founding member of the Southern Baptist denomination[789]

By the unknown sin ... I mean acts which were not known to be sins; acts for which no vocabulary existed to denominate them as sins; acts participated in by upright men and women, by popes and dedicated members of religious orders and canonized saints; acts now regarded with horror as the blackest kind of affront to the human person and among the most serious derelictions of duty to God, whose image is the person.

> —**John T. Noonan Jr.** (1926-2017), Catholic historian and federal judge discussing slavery and other historic Catholic moral blind spots[790]

While perhaps surprising to many modern believers, the early church was not opposed to the institution of slavery. Although manumission was seen as admirable[791] and slaves were typically regarded as equal in the sight of God (Gal. 3:27-28), there was no impulse towards abolitionism or wholesale emancipation in early Christianity. Condemnation of slavery by both Christian Scripture and early saints rather pertains to abuses.[792] In many ways, the history of Christian slavery can be understood as an outworking of the incompatibility of the golden rule and biblical passages which support or regulate slavery. While two pre-Christian Jewish sects as well as some Greeks had eschewed all slave ownership as immoral,[793] it was not until the modern era that the majority of Christians came to see slavery as a categorical sin that required a blanket rejection.[794]

The support for slavery in the Bible is considerable. Although there are some relatively progressive provisions in the Old Testament Law instructing that escaped slaves should not be returned to their masters (Deut. 23:15-16), that kidnapping for the purposes of selling into slavery was forbidden (Exod. 21:16), and that Israelite slaves could only be held for a limited period (Exod. 21:2, cf. Exod. 6:6), it is clear that foreign slaves could be held in perpetuity: "You may keep them as a possession for your children after you, for them to inherit as property" (Lev. 25:44-46a). Tellingly, it was also permissible under the Law, with certain restrictions, to sell one's daughter as a slave (Exod. 21:7). Servitude is part of the divine plan for the conquest of Canaan, and the labor force of conquered cities was to be enslaved (Deut. 20:10-16). Likewise, sex slavery appears permissible at points; Israelite soldiers are even ordered by Moses to kill all children and married women, but the virgins they are to "keep alive for [them]selves" (Num. 31:17-18). The Ten Commandments, often considered to be the basis of the Christian moral system, declared the coveting of a slave to be sinful; however, it made no suggestion that being a slaveholder was (Exod. 20:17).[795] While beatings that caused the loss of an eye or tooth could result in a slave's freedom (Exod. 21:26-27), severe corporal punishment that did not result in a slave's immediate death were not considered to be problematic (Exod. 21:20-21). Cited by some antebellum American pastors as warrant for the whip, Proverbs 29:19 likewise implies that corporal punishment is necessary for troublesome servants—just like other Proverbs state it is for disobedient children (cf. Prov. 13:24, Prov. 22:15, etc.).[796] Though Solomon was the wisest man in the Bible (1 Kings 3:12), he apparently did not realize that servitude was immoral and used slave labor for his building projects (1 Kings 9:21; cf. 2 Chron. 8:8). While Solomon's idolatry is condemned in Scripture (cf. 1 Kings 11:2), his attitudes regarding slavery are not. Likewise, Job is a slaveholder in Holy Writ; he does not worry that slaveholding itself may be immoral, but only has concerns about the mistreatment of slaves (Job 31:13). As another example, the prophet Jeremiah demands the release of all Hebrew slaves—but gives no such requirement for slaves from other nations (Jer. 34:8ff). Tellingly, Yahweh himself is said to sell people into slavery (Joel 3:8, Lam 1:3-5).

Certain books in the Roman Catholic Apocrypha, generally accepted as canonical by non-Protestant Christians, similarly provide support for slavery. The book of Sirach recommends the use of yokes, thongs, racks, tortures, and fetters for disobedient slaves (Sir. 33: 25-30); it further counsels that no shame should be felt for "drawing blood from the back of a wicked slave" (Sir. 42:5).[797] Without a word of disapproval, the Book of Tobit has the righteous Tobias receive gifts of male and female slaves (Tob 10:10). Likewise, the heroine Judith held both male and female slaves without stain to her reputation for holiness—"No one spoke ill of her, for she feared God with great devotion" (Judith 8:7-8).

While the New Testament picture is perhaps less graphic and disturbing than the Old, there is no call for a general emancipation nor the eradication of slavery in its pages. It seems that the writers of the New Testament simply did not comprehend the full moral implications of slavery. "Believing masters" were in full fellowship in New Testament churches; they were to be treated as both "believers and beloved" (1 Tim. 6:2). Of course, the failure to name slaveholding as a sin in the New Testament is not due to an unwillingness to name sinful behavior. The New Testament condemns a tremendous number of specific sins that seem far more trivial[798] than denying a person's basic freedoms—among them worrying about life (Matt. 6:25), making oaths (Matt. 5:34-37; James 5:12), failing to wear a head covering, having the wrong hair length (1 Cor. 11:4-15), wearing gold jewelry, having hair braids, wearing expensive clothes (1 Pet. 3:3, 1 Tim. 2:9), filing lawsuits against other Christians (1 Cor. 6:1-8), enviousness, quarrelling, anger, strife, drunkenness (Gal. 5:19-21), holding incorrect religious opinions (2 John 10, Gal. 1:9, 1 John 4:1-3, etc.), disobedience to parents and husbands (1 Pet. 3:1, Eph. 6:1), vulgar or silly talk, greediness (Eph. 5:3-4), lustful thoughts (Matt. 5:28), selfishness, pride (Rom. 12:16, Phil. 2:2), disorderly worship (1 Cor. 14:39-40), acting like a busybody, being idle (2 Thess. 3:11), gossiping (Rom. 1:29), eating blood or food sacrificed to idols (Acts 15:28-29), praying or giving alms publicly (Matt. 6:1-6), divorcing (Mark 10:11-12, Luke 16:18), speaking in church by women (1 Cor. 14:34), and the holding of leadership positions by women (1 Tim. 2:11-12).

The lack of abolitionism in the New Testament does not mean that its general teachings on slavery were not relatively progressive for their time. There are injunctions for masters to be kind and just (Col. 4:1), a condemnation of slave traders (1 Tim. 1:9-10), and a possible indication that one particular slave should be freed (Philem. 15:16). However, the ethics of the New Testament did not require manumission; the general assumption seems to be that slavery was part of the earthly state of affairs. Often quoted by masters through the centuries, slaves were repeatedly admonished to serve their owners with respect and fear (Eph. 6:5, Col. 3:22-25, 1 Tim. 6:1-2).[799] They are also instructed to not worry about gaining their freedom, noting that Christ gives spiritual freedom to the slave—and that every believer is in fact a "slave of Christ" regardless of status (1 Cor. 7:20-22). In fact, 1 Peter even suggests that a slave can deserve beatings—and that unmerited corporal punishments can be a way to gain God's good favor: " If you endure when you are beaten for doing wrong, where is the credit in that? But if you endure when you do right and suffer for it, you have God's approval" (1 Pet. 2:20).[800] The Epistle to Titus asks slaves to not "pilfer" from or talk back to their masters so that they can "be an ornament to the doctrine of God" (Tit. 2:9). However, there is no mention of how slaveholders should honor slaves by manumission, how depriving another of freedom is far worse than petty theft or backtalk, or how owning another human being is inherently sinful or at odds with the golden rule.[801] In short, the New Testament does expose the incompatibility of the institution of slavery with the law of love.[802]

Likewise, Jesus' parables often draw on the reality of beatings and harsh treatment that were a common part of the life of a slave in the ancient world—but do not bring a word of criticism about such treatment.[803] In fact, his parables would seem to assume that disobedient slaves are getting punished appropriately—otherwise, it is difficult to understand how his hearers would not find fault with God's sense of justice.[804] In the Parable of the Faithful or the Unfaithful Slave, for instance, Jesus teaches that God will treat disobedient people like masters treat irresponsible slaves: "That slave who knew what his master wanted, but did not prepare himself or do what was wanted, will receive a severe beating[48] " (Luke 12:47). (Former slave and abolitionist Frederick Douglass mentioned one cruel master that quoted this very verse as he applied the whip.[805]) In Matthew's Parable of the Unforgiving Servant, the "wicked slave" was "handed over to be tortured" (Matt. 18:23-35). God is portrayed as just as severe as the story's brutal slaveholder: "So my heavenly Father will also do to every one of you, if you do not forgive your brother or sister from your heart." In another analogy concerning God's judgment, the master issues this order for a wicked slave: "cut him in pieces and put him with the hypocrites, where there will be weeping and gnashing of teeth" (Matt. 24:45-51).[806] These slave parables suggest that the moral blind spot pertaining to slavery in the New Testament is tied in some ways to the inconsistencies in the moral character of the Christian God himself. God, at least at times, is portrayed as the moral equivalent of a stern slave master—controlling, brutal, abusive, and asserting his authority with threats and violence. Thus while it is often asserted by traditional Christian apologists that Hebrew slavery or early Christian slavery was not as harsh as the slavery in the American South before the Civil War, this opinion appears to be overstated.[807] It is true, of course, that there were racist elements of American slavery that gave it some especially toxic features. Additionally, in some cases, there were also greater chances for upward mobility and emancipation for slaves in the ancient world. Nevertheless, Christian Scriptures show "biblical" slavery as an oppressive condition marked by a basic denial of freedoms, a general lack of legal protection, and the threat of physical violence for disobedience.

This qualified acceptance of slavery is seen in the earliest non-canonical Christian writings as well. It was "spiritual slavery," or slavery to sin, that the early Church uniformly condemned. Apostolic father Ignatius of Antioch (c.35-c.107) urged that slaves should accept their place and not ask for the church to buy their freedom. His pastoral concern was not focused on emancipation, but rather on a fear that those in bondage might be "found slaves to their own desires."[808] In the Acts of Thomas, Jesus himself sells the apostle Thomas into slavery.[809] The Didache, which was considered canonical by some prominent early Catholic believers, condemns a very wide range of behaviors—but there is no suggestion that Christians should not own slaves. Rather, Christian masters are urged not to "be harsh in giving orders to your slaves" and slaves are urged to obey their masters.[810]

In the Apocalypse of Peter, a book also deemed canonical by some early Catholics, slaves were threatened with eternal torment in hell for disobedience to their masters.[811] Early father Athenagoras (d.c.190) described slavery as commonplace among believers, noting simply that Christians "have slaves, some more and some fewer."[812] St. Peter of Alexandria (d.311), a bishop martyred in the Diocletian persecution, ordered that slaveholders be given three years' penance if they forced their slaves to offer incense on their behalf—forcing a slave to offer a disingenuous sacrifice was thus deserving of a stern chastisement, owning another person was not.[813]

Standouts like St. Ambrose (c.333-397), St. Gregory Nazianzus (c.330-c.390),[814] and St. Jerome (347-419)[815] also accepted slavery. Pope and saint Gregory the Great (c.540-604) utilized hundreds of slaves on papal lands.[816] Touted as the "mouthpiece of Christ and pillar of the Church" in the Eastern Orthodox tradition,[817] St. Basil the Great (330-379) also supported the institution, both owning slaves and gifting them to others.[818] St. John Chrysostom (c.347-407), eminent Greek Father,[819] even pronounced that physical slavery could potentially be "no harm but rather an advantage" for spiritual growth. Chrysostom describes the general thrust of the teachings of the Fathers: slaves should be obedient, masters should be fair and not overly harsh, and sin was actually "the worst form of slavery."[820] Foremost Western Father St. Augustine (354-430) also attested to the commonplace of Christian slaveholding, regarding slavery as an appropriate but unfortunate state of affairs resulting from Adam's fall from grace. Even remarking that "masters ought to feel their position of authority a greater burden than servants their service," he viewed slavery as the just judgment of God against sin and advised slaves to accept their lot:

> The prime cause, then, of slavery is sin, which brings man under the dominion of his fellow—that which does not happen save by the judgment of God, with whom is no unrighteousness, and who knows how to award fit punishments to every variety of offence.[821]

The early councils of the Church likewise approached slavery as something to regulate, not eradicate. The 4th-century Council of Gangra anathematized any who encouraged slaves to run away.[822] The Code of the Canons of the African Church (419) did not call for abolition, but rather forbade slaves from bringing any accusations in criminal proceedings.[823] The

Fourth Ecumenical Council of Chalcedon (451), while supposedly capable of parsing the most intricate of Christological definitions, was apparently unable to understand the immoral nature of slavery. Their only counsel on slavery was to threaten excommunication for anyone who allowed a slave to be accepted as a monk without the permission of his owner.[824] The Seventh Ecumenical Council of Nicaea (787) declared that Jews should not be allowed to "purchase or possess a slave" and threatened to depose any bishop who kept a female slave; no condemnations were issued for the Christian laity holding slaves or for bishops holding male slaves.[825]

Fortunately, this general thrust of the early Church was not the whole story. As mentioned, some devoted believers emancipated their slaves as a voluntary act of love; there are countless examples of Christians being kind to slaves.[826] For example, St. Aidan (d.651) took money given to him by the wealthy to ransom Christian slaves.[827] Likewise, St. Wilfrid (634-709) released 250 Christian men and women from slavery[828] and St. Theodore of Studium (759-826) urged monks to avoid slaveholding, describing slavery as "an indulgence ... only for those who live in the world."[829] There was also a growing realization in the early Christian centuries that slaves should be given full rights to marry.[830] Seemingly an isolated example in the early Church, St. Gregory of Nyssa (c.335-394) actually made a categorical condemnation of slavery. In one of his homilies, Gregory critiques slavery as an institution, attributing fault to slaveholders in a general way: "You condemn man who is free and autonomous to servitude, and you contradict God by perverting the natural law."[831] Though Gregory did not overtly call for abolition of slavery or the ecclesiastical censure or excommunication of slaveholders, his general opinion of slaveholding was clearly negative and way ahead of its time.

While Jews, Muslims, and pagans were susceptible to different treatment,[832] the medieval Church had a strong developing sense that it was sinful to enslave fellow Catholics.[833] Consequently, slavery significantly diminished in medieval Christendom with some countries even eradicating the practice.[834] However, the institution remained common in many parts of Europe,[835] especially around the Mediterranean.[836] As examples of slavery's tenacity, preeminent theologian St. Thomas Aquinas (1225-1274) did not forbid servitude in his writings[837] and the Fourth Lateran Council (1215) denounced "false and ungodly Christians" who traded with Muslims, decreeing that "their possessions be confiscated and they themselves become the slaves of their captors."[838] Both the Spanish Inquisition (1478-1834) and the Portuguese Inquisition (1536-1821) used slavery as a form of punishment.[839] In his bull *Romanus Pontifex* (1455), Pope Nicholas V gave authority to "subdue all Saracens and pagans whatsoever ... and to reduce their persons to perpetual slavery."[840] Tellingly, St. Thomas More described the perfect society in his *Utopia* (1515) as one that allowed for the enslavement of adulterers, prisoners of war, criminals from other countries, the foreign poor who asked to be enslaved, and the perpetrators of serious crimes.[841]

As the Reformation and colonial eras dawned, however, some Western Christians began to reach new levels of clarity about not only fellow Christians but about all of humanity. Bartolomé de las Casas (1484-1576),[842] the Mennonites[843] and the Amish,[844] Roger Williams (1603-1683) and the Rhode Island colony,[845] and Quakers[846] were early voices for emancipation. As time progressed, there became more and more mainstream Christians who advocated for abolition.[847] Founding Methodist John Wesley (1703-1791)[848] and prominent evangelist Charles Finney (1792-1875) were outspoken in their condemnations of slavery[849] as were persistent Anglican abolitionists William Wilberforce (1759-1833) and Thomas Clarkson (1760-1846).[850]

However, this new surge of conscience was unfortunately countered by the resistance of a large number of prominent Christian leaders, canonized saints, leading pastors, and Christian nations. Despite his admirable commands that Native Americans should not be enslaved,[851] Pope Paul III (1468-1549) affirmed that people in Rome could "freely and lawfully buy and sell publicly any slaves whatsoever of either sex"[852] and threatened Englishmen who left the Catholic Church during the reign of Henry VIII with slavery.[853] Likewise pope and canonized saint Pius V accepted 558 Muslim slaves after the Battle of Lepanto in 1571.[854] Puritan Oliver Cromwell enslaved hundreds of Royalists in 17th-century Britain; most went to sugar plantations in the Caribbean.[855] The Massachusetts Bay Colony, believing they were setting up a society based on Scripture, issued the 1641 "Body of Liberties" which allowed slavery for those obtained by "just wars, and such strangers as willingly sell themselves or are sold to us."[856] Despite their significant role in emancipation later, 18th-century Anglicans traded slaves "with the blessing of the church, the government, the monarchy, and the public."[857] Although leading lights of the Great Awakening in America, Calvinist leaders George Whitefield (1714-1770) and Jonathan Edwards (1703-1758) had not awoken to the evils of servitude—both owned slaves and defended the institution.[858] Pope Pius VII held slaves as late as 1807.[859] Influential Presbyterian theologian Charles Hodge (1797-1878) argued forcefully for slavery's acceptability.[860] Spain, a bastion of Roman Catholic orthodoxy, did not abolish slavery at home until 1837[861] and likewise Brazil held out until 1888.[862]

Unfortunately, the strong pro-slavery contingent among Western Christians was able to garner much of the aforementioned biblical material to make a strong case that Scripture did not recommend nor require abolitionism. In his 1845 dialogue with an anti-slavery minister, Southern Baptist founder Rev. Richard Fuller (1804-1876) provides a clear example of how the Bible contributed to the slow demise of the existence of slavery in the West. Basing his position on the authority of biblical texts, he notes that Scripture condemns the abuses of slavery but not the institution, that Christian slaveholders had existed from earliest times with no suggestion that they were unfit members of the church, that Paul "kept back nothing" when condemning sin (cf. Acts 20:20, 27), and that abolitionism exults a "lurking principle" over a plain teaching. Taking the whole of Scripture, Fuller found it wholly apparent that the golden rule was to be applied in the context of the *acceptance* of the institution of slavery—and that absolute abolitionism was a "novel doctrine" that was foreign to the Scriptures and church history:[863]

> But slavery was everywhere a part of the social organization of the earth; and slaves and their masters were members together of the churches; and minute instructions are given to each as to their duties, without even an insinuation that it was the duty of masters to emancipate. Now I ask, could this possibly be so, if slavery were "a heinous sin?" … What, then, are we to think of those who revile us as pirates and thieves, and fulminate anathemas and excommunications against every Christian at the South, no matter what his conduct or character, simply because he will not submit to the arrogant behests of mortals who at best are, like himself, loaded with imperfections;

and because he esteems the Bible a safer directory than the dogmas of men.[864]

While it is right to name the shortcomings of Scripture and Western Christians as pertains to slavery, it would be unfair to single them out as guilty of some unique moral failing regarding human bondage. Slavery has been a near-universal stain among people groups. Aztecs, Incas, and the Maori of New Zealand held slaves.[865] Slavery existed in Africa before the arrival of Europeans.[866] India has had slave societies, as did China, Korea, Thailand, Japan,[867] and the Mongol Empire.[868] Muhammad took slaves in warfare[869] and Muslims have at times been enthusiastic slavers, obtaining both Christians from Europe and especially sub-Saharan Africans.[870] Some Native Americans held slaves before the arrival of Europeans; others held blacks as slaves in the American South.[871] On rare occasions, free blacks in the West Indies and in the United States even owned slaves.[872] Greeks,[873] Romans, Egyptians, Babylonians and other polytheist cultures have held slaves.[874] Barbarians attacking the Roman Empire took Roman citizens as slaves.[875] The Vikings held slaves, often gathering them in their infamous raids.[876] Slavery was likewise licit and commonplace in the Eastern Orthodox Byzantine Empire until its fall in 1453.[877] Eastern Orthodox Russia's slaveholding society was well established into the 17th century until it gave way to serfdom.[878] Founding Fathers like George Washington (1732-1799) and Thomas Jefferson (1743-1826) held slaves until their deaths.[879] Theologically progressive Unitarian John C. Calhoun (1782-1850) was a militant advocate of slaveholder's rights.[880] Christian Ethiopia was not allowed into the League of Nations until as late as 1923 for its slowness in emancipation.[881] Saudi Arabia, Bahrain, Kuwait, Qatar, and Oman all abolished servitude only in the 20th century.[882] Sadly, slavery still exists and even flourishes in some places in the world today.[883] The demise of government-sanctioned slavery has been a slow and painful process. Even otherwise admirable people can have significant flaws, and a fair-minded modern should consider the times and recall the benefits of hindsight when they render criticism against peoples of the past.

Although factors besides ideology played a role in the demise of Western slavery, the moral impetus behind abolition is perhaps best described as a combination of a growing and significant Enlightenment influence and the mounting realization among Western Christians of the incompatibility of the golden rule and slavery.[884] Once converted to the cause, Western believers were crucial in bringing "the energy and zeal" that was necessary for abolition to become a reality.[885] While it is true that Scriptural teachings made slavery more intractable in Western societies, the lives of many heroic believers serve as a reminder of the significant positive contributions that Christians have made to history. Furthermore, despite its tragic failings in this regard, it is also important to note that the West is in fact the cradle of modern abolitionism. Great Britain may be the best example of this reality, changing from an enthusiastic supporter of African bondage to a trailblazing nation that ended their slave trade as early as 1807, enacted general emancipation by 1833, and went on to pressure other nations around the world to end the practice in the decades and centuries to come. Perhaps an odd symbol for both humanity as a whole and the wide range of biblical ethics, Britain has been a brutal colonizer and eager slaver along with being a great force for abolition, democracy, and justice.

[20] All Things Are Permissible
...Torture and persecution in Christian history

> Without even being aware of it, many people believe in a cruel God, and they are consequently cruel when it comes to religion.
>
> —**Baron d'Holbach** (1723-1789), Enlightenment philosopher[886]

> Certainly anyone who has the power to make you believe absurdities has the power to make you commit injustices.
>
> —**Voltaire** (1694-1778), Enlightenment philosopher[887]

Russian novelist Fyodor Dostoevsky (1821-1881) is often attributed with the saying "Without God, all things are permissible."[888] Many Christian apologists have used the reasoning behind Dostoevsky's sentiment to argue that a traditional view of God is necessary for an objective and "absolute" moral code to exist—and that its absence inevitably leads to moral disintegration and chaos.

While certain aspects of traditional forms of Christianity have certainly been a motivation for moral growth and the humanitarian impulse, common Christian dogmas have also served to retard the ethical development of Western society historically in fundamental ways. As Scripture contains numerous passages in which a supposedly perfectly righteous God either commands or commits the most malicious types of actions (see prior meditations for discussion),[889] Christians have easily found justifications for acting in direct opposition to the golden rule. As the reasoning of St. Thomas Aquinas (1225-1274) demonstrates, a simple appeal to a divine command can be used to reject ordinary methods of moral discernment and excuse what would otherwise be recognized as grossly unethical behavior:

> God is Lord of death and life, for by His decree both the sinful and the righteous die. Hence, he who at God's command kills an innocent man does not sin, as neither does God Whose behest he executes: indeed, his obedience to God's commands is a proof that he fears Him.[890]

Reviewing the history of Christian ethics then, Dostoevsky's statement is perhaps more germane in the negative. Is there any behavior—no matter how cruel or misanthropic—that it is not permissible for God to command or allow? With God, are all things in fact permissible?[891]

Persecution and torture are commonly regarded as among the vilest of human crimes. The long history of the Christian dogmatic justification for such acts exposes both a great weakness of the Christian Scriptures and the tremendous moral blind spots of some of the greatest heroes of the faith. Relatedly, common traditional beliefs regarding the Last Judgment and the everlasting torment of "heretics" and unbelievers demonstrate how cruelty and malice have been interwoven into the fundamentals of traditional forms of Christianity.

The earliest Christians were at times subject to oppression, torture, and martyrdom because of their faith; they seem to have generally had neither the desire nor the ability to persecute others.[892] Although having some significant blind spots (regarding slavery for instance), their ethical insights on the torture and execution of theological opponents were generally much clearer than Christians of the medieval or Reformation periods. For example, early father Tertullian (c.155-c.220) called the freedom of worship "a fundamental human right," noting that "It is assuredly no part of religion to compel religion."[893] The early apologist Lactantius (c.250-c.318), a tutor to the emperor Constantine's son, likewise insisted that religion is "polluted and profaned" when it is wed to violence.[894] Athenagoras (c. 177), however, provides one notable exception to such noble ideals among the early fathers. As is widely known, early Christians were often charged as "atheists" for rejecting the Roman pantheon.[895] In his refutation of this supposedly ignominious label, Athenagoras suggests that persecution could in fact be rightly doled out to those who denied the existence of gods: "If we shared the views of [the atheist] Diagoras when we have so many good reasons to adore God ... we should rightly be charged with impiety and there would be due cause to persecute us."[896]

While noting that the persecution of dissenters was unacceptable in the current age of the church, St. Cyprian (c.200-258) did not reject its legitimacy in all situations, reminding his readers that it was clearly licit in ancient Israel. Specifically, he acknowledged that God had indeed commanded the deaths of those disobedient to Old Testament priests (Deut. 17:12). Further, he made it clear that current ecclesiastical restraint was not due to the inherent evil of persecution or because such treatment was not deserved. Rather, he urged that those who did not obey bishops were to be chastised instead by spiritual violence: "the proud and contumacious are slain with the sword of the Spirit, in that they are cast out of the Church." Although a seemingly less harsh sentence, to Cyprian excommunication meant literal damnation and future everlasting torment, firmly believing that there was "no salvation to any except in the Church."[897] Cyprian was here expressing a common sentiment, and it was customary for those deemed to be "perverted and sinful" to be condemned and excluded from fellowship (Titus 3:9-11; cf. 1 Cor. 5:11-13, Matt. 18:15-18). Relatedly, St. Athanasius's hagiographic account of the revered St. Antony of Egypt (c.251-c.356) shows an example of how even openly despising rival Christians was to become consistent with saintly ideals. When it came to his theological rivals, St. Antony reportedly would never "bestow friendly words" on them, "spoke out against friendship with them," "loathed the Arians,"[898] and even counseled his followers to "imitate me in hating" them.[899] The pious permissibility of such attitudes would bear tragic fruit in the age of Christendom to come.

As Cyprian's sentiments about damnation would suggest, the most prominent example of the legitimacy of persecution in early Christian thought was connected to the Lord's wrath in the afterlife. From their earliest writings, in fact, it is clear that Christians in part found the strength to endure torture and martyrdom because of a belief that God would inflict more severe torments on them if they did not remain faithful (Luke 12:4-9, Heb. 10:26-31).[900] Early martyr Polycarp is said to have reasoned that he was much less concerned "with a fire that burns only briefly" during execution than the eternal fire of damnation.[901] The Letter of the Churches of

Vienne and Lyons (c.177) described a similar dynamic of one martyr: "But on the rack she came to her senses, and, so to speak, awoke out of a deep sleep, reminded by the brief chastisement of the eternal punishment in hell."[902] In an illustration of how the doctrine of a literal hell can warp the conscience, some early Christians even looked forward to watching the agony of the damned. Tertullian, despite his aforementioned lucidity about freedom of religion, described how he would have "joy" and "exultation" in heaven when he sees non-believers being tormented in the afterlife.[903] Likewise 2 Clement, a second-century work regarded as Scripture by some early Catholics, describes how the faithful will give "glory to God" upon seeing the unfaithful in hell being "punished with grievous torments in fire unquenchable" (cf. Rev. 19:1-3).[904] Perhaps predictably, it seems the concept of a perfect God exercising his wrath against the "ungodly" suggested to many that there must be people who were in fact deserving of abuse.

Hence, early Catholic Christians largely limited their misanthropic behavior to rebuke, scorn, social dissociation, and the psychological threat of eternal tortures in an age to come. Unfortunately, these inherent vices in the Christian foundation rapidly grew to include physical intimidation and persecution when faith transitioned to political power. The first Christian emperor Constantine (c. 272-337), a canonized saint in the Eastern Orthodox tradition,[905] ordered Arius's works to be burned; those who refused to hand them over were to be executed.[906] Both Arian and Nicene Catholics subjected each other to imprisonment and exile in the controversies of the fourth century; violence among rival Christian factions was in fact becoming somewhat proverbial.[907] Contemporary Roman historian Ammianus (c.330-395) even remarked that "no wild beasts are so hostile to men as Christian sects in general are to one another."[908] By an edict of the emperor Theodosius in 380, Catholic Christianity became the official religion of the Empire—and capital punishment was deemed a suitable penalty for certain heretics.[909]

St. Augustine (354-430) is perhaps the embodiment of this transitional period in the early Catholic Church. He remained against the death penalty for heresy,[910] but changed his position on persecution after seeing its effectiveness against Donatist Christians. Although initially against coercion with regard to the "lapsed," he later found biblical endorsement for persecution in the Parable of the Great Dinner (Luke 14:22-23), believing that it was wholly proper for the Catholic Church to "use force in compelling her lost sons to return."[911] Augustine also saw Christ's temporary blinding of Paul and knocking him to the ground as Scriptural warrant for physical violence against the spiritually wayward (Acts 9:1-8).[912] Often thought to be among the greatest teachers of early Christianity by Protestant and Roman Catholic alike, the North African saint found that force and fear were valuable tools in reclaiming the erring:

> For many have found advantage (as we have proved, and are daily proving by actual experiment), in being first compelled by fear or pain, so that they might afterwards be influenced by teaching, or might follow out in act what they had already learned in word.[913]

While Augustine's conclusions were horrifying and would in some part[914] lead to untold suffering in the Middle Ages and beyond,[915] his position was somewhat understandable within the context of foundational Catholic beliefs about the Last Judgment and damnation. It does not seem that Augustine delighted in the idea of inflicting suffering on others; however, he believed that all non-Catholics would be tormented eternally in hell after death.[916] His discovery that persecution led to conversion had him conclude that he was, in the long view, acting in a more compassionate manner.

Also a transitional figure, Eastern Orthodox pillar St. John Chrysostom (c.347-407) denounced the killing of dissenters but approved of lesser forms of persecution, noting that God allowed "checking heretics, and stopping their mouths, and taking away their freedom of speech, and breaking up their assemblies and confederacies, but [not] our killing and slaying them."[917] St. Cyril of Alexandria (c.376-c.444), a canonized saint and Doctor of the Roman Catholic Church, bribed government officials and used a "private army of monks" to thwart his theological adversary Nestorius.[918] He also caused rival Novatian churches to be closed and their sacred vessels to be confiscated; furthermore, he was instrumental in driving the Jews out of Alexandria.[919] Under Christian emperor Justinian I (483-565), the persecution of religious dissidents became enshrined in the law code and the death penalty was deemed appropriate for apostasy.[920]

In the anti-iconic zeal of the Iconoclastic Controversy in the eighth and ninth centuries, monks were forced to wear lay clothes, hold hands with women, and get married. Others had their beards singed off and their nostrils sliced—some monks even had Bible verses burned into their foreheads.[921] Iconoclastic believers, who cited Isaiah 60:12 to prove that their theological rivals deserved to "be utterly laid waste," also argued from New Testament language that those who disobey God "deserve to die" (Rom. 1:32).[922] Around 100,000 Christians are said to have been injured or killed in these holy controversies of the Orthodox East.[923]

Roman Catholic and Eastern Orthodox Christians in the medieval and post-medieval periods participated in many vicious pogroms against Jews, often believing that they were killing men, women, and children with God's full approval. In addition to murder and violence, Jewish property was frequently stolen or destroyed. In many pogroms the dead numbered in the hundreds or even thousands.[924] St. Thomas Aquinas (c.1225-1274), known in Catholic theology as the "Angelic Doctor" and traditionally held "in singular honor" by the later Church for his orthodoxy,[925] unabashedly taught that the spiritually wayward should be executed after a third instance of heretical belief.[926] Continuing a sentiment from the early Church, he also thought that being "allowed to see perfectly the sufferings of the damned" would be a cause of joy in heaven.[927] In addition to calling for a crusade, the Ecumenical Council of Vienne (1311-1312) gave regulations for how to licitly conduct persecution and inquisition—including the regulation of prisons for those who had committed "the crime of heresy."[928] Relatedly, a number of inquisitors have even been sainted by the Roman Catholic Church.[929] Among them are St. Raymund of Penafort (1175-1275),[930] St. John Capistrano (1386-1456),[931] St. Turibius (1538-1606),[932] and St. Pedro de Arbués (c.1441-1485).[933] Founding Jesuit and canonized saint Francis Xavier (1506-1552), famous for his evangelization efforts in the Far East, requested that the Inquisition come to Goa in India in 1546.[934] Pope St. Pius V (1504-1572) was a Grand Inquisitor before his pontificate, gaining his office in large part through the support and approval of St. Charles Borromeo (1538-1584). Pius's deadly cruelty towards Protestants is well known.[935] While Lord Chancellor in England, St. Thomas More (1478-1535), hailed as a martyr and called the "heavenly patron of statesmen and politicians" in the Roman Catholic tradition,[936] had Protestants persecuted and executed because of their "heresies."[937]

It is generally held that the "immense majority of sensible Christian divines" of the Protestant Reformation advocated civil penalties for perceived heresy and errors of doctrine. Even more moderate Protestant leaders usually advocated the punishment of atheists and blasphemers.[938] As the early 20th-century scholar and believer Philip Schaff further explained, "To the great humiliation of the Protestant churches, religious intolerance and even persecution unto death were continued long after the Reformation."[939] John Calvin's Geneva, seeking to rout out immorality and irreligion, outlawed such things as missing church services, singing crass songs, gambling, wearing improper head coverings (by women), drunkenness, improper dress, impious laughter or remarks, and dancing. Capital punishment and banishment were penalties for heresy, habitual adultery, and blasphemy. Torture was lawful.[940] Regarding the infamous 1552 execution of Michael Servetus on charges of heresy, Calvin never repented of the slaying, even noting in 1562 that "posterity owes me a debt of gratitude for having purged the Church of so pernicious a monster."[941] Calvin also asserted that magistrates who did not fulfill his counsel of killing apostates would be guilty "of the greatest perfidy and cruelty" for allowing true religion to be undermined and eternal souls be put in jeopardy.[942] While Martin Luther is generally thought to have had more restraint than Calvin in such matters, he nevertheless penned the infamous and disturbingly anti-Semitic *On the Jews and Their Lies*. Therein, Luther laid out reasons for the burning of synagogues, the confiscation of Jewish property and religious writings, the denial of safe conduct for travel, forced labor, forced exile, and the death penalty for the teaching of Judaism in public.[943] Reformer Ulrich Zwingli (1484-1531) subjected Anabaptist Balthasar Hubmaier to torture to obtain a recantation.[944] Reformers in Zurich, Berne and other cities banished, drowned, burned, or otherwise executed significant numbers of Anabaptist men and women.[945] According to Christian historian Justo González, the thousands of Anabaptist martyrs during the Reformation period likely totaled more "than those who died during the three centuries of persecution before the time of Constantine."[946]

Canonized Eastern Orthodox saint Joseph of Volokolamsk (1439-1515) also advocated persecution—advising jail, torture, and execution for "stubborn" heretics.[947] The Russian Patriarch Nikon (1605-1681) invoked the civil authorities against the Old Believer sect who were often then exiled, imprisoned, or burned at the stake.[948] It is believed that Roman Catholics and Protestants together killed at least tens of thousands of "witches" in the medieval and early modern eras, often by burning them to death.[949] 14th-century popes John XXII and Benedict XII encouraged the persecution of witches in France. Pope Innocent VIII promulgated a bull in 1484 that confirmed the reality of witchcraft, officially validating and perpetuating this combined tradition of superstition and cruelty.[950] The Puritan *Massachusetts Body of Liberties* (1641), while progressive for its day, still provided for capital punishment for witchcraft, the worship of other gods, blasphemy, and homosexual acts. It also allowed dismemberment as a form of execution, torture to find out information about co-conspirators, and whipping for certain crimes.[951] Quakers are known to have been persecuted, mutilated, and killed in the Massachusetts colony due to their perceived unorthodoxy.[952] One of the foremost leaders of the American Great Awakening, Jonathan Edwards (1703-1758) echoed St. Thomas Aquinas in chillingly believing that the "view of the misery of the damned will double the ardor of the love and gratitude of the saints in heaven."[953] As late as 1832, Pope Gregory XVI declared in his bull *Mirari Vos* that liberty of conscience was an "absurd and erroneous proposition." He also denounced freedom of the press and advocated book burning by citing Acts 19:18-20. Gregory further opposed the separation of Church and State, denouncing its advocates as "shameless lovers of liberty."[954]

This approval of oppression and cruelty by stalwart and even foundational Christian figures is not just an exercise in the airing of dirty laundry. Truly weighty questions arise. How can we trust the spiritual guidance of the great heroes of the faith, knowing that their moral sensibilities were at times so profoundly and gravely warped and mistaken? Can prominent saints like John Chrysostom, Augustine, Cyril, Aquinas, Luther, Zwingli, and Calvin be trusted on questionable and unverifiable theological doctrines such as the revelatory character of the Bible, the nature of God, the reality of miracles, the means of salvation, and the existence of the afterlife when they failed to understand that the persecution or even murder of others for supposedly mistaken theological opinions is profoundly immoral and misguided?

Of course, dogmatic Christians are by no means the only ones guilty of cruelty and oppression. The annals of history teach the ruthlessness of Romans and Greeks, of Babylonians and Mongols, of Muslims and Buddhists, of Hindus and Zoroastrians. While moderate forms of secular humanism have brought untold benefits to human societies, strident anti-religious and atheistic political movements have also had the most thorough of dark sides. The blackest days of the anti-Catholic 18th-century French Revolution saw the execution of thousands.[955] The horrors of the Inquisition and witch-hunts were far less destructive and oppressive than the totalitarian atheistic regimes of the 20th century.[956] The governments of men like Joseph Stalin, Pol Pot, and Mao Zedong have arguably caused humanity's greatest self-inflicted wounds. Stalin particularly was brutal towards all manner of dissidents—traditional Christians were indubitably treated savagely in Russia and unknown numbers were martyred for their faith. Many showed incredible courage.[957]

While the cruelties of Christian history and Scripture should not be forgotten nor dismissed, there have been many examples of traditional believers who were way ahead of their times. Early Church examples like Lactantius and Tertullian (aside from their visions of hell) have already been mentioned. While an exception to the rule, Gerbert of Aurillac (Pope Sylvester II, c. 945-1003) was known to detest capital punishment.[958] St. Bernard of Clairvaux (1090-1153), although enthusiastically urging the Second Crusade, nevertheless "stood out from his contemporaries" by denouncing the maltreatment of Jews.[959] Like most other Anabaptists,[960] Menno Simons (1496-1561), despite his literal views on hell, denounced religious persecution.[961] Roman Catholic scholar Erasmus (1466-1536) was a voice against violence in a violent age.[962] American colonial leader and human rights pioneer Roger Williams (c.1603-1683) forbade magistrates to punish people for religious dissent and declared that freedom of religion was to be granted to "the most paganish, Jewish, Turkish, or anti-christian consciences."[963] In the Eastern Orthodox tradition, St. Nilus of Sora (1433-1508) condemned religious persecution while opposing the aforementioned St. Joseph of Volokolamsk. As Eastern Orthodox historian Timothy Ware rightly explains, "One only has to recall how Protestants and Roman Catholics treated one another in Western Europe during the Reformation, to realize how exceptional Nilus was in his tolerance and respect for human freedom."[964] Of course, countless other Christians have been inspired to seek justice and to love others in both small and great ways. Professional skeptic Michael Shermer (b.1954) seems to put religion's atrocities in their proper balance:

> However for every one of these grand tragedies there are a thousand acts of personal kindness that go unreported. ... Religion, like all social institutions of such historical depth and cultural impact, cannot be reduced to an unambiguous good or evil.[965]

Thankfully, the vast majority of modern believers are "dissenters" to the Churches of centuries past. Being repulsed by a good deal of Christian tradition and history surrounding this issue of persecution, even very dogmatic traditionalists often find the persecutorial mindsets of many of their spiritual forebears to be untenable and even unconscionable. Many otherwise traditional believers have even softened or abandoned a literal belief in an eternal hell, rejecting the retributive and cruel dogma that has so tainted Christianity since its earliest expressions.[966]

Whether religious or not, absolutism has repeatedly shown itself to be a poor bedfellow of ethics. The worst crimes of the religious and the irreligious alike are often committed when absolute beliefs are joined with the willingness to inflict or condone violence. The Christian tradition exalts the love of others as equivalent to the love of God (cf. 1 John 4:7-8; Matt. 22:37-40). When following this ethic, traditional Christians have done wonderful, kind, just, and noble things. Conversely, Christendom's faithful have committed their worst sins when their metaphysical beliefs were used to rationalize coercion and cruelty. Exaggerated and unsubstantiated notions of biblical or ecclesiastical rectitude contributed to both a profound ethical blindness and the sanctification of certain aspects of ancient Middle Eastern moral primitivism and barbarity.

In Muslim thought, human history before the revelation of the Qur'an is known as the "period of ignorance."[967] In the Christian tradition, the world lay unawares until the "fullness of time" (Gal. 4:4; cf. Acts 17:23), when the Incarnation revealed hidden truths to humanity. Likewise, whether there is no "absolute truth," whether it will forever be beyond human reach, or whether some great discovery still awaits humanity, the wounds from its absence are in no way healed by professing to have a balm we don't possess. The golden rule, found nearly universally in some form in human societies, may be the best approximation of an absolute morality that we can find. "Objective" morality may mean only what people can reasonably perceive will promote the most human flourishing and the least suffering. Whether there is a God or not, this appears to simply be the best way to live. And if perchance some god ordered humanity to flout or contravene the golden rule, it might be fairly asked whether such commands were worthy of being heeded by a perpetually fragile and afflicted human race.

[21] Resurrection Reflections
...Why a literal Resurrection is improbable

When anyone tells me that he saw a dead man restored to life, I immediately consider with myself whether it be more probable that this person should either deceive or be deceived, or that the fact which he relates should really have happened. ... If the falsehood of the testimony be more miraculous than the event that he relates; then, and not until then, can he pretend to command my belief or opinion.

—**David Hume** (1711-1776), *Of Miracles*[968]

A thing which everybody is required to believe, requires that the proof and evidence of it should be equal to all .... Instead of this, a small number of persons ... are introduced as proxies for the whole world, to say they saw it, and all the rest of the world are called upon to believe it. But it appears that Thomas did not believe the resurrection; and, as they say, would not believe without having ocular and manual demonstration himself. So neither will I; and the reason is equally as good for me, and for every other person, as for Thomas.

—**Thomas Paine** (1737-1809), *The Age of Reason*[969]

While skeptics of a literal Resurrection have brought forth many challenges, some of the most penetrating questions pertain to the problematic nature of the Gospel sources themselves. As is well known, there are significant differences in the Gospel Resurrection accounts and many of them seem irreconcilable.⁹⁷⁰ Furthermore, it is often overlooked that the four canonical Gospels are anonymous works—none of them names its author and their titles are the products of later tradition.⁹⁷¹ Likewise, the authors do not name their sources nor give the places or dates of their composition.⁹⁷² Further, those later believers who claimed to know the identity of the authors of the Gospels have questionable reliability themselves. For instance, the historian Eusebius of Caesarea (c.263-c.340) provides text he says is from Papias (c. 140) who evidently wrote that an "elder" or "presbyter" named John told him who authored Mark. Interestingly, Papias wrote that Mark related not his own but rather St. Peter's memories (although in the wrong order)—making Mark a non-eyewitness even in this earliest recorded hearsay attribution. While not naming his source, Papias also apparently asserted that Matthew was written in the "Hebrew dialect"— providing a further apparent difficulty since the canonical Gospel of Matthew was composed in Greek.⁹⁷³ Interestingly, Papias evidently made no reference to the Gospels of Luke and John—it therefore may be that he did not know about these works or did not accept them as authentic.⁹⁷⁴ The attestations for the authorship of Luke and John come decades later from the bishop Irenaeus of Lyons (c. 180), who unfortunately does not name his specific sources.⁹⁷⁵ John, typically thought to be the last of the Gospels written, was heavily challenged as inauthentic in both Rome and Asia Minor;⁹⁷⁶ critical scholars generally reject the notion that it was written by the apostle.⁹⁷⁷ Even according to tradition, Luke is not an eyewitness of Jesus but rather a companion of St. Paul (who also never met the historical Jesus anyway). Lastly, the Gospel of Luke itself asserts that there were "many" accounts in circulation at the time of its composition (Luke 1:1)— and thus it seems that we are missing other narratives which contained additional (and perhaps different) information.

While the above issues certainly provide ample reason for doubt, the miraculous nature of a literal, bodily resurrection itself is perhaps the weightiest consideration for doubting its historicity. While anything approaching a modern history of the life and death of Jesus of Nazareth is probably doomed to failure,⁹⁷⁸ the information that we do have would seem to amply allow for reasonable speculation on non-miraculous alternatives.[979] With anonymous, unreliable documents being our only source material, a host of options is possible. Here are a few:

Misinterpretation. The Resurrection story may have been initially intended by a disciple or disciples as metaphorical, but this more symbolic understanding became lost during oral or written transmission and development. Modern New Testament scholar and progressive Christian Marcus Borg (1942-2015) could in fact be correct in his interpretations of these stories—that they were actually not meant to be literal accounts but rather "powerfully true metaphorical narratives."[980] Although the lives and deaths of the disciples introduced in Scripture are murky (and it incidentally seems conjectural that any were specifically martyred for a belief in a literal resurrection),[981] perhaps any who were devoted to a metaphorical truth were eventually followed by those who were devoted to a literal one. A metaphorical resurrection could also explain how disciples like Thomas would have supposedly seen Jesus perform many stunning miracles over nature and illness, beheld him raise others from the dead (John 11:43-33, Luke 7:13-15, Matt. 9:24-26), heard him command his disciples to raise the dead (Matt. 10:7-8), felt the earthquake at Jesus' death and witnessed the resulting resurrection of many saints (Matt. 27:51-53), and known that he predicted his own death and resurrection many times (Matt. 16:21, Matt. 20:17-19, Luke 18:31-34)—and could still be so incredulous about the source of such miraculous power being resurrected himself! (See also Luke 24:10-11, John 20:24-29.) Perhaps the Gospel of Matthew itself retains a tradition of metaphor in noting that the Resurrection is just as sure an event as the story of Jonah and the Fish (Matt. 12:40), a tale that even C. S. Lewis regarded as non-historical.[982]

Confusion/Delusion. There are many passages in the Gospels that show that Jesus' closest disciples were prone to confusion and misunderstanding. This occurred both before and after they were supposedly given the Holy Spirit to guide them (Acts 2:1-4). For example, disciples are described as having trouble understanding parables (Mark 4:10-14), not recognizing Judas as a betrayer (John 13:21-29), being confused about whether one should eat with Gentiles (Gal. 2:11), and not understanding that God accepted Gentiles (Acts 10). Perhaps some of the original disciples—or even the disciples of these disciples—simply became confused about what actually happened. Instead of initially not recognizing the crucified Jesus in a short encounter (John 20:15-16, John 21:5-7, Luke 24:13-27), perhaps one or more mistook someone else for Jesus after a brief meeting. Or perhaps instead of mistaking Jesus for the gardener (John 20:15), an exhausted and heart-broken Mary Magdalene mistook the gardener for Jesus. Although, as mentioned, the Gospel accounts are probably not the work of witnesses, the known, common tendency of even eyewitnesses to be confused or mistaken is further reason for pause.[983] And as the history of religions and other psychological phenomenon show, delusions can be passed from one person to another with some rapidity, especially if they are in close relationships and it is a time of stress or excitement. Perhaps one or more influential disciples became deluded, and the false belief spread.[984]

Body stolen. As is suggested in Matt. 27:62-66 and Matt. 28:11-15, some (perhaps lesser) disciples may have stolen the body in order to claim that a literal resurrection occurred. The Jews who told this story may have actually been honest and were misrepresented by the author of the Gospel of Matthew—who made the mistake of trusting a devout but unreliable source. Or perhaps someone else stole the body for some other reason. According to the Gospel of John, Mary Magdalene originally thought the body was stolen (John 20:2). Perhaps a gardener stole the body of Jesus as was asserted by some Jews—and mocked by church father Tertullian (c.155-c.220).[985]

Body moved and then discarded. As New Testament scholar Bart Ehrman has suggested as an (admittedly) unlikely possibility, two of Jesus' family members could have moved the body because they were upset about where it was buried. When discovered, they might have been killed by Roman soldiers and put with Jesus in an unmarked grave.[986] The other disciples were unaware of this incident and ecstatically proclaimed that a resurrection occurred.

Wrong tomb. Unbeknownst to the disciples, the body of Jesus may have been placed in the wrong tomb. Assuming he's a historical person, Joseph of Arimathea may have owned multiple tombs—or those doing the deed might have misunderstood which tomb they were supposed to use. The stone may have appeared to be rolled away because the tomb had never been closed.

Animals ate the body/Tomb not used. As New Testament scholar John Dominic Crossan has suggested,[987] wild animals may have torn up and ate the body of Jesus during or after crucifixion. So perhaps while the fleeing disciples (Mark 14:27) expected Jesus to be buried in a particular tomb, it was actually never used. As no recognizable body existed and the tomb was empty, some resurrection stories could have subsequently developed proclaiming the undying spirit of the apocalyptic preacher. As many Mormons find their unlikely beliefs verified by a "burning in the bosom,"[988] so too early disciples may have become confident of their resurrection beliefs due to psychological feelings that they thought evidenced the witness of the Holy Spirit.

Dreams. Perhaps after the body was decayed beyond recognition (i.e., after several days in a warm climate), a notable disciple or disciples of Jesus had vivid dreams about Jesus being alive and walking among them. In early Christianity, as in the history of many other religions, dreams were widely believed to be vehicles of divine messages (Matt. 1:20-21, Matt. 2:13, Matt. 2:19-20, Acts 8:26, etc.). Disciples may have believed that these dreams were inspired by God directly—and therefore every bit as real and spiritually significant as if Jesus had actually been raised from the dead in their waking lives. Stories may have spread with differing details in part because different individuals had dreams with differing content—and in part due to the typical alterations that take place in oral storytelling.[989]

Visions/Hallucinations. Perhaps the literal belief in a bodily resurrection grew out of experiences like St. Paul on Damascus Road (1 Cor. 15:7-9)—which were not interactions with a historical Jesus but with a supposedly heavenly one. Studies in the psychology of religion have found that certain extreme religious practices can lead to altered states of consciousness, hallucinations, and hyper-suggestibility.[990] Perhaps zealous and susceptible individuals who had been fasting, depriving themselves of sleep and stimulus deprivation in "night vigils," distraught and exhausted over the loss of their beloved teacher, and/or were affected by fear-inducing preachments about damnation had visual, auditory, and/or tactile hallucinations which were misconstrued as actual events in the real world.[991] It should also be noted that visions of loved ones after their deaths are well-documented in psychological literature.[992] Further, there is some evidence that similar hallucinations can occur between individuals with shared delusions.⁹⁹³ When the Gospel of Matthew notes that some disciples doubted when there was an appearance of Jesus (Matt. 28:16-17), perhaps that indicates that the appearance of Jesus was not seen by everyone there. Jesus may have just been seen by one or two of them—or perhaps hallucinations with slightly different content were seen by some and nothing was seen by others. Perhaps then tales of separate visions were misremembered as group appearances as resurrection stories spread.⁹⁹⁴ The supposed apparitions of St. Mary at Medjugorje could be a modern example of the general phenomenon, wherein some claim to see a dead person while others cannot see or hear anything (nor can video or audio equipment detect anything).⁹⁹⁵ Some visionaries at Medjugorje even claim that they touched Mary's robe, much like disciples were supposed to have touched the risen Christ (Luke 24:40-43, John 20:27).⁹⁹⁶ Furthermore, it is also worth noting that there is some overlap between biblical visions and dreams (Num. 12:6; Job 4:13, Acts 2:17)—so that many of the issues pertaining to dreams may apply to visions as well.⁹⁹⁷

Survived crucifixion. According to the ancient historian Herodotus, a man named Sandoces was crucified by King Darius but then removed from the cross and survived. He recovered enough to be the commander of a Persian squadron.⁹⁹⁸ Likewise, the ancient Jewish historian Josephus recounts that he pleaded with the Roman emperor Titus to take down three men from crosses; Titus agreed, and one of them apparently survived.⁹⁹⁹ In the 18th century, radical Jansenists known as *convulsionnaires* were known to have themselves ritually crucified for up to hours at a time as extreme acts of piety.¹⁰⁰⁰ Some modern Filipinos, despite the discouragement of church officials, have likewise been ritually crucified and routinely survive.¹⁰⁰¹ Furthermore, modern Syrians have been said to survive crucifixions at the hand of ISIS.¹⁰⁰² Perhaps Jesus recovered after his crucifixion as well. It may be that the story of the spear being thrust into his side, told only in the Gospel of John (John 19:31-37), is a later accretion that was added in order to claim a prophetical fulfillment had occurred (cf. Zech. 12:10). Or maybe he was removed from the cross earlier than the canonical gospels suggest (perhaps in an unconscious state) and then later revived.¹⁰⁰³ Spiritual stories could have then grown up around the remarkable survival of a charismatic apocalyptic preacher.

Non-historical myth. Although in opposition to the great majority of historians,[1004] mythicists like Richard Carrier (b. 1969), Earl Doherty (b. 1941), and Bertrand Russell (1872-1970) could be correct that Jesus of Nazareth never actually existed.[1005] The true explanation of all the Jesus stories would lie in the creativity of the human religious imagination—which is elsewhere demonstrated in the immense varieties of religions, sects, doctrines, myths, metaphysical ideas, miraculous tales, and purported revelations that appear throughout recorded history. Or more likely, some events or details from the Gospels may be accurate, but historically speaking the Resurrection itself may just be the "idle tale" that we are told some of the disciples originally understood it to be (Luke 24:11). Furthermore, the position that the Resurrection was mythical has actually been shared by devout believers (albeit for different reasons). Followers of the Manichaean faith, though believing themselves to be followers of Jesus, thought a literal resurrection was a fable[1006] —as did many Gnostic Christians.[1007]

It is true that all these admittedly speculative explanations may well be inaccurate in part or in whole (and some are surely less plausible than others). Nevertheless, they would all seem more likely than a literal, bodily resurrection. The following explanation from New Testament scholar Bart Ehrman about the plausibility of Jesus' body being stolen by family members could be applied to any of the above:

> Is this scenario likely? Not at all. Am I proposing this is what really happened? Absolutely not. Is it more probable that something like this happened than that a miracle happened and Jesus left the tomb to ascend to heaven? Absolutely! From a purely historical point of view, a highly unlikely event is more probable than a virtually impossible one.[1008]

Stated differently, hallucinations, dreams, mistaken identities, grave-robbing, misapprehensions, deceptions, delusions, tall tales, legends, myths, embellished stories, false memories, miscommunications, errors, misinterpretations, and the like are all verifiably part of human experience. They have been studied by social scientists, historians, and psychologists. They are observable in human experience. In a definitional sense, it would not be a miracle if any of these other explanations were true. Conversely, literal resurrections would have to be regarded as extremely improbable events—which may even be outside the realm of possibility.

[22-24] The Great Grab Bag

> It's a vast array of things that people believe. ... There's a grab bag of religious alternatives.
>
> —**Carl Sagan** (1934-1996), American astrophysicist[1009]

The tremendous range of religious diversity is one of the greatest reasons for skepticism towards any particular religious belief. In the next three meditations, this general problem of diversity will be explored through the presentation of various anecdotes, examples, and numerical data. While these meditations are interrelated, coming at the issue from different angles—as well as exploring specifics as opposed to just generalities—provides a much deeper understanding of the extent of the problem. This three-part series will thus focus on the following implications of religious diversity: (1) that subjective supernatural leadings are probably unreliable, (2) that the prodigious human propensity to err appears to be even more pronounced in religious contexts, and (3) that the sheer number of options suggests that any particular individual is very unlikely to have accurate religious opinions—especially in any way that could be deemed comprehensive.

[22] The Great Grab Bag (pt.1): Led by the Spirit

...The unreliability of subjective Christian leadings

Many of those, however, who profess to believe in Christ, hold conflicting opinions not only on small and trivial questions, but also on some that are great and important.

—**Origen** (c.185-c.254), Egyptian early church father[1010]

Learning to accurately distinguish the leading of the Holy Spirit is perhaps the greatest challenge we can face.

—**Kenneth Copeland ministries**, American televangelist organization[1011]

The immense variety of Christian opinions and practices throughout history often goes unrecognized. Scholar Elaine Pagels has asserted that "Contemporary Christianity, diverse and complex as we find it, actually may show more unanimity than the churches of the first and second centuries."[1012] While there are no doubt some difficulties in making this comparison, it is nonetheless clear that Christianity was already profoundly diverse even by the late second century. In fact, leading early bishop Irenaeus of Lyons (fl. c. 175-195) proclaimed in his lengthy *Against the Heresies* that he could not even catalogue all the many divergences in belief. From his own perspective, "It is impossible to tell the number of those who have fallen away from the Truth in various ways."[1013] Of course, this proclamation was made centuries before all the developments and changes that came with the Middle Ages, the Reformation, and worldwide attempts to spread various versions of Christianity in a variety of different cultural and historical contexts.

What all this suggests is that there is no "faith that was once for all entrusted to the saints" (Jude 1:3)—but that the doctrines of even professedly "orthodox" forms of Christianity are constantly changing, developing, reforming, and disappearing. Claiming exact kinship to believers in other times and places typically seems forced.[1014] Strict standards of belief and practice throughout time, culture, and geography appear to be more of a product of imagination than careful comparison. As scholar and former Archbishop of Canterbury Rowan Williams (b. 1950) himself confessed, "Proclaiming *now* the same gospel as before is a great deal less easy than it sounds."[1015]

Building on the Christian diversity presented in past meditations, what follows is a somewhat random sampling of some of the odd, conflicting, violent, colorful, and fantastic beliefs and practices that have arisen in world Christianity. What is striking is not only the profound variety, but also the common belief that inspiration came from the same Divine Source.

Although the beliefs of the early church are often unknown to moderns, early believers often had strong convictions about God that are sometimes no longer even part of the Christian landscape. While examples abound, a few provide an inkling of the diversity of thought and practice. As witnessed by the 2nd-century scripture called the *Infancy Gospel of Thomas*, some early Christians believed that the child Jesus was not that "meek and mild"—but rather vindictive and cruel. After crippling, blinding, or killing people who he found vexing,[1016] Jesus' father Joseph became distraught and instructed Mary: "Do not let him go outside the door, because anyone who angers him dies."[1017] In another interesting example, certain Gnostic believers in the early Christian centuries thought that the God of the Old Testament was ignorant and immoral. This, they asserted, was proved by his jealousy, violence, and propensity for cursing and killing people.[1018]

Many early Christians felt that there was only one ecclesiastical group that had valid sacraments and through which people could be saved.[1019] Described by modern scholars with the terms *fruhkatholizimus* or "early catholicism," these Christians—who were a recognizable body by the early second or perhaps even the late first century—had a fixed structure that put great stress on the authority of bishops.[1020] Relatedly, the second-century *Acts of Thecla* seems to support the emergence of early examples of what Protestants later derided as "Romanism" or "popery"—where the virtues of lifelong virginity, prayer for the dead, and making the sign of the cross are all described.[1021] The Martyrdom of Polycarp, a second-century account of a bishop and martyr, likewise shows how some early Christians desired relics and wanted to touch the "holy flesh" of dead saints.[1022] While divorce and remarriage was denounced in the early catholic tradition, the third-century *Didascalia* even advised that God disapproved of widows who remarried. While a second marriage for a widow was not laudatory, the *Didascalia* pronounced that upon marrying a third time a widow was "(to be accounted) a harlot."[1023] While vandalizing non-Christian religious property is generally seen as sinful by modern Christians, St. Martin of Tours (d.397) was reportedly convinced that God wanted him to tear down pagan temples, statues, and shrines.[1024]

Traditional Eastern Orthodox spirituality claims that St. Luke was not only the inspired writer of the third Gospel but also the first painter of icons. While the first record of this tradition does not appear until the sixth century,[1025] it is a common belief among the Eastern Orthodox, who strongly believe in the divine power of these stylized paintings. The icon of the Virgin Hodegetria at the Golden Gate in Constantinople, which was greatly revered for its holiness, was in fact regarded as St. Luke's creation.[1026] Early church fathers often gauged the leadings of God differently, however, often speaking disparagingly of religious images and statues.[1027] Even as late as the fifth century, St. Augustine remarked agreeably in his *City of God* to the notion that God "should be worshipped without an image."[1028]

Church father Origen, who was both extremely devout and perhaps the premier biblical scholar of the early church, held that contradictions, absurdities, or immoral content in the Scriptures were in fact an indication that God was attempting to communicate a deeper meaning.[1029] While uncommon today, early Catholic Christians often enforced long penitential periods for what they considered to be grave sins. For instance, a rigorist element in early Catholicism thought that those who had offered incense to the emperor during persecution could not be restored to fellowship—but must rather live a life of penance and only hope for God's mercy in the afterlife.[1030] Canon 11 of the famous Council of Nicaea (325) laid out an 11-year penitential period for those who renounced the faith and then wished to return.[1031] Likewise, and in contrast to the relative leniency often given to abusive priests in the modern Roman Catholic Church, the Council of Elvira in the fourth century declared that pedophiles could not receive communion even at the point of death.[1032] Voluntary lives of penance were also fairly common. Some highly revered Christian ascetics in the earlier periods of the Catholic Church even believed that God wanted them to live their lives on top of pillars. The highly esteemed St. Simeon the Stylite (c.390-459) is said to have spent 36 years on the top of a pillar[1033] while St. Daniel the Stylite (409-493) is said to have spent 33 years doing the same.[1034]

While the belief that Jesus is fully God became a hallmark of Roman Catholicism, Eastern Orthodoxy, and most forms of traditional Protestantism, for a time a lower Christology was very prominent in the Christian landscape. Early Jewish Christians, who claimed their beliefs came from the apostle Peter and Jesus' brother James, denied the pre-existence and divinity of Jesus—and many rejected the Virgin Birth as well.[1035] As St. Jerome (347-419) famously once lamented about the prevalence of one non-Trinitarian strain of Christological belief, "the whole world groaned and marveled to find itself Arian."[1036]

Another notable group of believers was the dualistic Manichaeans, who held themselves to be true followers of Jesus Christ and in fact called themselves the "Church of the Holy Spirit." Lasting from the 3rd to perhaps the 17th century,[1037] Manichaeans professed that it was Jesus and not Satan who encouraged Adam to eat from the Tree of Knowledge.[1038] The Circumcellions were a violent and fanatical wing of the Donatist Church that thrived in North Africa before the Islamic conquests of the seventh century. In an interesting parallel to radical Islamic terrorism in the modern era, Circumcellions killed and maimed adversaries, revered martyrdom, and would often shout "Praise to God!" when inflicting their terrors. St. Augustine (354-430) is said to have narrowly escaped one of their ambushes.[1039] One obscure group of Monophysite Christians, who have generally been known for believing that Christ had only one nature, were known as the Halacephalites. Interestingly, these believers held that if they hung down their heads for a certain number of hours every day for twenty days, God would purify them from evil.[1040] St. Augustine provides evidence of the strong belief in God's miraculous intervention that is often absent in modern Christians. For example, he maintained, based on "very respectable and trustworthy witnesses," that God had granted a slave named Christianus "full knowledge of the art of reading simply through prayer."[1041] Giving an early example of a strong belief in faith healing, St. Jerome recounted that revered ascetic St. Hilarion (c.291-371) told a chronically ill woman that "If you had given to the poor what you had wasted on doctors, Jesus, the true doctor, would have healed you."[1042]

While Christianity greatly extended its reach through missionary endeavors in the Middle Ages, it was also commonly spread by coercion and threats of violence. For instance, the Viking King Olaf Trygvesson (960's-1000) believed that he was on a holy errand to have all Norwegians baptized, reportedly remarking that "All Norway will be Christian or die." He was good to his word, using threats, torture, banishment, and massacres to accomplish his goal.[1043] While Olaf is an extreme example, forced conversions were not uncommon in the medieval period. The Frankish emperor Charlemagne (742-814), for instance, compelled the Frisians and Saxons to be baptized against their will.[1044] Likewise, St. Stephen of Hungary (977-1038) forcibly converted his subjects[1045] as apparently did St. Vladimir of Kiev (d. 1015).[1046] The 9th-century Eastern Empress Theodora ordered a campaign of persecution against the dualist Paulician sect; over 100,000 are thought to have been martyred during her reign.[1047] Another prominent example of persecution pertains to the pacifist Christian sect known as the Cathars. Since they were resistant to rejoining the Roman Catholic Church, Pope Innocent III inaugurated a brutal crusade (1209-1229) which resulted in the deaths of as many as one million people from the region in total.[1048] While such behavior is usually considered an abomination to modern Christians, captured Cathars were cruelly tortured or burned at the stake both in the midst of the campaigning and afterwards, when the newly established Inquisition was called into existence to finish the "cleansing" that the crusade had failed to accomplish.[1049] Tragically, in a different way, some Cathars lost their lives not to persecution but to voluntarily starving themselves to death in the *Endura* rite.[1050]

The preaching of the First Crusade in 1095 was met with the cries of "Deus vult" ("God wills it") from the laity.[1051] While there were some rare voices of concern, the Crusades of the Middle Ages were commanded by the Magisterium of the Roman Catholic Church through popes and Councils,[1052] exhorted by many prominent saints like St. Bernard of Clairvaux (1090-1153),[1053] St. Catherine of Siena (1347-1380),[1054] and St. Albert the Great (1206-1280),[1055] and approved by the general "sense of the faithful."[1056]

While Catholic authorities were at times decisive and quite heavy-handed, at other points they gave unclear or even conflicting directions about God's will. A major example is in the Great Schism of 1054, when Greek East and Latin West separated and denounced each other's teachings on various things including the extent of papal authority, whether it was correct to say that the Holy Spirit proceeded from the Father only or from both Father and Son (*filioque*), and whether the bread in the eucharist should be unleavened. Another prime example of division is the Roman Catholic Great Schism of 1378-1417, when there were as many as three men who claimed to be the Vicar of Christ on earth.[1057] Even canonized saints held different opinions about which pope was God's anointed.[1058] Interestingly, St. Bernard of Clairvaux (1090-1153), though an official Doctor of the Roman Catholic Church due to the perceived excellence of his teachings, rejected the doctrine of the Immaculate Conception of Mary even though it was to later become a dogma of the Roman Catholic Church in 1854.[1059]

While he did not believe in the central Protestant doctrine of justification by faith alone,[1060] the so-called "Morning Star of the Reformation" John Wycliffe (c.1320-1384) thought the Spirit urged the authority of Scripture over the Church and the translation of the Bible into the vernacular. Furthermore, Wycliffe urged the rejection of image veneration, clerical celibacy, transubstantiation, praying for the dead, and papal claims pertaining to spiritual authority. Although he was protected while he was alive, forty-three years after his death Roman Catholic authorities thought his teachings were corrupt enough that they dug up his corpse, burned it, and threw his remains into a river.[1061] Another example of divergent thought in the Middle Ages is seen with Jan Huss (c.1369-1415), another prominent forerunner of the Reformation. While he also did not believe that faith alone saved,[1062] Huss thought God advocated the end of indulgences, wanted the restoration of communion with both bread and wine, gave the Bible as an authority over pope and council, and wished for the end of simony and clerical wealth.[1063] After being given assurances of safe conduct, Huss was burned alive by the Council of Constance (1414-1418) which declared that it had "legitimately assembled in the holy Spirit" and had "power immediately from Christ."[1064] Interestingly, the Council not only condemned the teachings of Wycliffe and Huss and helped bring about the end of the Roman Catholic Church's Great Schism, but also espoused a view of conciliar authority that was eventually declared heretical by the 1870 Vatican I Council.[1065]

Confusion about the Spirit's leadings are also connected to famous medieval visionaries and theologians. St. Bridget (d.1373) wondered for a time if her visions were from God, the devil, or her imagination. Likewise, St. Hildegard (1098-1179), known chiefly for her revelations and prophecies, was thought by some of her contemporaries to be demon-possessed and a fraud.[1066] St. Thomas Aquinas (1225-1274), whose work was deemed to be the quintessential expression of Roman Catholic truth by Pope Leo XIII in 1879,[1067] is said to have stopped writing his famous *Summa Theologiae* a few months before his death after experiencing an intense sense of ecstasy at Mass. He supposedly said: "I can write no more. All that I have written seems like straw."[1068]

Perhaps the most entertaining aspects of medieval faith are its more extreme and outrageous characteristics. While frequently considered bogus today, medieval relics included the axe used by Noah to build the ark, the tunic and hair of St. John the Baptist,[1069] the foreskin of Jesus, and even the breastmilk of the Virgin Mary.[1070] The faithful in the Middle Ages often went to great lengths to obtain relics due to their perceived spiritual power.[1071] Some of the most coveted relics belonged to St. Nicholas of Myra, the beloved 4th-century bishop who became the basis of later Santa Claus myths.[1072] In an apparently successful attempt to rid himself of all lustful thoughts, St. Benedict of Nursia (480-547), author of monasticism's famous Benedictine Rule, is said to have thrown himself naked into "sharp thorns and stinging nettles" and then rolled "around in them for a long time."[1073] As related by the English church historian Bede (d. 735), a man named Drythelm stood out in icy waters for long periods as severe penance after seeing a vision of hell—and by his example "helped many people to salvation."[1074] Eschewing the notion that "cleanliness is next to godliness," St. Symeon the New Theologian (949-1022) felt that monks would be closer to God if they did not take baths—even if urged to by their fellow monks! Symeon also advised that every monk should wash his outer garment twice every year—but only "if" it gets dirty.[1075] Described as having an "abundant anointing of the Holy Spirit,"[1076] St. Francis of Assisi (1181-1226) is said to have mixed ashes into his food to ruin its taste, used a piece of wood or stone for a pillow, thrown himself into icy ditches, jumped naked into deep snow, fasted for forty days at a time, and preached to attentive flocks of birds.[1077] St. Thomas Aquinas and St. Bonaventure (1221-1274) both believed that humans could have sexual intercourse with demons.[1078] In the 14th-century Hesychast Controversy, the Eastern Orthodox quarreled over whether the spiritually advanced were able to see the Divine and Uncreated Light of God with their bodily eyes.[1079] St. Catherine of Siena (1347-1380) engaged in such frequent fasting that today she would likely be diagnosed with anorexia. Following what she perceived as the stern leadings of the Spirit, she also routinely deprived herself of sleep and was known to flagellate herself with iron chains up to three times a day for one and a half hours at a time.[1080] St. James, son of Zebedee and one of the twelve disciples, became known as Matamoros ("the Moor Slayer") in medieval Spain during the Reconquest. Oddly enough, the long-dead fisherman-turned-apostle was believed to have personally killed thousands of Muslims on the battlefield.[1081] Like the Counter-Reformation Catholics that followed them, the medieval faithful believed that saints filled with the Spirit of God performed frequent miracles. Examples include nuns floating during prayer, heavenly light shining from saints' faces, sores mimicking the wounds of the Crucifixion (stigmata), hearts becoming so "inflamed" with love that they literally became as hot as fire, and strict fasts lasting for years without respite. The relics of some dead saints have been thought to cure disease and their corpses were sometimes believed to be incorrupt or pleasant-smelling.[1082]

The turmoil and enthusiasm of the Reformation highlights the diverse nature of the Spirit's leadings. While lamenting the "pernicious poison" of Lutherans who interpreted the Bible "otherwise than the Holy Spirit demands," Pope Leo X (1475-1521) declared in his bull *Exsurge Domine* that it was gravely erroneous to assert that the burning to death of heretics was "against the will of the Spirit."[1083] Claiming to know God's plan for the

Jews and failing to predict the 1948 rise of the Israeli state, Martin Luther (1483-1546) confidently asserted that he would get circumcised if Israel ever became a nation again.[1084] In contrast to most forms of Christian worship today, early Calvinists often rejected the use of musical instruments and insisted that only the book of Psalms should be used when singing hymns.[1085] Anabaptist radical Jan van Leyden (1509-1536) inaugurated his kingship of Munster, the "new Jerusalem," by running through the town nude in an ecstatic religious state.[1086] Early English Separatist John Smyth (c.1570-1612) thought that the Church of England was "the Church of the Antichrist." Since he could find no true church remaining on earth, he felt God wanted him to baptize himself.[1087] In contrast to modern sensibilities, both Protestant and Roman Catholic authorities believed it was God's will to censor books during the Reformation period.[1088] Thinking that the Lord only permitted things specifically mentioned in Scripture, 17th-century Puritans concluded that celebrating Christmas was sinful.[1089] The wars of Puritan Oliver Cromwell in Britain in the seventeenth century are in some ways analogous to medieval crusades. Cromwell's army was convinced that he was conducting a holy war; his soldiers were in fact known to sing hymns while running into battle.[1090] The campaigns in Ireland are remembered as particularly brutal—not only laymen, but priests, women, and even children were sometimes massacred.[1091]

While many traditional Protestants have questioned whether Roman Catholics could be regarded as true Christians and have considered Catholicism to be clearly false and corrupt, French mathematician Blaise Pascal (1623-1662) thought the Roman Catholic Church was an obvious product of the Holy Spirit. He once remarked, "Those who love God with all their hearts cannot possibly fail to recognize the Church, plain as it is. Those who do not love God cannot possibly be convinced of the Church."[1092] While perhaps more reminiscent of fundamentalist Protestantism than Catholicism, St. John Vianney (1786-1859) was a stern moralist who believed that God was extremely concerned about the sinfulness of dancing. He was known to refuse absolution in the confessional to those who would not resolve to quit dancing forever![1093] St. Rose of Lima (1586-1617) believed God was pleased when she inflicted severe pain on herself. She reportedly engaged in strict and frequent fasts, wore a spiked metal crown and an iron chain about her waist, rubbed her face with pepper to ruin her complexion, and slept on "a bed constructed by herself, of broken glass, stone, potsherds, and thorns."[1094] A group of ecstatic Jansenists in 18th-century France called *convulsionnaires* believed that their screaming, trembling, contorting, speaking in tongues, giving sermons in dream-like trances, and healings were all proof of the Holy Spirit's presence. In their gatherings participants were dragged, jumped on, poked with sharp objects, choked, and beaten; they believed their ability to endure pain was a sign of God's miraculous power and an encouragement for the coming of the Last Days.[1095] Excommunicated Roman Catholic modernist Alfred Loisy (1857-1940), who looked back on his traditional theological training as a kind of "mental and moral torture," was taught by a professor of Scripture that the book of Revelation predicted the first Vatican Council.[1096]

In more modern times, papal remorse for the Crusades[1097] and the current Roman Catholic teaching on warfare[1098] suggest that the Spirit was gravely misunderstood for centuries. Relatedly, traditionalist Roman Catholics today largely lament the changes in doctrine and practice that have entered the modern Catholic Church since Vatican II (1962-1965), claiming that they are outside Holy Tradition and thus not part of God's will. Some of these changes pertain to views on capital punishment, the freedom of religion and conscience, the cremation of the dead, the doctrine of Limbo,[1099] the permissibility of mass in vernacular languages, whether the "perfidious Jews" need to convert,[1100] the use of altar girls in Mass, the neglect of head coverings by women in Mass, receiving the Host in the hand instead of on the tongue, the abandonment of literal and historical nature of Genesis, the decreased interest in missionary work and evangelization, and the recent practices of worshipping with non-Christians or with other types of Christians. In the words of one traditionalist source, modern Roman Catholics now "gladly defend and practice a form of Catholicism that would have horrified any Pope before 1960."[1101] Some traditionalist Roman Catholics called sedevacantists also hold that recent popes since the Vatican II Council (1962-1965) are not legitimate leaders due to their departure from traditional Catholic teachings.[1102] Inspired by a Marian vision at Palma de Troya in Spain, the separatist Palmarian Catholic Church has actually been crowning its own popes since 1978—and has continued the use of the traditional Latin Tridentine Mass.[1103] Incidentally, there have been many other different churches using the title

"Catholic" and following God in their own (often very different) ways today. These include various Old Catholic, Liberal Catholic, and Independent Catholic Churches with intriguing names like the Polish National Catholic Church, the Liberal Catholic Church, the Catholic Apostolic Church, the Catholic Church of the Apostles of Latter-Day Times, the United American Catholic Church, the Traditional Independent Roman Catholic Church, the Orthodox Catholic Church of America, the Orthodox Catholic Church, the Free Catholic Church International, and the Friends Catholic Community Church.[1104]

Starting with the "camp meetings" of the Second Great Awakening in the early nineteenth century, American Protestantism has often had an ecstatic dimension that was believed to be inspired by the Holy Spirit. Trances, spasmodic "jerks," holy laughter, weeping uncontrollably, speaking in tongues, barking on all fours to "tree the devil," falling down, seeing visions, rolling over continuously, and shouting are some of the more colorful behaviors that have found expression.[1105] Likewise, 19th-century Amish Mennonite "sleep preachers" gave sermons in a deep trance, believing that they were communicating messages directly from God. Some claimed that they could not afterwards remember anything that they had spoken.[1106] The Rev. Edmund Massey (1690-1765) preached a sermon in 1722 in which he urged that while scoffers and unbelievers might inoculate to prevent disease, Christians could not do it without sin. He reasoned that people should "bless God for the Afflictions which he sends" rather than try to "sinfully endeavour to alter the Course of Nature."[1107] Similarly, Dr. Timothy Dwight (1752-1817), president of Yale and a leading divine, objected to vaccinations as an interference with God's providence.[1108] Early 20th-century Pentecostal Christians in the United States were known to speak in tongues, fall in to trances, laugh uncontrollably—and allegedly even levitate.[1109]

In stark contrast to the meekness championed by some expressions of Christianity, American Protestant bodybuilder-evangelists known as "The Power Team" combine feats of strength with proselytization. Focused primarily on impressing teenagers, the Power Team has been known to bend metal bars, rip telephone books in two, and blow up hot water bottles until they burst open.[1110] In contrast to most Protestants, the Amish have generally seen insurance as worldly and a failure to have faith in God's provision.[1111] "The Family," also called the "Children of God" or "The Family of Love," is a fundamentalist and apocalyptic Christian group that believed God wanted them to use religious prostitution ("flirty fishing") to win converts. They carried on this practice from around 1978 until 1987—when fears of the growing AIDS epidemic ended the tradition.[1112] In contrast, the once-thriving Shaker sect, named for its early practice of shaking during worship ceremonies, as of 2017 is down to just two members. No doubt a primary reason is their belief that God enjoins a complete rejection of sexual relations.[1113] As parodied in the 2002 hit movie *My Big Fat Greek Wedding*, the Eastern Orthodox are known to "spit on the devil" during the service of Baptism.[1114] The Ethiopian Orthodox hold that it is God's will to observe the Sabbath, practice circumcision, avoid "unclean" meats,[1115] and fast between 110 and 150 days a year.[1116] Ethiopian piety also commonly holds that God has made them guardians of the original ark of the covenant, which they believe is kept in the town of Aksum.[1117]

In all periods of Christianity, individual believers have felt led by the Holy Spirit to switch sectarian affiliation—in almost every conceivable direction. Second-century scholar Aquila converted from paganism to Christianity—but then to Judaism.[1118] Church father Tertullian (c.155-c.220) lost his fervor for early Catholicism and converted to Montanism. In the 15th century, Roman Catholics made statements of unity with Armenian, Coptic, Syrian, Chaldean, and Maronite Christians.[1119] Great numbers of Eastern Orthodox became Roman Catholic in 1596 at the Union of Brest-Litovsk while many Nestorian Christians have joined the Roman Catholic Church since the 16th century.[1120] To the distress of his English brethren, John Henry Newman (1801-1890) converted from Anglicanism to Roman Catholicism.[1121] Many other 19th- and 20th-century intellectuals followed suit[1122] –including G. K. Chesterton (1874-1936). 19th-century Frenchman Jules (Raymond) Ferrette changed from Protestantism, to Roman Catholicism, and back to Protestantism—before he was ordained as a bishop in an Oriental Orthodox church.[1123] *First Things* editor Richard Neuhaus (1936-2009) switched from being a Lutheran pastor to a Roman Catholic priest. The Coming Home Network International boasts converts to Roman Catholicism from Anglican, Baptist, Methodist, Pentecostal, Lutheran, Church of Christ, Quaker, Mennonite, Jehovah's Witness, and other Christian affiliations.[1124] Similarly, the Journey to Orthodoxy website chronicles conversions to Eastern Orthodoxy from Roman Catholicism and a variety of other Christian perspectives.[1125] Peter Gillquist and other staff workers at the evangelical parachurch organization Campus Crusade for Christ converted to Eastern Orthodoxy in 1987; radio personality and "Bible Answer Man" Hank Hannegraaff did the same in 2017.[1126] Apologist William Webster converted from Roman Catholicism to evangelical Protestantism;[1127] numerous former Roman Catholic priests have likewise linked their salvation with doing the same.[1128] Likewise, Latin Americans have left the Roman Catholic Church in droves in recent decades to become Protestant.[1129] American preacher Billy Graham (1918-2018) changed from Reformed Presbyterian to Southern Baptist.[1130] Frank Schaeffer, son of prominent evangelical Presbyterian Francis Schaeffer, converted from Calvinism to Eastern Orthodoxy—and now calls himself "an atheist who believes in God."[1131] A good number of Russian Orthodox believers have converted to various types of Protestantism or to Roman Catholicism.[1132] Protestants commonly move around between charismatic, fundamentalist, nondenominational, Calvinist, liturgical, and progressive orientations.[1133] While more mundane reasons can accompany such interdenominational conversions, a heartfelt belief in divine promptings is a common explanation. (And while it seems somewhat absurd looking back, I myself believed that God was leading me every time I made a transition—from a nominal Roman Catholic with charismatic leanings, to attending a Southern Baptist church, to joining a Presbyterian church and going to Presbyterian seminary, to considering becoming Anglican or Eastern Orthodox, and then briefly rejoining the Roman Catholic Church.)

While interesting and at times even somewhat astonishing, knowledge of the diversity of Christian beliefs about the Holy Spirit's leadings also has a practical application. It provides a potential window into the tenuousness of individual Christian claims to supernatural guidance—and thus an antidote to various forms of religious manipulation. Despite the sincere earnestness and confidence of individual believers, preachers, and priests, the divergent and often contradictory paths of the supposed leadings of God seem to reflect more the human propensity for imaginative thinking than a true connection to an omniscient and ineffable Source. In the words of Unitarian Universalist minister Roger Christan Schriner,

Often when people say "*God wants this*" they are merely expressing their own biases. "*Thus saith the Lord*" sounds more impressive than "*Thus saith me*," but it may amount to the same thing.[1134]

[23] The Great Grab Bag (pt.2): Reasons of the Heart
...Worldwide religious diversity and human error

> The heart has its reasons of which reason knows nothing: we know this in countless ways.
>
> —**Blaise Pascal** (1623-1662), French mathematician and Roman Catholic philosopher[1135]

> The easy confidence with which I know another man's religion is folly teaches me to suspect that my own is also.
>
> —**Mark Twain** (1835-1910), American satirist and novelist[1136]

Although the diversity of Christianity is quite vast, it is miniscule compared to the varieties of belief and practice in the entirety of the human religious experience. While Christians have of course generally held that their particular religious expressions were based on the leadings of their god, countless other believers from multitudes of other religions have felt that they have known and understood mystical realities from other divine sources. Though it is difficult to provide a representative picture of the scope of this diversity, it has been so broad that it seems fair to say that it has only been restricted, in the words of one psychology of religion text, "by the structure and capacities of the human body and by the outer boundaries of human inventiveness."[1137]

While the following religious facts and anecdotes are presented in a similar manner to the last meditation, examples are now garnered from the beliefs and practices of various non-Christian religions. Furthermore, they are presented as a forum to consider further whether emotive or spiritual "reasons of the heart" are sufficient grounds to maintain beliefs that seem otherwise divorced from reason and evidence.

There are likely an immense number of religions whose beliefs have been lost in pre-history. Over 100,000 years ago, the Neanderthals of central Europe are thought to have buried their dead with food for the afterlife. In fact, religious ritual has been projected by some scholars to be possibly as old as 500,000 years.[1138] *The ruins of the oldest known temple in the world*, Göbekli Tepe, can still be seen in southern Turkey. It is believed that the site is 11,600 years old—seven thousand years older than the Great Pyramid of Giza. The religious beliefs of Göbekli Tepe's worshippers are long-forgotten and largely unknown.[1139]

Like the later Mosaic Law, the Babylonian Code of Hammurabi (c.1750 BCE) was said to have been given by a god.[1140] Ancient Babylonian religion also provides several parallels to later biblical stories. These include the myth of a primordial paradise and the creation of humanity from clay by divine word. Perhaps most strikingly is a flood myth wherein a deluge is sent as divine judgment on humanity. The patriarchal figure of the story, after being given divine warning, builds a boat to save his family and animals. When his ship comes to rest on a mountaintop, he dispatches birds.[1141]

In addition to the casting of lots and speaking with the spirits of the dead, ancient Greeks examined entrails, ripples in the water, fire, trees, vegetables, word patterns, mirror reflection patterns, stars, and even sneezing to determine the will of the gods. The priestess at the temple of Apollo in Argos would drink the blood of sacrificed animals in order to prophesy.[1142] Ancient Greek piety included the notion that statues of gods could be induced to smile or nod their heads through the use of chants, incense, and herbs.[1143] While celibate religious expressions are well known, religious prostitution was also common in the ancient world. The Temple of Aphrodite in Corinth, by way of example, is said to have had 1,000 temple prostitutes at its height.[1144] Pagan oracles like the one at Delphi claimed to proclaim the truths of the gods; believers thought that their track record of accurate predictions proved their validity.[1145] During the rise of Christianity, some oracles gave anti-Christian messages claiming that the new faith was false and that it sullied the purity of paganism.[1146]

In the Roman mystery religion of Cybele, baptism in bull's blood was thought to bring eternal life.[1147] In addition to the classic Roman pantheon, the ancient peoples of the Roman Empire worshipped a large variety of other deities. One prominent goddess, often referred to as the "Great Mother," had some radical devotees who would castrate themselves as an act of piety.[1148] While the Roman Empire is well known for its classical gods, the emperor Aurelian established the sun god as the supreme deity of Rome in 274.[1149] (Constantine the Great was himself a sun-worshipper before converting to Catholic Christianity.[1150]) The Norse berserks fought naked and in a state of frenzy, claiming to derive their power from the god Odin.[1151] Perhaps in an attempt to harness spiritual power, ancient Celts were head-hunters and often displayed skulls in niches in their temple doorways.[1152]

The Vietnamese Cao Dai hold French novelist Victor Hugo, most famous for writing *Les Misérables*, as either one of their prophets or one of their divinities.[1153] Many Hindus believe that the miraculous powers of the elephant-headed god Ganesha were displayed when he devoured the milk offerings of his devotees around the world on September 22, 1995.[1154] The Sikhs of India believe in reincarnation but are also strictly monotheistic; they also have an initiation ceremony of baptism.[1155] Among the cardinal sins of orthodox Sikhism are cutting one's hair, consuming meat killed in the Muslim fashion (*halāl*), and smoking.[1156] Mongolian shamans once prophesied by interpreting the cracks in the burned shoulder blades of sheep.[1157]

Tibetan Buddhists have been known to dismember their dead and leave the body parts to feed wild animals.[1158] Based on a belief in the spiritual power of cows, Hindus have been known to drink cow urine, use soaps and other "health" products made with cow feces, and even pave the floors of their homes with bovine dung.[1159] Nepalese dwelling in the Kathmandu Valley select prepubescent girls to be "kumaris" or living goddesses. They believe that the girls are indwelt by a female Buddha named Vajradevi or the Hindu goddess Taleju. While the goddesses are thought to remain with the girls until they start their menstrual cycles, it is believed that if a girl bleeds for any other reason before puberty that the divine being will leave early. Former kumaris often have trouble marrying later in life— some even believe that snakes come out of their vaginas to devour any man who has sexual intercourse with them![1160] Taoists often believe that their sages have learned sexual secrets, ingested mercury compounds, and practiced mystical processes of "internal alchemy" to greatly extend their lifespans. Likewise, their masters are said to have controlled animals and ghosts, made themselves translucent, healed broken bones and diseases, shrunk the size of the earth, and made spiritual journeys to the Big Dipper constellation so that its gods could inhabit their bodily organs.[1161] In an interesting parallel to the future savior Buddha Maitreya, some Taoists have believed in a messianic figure named Lord Li who will come to bring political and cosmic redemption.[1162]

The often cryptic and even illogical Zen koans seek to provide a medium for insight and enlightenment. One example from the collection known as *The Gateless Gate* colorfully illustrates this unusual form of spirituality: "A monk asked Ummon, 'What is Buddha?' Ummon replied, 'Kanshiketsu!'" ("Kanshiketsu" means "shit-stick.")[1163] The current Dalai Lama believes that the karmic cycle is not limited to the planet earth. Rather, he holds that reincarnation was taking place before the earth was formed—on other planets. He also thinks that the cycle has been so long that all beings in existence have at one time been every other person's mother.[1164]

A Japanese religious practice encourages believers to write their prayers on pieces of paper, chew on them, and throw them to the ceiling of the temple. If they stick, it is believed that the prayers will be heard.[1165] The Oomoto religion, one of the "new religions" of Japan, holds to a syncretistic view of God that has been described as a kind of combination of monotheism, pantheism, and polytheism. The religion started in 1892 with the revelations of a supposedly illiterate widow. It is claimed that she took down over 200,000 pages of revelations through automatic writing after being possessed by the divine spirit Ushitora no Konjin. Oomoto adherents believe that all religions of the world are merely forerunners of their faith.[1166]

The Jain saint Mahavira, who may have been a contemporary of the Buddha, is said to have reached a state of omniscience. Tradition also holds that he went around naked for 12 years in a demonstration of asceticism and achieved a state of nirvana at the age of 72. Like the Buddha, he was said to have attained enlightenment while meditating under a tree.[1167] Jains, who are renowned for their charitable deeds, do not believe in a creator god or a god that can provide salvation.[1168] Holding non-violence (*ahimsa*) as one of the cardinal virtues,[1169] some Jains have been known to wear masks, sweep the path before them, and refrain from eating after dark to avoid the accidental killing of insects.[1170] More extreme adherents of Jainism have even been known to starve themselves to death as a supreme act of *ahimsa*.[1171]

Elijah Muhammad (1897-1975), African-American leader of the Nation of Islam (Black Muslims), claimed that African Americans could trace their lineage back to people living 66 trillion years ago on the moon! Muhammad's predecessor in the movement, Wallace Fard (c.1877-1934?), was believed by some to be the incarnation of Allah himself.[1172] Known as "Brides of the Koran," some girls and young women have literally married Islam's holy book—thereafter living lives of seclusion.[1173] In the Shi'a Muslim Ashura festival, the devout punch their own chests, cut themselves with knives, and inflict other forms of self-injury.[1174] Although rejected by mainstream Islam, the 'Alawite Shi'a sect has traditionally regarded Ali, Muhammad's cousin and son-in-law, as a divine incarnation.[1175] While Muslims generally agree that images are inappropriate and even offensive in places of worship, many believers in Iran, Turkey, Central Asia, and India nonetheless depict the Prophet Muhammad in pious pictures.[1176]

The writings of the Sufi Hafiz of Shiraz (14th c.) are held in such high esteem that many devotees select random passages to help them make decisions in everyday life situations.[1177] Sufi ascetics in the Qalandar movements were known to beg for their food, reject property, practice celibacy, wear iron chains and odd hats, and shave all hair off their heads (including their eyebrows). Many were also known for using intoxicants and hallucinogens. Some went about in rough wool clothing, others completely naked.[1178] Traditional Sufi piety holds that true saints can perform extraordinary miracles of healing, resurrect the dead, and fly.[1179] After ten years of intense spiritual practice, Muslim scholar Al-Ghazali (c.1058-1111) claimed that he knew "with certainty" that the Sufi way was the most ethically pure and spiritually enlightened, such that "were one to combine the insight of the intellectuals, the wisdom of the wise, and the lore of scholars versed in the mysteries of revelation in order to change a single item of Sufi conduct and ethic and to replace it with something better, no way to do so would be found!"[1180]

The Islamic hadith, which recount traditions of Muhammad and other early Muslim figures, often show a great deal of specificity about faith and practice. In one somewhat amusing example, Muhammad gives instructions about flatulence, suggesting that a worshipper "should not leave his prayers unless he hears sound or smells something."[1181] In another hadith, Satan is said to "pass wind with noise" in order to avoid hearing the Muslim call to prayer![1182] In yet others, Satan urinates in people's ears to keep them asleep and absent from morning prayers,[1183] causes yawns and bad dreams, stays in the upper part of people's noses at night,[1184] and touches newborn babies to make them cry.[1185]

Jinn are powerful supernatural beings described in the Qur'an. There are good and evil jinn—and Satan is described as a jinn that turned bad.[1186] While Calvinism is famous for advocating a Christian form of predestination, Islam has a similar tenet which attributes unbelief to Allah's inscrutable choice. According to the Qur'an, "The man whom Allah guides is rightly guided, but he who is led astray by Allah shall surely be lost. We have predestined for Hell many jinn and many men" (Sura 7:178-79; cf. 35:8).[1187]

Marrying up to four wives is traditionally licit in Islam. Muhammad himself is known for not only having nine or more wives but also keeping sex slaves or concubines.[1188] While there is a heated dispute on this point among the faithful, one hadith startlingly notes that Muhammad married his wife A'isha "when she was six years old and he consummated his marriage when she was nine years old."[1189] Some early Islamic teachings seem to support practices which are considered to be cruel and even barbaric according to modern standards of justice. The Qur'an famously gives instructions for the beating of disobedient wives (Sura 4:34).[1190] The hadith give an injunction for the killing of apostates,[1191] allows forced servitude including the taking of sex slaves,[1192] and tells a story of Muhammad commanding torture.[1193] In the early biography of Muhammad by Ibn Ishaq, waging war against unbelievers is presented as a duty of Islam.[1194] Muhammad is described as both reinstituting the Jewish law of stoning for adultery[1195] and ordering the torture of a man to determine the location of treasure.[1196] Just as modern Jews and Christians usually reject the applicability of violence in the Bible to modern society, however, so too 21st-century Muslims commonly denounce interpretations of the Qur'an that encourage bloodshed. In May 2018, for example, 70 Muslim clerics issued a fatwa against violent acts of terrorism; in January of the same year, 1,800 clerics in Pakistan denounced suicide bombings as forbidden by Islam.[1197]

The native American Sioux were known to participate in a Sun Dance ritual that included acts of painful self-mutilation that were thought to encourage communion with the Great Spirit. The rituals could include fasting, cutting off pieces of flesh, hanging buffalo skulls from the skin using skewers, or using skewers to either hang from or otherwise be tethered to a cottonwood pole. The ordeals involving skewers ended when they ripped free from the body.[1198] Tlazolteotl, Aztec goddess of unbridled sexuality, was thought to eat filth and hear confessions of sexual misdeeds.[1199] In a gruesome act of worship of the Aztec god Xipe Totec ("the Flayed One"), sacrificial victims had their hearts cut out and were then flayed. Warriors then greased themselves, donned the skins, and ran through the city streets.[1200]

The Mandaeans, a small group that still has some adherents in the Middle East, claim to be descended from John the Baptist. Mandaeans hold that Christianity and Judaism are false religions that inhibit the soul's liberation. They also claim that baptism is essential to salvation and that certain rites at death are necessary to allow the soul's passage to the world of light. The sect, which may predate Christianity, is often thought to be a remnant of Gnosticism.[1201] Baha'i moral teachings emphasize, among other things, the need to abstain from alcohol, the need for parental consent before marriage, the value of pilgrimage to Haifa in Israel, and the rejection of participation in the political process apart from voting.[1202] Though illiterate, Mughal emperor Akbar the Great (1542-1605) was a diligent student of comparative religion and came to espouse a syncretistic religion which incorporated ideas from Christianity, Islam, and Hinduism. According to the account of his reign called the *Akbar-Nama*, one of Akbar's forefathers was conceived when his widowed mother was impregnated by a miraculous ray of light.[1203]

Glossolalia, or speaking in tongues—a type of prayer that I once engaged in myself—is a spiritual practice in many religions around the world.[1204] In addition to charismatic and Pentecostal Christians, Sufi Muslims and African and Asian shamans are known to engage in it.[1205] (Psychologists of religion regard the practice as the speaking of "pseudo-languages" which imitate certain linguistic patterns.[1206]) A personal union with a god is not just a Christian concept. Greek philosopher Plotinus (205-270 CE) claimed to have experienced a mystical union with God.[1207] Among others, Hindus, Sikhs, Sufi Muslims, and Jewish mystics have also claimed this experience.[1208] Human sacrifice was a common religious practice in the ancient world. Indians, Chinese, Aztecs, Mayans, Incas, the Chimú, Celts, Dacians, Germans, Scythians, Thracians, Taurians, Carthaginians, Britons, Vikings, Berbers, and Swedes, among others, are known to have killed humans in attempts to appease their gods.[1209]

While fundamentalist claims about the inerrancy of the Bible are well known in the West, other religious traditions make lofty claims about divinely inspired communication. For instance, the founder of the Ratana Church of the Maoris in New Zealand was reputed to be "God's direct mouth-piece."[1210] The Aborigines of Australia believed that their chanted spiritual verses were composed by supernatural beings.[1211] Traditional Muslim piety holds that the words of the Qur'an are eternal and uncreated.[1212] Likewise, the *Vedas* are so esteemed in Hinduism that they are often deemed to "not originate at a particular time in history but [to be] eternal and of divine origin."[1213] Taoists have often regarded their Scriptures as communications from gods that pre-existed time; the famous *Tao Te Ching* has been believed to be a manifestation of the eternal Tao itself.[1214] Sikhs, who prefer the name Akāl Purakh ("The One beyond Time") for their God, have perhaps the highest view of Scripture among all the world's religions. They not only regard it as infallible,[1215] but are also known to bow to the *Adi Granth* and even pray to it![1216]

While the old maxim that "to err is human" finds few detractors, the predicament is drastically compounded by the human capacity to forget or avoid the implications of this reality. As one Unitarian Universalist minister explains,

> I think most people are grossly overconfident about their own knowledge. People who have trouble balancing their checkbooks think they know how to fix the economy. Folks who can't cope with irritable spouses figure if they were President they could make peace in the Middle East. And even well-informed individuals disagree about

religion, psychology, psychotherapy, child rearing, education, nutrition, medicine, economics, and criminal justice.[1217]

While this genuine assessment appears beyond reproach, it seems fair to expect that supernatural beliefs—by virtue of their typically speculative, otherworldly, non-material, and non-verifiable character—would be even more likely to be erroneous than conclusions in other areas of thought. As journalist and author Nicholas Wade explains, there may be particular evolutionary reasons why humans are often stridently attached to religious beliefs despite their often-dubious connection to reality:

> A distinctive feature of religion is that it appeals to something deeper than reason: religious truths are accepted not as mere statement of facts but as sacred truths, something that it would be morally wrong to doubt. This emotive quality suggests that religion has deep roots in human nature, and that just as people are born with a propensity to learn the language they hear spoken around them, so too they may be primed to embrace their community's religious beliefs.[1218]

This sentiment jives with some scientific research that has suggested that human reason was largely developed to resolve problems inherent in social groups. Apparently, our strong predispositions toward sociability may make us particularly vulnerable to societal pressures and influences when arriving at beliefs. In other words, our social tendencies can lead us to believe that we know things that we actually do not.[1219] This, in essence, could be a source of the "reasons of the heart" that encourages such powerful emotive sensations of religious truth even when in all likelihood it has not actually been found.[1220]

[24] The Great Grab Bag (pt. 3): By the Numbers

...Quantified religious diversity and doubt's universality

> Man ... is the only animal that has the True Religion—several of them.
>
> —**Mark Twain** (1835-1910), American satirist and novelist[1221]

> There's no subject on which there is more difference of opinion among both the learned and the ignorant. But in this medley of conflicting opinions one thing is certain. Though it is possible that all of them are false, it is impossible that more than one of them is true.
>
> —**Cicero** (106-43 BC), Roman statesman and philosopher[1222]

Confidence in religious belief begs to be reconsidered when the sheer diversity of religious thought and practice is understood.[1223] While enumeration of the groups, sects, schools, doctrines, gods, scriptures, and practices of religions is inherently imprecise and subject to reclassification, it is nonetheless true that there have been many thousands of religious manifestations with myriads of differing supernatural beliefs positing thousands upon thousands of divinities. While individual believers are often called to confidence or even certainty in specific religious beliefs or expressions, the innumerable variety of choices would seem to render the likelihood of reliable, comprehensive religious opinions as statistically negligible—even assuming that one of the options was known to be correct.[1224]

The Great Grab Bag (pt. 3): By the Numbers

What follows is a somewhat eclectic list of facts and numbers which help quantify the incomprehensibly vast and complex religious alternatives that have been part of human religious experience:

- **0**—There are multitudes of religions and sects that have appeared and thrived only to eventually lose all their adherents. Among the many dead world religions are the ancient Greek, Scythian, Babylonian, Hittite, Norse, Mithraic, and Celtic religions. One interesting defunct Christian group is the Messalians, a Trinitarian sect that eschewed the sacraments, devoted themselves assiduously to prayer, and existed from the fourth to perhaps the ninth century.[1225] From the Protestant tradition, one quirky example is the Muggletonians, a non-Trinitarian sect from England that lasted from 1652 to 1979.[1226]

- **2**—A schism in Jainism between the Digambaras (sky-clad) and the Shvetambaras (white-clad) focused on whether it was permissible for monks to wear clothes and which scriptures were authentic.[1227] Two major historical sects within Zoroastrianism were Zurvanism and Mazdakism.[1228]

- **3**—The Donatist Church of North Africa, which held that salvation was only possible within its fold, had at least three schisms: the Maximianists, the Rogatists, and the Claudianists. Not an insignificant sect, as many as 310 Donatist bishops gathered to denounce the Maximianist subsect in 394.[1229]

- **5**— The Digambara Jains are divided into at least five subsects—Bisapantha, Terapantha, Taranapantha, Gumanapantha, and Totapantha.[1230] The ancient Sumerians had a great number of gods—but the five chief among them were the sky-god An, air-god Enlil, water-god Enki, mother-goddess Inanna, and her consort Dummuzi.[1231]

- **7**—Though frequently described as monotheistic, Zoroastrianism has a group of seven lesser or derivative divine beings known as the Heptad or the *amesha spentas*.[1232] There are seven general categories of texts in the immense Hindu canon of Scripture: Vedas, Brahmanas, Aranyakas, Upanishads, Epics, Sutras, and Puranas.[1233]

- **8**—Ancient Egyptians had a large pantheon of gods that included these eight: Anubis (the jackal-headed god), Horus (the falcon-headed god), Thoth (the ibis-god), Amon-Re (the sun-god), Osiris (a god of vegetation), Set (Osiris' step-brother), Isis (the wife of Osiris), and the Pharaohs.[1234] The Baha'i religion, traditionally believed to be founded in 1844, believes in the following eight prophets or "Manifestations of God": Abraham, Krishna, Moses, Zoroaster, Buddha, Jesus, Muhammad, and Baha'u'llah (1817-1892).[1235]

- **13**—There are thirteen main sects in "sectarian" Shinto. Dozens of movements have emerged from these thirteen forms.[1236] Some examples are the ascetical Shugendo, the Urabe, the Watarai, the Confucian-oriented Yoshikawa, Kurozumi-kyo, Suiga, Sanno-ichijitsu, and Minkan.[1237]

- **14**—According to one enumeration, there were at least fourteen creeds created during the 4th-century Arian controversies in the Catholic Church. These include not only the original Nicene Creed, but also four different creeds of Sirmium and four different creeds of Antioch. One creed with Arian tendencies was known as the "Blasphemy of Sirmium" by its detractors.[1238]

- **16**—There have been many different Sikh sects and movements including the following sixteen: Khalsa, Sanatan, Namdharis, Nirmalas, Udasis, Seva-panthis, Asali Nirankaris, Nakali Nirankaris, Radnasoamis of Beas, Sahaj-dharis, Nihangs, Bhai Randhir Singh da Jatha, Damdami Taksal, Sikh Dharma of the Western Hemisphere, Sant Nirankari Movement, and various Sant movements.[1239]

- **18**—The traditional number of original Buddhist sects numbered eighteen. Only the Theravada school remains out of these original groups.[1240] Mahayana Buddhism was a later development—and there are now a vast variety of sects and communities in Mahayana Buddhism which include the major groupings of Pure Land, Tantric, and Zen schools.[1241]

- **20**—Known for believing that Christ only had one nature, Monophysite Christians in the sixth century were divided into as many as twenty sects.[1242]

- **21**—The Roman Catholic Church recognizes 21 Ecumenical Councils. (The Eastern Orthodox recognize seven, Oriental Orthodox three, and Assyrian Church of the East only one.)[1243] There are 21 "main groups" or denominations of Amish and Mennonites in Lancaster County, Pennsylvania.[1244]

- **23**—There were 23 Methodist denominations in the United States in 1995.[1245]

- **24**—The Talmud describes 24 competing Jewish sects.[1246]

- **Dozens**—There have been dozens of Taoist schools and sects over the centuries. Among these are the Celestial Masters school, the Perfect Realization school, the Great Purity School, the *Ling Bao*, Heavenly Mind, Divine Highest Heaven, Great Oneness Taoism, the Five Pecks of Rice sect, the Sacred Jewel sect, the Heavenly Masters sect, the Highest Pure sect, and many other groups collectively described as Spirit Cloud Taoists.[1247]

- **27**—A 1995 source recognized 27 Baptist denominations in the U.S., but also cited over 100,000 independent Baptist congregations.[1248] A 1998 source recognized 52 kinds of Baptists in the United States.[1249] Theological differences include the predestinarian beliefs of Primitive Baptists, the Sabbatarian views of Seventh Day Baptists, progressive gender and sexuality beliefs of the Alliance of Baptists, the charismatic leanings of the Pentecostal Free Will Baptist Church, and the civil rights focus of the Progressive National Baptist Convention.[1250]

- **33**—There numbered 33 gods in early Vedic Hinduism.[1251] Among these were Indra (warrior and storm god), Agni (fire god), and Varuna (sky and water god).[1252] Modern Hinduism posits thousands of deities—although some conceptions of the faith describe it as monotheistic.[1253]

- **40**—A bronze model of a sheep's liver made by the Etruscans, known as the liver of Piacenza, is divided into forty regions—each one belonging to a different god.[1254] The number of Sufi orders has been traditionally numbered at 40—although there are certainly more.¹²⁵⁵ There are also approximately 40 different types of Amish affiliations.¹²⁵⁶

- **46**—Scholar Yu-hsui Ku (1902-2002) noted 46 sects of Zen Buddhists in Japan.¹²⁵⁷

- **70**—Over 70 different indigenous religious movements have been recorded in Irian Jayra in Indonesia since the 1850's. These movements are related to the hundreds of "Cargo Cults" of Micronesia which frequently contain beliefs that "spiritual agents will, at some future time, bless the believers with material prosperity (which, in turn, will usher in an era of peace and harmony)." Perhaps the most famous cargo cult is that of John Frum, whose adherents build faux landing strips in hopes of being blessed with material goods.¹²⁵⁸

- **70+**—Muslim scholar Al-Ghazali (c.1058-1111) noted that there were "seventy-odd sects" in Islam, but only one would be saved.¹²⁵⁹ The two main divisions in Islam are the Shiites and Sunnis. Shia or Shiite Muslims have multiple groupings and subgroupings such as the "Fivers" (Zaydis), "Seveners" (Ismailis), and "Twelvers" (Imami). Sufis, typically regarded as the mystics of Islam, have often been at odds both theologically and devotionally with their stricter and more legalistic co-religionists; however, they have operated in the bounds of both the Shiite and Sunni umbrellas.¹²⁶⁰ Other Islamic groups have included the Kharijites (which at one point were divided into as many as 20 different groups),¹²⁶¹ Ahmadis (who believe that Mirza Ghulam Ahmad was the Mahdi and Messiah),¹²⁶² black Muslim groups in the United States like the "Nation of Islam," Quranists (who reject the hadith), Khubmesihis (who thought that Jesus was more important than Muhammad),¹²⁶³ Qadarites (who believe in free will), and the more rationalist Mu'tazilites.¹²⁶⁴ There are also various believers who have been more influenced by Western values who term themselves "Progressive Muslims." According to one religion text, there have been "literally thousands of sectarian groups" within the general confines of Islam.¹²⁶⁵

- **80**—Church father Epiphanius (c.315-403) cites 80 different types of heresies in his *Panarion*.¹²⁶⁶

In his 1864 *Syllabus of Errors*, Pope Pius IX outlined a series of 80 errors and heresies pertaining to modern liberal ideas and philosophies (like freedom of religion and the press).[1267] Interestingly, some of these claimed errors appear to be embraced in the teachings of the Vatican II Council (1962-1965).[1268]

- **98**—The Tibetan Buddhist Canon has 98 volumes with over 600 texts.[1269]
- **100**—Baha'u'llah (1817-1892) produced over 100 volumes of script that Baha'is regard as sacred.[1270]
- **100+**— There are perhaps 100 to 200 Presbyterian denominations in Korea. Controversies related to Shintoism, theological liberalism, ecumenism, and clergy corruption have all apparently contributed to the schisms.[1271]
- **103**—According to Liu Xiang (77-6 BCE), there were 103 Confucian schools of thought in the 1st century BCE.[1272]
- **112**—The Hindu Scriptures known as the Upanishads are about 112 in number. If all the known Upanishads were gathered together, they would be about as long as the Bible.[1273]
- **128**—In the fourth century, the bishop Filastrius of Brescia catalogued 128 heretical groups.[1274]
- **200**—The 1995 edition of *Handbook of Denominations in the United States* describes approximately 200 U.S. Christian denominations. The author also notes that there are "several dozen" that have not been mentioned due to concerns of brevity and accessibility of information. Furthermore, he notes that there are 20 independent groups called the "Church of Jesus Christ" and that the name "Church of God" is used by over 200 traditional Protestant groups.[1275]
- **211**—Noting that its list is "substantially incomplete," *CatholicHierarchy.org* lists 211 Orders of the Catholic Church. A 1995 source maintains that there are 131 religious orders of priests and brothers in the U.S. and more than 400 for nuns.[1276] Examples of such orders

include Franciscans, Dominicans, Trappists, Jesuits, Cistercians, Augustinians, and Carmelites.

- **Hundreds**—There are "literally hundreds" of small, independent sacramental groups in the United States that have branched off from Catholic, Orthodox, and Anglican communions—and that show a variety of traditionalist, feminist, New Age, Quaker, Gnostic, Protestant, charismatic, and other influences.[1277] There are also many hundreds of extant African religions.[1278]

- **370**—Although some could be variant names for the same deities, there are over 370 known names of Celtic gods and goddesses.[1279]

- **400**—The Mormons have had at least 400 different denominational groups since 1830. The five most prominent of these are the Church of Jesus Christ of Latter-Day Saints (main or Brighamite group), Church of Jesus Christ (Bickertonites), Church of Christ (Temple Lot), Church of Jesus Christ of Latter-Day Saints (Strangites), and the Reorganized Church of Jesus Christ of Latter-Day Saints or Community of Christ (organized by Joseph Smith's son, Joseph Smith, Jr.).[1280]

- **401**—There are 401 Orishas or gods in the myths of the Yoruba people of Nigeria.[1281]

- **1,500**—The Taoist canon known as the *Daozang* is comprised of approximately 1,500 separate works.[1282]

- **2,290**—Not to be confused with the lengthy Pāli Canon of Theravada Buddhism or the extensive Tibetan Buddhist Canon,[1283] the immense Chinese Mahayana Buddhist Canon, commonly called the *Taishō Shinshū Daizōkyō, contains approximately 2,290 works.*[1284]

- **8,000**—According to one reckoning, Sub-Saharan Africa has produced some 8,000 Christian and quasi-Christian movements.[1285]

- **10,000**—According to the 2001 *World Christian Encyclopedia*, there are "at least 10,000 distinct and different religions" currently in existence.[1286]

- **36,000**—The ancient Chinese concluded that 36,000 gods dwelled in the human body.[1287]
- **47,000**—According to a 2017 report from Gordon-Conwell Seminary's Center for the Study of Global Christianity, there are currently 47,000 Christian denominations in existence and there will likely be 70,000 by 2050.[1288]
- **8 million**—Traditionally, Japanese believers have claimed that there are 8 million Kami, or divine beings of Shintoism.[1289]
- **Countless/uncountable**—There are innumerable Buddhas and Bodhisattvas in Mahayana Buddhist belief—among the most popular are Amitabha, the future "messiah" figure Maitreya, Avalokiteśvara, Samantabhadra, and Mañjuśrī.[1290] Buddhism and Jainism are the only two of "countless ascetic movements" that survived from ancient India.[1291] Traditional African religion posits "countless gods"[1292] and the number of gods in the Chinese Pantheon has been described as "impossible to count."[1293]

These types of religious statistics demonstrate that all people—albeit in differing degrees and in different ways—have religious doubts. Even those who are very religiously or supernaturally inclined could of course not accept all the religious ideas and perceptions stated or implied by such data—in part because many aspects of different religions are distinct, discordant, or even flatly contradictory. And while broader and more ecumenical perspectives endeavor to be more inclusive, they not only lack uniformity among themselves, but are also necessarily at odds with multitudes of more narrow approaches that deny such liberality. In other words, a significant degree of religious doubt is a universal human trait. So, while doubting specific religious teachings can at times make one feel like an outsider in a particular community, it is helpful to remember how natural and even inevitable religious doubt is to the human experience. The famous words of Enlightenment philosopher and author Voltaire (1694-1778) seem to provide a proper perspective on this perennial human struggle: "Doubt is not a pleasant condition, but certainty is an absurd one."[1294]

Part II
The Contemplative Skeptic's Path

[25] The Prayer of St. Spurious

...The Peace Prayer of St. Francis and the unimportance of origins

Of these [works attributed to St. Francis], some twenty-four or more are found to be either doubtful or clearly not authentic, including the Prayer for Peace— "Lord make me an instrument of your peace," ascribed to St. Francis in the last forty years or more.

—**John Vaughan**, modern Franciscan scholar and priest[1295]

Do not let the authority of the author irk you, whether he be of great learning or little, but let the love of every pure truth stir you to read. Ask not: Who said this; but heed well what is said.

—**Thomas à Kempis** (c. 1380-1471), *The Imitation of Christ*[1296]

Perhaps the most famous composition connected to St. Francis of Assisi (1182-1226) is the beautiful "Peace Prayer of St. Francis." Curiously, the prayer has no actual link to the saint, not appearing in print until some seven centuries after his death.[1297] Apparently first published anonymously in French in 1912,[1298] the prayer was not attributed to Francis until 1927. Since that time, it has circulated widely in the English-speaking world in different versions and translations. Some versions are even slightly longer than others—the original French has two additional lines of text than the most common English version.[1299]

These types of issues, which tend to plague all searches for religious purity (textual or otherwise), also highlight why adapting and borrowing from traditional religions is an appropriate endeavor for the skeptically-minded. Regardless of the prayer's history, it has some beautiful and inspiring sentiments. Although some of its metaphysical content may be misguided, there appears to be little doubt that the world would be a better place if more people sought after its ethical ideals. Furthermore, meditative prayer has shown signs of providing psychological benefits in research studies[1300] —and there is no reason to think that certain aspects of prayer cannot be adopted by those with a vaguely spiritual or non-supernatural view of reality.[1301]

So, use the Prayer of St. Francis—even if it was not written by St. Francis, even if it was misattributed, even if its texts and its translations differ. Here is a suggested adaptation:[1302]

> Let me be an instrument of peace.
> Where there is hatred, let me bring love.
> Where there is offense, pardon.
> Where there is discord, harmony.
> Where there is pride, humility.
> Where there is despair, hope.
> Where there is darkness, light.
> Where there is sadness, joy.
>
> Let me not seek as much
> to be consoled as to console,
> to be understood as to understand,
> to be loved as to love.
> For it is in giving that one receives,
> it is in pardoning that one is released,
> it is in dying to selfishness that one becomes fully alive.

[26] Light in the Dark Night
...Finding solace while leaving dogmatic religion

> [Richard] Yao (1987) delineates a complex of symptoms he calls the "shattered faith syndrome": chronic guilt, anxiety, and depression; low self-esteem; loneliness and isolation; distrust of other people or groups; aversion to any structure of authority; bitterness and anger over lost time; distressing recurrences of fundamentalist consciousness; lack of basic social skills; and, in some instances, sexual difficulties, including guilt and anxiety about sex if not actual sexual dysfunction.
>
> —Description of "Shattered Faith Syndrome" by **David Wulff**, contemporary psychologist of religion[1303]

> It remains to be said, then, that even though this happy night darkens the spirit, it does so only to impart light concerning all things.
>
> —**St. John of the Cross** (1542-1591)[1304]

Anyone familiar with the life of faith knows that religiosity does not necessarily bring peace of mind. However, it must also be said that skepticism is not necessarily a recipe for a happier existence either. In fact, even though fundamentalism is generally associated negatively with psychological well-being, there is some evidence to suggest that a milder form of spirituality can be an indicator of greater mental health.[1305] Perhaps the best path is therefore to reject many of the negative aspects of traditional religion—such as authoritarianism, excessive guilty feelings, threats of damnation and divine punishment, and an unrealistic metaphysical rigidity[1306]

—while embracing some of the more positive aspects which encourage wholeness, authenticity, patience, forgiveness, honesty, simplicity, humility, moral courage, compassion, and community.[1307]

While his traditional Roman Catholic theology would no doubt be deemed "fundamentalist" by today's standards, 16th-century Spanish monk and mystic St. John of the Cross spent much time and effort pondering negative feelings and thoughts and attempting to discover their potential value for his spiritual life. Contemporary Benedictine theologian Kieran Kavanaugh describes the condition that St. John was attempting to make sense of:

> What the person undergoing the dark night experiences is a painful lack or privation: darkness in the intellect, aridity in the exercise of love in the will, emptiness in the memory of all possessions, and affliction and torment as a consequence and general state. Such persons receive a vivid understanding of their own misery and think they will never escape from it. Their faculties seem powerless and bound; all outside help appears useless; they feel no hope for any breakthrough or remedy in the future.[1308]

Perhaps ironically, some of St. John's observations can be useful for the distressing experience of leaving a conservative expression of faith. The pain of "purgation" noted in St. John's "dark night of the soul" is felt at times by the defector from traditional religion as well—feelings of emptiness, confusion, isolation, rejection, lack of direction, and anxiety. In the words of psychologist Marlene Winell: "In general, leaving a cherished faith is much like the end of a marriage. The symptoms of separation are quite similar—grief, anger, guilt, depression, low self-esteem, and social isolation."[1309]

St. John reminds us that suffering, while unpleasant and at times even odious or debilitating, can have a hidden value. Purging the mind of ingrained habits and attachments is unfortunately often the necessary path to a better life. The privation of feelings of a particular god's supposed presence—with all its positive and negative manifestations—becomes a permanent loss. But, like many losses, it is also the start of new possibilities. There are new paths to the light that can be sought out and followed which allow for growth in authenticity and maturity—and even patience and compassion. With all the faults of fundamentalism, there yet remains a potential redemptive value in suffering.

The way ahead is forward. With very rare exceptions, those who leave fundamentalist or traditionalist faiths find that they cannot return. Once the veil falls away, many things cannot be unseen or unlearned. In the words of British de-convert John Ruskin (1819-1900), "The unbeliever may be taught to believe, but not the Julian the Apostate to return."[1310] Knowing that one cannot return once certain illusions are exposed, the load is actually lightened as the choices are narrowed. As African-American abolitionist Frederick Douglass (1818-1895) remarked in an autobiography full of sufferings and triumphs: "A man's troubles are always half disposed of when he finds endurance the only alternative."[1311]

In essence, suffering caused by religion can be redeemed only in the ways that other types of suffering can be redeemed. As Rabbi Harold Kushner (b. 1935) explained in his *When Bad Things Happen to Good People*, it is each person's "sacred" responsibility to find potential meaning, purpose, and direction in the aftermath of life's difficulties and tragedies. In words that could be placed in the mouth of any skeptic:

> Let me suggest that the bad things that happen to us in our lives do not have a meaning when they happen to us. They do not happen for any good reason which would cause us to accept them willingly. But we can give them a meaning. We can redeem these tragedies from senselessness by imposing meaning on them. The question we should be asking is not, "Why did this happen to me? What did I do to deserve this?" That is really an unanswerable, pointless question. A better question would be "Now that this has happened to me, what am I going to do about it?"

[27] True Believers Anonymous[1312]
...A 12-step program for faith addicts

> Anguish emerges from craving for life to be other than it is. In the face of a changing world, such craving seeks consolation in something permanent and reliable, in a self that is in control of things, in a God who is in charge of destiny. The irony of this strategy is that it turns out to be the cause of what it seeks to dispel. ... We find ourselves spinning in a vicious circle. The more acute the anguish, the more we want to be rid of it, but the more we want to be rid of it, the more acute it gets. Such behavior is not just a silly mistake we shrug off. It is an ingrained habit of addiction.
>
> —**Stephen Batchelor** (b.1953), secular Buddhist[1313]

> Faith in a holy cause is to a considerable extent a substitute for lost faith in ourselves.
>
> —**Eric Hoffer** (1898-1983), *The True Believer*[1314]

Dogmatic religion can act like an addiction. While some elements of religions address actual human problems, more doctrinaire faiths many times generate perceived needs that otherwise would not exist. Roman Catholicism perhaps illustrates this best with its elaborate systems of rewards and punishments intertwined with sacraments, rituals, indulgences, penances, and purgatory. However, traditional Protestant preaching is often geared in a similar way. The "good news" of the gospel is typically presented with the horrible news that a god demands an absolute and unattainable moral perfection—or a firm belief in a particular formula of speculative dogmas—to avoid eternal torment. Even for the many taught that salvation is a gift of free grace, the accompanying threats that believers could have false assurance,[1315] or fall away, or that their friends and family could be damned, or that God could punish them horribly for transgressions in this life all still remain. The carrot-and-stick approach is an integral part of these religious systems; a "metaphysics of fear and hope"[1316] can force the faithful into a desperate and anxious cycle.

As Kenneth Pargament notes in his *Psychology of Religion and Coping*, dogmatic religion can operate much like other types of addiction. While the problems inherent with drug and sex addiction are well known among the faithful, religious compulsions probably belong to the same general family of behavior:

> A life devoted to drugs or sex may prove to be empty, and the transition to a life of spiritual devotion may provide immediate relief. However, unless a way can be found to integrate spiritual needs with personal and social ones, the religious solution is likely to fail and the cycle is likely to continue as the individual jumps to yet another one-sided solution.[1317]

Recognizing that a problem exists is an essential part of the traditional 12-step program in Alcoholics Anonymous (AA).[1318] In the realm of dogmatic religion, this recognition would involve admitting that devotion to a particular faith community or dogmatic perspective was causing significant, personal harm. Likewise, AA requires complete honesty—and so too the religious "addict" should give a frank acknowledgment of when fears of divine wrath or social rejection have taken precedence over cognitive congruence or psychological well-being. Finally, AA encourages an open acknowledgment of individual limitations and weaknesses. And so, the "true believer" should be encouraged to ask whether confident belief in certain ancient miracle stories or in any particular set of widely disputed, unverifiable, and speculative metaphysical doctrines is either realistic or commensurate with a finite and fallible human nature.

A 12-Step Program for Religious Addiction

1. We admitted that we had become powerless over a certain religious perspective or community, even while recognizing the harm it was doing to us.

2. We recognized that there were resources and people that could help us consider better and more helpful ways of thinking and acting.

3. We decided to both admit our personal fallibility and to still trust that being open and genuine is the best approach.

4. We made a searching and fearless moral inventory of ourselves, our cognitive abilities, and our capacity to make reliable speculative metaphysical determinations and extra-sensory perceptions about divine leadings.

5. We admitted to ourselves without reservation, and to another human person, that despite the internal psychological pain and the friction it could cause with others, we needed to have the courage to make a change.

6. We acknowledged our defects of character and our unrealistic claims to know speculative conjectures about the divine and the metaphysical. We were ready to accept help from "unorthodox" books and "heretical" people—as long as their counsel seemed both objectively true and personally helpful to the best of our knowledge and understanding.

7. We humbly and with openness sought to give up our religious addiction.

8. We made a list of all persons we had harmed by evangelism or other forms of religious manipulation. We became willing to make amends to them all if and when appropriate.

9. We made direct amends to such people if and when appropriate, except when to do so would injure them or others.

10. We continued to take personal inventory and when we were wrong about some aspect of a religion (or didn't know if we were right or

wrong), promptly admitted it. We sought neither to demonize nor glorify religious people or human religious experience in general.

11. We sought through reflection, study, and meditation to improve our contact with reality, understanding that it is proper to admit when we don't know or can't comprehend things.

12. Having had an "awakening" as the result of these steps, we tread with care when trying to communicate our new perspective to others, never forgetting our own ability to err and our own never-ending process of learning. We recognize the fact that different approaches work for different people, and that attempting to force perspectives on others is often both disrespectful and unhelpful.

The rejection of traditional dogmas does not need to lead to a vacuum. While professing uncertainty and refusing labels is often an appropriate approach, alternative perspectives can also be adopted loosely. Here are some possibilities:[1319]

- **Nondogmatic atheism**: A position characterized by non-belief in the divine but also marked by a degree of uncertainty and a lack of dogmatic attachment.[1320]

- **Agnosticism**: Lack of knowledge concerning the existence or non-existence of God or gods; or, being unable to commit to belief or disbelief in the divine.[1321]

- **Deism**: The belief in a non-interventionist deity. While deists have a wide range of opinions, they tend to have rationalist and nondogmatic spiritual views.

- **Pandeism**: The belief that the divine became the universe. This perspective tends to combine deism and pantheism, seeking to retain the most satisfying aspects of both.[1322]

- **Pantheism**: The belief that the divine is the universe. While pantheistic approaches are common in Eastern religious perspectives, rational pantheism generally rejects supernaturalism.

- **Religious humanism**: An approach to religion that discounts the supernatural. It has been described as focusing on "mystery, a sense of oneness with all things, values, a sense of meaning, community, and gratitude."[1323]

- **Theological liberalism**: While having a tremendous range of perspectives, theological liberalism at its best can be defined by openness to new ideas, a distrust of dogmatism and certainty, and a focus on humanitarianism. Such liberalism, which has no necessary connection to political liberalism, may or may not include the understanding of divinity in more metaphorical terms.[1324]

[28] Reflections on a Buddhist Atheist

...Insights from secular Buddhist Stephen Batchelor

> It is counterintuitive to accept that ... happiness in this world is only possible for those who realize that this world is incapable of providing happiness; that one becomes a fully individuated person only by relinquishing beliefs in an essential self.
>
> —**Stephen Batchelor** (b.1953)[1325]

> Great Doubt: great awakening. Little Doubt: little awakening. No Doubt: no awakening.
>
> —**Zen aphorism**[1326]

Searching for a salve for what he calls "the bewildering, stomach-churning insecurity of being alive,"[1327] native-born Englishman Stephen Batchelor journeyed east in 1972 and became a Buddhist monk. His *Confession of a Buddhist Atheist* is a personal account of not only his travels, but also his intellectual attempts to reconcile a growing doubt in Buddhist dogmas with a profound appreciation of many Eastern spiritual practices and perspectives. Engaging and broadening, Batchelor's *Confession* is a fascinating combination of travel log, primer on Buddhist belief and practice, review of modern Western philosophy, and search for the "historical Buddha." Above all, the author provides a fresh framework for reflection on the deep contradictions that have frequently accompanied dogmatic religious expressions—advocating truthfulness, but often opposing honest inquiry;

promoting compassion, but threatening hell and engendering divisive disputes; praising humility, yet assured of enigmatic and unverifiable metaphysical doctrines; fostering a search for inner peace, but stirring up deep cognitive dissonance and agonizing doubts.

Among other things, Batchelor's memoir is a reminder of the dubious notion that indiscriminately posits a gentle Eastern mysticism as a foil to an oppressive Western dogmatism. While recounting some interesting (and bitter) doctrinal controversies in contemporary Buddhism, the former monk reminds his readers that the accusation of "heresy" is by no means an exclusively Western woe. While relating his own spiritual struggles, Batchelor starkly describes the threats levied against those who doubt the law of karma:

> To believe there is no rebirth and no law of moral causation is an evil mental act that will lead to confusion and anguish in this life and hellfire in the world to come. ... Such "wrong view" is a thought crime, listed in the classic texts alongside murder, robbery, and rape. Indeed, it is often said to be the heaviest of all evil actions, since it establishes the viewpoint from which every other misdeed stems.[1328]

Perhaps most central to Batchelor's journey is a dawning awareness of the affectation and artificiality of his dogmatic belief. Although initially finding it impossible to resist the allure and mysticism of Buddhist monasticism, the author ultimately embraces a perspective that is analogous to Western existentialism: insistent on the value of free intellectual inquiry, unrelenting in the pursuit of honesty, and unyielding in its positive humanistic approach. Finding affinity in a phrase traditionally attributed to the Buddha (563-483 BCE?) himself, the author explains how persisting in his monastic path eventually became an uncomfortable exercise in "eel wriggling"—using equivocations or dubious rationalizations to avoid a frank and honest appraisal of the most likely descriptions of reality.[1329]

In what provides an interesting parallel to the search for the historical Jesus in the West, Batchelor's quest for the historical Buddha (Siddhattha Gotama or Siddhartha Gautama) also adds another intriguing dimension to the book. After an extensive review of the most ancient Buddhist scriptures (the Pāli Canon), Batchelor determined that an important clue to Gotama's original teachings could be found in those texts that most diverge from the traditional doctrines of Hinduism. His conclusions present the Buddha as a religious revolutionary:

> Siddhattha Gotama was a dissenter, a radical, an iconoclast. He wanted nothing to do with the priestly religion of the Brahmins. He dismissed its theology as unintelligible, its rituals as pointless, and the social structure it legitimated as unjust. Yet he fully understood its visceral appeal, its addictive hold on the human mind and heart.[1330]

While the former monk classifies Gotama as an "ironic atheist,"[1331] it becomes clear that Batchelor thinks it unlikely that the Buddha was fully atheistic in the modern sense of the term. He remarks that the historical Buddha "acknowledged the presence of the gods" but "marginalized them,"[1332] regarding them as essentially irrelevant to human existence.

Batchelor has apparently received some significant criticism in the Buddhist community for his historical methods. The author himself is candid about his fallibility and admits that his appeal to the Pāli canon may well be overly selective. His search is clearly as spiritual as it is historical; he is clearly intent on not only "demythologizing" Buddhism, but also reapplying some of its insights and practices to the modern human condition. Batchelor's secular "enlightenment" is thus ultimately a form of non-theistic humanism—albeit both informed and influenced by Buddhist sensibilities pertaining to such matters as impermanence, the importance of mindfulness and meditation, and the suffering that arises from misguided desire.

Although the book's title might suggest otherwise, the author tends to describe his own beliefs in terms of a "deep agnosticism" as opposed to a strict atheism.[1333] Like his Buddha, Batchelor suggests that the search for hidden divinities is an unhelpful distraction. Being wary of aggressive forms of "anti-theism," he rather recommends detachment from god-concepts as the best way to foster both intellectual integrity and the relinquishment of illusion:

> This deep agnosticism is more than a refusal of conventional agnosticism to take a stand on whether God exists or whether the mind survives bodily death. It is the willingness to embrace the fundamental bewilderment of a finite, fallible creature as the basis for leading a life that no longer clings to the superficial consolations of certainty.[1334]

Stephen Batchelor's *Confession* is an embodiment of the tension of the modern existential journey. It is a story of developing insight and honesty, an emerging realization of the harmfulness of the "craving to believe,"[1335] and an embracing of personal limitations and fallibility. The story will likely resonate with many people who have found significant psychological and intellectual stimulation in traditional religions, but have also concluded that much of their metaphysical content is too speculative and improbable to be maintained. Batchelor has provided a vivid picture of how a life can be both enriched and impoverished by religious traditions. Perhaps ironically, he has also presented dogmatic faith as a potential wellspring of both moral failure and suffering—in Western terms, an eighth deadly sin.

[29] Einstein's Creed, Spinoza's God
...Skeptical and subtle divinity in Einstein and Spinoza

I believe in Spinoza's God, who reveals himself in the lawful harmony of all that exists, but not in a God who concerns himself with the fate and the doings of mankind.

—**Albert Einstein** (1879-1955)[1336]

Except God no substance can be granted or conceived.

—**Benedict Spinoza** (1632-1677)[1337]

Renowned physicist and winner of the 1921 Nobel prize for his work on the photoelectric effect, Albert Einstein is best known for his theories of special and general relativity. He also wrote at some length about religion, giving his opinions on a variety of topics and doctrines.

It is abundantly clear that Einstein was not a "fundamentalist" or traditional believer. For instance, he denied the existence of a personal god, an afterlife, miracles, and the efficacy of prayer. Staunch atheists like Richard Dawkins can make a fair case that Einstein uses the term "God" in a "metaphorical, poetic sense."[1338] Christopher Hitchens rightly calls Einstein a "humanist and humanitarian" who cannot be easily drafted into the ranks of theists.[1339] Nonetheless, Einstein's typical avoidance of the term "atheist" and his positive comments about certain aspects of religion seem to put him in a somewhat different camp than anti-theists like Dawkins and Hitchens. In his own words:

> I have repeatedly said that in my opinion the idea of a personal God is a child-like one. You may call me an agnostic, but I do not share the crusading spirit of the professional atheist whose fervor is mostly due to a painful act of liberation from the fetters of religious indoctrination received in youth. I prefer an attitude of humility corresponding to the weakness of our intellectual understanding of nature and of our own being.[1340]

In addition to distancing himself from aggressive atheists, Einstein also expressed some affinity with philosopher Benedict Spinoza's pantheistic views. Spinoza himself talked frequently of God, espousing a form of rational pantheism that rejected a personal deity and equated God with Nature.[1341] In his own words from his *Ethics*: "Whatever is, is in God, and nothing can exist or be conceived without God."[1342] While one interpreter has called Spinoza "God-intoxicated" and he has been thought to possess a form of rational mysticism, many others have claimed that he did not believe in God at all.[1343]

Spinoza is famously difficult to interpret[1344] —and so perhaps it should come as no surprise that Einstein, who so admired Spinoza's conception of God, has some obscurity in expression at times as well. While there is admittedly some tension in Einstein's beliefs about religion, what follows is what seems to be an accurate "creed" of the self-professed "deeply religious nonbeliever."[1345]

- **I do not believe in a personal god.**
    - "In their struggle for the ethical good, teachers of religion must have the stature to give up the doctrine of a personal God, that is, give up that source of fear and hope which in the past placed such vast power in the hands of priests. ... And so it seems to me that science not only purifies the religious impulse of the dross of its anthropomorphism but also contributes to a religious spiritualization of our understanding of life."[1346]
    - "The idea of a personal God is quite alien to me and seems even naïve."[1347]

- **I deny the existence of miracles and the efficacy of prayer.**
  - "Through the reading of popular scientific books, I soon reached the conviction that much in the stories of the Bible could not be true. The consequence was a positively fanatic orgy of freethinking coupled with the impression that youth is intentionally being deceived by the state through lies; it was a crushing impression."[1348]
  - "Scientific research is based on the idea that everything that takes place is determined by laws of nature, and this holds for the actions of people. ... For this reason, a scientist will hardly be inclined to believe that events could be influenced by prayer, i.e. by a wish addressed to a supernatural Being."[1349]
- **I don't believe in the afterlife.**
  - "I do not believe in the immortality of the individual, and I consider ethics to be an exclusively human concern with no superhuman authority behind it."[1350]
  - "I cannot imagine a God who rewards and punishes the objects of his creation .... Neither can I believe that the individual survives the death of his body, although feeble souls harbor such thoughts through fear or ridiculous egotisms."[1351]
- **I typically call myself an agnostic and have affinity for Spinoza's pantheism. I adhere to what I call "cosmic religion."**
  - "My position concerning God is that of an agnostic."[1352]
  - "My views are near those of Spinoza: admiration for the beauty of and belief in the logical simplicity of the order which we can grasp humbly and only imperfectly."[1353]
  - "I am satisfied with the mystery of life's eternity and with the awareness of—and glimpse into—the marvelous construction of the existing world together with the steadfast determination to comprehend a portion, be it ever so tiny, of the reason that manifests itself in nature. This is the basis of cosmic religiosity, and it appears to me that the most important function of art and science is to awaken this feeling among the receptive and keep it alive."[1354]

- **As far as fundamentalist or traditional concepts of God go, I am an atheist.**
  - "From the viewpoint of a Jesuit priest I am, of course, and always have been an atheist. ... It is always misleading to use anthropomorphical concepts in dealing with things outside the human sphere—childish analogies. We have to admire in humility the beautiful harmony of the structure of the world as far as we can grasp it. And that is all."[1355]

- **I am not an anti-theist or a strident atheist.**
  - "What separates me from most so-called atheists is a feeling of utter humility toward the unattainable secrets of the harmony of the cosmos."[1356]
  - "In view of such harmony of the cosmos which I, with my limited human mind, am able to recognize, there are yet people who say there is no God. But what makes me really angry is that they quote me for support of such views."[1357]
  - "The fanatical atheists ... are like slaves who are still feeling the weight of their chains which they have thrown off after hard struggle. They are creatures who—in their grudge against traditional religion as the 'opium of the masses'—cannot hear the music of the spheres."[1358]

- **I am not a nihilist. I believe that morality is very important—although it is the domain of humanity and not of any god.**
  - "Man's ethical behavior should be effectively grounded on compassion, nurture, and social bonds. What is moral is not of the divine, but rather a purely human matter, albeit the most important of all human matters."[1359]

- **I find the universe mysterious and in many ways beyond my comprehension.**
  - "The most beautiful and deepest experience that a man can have is the sense of the mysterious. It is the underlying principle of

> religion as well as of all serious endeavor in art and science. He who never had this experience seems to me, if not dead, then at least blind. To sense that behind anything that can be experienced there is a something that our minds cannot grasp, whose beauty and sublimity reaches us only indirectly: this is religiousness. In this sense I am religious. To me it suffices to wonder at these secrets and to attempt to grasp with my mind a mere image of the lofty structure of all there is."[1360]

While it may be legitimate to call Spinoza's or Einstein's views a form of "sexed-up atheism,"[1361] it nonetheless appears more straightforward to conclude that there is a genuine (although skeptical and limited) mystical sensibility in their approaches. As such, they provide an example of a path for those who are skeptical and devoted to rational thought, but still have a vague or subtle sense of the divine.

Perhaps more importantly, both men believed that the strongest affinity could exist between persons of differing beliefs if they possessed a similar spirit of honesty and charitableness. Einstein, who noted his own "insuperable distaste" for fanatical approaches,[1362] seems to be of one mind again with Spinoza in the philosopher's following redefined notion of faith:

> Faith allows every man the utmost freedom to philosophize, and he may hold whatever opinions he pleases on any subjects whatsoever without imputation of evil. It condemns as heretics and schismatics only those who teach such beliefs as promote obstinacy, hatred, strife and anger, while it regards as the faithful only those who promote justice and charity to the best of their intellectual powers and capacity.[1363]

True faithfulness, according to both Spinoza and Einstein, posits a compassionate and respectful attitude as perhaps the most essential part of any worthwhile human creed. It is partly in this sense it seems that we may fully understand Einstein's famous remark that "science without religion is lame, religion without science is blind."[1364]

[30] There Is Yet Something in It

...Leo Tolstoy's mildly supernatural and non-traditional theism

And what can be more immoral than that awful theology according to which God is cruel and revengeful, punishes all men for the sin of Adam, and to save them sends His Son to earth knowing beforehand that men will kill him and will be cursed for doing so; and that the salvation of men from sin consists in being christened [baptized], or in believing that all this is actually true, that the Son of God was killed by men for the salvation of men, and that those who do not believe this will be punished by God with eternal torments?

—**Leo Tolstoy,** Russian novelist and unorthodox theologian (1828-1910)[1365]

I do not live when I lose faith in the existence of a God; I should have long ago killed myself, if I had not had a dim hope of finding him. ... "To know God and to live are one. God is life."

—**Leo Tolstoy,** on his subjective experience of faith[1366]

Leo Tolstoy is perhaps most famous for his novels, particularly *War and Peace* and *Anna Karenina*. But the Russian's lasting influence is in many ways more connected to his views on religion, which both inspired such men as Mohandas Gandhi, Martin Luther King, Jr., and Zen master Thich Nhat Hanh[1367] and also earned him an excommunication from the Russian Orthodox Church in 1901.[1368] Tolstoy's ideas are valuable in part due to their originality and have been described as "unique in that they belong to no recognizable school of philosophical thought."[1369]

Tolstoy's faith was an interesting collection of principles and practices that he felt were born from his reflection and his experience. He believed in the equality of all people, wore simple dress, became a strict vegetarian, emphasized non-violence, found an ideal in the life of the poor, and believed in the great value in physical labor. Though he fathered thirteen children, towards the end of his life he sought to live with the complete absence of sexual desire.[1370] The focus of Tolstoy's spiritual praxis centered in many ways around self-sacrifice. In fact, he claimed that Christianity, Buddhism, Confucianism, and Zoroastrianism all had recognized this truth.[1371] Such considerations, however, did not descend into a pure asceticism, but rather focused on a deeply personal and sensitive degree of care towards others. In a striking passage reminiscent of Buddhist teachings on mindfulness, Tolstoy wrote:

> Remember that there is only one important time and that is now. The present moment is the only one over which we have dominion. The most important person is always the person you are with, who is right before you, for who knows if you will have dealings with any other person in the future? The most important pursuit is making the person standing at your side happy, for that alone is the pursuit of life.[1372]

The great Russian also had a significant degree of agnosticism in his general approach. To Tolstoy, the universe was ultimately a mystery that could not be fully understood. He confessed that "the explanation of the whole, like the beginning of all things, was hidden in infinity."[1373] However, he regarded religious belief as a pragmatic necessity, confessing that he could not hold off a sense of despair and meaningless without holding to some concept of God and faith.[1374] Tolstoy himself summed up his religious beliefs as follows:

> And these principles are very simple, comprehensible, and not numerous. They assert that there is a God, the source of all; that in man there is a particle of this divine element which he can either diminish or increase by his life; that to increase this element man must suppress his passions and increase love in himself; and that the practical means to attain this is to act with others as one wishes others to act towards oneself.[1375]

One of the most striking elements of Tolstoy's theology was his condemnation of traditional dogmas on both ethical and rational grounds. He rejected what he called the "absurdities of the Old Testament," denying the credibility of a 6,000-year-old earth, the historicity of Noah and the ark, and "various immoral abominations" like the killing of children and the destruction of cities.[1376] He also discarded any aspects of spirituality that he felt descended into "supernaturalism and senselessness,"[1377] denying dogmatic approaches that he felt confused mystery with obfuscation and irrationality. In his own stinging words:

> From earliest childhood, the age most receptive of suggestion, at the very time when the educator cannot be too careful about what he transmits, senseless and immoral dogmas of the so-called Christian religion, incompatible with reason or knowledge, are instilled into the child. … And so by degrees the man becomes accustomed (and in this the theologians vigorously support him) to the idea that one cannot trust in reason and that therefore everything is possible in the world, and that in man there is nothing by the aid of which he can distinguish for himself good from evil and falsehood from truth; and that in what is most important from him—his conduct—he must be guided, not by his reason, but by what other men tell him.[1378]

Tolstoy's approach to atheism was, perhaps not surprisingly, a combination of both admiration and concern. He was quite sympathetic to those who left dogmatic traditional religions for an non-religious perspective, noting that it took a person of "strong personality" to leave fundamentalism and that freedom from its grip could only be attained "with great difficulty and suffering."[1379] Nonetheless, he personally saw common expressions of atheism as natural but unfortunate overreactions: "Having freed himself from the hypnotism of this deceit, such a man, hating the lie from which he has just escaped, will naturally adopt that theory of the leaders in which all religion is regarded as one of the obstacles to humanity along the way of progress."[1380] A 21st-century Tolstoy would likely be an opponent of both the fundamentalist and the anti-theist.

While parts of his system of thought may not be fully satisfying,[1381] Tolstoy's profundity, existential honesty, and moral courage provide a vivid example of but one spiritual path which takes a skeptical approach to traditional theism.[1382] Although Tolstoy recognized that he could not prove the existence of God, goodness, or freedom on a rational basis,[1383] he maintained that he had come to realize the most satisfying and authentic way in which he personally could live. For Tolstoy, religion is not wholly corrupt. Despite its many warped manifestations, "there is yet something in it."[1384]

[31]   A Euthanasia of Fanaticism

...Thomas Jefferson and the freedom of religious thought

> For here we are not afraid to follow truth where it may lead, nor to tolerate any error so long as reason is left free to combat it.
>
> —**Thomas Jefferson** (1743-1826) on his vision for the University of Virginia[1385]

> In the first place divest yourself of all bias in favor of novelty and singularity of opinion. ... Question with boldness even the existence of a god; because, if there be one, he must more approve of the homage of reason, than that of blindfolded fear.
>
> —**Thomas Jefferson**[1386]

Thomas Jefferson was the author of the Declaration of Independence, founder of the University of Virginia, third President of the United States, and a consummate defender of religious liberty. His genius engaged a wide variety of subjects and disciplines; he is sometimes thought to be the greatest intellect that ever occupied the White House.

Jefferson's religious thought, often described as a form of deism or Unitarianism,[1387] not only celebrated the freedom of conscience but also had a high esteem for the ethical teachings of Jesus of Nazareth. Although he expressed that the universe had a divine Creator, he also believed that God did not intercede in human affairs[1388] and that reliance on divine intervention was both misguided and a common occasion for human folly. Though God's existence appears to have been a "hypothesis" rather than a dogma for Jefferson, he marveled at the order and majesty of the cosmos and held that there were "evident proofs of the necessity of a superintending power to maintain the Universe." To Jefferson, a "self-existent Universe" was simply a less likely proposition.[1389] Furthermore, the founding father thought that the affirmation of atheism or theism was far less important than the rejection of "servile prejudices," a commitment to diligent inquiry, and a pursuit of personal honesty.[1390] In contrast to many of the confessions and creeds of Christendom, Jefferson welcomed diversity in thought and found uniformity of religious opinion neither possible nor even desirable. Of the individuality of his own religious beliefs he once remarked, "I am of a sect by myself, as far as I know."[1391]

Many theologically liberal Christians have found common ground with Jefferson over his approach to Jesus and the Scriptures. Often called the "Jefferson Bible," the founding father compiled *The Morals and Life of Jesus of Nazareth* by removing sections from the Gospels that he thought were spurious, irrational, or otherwise tainted with supernaturalism.[1392] In line with other Enlightenment thinkers, Jefferson counseled distrust whenever the Bible related miraculous events. He thought it fair to judge the relative likelihood of the "pretensions" of any biblical author to divine inspiration and suggested that a careful analysis of miraculous stories be made to determine "whether the evidence is so strong as that it's falshood would be more improbable than a change of the laws of nature in the case he relates."[1393] Interestingly, Jefferson was particularly dismissive of the book of Revelation, once remarking that it was "merely the ravings of a maniac" and in essence a waste of time to study.[1394]

The "Sage of Monticello" was at times quite blunt in rejecting traditional orthodoxies. He thought that systematic theology was typically an exercise in "a system of fancy absolutely incomprehensible" and hoped that the belief in the Virgin Birth would be one day "classed with the fable of the generation of Minerva in the brain of Jupiter."[1395] He also rejected such dogmas as the divinity of Christ, the Trinity, original sin, and the Atonement, while also denying that Jesus of Nazareth had any supernatural powers. Deeply concerned with the amount of strife and bloodshed caused by religious controversies, he wished for a "quiet euthanasia of the heresies of bigotry and fanaticism" which he believed had squelched rational thought and "deeply afflicted mankind."[1396] Perhaps in large part due to his insistence on human liberty, Jefferson had an especially strong dislike of what he called the "atrocious attributes" of Calvinism. Explicitly rejecting the predestinarian "Five Points" of Calvinist doctrine, Jefferson even asserted that Calvinism's object of worship was not divine but rather a "daemon of malignant spirit."[1397]

Jefferson's hostility to Calvinism was no doubt in part due to its strong positions on both divine sovereignty and human spiritual bondage. In Jefferson's own words, he had "sworn upon the altar of God, eternal hostility against any form of tyranny over the mind of man."[1398] It was clearly not just mental bondage that he was concerned about, however, knowing the role that dogmatic forms of Christianity like Calvinism played in the sectarian strife in the European wars of religion. In his *Notes on the State of Virginia*, Jefferson bluntly gave his perceptions on the tragic history of coercive forms of religion:

> Millions of innocent men, women, and children, since the introduction of Christianity, have been burnt, tortured, fined, imprisoned; yet we have not advanced one inch towards uniformity. What has been the effect of coercion? To make one half the world fools, and the other half hypocrites.[1399]

It was with such concerns that Jefferson came to believe that governments should only be concerned with the actions of their citizens—and not their religious beliefs. In a letter to some Connecticut Baptists who were concerned about maltreatment by other Christians, Jefferson famously remarked that there should be a "wall of separation between Church & State" in order to preserve the freedom of religion.[1400] In his view, only erroneous religious systems needed governmental support because "Truth can stand by itself."[1401]

Like all people, Jefferson was not without his shortcomings—and we can perhaps learn as much from his failings as from his genius. While his original draft of the Declaration of Independence sought to outlaw human bondage, Jefferson was compelled to change the document in order to assure its adoption.[1402] And although he did sign an act in 1807 which banned the foreign slave trade,[1403] he sadly could never bring himself to emancipate his own slaves—apparently for chiefly economic reasons. While of course more understandable for a man of his time, his moral failure in this area is a resounding blight on an otherwise shining example of humanity. Author and outspoken atheist Christopher Hitchens (1949-2011), who referred to Jefferson as one of his heroes in speeches,[1404] nonetheless gave a very frank analysis of the founding father's flaws in his biographical work *Thomas Jefferson: Author of America*:

> At the end, his capitulation to slave power that he half-abominated was both self-interested and a menace to the survival of the republic. This surrender, by a man of the Enlightenment and a man of truly revolutionary and democratic temperament, is another reminder that history is a tragedy and not a morality tale.[1405]

[32] Crying Out in the Wilderness
...The Desert Fathers and the good and bad in dogmatic religion

> The abbot Antony said, "who sits in solitude and is quiet hath escaped from three wars: hearing, speaking, seeing: yet against one thing shall he continuously battle: that is, his own heart."
>
> —**St. Antony of Egypt** (c.251-c.356)[1406]

> A dog is better than I am, for he has love and does not judge.
>
> —**Abba Xanthius**, The Sayings of the Desert Fathers[1407]

With the age of martyrdom coming to a close, Christian men and women of the fourth and fifth centuries took to the deserts of Egypt, Palestine, and Syria in an effort to renew the call to ultimate self-sacrifice. Although the lives of these monks and hermits are often little known in the West, they left an enduring mark on the development of Christian orthodoxy and practice. Frequent fasts, strict celibacy, lengthy night prayer vigils, the rejection of earthly possessions, and obedience to particular teachers ("abbas" and "ammas") were the staples of desert monasticism. The birth of the medieval ideals of poverty, chastity, and obedience was in the Egyptian desert.[1408]

There have certainly been many fringe movements in the history of Christianity, but desert monasticism should probably not be considered one of them. Along with the early martyrs, these monks were held by many in the early Catholic Church as the embodiment of the Christian ideal. St. Athanasius of Alexandria (c.296-373), stalwart defender of Nicaean orthodoxy and the first to list the canonical books of the New Testament in their common Catholic form, wrote his *Life of Antony* in praise of the virtues and orthodoxy of one of the most prominent of these ascetics.[1409] When he was on the run from the secular authorities during the Arian Controversy, Athanasius lived with the desert monks who successfully kept him hidden for an extended period.[1410] St. Basil the Great (330-379), who had a profound effect on the establishment of Nicaean orthodoxy in the Eastern Church, spent some years in the desert as a monastic and wrote the basis of two monastic rules;[1411] his harsh ascetic living is thought to have largely ruined his health and shortened his lifespan.[1412] Standout scholar and translator of the Vulgate, St. Jerome (347-419) was deeply impacted by the desert fathers, wrote a short but glowing biography of the early desert father St. Paul of Thebes,[1413] founded a monastic community at Bethlehem in 386,[1414] and was himself a "ferocious ascetic" who spent three intense years mortifying his passions in the desert.[1415] Bishop and eminent theologian St. Augustine (354-430), who founded his own religious community in North Africa at Thagaste and had a great affinity for monasticism,[1416] writes of St. Antony of Egypt as a "just and holy man" who memorized and understood the Scriptures.[1417] St. John Cassian (c. 360-435) lived for several years in the Egyptian desert before he founded a monastery in Marseilles. Cassian's interpretations of the teachings of the desert were to have a significant influence on the development of the Benedictine Rule in particular and Western monastic life in general.[1418] Although largely rejected by Protestantism, the enduring ideal of the desert hermits and monks is clear in medieval Catholic piety in both east and west—and survives to the present day in monastic models and standards. The traditions surrounding St. Francis of Assisi (1182-1226), perhaps the ultimate ideal of Christian saintliness in the West, provide just one example of how the desert ideal of poverty, chastity, and obedience—attended by miracles—has been a lasting paradigm of Christian holiness.[1419]

There is a vein in the traditions of the desert fathers and mothers that appears positively fanatical to moderns. Sometimes self-inflicted misery is presented as the only sure means of consoling an angry God. In the words of one desert abba, "All bodily comfort is an abomination to the Lord."[1420] According to the *Sayings*, individual monks at times are said to have kept the following practices: putting a stone in the mouth for three years to learn silence; holding up hands in prayer from sunset to sunrise; eating meager meals once per day (or less); spending years living on top of a column;[1421] not lying down for fourteen years; not leaving a cell for thirty years; helping thieves to steal one's own possessions; standing in water for hours until the skin had the appearance of leprosy; maintaining total separation from spouse, parents, and children; eschewing contact with any visitors for extended periods; wearing only rags; completely abstaining from wine and meat; the wearing of hairshirts; sleeping only one hour per night; and weeping so much that the eyelashes fell out. While one is probably wise to remember the common hyperbole in hagiography, there can be little doubt that the desert monks frequently lived lives of extreme asceticism and suffering. Many seem to have adopted that persistent Christian malady of assuming that God is most pleased when his followers voluntarily undergo the greatest pain and discomfort. As one desert father expressed, "he is a monk who does violence to himself in everything."[1422] Some unfortunately also turned this violence outwards at times, acting as "shock troops" against both pagans and those they perceived to be heretics.[1423]

The modern psychological community would likely use terms like obsessive-compulsive disorder, anorexia, self-harm, and delusional thinking to characterize much of this activity—with evidence that in some cases neurosis had likely taken a turn towards a psychotic break with reality. In addition to the extremes of mortification, tales of the miraculous also abound in the sayings: the immediate bodily "teleportation" from one location to another, angelic and ecstatic visions, the hearing of divine voices, physical altercations with demons, healing the sick, raising the dead, control of the weather, having conversations with corpses, predicting the future, casting out devils, and even a lizard bursting as an answer to prayer. While these more fantastic stories can just be viewed as legends or tall tales, they also may be evidence of the volatile psychological combination of dogmatic spiritual beliefs and extreme fasting and sleep deprivation. As psychologist of religion David Wulff explains, fasting individuals are in fact more prone to visions and intense dreams—thus making the practice in fact "a means of seeking prophetic revelations."[1424] Regarding sleep deprivation, Wulff further notes:

> The potentially dramatic effects of sleep deprivation have been vividly demonstrated by contemporary research. Some subjects who

undergo total sleep deprivation will exhibit psychotic symptoms, including delusions and visual or tactile hallucinations, after only three or four days. Such striking reactions are likely to occur among persons with a history of psychiatric disorder or those that fall at the extremes of temperamental disposition—as may well be the case with a number of saints or mystics.[1425]

Despite all that is the dubious and fanciful in the *Sayings*, however, it is important not to lose sight of the more practical and understandable aims of the desert. Although it does seem that many sayings offer bad advice and many more could only have value when taken as metaphor or hyperbole, there is good reason to think that the relentless pursuit after possessions and desires can often be more of a source of pain than pleasure—and that people frequently spend all their energies striving after things that, when attained, do little to assuage their existential angst or give them peace of mind. Here is a sampling of what I consider to be some of the more thought-provoking sayings of the desert:

- "For this is humility, to see yourself to be the same as the rest."[1426]
- "A brother asked Abba Sisoes, 'What shall I do, abba, for I have fallen?' The old man said to him, 'Get up again.'"
- "Vigilance, self-knowledge and discernment; these are the guides of the soul."
- "Do not give your heart to that which does not satisfy your heart."
- "Abba Poemen was asked for whom this saying is suitable, 'Do not be anxious about tomorrow.' (Matt. 6.34) The old man said, 'It is said for the man who is tempted and has not much strength, so that he should not be worried, saying to himself, 'How long must I suffer this temptation?' He should rather say every day to himself, 'Today.'"
- "Abba Sisoes said to a brother, 'How are you getting on?' and he replied, 'I am wasting my time, father.' The old man said, 'If I happen to waste a day, I am grateful for it.'"
- "If you take little account of yourself, you will have peace, wherever you live."

It is also important to keep in mind that two of the highest goals of the desert mystics were *hesychia* and *apatheia*—the development of the inner peace and the calming of the passions. Although it appears that the extremes of ascetical life did little to help cast off guilt and fears of divine punishment for some,[1427] others seem to have found a sense of joy in the solitude and simplicity. There are certainly sayings that enjoin what appears to amount to self-torture, but there is also a clear vein of teachings that encourages moderate eating, moderate sleep, and a simple love of fellow men and women. The sayings taken as a whole can be a microcosm of a proper way to look at dogmatic Christianity in general —sometimes harmful, sometimes delusional, but at times also containing pragmatic advice and thoughtful observations about how to satisfy the yearnings of the soul. The desert monks can thus be a source of wisdom in two ways: as a stark reminder of the harm that religion can inflict and as a poetic example of the heights that people have reached when attempting to love one another amid hardship.

[33] The New Apatheism

...Giving up strident views on religion or a-religion

> If ... we are willing to participate in a culture of generosity that affirms that *all* of our traditions contain verses, teachings, and practices that are at first glance—and sometimes at second and third glance—profoundly problematic, and that we must come to terms with them, and that all of our traditions also contain profound beauty and wisdom, then there is a journey we can take together.
>
> —**Omid Safi**, professor of Islamic Studies at UNC-Chapel Hill[1428]

> The truly great gap is not between belief and unbelief. It is between those who dedicate their lives to a greater purpose and those who care little for the common good.
>
> —**Roger Christan Schriner**, Bridging the God Gap[1429]

In traditional Christian theology, one of the prime goals of the monastic life was *apatheia*. Literally meaning "without passion," *apatheia* was the state of the soul that had mastered negative impulses and cravings. Ironically, this worthwhile pursuit has often been crippled by an overlooked passion that is one of the most dangerous of them all—dogmatism.

Just as excessive anger, lust, greed, pride, envy, and the like can be a source of profound human suffering, so also has the dogmatic insistence about the truth or falsehood of certain speculative metaphysical beliefs. Crusades, civil wars, sectarian violence, torture, executions, riots, various types of discrimination, fractured friendships, broken families, crippling anxieties about hell and purgatory, and a host of other tragedies have been fueled by people's religious and philosophical dogmatism. There have been great conflicts between religious groups, inside religious groups, and against religious groups that have been fueled by this passion. As Thomas Jefferson suggested, the level of emotion underlying such conflicts has often been both irrational and counterproductive: "But it does me no injury for my neighbor to say there are twenty gods, or no gods. It neither picks my pocket nor breaks my leg."[1430]

The goal of a "New Apatheism" would in no way suggest a lack of interest in religion or an indifference towards religious people. "Apathy" towards people is of course not a goal to be espoused. Rather, a New Apatheism would only suggest that religion (or a-religion) has no necessary relationship to intelligence or ethical rectitude and is not a valid basis for depriving anyone of respect or compassion. It would also insist on the recognition that human beings—by their very nature—have an irrational component and to become angry or overly upset about that is often to feed rather that diminish such irrationality. Furthermore, an emotional stance either for or against religion can inhibit worthwhile dialogue and the ability to appropriate insights from others.

People's belief or unbelief about gods has been given far too much import. Early Christians were often called "atheists" by their detractors. They rightly complained that their maltreatment was unfounded since it was not tied to any criminal activity. Today, many nonbelievers are overly suspicious of and disrespectful toward people of faith. Likewise, many believers have a profound distrust of atheists, making a moral assessment of a position that has no necessary connection to morality—and has been held by many extremely brave, admirable, and compassionate human beings.[1431] As the early Christian philosopher Justin Martyr (c.100-c.165) explained while pleading for an end to Christian persecution:

> For from a name neither praise nor punishment could reasonably spring, unless something excellent or base in action be proved. … Justice requires that you inquire into the life both of him who confesses and of him who denies, that by his deeds it may be apparent what kind of man each is.[1432]

Eleven principles of this New Apatheism could therefore include the following:

1. That a person's beliefs or non-beliefs about gods, in and of themselves, need not be considered to be of great importance.
2. That simple labels are typically not adequate descriptors of people due to the diversity of opinions and attitudes within religious and non-religious belief systems.
3. That neither "believer" nor "unbeliever" is a necessarily a meaningful categorization for morality or for ethical character.
4. That the wealth of human knowledge includes valid and valuable insights from both believer and unbeliever.
5. That one can be interested in someone's religious or a-religious beliefs without being emotionally upset or angered by them.
6. That neither belief nor unbelief necessarily "poisons everything"[1433] —rather, there are ways of both believing and not believing that can be poisonous.[1434]
7. That compassion, humility, curiosity, honesty, and other virtues are much more significant than religious or a-religious belief.
8. That threats, manipulation, shame, and guilt are inappropriate (and often counter-productive) means for encouraging truth-seeking.
9. That expressing ignorance or indecision about complicated and mysterious issues can be an appropriate—or even the most appropriate—attitude for finite and fallible people.
10. That people should resist violent, demeaning, disrespectful, destructive, inhumane, and prejudicial attitudes and behaviors regardless of their source.
11. That reliance on faith or other subjective feelings of certitude, no matter how strong, do not remove or diminish human fallibility.

For those inclining towards more strident forms of skepticism, humanist chaplain and former evangelical minister Bart Campolo offers a helpful perspective on the benefits of having goals that supersede one's stance on religion:

Look, everybody knows there are bunches of angry atheists running around out there, openly mocking the church and loudly proclaiming that organized religion poisons everything, but I will never be one of them. ... After all, my goal isn't to destroy Christianity; my goal is to help as many people as possible commit themselves to loving relationships, meaningful work, and an ever-deepening sense of love and gratitude.[1435]

[34] Hearsayings of the Prophet
...Selective value in the hadith of Islam

> Muslim jurists and *ulamā* [scholars] have developed elaborate methodologies for the authentication of hadith with the purpose precisely to enhance the scope of scientific objectivity in their conclusions. This they have done in full awareness that in no other branch of Islamic learning has there been as much distortion and forgery as in hadith.
>
> —**Mohammed Hashim Kamali**, modern Muslim scholar[1436]

> In (kindness to) every living being there is a reward.
>
> —**Saying attributed to Muhammad** (570-632 CE)[1437]

According to Islamic tradition, there were at one time perhaps 600,000 purported sayings of the words and deeds of the Prophet Muhammad (hadith) in existence. Islamic scholars al-Bukhari (810-870 CE) and Muslim (c.817-875) each made collections of about 4,000 hadith, purging hundreds of thousands that they thought were not genuine. Out of many collections, eventually four additional hadith collections achieved the most authoritative status in Islam.[1438] The hadith sayings originally were passed down orally before they were committed to writing. The authoritative collections are supposedly confirmed by a chain of reliable individuals and written down across many decades after the death of Muhammad.[1439]

In legal terms, hadith are what is typically referred to as "hearsay." While it is of course possible for the content of hearsay to be accurate, the process is tenuous enough that courts of law usually consider it to be inadmissible as evidence. This general suspicion about the reliability of hearsay would seem to be magnified with the longer chains of individuals in the hadith process. Even if the final "link" in the chain was very reliable, the possibilities of corruption through mistaken memory, misspeaking, mishearing, wishful thinking, errors in transcription, and other frailties of human cognition and communication would seem undeniable.[1440]

While a skeptical approach would generally question the reliability of the whole hadith collection and selection process (not to mention the likelihood of a divine "source"), the value of a subset of sayings in the collections seems clear regardless of the reliability of their connection to Muhammad. The origin of any religious teaching appears insignificant in comparison with its practical power to encourage compassion and a sense of justice. These sorts of sayings are always worthy to be both valued and shared. Here is a small sampling of such sayings from the Islamic tradition:

- "A man will follow the way of his close friends, so let one of you look to whom he takes as a close friend."[1441]

- "Every act of kindness is a charity."

- "Give the worker his wages before his sweat dries."

- "Do not regard any act of kindness as insignificant, even meeting your brother with a cheerful countenance."

- "The best amongst you is he who repays his debts in the most handsome way."[1442]

- "There should be neither harming nor reciprocating harm."

- "Whoever among you wakes up in the morning and is safe in his home, in good health and has enough provision for the day, it is as if he has all the good things of this world."

From a nondogmatic perspective, true sayings are not those that are uttered or approved by any particular person, but only those that help us to become more compassionate, more just, more humble, and more content amidst the difficulties of life. For those who see no shame in doubt, there is thus no "orthodoxy" beyond what is wise, what is true, and what inspires authentic personal growth:

I'm sorry if I seem impatient, but this is simply the way it is.

If you want to grow your soul,
you have to do your own hard work. ...

A wise man does not gain his wisdom
because a jinn poured it into his ear as he slept,
but from a lifetime of observation and study.

It is the same with the soul.
Najat knows this is not what you want to hear,
But sometimes it is kind to say the hard thing.[1443]

[35] A Partial Imitation of Christ
...Insights from Thomas à Kempis

> It is good to hear every man's counsel; not to agree with it, when reason demands agreement, is a sign of great isolation of mind and of much inward pride.
>
> —**Thomas à Kempis** (c.1380-1471)[1444]

> I sought for rest but never found it, save in a little corner with a little book.
>
> —A favorite saying of **Thomas à Kempis**[1445]

One of the most widely translated and deeply cherished works of Christian devotion, the *Imitation of Christ* is generally attributed to the German monk Thomas à Kempis.[1446] Not surprisingly, Thomas was known as a quiet and reflective man who aimed to live a good life. He took the vows of a brother in his mid-twenties and was ordained priest at the age of thirty-three; he eventually rose to become a superior of a monastery. Although a great lover of books and a skilled author,[1447] he counseled against forms of learning that led to intellectual pride. For Thomas, helpful knowledge was only that which fostered growth in character (1.3).

Not surprisingly, Thomas was steeped in the Roman Catholic theology and practice of the late Middle Ages. Holding the doctrines of the medieval Church supreme, he asked readers to let faith rule over reason (4.18) and had a general suspicion of curiosity (1.1, 3.43). Unfortunately, Thomas' attachment to Roman Catholicism included some of its less savory characteristics, most notably the doctrines of a literal hell and purgatory. In his *Imitation*, the monk even felt compelled to give grotesque details about specific torments for sinners, such as prodding with "burning prongs of iron" and being "filled with burning pitch and brimstone" (1.24). He also at times seems to conflate humility and self-loathing (2.12, 3.8), even advocating calling oneself a "most abject worm" (3.3).[1448] Thomas was also perhaps too fearful of "earthly" pleasures (1.1, 1.20, etc.) and goes overboard when warning of the dangers of a cheerful attitude and "indiscreet mirth" (1.21). Despite such problematic tendencies, Thomas is surely a man who has things to teach skeptic and believer alike. Beloved and even translated into English by Protestant standout John Wesley (1703-1791),[1449] the *Imitation* is full of helpful and perceptive observations for those wishing for the sense of quietude that can be found in a pragmatic and measured approach to life.

Thomas had much to say of the deceptive nature of desire, extolling the benefits of moderation (1.22) and finding inordinate attachments to be a common cause of restlessness of mind (1.6). Perhaps his most insightful comments on this general theme of excessive attachment revolve around the misdirected longing to please people. Thomas held that those who had overcome this inclination would have a "great plenty of peace," maintaining that "all disquiet of heart and restlessness of mind come from inordinate love and groundless fear" (3.28). He noticed the rather obvious but largely overlooked fact that people's judgments about others have no necessary connection to reality, and that an accurate self-perception allowed for the disregard of both false flattery and unfair criticism:

> You are not the better because you are praised, or the worse because you are blamed, for as you are, you are …. If you behold well what you are inwardly, you will not care much what the world says of you outwardly. (2.6)

Thomas gave further insightful counsel on interpersonal relationships, sometimes in words that are reminiscent of cognitive therapy. While false or malicious insults can sting, the monk counseled that they should be allowed to pass rather than be dwelled upon. The mind that disregards slights can diminish their relevance, for "what hurt would they bring, if you suffered them to pass and go away?" (3.46). To combat an inclination towards judgmentalism, Thomas recommended that one remember one's own shortcomings and flaws:

> Study always to be patient in bearing other men's defects, for you have many in yourself that others suffer from you, and if you cannot make yourself as you would, how may you then look to have another regulated in all things to suit your will? (1.16)

Relatedly, Thomas counseled the importance of an honest and humble look at the nature of human existence. Beauty and strength should not be a cause of pride, because life constantly shows how illness can quickly make physical vigor diminish (1.7). Even the most learned have significant gaps in knowledge, so one should ask for the counsel of others and not despise differing opinions (1.9). Similarly, Thomas warned against being overly inclined to offer advice, concerned that it could not only be mistaken, but also could lead to unnecessary interpersonal conflict and inner turmoil (1.11).

Thomas thought that suffering was an inescapable part of reality for everyone. He noticed that those who did not accept this truth inevitably became more prone to irritability, anger, and hypercriticism— thereby ironically compounding their own troubles and difficulties. Those, therefore, who did not learn to suffer well would consequently suffer most, whereas a person "who can suffer best will have the most peace" (2.3). To find the strength to carry the burden of suffering, Thomas counseled that love was the best and surest aid: "Love bears a heavy burden and does not feel it, and love makes bitter things tasteful and sweet." In short, love was the greatest resource in ameliorating the human condition: "Nothing, therefore, is sweeter than love; nothing higher, nothing stronger, nothing larger, nothing more joyful, nothing fuller …." (3.5).

The greatest insights of Thomas revolve around the value of a reflective and deliberate life. The monk clearly understood that the human mind is subject to a frustrating inconstancy and disconcerting changes of emotion, and recognized the simple truth that a premeditated path of being was indispensable for maintaining direction amid the turmoil of existence:

> As long as you live, you will be subject to change, whether you will it or not—now glad, now sorrowful; now pleased, now displeased; now devout, now undevout; now vigorous, now slothful; now gloomy, now merry. But a wise man who is well taught in spiritual labor stands unshaken in all such things, and heeds little what he feels, or from what side the wind of instability blows. (3.33)

[36] Invincible Ignorance
...*The relative ignorance of everyone*

> Invincible ignorance, whether of the law or of the fact, is always a valid excuse and excludes sin.
>
> —**The Catholic Encyclopedia**[1450]

> One thing each of us knows for certain is that reality vastly exceeds our awareness of it.
>
> —**Sam Harris** (b.1967), neuroscientist and atheist[1451]

In Roman Catholic theology, the concept of "invincible ignorance" is used to describe those who are not morally culpable due to their lack of information or understanding. Reinterpreted more broadly, such a concept could be used as an apt descriptor for the entire human race. Human knowledge is always partial, affected by bias, and marked by ignorance.

The operations of the United States Library of Congress bluntly show this reality. As of 2013, the Library had over 830 miles of bookshelves. The largest library in the world, it now houses approximately 168 million items in 470 languages and accepts approximately 12,000 new items each business day.[1452] Even discounting all human proclivities to misinterpret, forget, and distort information, constant reading and study at the Library would render an ever-growing deficit of untouched material at the end of each day's labors.

Today, books are being printed, websites and letters are being generated, speeches are being delivered, debates are being held, magazines and articles are being published, and reports are being created. History is unfolding; science is experimenting and exploring. The collective knowledge of the human race is expanding at a rate immeasurably faster than we can even conceptualize. Who knows what extraordinary things dwell in other worlds in other galaxies, never to be revealed to human minds?

[37] Experiments with Truth
...A selection of Gandhi's religious reflections

No knowledge is to be found without seeking, no tranquility without travail, no happiness except through tribulation. Every seeker has, at one time or another, to pass through a conflict of duties, a heart-churning.

—**Mohandas "Mahatma" Gandhi** (1869-1948),
The Bhagavad Gita According to Gandhi[1453]

I have gone through deep introspection, searched myself through and through, and examined and analysed every psychological situation. Yet I am far from claiming any finality or infallibility about my conclusions.

—**Mohandas Gandhi**, *Autobiography: The Story of My Experiments with Truth*[1454]

Mohandas Gandhi was one of the most beloved religious leaders of the 20th century. Often known by the title "Mahatma" or "Great Soul," the native of the Gujarat region of India is well known for his heroic virtue, deep sense of compassion, and non-violent struggle for Indian independence. What makes the Hindu leader such a fascinating historical and spiritual figure, however, is that his formidable moral force was coupled with some idiosyncratic behavior, unusual perspectives, and very ordinary human struggles.

Despite eventually talking to large audiences, Gandhi was intensely shy in his youth and young adulthood, having great difficulties with public speaking.[1455] While he became a world-renowned spiritual leader, his political effectiveness was in part due to his rather "worldly" and Western legal training in London's prestigious Inner Temple.[1456] Although sometimes called the "Father of the Nation" in India, he had a very strained relationship with his own son Harilal, a heavy drinker who eventually apostatized from Hinduism and converted to Islam.[1457] In what would be seen as irresponsible behavior in Western society, Gandhi refused to buy insurance coverage for his family, believing that it was morally and spiritually suspect.[1458] He also quarreled with his wife, forcing her to give up jewelry[1459] and at times suspecting her fidelity.[1460] While his fellow Indians delighted in calling him Mahatma, he disliked the title and became greatly offended when he discovered that some people were worshipping him as a god.[1461]

Gandhi's relationship to food and sex often gravitated towards ascetic extremes. While his last name indicates that he was from a grocer caste,[1462] Gandhi at one point adopted a strict diet and avoided not only meat but also such staple groceries as tea, coffee, wine, beans, peas and cereals.[1463] Despite his great efforts for humanity, he believed that animal life and human life were of equal value, once remarking about animal sacrifice, "To my mind the life of a lamb is no less precious than the life of a human being."[1464] Although known for some puritanical inclinations at times, he also walked about in only a loincloth, thus earning the nickname of "the naked fakir."[1465] While not an uncommon stance in even Western nations at the time, he objected to the use of contraception on ethical grounds.[1466] Although Gandhi was married at the age of 13,[1467] by age 37 had taken a vow of perpetual celibacy (*brachmacharya*). In a rather unorthodox quest to test and purify himself, he even slept naked with young women for a time.[1468]

Gandhi is also interesting because of his perspectives on different religions, many of which are found in his autobiography *The Story of My Experiments with Truth*. His philosophical and spiritual conclusions were primarily forged in his investigations of the religious landscape of his native India—although he also lived for a time in Britain and South Africa as well. He was familiar with the teachings of Hinduism, Jainism, Buddhism, Islam, Zoroastrianism (in the Parsis), and Christianity; he drew from them all.[1469] It is perhaps in part the many personal contacts with different types of believers that most informed his eclectic approach. He knew from experience that there were individuals of varying stages of ethical development and spiritual attainment in every faith, and noted that "conversions" or reformed lives could be found in a variety of religious traditions.[1470]

While frequently noted for his non-violent, "Christ-like" character, Gandhi himself remarked that the Buddha had greater compassion than Jesus of Nazareth. When comparing the lives of the two sages, Gandhi commented that the Buddha's kindness extended to all creatures whereas "One fails to notice this love for all living things in the life of Jesus."[1471] Despite somewhat of a distaste for the Old Testament, Gandhi noted that "the New Testament produced a different impression, especially the Sermon on the Mount which went straight to my heart."[1472] His central concept of *satyagraha*, or "soul-force," was influenced by the Christian concept of changing others' moral sensibilities through the power of suffering love.[1473] Interestingly, he was not as fond of the writings of St. Paul and thought that the apostle had altered Jesus' teachings.[1474] For reasons reminiscent of those forwarded by many skeptics, Gandhi also had an extreme distaste for the traditional Christian and Muslim views of hell. He viewed these retributive realms as not only logically incoherent, but morally unacceptable as well:

> Let us not seek to prop virtue by imagining hellish torture after death for vice and houris [the heavenly virgins of Islam] hereafter as a reward for virtue in this life. If virtue has no attraction in itself, it must be a poor thing. ... The wise are unaffected either by death or life. These are but faces of the same coin.[1475]

While Gandhi regarded all religions as both insightful and flawed,[1476] he had a special love for the Hindu *Bhagavad-Gita* and once remarked that it was "an infallible guide of conduct."[1477] Clearly a source of personal solace and contemplation, Gandhi explained that when troubled he could always find a comforting verse and would "immediately begin to smile in the midst of overwhelming sorrow."[1478] It is clear that strong Jain influences played prominently on the Indian sage, most notably in the religion's focus on non-violence.[1479] His synthesis of religions focused on what one biographer seems to aptly describe as "the novel idea of an active and positive but detached and non-emotive love."[1480]

Perhaps in large part because of the manifold religious influences in his life, Gandhi tended to reject doctrinaire approaches to religious metaphysics. Although it is true that he displayed some moral rigidity and idealism,[1481] he also expressed some suspicion of dogma and certainty and favored approaches that were pluralistic and open. In his better moments, Gandhi also expressed an inclination towards compromise due to an appreciation of his own fallibility.[1482] Preferring to focus on ethics rather than doctrine,[1483] he once remarked: "Amongst the many untruths that are propounded in the world one of the foremost is theology. ... I know two good Christian friends who gave up theology and decided to live the gospel of Christ."[1484] Interestingly, he also described himself in terms of a seeker:

> There are innumerable definitions of God, because his manifestations are innumerable. They overwhelm me with wonder and awe and for a moment stun me. But I worship God as Truth only. I have not yet found Him, but I am seeking after Him. ... But as long as I have not realized this Absolute Truth, so long must I hold to the relative truth as I have conceived it.[1485]

Although he thought that religion was central to human life, even remarking that "Truth is God,"[1486] Gandhi also believed in the separation of church and state.[1487] He also had a rather broad-minded attitude towards non-believers, and even had a flirtation with atheism early in life.[1488] As biographer Bhikhu Parekh explains, "Gandhi knew many atheists with deep spiritual and even mystical feelings, and was anxious to not put them outside the pale of religious discourse."[1489] Indian atheist and social activist Shri Goparaju Ramachandra Rao (1902-1975) claims that he had a series of conversations with Gandhi over a period of four years. During one of their conversations, Rao maintains that Gandhi showed great patience in listening and looked for common ground based on a shared love of humanity. In perhaps an ideal example of theist-atheist debate, Rao relates the following words of the man that many Hindus have endearingly called "Bapu" or "father":

> Yes, I see an ideal in your talk. I can neither say that my theism is right nor your atheism is wrong. We are seekers after truth. We change whenever we find ourselves in the wrong. I changed like that many times in my life. I see you are a worker. You are not a fanatic.

> You will change whenever you find yourself in the wrong. There is no harm as long as you are not fanatical. Whether you are in the right or I am in the right, results will prove. Then I may go your way or you may come my way; or both of us may go a third way. So go ahead with your work. I will help you, though your method is against mine.[1490]

Oftentimes spiritual inquiry and searching are expected to lead to definitive resolutions, otherworldly insights, and a saintly self-mastery. While marked by growth, insight, and great courage, Gandhi's life is a reminder of the perhaps comforting truth that even the most exemplary spiritual and ethical quests are incomplete and hampered by the congenital flaws and finitude of each human life.

[38] The Noble Fundamentalist
...Remembering exemplary traditional Christians

> For him who is perfect in love and has reached the summit of dispassion, there is no difference between his own or another's, or between Christians and unbelievers, or between slave and free, or between male and female. But because he has risen above the tyranny of the passions and has fixed his attention on the single nature of man, he looks on all in the same way and shows the same disposition to all.
>
> —**St. Maximos the Confessor** (580-662)[1491]

> A paltry man and poor of mind
> At all things ever mocks;
> For never he knows, what he ought to know,
> That he is not free from faults.
>
> —*The Poetic Edda* (ancient Norse verse)[1492]

Much of the history of the most influential and largest Christian denominations and sects has largely been one of fundamentalism. Of course, this is not to say that the most widespread forms of historical Christianity have been "fundamentalist" in the precise sense of the "Fundamentals" of 20th-century American Protestantism.[1493] Nor is it to say that even very traditional Christians have been uniformly morally strict with issues like dancing, cards, or other such amusements. Rather, it is just that the largest groups of Christians—early Catholics, Roman Catholics, Eastern Orthodox, Oriental Orthodox, Lutheran, Calvinist, Anglican, Anabaptist, and the like—have historically had views of creeds, theological doctrines, miracles, and Scripture that would largely be considered to be overly rigid and literalistic not only by skeptics, but by many modern believers as well. Attitudes on freedom of conscience, women's rights, corporal and capital punishment, the age of the earth, the evolution of life, literal hellfire, the general historical accuracy of biblical stories, the existence of witches, the efficacy of relics, and the like have greatly moderated in the last two to three centuries. As Neill and Wright wrote about 19th-century English Christians, for example, "It must be remembered that at that time almost all good Christians in England were what would now be called 'fundamentalists.'"[1494] An investigation of historical creeds and confessions of the largest and most influential churches largely confirm this reality.[1495]

While it is true that the most prominent historical forms of Christianity have been significantly dominated and defined by such fundamentalist tendencies, it is nonetheless also true that there have been and still are large numbers of Christian "fundamentalist" individuals and groups that are among the most inspiring and noble of human beings. Put another way, there are heroes of traditional forms of Christianity who, despite some of their rigid metaphysical tendencies, have been superior people in almost every conceivable category—serving both as models of human behavior and exposing the inherent difficulties with being overly dismissive of the adherents of any particular religious expression. In one poignant example of this reality, Voltaire (1694-1778), while a fierce critic of Roman Catholicism himself, still felt that honesty required him to praise the selfless and altruistic service of nuns in hospital work:

> Perhaps there is nothing greater on earth than the sacrifice of youth and beauty, often of high birth, made by the gentle sex in order to work in hospitals for the relief of human misery, the sight of which is so revolting to our delicacy.[1496]

While fundamentalist doctrines (in their many varieties) may still show every sign of being dubious, there have nonetheless been traditional or fundamental believers who have been superior people intellectually, morally, and civically. They have been better parents, better siblings, and better spouses. They have been more generous, less judgmental, more humble, more patient, more courageous, more compassionate, more honest, and more principled. They have been better athletes, better linguists, better mathematicians, and even better scientists. Furthermore, the vast diversities in people of faith show that people who are traditional in one area of doctrine or practice can at times be more broadminded or "progressive" than even many skeptics in another—and that significant diversity exists even among those who espouse the same sectarian definitions of orthodoxy.

In one proverbial example, many Christians have been known for their courage in the face of persecution and torture. While accounts of martyrs and confessors are often idealized, there is no question that there have been many thousands of brave martyrs from a variety of different "orthodox" and "heretical" denominations and sects, from a host of different countries and time periods. While the sufferings of the early church are well known, St. Maximilian Kolbe (1894-1941), who offered himself up for another man in a Nazi concentration camp, provides but one example of individual courage.[1497] In the 21st century, many marginalized but committed Coptic Christians in Egypt have been killed by Muslim jihadis.[1498] Many Roman Catholics, Anglicans, Calvinists, Lutherans, and especially Anabaptists died for their convictions in the Reformation period.

Christians throughout history have also been shining examples of caring for children, the sick, and the elderly. Early Catholic Christians in Rome are known to have supported 1,500 widows in 250 CE.[1499] St. Catherine of Siena (1347-1380) remained to comfort and care for the sick during an outbreak of the plague. She is remembered in general for her care of the poor and prisoners.[1500] St. Louis (1214-1270) is often regarded as an ideal Christian king. He visited the poor and sick, even changing bedpans.[1501]

St. Martin de Porres (1579-1639) is remembered for his extensive work among orphans, the sick, slaves, and the animals of Peru.[1502] The evangelical World Vision organization, while controversial due to their opposition to gay marriage, sponsored 3.4 million children and helped 420 million children in 2014.[1503] Relatedly, early Franciscans like St. Francis of Assisi (1182-1226) and St. Clare of Assisi (1194-1253) left behind lasting ideals of patience, generosity and simplicity, inspiring multitudes to acts of service.[1504]

Traditional Christians have famously championed education and literacy as well. For example, medieval monks painstakingly copied the Bible and many other books by hand, thereby helping to preserve large numbers of writings from antiquity. Many Protestant ministers, missionaries, and laymen have labored tirelessly for literacy and education.[1505]

Christians with fundamentalist leanings have been advocates of human rights in a variety of contexts. Christian Kievan Russia for a time was successful in halting capital punishment, torture, and mutilation.[1506] St. Nilus of Sora (1443-1508) was a pioneering Eastern Orthodox believer who fought against the religious persecution advocated by his co-religionists.[1507] St. Pedro Claver (1580-1654) offered food, medical care, and spiritual guidance to slaves and blacks in Cartagena in South America, acting as a beacon of justice against the overtly racist attitudes that prevailed at the time.[1508] Dorothy Day (1897-1980), currently under consideration for sainthood, fought tirelessly for rights and protections for workers.[1509] Traditional Christians were also crucial forces in emancipation and ending the slave trade. St. Wulfstan (c.1008-1095) is known for his successful efforts to eradicate the slave trade in Bristol, England.[1510] William Wilberforce (1759-1833) introduced nine bills against the slave trade between 1789 and 1805.[1511] Harriet Tubman (c.1822-1913) helped deliver at least 300 slaves to freedom, risking her own freedom and her very life for others.[1512]

Christians have also been prolific and learned authors. The surviving works of Origen (c. 185-c.254) contain more script than the total of all other Christian authors of the first through third centuries combined. A devoted linguistic scholar, his knowledge of the Hebrew Bible is proverbial.[1513] St. Augustine of Hippo (354-430) is said to have written the equivalent of a 300-page book every year for about 40 years.[1514] According to his biographer Possidius, Augustine wrote more than 1,000 total works, including 242 books;[1515] biographer Gerald Bonner calls him "not merely one of the most prolific of the Fathers, but also one of the most voluminous writers of all time."[1516] St. Isidore of Seville (d.636), also an industrious writer, penned not only many theological works, but also books about astronomy, geography, and history.[1517] St. Anthony Claret (1807-1870) is said to have preached more than 10,000 sermons and written over 200 books and pamphlets.[1518] Relatedly, traditional Christians have been superb novelists. Fyodor Dostoevsky (1821-1881), regarded as a genius due to novels such as *Crime and Punishment* and *The Brothers Karamazov*, was a devout (albeit troubled and often wayward) Eastern Orthodox Christian.[1519] J.R.R. Tolkien (1892-1973), beloved for his stories of *The Hobbit* and

The Lord of the Rings, was a committed Roman Catholic who disliked the modernizing tendencies of Vatican II.[1520]

While fundamentalism has often been at odds with evolution and geology, traditional Christians have made invaluable contributions to mathematics and science. A prime example is the brilliant Blaise Pascal (1623-1662), who invented the first calculating device (at age 19), developed a law of hydraulics and a probability theory, and invented the syringe and the hydraulic lift.[1521] Another example is Gregor Mendel (1822-1884), an Augustinian monk and abbot who was also a pioneer in the field of genetics.[1522] A last example is Sir Isaac Newton (1642-1727). Among the most celebrated of scientists, Newton wrote widely on theology. Though a non-Trinitarian, he was fascinated with the Second Coming and did some of his own "apocalyptic number-crunching"![1523]

Christian orators and public speakers have also been famously gifted. St. John Chrysostom (c.347-407), whose name means "golden-tongued," is regarded by many as one of the most eloquent preachers of the early Church. Many of his sermons still survive.[1524] George Whitefield (1714-1770) was a mesmerizing preacher who helped bring on the Great Awakening in colonial America. Even Benjamin Franklin, despite his heterodox and largely skeptical religious opinions, felt compelled to give a donation after hearing him preach. Franklin even once noted that Whitefield was "a perfectly honest Man."[1525] There have of course been many remarkable Christian artists, architects, and musicians as well. Untold numbers of paintings, mosaics, and cathedrals provide proof of this reality. Known chiefly for his Pieta, David, and the Sistine Chapel ceiling, one standout example is Michelangelo (1475-1564), widely regarded as one of history's greatest artists.[1526] Johann Sebastian Bach (1685-1750) for a period wrote an average of one cantata per week—202 survive. In all, he composed about 1,000 musical pieces.[1527]

Christianity has produced many able diplomats and administrators. By way of example, St. Leo the Great (c.400-461) convinced Attila the Hun to withdraw from Rome and persuaded the Vandal Gaiseric not to burn the eternal city or slaughter its inhabitants.[1528] St. Gregory the Great (c.540-604) made peace with the Lombards, recovered citizens sold into slavery, took active steps for the military defense of Rome and other Italian cities, provided for the poor, and preserved the grain supply.[1529]

Traditional Christians have also been amazing linguists. William Tyndale (1494?-1536), who could speak seven languages, is best known for his translation of the Bible into modern English during the Reformation—and his martyrdom at the hands of Roman Catholic authorities.[1530] St. Laurence of Brindisi (1559-1619) knew at least six languages, and St. John Neumann (1811-1860) was proficient in eight.[1531] Famed Protestant missionary William Carey (1761-1834), who was also instrumental in putting an end to the practice of widow-burning (sati) in India, translated at least parts of the Bible into 35 different languages![1532]

Fundamentalists have often been world-class athletes. Olympic runner and missionary Eric Henry Liddell (1902-1945), American football quarterback Kurt Warner (b. 1971), and gold medalist Gabby Douglas (b. 1995)[1533] are just three of many examples.

The thrust of this general line of thinking seems to be a reminder of the rather clear but often forgotten truth that all people are a mixture of folly and insight, of faults and strengths. Rejecting this reality, either through excessive praise or excessive blame, is in many ways to be one of the defining negative characteristics of fundamentalism itself—and thus out of accord with a more balanced and healthy approach to life. Another Norse saying seems to provide a fitting conclusion:

> None so good is found that faults he has not,
> Nor so wicked that nought he is worth.[1534]

[39] The Most Excellent Way
...Love and 1 Corinthians 13

Love is sufficient for itself; it gives pleasure to itself, and for its own sake. It is its own merit and own reward. Love needs no cause beyond itself, nor does it demand fruits; it is its own purpose.

—**St. Bernard of Clairvaux** (1090-1153)[1535]

Judging others makes us blind, whereas love is illuminating.

—**Dietrich Bonhoeffer** (1906-1945), German pastor and theologian[1536]

After leaving a traditional Christian perspective, there can be an exaggerated impulse to devalue the content of the Bible. Although there is much in Christian Scripture that is unsavory, there is also some material that is fruitful for meditation and personal growth. Legitimate biblical insights—which are often found in other religious and philosophical perspectives—should not be dismissed due to a bias against their source.

Perhaps more than any other text, 1 Corinthians 13 shows the truth of this sentiment. Although the value of love and compassion is expressed in many religious and secular schools of thought, the "definition" of love that comes here is among the most engaging and complete. If looked at in a certain light, the passage also provides a critique of religious dogmatism. For if adherence to the "law of love" is of such import that metaphysical knowledge, miraculous power, and supernatural faith are "nothing" in comparison, it would seem that a large part of Christian history has been an exercise in distraction and misguided effort. And while most of the rest of Scripture may not live up to the sentiments of 1 Corinthians 13, it is easy to see how there is little else that does either:

> And yet I will show you the most excellent way.
>
> If I speak in the tongues of men or of angels, but do not have love, I am only a resounding gong or a clanging cymbal. If I have the gift of prophecy and can fathom all mysteries and all knowledge, and if I have a faith that can move mountains, but do not have love, I am nothing. If I give all I possess to the poor and give over my body to the flames, but do not have love, I gain nothing.
>
> Love is patient, love is kind. It does not envy, it does not boast, it is not proud.
>
> It does not dishonor others, it is not self-seeking, it is not easily angered, it keeps no record of wrongs.
>
> Love does not delight in evil but rejoices with the truth.
>
> It always protects, always trusts, always hopes, always perseveres.
>
> Love never fails (1 Cor. 12:31b-13:13, NIV).

[40] Inordinate Attachment and the Ordered Life

...The poisonous and practical in St. Ignatius of Loyola

> For just as taking a walk, journeying on foot, and running are bodily exercises, so we call Spiritual Exercises every way of preparing and disposing the soul to rid itself of all inordinate attachments ....
>
> —St. Ignatius of Loyola (1491-1556)[1537]

> If we wish to proceed securely in all things, we must hold fast to the following principle: What seems to me white, I will believe black if the hierarchal Church so defines.
>
> —St. Ignatius of Loyola[1538]

The Spanish Roman Catholic saint Ignatius of Loyola had an intensity that marked all the seasons of his life. In his earlier days, he had a reputation as a reveler, delighting in expensive clothes and the company of women. His unflagging bravery as a soldier resulted in his refusal to surrender against overwhelming odds in battle; in 1521, such courage resulted in a shattered leg from a cannonball and the end of his military career. During his extended convalescence, Ignatius had a spiritual change of direction—even if no change in vigor. He discarded his finery and took on the garments of a beggar, living in a cave for a time in extreme austerity as he struggled with severe pangs of conscience. The heights of his newfound zeal were even looked at with concern by the Inquisition, who put him in jail for some weeks to examine his orthodoxy.

The eventual result of his fervor was the establishment of the Society of Jesus in 1534, which he believed was entrusted to him by a heavenly vision. His organization was intent on bringing new strength to the Roman Catholic Church through absolute obedience to the pope. More commonly known as the Jesuits, his Society was given papal approval in 1540 and became a significant force in both worldwide missions and in the Counter-Reformation in Catholic Europe.

One of Ignatius' chief legacies to Roman Catholicism is his *Spiritual Exercises*. The principal devotional work of the Jesuit Order, the *Exercises* place supreme emphasis on the structured spiritual life. The work is in essence a month-long retreat manual, giving the director a systematic approach for the dispensing of spiritual guidance. Filled with advice on self-examination, structured meditation, devotional reading, penance, and prayer, Ignatius' goal for the participant was the renunciation of sinful behavior, growth in the sense of service towards humanity, a submission to Roman Catholic orthodoxy, and a renewed sense of communion with God. The direct and simple style of the *Exercises* reflects the spirit of Ignatius himself and embodies his intensity, love of order, and unyielding focus.[1539]

The strengths of the *Exercises* lie, as monk and author Thomas Merton noted, in their practical nature.[1540] Ignatius recognized that training was as essential to the spiritual life as to athletics. He created a practical program to address the attitudes and behaviors necessary to foster a more deliberate and purposeful existence. His willingness to consider individual differences makes his *Exercises* adaptable to all types of people. Moreover, his suggestions regarding the modification of sleep and diet, rhythmic breathing, scheduled times of meditation, measured decision-making, the power of the imagination, the need for edifying reading, and the development of specific goals allow for a broad opportunity for selective appropriation of his ideas.

Perhaps most poignantly, Ignatius is thoroughly concerned with the problem of "inordinate attachments," whereby individuals lose their focus and moral strength by being overly attached to particular people, places, comforts, or beliefs.[1541] In fact, avoiding attachments is an expressed reason for the development of the *Exercises*. As he describes in a subtitle, the *Exercises* "have as their purpose the conquest of self and the regulation of one's life in such a way that no decision is made under the influence of an inordinate attachment."[1542]

While Ignatius' spirituality draws much of its strength from its zealous adherence to the authority of the Church, his strict obedience to Roman Catholic dogma seems to epitomize the "inordinate attachment" that he otherwise so strongly warns against. In effect, he utilizes his program to eradicate any distraction that interferes with his own primary inordinate attachment.[1543] His blind passion for the Church shows itself most clearly in his belief that "What seems to me white, I will believe black if the hierarchal Church so defines,"[1544] a notion which is as dehumanizing as it is disturbing—and which in exaggerated form presents one of the most tragic flaws of fundamentalist Christianity at large.[1545]

Although unswerving deference to authority is often touted as an example of perfect humility in traditional forms of Christianity, such unqualified obedience ironically seems to demand the highest estimation of one's own skills of metaphysical discernment concerning religious authority. For Ignatius, the individual was "a source of corruption and contamination from which has issued countless sins and evils and the most offensive poison."[1546] Nonetheless, the sinful exercitant is asked to "put aside" all personal judgment in complete reliance on the Roman Catholic Church.[1547] Inexplicably, the depraved soul need not consider any other religious or secular authorities as possibilities. Personal vileness and weakness thus affect all judgments save one—which is rendered completely unassailable. Reason is utilized only after this preordained framework is established. All the intellect is used only to justify the Church's rectitude, no matter what evidence there may be to the contrary: "Finally, we must praise all the commandments of the Church, and be on the alert to find reasons to defend them, and by no means in order to criticize them."[1548]

Ignatius also at times dismisses his own warnings of the dangers of making major decisions in a state of anxiety or distress. He urges the usage of shame and guilt as motivators for what he deems to be proper belief and behavior.[1549] More specifically, the summoning of "sorrow, suffering, and anguish" is specifically recommended for the exercitant, as is the need to make a "great effort to strive to grieve, be sad, and weep" and to generally "feel pain" psychologically.[1550] He strikingly and explicitly recommends the evoking of the fear of eternal torment to exercitants, noting that such musings should be utilized in part to "rouse more deeply the emotions" and to elicit the appropriate response.[1551] Ignatius no doubt understood the power of evoking such fears and used the full realm of the imagination to make all Roman Catholic metaphysical speculations seem as vivid as possible. In one exercise, the exercitant is told not only to "Recall to memory [the pain] of those who are in hell," but to personally "beg for a deep sense of the pain that the lost suffer" for oneself. All five senses are specifically named to make eternal damnation appear as real and graphic as possible:

- "to *see* ... the souls enclosed, as it were, in bodies of fire"
- "To *hear* the wailing, the howling, the cries" of the damned
- "With the sense of *smell* to perceive the smoke, the sulphur, the filth, and corruption"
- "To *taste* the bitterness of tears, sadness, and remorse of conscience"
- "With the sense of *touch* to feel flames which envelop and burn souls."[1552]

The value of confessions under threat of torment has been widely dismissed in Western systems of justice, but that is not because such threats provide no effectiveness in behavioral control. Desperation and fear can bring obedience and confessional orthodoxy, but they often do so at the immeasurably high cost of personal honesty, integrity, intellectual curiosity, and peace of mind.

This dimension of the *Exercises* is reminiscent of Inquisitional methods, especially when the need to promote psychological anguish turns physical. "Exterior penance," so Ignatius counsels, "consists in inflicting punishment on ourselves for the sins we have committed."[1553] Although he instructs that bodily penances should "not penetrate to the bones, so that it inflicts pain, but does not cause sickness," this slight degree of moderation does little to soften the sense that Ignatius' inordinate attachment to Roman Catholicism had reached an unhealthy extreme:

> The third kind of penance is to chastise the body, that is, to inflict sensible pain on it. This is done by wearing hairshirts, cords, or iron chains on the body, or by scourging or wounding oneself, and by other kinds of austerities.[1554]

A critical look at the *Exercises* thus reveals a program for indoctrination rather than an effort to encourage either true existential searching or intellectual integrity. The encouragement of extreme emotional vulnerability, the insistence on ideas promoting excessive guilt, the doctrinaire attitudes on authority, and the psychological manipulation offer with rare clarity some of the darkest elements of Christian traditionalism. Although absolute obedience to an authority can bring a sense of existential comfort, the dogmatic aspects of Ignatian spirituality, as with many forms of Abrahamic dogmatism, are ultimately a desperate attachment to the "myth of certainty"[1555] and a squelching of the endeavor to reach Ignatius' professed goal of "an intimate understanding and relish of the truth."[1556]

The *Spiritual Exercises* thus serve as a window into why many forms of traditional Christianity have been both a source for good and for suffering in the world. Some of Ignatius' practical advice can be quite helpful in efforts to build a more ordered and contemplative life. His counsel on such things as measured breathing, meditation, devotional reading, sleep, diet, helping others, and daily schedules can be perceptive. His doctrinaire attitudes and more abusive spiritual guidance, while not instructive in their own right, provide a rare opportunity to understand more clearly the darker side of traditional Christian spirituality. In essence, Ignatius' frank and direct approach clearly reveals how dogmatic faith can provide not only a powerful medium for order, focus, vitality, and consolation, but also be a potent means of inflicting harm on oneself and others.

[41] A More Balanced Way

...Light from the Tao Te Ching; Darkness in The Divine Panorama

> I have three treasures that I hold and cherish:
> One is called "compassion"
> Another is called "moderation"
> And the third is called "daring not to compete."
> With compassion, one is able to be brave.
> With moderation, one has enough to be generous with others.
> Without competition, one is fit to lead (no. 67).
>
> —*Tao Te Ching*[1557]

According to tradition, the *Tao Te Ching* ("The Way and Its Power") was penned by Chinese philosopher Lao Tzu in the sixth century BCE. Although there is some question as to whether Lao Tzu was an actual historical figure, he is usually described as an archivist in the imperial library and a contemporary of Confucius. Legends tell us that he was born of a virgin,[1558] spent seventy-two years in his mother's womb, had an old man's white hair at birth, and lived for more than 200 years.[1559] It is even believed by some Taoists that he is the Creator of the universe.[1560]

Although its reputed author may be shrouded in myth, the main thrusts of the *Tao Te Ching* seem clear—the importance of humility, the benefits of moderation and simplicity, the usefulness of flexibility, and the value of compassion.[1561] While reading the volume is the only way to get the full depth of this time-honored spiritual classic, a few excerpts should help show its relevancy for the modern age. In terms that could easily be applied to both obsessive internet behavior and the frantic pace of modern life in general, there is a warning of the effects of excessive stimulation:

> Too many colors tax people's vision.
> Too many sounds deaden people's hearing.
> Too many flavors spoil people's taste.
> Thrill-seeking leads people to do crazy things.
> The pursuit of wealth just gets in people's way.
> Therefore, the Sage provides for her needs, not her desires.
> She renounces the latter, and chooses the former (no. 12).

In an era of materialism, probing questions are asked about whether acquisition may not many times result in a more profound kind of deprivation:

> Fame or self: which is more important?
> Your possessions or your person: which is worth more to you?
> Gain or loss: which is worse?
> Therefore, to be obsessed with "things" is a great waste,
> The more you gain, the greater your loss.
> Being content with what you have been given,
> You can avoid disgrace.
> Knowing when to stop,
> You will avoid danger.
> That way you can live a long and happy life (no. 44).

In a world where displays of power are honored, restraint and humble achievement are praised:

> A good leader accomplishes only what he has set out to do
> And is careful not to overestimate his ability.
> He achieves his goal, but does not brag.
> He effects his purpose, but does not show off.
> He is resolute, but not arrogant.
> He does what he must, though he may have little choice.
> He gets results, but not by force (no. 30).

While there is much in the *Tao Te Ching* that is beneficial and even beautiful, a note of caution about the larger umbrella of Taoism seems in order. Going far beyond some of the tamer forms of superstition and speculation in the largely nondogmatic *Tao Te Ching*, the popular[1562] Taoist Scripture known as *The Divine Panorama* indulges in the grossest forms of mythology, fearmongering, and spiritual manipulation. In a discussion of the "Ten Courts" of damnation that await those guilty of thought-crimes and other misdeeds, *The Divine Panorama* provides an utterly sadistic description of a series of torture chambers that has an all-too-familiar resemblance to the hells of other faiths.[1563] In but one example of such fictitious horrors, the sixteen wards of the "Eighth Court" of the netherworld are described with sadistic creativity:

> In the first [ward], the wicked souls are rolled down mountains in carts. In the second, they are shut up in huge saucepans. In the third, they are minced. In the fourth, their noses, eyes, mouths, etc. are stopped up. In the fifth, their uvulas are cut off. In the sixth, they are exposed to all kinds of filth. In the seventh, their extremities are cut off. In the eighth, their viscera are fried. In the ninth, their marrow is cauterized. In the tenth, their bowels are scratched. In the eleventh, they are inwardly burned with fire. In the twelfth, they are disemboweled. In the thirteenth, their chests are torn open. In the fourteenth, their skulls are split open and their teeth are dragged out. In the fifteenth, they are hacked and gashed. In the sixteenth, they are pricked with steel prongs.[1564]

While doubters are often painted with a dark brush in religious faiths (and "non-worshippers and sceptics" are predictably promised their own torments in the Fifth Court in *The Divine Panorama*),[1565] there is good reason to think that those who resist such blatant attempts at religious intimidation may in fact be answering a higher calling. While "His Infernal Majesty" Tu Shih may promise rewards and safety to those who believe and disburse the teachings of the *Panorama*,[1566] a more authentic approach rather suggests that His Majesty is mythical, his threats and promises baseless, and his followers ill with the sickness of those that pretend to know but do not (*Tao Te Ching*, no. 71). Compassion and honesty cry out for a Way that rejects the intentional infliction of fear and anxiety through ideas that are wholly unsupported by evidence. While threats like those in *The Divine Panorama* no doubt have brought about some cowering obedience to social and religious norms, there appears to be little doubt that its methods are a poor way to build a more benevolent and ethical society. As the moral arc of human progress would seem to suggest,[1567] the more balanced path suggested in the *Tao Te Ching* is likely not only more ethical, but more liable to be effective in the long run:

> To foster gentleness is true strength.
> Choose to do what is wise and return to wisdom
> Then you will avoid life's troubles (no. 52).

[42] Sinners of Light, Saints of Darkness

...Virtues and flaws of Mother Teresa and Christopher Hitchens

If I ever become a Saint—I will surely be one of "darkness."

—**Mother Teresa of Calcutta**, (1910-1997)[1568]

I do not set myself up as a moral exemplar, and would be swiftly knocked down if I did ....

—**Christopher Hitchens**, (1949-2011)[1569]

Christopher Hitchens and Mother Teresa are rarely jointly held in high esteem. To many, they represent irreconcilable views of humanity, foils that could never be mutually admired or appreciated. Hitchens is often maligned for his uncharitable comments, his heavy drinking, and his insulting invective against political figures and traditional believers. Mother Teresa is often held up as the pious nun who spent a life loving God and "the poorest of the poor," demonstrating to all that the religious life is the ultimate expression of human goodness. I believe that these sorts of views, when taken uncritically, are distortions of the life and legacy of both individuals. Saints and fiends alike often seem to be figments of the imagination, distortions of flesh and blood.

Angel of Misery

Mother Teresa was a devoted, driven, courageous, and intelligent woman. She was well versed in Roman Catholic theology and conversant in five languages.[1570] She left her family and homeland of Albania in order to serve the poor; she clearly undertook many hardships to follow her faith. Although Christopher Hitchens might have disagreed,[1571] in my mind there is no reason to doubt that she was sincere in her desire to live a good life and help others. The order she founded made many efforts to help feed, clothe, educate, and care for many who may not have received any assistance otherwise. She drew attention to the plight of the destitute, and the symbol of her life indubitably led many to help the less fortunate. In many significant ways, she was an amazing and admirable person.

But to accept a purely hagiographic view of Mother Teresa is to miss some substantial and systemic problems with her approach to both the poor and to suffering in general. Although I think Hitchens goes much too far in reducing her to a mere "fanatic, a fundamentalist, and a fraud,"[1572] his recognition of a poisonous dimension of Mother Teresa's religious beliefs is compelling. Despite her admirable qualities and achievements, her dogmatic adherence to a particular expression of Roman Catholicism appears to have significantly diminished her extraordinary ministry and inflicted unnecessary suffering on herself, the nuns of her order, and some of the "poorest of the poor" under her care. Although she may not have been the caricatured "Hell's Angel" that Hitchens claimed,[1573] her legacy seems to be one of both light and darkness.

In Brian Kolodiejchuk's very sympathetic collection of her letters (*Mother Teresa: Come Be My Light*), there appears to be significant evidence that Mother Teresa was at times more concerned with proselytizing than caring for the poor, was often racked with guilt and driven by fears of mortal sin, had a theological stance that often promoted suffering, and adhered to a metaphysical system that in many ways valued the horrible systemic poverty that so plagues India and other parts of the world. Her intense desire to suffer and her glorification of the sufferings of others is at times disturbing; there seems to be a direct connection between her morbid theological outlook and the now famous dark descriptions of her interior life:

> Please pray specially for me that I may not spoil His work and that Our Lord may show himself—for there is such terrible darkness within me, as if everything was dead. It has been like this more or less from the time I started "the work."[1574]

One of the most striking characteristics of this dark side of Mother Teresa's worldview is its intense and gloomy preoccupation with misery. Although Kolodiejchuk spiritualized her psychological pain in terms of the "dark night of the soul,"[1575] in my reading the "darkness" is an almost necessary corollary to certain aspects of her understanding of the divine. Her mission in life was, in her own words, to "take away from the Heart of Jesus His continual suffering"[1576] and she seems to have believed that God was most pleased when she experienced pain.[1577] Her desire to both suffer and spread suffering fills her letters. It is but a part of the set of contradictions that defined Mother Teresa—smiling yet dejected, dedicated to the plight of the poor yet encouraging misery, living a life of faith yet racked with doubt, carrying a message of love but believing in a stern God who constantly demanded her personal anguish. Although the themes of suffering run throughout Kolodiejchuk's book, perhaps these examples are the most illuminating:

- She believed that Christ showed His love by intensifying suffering in people's lives: "Sorrow, suffering, Eileen, is but a kiss of Jesus—a sign that you have come so close to Jesus that He can kiss you. —I think this is the most beautiful definition of suffering. —So let us be happy when Jesus stoops down to kiss us."[1578]

- She believed that Jesus still suffered and asked her to unite in suffering with Him. She thought Jesus told her: "You will suffer and you suffer now—but if you are my own little Spouse—the Spouse of the Crucified Jesus—you will have to bear these torments on your heart. —Let me act—Refuse me not—Trust me lovingly—trust me blindly. … How it hurts—if you only knew—to see poor children soiled with sin."[1579]

- She believed that God had an unquenchable thirst for suffering and sacrifice: "He spoke of His thirst—not for water—but for love, for sacrifice. Jesus is God: therefore, His love, His thirst is infinite. Our aim is to quench this infinite thirst of the God made man."[1580]

- She desired that her nuns suffer, asking them to become "victims for India," "living holocausts," and to pursue their own "continual immolation for souls." She campaigned for and encouraged their "rigorous poverty."[1581]

- She expressed willingness to suffer eternal torture herself if it would please God: "And if the night becomes very thick—and it seems to me as if I will end up in hell—then I simply offer myself to Jesus. If He wants me to go there—I am ready—but only under the condition that it really makes Him happy."[1582]
- She came to love suffering herself: "For the first time in this 11 years—I have come to love the darkness—for I believe that it is a part, a very, very small part of Jesus' darkness & pain on earth."[1583]

It is not difficult to see how the promulgation of such ideas could encourage human pain and misery. God is at times portrayed in Mother Teresa's letters in the imagery of an Omnipotent Sadist, delighting in and yearning for the suffering of others. Mother Teresa seems herself to often play the part of the masochist, longing for suffering and humiliation. Her outlook on suffering lends significant credence to the claims, both by Hitchens and those in the medical profession, that Mother Teresa did not provide necessary painkillers or sufficient medical care despite a large amount of accumulated donations.[1584] The allegations would seem to fit all too well into her theological framework.

One in fact feels a bit "cheated" by Mother Teresa's common outer appearance of joy. Although she revealed her inner struggles to her confessors, she gave no indication either to her nuns or to the outside world of her intense struggle with doubt, her feelings of distance from God, and her frequent tendency to mask intense psychological pain with a smile. In her own words:

> The whole time smiling—Sisters & people pass such remarks. —They think my faith, trust & love are filling my very being & that the intimacy with God and union to His will must be absorbing my heart. —Could they but know—and how my cheerfulness is the cloak by which I cover the emptiness and misery.[1585]

With all her interior shadow and anguish, Mother Teresa's drive to rid others of the "darkness of unbelief"[1586] often seems like the peddling of a false bill of goods. She herself starkly noted, "It is only that blind faith that carries me through for in reality to me all is darkness."[1587] Mother Teresa's interior life is thus strongly suggestive of the fact that dogmatic belief, with all its inconsistencies and difficulties, can be both a source of solace and a fount of suffering. The incongruities of her faith highlight humanity's great challenge in striving to retain the beautiful light in spirituality while expelling its deep darkness.

Sinful Sage, Combative Comforter

Christopher Hitchens was a highly intelligent man with an indomitable spirit. A product of private schools and a graduate of Oxford University, there is no doubt Hitchens developed a flair for both rhetoric and writing. Although perhaps best known for his writings and speeches on religion, he also wrote extensively on political, historical, and other matters.[1588] His level of knowledge on a wide range of topics was astounding.

Although Hitchens never touted himself as a moral example, his courage and sharp tongue were often a salve to those wounded by the more horrific claims of certain traditional forms of faith. Hitchens was a firm foe of religious dogmatism, demanding the death of the creeping fear that a vengeful god was waiting to torture those who doubt the incredible and resist the irrational. Perhaps his brazenness and aggressiveness were so welcome to so many because he dared to point out bluntly the severe problems that have been inextricably tied to so many forms of fundamentalism—scientific and academic obscurantism, unsubstantiated authoritarianism, ethical inconsistency, and a lack of metaphysical and philosophical humility. Unfortunately, he himself at times took on an attitude that smacked of the traditional evangelist: too quick to demonize, too comfortable with ridicule or insult, and too easily forgetful of the ubiquity of human fallibility and pain. However, it is unfair to reduce him to a mere "drink-soaked former Trotskyist popinjay"[1589] or a "self-serving, fat-ass, chain-smoking, drunken, opportunistic, cynical contrarian."[1590] Even less is it justified to write him off as simply a "wicked" and "evil" man who wasted his life and perpetrated "devastating harm" on society.[1591] Though all his words and deeds may not be praiseworthy, I believe the world is a better place because of Christopher Hitchens. Hitchens' own general analysis of human nature from his biography of Thomas Jefferson seems fitting here: "[I]t would be lazy or obvious to say that he contained contradictions or paradoxes. This is true of everybody, and of everything."[1592]

Both Together

Hitchens' zeal at times led him to exaggerate failings and gloss over the merits of his adversaries. If Mother Teresa was "a fanatic, a fundamentalist, and a fraud" in some senses, it would seem entirely too dismissive and too militant to say that was all she was. To call her a "thieving, fanatical Albanian dwarf"[1593] was even less constructive—and seems to be an ad hominem attack that betrays a level of prejudice similar to those who regarded her as an immaculate saint. His titles of "Hell's Angel," *The Missionary Position*, and "Mommie Dearest" for his commentaries on Teresa suggest an emotional bias, and should serve as a call for caution and the consideration of other perspectives. Mother Teresa was a complicated figure and his reduction of her to a fraud and a charlatan appears to be overstated devaluation of her humanity—and unfortunately an opportunity for her more ardent supporters to dismiss Hitchens' fairer criticisms without thoughtful deliberation. To say without qualification that Mother Teresa made no noble sacrifices and brought no comfort to the lives of the poor borders on the absurd. To mark her as one of the world's villains seems rather preposterous.

Both Christopher Hitchens and Mother Teresa were both light and darkness in a gray world. They can and should both be admired and emulated for their strengths; neither needs to be categorized as wholly saint nor sinner. Mother Teresa should continue to be an inspiration for us to serve others and examine our self-centeredness. We should strive to emulate her best, recalling that there is an elegant beauty in selflessness and that ideally "Love has no other message but its own."[1594] Christopher Hitchens should spur us to continually reexamine our sacred cows and dogmas, remembering that humanity is "only partly rational"[1595] and that we "now know things about our nature that the founders of religion could not even begin to guess at, and that would have stilled their overconfident tongues if they had known of them."[1596] Perhaps the best approach would be to emulate some odd amalgamation of them both: determined, engaged, compassionate, brave, searching, questioning, relentless, and intent on making the world a better place.

[43] Praising Jesus, Reforming Christ

...Following a greater Jesus

> To the corruptions of Christianity I am, indeed, opposed; but not to the genuine precepts of Jesus himself. I am a Christian, in the only sense in which he wished anyone to be; sincerely attached to his doctrines, in preference to all others; ascribing to himself every *human* excellence; and believing he never claimed any other.
>
> —**Thomas Jefferson** (1743-1826), 3rd president of the United States[1597]

> It is quite possible that we can do greater things than Jesus, for what is written in the Bible is poetically embellished.
>
> —**Albert Einstein** (1879-1955)[1598]

Even some famous opponents of traditional Christianity have felt drawn to the figure of Jesus of Nazareth. In addition to Jefferson and Einstein, atheistic scientist Richard Dawkins,[1599] ancient philosopher Porphyry, modern musician Jackson Browne, novelist Leo Tolstoy, and Hindu Mohandas Gandhi are among the many diverse figures who have praised the teachings of Jesus.[1600] The lessons that can be learned from Jesus as presented in the New Testament are legion, but include an expression of the golden rule (Matt. 7:12), the value of nonjudgmentalism and forgiveness (Matt. 7:1-5, Matt. 18:21-22, John 7:53-8:11), the dangers of materialism (Matt. 6:21), the importance of caring for the oppressed and unfortunate (Matt. 25:35-40, Luke 14:12-14), the benefits of humble service (Matt. 23:11-12, Mark 10:42-

45), and the centrality of love and compassion (Matt. 5:43-46).[1601] Perhaps the best summation of the core of such teachings comes from the Gospel of John:

> I give you a new commandment, that you love one another. Just as I have loved you, you also should love one another. By this everyone will know that you are my disciples, if you love one another (John 13:34-35).

While even a skeptical stance may affirm Jesus' profundity and dignity in many New Testament sayings and stories, certain teachings attributed to him appear to fall short of his profounder insights. Namely, it seems fair to say that the Jesus of the New Testament had some faulty and damaging supernatural beliefs, promoted certain ethical positions that were harmful and overly dogmatic, and had views of the Old Testament that were both unrealistic and ultimately injurious to human society.

It seems clear that the Jesus of the New Testament held some dubious and poisonous supernatural beliefs. He is presented as believing that God reliably answers persistent prayer (Matt. 7:7-10, Matt. 18:19), that nothing is impossible for those with faith (Matt. 21:21),[1602] and also that petitions to God would give people miraculous powers (Matt. 21:18-22, John 14:13-14, John 16:23-24). Millions have dedicated themselves to prayer and thereby often misdirected their efforts, failing to avert tragedies and discovering that those who ask for good things with faith often do not receive.[1603] Jesus is further represented as claiming that he was coming back soon in glory (Luke 21:25-33, cf. Rev. 22:20), giving generations of believers false fears and hopes about an approaching end of the world. Lastly and perhaps most tragically, Jesus may have rejected the golden rule and the forgiving attitude that he taught elsewhere, encouraging people to believe that God would inflict everlasting torments after death on either themselves or their loved ones (Mark 9:43-48, Matt. 13:41-42, Matt. 25:41).[1604] Reflecting upon how this New Testament doctrine of hell would likely be applied to many of his own beloved family members and friends, biologist Charles Darwin (1809-1882) judged that this aspect of Jesus' gospel was in no sense good news, but rather "a damnable doctrine" of cruelty.[1605]

The Christ of the New Testament is also presented as giving harmful and overly rigid ethical teachings. By asking followers to put their devotion to him above family (Matt. 10:34-39, Matt. 19:29, Matt. 7:13-14), Jesus encouraged untold numbers to make imprudent decisions that fractured relationships, neglected the needs of relatives, and compromised personal welfare. The lives of generations of monks and missionaries provide volumes of evidence to confirm this reality.[1606] Jesus' teachings on divorce and remarriage also appear overly and unreasonably strict (Mark 10:11-12, Matt. 5:31-32; Matt. 9:9-12), not taking into account the many interpersonal and social dynamics which can make divorce a difficult but ethical decision (e.g., spousal and child abuse, serious financial mismanagement, mental illness, various irreconcilable differences, etc.). It is hard to imagine the amount of human suffering that the guilt-induced preservation of bad marriages and the ostracism of divorced persons has created.[1607] Lastly, Jesus appears to have carelessly taught that it was praiseworthy to give away funds beyond one's means or even all one's possessions (Mark 12:41-44, Matt. 19:21, Luke 14:33), causing suffering for untold numbers of followers and giving an easy avenue for manipulation by corrupt ministers and priests.

Jesus' recorded understandings of the Old Testament are also quite problematic. He is shown supporting cruel Old Testament laws (Matt. 15:3-4) and generally upholding a wrong-headed notion of Old Testament moral excellence (Matt. 5:18, Luke 16:17, John 7:19), thereby encouraging many of his followers in later centuries to follow a path of injustice and oppression. The derivative attempts to preserve Old Testament Law in Catholic, Orthodox, and Protestant societies were a steady thorn in the progress of justice and human rights.[1608] Promoting a naïve view of history that still infects many modern believers, Jesus also appears to have mistakenly thought that stories such as Jonah and the Fish and Noah's ark were historical in nature (Matt. 12:40-41, Matt. 24:37-39). It seems unmistakable that such beliefs have encouraged obscurantism and Christian opposition to scientific discoveries both in the past and even still in the present day.[1609]

While such realizations may be disturbing on one level, it also seems fair to say that the Jesus of history, in both his deeds and his words, is largely one of speculation. As the *Handbook of Biblical Criticism* reminds, "historical research can never achieve more than approximate and probable knowledge of any figure in the past."[1610] We really don't know enough about the Nazarene to know exactly who he was or what he believed—and even less about how he would conduct himself in a modern society. Bart

Campolo, humanist chaplain and son of prominent evangelical minister Tony Campolo, claims convincingly that no one alive today can really say that they know Jesus of Nazareth in anything that resembles an intimate way. The Gospels seem unreliable and sometimes contradictory, numerous denominations and Christian teachers have applied Jesus' teachings in radically different and even opposing ways, and it is very difficult to determine how the Jewish preacher would have responded to modern ethical questions and scientific discoveries that were beyond not only his knowledge, but likely his imagination as well. Unlike the way that we know the friends and family members in our own lives, Jesus of Nazareth seems to be someone who is largely out of reach:

> To me, however, Jesus is almost entirely inaccessible. I've never seen his photograph, listened to a recording of his voice, or read a single sentence that can be surely ascribed to him, let alone met him in person or known someone else who did. ... Among the many important things I don't know about Jesus: whether he was a good carpenter; ... his sexual orientation; his perspectives on slavery, abortion, and just war; his favorite kind of anything; his sense of humor; his best friend .... [E]very Christian church and individual believer sees Jesus differently than all the rest, and each one of them is convinced that, thanks be to God, their vision is the fairest of them all.[1611]

From a more skeptical perspective, however, such considerations are not necessarily that germane. The Christ worthy of praise would not be a historical but a romanticized figure, ideally embodying the most noble and compassionate values of each age and culture where he is followed.[1612] As Jesus himself is also said to have repudiated certain Old Testament laws as morally deficient (Matt. 5:21-48),[1613] so also theological liberals and skeptics following the "spirit" of Jesus may conclude that some of the teachings ascribed to him are either misguided or ethically problematic, especially when strictly or literally interpreted. While this is perhaps not quite what Jesus meant when he supposedly said that his followers would do greater things than he did (John 14:12), following his reforming spirit may necessitate the rejection of many New Testament teachings that reason and conscience would find to be at odds with justice, compassion, or the golden rule.

[44] Wonder with Me

...Cultivating wonder through the lorica form

> The fact that the universe is illuminated where you stand—that your thoughts and moods and sensations have a qualitative character in the moment—is a mystery, exceeded only by the mystery that there should be something rather than nothing in the first place.
>
> —**Sam Harris** (b.1967), *Waking Up: A Guide to Spirituality Without Religion*[1614]

> Everything is full of gods.
>
> —**Thales of Miletus** (c.624 BC – c.546 BC)[1615]

Filled with a sense of awe in the natural and supernatural worlds, loricas are ancient Christian prayers believed to have been heavily influenced by the conventions of Druidic incantations. They were numerous in the early Irish church and were thought to be a protection from evil forces and dark magic.

Although there may be good reason to be skeptical about magic and supernaturalism, there is no need to reject the power of awe and the value of wonder. In the words that philosopher-theologian Rudolf Otto (1869-1937) used to describe the experience of the Holy, the universe is both a *mysterium tremendum* and a *mysterium fascinans*—an astounding and fascinating mystery.[1616]

What follows is somewhat loosely based on "The Breastplate of St. Patrick," a famous lorica traditionally (and likely erroneously) attributed to the great Irish saint (387-461):[1617]

I arise today
  With a renewal of Focus,
  With a remembrance of Wonder,
  With an openness to Reality.

I stand in awe today of
  The majesty of the Heavens,
  The brilliance of the Sun,
  The whiteness of Snow,
  The radiance of Fire,
  The flashing of Lightning,
  The rushing of Wind,
  The depth of the Sea,
  The stability of the Earth,
  The hardness of Rocks.

I am spellbound today by
  The numbers of the Stars,
  The glories of the Sunset,
  The blackness of Caverns,
  The shine of the Harvest Moon,
  The glow of the Aurora,
  The eruption of the Volcano,
  The roar of the Gale,
  The quiet of falling Snow.

I marvel today at
  The sprouting of Seeds,
  The spreading of Forests,
  The chattering of Insects,
  The soaring of the Hawk,
  The jumping of the Fish,
  The running of the Deer,
  The howling of the Wolf,
  And the thoughts of Humanity.

Wonder with Me

There is Wonder within me, Wonder before me, Wonder after me,
Wonder under me, Wonder above me,
Wonder at my right, Wonder at my left,
Wonder in lying down, Wonder in sitting, Wonder in rising.

Wonder in every mind that thinks,
Wonder in every mouth that speaks,
Wonder in every eye that sees,
Wonder in every ear that hears.

May this sense of Wonder be with me always.

[45] The Compass of Compassion
...Gandhi's guiding principle

True Ahimsa should mean a complete freedom from ill will and anger and hate and an overflowing of love for all.

—Mohandas "Mahatma" Gandhi (1869-1948)[1618]

This *ahimsa* is the basis for the search for truth. I am realizing every day that the search is vain unless it is founded on *ahimsa* as the basis. It is quite proper to resist and attack a system, but to resist and attack its author is tantamount to resisting and attacking oneself.

—Mohandas Gandhi[1619]

Mohandas Gandhi's ethics were grounded in the notion of *ahimsa*. His favored term for the principle of compassion, *ahimsa* literally means "non-hurting" or "non-violence." In practical terms, Gandhi believed that compassion should be "the spring of all his actions."[1620] He thought that true *ahimsa* meant the full consideration of perspectives of others, a willingness to change one's mind, and a heartfelt attitude of respect based on a notion of the intrinsic worth of every person.[1621] When he disagreed with others, he believed that he must make every effort to cultivate a deep sense of empathy for those who opposed him. While concern for the welfare of every individual was an unalterable goal for Gandhi, he also believed that hurting others was in fact a form of self-harm.[1622]

Interestingly enough, even Gandhi's epistemology was grounded in the sense of compassion. Although he thought that his beliefs were always clouded and imperfect, he had become convinced that he would only know if something was true if he could see its relation to *ahimsa*:

> The little fleeting glimpses, therefore, that I have been able to have of Truth can hardly convey an idea of the indescribable lustre of Truth, a million more times intense than that of the sun we daily see with our eyes. In fact what I have caught is only the faintest glimmer of that mighty effulgence. But this much I can say with assurance, as a result of all of my experiments, that a perfect vision of Truth can only follow a complete realization of Ahimsa.[1623]

While some might consider Gandhi's ideas about *ahimsa* to be overly romantic, it is perhaps worthwhile to consider how central the concept of compassion has become in counseling and psychology. There is a significant body of psychological research which suggests that the empathic approach of Person-Centered (or Rogerian) Therapy is a core value that has utility and application across a broad spectrum of therapeutic approaches and techniques.[1624] While a therapist's compassionate and empathic attitude may not be a fully sufficient condition for psychological growth and healing, it appears to be a largely necessary one. Hence it might be said that when looking for ways to lessen the psychological suffering of others, approaches that are devoid of compassion may largely be ineffective—and in that sense a faulty and false path as far as human well-being is concerned. As noted in one counseling text, Person-Centered principles have a truly broad application in human interactions:

> People without advanced psychological education are able to benefit by translating the therapeutic conditions of genuineness, empathic understanding, and unconditional positive regard into both their personal and professional lives. The approach's basic concepts ... encourage locating power in the person, rather than fostering an authoritarian structure in which control and power are denied to the person. The core skills can be used by many people in the helping professions. These skills are also essential as a foundation for virtually all of the other therapy systems .... If counselors are lacking in these relationship and communication skills, they will not be effective in carrying out a treatment program for their clients.[1625]

[46] Children of the Moment
...Insights from the Sufis

> The sect of lovers is distinct from all others,
> Lovers have a religion and a faith of their own.
>
> —**Rumi** (1207-1273), Sufi poet[1626]

> At Being and Non-being fret not; but either with calm temper see:
> Non-being is the term appointed for the most lovely things that be.
>
> —**Hafiz of Shiraz** (14th c.), Sufi poet[1627]

Although Islamist extremists often grab the headlines, the gentler approach of Sufism is a welcome reminder that Islam is a complex and multifaceted set of religious expressions. Sufi teachings often reject stricter forms of dogmatism and legalism,[1628] warn of the dangers of attachments, exhort followers to ethical living and meditation, and encourage adherents to follow the path of love.[1629] Sufis typically regard the Qur'an as a mystical text—each passage is thought to have seven (or more) meanings.[1630] Sharing a sentiment common in many religious traditions, Sufis have traditionally sought to experience life in the present—and have sometimes referred to themselves as "children of the moment."[1631] Although the non-believer may not recognize their Beloved, Sufism at its best has embodied much of the beauty of the religious impulse. This poetic description of the Sufi path comes from the Muslim scholar Qushayri (d.1074):

> Sufism is entry into exemplary behavior and departure from unworthy behavior. ... The sign of the sincere Sufi is that he feels poor when he has wealth, is humble when he has power, and is hidden when he has fame. Sufism means that you own nothing and are

owned by nothing. … Sufism is a state in which the conditions of humanity disappear.[1632]

While there are certainly marked differences, there are also many parallels between Sufi spirituality and Catholicism. Sufis are known to venerate holy men and their tombs; saints are believed to have miraculous powers. Pilgrimages to sacred places are common. While strict celibacy is not a generally espoused practice, many Sufis have been ascetics and have embraced fasting and poverty. There are also numerous Sufi orders.[1633] While some of these orders have at times been focal points of political and even armed resistance against Western colonialism, they more typically have been regarded as promoters of peace.[1634]

Surprisingly perhaps, Sufism is a rather common historic expression of Islam. For many centuries and up until the early 1800's, prominent Muslim academics in Medina and Mecca often had a close connection with Sufism.[1635] Scholar Geoffrey Parrinder even holds that "[a]s late as the nineteenth century Sufism was, to all practical intents and purposes, the real meaning of Islam for the majority of ordinary Muslims."[1636] Despite the growing influence of Wahhabi fundamentalism in modern times, Sufism remains popular in the Islamic world and Sufis still hold that theirs is the fullest and truest expression of the faith.[1637]

While Sufi spirituality has a broad set of expressions, the following parable by renowned 12th-century Persian poet and storyteller Farriduddin Attar seems to be a fitting example. In this adapted and shortened version, Attar weaves a plot around a simple realization that he thought applied to all life's situations and stages.

> A wandering Sufi dervish finds himself reuniting with a man named Shakir over intervals of years. Alternately fabulously rich or destitute, Shakir's chief observation about his predicament is never one of great concern. He simply remarks, "this too shall pass." Shakir eventually dies, but even his grave is temporary—a flood washes it away without a trace. The dervish pondered frequently on Shakir's refrain, and eventually became well known as a wise man.
>
> After some years had passed, a king was seeking a ring that would always lift his spirits when he was sad while also helping him to

savor the pleasant experiences of life. After many failed to satisfy his request, the king sunk into a deep depression. Then the dervish was sought out—and a ring was made according to the sovereign's instructions.

When the king was presented with the ring, he put it on his finger and burst out laughing. His depression was gone and his wish had been fulfilled. The ring was inscribed with the simple phrase, "This too shall pass."[1638]

[47]   A Litany on Humility
...*Adaptation of a Roman Catholic litany*

I often go outside on a clear night and gaze at the sky glittering with the lights of thousands of stars, most of them larger than our sun. As I ponder the unimaginable vastness of what I am seeing …, I am overcome with awe and amazement and with a sense of how tiny the earth is and how infinitesimally small I am. I am cleansed of pride and arrogance and filled with a sweet sense of humility.

—**William R. Murray**, religious humanist[1639]

The mind finds peace in humility. Patience is its daughter.

—**Brother Giles** (c.1190- 1262), *The Little Flowers of Saint Francis*[1640]

The litany is a popular type of responsive prayer that appears to have originated in the Catholic Church in the fourth century in Antioch.[1641] Some popular examples in the Roman Catholic Church today include the Litany of Loreto, Litany of the Saints, Litany of the Sacred Heart, and the Litany of Humility—although there are a great number of others as well.[1642] In my own experience, the alternating repetitions and variations help to provide a sense of both rhythm and focus.

The "Litany of Humility," frequently attributed to Rafael Cardinal Merry del Val (1865-1930),[1643] stands as a giant among modern Roman Catholic devotions. The prayer helps the mind recall its tendencies towards pettiness and pride—while at the same time serving as a reminder that many of life's struggles are linked to a destructive tendency to desperately want the approval of others.

Humility, it would seem, should mean something quite different from self-loathing or adopting a sense of worthlessness. There is nothing wrong with being loved and complimented. We should not wallow in or exaggerate our shortcomings. Nevertheless, attempting to maintain a sense of superiority over others is an exhausting and fruitless endeavor. Perhaps paradoxically, it also seems to erode our sense of contentment.

Here is a revised form of the Litany, expunged of Roman Catholic dogma (and a couple of lines that appear a bit too self-deprecating):

Today, may I let go.

> Of the desire of being esteemed, **Let go.**
> Of the desire of being honored, **Let go.**
> Of the desire of being praised, **Let go.**
> Of the desire of being preferred to others, **Let go.**
> Of the desire of being consulted, **Let go.**
> Of the desire of being approved, **Let go.**
>
> Of the fear of being humiliated, **Let go.**
> Of the fear of being despised, **Let go.**
> Of the fear of suffering rebukes, **Let go.**
> Of the fear of appearing foolish, **Let go.**
> Of the fear of being forgotten, **Let go.**
> Of the fear of being ridiculed, **Let go.**
> Of the fear of being wronged, **Let go.**
> Of the fear of being suspected, **Let go.**
>
> So if others are more loved, **I may be fully satisfied.**
> If others are more esteemed, **I may be fully satisfied.**
> If others are more important, **I may be fully satisfied.**
> If others are chosen, **I may be fully satisfied.**
> If others are praised, **I may be fully satisfied.**
> If others are preferred, **I may be fully satisfied.**

Today, may I be fully satisfied.

[48] Wonders of the Worlds
...Awe of the universe as spiritual discipline

The human mind, no matter how highly trained, cannot grasp the universe.

—**Albert Einstein** (1879-1955)[1644]

Everyone should have their mind blown once a day.

—attributed to **Neil deGrasse Tyson** (b.1958), American astrophysicist[1645]

One of the most reliable ways to engender a sense of wonder is to consider the marvels of the universe. Although even the more mundane experiences of life can have an astonishing quality, it is frequently the more exotic, bizarre, and startling facts of the cosmos that bring its full wonder into conscious view.

The earth travels an astonishing 108,000 km/hr through space.[1646] Mercury, however, travels 65,000 km/hr faster than the earth.[1647] The sun, which loses more than a million tons of material every second through the phenomenon of "solar wind," is a blistering 15 million degrees Celsius (27 million°F).[1648] The surface of the planet Mercury ranges from 427 degrees Celsius (800°F) on the sunlit side to -183 degrees Celsius (-297°F) on the dark side.[1649] While areas of the moon's south pole may never get warmer than -238 degrees Celsius (-460°F), Venus has an average temperature of 480 degrees Celsius (900°F).[1650] Mars has both the largest canyon and the biggest mountain in the solar system. Its Valles Marineris is more than 4,000 km long and averages 6 km deep; its Olympus Mons is three times the height of Mt. Everest.[1651] Saturn, known to have at least 53 moons,[1652] is less dense than water—and would float if placed on a sufficiently large ocean.[1653] Jupiter, known to have at least 79 moons,[1654] has an anticyclonic storm known as the "Great Red Spot" which has been observably active for over 300 years.[1655] Neptune's winds reach an astonishing 1,600 miles per hour;[1656] for perspective, hurricanes on earth qualify for the highest level of Category 5 if they have sustained winds of only 157 miles per hour.[1657] While more than 1,300 earths would fit inside Jupiter,[1658] an amazing one million earths could fit inside the sun.[1659] The largest known star dwarfs the sun, however, and is believed to be about 1,700 times greater in size.[1660] One 2013 estimate suggests that there could be as many as 17 billion "earth-like" planets (rocky planets of approximately earth's size) in the Milky Way galaxy alone.[1661] The 100-billion-star Milky Way galaxy is so large that light takes 100,000 years travelling 300 million meters per second to cross it.[1662] Believing that prior estimates have been wrong by a factor of ten, scientists now estimate that there are as many as two trillion galaxies in the universe.[1663] By one reckoning, there are by far more stars in the universe than there are grains of sand on the entire earth.[1664] More mind-boggling still, one astrophysicist has claimed that planets probably outnumber stars "by anywhere from a factor of 100 to 100,000."[1665] When high-mass stars explode in a supernova, they be brighter than a billion suns for more than a week. Small, extremely dense stars known as pulsars rotate over one thousand times per second.[1666] Perplexingly, scientists believe that roughly four to five percent of the universe is made up of things like stars and planets—the rest is classified under the rather vague concepts of "dark matter" and "dark energy."[1667] Equally intriguing is the world of (at least) 17 subatomic particles; for instance, 100 billion neutrinos are said to pass through a human fingernail every second.[1668] While noting the huge strides in knowledge that humanity has made in modern times, one popular science book notes that "mind-blowing mysteries still abound" and urges that "our mastery applies only to a small corner of the universe, and we are surrounded by a vast ocean of ignorance."[1669] While our universe is thought to be an incomprehensible 14 billion years old, it is unclear what might have happened before it all began. In the words of one professional stargazer: "Astrophysicists have no idea."[1670] Furthermore, some scientists have speculated that there could even be multiple universes of an unknown number—all with unknown contents and properties.[1671]

The earth's waters are an immense catalog of marvels. The six-eyed spookfish, a deep-sea anomaly unknown to science until 1958, has six total organs of vision; it has two common eyes, two additional eyes with lenses and retinae, and then two more organs that lack retinae but help direct incoming light to the primary eyes.[1672] The barreleye fish has a see-through head—which it can gaze through in search of prey.[1673] Oddly enough, the forehead of a fish known as the pointy-nosed blue chimaera has retractable sexual organs.[1674] The electric eel, which can grow up to 8 feet in length, can create more than 600 volts of electricity—which is enough to power ten 60-watt bulbs.[1675] Anemonefish, Parrotfish, and Hawkfish are known to change their gender, actually becoming the opposite sex.[1676] Bioluminescent life in the sea comes in many varieties and includes plankton, algae, bacteria, jellyfish, sea stars, squid, and several types of fish.[1677] While red blood cells can generally be found in all vertebrates, there are approximately 15 species of Antarctic ice fish that have evolved to live in sub-freezing waters and totally lack red blood cells.[1678] While flying fish are well known, some of the members of the Ommastrephidae family of squid have been known to propel themselves out of the water for up to 110 feet.[1679] The axolotl, an odd-looking Mexican salamander, can regrow its limbs, spinal cord, heart and even brain.[1680] It is believed that one species of cave-dwelling crayfish can live to up to 175 years,[1681] that the Greenland shark can live 400-500 years,[1682] that certain species of sponges survive for thousands of years,[1683] and that nematode worms in Siberia have revived after being frozen in permafrost for over 40,000 years![1684]

Our planet's land-dwellers are no less amazing. Whiptail lizards of the genus *Aspidoscelis* are one of the 70 vertebrate species that reproduce asexually; they are all female, and reproduce parthenogenetically by giving their eggs twice the number of chromosomes.[1685] The basilisk lizard of Central America is also referred to as the "Jesus Christ lizard;" its alternate name was given due to its ability to run across water on its hind legs.[1686] Australia's Mary River turtle, which grows green algae on its head that resembles hair, breathes through its genitals and can stay submerged under water for 72 hours.[1687] Perhaps as many as 550 million monarch butterflies migrated as much as 3,000 miles in the fall of 2004. The artic tern vastly outdoes the monarch, though—it is estimated that it flies over 44,000 miles per year in meandering routes between Greenland and Antarctica.[1688] Bilateral gynandromorphs, animals that are split between male and female characteristics along the midline, have been found among butterflies, birds, and crustaceans.[1689] Among some 46,000 known species of spiders in the world, the Giant Huntsman of Laos has the largest leg span—over one foot. The biggest spider by mass is the Goliath Birdeater Tarantula of South America—it has one-inch long fangs, hisses, and has been recorded as being the size of a puppy.[1690] "The President," a 247-foot massive sequoia tree that lives in the Sierra Nevada Mountains in California, is believed to be at least 3,200 years old.[1691] The largest living organism may be the "humongous fungus" near Crystal Falls, Michigan; it is believed to be 2,500 years old and weigh 440 tons (as much as three blue whales).[1692] In one example of the many bizarre instances of animals becoming "zombies," an Amazonian ant infected with a parasitic fungus is driven from the forest floor to the treetops; fresh fungus spores are then released and rain down on other ants below, renewing the cycle.[1693] The Dracula ant, found in tropical regions of Africa, Asia and, Australia, is thought to have the quickest jaws in the animal world; it can snap them shut 5,000 times faster than a human eye can blink.[1694] Orangutans share 96.4% of DNA with humans, gorillas 97.7%, and chimpanzees and bonobos 98.4%. Humans can actually receive a one-time blood transfusion from chimps.[1695] A group of three-foot tall pygmy *homo erectus* humans lived until about 13,000 years ago on the Indonesian island of Flores; other inhabitants of the island included giant rats and pygmy elephants.[1696] There are over 33,000 different species of bacteria that inhabit the human large intestine; there are also trillions of bacteriophages (bacteria-infecting viruses) in every human body.[1697] There are approximately 7,000 languages spoken today in the world—approximately one dies every 14 days.[1698] Based on the evolutionary history of the body louse, it is believed that humans have worn clothes for approximately 72,000 years.[1699] About one out of every 200 humans on earth is blind—in 2016, an estimated 39 million people.[1700] According to one 2011 estimate, there have been 108 billion human beings that have lived on earth during the past 50,000 years.[1701]

The sheer diversity of life is perhaps most striking. Scientists have already identified about 1.6 million different species that are alive today; many more are yet to be catalogued.[1702] Remarkably, biologists generally estimate that over 99% of all species that have lived on earth have become extinct.[1703] While modern humans are generally thought to have been around for less than 200,000 years, dinosaurs held dominion over the earth for some 135 million years.[1704] Over 1,000 types of dinosaur genera have been identified—there are of course many, many more dinosaur species.[1705] The types of life in ancient periods of the earth are striking for many reasons, perhaps most famously for their often large sizes. The ancient millipede Arthropleura grew to approximately 8.5 feet in length.[1706] The largest pterosaurs, or winged reptiles, could be as large as small aircraft.[1707] Megalodon sharks are estimated to have been 52 to 65 feet long—three times longer and thirty times heavier than the modern great white shark.[1708] The *Sarcosuchus imperator* or "SuperCroc" is an extinct form of ancient crocodile that grew to be up to 39 feet long. First discovered in Niger in 1997, its jawbone was as long as a modern human.[1709] Perhaps the biggest land animal to have ever lived, the giant Argentinosaurus is a titanosaurid dinosaur of the Cretaceous period; it is believed to have been about 26 feet high, 121 feet long, and to have had a top speed of only about 3 miles per hour.[1710]

Many philosophers have been stumped as to why there is something rather than nothing. One can further ponder why the "something" that exists is so incomprehensibly vast, varied, amazing, and even mysterious. Some who consider such wonders are led to think that there is perhaps some sort of mystical or even inexplicable dimension to reality. Others conclude that there is probably not—but still marvel at all the magnificence of the universe that they very incompletely understand.

Regardless of how one thinks about such matters, perhaps it is best to hold such viewpoints with a detached frame of mind. As was noticed by some ancient skeptics, feeling compulsion to believe that one has discovered answers to perplexing questions can be a source of psychological angst. Accepting the limitations of one's own perspective, perceptions, and reasoning powers can even be a liberating experience, leading to peace of mind.[1711] In the words of Sextus Empiricus (3rd c.), "We assert still that the skeptic's end is quietude in respect of matters of opinion and moderate feeling in respect of things unavoidable."[1712] Put simply, when in the face of the wondrous, it can be a calming experience to have no compulsion to arrive at conclusions.

[49] Undesirable Desire
...The danger of desire in the Bhagavad-Gita

> I owed ... a magnificent day to the *Bhagavat Geeta*. It was the first of books; it was as if an empire spoke to us, nothing small and unworthy, but large, serene, consistent, the voice of an old intelligence which in another age and climate had pondered and thus disposed of the same questions which exercise us.
>
> —**Henry David Thoreau** (1871-1852), American transcendentalist[1713]

> The Gita says: "Do your allotted work but renounce its fruit—be detached and work—have no desire for reward [,] and work." ... He who gives up action falls. He who gives up only reward rises.
>
> —**Mohandas "Mahatma" Gandhi** (1869-1948)[1714]

Much of the pursuit of happiness is focused on fulfilling longings: gathering money or material objects, satisfying impulses and urges, and gaining the approval of others. To the famous Hindu Scripture known as the *Bhagavad-Gita* ("Song of the Lord"), chasing after such things only creates "mines of misery."[1715] While seeking joy, we can actually chase contentment away. For the *Gita*, it is only when desires are diminished that a person can "find satisfaction in the self alone"[1716] and thereby gain a greater sense of inner peace:

> A person who is not disturbed by the incessant flow of desires—that enter like rivers into the ocean, which is ever being filled but is always still—can alone achieve peace, and not the man who strives to satisfy such desires.[1717]

Undesirable Desire

Instead of spending energy to satisfy cravings, the *Gita* therefore proposes that efforts be made to lessen the grip of desire of itself. This journey is a struggle which begins with the realization that desire is often deceitful and does not bring the joy or peace it so persistently promises.

But the detachment or desirelessness counseled by the *Gita* is not an encouragement to listlessness or aimlessness. Detachment is rather grounded in action and duty—in ethics and social responsibility. In the words of Gandhi, "Fulfillment of one's duty in the spirit of detachment or selflessness leads to Freedom."[1718] It is not that goals and aspirations are not considered valuable, but rather that a healthy and measured spiritual path becomes the constant focus—and thus the ends and the means become almost the same thing.[1719]

[50] Memento Mori

...Remembrance of death as spiritual discipline

> Whenever possible, we should always remember death, for this displaces all cares and vanities, allowing us to guard our intellect. ... Indeed, it is the source of every virtue.
>
> —**St. Hesychios the Priest**, (8th c.?)[1720]

> Mindfulness of death, when developed and pursued, is of great fruit and great benefit. ... Therefore you should train yourselves.
>
> —**The Buddha** (563-483 BCE?)[1721]

If you spend only two minutes reading this meditation, you will have missed the birth of 500 people.[1722] Chances are, of course, that you will never meet any of these 500 people before you die. You will know nothing of their joys and tragedies—nor they of yours. You will be totally insignificant to each other.

If you spend only two minutes reading this meditation, you will have also missed the deaths of over 200 people. Chances are that you not only have never met any of these people, but that you have never heard of any of them. They were wrapped up in their lives just as you are preoccupied with yours.

While some become melancholy with such considerations, it need not be that way. Ignorance and death are central to the human experience. There can be an odd sense of solace in these certainties. All struggles end. All pursuits and achievements are temporary.

Remembering these realities can have a calming effect. As the earth seems quiet and serene from space, so also a more measured approach looks beyond the constant drama of life. The *memento mori*, the reminder of death, has often been used as a spiritual practice to recall the fleetingness of life.[1723] When we remember death, we can gain some of the perspective we need to live well.

While focusing on death has been part of spiritual practice in both East and West, Buddhists have been known to even meditate on the subject in the presence of corpses. While this seems rather morbid at first consideration, there is little doubt that much existential angst is released when death becomes more familiar and is accepted as a normal and inevitable part of the human experience. As described in one Buddhist sutta on meditation, monks are encouraged to observe the different stages of bodily decay and composition to realize that one's own body "is just like that [corpse]; it has the same nature and will not escape this fate."[1724]

For those inclined to less intense practices, the Hebrew book of Ecclesiastes provides an alternate source of meditation on the subject of death. Often containing commentary that appears very existentialist and non-supernaturalist in tone,[1725] Ecclesiastes contains some of the most thought-provoking insights on death in the wisdom literature of the Bible.

Death has an absolute quality to the author of Ecclesiastes. It is not only the body that dies, but even the memory of those who have yet to live will be lost:

> The people of long ago are not remembered,
>   nor will there be any remembrance
> Of people yet to come
>   by those who come after them (1:11).

Since there are none that escape death, acceptance is the only option. The wisest and the most foolish all experience life's end (2:14), and humans with even great intelligence share the same fate as unreasoning animals:

> For the fate of humans and the fate of animals is the same; as one dies, so dies the other. They all have the same breath, and humans have no advantage over animals; for all is vanity. All go to one place; all are from the dust, and all turn to dust again (3:19-20).

Birth and death are the great equalizers, for all are born wearing nothing and can take nothing with them at the end of life (5:15). Since we cannot change our predicament, we should value our friends (4:9-12) and "eat and drink and find enjoyment" in our work—this is the most fitting way to make the most of the fleeting human experience (5:18). And while wisdom has its value, there are many aspects to life that are both unavoidable and unpredictable. When we remember death, we remember that things are ultimately beyond human control:

> Again I saw that under the sun the race is not to the swift, nor the battle to the strong, nor bread to the wise, nor riches to the intelligent, nor favor to the skillful; but time and chance happen to them all (9:11).

[51] The Noble Psycho-Ethical Path

...A (non-supernatural) Buddhist strategy to lessen suffering

> The religious life in simplest terms is a matter of taking hold of those factors that produce suffering and, by training one's mind, redirecting those factors towards freedom and happiness. Thus, the essence of the Buddhist path is psychological and ethical, rather than metaphysical or theological.
>
> —**John J. Holder**, Western Buddhist scholar[1726]

> "He abused me, he beat me, he defeated me, he robbed me,"—in those who harbor such thoughts hatred will never cease. ... For hatred does not cease by hatred at any time: hatred ceases by love, this is an old rule.
>
> —*The Dhammapada*[1727]

Early Buddhist teachings espouse a method of diminishing psychological suffering and improving ethical behavior simultaneously. These teachings have historically been called the Noble Eightfold Path. Interestingly, Western Buddhist scholar John J. Holder has described the content of the Path as an ancient form of "practical therapy" with the goal of "ethical and psychological transformation."[1728] While comparisons to modern cognitive-behavioral therapy could be taken too far, the importance of changing cognition and action in order to reduce mental suffering is clearly integral to early Buddhist thought.

The Eightfold Path is best viewed not as stages of growth but as an interrelated and mutually dependent web of activity.[1729] From a more non-supernatural perspective then,[1730] the Path can be viewed not as religious commandments or a method to achieve nirvana, but rather as guidelines for a way of being that simultaneously encourages peace of mind for oneself and fosters beneficial relations with others. The Eightfold Path[1731] may be categorized as follows:

1. *Right Speech*—abstaining from false, malicious, and harmful speech.

2. *Right Action*—refraining from killing, stealing, sexual abuse and manipulation, etc.

3. *Right View*—having a knowledge of the Four Noble Truths: (i) all life is tainted with dissatisfaction or suffering, (ii) dissatisfaction or suffering is commonly the result of craving, (iii) craving can be diminished, and (iv) a deliberate ethical-spiritual path can diminish craving.[1732] Along with this emphasis, a strain of early Buddhist teachings stresses the "wrong view" of attachment to speculative metaphysical or religious ideas.[1733]

4. *Right Effort*—stirring energy to produce willpower.

5. *Right Mindfulness*—observing mental states and feelings as they are, being aware of actions and thoughts.

6. *Right Intention*—intending not to hurt anyone; renouncing evil and unhelpful things.

7. *Right Livelihood*—avoiding employment or income that is generated from harm to self or others.

8. *Right Concentration*—cultivating calm and focused mental states through meditation.[1734]

The Eightfold Path's potential value can only be realized by verification through personal experience. It is "when you know for yourselves"[1735] that an activity or perspective is helpful that it should be adopted. For those looking for a sample of Buddhist pragmatic advice, I offer a few selections from the *Dhammapada*, a short but insightful collection of Buddhist aphorisms. The sayings of the *Dhammapada* should be seen as practical guidance for the Buddha's Noble Eightfold Path, the way of living thought to release humanity from suffering:

- "Do not speak harshly to anybody; those who are spoken to will answer thee in the same way. Angry speech is painful, blows for blows will touch thee." (X.133)
- "Victory brings hatred, for the conquered is unhappy. He who has given up both victory and defeat, he, the contented, is happy." (XV.201)
- "'They blame him who sits silent, they blame him who speaks much, they also blame him who says little; there is no one on earth who is not blamed.'

  There never was, there never will be, nor is there now, a man who is always blamed, or a man who is always praised." (XVII.227-8)
- "The fault of others is easily perceived, but that of oneself is difficult to perceive; a man winnows his neighbor's faults like chaff, but his own faults he hides, as a cheat hides the bad die from the gambler.

  If a man looks after the faults of others, and is always inclined to be offended, his own passions will grow, and he is far from the destruction of the passions. (XVIII.252-3)
- "He who, by causing pain to others, wishes to obtain pleasure for himself, he, entangled in the bonds of hatred, will never be free from hatred." (XXI.291)

In pursuit of a non-supernatural and practical Eightfold Path, it is important to remember that the spiritual life is a process of both progress and failure, full of alternating moments of authenticity and hypocrisy, bravery and cowardice, and insight and foolishness. The value of finding your path is not that it erases human fickleness and inconstancy, but rather that it provides a point of return and of focus during moments of confusion and misdirection. What has worked before can be remembered and embraced again—and even adjusted to square with changes in self and circumstances.[1736] As secular Buddhist Stephen Batchelor suggests in his practical manual *Buddhism without Beliefs*, the greatest stability on the path ironically comes from being grounded in the acceptance of its changing nature:

Grounded in awareness of transiency, ambiguity, and contingency, such a person values lightness of touch, flexibility and adaptability, a sense of humor and adventure, appreciation of other viewpoints, and a celebration of difference.[1737]

[52] Wisdom Cries Out

...Biblical proverbs and enlightened self-interest

Wisdom cries out in the street; in the squares she raises her voice.

—Proverbs 1:20

Live your lives with my words in your heart,
And you will live your lives with success.

—**Amen-em-ope**, Egyptian sage (c.1200-1000 BCE)[1738]

There is a wealth of material for meditation in the proverbs of the Bible. Among their many themes, perhaps the most striking is the clear link between self-interest and ethics. Those who engage in foolish behavior harm themselves as much as others. Kindness, self-control, temperance, generosity, patience, diligence, humility, and the like are not only ethical practices, but often bring bountiful rewards to those who practice them. As the Book of Proverbs itself declares, "To get wisdom is to love oneself; to keep understanding is to prosper" (Prov. 19:8).

The general value of this "enlightened self-interest" is found not only in biblical proverbs, but in the wisdom literature of other ancient peoples as well. The Assyrians and Egyptians had similar types of proverbs and sayings.[1739] In ancient Greek thought, happiness and virtue were also explicitly connected. As one author explains:

> The characteristic question of ancient ethics is "How can I be happy?" and the basic answer is "by means of virtue." … Being happy in this sense is living a life of what some scholars call "human flourishing."

Thus, the question "How can I be happy?" is equivalent to "How can I live a good life?"[1740]

By way of example, here are a few exemplary biblical proverbs that attempt to lay down some stones on this path of human flourishing:

- "Those who are kind reward themselves, but the cruel do themselves harm" (Prov. 11:17).
- "Evil will not depart from the house of those who return evil for good" (Prov. 17:13).
- "A soft answer turns away wrath, but a harsh word stirs up anger" (Prov. 15:1).
- "Those with good sense are slow to anger, and it is their glory to overlook an offense" (Prov. 19:11).
- "Like a city breached, without walls, is one who lacks self-control" (Prov. 25:28).
- "Those who are patient stay calm until the right moment, and then cheerfulness comes back to them" (Sir. 1:23).
- "When pride comes, then comes disgrace; but wisdom is with the humble" (Prov. 11:2).
- "Fools think their own way is right, but the wise listen to advice" (Prov. 12:15).
- "The simple believe everything, but the clever consider their steps" (Prov. 14:16).
- "The one who first states a case seems right, until the other comes and cross examines" (Prov. 18:17).

"The Teachings of Amen-em-ope," a work attributed to an Egyptian polytheist sage who lived c.1200-1000 BCE, contains many themes and counsels similar to those found in the Bible's wisdom literature. Widely believed to be a source for Proverbs 22:17-24:22,[1741] "The Teachings" describes itself as both "pleasing to the Gods"[1742] and instructive for human happiness. While one may doubt some of Amen-em-ope's advice (and few moderns would be tempted to take Amon-Ra as a "pilot" in life[1743]), this Egyptian polytheist provides yet another reminder that Wisdom speaks from many sources:

> Make honesty your guide to life,
> And you will sleep soundly, and wake happily.
> Better to be praised for loving your neighbor,
> Than loving your wealth.
> Better is bread eaten with a contented heart,
> Than wealth spent with sorrow ....[1744]

[53] Sayings of the Master
...Counsel from Confucius

> Ever since man came into this world, there has never been one greater than Confucius.
>
> —**Mencius** (379-289 BCE), Confucian philosopher[1745]

> Quietly to store up knowledge in my mind, to learn without flagging, to teach without growing weary, these present me no difficulties.
>
> —**Confucius** (551-479 BCE)[1746]

Widely known in the West for his pithy and pragmatic sayings, Confucius made little impact on his native China during his lifetime.[1747] After his death, however, his disciples faithfully spread his ideas until they obtained acceptance. Admiration of his teachings eventually grew to the point where Confucius was even deified and worshipped as a god.[1748] Confucianism, though not monolithic and subject to the variation and development that is characteristic of all religions, nonetheless dominated the Chinese religious and political landscape from the second century BCE until the Communist revolution in 1949.[1749]

Although perhaps too particular about decorum and societal norms, the Eastern master taught many principles and concepts that can be appropriated by the nondogmatic. While it would seem forced to call Confucius either non-religious or agnostic (at least in the modern sense), he nevertheless appears to have had little interest in miracles or mysticism.[1750] Furthermore, Confucius' thought typically has a pragmatic element that encourages rational analysis and rejects fanaticism and rigidity. Confucius did not present a revelation or a path to a blissful afterlife.[1751] Rather, he taught a Way that valued learning, benevolence, honesty, moderation, respectfulness, and the life of service for the betterment of society.

The following sample quotations are from *The Analects*, typically regarded as the most reliable collection of his teachings:[1752]

- "The Master said, 'Yew, shall I teach you what knowledge is? When you know a thing, to hold that you know it; and when you do not know a thing, to allow that you do not know it; — this is knowledge.'" (2.17)

- "Tsze-loo then said, 'I should like, sir, to hear your wishes.' The Master said, 'They are, in regard to the aged, to give them rest; in regard to friends, to show them sincerity; in regard to the young, to treat them tenderly.'" (5.25.4)

- "The Master said, 'He who speaks without modesty will find it difficult to make his words good.'" (14.21)

- "Tsze-kung asked, saying, 'Is there one word which may serve as a rule of practice for all one's life?' The Master said, 'Is not RECIPROCITY such a word? What you do not want done to yourself, do not do to others.'" (15.23)

- "The Master said … 'There is the love of being benevolent without the love of learning; — the beclouding here leads to a foolish simplicity. There is the love of knowing without the love of learning; — the beclouding here leads to dissipation of mind. There is the love of being sincere without the love of learning; — the beclouding here leads to an injurious disregard of consequences. There is the love of straightforwardness without the love of learning; — the beclouding here leads to rudeness. There is the love of boldness without the love of learning; — the beclouding here leads to insubordination. There is the love of firmness without the love of learning; — the beclouding here leads to extravagant conduct.'" (17.8)

Aspects of Confucian thought fit particularly well with more skeptical approaches because of the philosopher's pragmatic approach to supernaturalism. Confucius in general did not talk of spiritual beings (7.20), and when asked about the supernatural tended to draw the discussion back to matters within the realm of human experience and knowledge:

> Ke Loo asked about serving the spirits of the dead. The Master said, "While you are not able to serve men, how can you serve their spirits?" Kee Loo added, "I venture to ask about death?" He was answered, "While you do not know life, how can you know about death?" (11.11)

[54]   No Body but Yours
...The Stations of the Cross re-imagined

> Christ has no body but yours,
> No hands, no feet on earth but yours,
> Yours are the eyes with which he looks
> Compassion on this world,
> Yours are the feet with which he walks to do good,
> Yours are the hands, with which he blesses all the world.
> Yours are the hands, yours are the feet,
> Yours are the eyes, you are his body.
>
> —Attributed to **St. Teresa of Ávila** (1515–1582)[1753]

These words ascribed to the Carmelite nun and mystic St. Teresa of Ávila perhaps have an enlarged meaning for those skeptical about the supernatural. Our desperate world could well benefit from a benevolent, divine Savior—but in our tragedies, none appears. Jesus of Nazareth has no hands, no feet, no eyes, no body—likely no existence at all. Human societies must attempt to heal their own profound wounds. Although this prospect is daunting, it has been the glory of humanity that it has so often found ways to ameliorate its condition. In the words of the 19th-century great Robert Ingersoll (1833-1899):

> If abuses are destroyed, man must destroy them. If slaves are freed, man must free them. If new truths are discovered, man must discover them. If the naked are clothed; if the hungry are fed; if justice is done; if labor is rewarded; if superstition is driven from the mind; if the defenseless are protected and if the right finally triumphs, all must be the work of man.[1754]

The ability to fully participate in improving the world often begins with a focused mind. Although psychological studies suggest that intercessory prayer has doubtful efficacy,[1755] meditative forms of prayer have been shown to be beneficial for mental health.[1756] And so while Christ may have no body to help us, our own minds and bodies contain unrealized sources of strength. Evangelical Anglican C.S. Lewis suggested why prayer, even for the believer, can be much more about internal development than miraculous divine intervention anyway: "I pray because the need flows out of me all the time, waking and sleeping. It doesn't change God, it changes me."[1757]

The Roman Catholic devotional of the Stations of the Cross has provided countless worshippers with a structured activity to re-focus the mind on specific areas of spiritual growth.[1758] Fourteen different scenes from the life of Christ are typically portrayed in pictures, engravings, or statuary. In popular piety, each station is often matched with a virtue or theme that is thought to correspond with Christ's experience—patience, compassion, acceptance, mortality, and the like. Furthermore, the physical motion of the body between the stations helps fend off both drowsiness and distraction, somewhat paradoxically providing greater focus through variation.

One of my favorite spiritual exercises during my Roman Catholic days, I have adapted the Stations of the Cross to parts of the body. Like the scenes of Christ's life, different parts of the body can evoke virtues and provide the necessary variations to avoid distraction. Each part of the body should be focused on in turn in order to help center the mind. This exercise can be performed while sitting or while walking.

1. Hands and Arms: *Charity*

Hands and arms are the classic means of compassion. Let your arms bring support, your hands give generously.

2. Heart: *Quietness of Spirit*

Feel your heartbeat and remember its near-silent constancy. Listen to the gentle rhythm that gives you life.

3. Brain: *Rational thought*

Clear thinking is one of humanity's greatest assets and hopes. Avoid dogmatism, seek intellectual honesty, admit when you don't know things. Recall all the problems that you and others have solved by deliberate and patient analysis.

4. Back: *Conviction*

Let your backbone remind you of the power of holding to convictions. But remember even the back also has some flexibility.

5. Bones: *Mortality*

Below the surface are the ever-present reminders of mortality. Your life will end. Accept your fleeting nature. Enjoy and value today, remember all your troubles will one day be gone.

6. Shoulders: *Solidarity*

Try to shoulder the burdens of others with thankfulness, remembering the good things that you have and enjoy. Consider friends, family, neighbors, coworkers, teachers, medical professionals, and others who have helped or protected you.

7. Stomach: *Self-centeredness*

Traditional piety often calls the stomach the source of the passions.[1759] Craving can unsettle the mind by bringing inordinate urgency to things of secondary importance. The seven "deadly" passions of pride, avarice, gluttony, lust, sloth, envy, and anger often bring much greater harm and distress when they are surrendered to. Avoid people, media, and situations that inflame your self-destructive desires or self-centered attitudes.[1760]

8. Eyes: *Wonder*

Look at the amazing sights that surround you daily—light, color, movement, the majesty of the skies, and nature in general. Think of the incredible properties of the human eye and the benefits vision gives you.

9. Ears: *Listening*

Listen carefully to others, remembering the value of considering the most important person in your life to be the one you are with at that moment.[1761] Don't forget the value of music; listen to songs that lift your spirits.

10. Legs: *Perseverance and Patience*

Marathons, so demanding on the legs and joints, are a classic symbol of perseverance. Many things in life must likewise be patiently endured and accepted; troubles can multiply when trying to avoid the unavoidable.

11. Lungs: *Inner Calm*

Breathe naturally and quietly. Inhale deeply. Experience the peaceful rhythm.

12. Mouth: *Speech and Laughter*

Avoid harsh or dishonest speech. Be generous with words; give compliments before rendering criticism. Look for humor and seek out people and experiences that bring laughter.[1762]

13. Face: *Vanity*

Don't be preoccupied with the importance of looks. The beautiful are often not the happy. Appearances have no necessary correlation with contentment.

14. Feet: *Readiness*

Meditate on what makes you more ready and able to be a quick help to those in need.

The task of the contemplative skeptic is not only to jettison what is false or injurious in religious traditions, but also embrace those spiritual ideas and practices which lead to a more content and compassionate existence. While religion at times has encouraged dubious beliefs as well as pointless and even harmful practices, it has also been an encouragement to reject the trivial human preoccupations that distract from a more meaningful way of being. As the gentle and sometimes profound Roman Catholic priest and author Henri Nouwen (1932-1996) reminds, the ideal contemplative way has often been understood as a path of both reflection and hope:

> Contemplatives are not needy or greedy for human contacts but are guided by a vision of what they have seen beyond the trivial concerns of a possessive world. They do not bounce up and down with the fashions of the moment, because they are in contact with what is basic, central, and ultimate. ... More than anything else, contemplative critics will look for signs of hope and promise in the situations in which they find themselves.[1763]

[55] Anima Foci[1764]

...The importance of focus and a re-working of the Anima Christi

> I have often said that the sole cause of man's unhappiness is that he does not know how to stay quietly in his room.
>
> —**Blaise Pascal** (1623-1662), French mathematician and Catholic philosopher[1765]

> And I asked myself about the present: how wide it was, how deep it was, how much was mine to keep.
>
> —**Kurt Vonnegut** (1922-2007), American novelist[1766]

A favorite of Jesuit founder St. Ignatius of Loyola (1491-1556), the 14th-century prayer Anima Christi ("Soul of Christ") remains a popular devotional in the Roman Catholic Church today.[1767] While the doctrinal assumptions of the devotion may be of use only for the traditional believer, the need for a quiet moment of focus has no necessary correlation to religiosity. Centering is a welcome respite for any anxious soul. What follows is based loosely on the Catholic classic:

> Compassion invade me.
> Courage invigorate me.
> Joy inebriate me.
> Forgiveness release me.
> O Humility, heal me.

May all Wisdom nourish me
    That fear not deceive me
    Nor selfishness cripple me
Till death overtakes me.
So may it be.

[56] Taoist Training
...Insights from the Seven Taoist Masters

Methods are the inventions of people. The intelligent will come up with a way that will work best for them. The stubborn will stick to existing methods even though they are inappropriate.

—*Seven Taoist Masters*[1768]

Of those who have their hands and feet, and yet have neither minds nor ears, there are multitudes.

—**Lao Tzu** (6th c. BCE?)[1769]

Seven Taoist Masters is an anonymous work that originated during China's Ming Dynasty. Probably written about 1500 CE, it is part of the vast Taoist canon[1770] and has been thought of as a manual for Taoist training and an introduction to Taoism in general. Having the form of a folk novel, *Seven Taoist Masters* weaves Taoist principles and concepts into a colorful narrative. Central to the tales are the "three jewels" of Taoism: compassion, humility, and simplicity.[1771]

In an interesting parallel to the "seven deadly sins" of the Catholic tradition, Taoism traditionally regards "four obstacles" to the spiritual path: drunkenness, sexual desire, wealth, and anger.[1772] (Unfortunately, sometimes the warnings about excessiveness in such behaviors become puritanical or absolutized—ironically resulting in another form of "craving" or obsession.[1773]) Despite some rigid tendencies on these issues however, Taoism, like many other world religions, still rightly sees a connection between carelessness regarding such "obstacles" and interpersonal strife and personal anguish. Spiritual pitfalls in Taoism go beyond these four however—and the seven seekers in *Seven Taoist Masters* must each overcome their own particular difficulty: complacency, closed-minded intellectualism, impatience, lust, rigidity, pride, or a competitive attitude.[1774] While the sacrifices made are often significant, a richer and more rewarding life is described as a consistent result.

From a skeptical perspective, much of the content of the *Seven Taoist Masters* appears fanciful. Traditional Taoist teachings regarding karma and reincarnation are a mainstay of its theological landscape,[1775] and miracles and supernaturalism abound. Interestingly, there are several parallels to Christian miracles—including walking on water, ascending into heaven, walking through walls, mind-reading, predicting the future, drinking poison without harm, a spiritual realm of hell, and even a virgin birth (of Lao-Tzu).[1776]

Despite these frequent forays into the dubious, many of the teachings of the *Seven Taoist Masters* are quite thought-provoking and echo some of the richer themes of Buddhism. Its musings can be quite insightful and instructive:

- "If your compassion and charity are sincere, you will give without expecting anything in return."[1777]

- "If one cannot cut the ties to gain and loss and to social pressures; if one is concerned with whether one's appearance is appealing, whether one's food is the best, whether one's wealth is acknowledged, and whether one's property is large, then one has not learned to see through the illusions of material things. Craving breeds anxiety. If you crave, then you will be anxious to obtain what you desire. If you want to dissolve it, you must cut your ties to gain and loss."[1778]

- "It is not because I grasp the instructions of our teacher better, but because for a long time you closed your mind to learning new things. … Your intelligence became an obstacle to your training. Learning is limitless. Not many can fully grasp this idea."[1779]

Despite the mythical elements in the *Seven Taoist Masters*, it is an interesting, challenging, and even comforting book which provides a good reminder of the benefits that spiritual readings can provide to mind and mood. While life provides a fairly steady stream of difficulties, frustrations, and sorrows, it still seems to be the case that respite is usually as close as a good book in a quiet place. In the words of the Taoist sage Ch'en Tuan (d.989):

> For ten long years I plodded through
> > the vale of lust and strife,
> Then through my dreams there flashed a ray
> > of the old sweet peaceful life. ...
> But I love to seek a quiet nook, and
> > some old volume bring
> Where I can see the wild flowers bloom
> > and hear the birds in spring.[1780]

[57] Make Your Own Meditation
...Developing a reflective meditation practice

> Awareness begins with remembering what we tend to forget.
>
> —**Stephen Batchelor**, secular Buddhist[1781]

> Anything that inspires us to see what is true and do what is good is proper practice. You may call it anything you like.
>
> —**Achaan Chah** (1918-1992), Buddhist monk[1782]

Daily distractions keep us from living an intentional life. They scatter stillness and a sense of purpose. Much of meditation can thus be thought of as an attempt to return to a positive state of mind, an endeavor to remember and reenact a former psychological state.

To cultivate a remembrance of prior and more peaceful mental moods, I find it helpful to have a short list of themes in mind. For this particular meditation, I developed a mnemonic to help myself stay on course: **A-BAG-HAG-TAG-CC**.

A **Awe**—Consider the wonders of nature and the universe, the complexities of human society and language, the discoveries of science and the works of inventors, the markedly different ways that people have lived throughout history.

B **Breathe and Be Relaxed**—Breathe deeply, calmly. Slow down, let your mind go at a proper pace. Think of a slow-moving river, gentle breezes across a field, falling snow on a mountaintop, a peaceful and colorful sunset.

A **Awareness**—Be aware of the moment: sounds, smells, bodily sensations, and temperature.

G **Guilt and Fear**—Let go of fears and excessive and inappropriate guilt. Feel them leave your shoulders and your stomach. Remember how negative feelings affect your resolve and distract you from a better way of living.

H **Honesty**—Be candid about what you know and what you don't know. Be frank about both your faults and your strengths. Strive for an honesty that is unburdened with pretense, pride, or forced conclusions.

A **Appreciate**—Appreciate your family, friends, and resources. Recall to mind that which gives you joy. Express gratitude for all good things.

G **Guard**—Guard your senses. Avoid sights and sounds that unnecessarily agitate you. (Pictures, sounds, TV, internet, aggressive people, loud noises in general.) Guard your mind. Whenever possible, direct your mind to think about helpful things. Gently dismiss negative thoughts of people; focus on their positive attributes. Be watchful against judgmentalism, fear, dogmatism, anger, pride, and the like. Think of your own faults when judgmental ideas present themselves.

T **Time**—Whether this be a good or bad moment—"This too shall pass." Be watchful of thinking you can accomplish more in an amount of time than is reasonable.

A **Accept**—Accept yourself, your looks, your situation, your job, your family, and your flaws (especially those you cannot change). Accept the pain that is an unavoidable part of human experience. Don't fight against what cannot be conquered. Consider this maxim: "If you let go a little, you will have a little peace. If you let go a lot, you will have a lot of peace."[1783]

G **Generosity and Compassion**—Reflect on the many understandable reasons for your own flaws and failings; consider the diverse reasons that others have shortcomings and weaknesses too. Be generous with your time, resources, and words. Imagine others being happy; think of how you can contribute to their happiness.

C **Courage**—Recall to mind when you have been brave and have persevered through adversity in the past. Reflect on how you can summon that courage once again.

C Calm—Refocus on slow breathing again. Think of a willow gently swaying in the breeze, ripples in a clear pond, clouds slowing passing a bright moon.

When creating time for reflection and stillness, it is helpful to reject a false dichotomy that pits personal contentment against service to others. Meditation at its best will help foster both. As explained by Zen Master Thich Nhat Hanh (b. 1926):

> Interconnections between other beings and ourselves are intimate. When we are peaceful and happy, we will not create suffering in others. ... Practice is not just for ourselves, but for others and the whole of society.[1784]

[58] A Page from the Love Doctor
...Pragmatic advice from St. Francis de Sales

> Through his teachings he handed down the most insightful maxims …. And so Francis is regarded by all as both restorer and teacher of sacred eloquence.
>
> —**Pope Pius IX**, (1792-1878)[1785]

> You learn to speak by speaking, to study by studying, to run by running, to work by working; and just so you learn to love … by loving. All those who think to learn in any other way deceive themselves.
>
> —**St. Francis de Sales** (1567-1622)[1786]

St. Francis de Sales, often referred to as the "Doctor of Love" in the Roman Catholic tradition, was the titular bishop of Geneva during the Catholic Counter-Reformation period. Well known for his successful attempts to win thousands of Calvinists back to the Roman Catholic Church, he is also remembered for championing peaceful forms of evangelism in an often harsh and brutal age. "Love alone," he reportedly said, "will shake the walls of Geneva."[1787]

While de Sales and his Calvinist opponents would both be deemed fundamentalists by modern standards, this lesser-known St. Francis provides some helpful insights on treating others with kindness amid deep-seated conflict. He also imparts some common-sense counsel that shows a remarkable practicality—especially from a man who lived in a largely pre-scientific and superstitious age.

De Sales once remarked that "Our front lines must wield the weapons of Love."[1788] His "armory" thus tended to embrace the best of Christian spirituality while avoiding some of the more negative weapons of traditionalism—shame, intolerance, judgmentalism, and encouragements toward excessive self-recrimination. Though his Roman Catholic Church would eventually become much more hopeful for the fate of "heretics" and non-Catholics than he ever would, his words and insights can still be applied to the vitriolic nature of many religious and anti-religious disputations today.[1789] To get a better taste of St. Francis' approach, here are some exemplary lines from his classic, *Introduction to the Devout Life*:

- On being patient with yourself: "For though reason requires that we should be displeased and sorry for it when we commit a fault, yet we must refrain from a bitter, gloomy, spiteful, and passionate displeasure. For many make a great mistake in this respect, who, being overcome by anger, are angry for having been angry, and vexed for having given way to vexation, and fretful for having been fretful. … [W]e correct ourselves much better by calm and steady repentances than by those which are harsh, eager, and passionate; for repentances made with violence proceed not according to our faults, but according to our inclinations." (3.9)

- On multi-tasking: "Work done with too much eagerness and hurry is never done well. We must hasten leisurely, says the old proverb …. Take your affairs in hand quietly, and try to do them in order, one after another; for if you want to do them all at once, or in disorder, you will make efforts which will so overcharge and depress your spirit, that it will probably lie down under the burden without effecting anything." (3.10)

- On ridicule: "Nothing is so contrary to charity or devotion as scorn and contempt of our neighbour. But as derision or mockery are never without scoffing, therefore it is a very great sin; so that divines are right in saying that mockery is the worst kind of offense a man can be guilty of against his neighbor by words; for other offences may be committed with some esteem for the party offended, but this is committed with scorn and contempt." (3.27)

- On the counter-productiveness of anxiety: "Whenever, then, you are desirous to be freed from evil, or to attain some good, before all things settle your mind in repose and tranquility, calm your judgment and will; and then gently and quietly pursue your desire, taking in regular order the means which are most suitable." (4.11)

While theological insights are often touted as the key to peace of mind and human flourishing in certain faith communities, the benefits of religion for those of more skeptical orientation largely reside in practical counsel. It is here that Francis excels. The noblest sentiments of the bishop help underscore why, despite some marked differences, there is in fact a sizeable overlap between the best religious and secular ways of being. Certain practical habits and virtues—like kindness, patience, moderation, and humility—are a necessary and enriching part of any good life.[1790]

And to further that end, St. Francis reminds that the good life is not all gravity and productivity. In contrast to some more "gloomy saints,"[1791] the Roman Catholic bishop even professed it to be immoral to avoid relaxation—and that virtue even necessitated some frivolity:

> It is necessary sometimes to relax our minds as well as our bodies by some kind of recreation. ... It is doubtless a vice to be so rigorous, rough, and austere, as neither to be willing to take any recreation ourselves, nor allow it to others. (3.31)

[59] The Love of the Beautiful
...An adaptation from the Eastern Orthodox *Philokalia*

> The *Philokalia* is an itinerary through the labyrinth of time, a silent way of love and gnosis through the deserts and emptinesses of life, especially of modern life, a vivifying and fadeless presence. It is an active force revealing a spiritual path and inducing man to follow it. … The texts of the *Philokalia* are, then, guides to the practice of the contemplative life.
>
> **—G.E.H. Palmer, Philip Sherrard, and Kallistos Ware**, translators of the *Philokalia*[1792]

One of the greatest spiritual treasures of the Eastern Orthodox tradition is the *Philokalia*. Literally meaning "the love of the beautiful," this extensive 18th-century compilation contains classic Orthodox spiritual direction spanning from the 4th to the 15th centuries.[1793] The high regard for the *Philokalia* in Eastern Orthodoxy is described in *The Way of a Pilgrim*, a 19th-century Russian Orthodox spiritual text: "the Holy Bible is a shining light and the *Philokalia* is the necessary glass."[1794]

At the heart of the *Philokalia* is perhaps the Jesus Prayer, a short and simple prayer sometimes called a "Christian mantra."[1795] Although having varied forms and differing in length between two and four phrases, a traditional version of the prayer is as follows: "Lord Jesus Christ, Son of the Living God, have mercy on me, a sinner." In ways that are analogous to the devotional practices of other religions, the prayer is often said in harmony with the breath and the heartbeat. A prayer rope, which is similar to a string of rosary beads, is often used to help foster the practice.[1796] A favorite exercise of mine during a fairly brief romance with Eastern Orthodoxy, the

Jesus Prayer is thought to be a powerful path to union with God through a deepening in awareness of the divine majesty, the stilling of the passions, and the cultivation of humility. Eastern Orthodox great St. Simeon the New Theologian (949-1022) gives this concise guidance for the practice of the Jesus Prayer:

> Sit alone and in silence; bow your head and close your eyes; relax your breathing and with your imagination look into your heart; direct your head into your heart. And while inhaling say, "Lord Jesus Christ, have mercy on me," either softly with your lips or in your mind. Endeavor to fight distractions but be patient and peaceful and repeat this process frequently.[1797]

While the words of the Jesus Prayer will likely be distracting and unmeaningful for those uncomfortable with traditional Christian dogmas, some of the methods of the prayer can retain their value as a meditative practice. St. Simeon's directions regarding the breath, the posture, and the heartbeat remain helpful, especially when coupled with some verbiage that resounds with the broader themes of Philokalian spirituality—namely the inculcation of greater senses of wonder, stillness, and humility.

While for the Eastern Orthodox help comes from above, the more skeptically-minded draw strength from an understanding and utilization of the inherent properties of the brain. Meditation, which is often encouraged by psychologists and even stalwart atheists,[1798] is in significant part an exercise in developing the brain's natural powers. Although the brain may have some innate characteristics which encourage pride and a lack of self-awareness,[1799] it also has the capabilities to encourage greater psychological health. In effect, meditation in the format of the Jesus Prayer may be "praying" to one's own brain to change[1800] and an intentional fostering of a calm spirit and a therapeutic sense of wonder.

As with many spiritual practices, perseverance and a measure of realism are in order. Meditation and mantras are not "magic." Sometimes meditative practice is more productive than others. Some people are more naturally inclined to the exercise. As with most things in life, more experience brings greater proficiency. Furthermore, as *The Way of a Pilgrim* expresses, some variety can be beneficial: sitting or standing, speaking or chanting, or intermixing with other spiritual practices like reading are beneficial.

Manual labor, physical exercise, or some other activity may also be combined with the discipline.[1801] Distracting thoughts will arise; it is best to expect them and let them pass.[1802]

Although the *Philokalia* at times enjoins an unhealthy asceticism, a preoccupation with eternal punishment, and a morbid and superstitious fascination with literal demons, it also has many pithy sayings and perceptive insights. While the metaphysical assumptions of the Jesus Prayer may be dubious, there is little doubt that fostering senses of wonder, humility, and stillness can have a powerful psychological effect and can be a valuable tool in the pursuit of a more beautiful life.

What follows is a mantra inspired by the Jesus Prayer with commentary drawn from or inspired by the *Philokalia*:

> **Fill with Wonder,**
> **Rest in Stillness,**
> **Find refuge in Humility.**

Fill with Wonder:
The ability to recollect the wonders of the universe is an ever-present source of consolation and inspiration. Awe provides distance from mundane stressors and anxieties. While at times an experience of wonder can come upon us unexpectedly, it is also a sensibility that can be encouraged by conscious intention. A practice of wonder is the deliberate recognition of all the amazing things of life that can be obscured by familiarity or inattention.

Wonder is the constant companion of all that is complex and unknown. It can be summoned through the contemplation of nature and time. A host of amazing things surround our daily existence: human language, modern inventions, myriad examples of flora and fauna, the varieties of smell, taste, and color, and the complexities of social interactions and human traditions. A broader perspective recognizes thousands of religions and cultures, the peculiar passing of moments, innumerable stars (in billions of galaxies), the double helix of DNA, supernovas and black holes, tornadoes and waterspouts, tsunamis, supernovas, Venus fly traps, extinct saber-toothed cats and velociraptors, whirlpools, snow-capped mountains, cannibal tribes,[1803] soaring vultures, singing whales, gentle rains, glorious sunsets, changing chameleons, flying fish, bioluminescent plankton and fireflies, extinct mammoths preserved in ice, buried treasure, hidden tombs, lost cities and civilizations, and the shrouded thoughts of those all around us. Multitudes of people and other creatures are born and die daily, and have been doing so for periods of time that are unfathomable.

- "Great struggle and awe are needed to guard the soul." —A Discourse on Abba Philimon[1804]
- "By contemplating dispassionately the beauty and use of each thing, he who is illumined sees ... in all things the order, the equilibrium, the proportion, the beauty, the rhythm, the union, the harmony, the usefulness, the concordance, the variety, the delightfulness, the stability, the motion, the colours, the shapes, the forms, the reversion of things to their source, permanence in the midst of corruption. Contemplating thus all created realities, he is filled with wonder." —St. Peter of Damaskos[1805]

Rest in Stillness:
Stillness can be fostered through the tried and proven method of breathing and focus. The life of meditation has stillness as a chief aim. The *Philokalia* often envisions a sense of stillness coupled with a sense of watchfulness—reminding that both serenity and focus are the inextricable goals of the spiritual life. Meditation and contemplation are thus a marrying of active and passive processes and a striving for a "tranquility of watchfulness."[1806]

- "Be like an astute businessman: make stillness your criterion for testing the value of everything, and choose always what contributes to it." –Evagrios the Solitary[1807]
- "To speak generally, it is impossible to acquire all other virtues except through watchfulness."—St. Symeon the New Theologian[1808]
- "According to St. Basil the Great, nothing so darkens the mind as evil, and nothing so enlightens the mind as spiritual reading in stillness." —St. Peter of Damaskos[1809]

Find Refuge in Humility:
Although sometimes understood as a spiritual attainment, humility is more properly viewed as a simple admission of reality. Geniuses still suffer from bias and ignorance about innumerable things. Even the most beautiful become less attractive or even unsightly in illness or old age. The rich lose all their possessions in either an uncertain life or certain death. The strongest must confess their utter weakness compared to forces of machine, weaponry, natural disaster, disease, injury, or decrepitude.

While often associated with weakness, humility can provide shelter from the oppressive and anxiety-inducing pretenses and self-deceptions which so often define both internal and interpersonal conflicts. Humility is the path to overcoming the passions that can engulf the soul in self-centeredness—pride, greed, jealousy, anger, and the like.

Humility also provides a proper platform for approaching metaphysical speculation. Dogmatic religion, while often championing humility in many ways, also enjoins people to make confident religious choices despite a vast array of theological positions which often seem not only nonsensical, but also beyond a human capacity to even evaluate. Humility allows for the guileless recognition of the unknown, the unfathomable, and the dubious.

- "Nothing so strengthens these passions against us as arrogant thoughts, and nothing uproots the evil herbs of the soul so effectively as blessed humility. Hence humility is rightly called the executioner of the passions." —St. Theodoros the Ascetic[1810]

- "[H]e who is humble in heart is stronger than the strong." —St. Mark the Ascetic[1811]

- "The substance of gold is wealth; of virtue, humility. ... Truth without humility is blind. That is why it becomes contentious: it tries to support itself on something, and finds nothing except rancour." —Ilias the Presbyter[1812]

- "Again, the more knowledge one has, the more one thinks himself ignorant; and the more one is ignorant of their own ignorance and of the shortcomings in one's spiritual knowledge, the more one thinks one knows." —St. Peter of Damaskos[1813]

[60] A Look on the Bright Side
...Focusing on the positive as spiritual discipline

> That is [the satisfied person's] way of contentment: not so much by adding to what he has, not by adding more to his condition, but rather by subtracting from his desires to make his desires and his circumstances even and equal.
>
> —**Jeremiah Burroughs** (1599-1646), Puritan preacher[1814]

> When upon life's billows you are tempest tossed,
> When you are discouraged, thinking all is lost,
> Count your blessings, name them one by one ….
>
> —**Johnson Oatman, Jr.** (1856-1922), Protestant hymnodist[1815]

One of the great strengths of traditional Christian prayer and hymnody is a focus on and cultivation of a spirit of thankfulness. Life is always filled with good and bad things, with the bad often claiming an undeserved dominance in our minds. A change of perspective—rather than a change in circumstances—is often an easier way to foster a sense of contentment. This invaluable perspective, as prominent atheist and neuroscientist Sam Harris (b.1967) explains, has no necessary connection to religious dogma:

> And if, like many people, you tend to be vaguely unhappy much of the time, it can be very helpful to manufacture a feeling of gratitude by simply contemplating all the terrible things that have *not* happened to you, or to think of how many people would consider their prayers answered if they could only live as you are now.[1816]

This general observation has been made by observant souls for millennia. As the Greek philosopher Epictetus (c.55-135 CE) further remarked, people in very similar circumstances can often have drastically different mindsets: "Men are disturbed not by things, but by the views which they take of things."[1817] Our outlook seems to quickly change by merely remembering all the good things and circumstances we enjoy. While it would seem that scientific study of this reality would almost be unnecessary, preliminary studies have confirmed what many of us know from experience—gratitude can improve one's mood and motivation.[1818] St. Paul's Letter to the Philippians, whose authorship is often affirmed by even critical scholars, has often been described as having thankfulness as its most prominent theme.[1819] In the concluding chapter, Paul perceptively remarks how life becomes better when one's focus is on all its best and highest qualities:

> Finally, beloved, whatever is true, whatever is honorable, whatever is just, whatever is pure, whatever is pleasing, whatever is commendable, if there is any excellence and if there is anything worthy of praise, think about these things (Phil. 4:8).

It may help to make a checklist of positive people, situations, and circumstances. Living in the modern age alone (especially in the industrialized world) brings major advantages that are often forgotten. Advanced medicines and medical treatments prolong the lives and lessen the sufferings of millions. Common plagues and maladies such as leprosy, Black Death, smallpox, polio, malaria, typhus, and cholera have disappeared from scores of nations where they were once commonplace. Even repressive regimes of today are often milder than the tyrants of the past, and most countries are now free from the scourges of religious inquisition, pogroms, witch-burnings, and human sacrifice. Freedom of religion, speech, assembly, and the press are likewise common ideals. Modern travel conveniences make journeys that once took months now only take a few hours. Power tools and machinery make many tasks far simpler; heating and air conditioning make much of the population far more comfortable. Stable food supplies and modern irrigation techniques have removed famine from many societies. Modern psychiatry can ameliorate or even heal many mental conditions that were once lifelong sources of agony. Motion pictures allow us to escape into another world and see things before our eyes that were once only the visions and dreams of the imagination.

Of course, many other objects of thanksgiving are timeless, being independent of modern advances. Few can resist the infectious laughter of babies and small children. Positive relationships with siblings, parents, romantic partners, spouses, children, and friends often cheer our hearts. Beloved pets raise our spirits when human relationships fail us. Music can improve our moods and allows our minds to revel in pleasant distraction. The varieties of favorite foods and drinks provide great pleasure. Stories can inflame the delights of curiosity and provide soothing diversions. Vision lets us see the night sky, the pattern of clouds, running brooks, crashing waves, a beautiful array of colors, and the flora and fauna of the world.

Especially when joined with a sensitivity for the sufferings of others, a positive outlook can bring a more measured approach to the irritations and trials in our lives. When we inordinately focus on how life could be better, we can forget how it could also be much worse in a vast variety of ways. As the 5th-century BCE historian Herodotus reminds, often our lot is comparatively better than our minds have deceived us into believing:

> I do, however, know this much: if everyone in the world were to bring his own problems along to market with the intention of trading with his neighbors, a glimpse of his neighbors' problems would make him glad to take back home the ones he came with.[1820]

[61] Living in a Cloud of Unknowing
...Accepting a theology of ignorance

> The description of God by means of negations is the correct description .... With every increase in the negations regarding God, you come nearer to apprehension of God.
>
> —**Maimonides** (1135-1204), preeminent medieval Jewish scholar[1821]

> But you will ask me, "How am I to think of God himself, and what is he?" and I cannot answer you except to say "I do not know!" For with this question you have brought me into the same darkness, the same cloud of unknowing where I want you to be!
>
> —*The Cloud of Unknowing*[1822]

The *Cloud of Unknowing* is an anonymous latter 14th-century spiritual treatise of English origin. Written during the tumultuous times of the Black Death and the Hundred Years' War, the *Cloud* purports to teach a way to find peace in the midst of a life of confusion and turmoil. While (seemingly inconsistently) holding to a high view of the Roman Catholic Church's dogmatic authority, the author also suggests that people are intellectually unable to know God due to "a cloud of unknowing" that exists between creature and Creator.[1823] While this kind of approach to God is foreign to many Western Christians, the "negative" or "apophatic" theological approach has been a common perspective in the Christian East. St. Gregory of Nyssa (c.335-394) gives a wonderful summation of this more mystical perspective—which at times can sound almost skeptical or even nonsensical in tone:

> The true knowledge and vision of God exists in this – in seeing that He is invisible, because what we seek lies beyond all knowledge, being wholly separated by the darkness of incomprehensibility.[1824]

For the author of the *Cloud*, however, intellectual ignorance about God is not a reason for concern. Since direct, rational knowledge of God is impossible, love and humility are the two central aims of inner development. Humility is described less in terms of some profound spiritual ability than as an honest self-awareness, for "whoever truly saw and felt himself as he is, would truly be humble."[1825] Plain self-knowledge is not sufficient though; it must be coupled with the desire to love. All virtue is deemed worthless without love: "Without it a man may have as many virtues as he likes; every one of them will be tainted and warped, and to that extent imperfect."[1826]

Metaphysical ignorance need not lead to lack of direction, and *The Cloud of Unknowing* provides practical spiritual "dodges" to help us find our way. When past failures and present fears inhibit us from growing in love, we are enjoined to forget them.[1827] However, *The Cloud* particularly recommends two spiritual practices which intriguingly have some parallels to the concepts of mindfulness and acceptance touted in Acceptance Commitment Therapy (ACT)—namely, an adoption of a "counterintuitive idea of abandoning the battlefield rather than winning the war."[1828]

> **Looking Beyond.** Love can be restrained by guilt and anxiety about the past. The author reminds us to look beyond and past such distractions to regain present focus: "Try to look, as it were, over their shoulders, seeking something else …. If you do so, I believe that you will soon find your hard work much easier."[1829] Love is the emotion of the present.

> **Admitting Defeat.** The second dodge the author enjoins is to admit weakness, asking that we "pay special heed to this suggestion, for I think that if you try it out it will dissolve every opposition." Much inner wrestling involves the emotions of the fight. Perhaps the struggle itself is doing greater harm than what is being fought against: "When you feel that you are completely powerless to put these thoughts away, cower down before them like some cringing

captive overcome in battle, and reckon that it is ridiculous to fight against them any longer."[1830] In effect, some inner battles are not worth waging. Winning or losing isn't nearly as important as moving on to a different focus.

While appreciating the insights of the *Cloud*, an expanded "cloud of unknowing" may be a more appropriate resting place for the nondogmatic. Seeking for ultimate meanings on an intellectual level seems to inevitably lead to frustration or forced conclusions. In a variety of religious traditions, however, love and humility are deemed to be at the core of the spiritual life. Looking beyond the distractions of supernaturalism, it is perhaps just love and humility that should be sought anyway. In the words of *The Cloud*'s author, "For whoever has clearly got these needs no more: he has all."[1831]

In effect, a contemplative-skeptical approach may just be taking the "negative" or "apophatic" theological approach to its natural conclusion. Humility may require not only the confession of a lack of intellectual knowledge about God's essence—but also God's attributes and even existence as well. This, in fact, is the basis of the "Agnostic confession" of Thomas Huxley (1825-1895), who counseled simply that in religious matters people ought to "object to say that they know what they are quite aware that they do not know." Huxley further wondered if ethical behavior and general human flourishing would in fact be augmented by such thorough and honest expressions of religious ignorance:

> As to the interests of morality, I am disposed to think that if mankind could be got to act up to this last principle in every relation to life, a reformation would be effected such as the world has not yet seen; an approximation to the millennium such as no supernaturalistic religion has ever succeeded, or seems likely ever to succeed, in effecting.[1832]

[62] Spiritual Exercises for Contemplative Skeptics

...Spiritual disciplines without supernaturalism

There is now a large literature on the psychological benefits of meditation. Different techniques produce long-lasting changes in attention, emotion, cognition, and pain perception, and these correlate with both structural and functional changes in the brain. ... Spirituality *must* be distinguished from religion—because people of every faith, and of none, have had the same sort of spiritual experiences.

—**Sam Harris** (b.1967), neuroscientist and atheist[1833]

A growing literature demonstrates that exercise benefits both affective experience and cognitive performance.

—**Candace L. Hogan, Jutta Matta, and Laura L. Carstensen**, psychological researchers[1834]

In many ways this book is a non-traditional approach to the spiritual discipline of "devotional" reading, a practice that has been known for centuries to have the potential to calm the mind and help bring higher focus to daily life.[1835] In the context of devotional reading, many other ideas and practices have been suggested or recommended. These have included reflection on the present moment, the passing of time, mortality, ignorance, compassion, authenticity, honesty, simplicity, non-attachment, humility, contentment, stillness, nondogmatic thinking, wonder, and the like. Some specific techniques have also been discussed or mentioned—including various forms of meditation, non-supernatural "prayer," challenging unrealistic and harmful cognitive distortions, and the benefits of positive thinking.

For those who would like some further resources for non-supernatural spiritual disciplines, please consider the following brief list for exploration. Many of these are easily accessible on the internet— they are all possibilities for normal, everyday people seeking to make their lives a little bit better through psychological and spiritual exercises. Scientifically investigated and thought to be potentially efficacious for mental well-being,[1836] they are all adaptable for the non-religious and the religiously nondogmatic alike. (Please note that while I have a graduate degree in counseling, I am not a licensed counselor. Persons with more profound psychological issues may want to consult their psychologist or counselor before adopting any of the following exercises.)

Breathing exercises. Various breathing exercises have been shown to slow heart rate, decrease anxiety, and help instill a sense of calm.[1837] Techniques frequently focus on slow and rhythmic respiration.

- Paced Breathing (Android app).[1838]
- eXHALeR breathing application[1839]
- Lori Granger, YouTube, "Sitting with Breath"[1840]

Relaxation techniques. Progressive muscle relaxation (PMR) is a technique whereby different muscle groups are tensed and then relaxed to achieve a greater sense of calm and a reduction of stress. Its efficacy has been extensively supported in psychological literature.[1841] Likewise, other forms of guided relaxation have shown to be effective. Here are a few readily available examples:

- Beth Salcedo, MD, *Progressive Muscle Relaxation: 20 minutes to total relaxation*[1842]
- Mark Connelly, YouTube, "Progressive Muscle Relaxation Training"[1843]
- Dr. Jaan Reitav, YouTube, "Progressive Muscle Relaxation"[1844]
- Beth Freschi, MA, *A Time for Relaxation: Guided Relaxation, Techniques for Wellness*[1845]

Mindfulness Meditation. Mindfulness meditation appears to lessen anxiety and instill a sense of calm and well-being. There are also suggestions that mindfulness promotes empathy and compassion.[1846] While the internet and YouTube have many examples, here are a few suggestions:

- Aware: Your Personal Mindfulness Trainer (Android app)[1847]
- Dan Harris, YouTube video, "The Long Journey to Becoming '10% Happier'"[1848]
- Dan Harris and Joseph Goldstein, 10% Happier Meditation Tour[1849]
- Sam Harris, "The Mirror of Mindfulness: Two Guided Meditations"[1850]

Spiritual music and chanting. There are clear indications that music can bring many positive benefits to mood.[1851] While the research is less developed, there is also some indication that certain types of spiritual chants may bring mental health benefits.[1852] Personally, I find that the tones and cadence of certain spiritual compositions stimulate relaxation and a sense of calm. If interested, here are some samples to try:

- Tibetan Singing Bowls: *33 Bowls*[1853]
- Latin Gregorian chant: 99 *Most Essential Gregorian Chants*[1854]
- Sikh Chant: "Wahe Guru Wahe Guru Simran"[1855]
- Qur'anic recitation[1856]
- Foreign language liturgies:
  - *Divine Liturgy of St. John Chrysostom*, The Greek Byzantine Choir, directed by Lycourgos Angelopolous[1857]
  - There are also Christian liturgies in Russian, Coptic, Arabic, Latin, and a variety of other languages available on YouTube.

Exercise. While exercise is often undertaken for losing weight, gaining strength, improving appearance, or generally improving health, there is significant evidence that exercise improves general mood both immediately after activity and also generally.[1858] In short, research has found that "Physical activity is associated with improved affective experience and enhanced cognitive processing."[1859] From the standpoint of spirituality, exercise can thus be undertaken with ethical and spiritual emphases at the fore—including a desire to decrease anxiety, depression, irritability, anger, impatience, and the like. It is important to choose a type of exercise that you enjoy enough to do regularly. As with any spiritual practice, consistency brings the greatest benefits. Swimming, walking, running, gardening, golf, tennis, rowing, aerobics, cycling, weightlifting or strength training, walking stairs, or anything else that provides physical activity can be suitable. Exercising with others can help improve regularity and enjoyability. Exercise can also be combined with meditative practices. For example,

- Walking meditation (Android app)[1860]
- Tai chi and yoga[1861]

Awe of the universe. There is some suggestion among researchers that awe, when not dominated by fear, increases human proclivities toward pro-social behavior as well as engendering a sense of personal well-being.[1862] While there are many science and nature films and books that would be helpful here, I have these suggestions:

- *Cosmos: A Spacetime Odyssey*, narrated by Neil DeGrasse Tyson[1863]
- Jorge Cham and Daniel Whiteson, *We Have No Idea: A Guide to the Unknown Universe*
- There are numerous YouTube videos that exhibit the majesty and power of the natural world and the universe. Here are a couple that I find particularly impressive:
    - Morn1415, YouTube, "Star Comparison 2"[1864]
    - Carykh, YouTube, "The Scale of the Universe 2"[1865]

Above all, the contemplative life is simply a planned path for a life of contentment. Perhaps one of the greatest insights into spirituality is that its psycho-ethical benefits do not come magically. Growth is an interplay between increasing self-knowledge and the implementation of those practices and behaviors which bring the most personal benefit. Richard Foster (b.1942), famous Christian advocate of the spiritual disciplines, noted that "Spiritual direction is concerned with the whole person and the interrelationship of all of life."[1866] It is essentially this goal that contemplative-skeptical spirituality has at its fore—a congruent, coherent, and contented life.

An Afterword
...Doubt, humility, and love

> If there is one thing the contemplative life should provide, it is clarification by way of simplification.
>
> —**Robert H. King**, religion professor and biographer of Thomas Merton and Thich Nhat Hanh[1867]

> Reserve your right to think, for even to think wrongly is better than to not think at all.
>
> —**Hypatia** (c.355-415), ancient philosopher killed by a religious mob[1868]

While there have perhaps been some complex information and ideas in this book, the overall message is meant to be a simple one. In short, as suggested in the three quotations at the beginning of this work, contemplative skepticism is intended to be the pursuit of honest doubt, humility, and love. From my perspective, spiritual approaches have most often gone astray when speculative faith discourages honesty, dogmatic certainty overshadows humility, and religiously-inspired condemnation undermines love. I have grown to so value the combination of skepticism and the contemplative path because their intersection seems to be the best avenue for fostering psychological health, ethical development, and cognitive congruence—in short, a balanced way of being.

I hope this book has been as helpful for you to read as it has been for me to write. Some aspects of my spiritual journey have been painful, and it has helped tremendously to organize and reflect deeply on the varied facets of religion and religious experience. While I believe that I

An Afterword

have made some progress,[1869] I think the Roman Catholic monk Thomas Merton was probably right in saying that when it comes to spirituality, we should "be convinced of the fact that we will never be anything else but beginners, all our life!"[1870] Or put in more skeptical terms, growth in ethical character, wisdom, and psychological health always seem to be partial and imperfect—and sometimes even cyclical or temporary. Furthermore, honesty compels me to recognize that I am very much fallible, am unfortunately prone to mistakes and misjudgments, and know very little about a very complex universe. While these realities are in many ways daunting, I find them now to also be an odd place of security. Just as the Buddhist tradition speaks of a "groundless ground"[1871] where stability is discovered in the constancy of change, so too I have found significant existential relief in the truth that quite often the most defensible philosophical position on ultimate questions seems to be that of indecision or ignorance.

So let this be the end of the book but not of the search.
—**St. Bernard of Clairvaux** (1090-1153), *On Consideration*[1872]

Acknowledgments

I would like to thank the many readers who have offered advice and criticism in my writing process. Among them are thoughtful cousin Kevin McBride, humanist-with-heart extraordinaire Eric Townson, former fellow Bible-studier Marc Renault, dear and compassionate mother-in-law Frances Maxwell, ex-Anglican priest and indomitable seeker Larry James, the wise and well-read former Mennonite missionary Gary Isaac, first-rate former boss George Michaels, perceptive and beloved son Sam Evans, and especially fellow seminarians Dr. Steven Fink and Rev. George Ontko. Their time and candor have made this a more succinct and coherent work. I appreciate all their friendships more than I can say. I would also like to thank Bart Campolo for both his words of encouragement and his valuable advice for improving the introduction to the book. Likewise, I am grateful to Ken Daniels for noting some shortcomings and making some great final suggestions, especially regarding my analysis of biblical prophecy. Bart Campolo, Marlene Winell, Gary Isaac, and (much-loved daughter) Katie Evans also gave some helpful critiques on the book's subtitle—hopefully the final form is more fitting. Lastly, I'd like to express my sincere appreciation to Janeen Jones for her editing assistance and to Dr. John Mabry for all his advice, patience, and support during this project.

Endnotes

1. Denis Diderot, *Philosophic Thoughts*, in *Diderot's Early Philosophical Works*, ed. and trans. Marget Jourdain (Chicago: The Open Court Publishing Co., 1916), no. XXXI, p. 45. Avail. at: https://archive.org/details/diderotsearlyph00jourgoog/page/n60.
2. Lao Tzu, *Tao Te Ching: The Book of the Way and Its Power*, trans. John R. Mabry (Berkeley, CA: The Apocryphile Press, 2017), no. 71, loc. 786, Kindle. Quoted with permission. Lao Tzu's authorship and 6th c. BCE date are disputed by modern scholars. See James Miller, *Daoism: A Short Introduction* (Oxford: Oneworld, 2003), p. x; Geoffrey Parrinder, ed., *World Religions: From Ancient History to Present* (New York: Facts on File, 1985), p. 328.
3. Augustine of Hippo, Homily 7 on the First Epistle of John, *Homilies on the First Epistle of John*, in *Nicene and Post-Nicene Fathers*, vol. 7, ed. Philip Schaff, trans. H. Browne (Buffalo, NY: Christian Literature Publishing Co., 1888), no. 8, http://www.newadvent.org/fathers/170207.htm.
4. Ibid.
5. As a possible exception, my meditation on Tolstoy discusses a perhaps subtle and skeptical form of supernaturalism. Regardless, I would personally put Tolstoy under the broader umbrella of freethought. For a broader definition of freethinking, see Fred Edwords, "The Saga of Freethought and Its Pioneers: Religious Critique and Social Reform," *American Humanist Association*, 2 Apr. 2005 (lecture, American Humanist Association, Washington, DC), accessed 8 Oct. 2019.
6. John F. Thornton and Susan B. Varenne, "About the Vintage Spiritual Classics," in *The Spiritual Exercises of St. Ignatius*, by Ignatius of Loyola, trans. Louis J. Puhl (New York: Random House, 2000), p. xii.
7. Unless otherwise noted, all Scripture quotations are from *The NRSV Notetaker's Bible: New Revised Standard Version with the Apocrypha* (New York: Oxford Univ. Press, 2009). Used by permission according to Licensing and Permissions, New Revised Stand Version, 2015, https://nrsvbibles.org/index.php/licensing/ (accessed 25 Jan. 2019). All rights reserved worldwide. NRSV links are also provided to the Oremus Bible Browser, http://bible.oremus.org/.

8   Hafiz of Shiraz, *The Divan*, in *Persian Literature, Volume 1, Comprising The Shah Nameh, The Rubaiyat, The Divan, and The Gulistan* (1909; Project Gutenberg eBook: 26 Nov. 2003), no. CI, loc. 5941, Kindle. Cf. Hafiz of Shiraz, "The Daughter of the Grape," *The Tangled Braid: Ninety-Nine Poems by Hafiz of Shiraz*, trans. Jeffrey Einboden and John Slater (Louisville, KY: Fons Vitae, 2009), p. 72. For a discussion of the traditional "seventy-odd sects" in Islam, see below in The Great Grab Bag (pt. 3): By the Numbers.

9   *Discourse to the Kālāmas (Kālāma Sutta)*, in *Early Buddhist Discourses*, ed. and trans. John J. Holder (Indianapolis: Hackett Publishing Co., 2006), no. 3, p. 21. Traditional dates of Siddhatta Gotama (the "Buddha") are given here.

10 I am not suggesting here that Buddhist perspectives always heed this advice. For an interesting discussion of metaphysical beliefs from a former Buddhist insider, see Stephen Batchelor, *Confession of a Buddhist Atheist* (New York: Spiegel and Grau, 2011), pp. 100-1, etc.

11 Hew McLeod, *Sikhism* (London: Penguin, 1997), p. xxiv.

12 Peter Abelard, *Yes and No: The Complete Translation of Peter Abelard's* Sic Et Non, trans. Priscilla Throop, 2nd ed. (Charlotte, VT: Medieval MS, 2008), Prologue, p. 25. For a short description of the controversy regarding *Sic Et Non* see Justo L. González, *The Story of Christianity: The Early Church to the Dawn of the Reformation*, vol. 1 (San Francisco: HarperSanFrancisco, 1985), p. 314.

13 See Batchelor, *Confession of a Buddhist Atheist*, p. 66 for a description of the human as a "finite, fallible creature." I use variants of this helpful phrase a few times in the book.

14 Corey, p. 338.

15 For fundamentalism as psychological malady, see David Wulff, *Psychology of Religion: Classic and Contemporary* (Hoboken, NJ: John Wiley and Sons, Inc., 1997), pp. 636, 244-9; Richard Yao, *Fundamentalists Anonymous: There Is a Way Out*, 3rd ed. (New York: Luce Publications, 1985), p. 2.

16 The inspiration for this title comes from Daniel C. Dennett, *Breaking the Spell: Religion as a Natural Phenomenon*, (New York: Viking, 2006). Dennett does discuss heaven and hell on pp. 279-83 of his book—but there is little overlap with the content here.

17 Christopher Jay Johnson and Marsha G. McGee, eds., *How Different Religions View Death and Afterlife*, 2nd ed., (Philadelphia: The Charles Press, 1998), p. 277. The response here is to the question: "Who goes to hell?" (p. 275). It is not clear whether the response is from the editors or the

Zoroastrian scholar who contributed a chapter to the book, Jamsheed K. Choksy. Choksy provides the same general answer on p. 257.)

18 Al-Ghazali, *Path to Sufism, His Deliverance from Error* (Al-Munqidh min al-Dalal), trans. R.J. McCarthy, 3rd ed. (Louisville, KY: Fons Vitae, 2006), p. 18. (The quotation within the text is from the Koran. See Sura 23:53, p.222).

19 Blaise Pascal, *Pensées*, rev. ed. (New York: Penguin Books, 1995), series 2, no. 418, p. 123.

20 A.J. Krailsheimer, introduction to *Pensées*, by Blaise Pascal, p. xxvi.

21 These sorts of sentiments are found throughout the *Pensées*. For example, see Jews (no. 102, p. 26; no. 838, p. 260); Chinese, Romans, Egyptians (no. 454, p. 148; no.281, p. 90); Calvinists/Huguenots (no. 733, p. 225; no. 791, p. 239; no. 571, p. 195); deists (no. 449, p. 140); Arians and other "heretics" (no. 733, pp. 226-7; no. 830, pp. 255-7; no. 840, p. 262; no. 662, p. 213); Muslims and members of other religions (no. 149, p. 47; nos. 203-209, 218-219, pp. 66-70, no.735, p. 228). For some remarks on Catholic exclusivity, see no. 706, p. 221; no. 856 and no. 858, p. 269; no. 881, p. 274, and no. 991, p. 329.

22 Gerald Corey, *Theory and Practice of Counseling and Psychotherapy*, 5th ed. (Pacific Grove, CA: Brooks/Cole Publishing Co., 1996), pp. 321-4. Ellis developed a brand of cognitive-behavioral theory known as REBT—Rational Emotive Behavior Therapy. Corey describes other forms of cognitive/cognitive behavioral theory in this chapter.

23 See Wulff, pp. 136-7.

24 Pascal, no. 419, p. 125.

25 See John Shelby Spong, *The Easter Moment* (San Francisco: Harper and Row: 1980), pp. 215-6, 221-2; Marcus J. Borg, *The Heart of Christianity: Rediscovering a Life of Faith* (New York: HarperCollins, 2003), pp. 10, 171-2, 181-4. Borg calls for a new paradigm focusing on salvation in this life and de-emphasis on the afterlife in general (pp. 171-2).

26 Robert Ingersoll, "Morality," *The Ingersoll Times*, n.d., http://www.theingersolltimes.com/morality/ (accessed 6 Aug 2018). See also Susan Jacoby, *The Great Agnostic: Robert Ingersoll and American Freethought* (New Haven: Yale Univ. Press, 2013), pp. 8-9.

27 *Jewish Encyclopedia*, 1906 ed., s.v. "Jesus of Nazareth," http://www.jewishencyclopedia.com/articles/8616-jesus-of-nazareth (accessed 5 Nov. 2017). See "The Resurrection" section: "Jesus is accordingly, in the following curious Talmudic legend, thought to sojourn in hell. ... [I]t was the degrading fate of those who mock the wise (Gi . 56b-57a)." See also Babylonian Talmud, Tractate Gittim, ed. Rabbi Dr. I. Epstein, trans. Maurice

Simon, http://www.halakhah.com/gittin/gittin_57.html (accessed 5 Nov. 2017), Git. 56b-57a: "Whoever mocks at the words of the Sages is punished with boiling hot excrement." Cf. Christopher Hitchens, god is Not Great: How Religion Poisons Everything (New York: Twelve, 2007), p. 111. Not all modern Jews believe in an afterlife, but a hell of torment is a common traditional opinion. See The Jewish Encyclopedia, 1906 ed., s.v. "Gehenna," http://www.jewishencyclopedia.com/articles/6558-gehenna (accessed 10 Jul. 2018).

28   Dante, The Divine Comedy: Inferno, trans. Henry Wadsworth Longfellow (Project Gutenberg eBook: 12 Apr. 2009), canto XXVIII, https://www.gutenberg.org/files/1001/1001-h/1001-h.htm#CantoXXVIII (accessed 14 Feb. 2018). For discussion, see Omid Safi, Memories of Muhammad: Why the Prophet Matters (New York: HarperOne, 2009), p. 7.

29   Raymond Van Over, ed., The Divine Panorama, in Taoist Tales (New York: Meridian, 1984), p. 122: "Those who ... disbelieve the doctrine of Cause and Effect [karma] ... are handed over to the everlasting tortures of hell." For some particularly gruesome tortures in Taoism's non-eternal hells, see pp. 125-36. For the fate of those who deny the law of karma in Buddhism, see Batchelor, Confession of a Buddhist Atheist, p. 45.

30   See Sûtrakritâṅga, in Jaina Sutras: Part II, ed. F. Max Müller, trans. Hermann Jacobi (Oxford: The Clarendon Press, 1895), bk. 1, lect. 5, ch. 1:3-5 http://www.sacred-texts.com/jai/sbe45/sbe4552.htm (accessed 31 Oct. 2018); see also bk. 1, lect. 2, ch. 3:9 www.sacred-texts.com/jai/sbe45/sbe4545.htm and bk. 1, lect. 5, ch. 2: 24 http://www.sacred-texts.com/jai/sbe45/sbe4553.htm.

31   Synodical Letter of the Council of Gangra, The Seven Ecumenical Councils of the Undivided Church, in Nicene and Post-Nicene Fathers of the Christian Church, Series 2, vol. 14, ed. Phillip Schaff and Henry Wace, trans. Henry R. Percival (Oxford: Benediction Classics, 2011), pp. 156-7. Orig. pub. date not given. See also The Catholic Encyclopedia, 1907-1912 ed., s.v. "Eustathius of Sebaste," http://www.newadvent.org/cathen/05628b.htm (accessed 8 Jul. 2013); Jennifer A. Glancy, Slavery in Early Christianity, (Minneapolis: Fortress Press, 2006), p. 90; Encyclopedia Britannica Online, s.v. "Eustathius, Bishop of Sebaste," http://www.britannica.com/EBchecked/topic/196672/Eustathius (accessed 8 Jul. 2013).

32   The Anathetisms of the Emperor Justinian against Origen, The Seven Ecumenical Councils of the Undivided Church, no. V, p. 464.

33   The Definition of the Faith of the Council of Chalcedon, The Seven Ecumenical Councils of the Undivided Church pp. 386-9. For similar beliefs of St. Cyril of Alexandria (c.376-c.444), see Anathematisms of St. Cyril against

Nestorius, ibid., no. 1, p. 312. See also Leo Donald Davis, *The First Seven Ecumenical Councils (325-787): Their History and Theology* (Collegeville, MN: Liturgical Press, 1990), pp. 186-8; Christopher Bellitto, *The General Counsels: A History of Twenty-One Church Councils from Nicaea to Vatican II* (New York: Paulist Press, 2002), pp. 22-3. The Greek term for Mary here is "Theotokos" or "God-Bearer."

34 Capitula of the Council, Second Council of Constantinople, *The Seven Ecumenical Councils of the Undivided Church*, no. 2, p. 453.

35 The Sentence against the Monothelites, *The Seven Ecumenical Councils of the Undivided Church*, pp. 491-2. Pope Honorius is specifically mentioned here as being anathematized. See also *The Concise Oxford Dictionary of the Christian Church*, 3rd ed., s.v. "Honorius I," p. 266; Justo L. González, *The Story of Christianity: The Reformation to the Present Day*, vol. 2 (San Francisco: HarperSanFrancisco, 1985), p. 299. The case of Honorius is often used as an example against the doctrine of papal infallibility. Many Roman Catholics objected to the doctrine of papal infallibility and it has been described as "an affront to the historical intelligence." See Patrick Allitt, *Catholic Converts: British and American Intellectuals Return to Rome* (Ithaca, NY: Cornell Univ. Press, 1997), pp. 39, 102-3. William Lane Craig, "#75 Monotheletism," *Reasonable Faith with William Lane Craig*, n.d., http://reasonablefaith.org/monotheletism (accessed 29 Jun. 2016).

36 Jerome, *Life of Paul of Thebes*, in *Early Christian Lives*, ed. and trans. Carolinne White (London: Penguin Classics, 1998), no.17, p. 8. Cf. González, vol. 1, p. 134 on how early Christians worried if "it was possible for a rich person to be saved."

37 "The Sigillion of the Pan-Orthodox Council of Constantinople, 1583," *Confessor*, no. 7 (25 Aug. 2017), http://www.omologitis.org/?p=1517 (accessed 8 Nov. 2017). Cf. Michael Azkoul, "The Gregorian Calendar is a Deviation from the Faith," *Orthodoxyinfo.org*, n.d., http://orthodoxyinfo.org/deviate.htm (accessed 3 Nov. 2013); Timothy Ware, *The Orthodox Church*, new ed. (New York: Pelican, 1997), pp. 302-3. Many of the condemnations from the Catholic traditions are done in a formulaic statement either by using the word "anathema." Although technically speaking ultimate judgment was thought to be in God's hands, such strong condemnations were undoubtedly meant to indicate extreme spiritual peril and an expectation of damnation if there was no repentance and restoration. For discussion, see *The Concise Oxford Dictionary of the Christian Church*, s.v. "anathema," p. 20; *The Catholic Encyclopedia*, s.v. "Anathema," http://www.newadvent.org/cathen/01455e.htm (accessed 6 Feb. 2013) and ibid.,

s.v. "Excommunication," http://www.newadvent.org/cathen/05678a.htm (accessed 10 Jul. 2018).

38 *The Garuda Purana*, trans. Ernest Wood and S.V. Subrahmanyam, 1911, *Internet Sacred Text Archive*, ch. IV, no. 36, p. 34, http://www.sacred-texts.com/hin/gpu/gpu06.htm. Ch. IV is filled with reasons for "certainly" being damned. For the specific torments of these hells, see ch.III, nos. 35-60, http://www.sacred-texts.com/hin/gpu/gpu05.htm (accessed 14 Jul. 2018). For a further description of Hindu hells, see Anne Pearson, "Hinduism," in *How Different Religions View Death and Afterlife*, p. 123.

39 Mary Boyce, ed. and trans., *Textual Sources for the Study of Zoroastrianism* (Chicago: Univ. of Chicago Press, 1990), pp. 88-9. Boyce cites a 9th-c. CE Zoroastrian text called the *Arda Viraz Namag* (6.3.16, ch. 58) which provides graphic and grotesque pictures of hell and describes a number of damnable sins.

40 Parrinder, ed., *World Religions*, p. 77 notes that the Aztec hell was a "horrible subterranean realm of the dead."

41 Ben Zion Bokser and Baruch M. Bokser, eds., *The Talmud: Selected Writings* (New York: Paulist Press, 1989), Tractate Avot, 1.5, p. 220.

42 Acts of Thomas, in *After the New Testament: A Reader in Early Christianity*, Bart D. Ehrman, ed. (New York: Oxford Univ. Press, 1999), ch. 56, p. 17.

43 John Knox, *The First Blast of the Trumpet Against the Monstrous Regiment of Women*, ed. Edward Arber (Grand Rapids, MI: Christian Classics Ethereal Library, orig. pub. 1558), no. 2, p. 26, https://www.ccel.org/ccel/knox/blast.pdf (accessed 18 Nov. 2016).

44 Peter Harvey, *An Introduction to Buddhism: Teachings, History and Practices* (New York: Cambridge Univ. Press, 1990), p. 167; see also pp. 152-3, 164, etc.

45 Jamsheed Choksy, "Zoroastrianism," *How Different Religions View Death and Afterlife*, p. 257. (See also pp. 277, 286.) See also Henry Lord's 17th-c. account of the Parsis: "upon pain of damnation, to believe no other law than that which was brought by Zardusht [Zoroaster]" (Boyce, ed., p. 127; cf. p. 88). Apostasy was thought to be a damnable offense, being cited in Zoroastrian polemics against Islam. See Jenny Rose, *Zoroastrianism: An Introduction* (London: I.B. Tauris, 2012), p. 164.

46 Grant Underwood, "'Saved or Damned': Tracing a Persistent Protestantism in Early Mormon Thought," *Brigham Young University Studies*, 25:3 (Summer 1985): pp. 85ff., https://byustudies.byu.edu/PDFLibrary/25.3UnderwoodSaved-861c2b45-a4e1-4d0d-81af-e7d7c15f9d8b.pdf (accessed 1 Nov. 2013). The contemporary Mormon view is more generous, only

damning those who knew Mormonism was true but then "willfully sinned against the Holy Ghost by rejecting it." See Richard Eyre, "The Church of Jesus Christ of Latter-Day Saints," *How Different Religions View Death and Afterlife*, p. 99. See also p. 277 in same volume.

47 Justin Marytr, *Dialogue with Trypho*, in *After the New Testament*, ch. 19, p. 110, who quips: "as you claim, circumcision had been necessary for salvation." (See also ch. 47, p. 113). Henry Chadwick, *The Early Church*, rev. ed. (New York: Penguin Books, 1993), p. 11. Chadwick also notes that in the 1st c. a "formal anathema" against Christians was added to the synagogue liturgy (p. 21).

48 See Al-Ghazali, p. 18; Ibn Warraq, *Why I Am Not a Muslim* (Amherst, NY: Prometheus Books, 2003), p. 176: "the orthodox Muslim position ... that salvation outside of Islam is not possible." See also "The Majority Group – The Group of Salvation," *Imam Ahmed Raza Academy*, 2009, https://www.raza.org.za/publications_group_of_salvation.html (accessed 11 Jul. 2018). While there is debate in the Muslim community, many Quran'ic passages that have often been read to mean that only Muslims can be saved. See *The Koran*, trans. N.J. Dawood (New York: Penguin Books, 1974), Sura 3:85, p. 415; Sura 5:72, p. 395; Sura 40:70-72, p. 168; Sura 57:19, p. 108; Sura 47:34, p. 126. There are some Muslims who see the issue differently because of other verses which seem more generous: Sura 5:69, p. 395; Sura 2:62, p. 338. An on-line version can be found at *The Noble Qur'an*, Sahih International Version, 2016, https://quran.com/. For a more moderate view, see Jane Idleman Smith, "Islam," *How Different Religions View Death and Afterlife*, p. 143; cf. p. 285. For some hadith passages which suggest Muslim-only salvation, see Muhammad al-Bukhari, *Sahih al-Bukhari, Sunnah.com*, trans. M. Muhsin Khan, n.d., bk. 23, no. 2 (2.23.330), https://sunnah.com/bukhari/23/2; bk. 23, no. 94 (2.23.422), http://sunnah.com/bukhari/23/94; bk. 23, no. 110 (2.23.438), http://sunnah.com/bukhari/23/110; bk. 56, no. 268 (4.52.296-7), http://sunnah.com/bukhari/56/268 (accessed 10 Oct. 2018). 4.52.296-7 expressly states that "None will enter Paradise but a Muslim …." For further discussion, see Ram Swarup, *Understanding the Hadith: The Sacred Traditions of Islam* (Amherst, NY: Prometheus Books, 2002), pp. 15, 18, 20, 21, 191, 212-13.

49 Parrinder, ed., *World Religions*, p. 498: "For the Shiah there is no hope of a proper life or reward hereafter, except through devotion to the *imam*."

50 *Mercer Dictionary of the Bible*, 1992 ed., s.v. "Dead Sea Scrolls" which notes that "God had called them to separate from those outside the community, … these would face eternal torment."

51 Eusebius of Caesarea, *Ecclesiastical History,* trans. C. F. Cruse (Peabody, MA: Hendrickson, 1998), 3.27, p. 93: "With them the observance of the law was altogether necessary, as if they could not be saved only by faith in Christ and a corresponding life." Davis notes that Ebionites insisted that "the Law remained the true way to salvation" (p. 34). Cf. Ehrman, ed., *After the New Testament,* p. 96.

52 Walter Klaassen, "A Fire that Spread Anabaptist Beginnings," *Christian History,* 4.1, issue 5 (1985): p. 8: "Like their contemporaries in other Christian groups, Anabaptists were pretty certain that all other groups would inherit not the kingdom of God but his fierce wrath for their intractable stubbornness in rejecting the truth that the Anabaptists had found." See William Estep, *The Anabaptist Story: An Introduction to Sixteenth-Century Anabaptism,* 3rd ed. (Grand Rapids, MI: William B. Eerdmans, 1996), p. 231, etc. Cf. Steven M. Nolt, *A History of the Amish,* 3rd ed. (New York: Good Books, 2015), pp. 28, 34-5, 41. Further, there have been diverse views among Anabaptists and controversies among different Anabaptist sects.

53 H. Chadwick, p. 220.

54 For discussions of early church and patristic expressions of the notion that one had to be a member of a singular "Catholic Church" to be saved, see H. Chadwick, pp. 41, 220; Gerald Bonner, *St. Augustine of Hippo: Life and Controversies* (Norwich: The Canterbury Press, 1986), pp. 261, 281; Elaine Pagels, *The Gnostic Gospels* (New York: Vintage Books, 1989), p. 121; I. Howard Marshall, *Luke: Historian and Theologian,* 3rd ed. (Downers Grove, IL: InterVarsity Press, 1998), pp. 81, 219-20; F.F. Bruce, *Paul: Apostle of the Heart Set Free,* 2nd ed. (Grand Rapids, MI: Wm. B. Eerdmans, 1998), p. 432. For some primary source examples see Augustine of Hippo, *On Baptism, Against the Donatists,* in *Nicene and Post-Nicene Fathers, First Series,* vol. 4, ed. Philip Schaff, trans. J.R. King, rev. Chester D. Hartranft (Buffalo, NY: Christian Literature Publishing Co., 1887), 4.18, http://www.newadvent.org/fathers/14084.htm (accessed 2 Feb. 2013). St. Cyprian (c.210-258) famously remarked: "You cannot have God as your Father if you do not have the church for your mother. If there was escape for anyone who was outside the ark of Noah, there is escape too for one who is found outside the church" (*On the Unity of the Catholic Church,* in *After the New Testament,* Bart D. Ehrman, ed., p. 342).

55 Ware, pp. 58-61, 98, 309, 315). Much of this discussion focuses around the patristic dogma that "outside the Church there is no salvation." See Archimandite (Metropolitan) Philaret, "Will the Heterodox Be Saved?" *Orthodox Life,* 34:6 (Nov.-Dec. 1984): pp. 33-6. Avail. at http://ortho-

doxinfo.com/inquirers/metphil_heterodox.aspx (accessed 30 Oct. 2013). George Mastrantonis, *A New-Style Catechism on the Eastern Orthodox Faith for Adults* (St. Louis: The OLOGOS Mission, 1969), pp. 27, 104, 112, 203, etc. "The Sigillion of the Pan-Orthodox Council of Constantinople, 1583," no. 1 (etc.), http://www.omologitis.org/?p=1517.

56 John Julius Norwich, *A Short History of Byzantium* (New York: Vintage Books, 1999), pp. 150-1; Ware, p. 55, 210ff; "The Sigillion of the Pan-Orthodox Council of Constantinople, 1583," no.1 http://www.omologitis.org/?p=1517. This clause is commonly called the "filioque" which means "and the Son."

57 Ware, p. 58; González, vol. 1, pp. 264-5.

58 Davis, pp. 196-9; 209. Certain patriarchs of Constantinople and Alexandria, other Monophysite Christian rigorists held this view. The Eastern Orthodox and non-Chalcedonian (or Monophysite) Churches have been out of communion since 451; the different parties condemned and anathematized one another at the time of the schism. For a look at modern developments see, Ware, p. 312; "Ecumenical Relations of the Syriac Orthodox Church" *Syriac Orthodox Resources*, 3 Dec. 2002, http://sor.cua.edu/Ecumenism/ (accessed 2 Nov. 2013).

59 The Definition of the Faith of the Council of Chalcedon, *The Seven Ecumenical Councils of the Undivided Church* pp. 338-9.

60 This is a common rigorist Protestant position. See R.C. Sproul, *Justified by Faith Alone* (Wheaton, IL: Crossway Books, 1999), pp. 9-10, 39. Abraham Calovius (1612-1686) is also an example; he taught that Lutheranism was necessary for salvation (González, vol. 2, p. 178; *The Westminster Dictionary of Theologians*, 2006 ed., s.v. "Calov, Abraham"). See also Martin Crusius (Ware, p. 94).

61 For a classic Roman Catholic expression of this, see *The Canons and Decrees of the Council of Trent*, trans. H. J. Schroeder (Rockford, IL: Tan Books and Publishers, 1978), sess. 6, can. 9-12, pp. 43-4. Some Anabaptists also hold that discipleship is necessary for salvation. For one example, see William R. McGrath, *The Anabaptists: Neither Catholics or [sic] Protestants*, (Crossreach Publications: 2015), loc. 588, Kindle.

62 Often described as the difference between being "of the same substance" as God the Father vs. being "of like substance" to the Father. Schaff gives this helpful description of the intensity of Arian debates: "council was held against council, creed was set forth against creed, and anathema was hurled against anathema" (Philip Schaff, *History of the Christian Church, Nicene and Post-Nicene Christianity A.D. 311-600*, rev. 5th ed., vol. III (Grand Rapids, MI: Christian Classics Ethereal Library, n.d.), p. 546

http://www.ccel.org/ccel/schaff/hcc3.pdf. See also Edward R. Hardy, ed., *Christology of the Later Fathers* (Louisville, KY: Westminster John Knox Press, 1954), p. 341; Norwich, p. 15; H. Chadwick, p. 139. See Rowan Williams, *Arius: Heresy and Tradition*, rev. ed. (Grand Rapids, MI: William B. Eerdmans, 2001) for a fascinating exploration of the Arian controversy. For the classic condemnation of Arians, see The Nicene Creed, Council of Nicaea (325), *The Seven Ecumenical Councils of the Undivided Church*, p. 39.

63 A common Churches of Christ view insists on adult immersion. See Thomas Olbricht, "The Churches of Christ," in *How Different Religions View Death and Afterlife*, p. 85; cf. p. 270 in this same volume. See also the Anabaptist *Schleitheim Confession of Faith* (1527) which calls infant baptism "the highest and chief abomination of the pope." *Schleitheim Confession of Faith, 1527*, trans. J.C. Wenger, University of Washington, http://courses.washington.edu/hist112/SCHLEITHEIM%20CONFESSION%20OF%20FAITH.htm (accessed 15 Feb. 2014). Orig. from *The Mennonite Quarterly Review*, 19:4 (Oct. 1945): pp. 247- 53.

64 *The Canons and Decrees of the Council of Trent*, sess.7, can.13, p. 54.

65 Augustine of Hippo, *On Nature and Grace*, in *Nicene and Post-Nicene Fathers*, vol. 5, ed. Phillip Schaff, trans. Peter Holmes and Robert Ernest Wallis, rev. Benjamin B. Warfield (Buffalo, NY: Christian Literature Publishing Co., 1887), ch.4, http://www.newadvent.org/fathers/1503.htm; Bonner, pp. 325, 345, 379, 392. (Augustine did hold that there were gradations of punishments in hell—and that infants received the mildest of the penalties.) For Eastern Orthodoxy, see Mastrantonis, p. 119; John H. Leith, ed., *The Confession of Dositheus*, in *Creeds of the Churches: A Reader in Christian Doctrine from the Bible to the Present*, 3rd ed. (Louisville: John Knox Press, 1982), decree XVI, p. 500. (For an online version see http://catholicity.elcore.net/ConfessionOfDositheus.html.) For Protestants, see John S. Oyer, "Sticks and Stones Broke Their Bones, and Vicious Names Did Hurt Them!: 16th-Century Responses to the Anabaptists," *Church History*, 4:1 (1985): p .19: "To the Reformers the denial of baptism to infants literally damned them…."

66 *The Casuist: A Collection of Cases in Moral and Pastoral Theology*, vol. II (New York: Joseph F. Wagner, 1908), pp. 36-7. Avail. at https://archive.org/details/casuistcollectio02unse/page/36. The Roman Catholic Church outlawed cremation until 1963—and currently does not allow the scattering of ashes. See Erin Blakemore, "The Vatican Just Banned Scattering Ashes," *Smithsonian.com*, 25 Oct. 2016, https://www.smithsonianmag.com/

smart-news/vatican-just-banned-scattering-ashes-180960907/ (accessed 30 Dec. 2018).

67 S.A. Nigosian, *The Zoroastrian Faith: Tradition and Modern Research* (Montreal: McGill-Queen's Univ. Press, 1993), pp. 36-8; Boyce, ed., p. 148; Philip Matyszak, *The Enemies of Rome: From Hannibal to Attila the Hun* (London: Thames and Hudson, 2004), p. 241. Rose notes in her description of the *Arda Viraz Namag* that hell is in part populated by "those sinners who have polluted water, fire, and earth with dead matter" (p. 129).

68 A Buddhist belief. See, for example, *Mahayana Lankavatara Sutra*, trans. Daisetz Teitaro Suzuki, Fodian.net, n.d., ch. 8, no. 11, http://www.fodian.net/world/0672_08.html (accessed 3 Nov. 2013).

69 Council of Gangra, *The Seven Ecumenical Councils of the Undivided Church*, can. 2, p. 159.

70 For a condemnation and "eternal anathema" by Eastern Orthodoxy of Calvinistic predestination, see Leith, ed., *The Confession of Dositheus*, in *Creeds of the Churches*, decree III, pp. 487-9. (Avail. at http://catholicity.elcore.net/ConfessionOfDositheus.html.) Cf. Owen Chadwick, *The Reformation* (New York: Penguin, 1990), p. 360. Cf. Council of Orange (529) for the "utter abhorrence" and anathema to those who belived that "any are foreordained to evil by the power of God" (Leith, ed., *Council of Orange*, in *Creeds of the Churches*, conclusion, pp. 44-5). Anabaptist Menno Simons (c.1496-1561) condemned Reformed Christians in general terms. See Menno Simons to Gellius Faber, *The Complete Works of Menno Simons*, ed. John Christian Wenger, trans. Leonard Verduin (Scottsdale, PA: Herald, 1956), p. 939. Simons also notes that the magisterial Reformers of his day were also commonly known to "violate and blaspheme and send each other to hell" (p. 678).

71 After the Synod of Dort (1618-1619), Arminians could be exiled, jailed, or fined heavily (González, vol. 2, pp. 181-2). González further notes that "At times, they even seemed to confuse doubt regarding the doctrine of predestination with actual reprobation and consequent damnation" (vol. 2, p. 184). See also *The Concise Oxford Dictionary of the Christian Church*, s.v. "Dort, Synod of." Dort at times suggests that Arminians may be damned: "Moreover, the Synod warns calumniators themselves to consider the terrible judgment of God which awaits them, for bearing false witness against the confessions of so many Churches; for distressing the consciences of the weak; and for laboring to render suspected the society of the truly faithful" (p. 30). There are also a few points in the canons where Arminians were accused of adhering to the heretical Pelagian position—which again has overtones of condemnation and damnation. See *Synod of Dort*

(Grand Rapids, MI: Christian Classics Ethereal Library, n.d.), http://www.ccel.org/ccel/anonymous/canonsofdort.pdf. For some modern discussions, see Steven Pribble, "Is Arminianism a damnable heresy?" *Grace Orthodox Presbyterian Church*, n.d., http://www.all-of-grace.org/pub/pribble/damnable.html (accessed 22 Jun. 2016); Christopher Adams, "Three Reasons Why Arminians Are Not Saved," *Outside the Camp*, Sovereign Redeemer Assembly, n.d., http://www.outsidethecamp.org/three.htm (accessed 22 Jun. 2016); "Are Arminians Saved?" *Reformation Theology*, 2008, http://www.monergism.com/thethreshold/articles/onsite/qna/arminians.html (accessed 22 Jun. 2016).

72 Council of II Nicaea (787), Extracts from the Acts, *The Seven Ecumenical Councils of the Undivided Church*, sess. I, pp. 762-3. See also Davis, p. 309; *The Canons and Decrees of the Council of Trent*, sess.25, p. 219; Leith, ed., *The Confession of Dositheus*, in *Creeds of the Churches*, Q.IV, p. 511.

73 Epitome of the Definition of the Iconoclastic Conciliabulum held in Constantinople, *The Seven Ecumenical Councils of the Undivided Church*, pp. 777-8; Davis, pp. 302-4. Its supporters called the 754 Council of Hieria an "Ecumenical" one.

74 "The Sigillion of the Pan-Orthodox Council of Constantinople, 1583," no.6, http://www.omologitis.org/?p=1517 (accessed 14 Jul. 2018); *Westminster Confession of Faith*, 1646, Center for Reformed Theology and Apologetics, 25.6, https://reformed.org/documents/wcf_with_proofs/index.html (accessed 21 Dec. 2018); Estep, p. 136.

75 Pope Boniface VIII, *Unam Sanctam*, in *Papal Encyclicals Online*, orig. pub. 18 Nov. 1302, http://www.papalencyclicals.net/bon08/b8unam.htm (accessed 14 Jul. 2018): "Furthermore, we declare, we proclaim, we define that it is absolutely necessary for salvation that every human creature be subject to the Roman Pontiff." See also *The Catholic Encyclopedia*, s.v. "Unam Sanctam," http://www.newadvent.org/cathen/15126a.htm (accessed 30 Oct. 2013). To contrast with modern Roman Catholicism, see *Catechism of the Catholic Church* (New York: Image/Doubleday, 1995), secs. 836-48, pp. 241-4.

76 For some especially rigid language, Ecumenical Council of Florence (1438-1445), *Eternal Word Television Network*, sess. 11, Bull of Union with Copts, https://www.ewtn.com/library/COUNCILS/FLORENCE.HTM (accessed 14. Jul. 2018). Taken from *Decrees of the Ecumenical Councils*, ed. Norman P. Tanner. Cf. Paul Halsall, ed., *Twelfth Ecumenical Council: Lateran IV 1215*, in *Internet Medieval Sourcebook*, Fordham University, Mar. 1996, can. 1, http://www.fordham.edu/halsall/basis/lateran4.asp (accessed 3 Jun. 2013): "There is one Universal Church of the faithful, outside of

which there is absolutely no salvation." From H. J. Schroeder, *Disciplinary Decrees of the General Councils: Text, Translation and Commentary* (St. Louis: B. Herder, 1937), pp. 236-96. See also Leo XII, *Ubi Primum*, in *Papal Encyclicals Online*, orig. pub. 5 May 1824, no. 14, http://www.papalencyclicals.net/Leo12/l12ubipr.htm (accessed 28 Aug. 2013); Julian of Norwich, *Revelations of Divine Love*, trans. Elizabeth Spearing (London: Penguin, 1998), no. 32, pp. 85-6; O. Chadwick, p. 367; Allitt, p. x. For a Roman Catholic historical review of this issue, see Francis A. Sullivan, *Salvation Outside the Church?: Tracing the History of the Catholic Response* (Eugene, OR: Wipf and Stock Publishers, 2002).

77   *Encyclopedia Britannica*, s.v. "Hell" https://www.britannica.com/topic/hell#ref924473 (accessed 13 Jul. 2018). This view of a "shady" and dismal existence is also a typical understanding of the Jewish concept of Sheol. See *Jewish Encyclopedia*, s.v. "Sheol" http://jewishencyclopedia.com/articles/13563-sheol. For a popular view of different ideas of hell throughout human history, see Alice K. Turner, *The History of Hell* (Orlando, FL: Harcourt, 1993)—Turner is a very interesting read with an array of colorful art but her facts need to be checked. The Greek and Roman conceptions of hell also included a paradisal state known as Elysia and a place of torment known as Tartarus. *The Penguin Dictionary of Religions*, s.v. "Afterlife (Ancient Near Eastern) notes that in Sumerian mythology the dead resided in "a dark underworld, where life would dimly reflect the joys of earthly existence."

78   *Encyclopedia Britannica*, s.v. "Niflheim," https://www.britannica.com/topic/Niflheim and s.v. "Hel" https://www.britannica.com/topic/Hel-Norse-deity (accessed 2 Oct. 2018). See also Turner, p. 106 and *The Penguin Dictionary of Religions*, s.v. "Hel" and s.v. "Vahalla."

79   See "What Do Jehovah's Witnesses Believe?" *JW.org*, n.d., https://www.jw.org/en/jehovahs-witnesses/faq/jehovah-witness-beliefs/, and "What Is Hell? Is It a Place of Eternal Torment?" *JW.org*, n.d., https://www.jw.org/en/bible-teachings/questions/what-is-hell/ (both accessed 9 Oct. 2017). This website explains that Eccles. 9:5 and 9:10 teach that there is no such thing as a "fiery hell"—a concept that would "violate God's justice" (Deut. 32:4). The Socians also believed in annihilation. See *The Catholic Encyclopedia*, s.v. "Socinianism" http://newadvent.org/cathen/14113a.htm (accessed 1 Oct. 2018).

80   Nolt, p. 192.
81   Bonner, p. 336.
82   C.S. Lewis, *The Great Divorce* (New York: MacMillian Publishing Co., 1946). In contrast, heaven is vibrantly and gloriously real. Individuals'

choices decide their fate. The preface of the novel (pp. 5-8) gives an indication that the story is meant to be fictional but yet still illustrative of Lewis' actual theological perspectives. For a popular evangelical's analysis of Lewis' view, see Timothy Keller, *The Reason for God* (New York: Riverhead Books, 2008), pp. 81-3.

83 Alexandre Kalomiros, *The River of Fire: A Reply to the Questions: Is God Really Good? Did God Create Hell?* (Seattle, WA: St. Nectarios Press, 1980), no. 4, p. 10. While a creative attempt to reframe traditional concepts of hell, it seems out of accord with patristic and historical Eastern Orthodox approaches. Cf. Rom. 12:19. For traditionalist rebuttal, see Vladimir Moss, "'The River of Fire' Revisited," *orthodoxchrisitianbooks.com*, rev. 20 Feb. 2014, http://www.orthodoxchristianbooks.com/articles/837/-river-fire-revisited/ (accessed 13 Jul. 2018).

84 For a discussion of the concept of "Socratic ignorance," see *Internet Encyclopedia of Philosophy*, s.v. "Socrates" http://www.iep.utm.edu/socrates/#SSH2bi (accessed 16 Feb. 2017); *The 100 Most Influential Philosophers*, s.v. "Socrates."

85 Plato, *The Apology* (*The Defense of Socrates*), in *Great Dialogues of Plato*, ed. Eric H. Warmington and Philip G. Rouse, trans. W. H. D. Rouse (New York: Mentor, 1956), p. 435. For a short biography on Socrates, see *Stanford Encyclopedia of Philosophy*, Speing 2010 ed., s.v. "Socrates" http://plato.stanford.edu/entries/socrates/ (accessed 8 Feb. 2013).

86 Mark Twain, *Letters from the Earth*, ed. Bernard DeVoto (New York: Harper and Row, 1974), lett. 6, p. 31.

87 As quoted in Edith Hamilton, *Mythology: Timeless Tales of Gods and Heroes* (New York: Mentor, 1969), p. 248.

88 While I assume that readers will get my general sense of the use of this term, even the concept of "literal" interpretation is not necessarily straightforward and has been understood in different ways. See *Handbook of Biblical Criticism*, 3rd ed., s.v. "Literal Sense."

89 The American Standard Version (ASV) translation reads: "For I shrank not from declaring unto you the whole counsel of God" (Acts 20:27).

90 See also Deut. 3:3-7, Josh. 6:20-21, Josh. 10:40.

91 Verses describing the annihilation of cities and the Flood would of course include pregnant women as well.

92 See also Isa. 42:24-25, Hosea 13:16.

93 See also Isa. 10:15-19, Num. 11:33.

94 See 1 Kings 18:22 for the number of prophets.

95 "Who Killed More People in the Bible—God or Satan?" *Religico*, 17 Dec. 2009, http://www.religico.com/2009/12/17/who-killed-more-people-in-

the-bible-god-or-satan/, (accessed 14 Jan. 2013). (This web address is no longer avail.; see https://web.archive.org/web/20150221190345/http://www.religico.com/2009/12/17/who-killed-more-people-in-the-bible-god-or-satan/.) See also Steve Wells, "How Many Has God Killed? Complete list and estimated killing (Including Apocryphal killings)," *Dwindling in Unbelief* (blog), 17 May 2013, http://dwindlinginunbelief.blogspot.com/2010/04/drunk-with-blood-gods-killings-in-bible.html, (accessed 7 Sep. 2013); and also "Who Has Killed More, Satan or God?" 09 Aug. 2006, https://dwindlinginunbelief.blogspot.com/2006/08/who-has-killed-more-satan-or-god.html (accessed 27 Sep. 2018). Of course, Satan is accused of generally corrupting people's behavior and all heinous crimes are perhaps thought to be with his participation in some sense (Luke 22:3, 2 Cor. 2:11, 1 Pet. 5:8-9, etc.). For confirmed murders of Satan, see Job 1:12-19 (although critical scholars assert that the "Satan" of Job is not the same character as the much more developed Satan of the NT).

96 See also Exod. 32:7-14, Deut. 7:9-11.
97 See also Matt. 18:8, Matt. 13:41-42, Matt. 25:41, Mark 9:43-48, Luke 16:24, Jude 7, Rev. 14:9-11, Rev. 20:14.
98 See also Josh. 6:26, Rev. 22:18-19.
99 I recognize that many Jews do not consider the description of Pharisees in the NT to be fair or accurate. I am using the term with the NT connotation.
100 Mark Twain, "Thoughts of God," in *The Portable Atheist: Essential Readings for the Nonbeliever*, ed. Christopher Hitchens (Philadelphia: Da Capo Press, 2007), p. 118. Hitchens notes that the selection is from Twain's *Fable's of Man*. Paine even called the belief that God is accurately presented in the Bible as a form of blasphemy. See Thomas Paine, *The Age of Reason*, in *Works of Thomas Paine* (Coyote Canyon Press, 2010), pt. 2, ch. 1, loc. 1237, 1277, Kindle.
101 Martin Luther, *The Bondage of the Will*, trans. Henry Cole (Legacy Publications, 2011), sec. 24, loc. 666ff., Kindle.
102 As quoted in Timothy Michael Law, *When God Spoke Greek: The Septuagint and the Making of the Christian Bible* (Oxford Univ. Press, 2013), p. 117, Kindle. (Source given as Augustine, *Speculum* 22). Also quoted and commented on in Edmund Louis Gallagher, *Hebrew Scripture in Patristic Biblical Theory* (Boston: Brill, 2012), p. 53.
103 Law, p. 60. Slavonic and Georgian Orthodox Churches are Eastern Orthodox. The others are Oriental Orthodox. For one attempt to classify these different canons in chart form, see *Wikipedia*, s.v. "Biblical Canon" http://en.wikipedia.org/wiki/Biblical_canon (accessed 12 Oct. 2014).

104 H. Chadwick, pp. 38-40.
105 *The Catholic Encyclopedia*, s.v. "Paulicians" http://www.newadvent.org/cathen/11583b.htm (accessed 23 Jan. 2017); *The New International Dictionary of the Christian Church*, 2nd ed., s.v. "Paulicians," p. 755; Norwich, p. 140. Stephen O'Shea, *The Perfect Heresy: The Revolutionary Life and Death of the Medieval Cathars* (New York: Walker and Co., 2000) notes that the Cathar view of Scripture attributed the OT to "the Evil One, the creator of matter" (p. 30) and describes Bogimils as predecessors of Cathars and not the same sect (p. 23). *The New International Dictionary of the Christian Church*, s.v. "Bogomiles" notes that the sect rejected "almost all of the OT" (p. 139) whereas the St. Pachomius Library, s.v. "Bogomils" http://www.voskrese.info/spl/Xbogomil.html (accessed 16 Jul. 2018) states that the Bogomils accepted only the Psalms from the OT. González, vol. 1, p. 300 identifies Bogomils with Cathars. The Manichaeans also rejected the OT. See Bonner, pp. 60, 215; González, vol. 1, p. 210. *The Catholic Encyclopedia*, s.v. "Manichaeism," http://www.newadvent.org/cathen/0951a.htm (accessed 2 May 2017).
106 Shomron and Osher Sassoni, *The Samaritan-Israelites and Their Religion:Educational Guide*, vol. 1 (Holon, Israel: 2004), ch.2, pp. 10-11, 29-30. Avail. at http://drshirley.org/rel402/samaritan-educationalguide.pdf; "The Samaritan number increase yearly," *The Samaritan Update*, 1 Jul. 2018 http://www.thesamaritanupdate.com/ (accessed 15 Jul. 2018).
107 Wolf Leslau, *Falasha Anthology: Translated from Ethiopic Sources* (New Haven: Yale Univ. Press, 1979), pp. xxxi-ii, xxxviii, etc.; Steven Kaplan, *The Beta Israel (Falasha) in Ethiopia: From Earliest Times to the Twentieth Century* (New York: New York Univ. Press, 1992), pp. 73-5, Kindle.
108 "Canon of the Bible," *Islamic-awareness.org*, n.d., http://www.islamic-awareness.org/Bible/Text/Canon/ (accessed 11 Aug. 2017). The word "apocryphal" refers to doubtful authenticity. In general, the term "Apocrypha" refers to books eventually rejected by mainstream Judaism and Protestantism but found to be canonical by other communions or believers. As this essay shows, there is some difference in usage of this word due to the variances between canons. The terms "Deuterocanon" and "*Anaginoskomena*" are also applied to this general category. For an Eastern Orthodox perspective, see Mastrantonis, pp. 28-9.
109 Lim, pp. 25, 50-3, 105, 175; *The Jewish Encyclopedia*, s.v. "Bible Canon," no. 11, http://www.jewishencyclopedia.com/articles/3259-bible-canon (Ezekiel, Proverbs, Ecclesiastes, Song of Solomon, and Esther are all mentioned here); Bruce Metzger, *The Canon of the New Testament: Its Origin, Development, and Significance* (Oxford: Clarendon Press, 1997),

pp. 109-10; Christine Hayes, "The Restoration: 1 and 2 Chronicles, Ezra and Nehemiah," Introduction to the Old Testament (lecture, Yale University, New Haven, CT) lect. 22, 13:20-14:20, http://www.youtube.com/watch?v=zDYJwHW1lsM&list=PLh9mgdi4rNeyuvTEbD-Ei0JdMUujXfy-Wi&index=22 (accessed 31 Jul. 2013); *Mercer Dictionary of the Bible*, s.v. "Canon" notes that "Ezekiel, Proverbs, Ecclesiastes, the Song of Solomon, and Esther occasioned debate." He also notes that Ecclesiasticus/Sirach "were excluded" without further description (p. 131). See also Alex Ozar, "Purim and the Exceptional Book of Esther," *First Things*, 9 Mar. 2012, http://www.firstthings.com/onthesquare/2012/03/purim-and-the-exceptional-book-of-esther (accessed 31 Jul. 2013). Sirach also does not reference Daniel—however, critical scholarship holds that Sirach was written about 200-175 BCE and Daniel between 167-164 BCE (NAB, pp. 771, 1021).

110   Lim, pp. 121, 175; *Mercer Dictionary of the Bible*, "Dead Sea Scrolls" ; Law, p. 25; *Handbook of Biblical Criticism*, s.v. "Dead Sea Scrolls." Although the remains of over 800 religious texts of various types were found at Qumran in the 20th century, the book of Esther was not only absent but is apparently never even referenced.

111   Law, pp. 59, 89-90; Lim, pp. 131-5, 143-4, 146-7. Jubilees and Enoch are authoritative in the Ethiopian Orthodox Church, per Emanuel Tov, *Textual Criticism of the Bible*, 3rd ed. (Minneapolis: Fortress Press, 2012), pp. 189-90, footnote 89.

112   Law, pp. 82-3: Froehlich, pp. 2, 6; *Handbook of Biblical Criticism*, s.v. "Apocrypha, The."

113   Bart D. Ehrman, *Jesus, Interrupted: Revealing the Hidden Contradictions in the Bible (and Why We Don't Know about Them)* (New York: HarperOne, 2009), p. 218. For the same basic conclusion, see Froehlich, p. 2; *Handbook of Biblical Criticism*, s.v. "Hebrew Bible (HB)."

114   Ecumenical Council of Florence (1438-1445), *Eternal Word Television Network*, sess. 11, Bull of Union with Copts, https://www.ewtn.com/library/COUNCILS/FLORENCE.HTM; *The Catholic Encyclopedia*, s.v. "Canon of the Old Testament" http://www.newadvent.org/cathen/03267a.htm.; Law, p. 60.

115   *The Catholic Encyclopedia*, s.v. "African Synods" http://www.newadvent.org/cathen/01199a.htm (accessed 6 Jun. 2014); Law, pp. 125; *Mercer Dictionary of the Bible*, s.v. "Canon."

116   Eusebius, 6.25, p. 214 which shows the Letter of Jeremiah and it seems "the Maccabees"; see Law, pp. 123-4 for acceptance of others. Law is drawing on other works besides the list in Eusebius. Contra Law, Lim states that

"clearly" Origen *excludes* the Maccabees (pp. 39,191-2)—the issue revolves around whether Origen is saying "outside these" or "besides these" when he ends his list with the Maccabees. Per Eusebius, Origen also accepted the story of Susannah in Daniel (which is rejected by Protestants). See 6.31, p. 218. *The Catholic Encyclopedia*, s.v. "Canon of the Old Testament" http://www.newadvent.org/cathen/03267a.htm affirms Law's position that Origen "employs all the deuterocanonicals as Divine Scriptures."

117 Eusebius, 6.13, p. 203. Clement of Alexandria quotes Sirach as Scripture in *The Educator*, in *After the New Testament*, 2.2, 2.5, 2.77, pp. 391-2.

118 Law, p. 189 (footnote). Likewise, Rufinus (345-411) referred to the books as "Ecclesiastical" but not "Canonical." See Rufinus, *A Commentary on the Apostles Creed*, in *Nicene and Post-Nicene Fathers, Series II*, vol. 3, ed. Philip Schaff (Grand Rapids, MI: Christian Classics Ethereal Library, n.d.), nos. 37-38, pp. 1434-5 http://www.ccel.org/ccel/schaff/npnf203.pdf.

119 *The Westminster Dictionary of Theologians*, s.v. "Jerome; *The New International Dictionary of the Christian Church*, s.v. "Jerome"; *The Concise Oxford Dictionary of the Christian Church*, s.v. "Jerome, St"; Jerome, "Preface to Proverbs, Ecclesiastes, and Song of Psalms," *The Principal Works of St. Jerome*, in *Nicene and Post-Nicene Fathers, Series 2*, vol. 6, ed. Philip Schaff, trans. M.A. Freemantle (Grand Rapids, MI: Christian Classics Ethereal Library, n.d.), p. 1056 http://www.ccel.org/ccel/schaff/npnf206.pdf. However, *The Catholic Encyclopedia*, s.v. "St. Jerome" http://newadvent.org/cathen/08341a.htm (accessed 31 Dec. 2018) rather that the issue is unclear as does Michael Barber, "Loose Canons: The Development of the Old Testament (Part 2)," *The Sacred Page* (blog), 6 Mar. 2006, http://www.thesacredpage.com/2006/03/loose-canons-development-of-old_06.html (accessed 12 Nov. 2018).

120 Augustine of Hippo, *On Christian Doctrine*, in *Nicene and Post-Nicene Fathers, First Series*, vol. 2, ed. Philip Schaff, trans. James Shaw (Buffalo, NY: Christian Literature Publishing Co., 1887), 2.8.13, http://www.newadvent.org/fathers/12022.htm. Augustine cites Baruch 3:35-37 as the words of the prophet Jeremiah and notes: "Some attribute this testimony not to Jeremiah, but to his secretary, who was called Baruch; but it is more commonly ascribed to Jeremiah." See Augustine, *The City of God*, in *Nicene and Post-Nicene Fathers, First Series*, vol. 2, ed. Philip Schaff, trans. Marcus Dods (Buffalo, NY: Christian Literature Publishing Co., 1887), 18.33, http://www.newadvent.org/fathers/120118.htm. *The Jewish Encyclopedia*, s.v. "Baruch, Book of" notes that it was sometimes included with Jeremiah in canonical lists and that Athenagoras, Clement of Alexandria, and other early Christians regarded it as "the work of Jeremiah and as sacred

Scripture." For further discussion of the Apocrypha in the early Church, see Eusebius, 6.31, pp. 218-9; 7.25, pp. 214-6; 6.13, pp. 203-4. Origen refers to the book of Wisdom as Scripture in his Homily 3, *After the New Testament*, ed. Bart D. Ehrman, ch. 4, p. 371.

121 Augustine, *City of God*, 18.36, http://www.newadvent.org/fathers/120118.htm.

122 *The Catholic Encyclopedia*, s.v. "Theodore of Mopsuestia" http://www.newadvent.org/cathen/14571b.htm (accessed 27 May 2014) which suggests that he rejected both Ezra and Nehemiah as a single combined book of "Esdras." For explanation, see s.v. "Esdras" www.newadvent.org/cathen/05535a.htm. *Encyclopedia Britannica* 1911 ed., s.v. "Theodore of Mopsuestia" https://www.studylight.org/encyclopedias/bri/t/theodore-of-mopsuestia.html (accessed 25 Mar. 2019) states that he rejected Chronicles, Ezra, and Nehemiah and "esteemed very lightly" Job and the "Solomonic writings." *Westminster Dictionary of Theologians*, s.v. "Theodore of Mopsuestia" states that he relegated Ezra, Job, and Songs of Songs to "second level books" with lesser authority. *The New International Dictionary of the Christian Church* just notes that he rejected the canonicity of some OT and NT books without specifics.

123 Athanasius, Letter 39, *Nicene and Post-Nicene Fathers*, Series 2, vol. 4, ed. Philip Schaff, trans. R. Payne-Smith (Buffalo, NY: Christian Literature Publishing Co., 1892), nos. 4 and 7, http://www.newadvent.org/fathers/2806039.htm. Law also states that Athanasius accepted Baruch and the Letter of Jeremiah (p. 124).

124 Lim, p. 38; Eusebius, 4.26.13-14, p. 140; Law, p. 123.

125 The Canons of the Holy and August Apostles, *The Seven Ecumenical Councils of the Undivided Church*, can. 85, p. 851.

126 The Canons of the CCXVII Blessed Fathers who Assembled at Carthage, *The Seven Ecumenical Councils of the Undivided Church*, can. 24, pp. 650-1. The "Five Books of Solomon" includes Wisdom and Sirach.

127 The Muratorian Canon, in *After the New Testament*, Ehrman, ed., pp. 311-12.

128 See Mar Abd Yeshua, "Index of Biblical and Ecclesiastical Writings," in *The Nestorians and Their Rituals*, vol. 2, by George Percy Badger, Appendix A, Part First, pp. 361-2. Avail. at https://archive.org/details/TheNestoriansAndTheirRituals/page/n395.

129 Martin Luther, *Table Talk*, trans. William Hazlitt (Grand Rapids, MI: Christian Classics Ethereal Library, n.d.), ch. XXIV, p. 27, http://www.ccel.org/ccel/luther/tabletalk.pdf.

130 Jonathan R. Seiling, "Solae (Quae?) Scripturae: Anabaptists and the Apocrypha," *Mennonite Quarterly Review*, 80:1 (Jan. 2006): pp. 5-34. The article concludes that "the early Anabaptists generally held the Apocrypha to be equal to the rest of the Scripture." See also Estep, p. 195. *Global Anabaptist Mennonite Encyclopedia Online*, s.v. "Bible" http://gameo.org/index.php?title=Bible&oldid=107164 (accessed 26 Aug. 2016) notes: "Some Anabaptists seem to have given the Apocrypha almost equal authority with the canonical books."

131 Seiling, p. 22. For one example see Thieleman J. van Braught, *Martyrs Mirror*, 1660 ed., trans. Joseph Sohm (Grand Rapids, MI: Christian Classics Ethereal Library, n.d.), 2nd part, An Account of Tide. Holy Baptism, art. VIII, p. 703, www.ccel.org/ccel/vanbraght/mirror.html.

132 Seiling, pp. 14-15. He somewhat confusingly seems to regard certain books in the Apocrypha as "Scripture" but still not "canonical."

133 Bokser and Bokser, eds., *The Talmud*, pp. 9, 21.

134 *Jewish Encyclopedia*, s.v. "Karaites and Karaism" http://jewishencyclopedia.com/articles/9211-karaites-and-karaism; *The Karaite Korner*, n.d., http://www.karaite-korner.org/ (accessed 17 Jul. 2018).

135 Lim, pp. 15, 189-90.

136 *NRSV Notetaker's Bible: New Revised Standard Version with the Apocrypha* (Oxford: Oxford Univ. Press, 2009), p. vi. The name "Esdras" can be confusing as it has been used to refer to just Ezra or a combined Ezra-Nehemiah. 1 & 2 Esdras can thus mean Ezra and Nehemiah. 1 Esdras, now typically not referring to Ezra or Ezra-Nehemiah, can also be called "2 Esdras" in the Slavonic tradition and "3 Esdras" in the Western tradition. It's also referred to as 2 Ezra (Mastrantonis, p. 29). 2 Esdras is often called "4 Esdras" in the Western tradition.

137 Mastrantonis notes the book as "debatable" (p. 29). See also *NSRV Notetaker's Bible*, pp. v-vi which calls 4 Maccabees part of an "Appendix to the Greek Bible." *Mercer Dictionary of the Bible*, s.v. "Maccabees, Fourth" rather notes: "It has not been regarded as canonical by any Christian community, though it is highly regarded in Eastern Orthodoxy."

138 Philaret of Moscow, "The Longer Catechism of the Orthodox, Catholic, Eastern Church," *The Creeds of Christendom with a History and Critical Notes*, ed. Philip Schaff, trans. R. W. Blackmore, nos. 31-35, http://www.pravoslavieto.com/docs/eng/Orthodox_Catechism_of_Philaret.htm#ii.xv.iii.i.p41 (accessed 3 Jun. 2018). See also *OrthodoxWiki*, s.v. "Philaret (Drozdov) of Moscow," 22 Dec. 2012, https://orthodoxwiki.org/Philaret_(Drozdov)_of_Moscow (accessed 3 Jun. 2018).

139 Ware, p. 200. See also Leith, ed., *The Confession of Dositheus*, in *Creeds of the Churches*, Q. III, p. 508, which lists The Wisdom of Solomon, Judith, Tobit, "The History of the Dragon," "The History of Susanna," "The Maccabees," and "The Wisdom of Sirach" as "undoubtedly delivered" Scripture.

140 *The Catholic Encyclopedia*, s.v. "Canon of the Old Testament" http://www.newadvent.org/cathen/03267a.htm. It would probably be more accurate to say that they retain some of the fluidity in their canons that was present in the early church—rather than suggesting they are unconcerned.

141 Vazken Movsesian, *The Bible in the Armenian Church* (Burbank, CA: Western Diocese of the Armenian Church: Department of Youth Ministries, 2003), pp. 9-10, 13. Avail. at http://armenianchurchlibrary.com/files/BibleintheArmenianChurchMovsesian.pdf.

142 "The Bible," *The Ethiopian Orthodox Tewahedo Church Faith and Order*, n.d., http://www.ethiopianorthodox.org/english/canonical/books.html (accessed 17 Jul. 2018). See also Metzger, *The Canon of the New Testament*, p. 226; Alemayehu Desta, *Introduction to the Ethiopian Orthodox Tewahedo Faith* (Bloomington, IN: AuthorHouse, 2012), pp. 2-6.

143 Ethiopian Maccabees have differing content from the standard books of the Maccabees.

144 Leslau, pp. xxxi-viii; Kaplan, pp. 73-5.

145 As explained above, 2 Esdras is often called 4 Esdras in the Western tradition.

146 Samaritans are not technically Jews but rather a related Semitic people.

147 Tov notes that there was no "council" as such or even "evidence of an authoritative meeting" (p. 177). However, he does suggest some sort of school or court was there and also that they may have found the Song of Songs and Ecclesiastes to be canonical.

148 See *New American Bible*, Saint Joseph Medium Size ed. (New York: Catholic Book Publishing Co., 1992), footnote, p. 750. For an interesting discussion of the possible relationships between Wisdom and Romans, see Lim, pp. 169-72. For a list of potential/alleged NT references to the Apocrypha from a modern Roman Catholic apologist, see James Akin, "Deuterocanonical References in the New Testament," *JimmyAkin.com*, n.d., http://jimmyakin.com/deuterocanonical-references-in-the-new-testament (accessed 20 Nov. 2014).

149 Randall McCraw Helms, *The Bible Against Itself: Why the Bible Seems to Contradict Itself* (Altadena, CA: Millennium Press, 2006), p. 41.

150 Eusebius, 3.25.3-5, p. 91.

151 Thomas Henry Huxley, "Agnosticism," in *Agnosticism and Christianity and Other Essays* (Buffalo, NY: Prometheus Books, 1992), p. 153. The term "Apocrypha" typically refers to disputed OT books, but it appears that Huxley is referencing NT apocryphal books here. Even if his terminology is a bit off, the point still seems valid.

152 John Calvin, *Institutes of the Christian Religion*, trans. Henry Beveridge (Grand Rapids, MI: Christian Classics Ethereal Library, orig. pub. 1845), 1.7.2, p. 75, http://www.ccel.org/ccel/calvin/institutes.html. Calvin is specifically addressing here why the authority of the Church is not needed to choose which books are Scripture. In contrast, Augustine thought the authority of individual Catholic Churches was necessarily for properly assembling the Bible. See Augustine, *On Christian Doctrine*, 2.8.12, http://www.newadvent.org/fathers/12022.htm.

153 Gnostic Christianity, which became prominent in the 2nd c. CE, was a diverse collection of groups and ideas which presented a great challenge to early catholicism. Chief among their beliefs was the idea that salvation came through knowledge ("gnosis") of humanity's true nature and the divine spark within. See *The Concise Oxford Dictionary of the Christian Church*, s.v. "Gnosticism." It may have had pre-Christian origins (Pagels, p. xxx).

154 Pagels notes how Gnostics held that they had "the charismatic gift of direct inspiration through the Holy Spirit" (p. 41). See also pp. 11, 25, 38, etc. where it is clear that Gnostics believed that they were inspired by God.

155 Bart D. Ehrman, *Lost Scriptures: Books That Did Not Make It into The New Testament*, (New York: Oxford Univ. Press, 2003), pp. 19-20, 35, 52. Elaine Pagels dates the Gospel of Thomas c. 140 but notes that some of the traditions in it may be older (pp. xvi-ii). Generally speaking, it would seem clear that Gnostic Gospels are to be dated after the four Catholic ones. However, Gnostics would no doubt assert that direct inspiration made proximity in time to the historical Jesus irrelevant.

156 Pagels, pp. xxiii, 12-16, 22, 29. For an interesting compendium of such other Scriptures, see *The Other Bible*, ed. Willis Barnstone (San Francisco: HarperSanFrancisco, 1984).

157 See Ehrman, *Lost Scriptures*, pp. 9-18 for text from these gospels. Ehrman believes that these three texts were written in the 1st or 2nd c. Ehrman, ed., *After the New Testament*, pp. 134-5 for a discussions with selections from the Gospel of the Ebionites. The Gospel of the Ebionites may be a kind of harmony of the Synoptic gospels. See Bart D. Ehrman, *Lost Christianities: The Battle for Scripture and the Faiths We Never Knew* (Oxford: Oxford

Univ. Press, 2003), p. 12. Ehrman notes in *Lost Scriptures* that there were "several Gospels used by various groups of Jewish Christians in the early centuries of the church" (p. 8); and that the *Gospel of the Nazareans* was either based on the Gospel of Matthew or perhaps an original composition in Aramaic (p. 9).

158 Eusebius, 3.27.4, p. 93.

159 Irenaeus, *Against Heresies*, in *Ante Nicene Fathers*, vol. 1, ed. Alexander Roberts, et al., trans. Alexander Roberts and William Rambaut (Buffalo, NY: Christian Literature Publishing Co., 1885), 1.27.2, http://newadvent.org/fathers/0103127.htm. See also Bart D. Ehrman, *Misquoting Jesus: The Story Behind Who Changed the Bible and Why* (San Francisco: HarperSanFrancisco, 2005), pp. 34-5. Ehrman notes that Valentinus used only John and that Marcion used a form of Luke.

160 See Metzger, *The Canon of the New Testament* for an invaluable study on this general topic. He notes that "there were dozens of other writings that in certain parts of the Church enjoyed temporary canonicity" (p. 163).

161 While dates for the Gospels are imprecise and often vary, the *New American Bible*, Saint Joseph Medium Size ed. provides the following: Matthew (80?), Mark (after 70), Luke (80-90), John (90-100). See pp. 10, 69, 96, 144. The Gospel of the Nazareans may have been in the late 1st or early 2nd c. according to Ehrman, *Lost Scriptures*, pp. 9. See also note on Papyrus Egerton 2, p. 29.

162 David Laird Dungan, *A History of the Synoptic Problem: The Canon, the Text, the Composition, and the Interpretation of the Gospels* (New York: Doubleday, 1999), p. 16.

163 While there is some lack of precision in these terms, I use the term "Catholic" as follows: 1st until late 2nd c. "early catholic," late 2nd c. through the Great Schism of 1054 "Catholic," and then "Roman Catholic" and "Eastern Orthodox" after that. Things appear a bit more fluid until fathers like Tertullian, Hippolytus, and Irenaeus arrive on the scene—where it then seems like a capital "C" should be used. I also consider the Oriental Orthodox and the Assyrian Church of the East part of the larger "Catholic" tradition.

164 Metzger, *The Canon of the New Testament*, p. 263. Cf. González, vol.1, p. 62: "Since there was no approved list, different Gospels were read in different churches, and the same was true of other books."

165 See H. Chadwick, p. 22; *Mercer Dictionary of the Bible*, s.v. "Canon"; Dungan, p. 3. Dungan also notes that Epiphanius described how the Alogoi disputed John's Gospel and also posits that Ignatius of Antioch and Polycarp did not regard it as authoritative as they never quoted from

it (pp. 23-4). *The Concise Oxford Dictionary of the Christian Church*, s.v. "Alogoi" gives the Alogoi a date of c. 175 and notes that they rejected both John and Revelation (p. 16). González notes John "was somewhat slower in gaining universal acceptance" (vol. 1, p. 63).

166   Epiphanius, *The Panarion of Epiphanius, Books II & III (Sects 47-80, De Fide)*, trans. Frank Williams (New York: E.J. Brill, 1994), 51.4.3, p. 28. See 51.3.3 (p. 27) for their rejection of Revelation and the Gospel of John.

167   Dungan, pp. 23-5; *The Catholic Encyclopedia*, s.v. "Alogoi" http://www.newadvent.org/cathen/01331b.htm (accessed 6 Apr. 2016).

168   See Ehrman's introductory remarks in *After the New Testament*, pp. 98, 244, 296, 310-11. See also Ehrman, *Lost Christianities*, p. 210 and note 21, p. 277; Metzger, *The Canon of the New Testament*, p. 218.

169   Metzger, *The Canon of the New Testament*, pp. 187-8. For an early discussion of the status of the Shepherd of Hermas, see Eusebius, *Ecclesiastical History*, 3.3.6, p. 68 where it is called "disputed"; 3.25.4, p. 91 where it is called "spurious." See also Ehrman, *Misquoting Jesus*, p. 47.

170   Eusebius, *Ecclesiastical History*, 2.23.25, p. 62, 3.3.1-4, p. 67, 3.24-25, p. 91. See also Origen, *Commentary on John*, in *After the New Testament*, pp. 314-15; Ehrman, *Lost Christianities*, p. 242.

171   For the text of the letter, see Eusebius, 1.13.9, p. 30. Eusebius appears to regard this as genuine.

172   Cyril of Jerusalem, *The Works of St. Cyril of Jerusalem: Lenten Lectures (Catecheses)*, in *The Fathers of the Church: A New Translation*, vol. 61, ed. Bernard Peebles et al., trans. L. P. McCauley and A. A. Stephenson, (Washington, DC: Catholic Univ. of America: 1969), 4.36, p. 137. See also Metzger, *The Canon of the New Testament*, p. 210.

173   Metzger, *The Canon of the New Testament*, p. 212.

174   From the Iambics of St. Amphilochius the Bishop to Seleucus, on the Same Subject, *The Seven Ecumenical Councils of the Undivided Church*, p. 876; Metzger, *The Canon of the New Testament*, p. 314.

175   The Canons of the Holy and August Apostles, *The Seven Ecumenical Councils of the Undivided Church*, can. 85, p. 851. See also Metzger, *The Canon of the New Testament*, pp. 216, 313.

176   Metzger, *The Canon of the New Testament*, pp. 214-9.

177   Ibid., pp. 237-8; *The Catholic Encyclopedia*, s.v. "African Synods" http://www.newadvent.org/cathen/01199a.htm (accessed 6 Jun. 2014); s.v. "Canon of the New Testament" http://www.newadvent.org/cathen/03274a.htm (accessed 24 Mar. 2013); *Mercer Dictionary of the Bible*, s.v. "Canon"; Ehrman, General Introduction to *After the New Testament*, p. 5; Ehrman, *Lost Christianities*, p. 231.

178	See Metzger, *The Canon of the New Testament*, pp. 18, 151, 214-5, 219-20. Metzger also notes that for the Syrian Orthodox, the 22-book Peshitta is exclusively used in their lectionary and "for the settlement of doctrinal questions." However, some Syrian Orthodox clergy "occasionally preach sermons" from other books (pp. 219-20). See also introduction to Nestle-Aland's *Novum Testamentum Graece*, 27th ed. (Stuttgart, Germany: Deutsche Bibelgesellschaft, 1993), p. 66; *The Concise Oxford Dictionary of the Christian Church*, s.v. "Peshitta"; *Encyclopedia Britannica*, s.v. "Peshitta" http://www.britannica.com/EBchecked/topic/453385/Peshitta (accessed 26 Jun. 2014); Paul D. Younan, "History of the Peshitta," *Peshitta.org*, 1 Jun. 2000, http://www.peshitta.org/initial/peshitta.html (accessed 12 Aug. 2018).
179	*The Catholic Encyclopedia*, s.v. "Theodore of Mopsuestia" http://www.newadvent.org/cathen/05628b.htm (accessed 27 May 2014). Cf. *Encyclopedia Britannica* (1911), s.v. "Theodore of Mopsuestia," https://www.studylight.org/encyclopedias/bri/t/theodore-of-mopsuestia.html; Metzger, *The Canon of the New Testament*, pp. 215-6. Metzger seems to agree about Theodore but also remarks there is some uncertainty about 1 Peter and 1 John.
180	"St. Augustine: Did You Know …" *Christian History Institute*, n.d., https://www.christianhistoryinstitute.org/magazine/article/augustine-did-you-know/ (accessed 19 Dec. 2015).
181	*The Catholic Encyclopedia*, s.v. "Paulicians" http://www.ne"wadvent.org/cathen/11583b.htm (accessed 23 Jan. 2017); *The New International Dictionary of the Christian Church*, s.v. "Paulicians"; Norwich, p. 140.
182	John of Damascus, *An Exposition of the Orthodox Faith*, in *Nicene and Post-Nicene Fathers, Second Series*, vol. 9, ed. Philip Schaff and Henry Wace, trans. E.W. Watson and L. Pullan (Buffalo, NY: Christian Literature Publishing Co., 1899), IV.17, http://www.newadvent.org/fathers/33044.htm: (accessed 1 Apr. 2019): "the Canons of the holy apostles, by Clement." I understand this to mean that John is affirming the *Apostolic Canons* in their acceptance of 1 & 2 Clement (see Metzger, p. 313).
183	Metzger, *The Canon of the New Testament*, p. 224 (see footnote as well).
184	Metzger, *The Canon of the New Testament*, pp. 223-4. Although see Movsesian who suggests that Revelation became part of the canon in 419 (p. 9).
185	Ibid., p. 224.
186	There is no Revelation, 2nd Peter, 2nd and 3rd John, nor Jude here; however, Tatian's Diatesseron is found. See Mar Abd Yeshua, "Index of Biblical and Ecclesiastical Writings," in *The Nestorians and Their Rituals*, pp. 362-3.

Avail. at https://archive.org/details/TheNestoriansAndTheirRituals/page/n395.

187　*Mercer Dictionary of the Bible*, s.v. "Canon." See also Metzger, *The Canon of the New Testament*, pp. 240-1.

188　*The Catholic Encyclopedia*, s.v. "Canon of the New Testament," http://www.newadvent.org/cathen/03274a.htm (accessed 31 Mar. 2019) which notes that the "Coptic-Arabic Church include with the canonical Scriptures the Apostolic Constitutions and the Clementine Epistles" and that the "Armenians have one apocryphal letter *to* the Corinthians and two *from* the same." Cf. Metzger, *The Canon of the New Testament*, p. 225 which suggests that Coptic canonical lists have not been entirely clear on 1 & 2 Clement and p. 223 which mentions 3 Corinthians in an appendix of an 1805 Armenian Bible. Movsesian, p. 13 does not cite 3 Corinthians as a part of the Armenian canon.

189　Metzger, *The Canon of the New Testament*, pp. 226-7; Ehrman, *Lost Christianities*, p. 231. Cf. Desta, pp. 6-8. "The Bible," *The Ethiopian Orthodox Tewahedo Church Faith and Order*, 2003, http://www.ethiopianorthodox.org/english/canonical/books.html (accessed 23 May 2014).

190　Metzger, *The Canon of the New Testament*, pp. 241-5; *Mercer Dictionary of the Bible*, s.v. "Canon"; Dungan, pp. 177-8. See also Martin Luther, Preface to the Revelation of Saint John, in *Works of Martin Luther—Prefaces to the Books of the Bible*, 1522, http://www.godrules.net/library/luther/NEW1luther_f8.htm (accessed 12 Aug. 2018).

191　Seiling, p. 14. Cf. *Mercer Dictionary of the Bible*, s.v. "Canon" which affirms this structure but notes that he "doubted the value of Revelation." See also Metzger, *The Canon of the New Testament*, p. 241.

192　See *Mercer Dictionary of the Bible*, s.v. "Peter, Letters of"; *The Concise Oxford Dictionary of the Christian Church*, s.v. "Peter, Epistles of"; Introduction in the *New American Bible*, p. 369. Ehrman singles out 2 Peter as being judged as pseudonymous by most scholars in general, *Lost Scriptures*, p. 4.

193　See Ehrman, *Lost Christianities*, pp. 10-11, 235. Neill and Wright note that the Pauline letters "generally agreed to be authentic" are 1 Thess., Gal., Rom., 1 & 2 Cor., Phil., and Philemon. See Stephen Neill and Tom Wright, *The Interpretation of the New Testament: 1861-1986*, 2nd ed. (Oxford: Oxford Univ. Press, 1988), p. 362. Soulen and Soulen cite the ones most frequently questioned books as 2 Thess., Col., Eph., 1 & 2 Tim., and Titus (*Handbook of Biblical Criticism*, s.v. "Deuteropauline").

194　See Dungan, p. 350; Craig Evans, "Directions: Doubting Thomas's Gospel," *Christianity Today*, 15 Jun. 1998 https://www.christianitoday.

	com/ct/1998/june15/8t7053.html (accessed 11 May 2016). Evans notes that the Jesus Seminar has promoted the value of the Gospel of Thomas as similar to that of Matt., Mark, Luke, and John.
195	Metzger, *The Canon of the New Testament*, p. 271.
196	Ware, p. 202; cf. Mastrantonis, p. 4: "The Church as a whole is infallible; that is, it is governed by the Holy Spirit to prevent the Church from formulating false teachings" (p. 4; cf. p. 19).
197	Michael Walsh, ed., *Butler's Lives of the Saints*, concise and rev. ed. (New York: HarperSanFrancisco, 1991), p. 127.
198	See Julian of Norwich, *Revelations of Divine Love*.
199	Estep, p. 171. His followers are apparently known as Davidians or Davidjorists. See also *Global Anabaptist Mennonite Encyclopedia Online*, s.v. David Joris https://gameo.org/index.php?title=David_Joris_(ca._1501-1556) (accessed 22 Jan. 2019).
200	González, vol. 2, p. 197.
201	Frank Mead and Samuel Hill, *Handbook of Denominations in the United States* (Nashville: Abingdon Press, 1995), pp. 281-3.
202	González, vol. 2, p. 203.
203	Pope Pius X, *Tribus Circiter*, Libreria Editrice Vaticana, no. 11 http://w2.vatican.va/content/pius-x/en/encyclicals/documents/hf_p-x_enc_05041906_tribus-circiter.html (accessed 23 May 2016); Mead and Hill, pp. 218-19.
204	Maureen Orth, "The World's Most Powerful Woman," *National Geographic* (Dec. 2015): pp. 40-1.
205	"The Testimony of Three Witnesses" and "The Testimony of Eight Witnesses," in *The Book of Mormon* (Salt Lake City, UT: The Church of Jesus Christ of Latter-Day Saints, 1989), 2nd page.
206	"Introduction," in *The Book of Mormon*, 1st page.
207	González, vol. 2, p. 258.
208	Eyre, "The Church of Jesus Christ of Latter-day Saints," in *How Different Religions View Death and Afterlife*, pp. 91-2; Mead and Hill, p. 166.
209	Mead and Hill, pp. 169-70. For other examples of Mormon scriptural and revelatory diversity, see Steven L. Shields, foreword to *The Scattering of the Saints: Schism within Mormonism*, ed. Newell G. Bringhurst and John C. Hamer (Independence, MO: John Whitmore Books, 2007), p. ix. The main Mormon denomination no longer holds to polygamy either.
210	Bonner, p. 159; González, vol. 1, p. 208.
211	Parrinder, ed., *World Religions*, p.189; Bonner, pp. 58, 159, 161. *The Catholic Encyclopedia*, s.v. "Manichaeism" http://www.newadvent.org/cathen/0951a.htm (accessed 2 May 2017) notes that Mani rejected the book of Acts

and that Manichaeans accepted the Gospel of Thomas, the Shepherd of Hermas, and the Teaching of Addas.

212 For the wording in the quotation, see *The Koran*, Sura 32:1-2, p. 187. Traditionally, Muslims say that the Qur'an (or Koran) is only the Word of God when in Arabic. Al-Ghazali notes "our infallible teacher is Muhammad" (p. 44).

213 Malise Ruthven, *Islam: A Very Short Introduction* (Oxford: Oxford Univ. Press, 1997),, pp. 20-21, 29, 76; Bloom and Blair, pp. 45, 55.

214 *The Bhagavad-Gita: Krishna's Counsel in Time of War*, trans. Barbara Stoler Miller, Bantam Classic reissue ed. (New York: Bantam Dell, 2004), 9.23, p. 88; 12.3, p. 109. See also Parrinder, ed., *World Religions*, p. 236; Shaunaka Rishi Das, "Jesus in Hinduism," *BBC*, 24 Mar. 2009, http://www.bbc.co.uk/religion/religions/hinduism/beliefs/jesus_1.shtml (accessed 5 Jun. 2016) for Jesus Christ in Hindu devotions.

215 John Hatcher, "Baha'i Faith," in *How Different Religions View Death and Afterlife*, pp. 15, 29; William S. Hatcher and J. Douglas Martin, *The Baha'i Faith: The Emerging Global Religion* (New York: Harper and Row, 1989), pp. 2-3, 82, 84, 119. See also "Writings of Bahá'u'lláh," *Bahá'í Reference Library*, n.d., https://www.bahai.org/library/authoritative-texts/bahaullah/ (accessed 29 Sep. 2019).

216 As quoted in George Townshend, ed., *The Glad Tidings of Bahá'u'lláh: Being Extracts from the Sacred Writings of the Bahá'ís*, rev. ed. (Oxford: George Ronald, 1975), p. 76. For further discussion of Baha'i Scripture and prophecy fulfillment, see pp. 4, 67, 70-77, etc.

217 For example see Herman Ridderbos, *Redemptive History and the New Testament Canon of Scripture* (Phillipsburg, NJ: Presbyterian and Reformed, 1988), pp. 8-11, 47. Ridderbos explains that (1) the Bible attests to itself, (2) the Holy Spirit witnesses about the truth of Scripture to the hearts of individual believers, and (3) no external factors can ultimately be used to verify its authenticity. While an attempt to avoid human subjectivity and fallibility, there is no way to resolve conflicting perceptions of the Holy Spirit's leadings within this framework (even if its questionable assumptions are accepted).

218 See John Calvin, *Institutes of the Christian Religion*. Among other expressions, Calvin describes humanity as filled with "injustice, vileness, folly, and impurity," "naturally prone to hypocrisy" (1.1.2, pp. 44-5) and "rottenness and a worm" (1.1.3, p. 46). Calvin also describes how "the depravity of the human mind lead[s] it away from the proper course of investigation" (1.2.2, p. 48), how there is "an immense flood of error with which the world is overflowed" (1.5.12, p. 66), and how man is generally "dull and

blind in heavenly mysteries" (1.5.12, p. 67). Sometimes this issue is referred to as the "noetic" effects of sin on the intellect.

219 The inspiration for this title came from John 10:35 in the KJV, which notes that "the scripture cannot be broken." See also ESV and RSV. Although in context the phrase suggests that the Scripture is unalterable in another sense, I think that the concept transfers over to the issue of textual criticism as well.

220 Ware, p. 200. See also Mastrantonis, p. 3. Per Lim, Philo also considered the Septuagint translation to be divinely inspired (p. 82).

221 Bruce Metzger, *The Text of the New Testament: Its Transmission, Corruption, and Restoration*, 2nd ed. (New York: Oxford Univ. Press, 1968), p. 246.

222 This is easily confirmed by looking at the textual apparatus of the Greek NT. See any page of the text of Nestle-Aland's *Novum Testamentum Graece* (Stuttgart, Germany: Deutsche Bibelgesellschaft, 1993) and you will note the variants at the bottom of the page. Ehrman notes that scholars generally hold that there are between 200,000-400,000 variants in the NT textual tradition (*Misquoting Jesus*, p. 89). Tov notes that there are more variants in the OT than the New (p. 342)—an unsurprising fact considering the different lengths. He also notes, for example, that scholars have traditionally noted 6,000 differences in the Masoretic and Samaritan Pentatuechs—but that he puts the total at 7,000 (footnote 126, p. 79).

223 Tov, p. 167 notes that sometimes due to "compositional stages" of development, "the textual evidence does not point to a single 'original' text, but a series of subsequent authoritative texts produced by the same or different authors. Each of these stages may be considered a type of original text" (p. 167).

224 Ehrman, *Misquoting Jesus*, p. 208; Tov, p. 22.

225 John Calvin, *Commentary on John*, vol. 1, trans. William Pringle (Grand Rapids, MI: Christian Classics Ethereal Library, org. pub. 1847), 8:3, p. 255, http://www.ccel.org/ccel/calvin/calcom34.pdf.

226 González, vol. 2, p. 176.

227 As quoted in Daniel C. Matt, *The Essential Kabbalah: The Heart of Jewish Mysticism* (Edison, NJ: Castle Books, 1997), p. 146. See source on p. 213.

228 As quoted in The Syriac/Aramaic/Assyrian Language, *Nestorian.org*, n.d., http://www.nestorian.org/the_syriac-aramaic-assyrian_language.html (accessed 16 Aug. 2018). Comments date from 5 Apr. 1957. The quotation is from Mar Eshai Shimum, a "Catholicos Patriarch of the East." This is also quoted by Paul D. Younan, History of the Peshitta, *Peshitta.org*, n.d., http://www.peshitta.org/ (accessed 16 Aug. 2018). A biography of Shimum

is also found at this same website: "Biography of His Holiness, The Assyrian Martyr, The Late Mar Eshai Shimum, XXIII."

229 Augustine, *On Christian Doctrine*, 2.11.16, http://www.newadvent.org/fathers/12022.htm.

230 H. Chadwick, p. 65, Law, p. 161; González, vol. 1, p. 204. *The Catholic Encyclopedia*, s.v. "Versions of the Bible" http://www.newadvent.org/cathen/15367a.htm (accessed 1 Jun. 2014).

231 González, vol. 2, p. 176.

232 Dogmatic Constitution on the Catholic Faith, Decrees of the First Vatican Council, 24 Apr. 1870, sess. 3, ch.2, no. 6. Avail. at http://www.papalencyclicals.net/Councils/ecum20.htm (accessed 29 Oct. 2013).

233 "Why the King James Version Bible is the Only Word of God," *Use KJV Only Ministries*, 2008, http://www.usekjvonly.com/tracts/Tracts-Web/kjvtractmain.html (accessed 13 Sep. 2013).

234 Augustine, *City of God*, 15.23, http://www.newadvent.org/fathers/120115.htm. See also reference in Law, p. 151; Augustine, *City of God*, 18.43, http://www.newadvent.org/fathers/120118.htm; Augustine, On *Christian Doctrine*, 2.15.22 and 4.7.15, http://www.newadvent.org/fathers/12022.htm; González, vol. 1., p. 12.

235 When citing the OT, NT authors appear to cite from Septuagint readings, Masoretic readings, and other readings that would seem to belong to neither textual tradition (Lim, pp. 157, 165-6). See also Law, p. 4.

236 Law, p. 2.

237 Notes on the Additions to Daniel can be found in the chart below. There are also six additions to Esther involving 107 verses that are included in the Roman Catholic, Greek Orthodox, Oriental Orthodox, and Assyrian Church of the East canons. The NAB notes that the additions are "equally inspired with the rest of the book" (p. 501). Law notes that the Septuagint and the "Alpha Text" both have additions but it is hard to tell which is shorter (p. 57) and that the additions add 107 verses to 194 verses already there (p. 62). Tov states that the additions to Esther make it 50% longer and that it then conforms to rest of Scripture by mentioning God (pp. 317, 243).

238 See further explanation in the chart below.

239 See *Handbook of Biblical Criticism*, s.v. "Septuagint" and Law, pp. 86, 146.

240 There have been varying opinions by scholars on this point. For one discussion see *Handbook of Biblical Criticism*, s.v. "Synoptic Problem (The)."

241 Neill and Wright, p. 127. (Note also p. 116: "the priority of Mark is generally accepted.")

242 See *Handbook of Biblical Criticism*, s.v. "Agrapha (sg. Agraphon)" which notes that "it is known that Jesus' teachings were first passed down orally."

243 See Neill and Wright, pp. 66-7; Nestle-Aland, *Novum Testamentum Graece*, pp. 52-7; Ehrman, *Misquoting Jesus*, pp. 45-69.

244 Norman Geisler, "A Note on the Percent of Accuracy in the New Testament Text," *normangeisler.com*, 2014, http://www.normgeisler.com/articles/Bible/Reliability/NoteOnPercentAccuracyOfNT.htm (accessed 14 Dec. 2014). Cf. Dungan for his assessment that 95% of Greek NT is in a reliable form (p. 300).

245 See *Handbook of Biblical Criticism*, s.v. "Oral Tradition" and s.v. "Form Criticism" which postulates that the OT "in many instances, has hundreds of years of oral tradition behind it."

246 Often called "autographs."

247 As noted, the Old Testament is a more difficult discussion due to its age and apparent periods of oral transmission.

248 Ehrman, *Misquoting Jesus*, p. 260.

249 I expect that if I personally had different editions of these translations that the footnotes on the texts could be different or more extensive. I have utilized translations that I own.

250 Cf. Metzger, The Text of *the New Testament*, pp. 226-9.

251 See Noah Feit, "A Snake Killed His Father in Church. Pastor Has also Been Bitten, New Documentary Shows," Lexington Herald Leader, 19 Aug. 2018, https://www.kentucky.com/news/nation-world/national/article216995475.html (accessed 15 Feb. 2019); "Kentucky Man Dies from Snake Bite at Church Service," CBS News, 28 Jul. 2015, https://www.cbsnews.com/amp/news/kentucky-man-dies-from-snake-bite-at-church-service/ (accessed 15 Feb. 2019).

252 Ehrman holds that some scribes probably took out Luke 23:34 because they did not like the implication that the Jews might be forgiven (Jesus, Interrupted, p. 188).

253 New American Bible, St. Joseph Medium Size ed, p.157, *footnote on John 7:53-8:11*. Metzger notes: "the case against it being of Johannine authorship appears to be conclusive" (*The Text of the New Testament*, p. 224).

254 Dungan, p. 93.

255 New American Bible, St. Joseph Medium *Size ed.*, p. 260.

256 See Ehrman, Misquoting Jesus, pp.183ff. For a short discussion of the different views regarding the authorship of the Pastorals, see New American Bible, St. Joseph Medium Size ed., pp. 321-2. The NAB notes that "Most scholars are convinced Paul could not have been responsible for the vocabulary and style, the concept of church organization, or the theo-

logical expressions found in these letters." For a key text regarding women in *the Pastorals, see* 1 Tim. 2:11-12. Outside the Pastorals, Eph. 5:22-24 is another key text regarding the submission of women. Neill and Wright also note that the Pauline letters do not include the pastorals (p. 362).

257   New World Encyclopedia, s.v. "*Bel and the Dragon*" http://www.newworldencyclopedia.org/entry/Bel_and_the_Dragon; "Deuterocanonical Books," St. Mary *and St. Antonious Coptic Church, 2009,* http://wiscopts.net/spiritual-library/dogma/145 (accessed 14 Dec. 2014).

258   The footnote for the Prayer states: "The church has always regarded them as part of the canonical Scriptures (NAB, p. 1025); remarks on chs. 13 and 14 include that "the church has always included them among the inspired writings" (NAB, p. 1039).

259   See Tov, pp. 21, 137, 287-8. Tov holds that the Septuagint is an older version of the text. This position appears to be bolstered by Qumran finds. Tov also notes the following: "Some biblical books, such as Jeremiah, reached a final state more than once, not just in [the Masoretic Hebrew text] but also at an earlier stage, as attested by some textual evidence" (p. 168). See also Mercer Dictionary of the Bible, s.v. "Jeremiah, Book of" which notes that the Hebrew text "is about 2,700 words longer" and the "best explanation for these variations is that two different Hebrew texts of Jeremiah existed in the last centuries B.C.E." Law agrees with and cites Tov regarding the "1/6" shorter text (pp. 28-9). Evangelical author Michael F. Bird describes this problem in "Inerrancy is Not Necessary for Evangelicalism outside the USA," in Five Views on Biblical Inerrancy, J. Merrick and Stephen M. Garrett, eds. (Grand Rapids, MI: Zondervan, 2013), p. 152.

260   NAB, p. 933.

261   Martin Luther, *Sermons on the Gospel of St. John Chapters 1-4, Luther's Works,* ed. Jaroslav Pelikan, vol. 22 (Saint Louis: Concordia, 1957), p. 160. Cf. Dungan, p. 180.

262   As quoted in Alec R. Vidler, *The Church in an Age of Revolution: 1789 to the Present Day* (New York: Penguin Books, 1990), p. 130.

263   Norman Geisler and Thomas Howe, *When Critics Ask: A Popular Handbook on Bible Difficulties* (Grand Rapids, MI: Baker Books, 1997), p. 11 (their italics).

264   Unlike Augustine, many stricter Protestant inerrantists discount allegorical approaches to biblical texts. See John R. Franke, "Response to Albert Mohler, Jr.," in *Five Views on Biblical Inerrancy,* p. 78. In this same volume, Michael F. Bird (p. 154) and Peter Enns (p. 181) also provide some discussion on whether its proper to call Augustine an "inerrantist." E.g.,

Augustine, *On Christian Doctrine*, 3.10.14, http://www.newadvent.org/fathers/12023.htm: "Whatever there is in the word of God that cannot, when taken literally, be referred either to purity of life or soundness of doctrine, you may set down as figurative."

265   Augustine of Hippo, *Reply to Faustus the Manichaean (Contra Faustum)*, in *Nicene and Post-Nicene Fathers, First Series*, vol. 4, ed. Philip Schaff, trans. Richard Stothert (Buffalo, NY: Christian Literature Publishing Co., 1887), 11.5, http://www.newadvent.org/fathers/140611.htm. This passage is also quoted by Geisler and Howe. Dungan discusses this dynamic in Augustine's approach to biblical interpretation—noting numerous principles and rules that allowed him to overcome apparent errors (pp. 118-39). For a strong contemporary view about the "allowability" of errors, see R. Albert Mohler, Jr., "When the Bible Speaks, God Speaks: The Classic Doctrine of Biblical Inerrancy," *Five Views on Biblical Inerrancy*, p. 51: "I do not allow *any* line of evidence from outside the Bible to nullify to the slightest degree the truthfulness of any text in all that the text asserts and claims." For a similar view from the Eastern Orthodox tradition, see St. Peter of Damaskos, *A Treasury of Divine Knowledge*, in *The Philokalia: The Complete Text*, vol. 3, ed. and trans. G.E.H. Palmer et al. (New Tork: Farrar, Straus and Giroux, 1984), pp. 144-45. For a pre-Vatican II Roman Catholic view, see Leo XIII, *Providentissimus Deus: On the Study of Holy Scripture*, in *Papal Encyclicals Online*, orig. pub. 18 Nov. 1893, no. 14, http://www.papalencyclicals.net/Leo13/l13provi.htm (accessed 23 Jun. 2014).

266   Peter Enns, "Inerrancy, However Defined, Does Not Describe What the Bible Does," in *Five Views on Biblical Inerrancy*, p. 114. See also p. 62 in the same volume where Enns notes that being unwilling to doubt a particular position on the Bible in the face of compelling evidence amounts to "an unhealthy and unrealistic assessment of one's own abilities" to make spiritual discernments.

267   Robert Burton, "The Certainty Epidemic," *Salon*, 29 Feb. 2008, https://www.salon.com/2008/02/29/certainty/ (accessed 24 Jun. 2018). See also a similar quotation and discussion in John Loftus, *Why I Became an Atheist: A Former Preacher Rejects Christianity* (Amherst, NY: Prometheus Books, 2012), p. 198, Kindle. Perhaps one should avoid feeling too certain about this conclusion though! Cf. Kathryn Schulz, *Being Wrong: Adventures in the Margin of Error* (New York: Ecco/HarperCollins, 2011), p. 71. However, emotions interestingly appear integral to the reasoning process. See William R. Murray, *Reason and Reverence: Religious Humanism for the 21st Century* (Boston: Skinner House Books, 2007), pp. 103-5.

268   John Calvin as quoted in Dungan, p. 182. Cf. John Calvin, *Commentary on Matthew, Mark, Luke*, vol. 1, trans. William Pringle (Grand Rapids, MI: Christian Classics Ethereal Library, orig. pub. 1845), Matt. 1:1, p. 123, http://www.ccel.org/ccel/calvin/calcom31.html. Calvin appears to ascribe "perfect agreement" among the Gospels here, but also notes lack of agreement in order of events in Matt. 4:18, p. 212 (cf. Matt. 4:5, p. 194). Evangelical author Michael F. Bird notes that Calvin is "much in the same ballpark" as modern American inerrantists who follow the Chicago Statement on Biblical Inerrancy ("Inerrancy Is Not Necessary for Evangelicalism Outside the USA," in *Five View on Biblical Inerrancy*, p. 154).

269   Sources used in this meditation included the following: Kurt Aland, ed., *Synopsis of the Four Gospels*, rev. English ed. (New York?: United Bible Societies, 1985); John W. Marshall, ed., *The Five Gospel Parallels*, 1996-2001, Dept. for the Study of Religion, University of Toronto, http://sites.utoronto.ca/religion/synopsis/ (accessed 7 Mar. 2016); Ehrman, *Misquoting Jesus*; Helms, *The Bible Against Itself*; *NIV Study Bible*; Geisler and Howe, *When Critics Ask*; Kenneth Daniels, *Why I Believed: Reflections of a Former Missionary* (Duncanville, TX: self-published, 2009); *New American Bible*, Saint Joseph Medium Size ed.; Bruce M. Metzger and Roland E. Murphy, eds., *The New Oxford Annotated Bible with the Apocrypha* (New York: Oxford Univ. Press, 1991); Donald Morgan, "Bible Inconsistencies – Bible Contradictions?" *Internet Infidels*, n.d., http://www.infidels.org/library/modern/donald_morgan/inconsistencies.html (accessed Apr. 2016); Steve Wells, *The Skeptic's Annotated Bible*, 1999-2016, http://skepticsannotatedbible.com/index.htm (accessed Apr. 2016); Matt Slick, "Bible Difficulties," *Christian Apologetics and Research Ministry*, n.d., https://carm.org/bible-difficulties (accessed Apr. 2016); NonStampCollector, "Quiz Show (Bible Contradictions)," YouTube video 9:52, posted 26 Apr. 2010, https://www.youtube.com/watch?v=RB3g6mXLEKk (accessed Apr. 2016).

270   The *NIV Study Bible* suggests that the resolution here is that God was not seen "in the fullness of his glory" when he was seen (p. 122, footnote on Exod. 24:10). From my perspective, this is not a satisfactory resolution—but rather an example of how imaginative and speculative reasoning can always provide speculative (if not probable) answers. This further note from the *NIV Study Bible* seems to point out the problems more than solve them: "Sometimes in the OT people are said to have seen God (e.g., Ex 24:9-11). But we are also told that no one can see God and live (Ex 33:20). Therefore, since no human being can see God as he really is, those who saw God saw him in a form he took on himself temporarily for the occasion" (pp. 1593-4, footnote on Jn 1:18).

271 *The New Oxford Annotated Bible* offers this explanation: "God's change of mind displays consistency of purpose, unlike human beings who manifest deceit and caprice." See *The New Oxford Annotated Bible*, p. 199, note on Num. 23:19. A question lingers—would a Perfect Being with "consistency of purpose" and who knew the future with certainty ever have the need to change his mind?

272 *The New Oxford Annotated Bible* notes regarding Ps. 115:17: "In early Israel it was believed that the dead in Sheol (*silence*) were separated from God (88.5-6)" (p. 775). Ben Zion Bokser notes in his introduction to The Tractate Sanhedrin in *The Talmud: Selected Writings*, "There is no explicit reference in the Bible to the resurrection of the dead and there were interpretations of Judaism that did not accept it. ... Through an ingenious interpretation of certain texts this teaching was read into the Bible" (p. 199).

273 The *NIV Study Bible* wrestles at length with this idea noting in a footnote on Ps. 6:4-5 that "resurrection was not yet part of the [the Israelite] communal experience with God" and "just how they viewed the condition of the godly dead is not clear" (p. 791). The NAB footnote on Ps. 6:6 notes regarding the phrase "For who among the dead remembers you?": "A motive for God to preserve the psalmist from death; in the shadowy world of the dead no one offers you praise. Sheol is the biblical term for the underworld where the insubstantial souls of dead human beings dwelt" (p. 606). See also *Jewish Encyclopedia*, s.v. "Sheol" http://jewishencyclopedia.com/articles/13563-sheol (accessed 1 Oct. 2018).

274 See Helms, p. 42.

275 The *NIV Study Bible* attempts to resolve the difficulty by asserting that "Although Scripture is clear that God does not tempt anyone to sin (Jas. 1:13-15), it is also clear that man's—and Satan's—evil acts are under God's sovereign control" (p. 461, footnote on 2 Sam. 24:1). The NAB rather notes on 1 Chron. 21:1 that it is due to a "changed theological outlook ... when evil could no longer be attributed directly to God" (p. 400). *The New Oxford Annotated Bible* seeks to explain the discrepancy by noting that "Satan" here is actually "the *satan*"—or an "adversary" or "accuser" that "was associated with evil and misfortune, but not as an enemy of God" (p. 526, footnote on 1 Chron. 21:1-22:1). The differing ways that such discrepancies are addressed seem to underscore the reality that potential resolutions of the problem are tenuous.

276 The *NIV Study Bible* notes: "According to 1 Sam 21:1, Ahimelech, Abiathar's father, was then high priest" (p. 1497). See also NAB, p. 73; *New Oxford Annotated Bible*, p. 51; Ehrman, *Misquoting Jesus*, p. 9.

277 This apparent discrepancy is often explained through the concept of "telescoping" where names are omitted. The *NIV Study Bible* notes: "Unimportant names are left out in order to relate an individual to a prominent ancestor, or possibly to achieve the desired number of names in the genealogy." (p. 581). The NAB notes that "Matthew is concerned with fourteen generations, probably because fourteen is the numerical value of the Hebrew letters forming the name of David" (footnote on Mt 1:17, p. 11). The NAB also notes another apparent problem here in that the last section only has 13 generations—which could be due to counting Jesus twice or a scribal error. *The New Oxford Annotated Bible* likewise notes that omitting names "was quite consistent with Jewish practice in forming genealogies" (note on Matt. 1, p. 2, NT). This may well be the case, but leaving out names when asserting significance in the number of generations appears to make the theological point invalid. So, it would seem probable that Matthew either made a mistake about the number of generations, or made an invalid theological point about the number of generations—or both.

278 *The NIV Study Bible* somewhat surprisingly remarks that "To emphasize a certain point the Gospel writers often bring various events together, not intending to give chronological sequence" (p. 1544, footnote on Luke 4:2). This seems to be an oblique admission of a chronological error. See also Calvin, *Commentary on Matthew, Mark, Luke*, Matt. 4:5, p. 194 who notes that "it was not the intention of the Evangelists to arrange" events chronologically.

279 Although the texts do not indicate this, The *NIV Study Bible* posits in a footnote on John 19:17 that "Somewhere along the way Simon of Cyrene took Jesus' cross (Mark 15:21), probably because Jesus was weakened by the flogging" (p. 1634). *The New Oxford Annotated Bible* makes a similar comment that Jesus carried the cross "*By himself*, until relieved by Simon of Cyrene" (footnote on John 19:17, p. 155, NT). But the text of John mentions nothing about Simon of Cyrene or anyone else helping but simply states that Jesus was "Carrying his own cross" (NIV) or "carrying the cross by himself" (NRSV) or "carrying the cross himself" (NAB) or "bearing his own cross" (NASB). The Greek eautō is rendered "for himself" by Max Zerwick and Mary Grosvenor, *A Grammatical Analysis of the Greek New Testament*, 5th ed. (Rome: Editrice Pontificio Istituto Biblico, 1996), p. 341. The NAB seems to have a more satisfying explanation about this issue that it is simply "a different picture from that of the synoptics, especially Lk 23, 26, where Simon of Cyrene is made to carry the cross, walking

behind Jesus. In John's theology, Jesus remained in complete control and master of his destiny (cf Jn 10, 18)" (p. 174, footnote on John 19:17).

280 See Ehrman, *Misquoting Jesus*, p. 10.

281 *The NIV Study Bible* attempts to resolve the problem by stating in the footnote that their translation of Matt. 28:2 as "There was a violent earthquake" should be understood as having a "sense of 'Now there had been.'" That the NIV itself does not translate the words in this manner should be cause for suspicion. Furthermore, no explanation is given why this understanding is preferable except for recourse to the other gospels (p. 1489, footnote on Mt 28:2). The NAB translates v. 2 "And behold [kai idou], there was a great earthquake ...." The phrase "kai idou"—meaning "and behold"—is not included in the NIV rendering. The NIV stance in the footnote thus appears to be a harmonization against the textual evidence—especially as v. 4 shows that the guards are afraid and v. 5 has the angel speaking to the women.

282 *The New Oxford Annotated Bible* acknowledges the discrepancy noting that "the sequence of events cannot be worked out. Each account is a separate summary of early Christian testimony to the fact of Jesus' resurrection" (footnote on Mt 28:8, p. 45, NT).

283 I find this explanation by Michael Shermer helpful: "Smart people ... are better able to give intellectual reasons justifying their beliefs that they arrived at for nonintellectual reasons" (Shermer, *Why People Believe Weird Things*, p. 299; see also pp. 273-313).

284 Schulz, pp. 293-4.

285 Rom. 4:3-8 was the inspiration for the wording of this title. Cf. James 2:21-24, where the same story of Abraham seems to make an opposing point about the relationship of faith and works.

286 *The Sayings of the Desert Fathers: The Alphabetical Collection*, trans. Benedicta Ward, rev. ed. (Kalamazoo, MI: Cistercian Publications, 1984), no. 17 from Abba Anthony, p. 4.

287 Tertullian, *Prescription of the Heretics*, in *After the New Testament*, ch.16, p. 214.

288 *American Heritage Dictionary*, Second College ed., s.v. "ambiguous."

289 According to *Wycliffe Bible Translators*, there are currently over 1,500 languages that have a NT translation and over 650 languages have a translation of the full Bible. See "Why Bible Translation," *Wycliffe.org*, n.d., https://www.wycliffe.org/about/why (accessed 13 Nov. 2014).

290 As quoted in William J. Bouwsma, *John Calvin: A Sixteenth Century Portrait* (New York: Oxford University Press, 1988), p. 100. See John Calvin, *Commentary on Genesis*, vol. 1, trans. John King (Grand Rapids, MI:

Christian Classics Ethereal Library, orig. pub. 1847), 2:8, p. 70 https://www.ccel.org/ccel/calvin/calcom01.pdf.

291 See Froehlich, pp. 5-8. See also "Allegorical Interpretation," *The Jewish Encyclopedia*, s.v. "Allegorical interpretation" http://www.jewishencyclopedia.com/articles/1256-allegorical-interpretation (accessed 17 Nov. 2014); *The Penguin Dictionary of Religions*, s.v. "Conservative Judaism"; Parrinder, ed., *World Religions*, pp. 385-419; Mead and Hill, pp. 160-5.

292 Maimonides, *The Guide of the Perplexed*, ed. Julius Guttman, trans. Chaim Rabin, abridged ed. (Indianapolis: Hackett Pub. Co., 1995), 2.25, p. 115.

293 Matt, pp. 4-5; 7-11; *The Penguin Dictionary of Religions*, s.v. "Kabbalah"; *The New International Dictionary of the Christian Church*, s.v. "Kaballah."

294 These three passages are noted as uses of allegory in *The Handbook of Biblical Criticism*, s.v. "Allegory." *The New International Dictionary of the Christian Church*, s.v. "Allegory" cites both Gal. 4 and 1 Cor. 10.

295 See *The Concise Oxford Dictionary of the Christian Church*, s.v. "Alexandrian theology" and s.v. "Antiochene theology." See also *The New International Dictionary of the Christian Church*, s.v. "Alexandrian Theology." Here, the Alexandrian approach is deemed to have reached its "highest peak of influence" with Origen; see also s.v. "Antiochene Theology" in the same volume. For Origen's views see Froehlich, p. 17.

296 Heiko Oberman, *Luther: Man between God and the Devil* (New Haven: Yale Univ. Press, 2006), pp. 251-2; Froehlich, pp. 28-9; *Catechism of the Catholic Church*, secs. 115-119, pp. 38-40. The anagogic sense, which typically involves an interest in the afterlife, seeks a heavenly or eternal sense of a text. According to Bonner, Augustine of Hippo also gave a four-fold sense: "historical, aetiological, analogical, and allegorical" (p. 216). The "aetiological" sense is described as "the cause by which a thing was written or done." According to the *Handbook of Biblical Criticism*, s.v. "Fourfold Sense of Scripture," John Cassian (c.360-435) first proposed this method.

297 Bernard of Clairvaux, Sermon 2: On the Kiss, Sermons on the Song of Songs, in *Bernard of Clairvaux: Selected Works* (New York: Paulist Press, 1987), I.2, p. 216. Cf. Maimonides, *The Guide of the* Perplexed, 3.51 excursus, pp. 194-5.

298 Augustine of Hippo to Januarius (Letter 55), *Letters of St. Augustine of Hippo*, in *Nicene and Post-Nicene Fathers, First Series*, vol. 1, ed. Philip Schaff, trans. J.G. Cunningham (Buffalo, NY: Christian Literature Publishing Co., 1887), 20.37, http://www.newadvent.org/fathers/1102055.htm. See also discussion in *The New Schaff-Herzog Encyclopedia of Religious Knowledge*, s.v. "Divination" https://www.ccel.org/ccel/schaff/encyc03/Page_451.html. Norwich, p. 147.

299 See the bestselling late 20th-c. book, Michael Drosnin, *The Bible Code* (New York: Touchstone, 1997).
300 Bokser and Bokser, eds., The Tractate Kiddushin, *The Talmud: Selected Writings*, 49a, p. 174.
301 Tovia Singer, "Outreach Judaism Responds to Jews for Jesus: Why Did Jews for Jesus Criticize Rabbi Tovia Singer's Audio Series," *Outreach Judaism*, n.d., Refutation V, http://outreachjudaism.org/outreach-judaism-responds-to-jews-for-jesus/ (accessed 16 Nov. 2014). Other critiques of what are described as "overzealous, fundamentalist" Christian theology can be found here. Interestingly, Ezekiel seems to contradict other OT passages like Exod. 20:5, Exod. 34:7, and Jer. 32:18 wherein children are punished for the sins of their parents.
302 Abbot Tryphon, "The Heresy of Penal Substitution," *Ancient Faith Ministries* (blog), 6 Jul. 2016, https://blogs.ancientfaith.com/morningoffering/2016/07/heresy-penal-substitution/ (accessed 22 Sep. 2018); Alexander J. Renault, *Reconsidering TULIP: A Biblical, Philosophical, and Historical Response to the Reformed Doctrines of Predestination* (Self-published, 2010), pp. 73-89. Renault cites the same Ezekiel passage as well as providing numerous other Scriptural citations incl. Jer. 31:29-30 and Deut. 24:16. *The Concise Oxford Dictionary of the Christian Church*, s.v. "Atonement" notes that "The general patristic teaching is that Christ is our representative, not our substitute ...." See also *The New International Dictionary of the Christian Church*, s.v. "Atonement."
303 E.g. Martin Luther, *Commentary on Galatians* (Grand Rapids, MI: Fleming H. Revell, 1988), p. 323: "So he [Arsenius] by the holiness and austerity of life had attained to nothing else but the fear and horror of death." Luther's holdout for his possible salvation was if he came to believe in a more Lutheran perspective at the end.
304 Athanasius, *Life of St. Anthony*, in *Nicene and Post-Nicene Fathers, Second Series*, vol. 4, ed. Philip Schaff and Henry Wace, trans. H. Ellershaw (Buffalo, NY: Christian Literature Publishing Co., 1892), no. 46, http://www.newadvent.org/fathers/2811.htm. This language is not found in Carolinne White's translation and I do not know which textual tradition is more reliable. Regardless, it is clear that Athanasius thought that Antony was an exceptional Christian approved of by God—and that whoever wrote these words believed that Antony was following the Scriptures. Cf. Jerome, *Life of Hilarion*, in *Early Christian Lives*, no.10, p. 93 as an example of the common claim that ascetic saints were very familiar with Scripture.
305 Augustine, *On Christian Doctrine*, Preface, no.4, http://www.newadvent.org/fathers/12020.htm; González, vol. 1, p. 211; *The Concise Oxford Dic-*

tionary of the Christian Church, s.v. "St. Augustine of Hippo"; Augustine, *The Confessions*, 8.12.29 and 8.6.13-15, http://www.newadvent.org/fathers/110108.htm; Law, p. 161; Bonner, p. 89-91.

306 *The Sayings of the Desert Fathers*, John the Persian, no. 4, p. 108.

307 Jerome, *Life of Paul of Thebes* in *Early Christian Lives*, no. 1, p. 75; no. 10, p. 80; no. 13, p. 82. See 1 Kings 17:1-7. Cf. NAB footnote on Matt. 3:4, p. 14: "The clothing of John recalls the austere dress of the prophet Elijah (2 Kgs 1,8)."

308 González, vol. 1, p. 137. Cf. The Canons of the 318 Holy Fathers Assembled in the City of Nice, in Bithynia, *The Seven Ecumenical Councils of the Undivided Church*, Canon I, pp. 44-5.

309 Bokser and Bokser, eds., The Tractate Yebamot, *The Talmud: Selected Writings*, Mishnah 6:6, 61b-64a, pp. 131-3.

310 Bokser and Bokser, eds., The Tractate Taanit, *The Talmud: Selected Writings*, 11a-11b, 22b, pp. 114-15. Cf. Bokser and Bokser, introduction, p. 46. Granted, the Proverbs citation seems a bit weak to me. Other rabbis supported fasting as an individual practice.

311 Hatcher and Martin, p. 118, footnote 27.

312 Hatcher, "Baha'i Faith," in *How Different Religions View Death and Afterlife*, pp. 27-8.

313 Hatcher and Martin, pp. 127-8, footnote 1.

314 Ibid., pp. 140-1.

315 Allitt, p. 321; *The Concise Oxford Dictionary of the Christian Church*, s.v. "Contraception, procreation, and abortion, ethics of" which notes that there was a "general patristic condemnation of contraception"; David Mills, "Onan's Onus," *Touchstone*, Jan./Feb. 2005, http://www.touchstonemag.com/archives/article.php?id=18-01-040-f (accessed November 30, 2014). Henri Troyat, *Ivan the Terrible*, trans. Joan Pinkham (New York: Dorset Press, 1987), pp. 52-3 recounts a Russian Orthodox decree that those who practiced "onanism" would be among those outside the Kingdom of God. For a traditionalist approach in Orthodoxy, see Taras Baytsar, "Eastern Orthodoxy and Contraception," *Orthodox Evangelical*, 2 Feb. 2014, http://www.orthodoxevangelical.com/2014/02/04/eastern-orthodoxy-and-contraception/ (accessed July 4, 2016). For a Roman Catholic apologetical tract, see "Birth Control," Catholic Answers, 19 Nov. 2018, https://www.catholic.com/tract/birth-control (accessed 31 May 2018).

316 John Calvin, *Commentary on Genesis*, vol. 2, trans. John King (Grand Rapids, MI: Christian Classics Ethereal Library, orig. pub. 1847), 38:10, p. 241 http://www.ccel.org/ccel/calvin/calcom02.pdf. Interestingly, Muslims have traditionally not been as strict on such issues (Safi, p. 110).

317 E.g., "Artificial Birth Control," Catholic Bible 101, n.d., https://www.catholicbible101.com/artificialbirthcontrol.htm (accessed 1 Jun. 2019).

318 E.g.,Matt Perman, "Does the Bible Permit Birth Control?" Desiring God, 23 Jan. 2006, https://www.desiringgod.org/articles/does-the-bible-permit-birth-control (accessed 31 May 2019).

319 For an American Baptist statement that includes traditional and moderate opinions, see "American Baptist Resolution Concerning Abortion and Ministry in the Local Church," American Baptist Churches USA, http://www.abc-usa.org/wp-content/uploads/2012/06/Abortion-and-Ministry-in-the-Local-Church.pdf (accessed 31 May 2019). For one atheist's evaluation, see Neil Carter, "What Does the Bible Say about Abortion?" Godless in Dixie, 23 Oct. 2016, https://www.patheos.com/blogs/godlessindixie/2016/10/23/what-does-the-bible-say-about-abortion/ (accessed 30 May 2019); cf. Rachels, pp. 64-9. For an early and explicit anti-abortion text, see the Didache, in *After the New Testament*, 2:2, p. 386. The *Catechism of the Catholic Church* cites both Scripture and Tradition in its argument (nos. 2270-75, pp. 605-8); cf. *The Catholic Encyclopedia*, s.v. "Abortion," http://www.newadvent.org/cathen/01046b.htm. See also *The Concise Oxford Dictionary of the Christian Church*, s.v. "Contraception, procreation, and abortion, ethics of" which confirms that "early Christian thinkers were united in their condemnation of infanticide and abortion." For a more progressive Christian argument, see Rachel Held Evans, "Why Progressive Christians Should Care about Abortion," Rachel Held Evans (blog), 2 May 2013, https://rachelheldevans.com/blog/why-progressive-christians-should-care-about-abortion-gosnell (accessed 30 May 2019). *Mercer Dictionary of the Bible*, s.v. "Abortion" states that the Bible "is silent on the subject" in any direct way so biblical principles of justice and compassion should hold sway. For a reviews of current religious groups and their stances, see David Masci, "Where Major Religious Groups Stand on Abortion," Pew Research Center, 21 Jun. 2016, https://www.pewresearch.org/fact-tank/2016/06/21/where-major-religious-groups-stand-on-abortion/ (accessed 2 Jun. 2019); David Masci, "American Religious Groups Vary Widely in Their Views on Abortion," Pew Research Center, 22 Jan. 2018, https://www.pewresearch.org/fact-tank/2018/01/22/american-religious-groups-vary-widely-in-their-views-of-abortion/ (accessed 2 Jun. 2019).

320 A law in Exod. 21:22-25 regarding the injury of a fetus and/or pregnant woman is claimed as support by both pro-life and pro-choice believers. The NRSV translation suggests that the fetus has a lower status than the pregnant woman while the NIV translation suggests that the fetus has a standing equal to a pregnant woman. See *The NIV Study Bible*,

Exod. 21:22-25 and esp. footnote, p. 118; cf. NAS. Rachels (p. 67) and *Mercer Dictionary of the Bible*, s.v. "Abortion" support the implications of the NRSV rendering; cf. NASB.

321 "Resolution on Abortion: St. Louis, Missouri- 1971," Southern Baptist Convention, http://www.sbc.net/resolutions/13/resolution-on-abortion (accessed 30 May 2019). The SBC is much more conservative on abortion now. See David Roach, "How Southern Baptists Became Pro-life," *Baptist Press*, 15 Jan. 2015, http://bpnews.net/44055/how-southern-baptists-became-prolife (accessed 30 May 2019); Matthew Miller, "How the Evangelical Church Awoke to the Abortion Issue: Convergent Labors of Harold O.J. Brown, Francis Schaeffer, and C. Everett Koop," *Reformation 21*, Mar. 2013, www.reformation21.org/articles/how-the-evangelical-church-awoke-to-the-abortion-issue-the-convergent-labors-of.php (accessed 30 May 2019).

322 Bokser and Bokser, introduction to *The Talmud: Selected Writings*, p. 36. Mishnah Ohalot 7:6 is quoted re: abortion. Yebamot 12b is cited here and given in the text on p. 136.

323 *The Westminster Confession of Faith*, 1.7, https://reformed.org/documents/wcf_with_proofs/index.html.

324 See Leith, ed., *The Confession of Dositheus*, in *Creeds of the Churches*, decree III, p. 489; decree XVII, p. 505; Q.4, p.511, etc. This confession is written against the perceived errors of Calvinism. Cf. O. Chadwick, p. 360.

325 1 Cor. 13:28 is erroneously cited here in an online version; it is a non-existent verse.

326 Ibid., Q. II, p. 507. For Scripture references, see online version at http://catholicity.elcore.net/ConfessionOfDositheus.html.

327 Menno Simons to Gellius Faber, *The Complete Works of Menno Simons*, p. 939.

328 John Calvin, *Treatises against the Anabaptists and against the Libertines*, ed. and trans. Benjamin Wirt Farley (Grand Rapids, MI: Baker, 1982), pp. 39, 41.

329 D. A. Carson, *Exegetical Fallacies*, 2nd ed. (Grand Rapids, MI: Baker Books, 196), p. 18.

330 Ibid., p. 141.

331 See "God as One vs. The Trinity," *Jews for Judaism*, n.d., http://jewsforjudaism.org/knowledge/articles/god-as-one-vs-the-trinity/ (accessed 19 Mar. 2018). Isa. 44:6 is also cited. Deut. 6:4 is translated as follows in the NRSV: "Hear, O Israel: The Lord is our God, the Lord alone." I use the NIV translation because that is essentially how Jews for Judaism renders

the verse. Cf. Tovia Singer, "The Trinity," Let's Get Biblical (Part 6 of 24), *Outreach Judaism*, n.d., https://outreachjudaism.org/the-trinity-audio/ (accessed 19 Mar. 2018); Bokser and Bokser, eds., The Tractate Sanhedrin, *The Talmud: Selected Writings*, 38a, p. 211.

332 Ehrman, *Jesus, Interrupted*, pp. 246-52.

333 Mead and Hill, pp. 36, 92, 237, 240. Adam Pastor, who was ordained by Anabaptist Menno Simons, taught that "Christ did not exist before the incarnation and was to be considered divine only in the sense that God dwelled in him" (Estep, p. 171). For the use of John 14:28, see "What Do Jehovah's Witnesses Believe?" *JW.org*, n.d., https://www.jw.org/en/jehovahs-witnesses/faq/jehovah-witness-beliefs/ (accessed 9 Oct. 2017).

334 Of course, Trinitarian Christians would disagree with these other voices. For one defense of the Trinity with Scripture citations, see *The Catholic Encyclopedia*, s.v. "The Blessed Trinity" http://www.newadvent.org/cathen/15047a.htm (accessed 18 Dec. 2014).

335 See "Myth 4: God Is a Trinity," *The Watchtower*, Nov. 2009, http://www.jw.org/en/publications/magazines/wp20091101/myth-god-is-a-trinity/ (accessed 18 Dec. 2014).

336 The Greek word in question here is αρχη which can mean "beginning" or "origin." See F. Wilbur Gingrich, *Shorter Lexicon of the Greek New Testament*, 2nd ed., rev. by Frederick Danker (Chicago: Univ. of Chicago Press, 1983), p. 27. The ESV renders αρχη as "beginning" and the NRSV renders it as "origin." See Mead and Hill, p. 156 for a Jehovah's Witnesses understanding of Rev. 3:14.

337 Williams, *Arius*, pp. 95-116 (esp. p. 109).

338 Pagels, p. 30.

339 Ehrman, ed., *After the New Testament*, p. 227: Gnostics thought Catholics "propounded absurd and ridiculous views about Christ based on a wooden reading of sacred texts that, as divinely inspired, cannot simply be understood as bare-bones descriptions of divine realities." For some condemnatory Gnostic views of early Catholics, see *The Coptic Apocalypse of Peter*, in *After the New Testament*, pp. 228-9; Pagels, pp. xv-xvi, xxxv.

340 Luma Simms, "Uncovering the Head Covering Debate," *Christianity Today*, Sep. 2013, www.christianitytoday.com/women/2013/septemeber/uncovering-head-covering-debate.html (accessed 24 Feb. 2017). See Nolt, p. 242 for comment on Amish. For various articles and resources, see *The Head Covering Movement*, www.headcoveringmovement.com (accessed 19 Aug. 2018). Calvin apparently viewed the issue with some indifference (Bouwsma, p. 138).

341   Froehlich, p. 3; Bokser and Bokser, introduction to *The Talmud: Selected Writings*, pp. 9, 21. The OT gives some indication of the need for an authoritative interpretation when reading Scripture (Neh. 8:8). Likewise, the NT seems to acknowledge this dynamic in places, as when the risen Christ found it necessary to explain his presence in the Jewish scriptures while talking with his own disciples on the road to Emmaus (Luke 24:13-27).

342   See Froehlich, p. 5; Neill and Wright, pp. 321ff; *Mercer Dictionary of the Bible*, s.v. "Dead Sea Scrolls."

343   Matt, pp. 1, 160-1; *The Penguin Dictionary of Religions*, s.v. "Kaballah"; *The New International Dictionary of the Christian Church*, 2nd ed., s.v. "Kabbalah."

344   Julius Guttman, introduction to *Guide of the Perplexed*, by Maimonides, pp. 20-1; Maimonides, 2.42, p. 146.

345   Bonner, pp. 23, 277.

346   Tertullian, *Prescription of the Heretics*, in *After the New Testament*, ch. 15, p. 214; González, vol. 1, p. 74.

347   See Augustine's requirement that Scripture be subjected to the "Rule of Faith" in *On Christian Doctrine*, 3.2.3, http://www.newadvent.org/fathers/12023.htm. See Dungan for discussion, p. 119. See also Tertullian, *Prescription of the Heretics*, in *After the New Testament*, chs. 13-14, pp. 213-14; Irenaeus, 1.10.1-2, http://www.newadvent.org/fathers/0103110.htm; 3.2.1-3 http://www.newadvent.org/fathers/0103302.htm; Hippolytus of Rome, *The Apostolic Tradition of Hippolytus*, trans. Burton Scott Easton (Ann Arbor, MI: Archon Books, 1962), 21:12-18, pp. 46-7; Froehlich, pp.12-15; *Handbook of Biblical Criticism*, s.v. "Rule of Faith."

348   González, vol. 1, p. 216.

349   Vincent of Lerins, *The Comminitory*, in *Nicene and Post-Nicene Fathers, Second Series*, ed. Philip Schaff and Henry Wace, trans. C. A. Heurtley, vol. 11 (Buffalo, NY: Christian Literature Publishing Co., 1894), 2.5, http://www.newadvent.org/fathers/3506.htm. This notion of a "unanimous consent of the Fathers" in scriptural interpretation is a cornerstone of traditional concepts of Catholicity. E.g. Leo XIII, *Providentissimus Deus: On the Study of Holy Scripture*, no. 14, http://www.papalencyclicals.net/Leo13/l13provi.htm.

350   A prominent interpretation of his thought known as the "Wesleyan Quadrilateral." s.v. http://www.umc.org/what-we-believe/glossary-wesleyan-quadrilateral-the (accessed 15 Aug. 2019). From *A Dictionary for United Methodists*, Alan K. Waltz, Copyright 1991, Abingdon Press.

351 Examples of this dynamic can of course be found throughout this section. For a description of where two types of Reformed Christians are at odds, see Jason A. Van Bemmel, "Baptists and Presbyterians: Why We Disagree," *The Aquila Report*, 2 Nov. 2015, https://www.theaquilareport.com/baptists-and-presbyterians-why-we-disagree/ (accessed 15 Aug. 2019). Often this debate has been conducted with less generosity than Van Bemmel has done here.

352 *The Way of the Pilgrim*, trans. Helen Bacovcin (New York: Image Books, 1992), p. 19.

353 González, vol. 2, pp. 260-1.

354 Karl Barth, *Church Dogmatics: The Doctrine pf the Word of God*, ed. G.W. Bromley and T.F. Torrance, trans. G.T. Thomson and Harold Knight (London: T&T Clark International, 2004), I.2, p. 525.

355 *The Concise Oxford Dictionary of the Christian Church*, s.v. "Liberation theology."

356 Ibid., s.v. "feminist theology"; Susan Brayford, "Reading Glasses: Feminist Criticism," *Teaching the Bible* (e-newsletter), The Society of Biblical Literature, n.d., https://www.sbl-site.org/assets/pdfs/TB7_FeministCriticism_SB.pdf (accessed 8 Jul. 2017).

357 Phyllis Trible, "Phyllis Trible on Feminist Biblical Interpretation," in *The Christian Theology Reader*, 2nd ed., ed. Alister E. McGrath (Oxford: Blackwell Publishing, 2001), pp. 149-54. Phyllis Trible, "Feminist Hermeneutics and Biblical Studies," *Religion-online.org*, n.d., http://www.religion-online.org/article/feminist-hermeneutics-and-biblical-studies/ (accessed 31 Dec. 2018). Orig. pub. in *Christian Century*, Feb. 1982, p. 116. Joyce Rupp, "Desperately Seeking Sophia," *U.S. Catholic*, n.d., http://www.uscatholic.org/church/scripture-and-theology/2008/07/desperately-seeking-sophia (accessed 8 Jul. 2017).

358 See for instance, John Shore, "Taking God at His Word: The Bible and Homosexuality," *johnshore.com*, 2 Apr. 2012 http://johnshore.com/2012/04/02/the-best-case-for-the-bible-not-condemning-homosexuality/ (accessed 2 Feb. 2013). Shore calls traditional Christian views on same-sex relationships as "morally reprehensible," "unbiblical," and suggests that they are not taking care to ensure that a faulty "lens does not distort our vision or understanding of God's sacrosanct word." Bishop Tim Cravens, an independent Catholic bishop, notes it as a repudiation of "one of the central messages of reconciliation in the Gospel." As quoted in John P. Plummer, *The Many Paths of the Independent Sacramental Movement* (Berkeley, CA: Apocryphile Press, 2006), p. 90. For a discussion, see Caleb Kaltenbach and Matthew Vines, "Debating Bible Verses on Homo-

sexuality," *The New York Times*, 8 Jun. 2015, https://www.newyorktimes.com/interactive/2015/06/05/us/samesex-scriptures.html?_r=0 (accessed 6 Jun. 2017).

359 For one discussion of David and Jonathan's relationship in homosexual terms, see David H. Jensen, *1 & 2 Samuel: A Theological Commentary on the Bible* (Louisville, KY: Westminster John Knox Press, 2015), pp. 128-31.

360 *Handbook of Biblical Criticism*, s.v. "Advocacy Criticism." See also these individual terms, ibid.

361 Ibn Ishaq, *The Life of Muhammad: Apostle of Allah*, ed. Michael Edwardes (London: The Folio Society, 2003), pp. 82-3. See also pp. 32-34, 76.

362 See Geisler and Howe, p. 133.

363 Ibid., pp. 269, 315, 419. For Mani, see Bonner, p. 159. For a general claim that the OT speaks of Muhammad, see Bukhari, bk. 34, no. 77 (3.34.335) http://sunnah.com/bukhari/34/77.

364 Bukhari, bk. 52, no. 46 (3.48.850) http://sunnah.com/bukhari/52/46.

365 The biblical terms for justification (δικαιοω and its cognates) can mean either "make righteous" (in a transformative sense) or "declare righteous" (in the sense of an acquittal in a court of law). See Gingrich, *Shorter Lexicon*, pp. 49-50. Although it seems that both definitions factor into Protestant and Catholic interpretations of Scripture, Catholicism tends to focus on the meaning of "make righteous" whereas Protestantism tends to focus on the meaning of "declare righteous." See Sproul, *Justified by Faith Alone*, for a short primer.

366 Alister McGrath, *Iustitia Dei: A History of the Doctrine of Justification*, 3rd ed. (New York: Cambridge Univ. Press, 2005), p. 208; Francis A. Schaeffer, *Escape from Reason*, rev. ed. (Downers Grove, IL: InterVarsity Press, 2006), pp. 27-8; Sproul, *Justified by Faith Alone*, p. 9. See also Luther, *Commentary on Galatians*, Declaration, p. 17: "If this doctrine is lost, then is also the whole knowledge of truth, life and salvation lost." Luther also calls it "the cheifest article of all Christian doctrine" (Gal. 2:11, p. 80). Concepts like the legal or "forensic" exchange of punishment in a substitutionary atonement, salvation by grace alone through faith alone, a "trust" in God that goes beyond mere intellectual assent to doctrine (although that is needed as well), imputed and "alien" righteousness, the exclusion of human merit, assurance of salvation, and a distinction between justification (being declared righteous) and sanctification (being made holy) are central to the classic Protestant understanding.

367 For similar conclusions, see A. McGrath, *Iustitia Dei*, pp. 213-16; Oberman, pp. 152-4, 177, 317.

368 In studying the Apostolic Fathers of the earliest decades of the catholic church, Protestant scholar T. F. Torrance described the teachings on justification as "a strange collection of both merit and bestowal." See Thomas F. Torrance, *The Doctrine of Grace in the Apostolic Fathers* (Grand Rapids, MI: Wm. B. Eerdmans, 1959), p. 53. For some examples from church fathers: Polycarp, Epistle of Polycarp to the Philippians, in *Ante-Nicene Fathers*, vol. 1, ed. Alexander Roberts, et al., trans. Alexander Roberts and James Donaldson (Buffalo, NY: Christian Literature Publishing Co., 1885), ch. 2.2, http://www.newadvent.org/fathers/0136.htm: "But He who raised Him up from the dead will raise up us also, if we do His will, and walk in His commandments, ..." Second Clement, in *Ante-Nicene Fathers*, vol. 9, ed. Allan Menzies, trans. John Keith (Buffalo, NY: Christian Literature Publishing Co., 1896), ch. 6, http://www.newadvent.org/fathers/1011.htm: "how can we hope to enter into the royal residence of God unless we keep our baptism holy and undefiled? Or who shall be our advocate, unless we be found possessed of works of holiness and righteousness?" Justin Martyr, *The First Apology*, in *Ante-Nicene Fathers*, vol. 1, ed. Alexander Roberts et al., trans. Marcus Dods and George Reith (Buffalo, NY: Christian Literature Publishing Co., 1885), ch. 12, http://www.newadvent.org/fathers/0126.htm: "each man goes to everlasting punishment or salvation according to the value of his actions." Cyprian of Carthage, *On the Unity of the Church*, in *Ante-Nicene Fathers*, vol. 5, ed. Alexander Roberts et al., trans. Robert Ernest Wallis (Buffalo, NY: Christian Literature Publishing Co., 1886.), no. 21, http://www.newadvent.org/fathers/050701.htm: "Confession [of faith] is the beginning of glory, not the full desert of the crown; nor does it perfect our praise, but it initiates our dignity; and since it is written, He that endures to the end, the same shall be saved, … whatever has been before the end is a step by which we ascend to the summit of salvation, not a terminus wherein the full result of the ascent is already gained." Cf. Cyprian of Carthage, *On the Lapsed*, in *Ante-Nicene Fathers*, vol. 5, ed. Alexander Roberts et al., trans. Robert Ernest Wallis (Buffalo, NY: Christian Literature Publishing Co., 1886), no. 35, http://www.newadvent.org/fathers/050703.htm.

369 Unlike Protestant creeds and confessions, the Apostles Creed and the Nicene Creed do not have a doctrine of justification by faith alone (but rather don't really address the issue). See *The Catholic Encyclopedia*, s.v. "Apostles' Creed" http://www.newadvent.org/cathen/01629a.htm (accessed 18 Oct. 2013). The so-called Athanasian Creed suggests that works are necessary: "At whose coming all men … shall give account for their own works. And they that have done good shall go into life everlasting, and

they that have done evil into everlasting fire. This is the Catholic Faith, which except a man believe faithfully and firmly, he cannot be saved." See *The Catholic Encyclopedia*, s.v. "The Athanasian Creed" http://www.newadvent.org/cathen/02033b.htm (accessed 19 Oct. 2013). In his explication of the Rule of Faith, Irenaeus (d. c. 202) includes much of the basic content of the Apostle's Creed and also writes that God grants salvation to "the righteous, and holy, and those who have kept his commandments, and have persevered in His love" (Irenaeus, 1.10.1, http://www.newadvent.org/fathers/0103110.htm). In his description of apostolic tradition and his presentation of the old Roman baptismal creed, Hippolytus also (c. 217) gives no indication that justification by faith alone was part of the early faith (Hippolytus of Rome, *The Apostolic Tradition of Hippolytus*, 21:12-18, pp. 46-7. See also pp. 33-5 for his comments on the priesthood and remission of sins).

370   See Alister McGrath, *Iustitia Dei*, pp. 49, 216; *The New International Dictionary of the Christian Church*, s.v. "Justification"; Augustine, *Later Works*, ed. John Burnaby (Philadelphia: Westminster Press, 1955), p. 229; B.B. Warfield, *Calvin and Augustine*, ed. Samuel Craig (Philadelphia: The Presbyterian and Reformed Publishing Co., 1956), pp. 315-22, 456-7; Bonner, pp. 107, 137, 261, 294, 325, 379, etc.; Augustine, *On Faith and Works*, in *The Fathers of the Church, St. Augustine: Treatises on Marriage and Other Subjects*, ed. Roy Deferrari, trans. Robert Russell (Washington, DC: The Catholic Univ. of America Press, 1969), 14.22, p. 248. While it is true that short, individual quotations of Fathers like Augustine can be found which sound sympathetic to classic Protestant statements on justification when taken out of context (see Thomas Oden, *The Justification Reader* [Grand Rapids: Wm. B. Eerdmans, 2002] as an example of what I believe to be this approach), they do not truly demonstrate such affinity when considered in light of their larger theological systems—especially when it is remembered that in traditional Catholic thought there is no merit of any type in the remission of sins in baptism.

371   John Chrysostom, Homily LXIX (on Mt 22:1-14), *Homilies on the Gospel of St. Matthew*, in *Nicene and Post-Nicene Fathers*, Series 1, vol. 10, ed. Philip Schaff (Grand Rapids, MI: Christian Classics Ethereal Library, n.d.), p. 735 http://www.ccel.org/ccel/schaff/npnf110.pdf; Gerald Bray, ed., *Ancient Christian Commentary on Scripture: James, 1-2 Peter, 1-3 John. Jude*, vol. XI (Downers Grove, IL: InterVarsity Press, 2000), Jas. 2:26b, p. 34.

372   Basil of Caesarea, Letter CCXCV (295), *Basil: Letters and Select Works*, in *Nicene and Post-Nicene Fathers*, Series 2, vol. 8, ed. Philip Schaff and

Henry Wace (Grand Rapids, MI: Christian Classics Ethereal Library, n.d.), p. 867, http://www.ccel.org/ccel/schaff/npnf208.pdf.

373 A review of the canons and the theological formulations of many of the early councils is instructive here. See *The Seven Ecumenical Councils*. The local Second Council of Orange (529), which I have heard cited as the most closely aligned with Protestant doctrine, has a firm condemnation of works-centered Pelagian theology, supports predestination, and insists on God's grace as the prerequisite of both the salvation of the believer and of any good work. Nonetheless, this council still does not hold to *sola* fide, as its concluding remarks would suggest: "all baptized persons have the ability and responsibility, if they desire to labor faithfully, to perform with the aid and cooperation of Christ what is of essential importance in regard to the salvation of their soul." (Leith, ed., *The Council of Orange*, in *Creeds of the Churches*, conclusion, p. 44.) As modern Protestant church historian Justo González relates, Lutheran Georg Calixtus (1586-1656) was forced to acknowledge that the Reformation understanding of justification by faith "was not part of the common faith of the first five centuries"—and thus in his view could not be considered a "heresy" but only an error (González, vol. 2, p. 178).

374 For Bede's love of the Scripture and enthusiasm for biblical commentary, see D. H. Farmer, introduction to *Ecclesiastical History of the English People*, trans. Leo Sherley-Price, ed. R.E. Latham, rev. ed. (New York: Penguin, 1990), pp. 21, 34; cf. Bede, *Ecclesiastical History of the English People*, 1.17, p. 66; 1.32, p. 95; 3.17, p. 17; 3.28, p. 197; 4.3, p. 210; 4.23, pp. 244-5; 5.15, p. 294; etc. Bede's clear belief in monasticism, celibacy, merit, penance, baptismal regeneration, Catholic ecclesiology, prayers and masses for the dead, devotion to Mary and the saints, the eucharist as sacrifice, shrines, pilgrimages, holy water, episcopacy, papal primacy, relics, and the like are a clear indication that he is a believer in Catholic and not Protestant theology. E.g., 3.14, p. 164; 3.18, p. 18; 3.22, p. 179; 3.27, p. 195; 3.30, p. 200; 4.19, p. 238; 5.12, pp. 287-8; etc.

375 Francis of Assisi comes across as a typical medieval Roman Catholic monastic on the issue of justification, advocating penance, obedience to the Roman Church and the Pope, Purgatory, praying to saints, praying for the dead, devotion to Mary, transubstantiation, and the like. He clearly taught the doctrine of mortal sin. For example, see his "The Second Version of the Letter to the Faithful" in *Francis and Clare: The Complete Works*, trans. Regis J. Armstrong and Ignatius C. Brady (New York: Paulist Press, 1982), pp. 66-73. For salvation tied to penance and forgiving others, see "The Earlier Rule," 21.3-8, p. 126. Likewise, early Franciscan tradition

shows no indication of a Protestant doctrine of justification. See *The Little Flowers of Saint Francis*, trans. Raphael Brown (New York: Image Books, 1958).

376   St. Bernard, canonized in 1174 and named a Doctor of the Roman Catholic Church in 1830, was "first and foremost a monk" and "an enemy of all theological innovation" (Gonzalez, vol. 1, p. 283). He was also an ardent supporter of the pope's power, quoted the Apocrypha as Scripture, ascribed to purgatory, and was a deep believer in asceticism and Marian devotion. His works also seem devoid of the notion of imputed righteousness. My reading of *Bernard of Clairvaux: Selected Works* also bears this out. See also *The Westminster Dictionary of Theologians*, s.v. "Bernard of Clairvaux"; *The New International Dictionary of the Christian Church*, s.v. "Bernard of Clairvaux"; *The New Schaff-Herzog Encyclopedia of Religious Knowledge*, s.v. "Bernard of Clairvaux" https://www.ccel.org/ccel/schaff/encyc02.html?term=bernard+of+clairvaux (accessed 31 Dec. 2018); *The Catholic Encyclopedia*, s.v. "St. Bernard of Clairvaux" http://www.newadvent.org/cathen/02498d.htm (accessed 6 Apr. 2018); entire issue of *Christian History* 8.4, issue 24 (1989) https://christianhistoryinstitute.org/magazine/issue/bernard-of-clairvaux-medieval-reformer-and-mystic (accessed 5 Apr. 2018). While Calvin and Luther admired Bernard to some extent, Bernard's focus appears to rather be on grace, love, and humility and not salvation by faith alone. Alister McGrath makes no exception for Bernard in his analysis of medieval theologians on justification (*Iustitia Dei*, pp. 213-16).

377   Thomas Aquinas, *The Catechetical Instructions of Thomas Aquinas*, trans. J. Collins (New York: Joseph F. Wagner, 1939), p. 44.

378   Philip Schaff, *History of the Christian Church, Vol. V: The Middle Ages A.D. 1049-1294* (Grand Rapids, MI: Christian Classics Ethereal Library, n.d.), sect. 84, pp. 387-8, http://www.ccel.org/ccel/schaff/hcc5.pdf.

379   Timothy George, "The Reformation Connection," *Christian History* 19.4, issue 68 (2000): p. 35; *The Catholic Encyclopedia*, s.v. "Hussites" http://www.newadvent.org/cathen/07585a.htm (accessed 13 Oct. 2013). The Hussite *Four Articles*, which summarized their chief complaints with Roman Catholicism, did not mention justification by faith alone.

380   Douglas C. Wood, *The Evangelical Doctor: John Wycliffe and the Lollards* (Welwyn, England: Evangelical Press, 1984), p. 113; *The Catholic Encyclopedia*, s.v. "John Wyclif" http://www.newadvent.org/cathen/15722a.htm (accessed 13 Oct. 2013). The Council of Constance condemned both Wycliffe and Huss, listing numerous articles of their teachings which they deemed heretical. However, a doctrine of justification by faith alone

was not among their criticisms. See "Council of Constance 1414-1418," in *Papal Encyclicals Online*, http://www.papalencyclicals.net/Councils/ecum16.htm (accessed 28 Sep. 2018). From *Decrees of the Ecumenical Councils*, ed. Norman P. Tanner. A. McGrath notes that Wycliffe and Huss are precursors to the Reformation in the areas of sacramental theology and ecclesiology, but not justification (*Iustitia Dei*, p. 216). Jacques Lefevre d'Etaples (1450-1536) is sometimes said to have believed in justification by faith alone before Luther. Assuming this is correct, the general issue of the lack of historical continuity with the doctrine would remain unchanged—especially as he was a rough contemporary of Luther. Rodney Stark, *For the Glory of God: How Monotheism Led to Reformations, Science, Witch-hunts, and the End of Slavery* (Princeton, NJ: Princeton Univ. Press, 2003), p. 87 names him as a believer in justification by faith alone before the Reformation—but tellingly names no one else.

381   As with both Eastern Orthodoxy and Roman Catholicism, both of these ancient communions regard penance as a sacrament, hold to a concept of mortal sin, say prayers for the dead, have a strong monastic and ascetic tradition, regard the eucharist as a Sacrifice that forgives sins, do not hold to imputed righteousness, and regard justification as both an act and a process. I have come across nothing in their traditions to suggest that they ever have thought differently. For an Assyrian Church of the East (a.k.a.) Nestorian view on the issue, see Mar Odisho, *The Book of Marganitha (The Pearl) On the Truth of Christianity*, Nestorian.org, IV.1 and IV.7, http://www.nestorian.org/book_of_marganitha_part_iv.html#partivchap1 (accessed 10 Oct. 2013); *The New International Dictionary of the Christian Church*, s.v. "Assyrian Church." For the Assyrian Church of the East website, see http://news.assyrianchurch.org/. For references to prayer for the departed and the sacrifice of the eucharist forgiving sins, see Paul Halsall, ed., *Selections from the Assyrian Liturgy*, in *Internet Medieval Sourcebook*, Fordham University, Jun. 1997, http://www.fordham.edu/halsall/basis/assyrlit.asp (accessed 11 Oct. 2013).

For an Ethiopian (Oriental) Orthodox description of justification by faith alone as an innovation, see Desta, p. 71. For an Coptic (Oriental) Orthodox view of salvation, see H. H. Pope Shenouda III, *Life of Faith* (Dar El Tebaa El Kawmia Pres, 1989) http://tasbeha.org/content/hh_books/faith/ (accessed 10 Oct. 2013). See esp. ch. 3 "Degrees and Kinds of Faith." For an Oriental Orthodox discussion of the sacrament of penance, see H. G. Bishop Mettaous, "Sacrament of Repentance and Confession," in *Sacramental Rites in the Coptic Orthodox Church*, 2nd ed., Coptic Orthodox Church

Network, 1998-2014, http://www.copticchurch.net/topics/thecopticchurch/sacraments/3_repentance_confesstion.html (accessed 31 Dec. 2018).

382   Daniel Clendenin, "Why I'm Not Orthodox: An Evangelical Explores the Ancient and Alien World of the Eastern Church," *Christianity Today*, 6 Jan. 1997, http://www.christianitytoday.com/ct/1997/january6/7t1032.html?paging=off (accessed 9 Oct. 2013); Daniel B. Clendenin, "What the Orthodox Believe," *Christian History* 16.2, issue 54 (1997): p. 35; Ware, *The Orthodox Church*, pp. 93-4; O. Chadwick, p. 358; St. Maximos the Confessor, *Four Hundred Texts on Love*, in *The Philokalia: The Complete Text*, vol. 2, ed. and trans. G.E.H. Palmer et al. (London: Faber and Faber, 1981), no. 39, p. 56; Leith, ed., *The Confession of Dositheus*, in *Creeds of the Churches*, decree XIII, pp. 496-7; Mastrantonis esp. pp. 100-1, 121-133, 157-9, 218.

383   W. R. McGrath, locs. 402, 544; Daniel Liechty, *Early Anabaptist Spirituality* (Mahwah, NJ: Paulist Press, 1994), p. 11; Thomas N. Finger, *A Contemporary Anabaptist Theology: Biblical, Historical, Constructive* (Downers Grove, IL: InterVarsity Press, 2004), pp. 112-32 (esp. pp. 131-2); *The Catholic Encyclopedia*, s.v. "Anabaptists" http://www.newadvent.org/cathen/01445b.htm (accessed 3 Feb. 2015); Phil Johnson, "The Anabaptists," *The Hall of Church History*, 2001, http://www.romans45.org/anabapt.htm (accessed 24 Aug. 2018); Estep, pp. 62-3, 82, 199); Nolt, p. 88; "Elbing Catechism," *Global Anabaptist Mennonite Encyclopedia Online* http://gameo.org/index.php?title=Elbing_Catechism&oldid=102182 (accessed 2 Sep. 2016).

384   C. S. Lewis, *The Joyful Christian: 127 Readings from C. S. Lewis* (New York: Collier Books, 1977), pp. 135-6: "Christians have often disputed as to whether what leads the Christian home is good actions, or Faith in Christ. … You see, we are now trying to understand, and to separate in watertight compartments, what exactly God does and what man does when God and man are working together." Anglo-Catholics typically express similar views.

385   The Council of Trent (1545-1563) brought the classic Roman Catholic denial of *sola fide*, claiming that it was against both a proper exegesis of Scripture and the teachings of the Fathers. Making over seventy citations of Scripture in its analysis of justification, the Council declared that the doctrine of *sola fide* was the cause of "the loss of many souls" and that believers in it were under the curse of "anathema." See *The Canons and Decrees of the Council of Trent*, sess. 6, introduction, p. 29; cans. 9, 11, etc., pp. 43ff. Trent maintained rather that "justification is not only a remission

of sins but also the sanctification and renewal of the inward man" (sess.6, ch. 7, p. 33).

386 See also Heb 5:9 "he became the source of eternal salvation for all who obey him" and 1 John 2:17 "those who do the will of God live forever." See also 1 Cor. 9:26-27, John 15:8-10, Rev. 22:12, 1 Tim. 5:8.

387 While many Protestants provide an alternate interpretation, linking John 3:5 to baptism was apparently common in the Fathers (e.g., Justin Martyr, *First Apology*, ch. 61, http://www.newadvent.org/fathers/0126.htm). Desta shows this understanding of John in the continued tradition of the Ethiopian Orthodox Church (p. 17). St. Peter of Damaskos cites John 6:53 and John 3:5, noting that both the eucharist and baptism at the hands of priests are necessary for salvation. See St. Peter of Damaskos, *A Treasury of Divine Knowledge* (book I), in *The Philokalia*, vol. 3, pp. 208-9. St. Francis of Assisi also links John 3:5 to salvation by baptism ("The Earlier Rule" 16.7, pp. 121-2). I have also seen 1 Pet. 3:21 and Mark 16:15-16 used as prooftexts.

388 Mastrantonis, pp. 118, 179; St. Peter of Damaskos, *A Treasury of Divine Knowledge*, p. 95.

389 Mastrantonis, p. 238.

390 Ibid., pp. 99-100 for Gal. 5:6b.

391 Ibid., p. 127. Mastrantonis says that partaking of the eucharist is essential for salvation and cites this verse (see above on baptism). See also St. Francis of Assisi's "The Admonitions" in *Francis and Clare: The Complete Works*, no. 8, p. 26.

392 Although it would be a mistake to describe the Catholic-Protestant debates over justification as merely a matter of semantics, there is some reason to believe that the differing Reformation positions on justification are not always as distinct as rhetoric might suggest. Martin Luther's full theological system, in contrast to many other Protestants, includes a type of baptismal regeneration, the Real Presence of Christ in the eucharist, and a de-emphasized form of auricular confession (O. Chadwick, p. 65; Oberman, pp. 226-33). Likewise, Calvin, unlike some of his Protestant descendants, stresses that "faith alone" can never in fact be alone (*Institutes of the Christian Religion*, 3.16.1, p. 641; cf. Bouwsma, p. 159) and described a "doctrine of rewards" based on works (*Institutes of the Christian Religion*, 3.18.1, p. 661). Likewise, the Council of Trent, contains some passages that can sound rather Protestant in tone: "namely, that we are therefore said to be justified by faith, because faith is the beginning of human salvation, the foundation and root of all justification, *without which it is impossible to please God* and to come into the fellowship with His sons; and we are

therefore said to be justified gratuitously, because none of those things which precede justification, whether faith or works, merit the grace of justification. For, *if by grace, it is not now by works, otherwise*, as the Apostle says, *grace is no more grace*" (sess.6, Decree Concerning Justification, ch.VIII, p.35). Much of this can be tied up in the concept of "mortal sins" which are believed to take someone out of a state of grace. For one short discussion, see Tim Staples, "Mortal and Venial Sin?" *Catholic Answers*, 14 Mar. 2014, https://www.catholic.com/magazine/online-edition/mortal-and-venial-sin (accessed 23 Dec. 2017).

393 See John T. Noonan, Jr., *A Church that Can and Cannot Change: The Development of Catholic Moral Teaching* (Notre Dame, IN: Univ. of Notre Dame Press, 2005), pp. 128-42, who notes both that any interest on loans was considered usury and that usury was considered to be a mortal sin. See also O. Chadwick, p. 183; Bellitto, p. 71; Apocalypse of Peter, in *After the New Testament*, ch. 10, p. 300; Excursus on Usury, *The Seven Ecumenical Councils of the Undivided Church*, p. 86; "The Council of Elvira," ed. Ken Pennington, *Catholic University of America*, n.d., can. 20 https://www.webcitation.org/6AS7rgB7f?url=http://faculty.cua.edu/pennington/canon%20Law/ElviraCanons.htm (accessed 24 Aug. 2018). Joseph Pérez, *The Spanish Inquisition: A History*, trans. Janet Lloyd (New Haven: Yale Univ. Press, 2005), p. 6 however notes that Christians just could not lend money at interest to other Christians—"But a Christian could charge a Jew interest on a loan, and vice versa."

394 The Bible notes at one point that David's only sin was "in the matter of Uriah the Hittite" (1 Kings 15:5)—suggesting again that David's polygamy was not problematic to God.

395 See O. Chadwick, p. 190; *Global Anabaptist Mennonite Encyclopedia Online*, s.v. "Batenburg, Jan van (1495-1538)" http://gameo.org/index.php?title=Batenburg,_Jan_van_(1495-1538)&oldid=111688 (accessed 23 Jan. 2014). "Unbelieving" here meant not believing in van Batenburg's interpretation of Christianity.

396 González notes that Luther, Melancthon, and Bucer "agreed that the Bible did not forbid polygamy" (vol. 2, p. 89). See also Oberman, pp. 284-9; *New World Encyclopedia*, s.v. "Martin Luther" http://www.newworldencyclopedia.org/entry/Martin_Luther (accessed 18 May 2013).

397 This is a traditional Roman Catholic teaching. For use of all these verses, see Christopher A. Ferrara and Thomas E. Woods, Jr., *The Great Façade: The Regime of Novelty in the Catholic Church from Vatican II to the Francis Revolution*, 2nd ed., (Kettering, OH: Angelico Press, 2015), approx. locs.

8968, 8994, 10074, 10159, Kindle. See Bede's discussion of The Synod of Hertford, 4.5 (pp. 214-5) for an example of this view.

398 Craig Kenner and William Heth, "Remarriage: Two Views," *Christianity Today*, 31 Aug. 2000, http://www.christianitytoday.com/ct/2000/august-web-only/48.0c.html?start=1 (accessed 24 Jul. 2016). The Catholic Church has traditionally held that remarriage is not valid. Protestants generally used to be stricter on this issue.

399 See Mastrontonis, pp. 3, 25 for 1 Tim. 3:15 citation. On p. 141, Mastrontontis affirms this general authority applies to the granting of divorces: "The Church grants ecclesiastical divorce …."

400 Ibid., p. 141.

401 Jean LeClercq, Introduction to *Bernard of Clairvaux: Selected Works*, p. 17; cf. "The Rule of Saint Clare" in *Francis and Clare: The Complete Works*, no. 3, p. 212. For the use of Luke 18:29-30 (among other verses) as a proof-text for the apostles leaving their wives, see Anthony Zimmerman, "The Logic of Priestly Celibacy," *EWTN*, 2001, http://www.ewtn.com/library/PRIESTS/CELIBACY.HTM (accessed 22 Feb. 2019). Orig. pub. *Homiletic and Pastoral Review* (Apr. 1995). For a discussion on different attitudes regarding divorce for aspiring western monastics, see Philip Lyndon Reynolds, *Marriage in the Western Church: The Christianization of Marriage in the Patristic and Early Medieval Periods* (Boston: Brill Academic Publishers, 2001), pp. 138-41.

402 Bokser and Bokser, introduction to *The Talmud: Selected Writings*, p. 35.

403 Jerome, *The Perpetual Virginity of the Blessed Mary*, in *Nicene and Post-Nicene Fathers, Second Series*, vol. 6, ed. Philip Schaff and Henry Wace, trans. W.H. Fremantle, et al. (Buffalo, NY: Christian Literature Publishing Co., 1893), no. 2, http://www.newadvent.org/fathers/3007.htm.

404 Luigi Gambero, *Mary and the Fathers of the Church: The Blessed Virgin Mary in Patristic Thought*, trans. Thomas Buffer (San Francisco: Ignatius Press, 1991), pp. 65-6.

405 Gambero, p. 221 (Augustine, Sermon 225, no. 2).

406 Ibid., pp. 177-9; John Chrysostom, Homily 5 on Matthew, in *Nicene and Post-Nicene Fathers, First Series*, vol. 10, ed. Philip Schaff, trans. George Prevost and M.B. Riddle (Buffalos, NY: Christian Literature Publishing Co., 1888), no. 5, www.newadvent.org/fathers/200105.htm.

407 Gambero, pp. 103-5.

408 Ibid., pp. 75-7; Origen, *Commentary on the Gospel of Matthew*, in *Ante-Nicene Fathers*, vol. 9, ed. Allan Menzies, trans. John Patrick (Buffalo, NY: Christian Literature Publishing Co., 1896), no. 17, http://www.newadvent.org/fathers/101610.htm.

409 See Calvin, *Commentary on Matthew, Mark, Luke*, vol. 1, no. 25, p. 107 (on Matt. 1:25). In this passage, Calvin seems to imply that it is better to believe in Mary's perpetual virginity—although suggesting that it is best not to discuss. See also Oscar Lukefahr, *"We Believe ... ": A Survey of the Catholic Faith* (Ligouri, MO: Ligouri, 1990), p. 68; Brantly Milligan, "A Protestant Defense of Mary's Perpetual Virginity," *Aleteia*, 10 Oct. 2013 http://aleteia.org/2013/10/10/a-protestant-defense-of-marys-perpetual-virginity/ (accessed 8 Sep. 2016). For Hubmaier, see Estep (p. 187). The Ethiopian Orthodox also hold that the Scriptures teach the perpetual virginity of Mary (Desta, pp. 39, 42-5).

410 Msgr. M. Francis Mannion, "Prosperity Gospel is a Travesty of the Good News of Christ," *Catholic News Agency*, 19 Oct. 2015, www.catholicnewsagency.com/column/prosperity-gospel-is-a-travesty-of-the-good-news-of-christ-3360/ (accessed 23 Feb. 2017); David W. Jones, "5 Errors of the Prosperity Gospel," *The Gospel Coalition*, 5 Jun. 2015, https://www.thegospelcoalition.org/article/5-errors-of-the-prosperity-gospel (accessed 23 Feb. 2017). See also Creflo Dollar, "Unlocking the Door to Financial Blessings," *Creflo Dollar Ministries*, 29 Aug. 2016, http://www.creflodollarministries.org/Bible-Study/Articles/Unlocking%20the%20Door%20to%20Financial%20Blessings (accessed 24 Feb. 2017); *The Concise Oxford Dictionary of the Christian Church*, s.v. "Prosperity Theology."

411 Athanasius, *Life of Antony*, in *Early Christian Lives*, no. 2-3, pp. 9-10; Cf. Ward, trans., *The Sayings of the Desert Fathers*, p. 1 (translator's introductory remarks on Antony the Great).

412 The editor notes Matt. 5:3, but Luke 6:20 appears to be the more appropriate reference. See source below.

413 Clare of Assisi, "The First Letter to Blessed Agnes of Prague," in *Francis and Clare: The Complete Works*, nos. 25-29, p. 193. The Matt. 19:24 rendering is from the text; Mark 10:25 is a parallel verse. Cf. González, vol. 1, p. 134.

414 Bonaventure, *The Life of St. Francis*, 3.1, pp. 199-200.

415 Bernard of Clairvaux, *On Loving God* in *Bernard of Clairvaux: Selected Works*, VI.21, p. 190. Cf. St. Francis of Assisi, "The Earlier Rule" in *Francis and Clare: The Complete Works*, nos. 1-5, p. 109. For a similar belief of St. Francis, see Bonaventure, *The Life of St. Francis*, 7.1, p. 240.

416 As quoted in O. Chadwick, p.193. Cf. Estep, pp. 98-9, 127-8 for Anabaptist "One-eyed" Jacob Wiedemann's view on the communal ownership of goods. See also Estep, p. 139; Nolt, p. 65.

417 For a Roman Catholic apologetic piece on this issue, see Tim Staples, "Is Purgatory in the Bible?," *Catholic Answers*, 17 Jan. 2014 http://www.catho-

lic.com/blog/tim-staples/is-purgatory-in-the-bible (accessed 24 Aug. 2018). Staples cites other verses as well.
418 Lewis, *The Joyful Christian*, p. 222. Lewis does not cite any Scripture here but clearly thinks that the doctrine accords with Scripture.
419 "The Sigillion of the Pan-Orthodox Council of Constantinople, 1583," no. 5, http://www.omologitis.org/?p=1517.
420 See *The Concise Oxford Dictionary of the Christian Church*, s.v. "dead, prayers for the" which describes "ample evidence" for the practice in the early fathers, the catacombs, and early Christian liturgies.
421 Augustine of Hippo, *The Care To Be Taken For the Dead*, in *The Fathers of the Church. St. Augustine: Treatises on Marriage and Other Subjects*, ed. Roy J. Deferrari, trans. John A. Lacy (Washington, DC: The Catholic Univ. of America Press, 1969), chs. 1-3, p. 353. For a Roman Catholic defense of purgatory, see *The Catholic Encyclopedia*, s.v. "Purgatory" http://www.newadvent.org/cathen/12575a.htm (accessed 5 Apr. 2019).
422 Robert Brom, "The Rapture," *Catholic Answers*, 10 Aug. 2004, www.catholic.com/tracts/the-rapture (accessed 18 Nov. 2016).
423 Fr. Anthony Coniaris, "The Rapture: Indisputable Christian Heresy," *Mystagogy Resource Center*, 22 Apr. 2010, http://www.johnsanidopoulos.com/2010/04/rapture-indisputable-christian-heresy.html?m=1 (accessed 20 Nov. 2016); Fr. Peter-Michael Preble, "Judgment Day: An Orthodox Christian Perspective," *Huffington Post*, 19 May 2011, http://www.huffingtonpost.com/fr-petermichael-preble/judgement-day-may-21st-an_b_863995.html (accessed 20 Nov. 2016); R.C. Sproul, "What is the Rapture?" *Ligonier Ministries*, 16 Jul. 2012, http://www.ligonier.org/blog/what-is-the-rapture/ (accessed 20 Nov. 2016). See also "The Rapture," *Ligonier Ministries*, n.d., http://www.ligonier.org/learn/devotionals/rapture/.
424 "Part II: Introduction to Church Sacraments," The Ethiopian Orthodox Tewahedo Church Faith and Order, 2003, no. 2 http://ethiopianorthodox.org/english/dogma/sacramentintro.html (accessed 24 Aug. 2016); Desta, p. 26.
425 Mastrantonis, p. 115.
426 See Bryan D. Spinks, "The Mystery of the Holy Leaven (*Malka*) in the East Syrian Tradition," *Issues in Eucharistic Praying in East and West: Essays in Liturgical and Theological Analysis*, ed. Maxwell E. Johnson (Collegeville, MN: Liturgical Press, 2010), pp. 63-70. "Holy Leaven (*Melka*)," *Holy Apostolic Catholic Assyrian Church of the East: Dioceses of Australia, New Zeland, and Lebanon*, n.d., https://assyrianchurch.org.au/about-us/the-sacraments/holy-leaven-melka/ (accessed 17 Mar. 2018). William Steuart McBirnie, *The Search for the Twelve Apostles* (Wheaton: Living

427 O. Chadwick, p. 65 (Luther had three: baptism, eucharist, a modified form of confession).
428 Bonaventure, *The Life of St. Francis*, 11.2, p. 281.
429 St. Francis of Assisi, "The Admonitions" in *Francis and Clare: The Complete Works*, no. 8, p. 26. See also in the same book: "The First Letter to the Custodians," no. 6, p. 53; "The Second Version of the Letter to the Faithful," nos. 33-35, p. 69.
430 Mead and Hill, pp. 74-5, 79, 112, 89.
431 Ibid., p. 109.
432 See *The Dordrecht Confession of Faith, 1632*, The Beachy Amish-Mennonites, n.d., XI. Of the Washing of the Saints Feet, http://www.beachyam.org/dortrecht.htm (accessed 2 Sep. 2016).
433 Mead and Hill, p. 299.
434 *The Canons and Decrees of the Council of Trent*, sess. 14, ch. 3, p. 101. For the four canons anathematizing contrary views on extreme unction, see sess. 14, cans. 1-4, p. 105.
435 As quoted in *The Concise Oxford Dictionary of the Christian Church*, s.v. "agape." For discussion of the agape meal, see *The New Oxford Annotated Bible*, p. 241 NT, footnote on 1 Cor. 11:20-21; p. 360 NT, footnote on Jude 12. See also *New American Bible*, p. 383 NT, footnote on Jude 12; *NIV Study Bible*, p. 1901, footnote on 2 Pet. 2:13.
436 Parrinder, ed., *World Religions*, p. 433.
437 For two discussions that show that there is diversity of opinion, see "Does a Christian Have to Tithe?" *Billy Graham Evangelistic Association*, 1 Jun. 2004, https://billygraham.org/answer/does-a-christian-have-to-tithe/ (accessed 10 Feb. 2017); John Ortberg, "Tithing: Law or Grace?" *Christianity Today*, Spring 2013, www.christianitytoday.com/pastors/2013/spring/tthing-law-or-grace.html (accessed 10 Feb. 2017). Roman Catholics generally do not require a literal 10% tithe. See "What is the Church's Position on Tithing?," *Catholic Answers*, 4 Aug. 2011, www.catholic.com/qa/what-is-the-churchs-position-on-tithing (accessed 10 Feb. 2017); Fr. William Saunders, "Straight Answers: Are We Required to Tithe?" *The Arlington Catholic Herald*, 19 Sep. 2016, www.catholicherald.com/Faith/Your_Faith/Straight_Answers/Straight_Answers_Are_We_Required_to_Tithe_/ (accessed 10 Feb. 2017). Saunders also mentions the 6th-c. advent of Christian tithing.
438 Basil of Caesarea, *De Spiritu Sancto* (*On the Holy Spirit*), in *Nicene and Post-Nicene Fathers, Second Series*, vol. 8, ed. Philip Schaff and Henry Wace,

trans. Blomfield Jackson (Buffalo, NY: Christian Literature Publishing Co., 1895) 29.71 and 27.66, http://www.newadvent.org/fathers/3203.htm (accessed 26 Aug. 2018). Basil cites 1 Cor. 11:2 and 2 Thess. 2:15 as support. See also Movsesian, p. 10 for use of this verse.

439 Tertullian, On the Crown, in *After the New Testament*, p. 352; Irenaeus, 3.2.1-2, http://www.newadvent.org/fathers/0103302.htm; Augustine of Hippo to Januarius (Letter 54), *Letters of St. Augustine of Hippo*, 1.1, http://newadvent.org/fathers/1102054.htm; *The Apostolic Tradition of Hippolytus* (c.217) was in large part an attempt to preserve what were claimed to be apostolic liturgical, sacramental and devotional practices as essentials of the Christian faith. For Scripture citations, see also John of Damascus, IV.16 http://www.newadvent.org/fathers/33044.htm. Cyril of Jerusalem is an example of a father who talks of the sufficiency of Scripture but also thought the Catholic Church was its faithful expositor. See Cyril of Jerusalem, *The Works of St. Cyril of Jerusalem: Lenten Lectures (Catecheses)*, 4.17; 18.23; 18.26.

440 See Mead and Hill, pp. 44-5, 125. See also remarks on American Evangelist Billy Sunday (1862-1935) in Mark Galli and Ted Olsen, eds., *131 Christians Everyone Should Know*, (Nashville, TN: Broadman and Holman, 2000), p. 75; Nolt, pp. 69, 177, 264-56; "Exclusive Brethren," *BBC*, last updated 11 Aug. 2009, http://www.bbc.co.uk/religion/religions/christianity/subdivisions/exclusivebrethren_1.shtml (accessed 4 Jan. 2015); "Doctrine: The Doctrine of Separation," *Plymouth Brethren Christian Church*, n.d., http://www.plymouthbrethrenchristianchurch.org/beliefs/doctrine/ (accessed 4 Jan. 2015); "The Amish," *BBC*, 23 Jun. 2009, http://www.bbc.co.uk/religion/religions/christianity/subdivisions/amish_1.shtml (accessed 26 Aug. 2018). Verses cited here include Rom. 12:2, 1 Cor. 5:11, and Rom. 16:17.

441 Mead and Hill, p. 45.

442 John Hamel, "The 'Jesus Drank Wine' Lie," *John Hamel Ministries*, n.d., http://www.johnhamelministries.org/wine_lie_Jesus.htm (accessed 28 Dec. 2014); John W. Mahaffy, "Wine or Grape Juice: Theological and Pastoral Reflections on the Fruit of the Vine in Communion," *Ordained Servant Online*, Feb. 2011 https://opc.org/os.html?article_id=237&issue_id=62 (accessed 10 Jul. 2018).

443 See, for example, "Question and Answer: Is Wearing Jewelry or Wigs Sinful?" *Orthodox Presbyterian Church*, n.d., http://www.opc.org/qa.html?question_id=469 (accessed 28 Dec. 2014).

444 Matt Slick, "Is It OK for Christians to Dance?" *Christian Apologetics and Research Ministry*, n.d., https://carm.org/christians-dancing (accessed

26 Aug. 2018); "Social Dancing," *Assemblies of God*, n.d., https://ag.org/Beliefs/Topics-Index/Dancing-Social-Dancing (accessed 18 Feb. 2017).

445 Bart Ehrman, *Misquoting Jesus*, p. 187. Cf. Allitt, pp. 145-6; *Handbook of Biblical Criticism*, s.v. "Quest of the Historical Jesus (The)."

446 Reader Gary Isaac put it this way: "all of us are hermeneutically constrained by our biological, experiential, and cultural context. There is no interpretation free of that."

447 Loftus makes a similar observation in *Why I Became an Atheist*, p. 278.

448 "Child Mortality Estimates," UN Inter-agency Group for Child Mortality Estimation, http://www.childmortality.org/ (accessed 4 Sep. 2013). See also "EveryChild," *UNICEFUSA*, 2012, no. 1, p. 11, http://www.unicefusa.org/news/publications/every-child/Every-Child-1-2012.pdf (accessed 4 Sep. 2013). For other alarming statistics on children, see 2012 Annual Report, *National Center for Missing and Exploited Children*, http://www.missingkids.com/en_US/publications/NC171.pdf (accessed 5 Sep. 2013).

449 Nicholas Shrady, *The Last Day: Wrath, Ruin and Reason in the Great Lisbon Earthquake of 1755* (New York: Penguin, 2008), p. 208.

450 "The Bloodiest Day in American History--Hope for Freedom," *Antietam National Battlefield*, updated 11 Jul. 2018, http://www.nps.gov/ancm/index.htm, (accessed 26 Aug. 2018).

451 "America's Wars," Department of Veterans Affairs, n.d., http://www.va.gov/opa/publications/factsheets/fs_americas_wars.pdf (accessed 4 Sep. 2013).

452 Garson O'Toole, "Be Kind; Everyone You Meet is Fighting a Hard Battle," *Quote Investigator: Tracing Quotations*, 29 Jun. 2010, http://quoteinvestigator.com/2010/06/29/be-kind/ (accessed 9 Dec. 2016).

453 Wilken, p. 203.

454 As quoted in Dungan, footnote 12, p. 431. See also Wilken, p. 197.

455 Ehrman, ed., introduction to *After the New Testament*, p. 3: "Most non-Christians, of course, completely rejected the Christian message; many scorned it as ludicrous, and some found it to be socially and religiously dangerous." See also González, vol. 1, p. 50.

456 Robert Louis Wilken, *The Christians As the Romans Saw Them*, 2nd ed. (New Haven, CT: Yale Univ. Press, 2003), pp. 92, 97. Galen also had these critiques.

457 Ibid., p. 97.
458 Ibid., p. 97.
459 Ibid., p. 112.
460 Ibid., p. 97.

461	Ibid., pp. 98-100. Celsus did not deny that Jesus worked miracles—he just thought this was common and did not show that Jesus was God. Asclepius is an example of supposed healing powers. See also Dungan, p. 60.
462	Wilken, pp. 111-12; Dungan, p. 60; Warraq, p. 150. While coming after Jesus, Apollonius of Tyana (c.15-c.100) was said to have miraculous powers; his disciples claimed that he was resurrected and ascended into heaven.
463	Wilken, p. 122 (Celsus, Plato and the golden rule); Adrian Murdoch, *The Last Pagan: Julian the Apostate and the Death of the Ancient World* (Rochester, VT: Inner Traditions, 2008), p. 133 for Julian's comments on the Ten Commandments.
464	Dungan, pp. 61-2 (Celsus). Porphyry had similar views (Wilken, pp. 146-7; Dungan, p. 95) as did Julian (Murdoch, p. 133). For discussions of Gospels as not being eyewitness accounts, see Ehrman, *Misquoting Jesus*, p. 199; Ehrman, *Jesus, Interrupted*, pp. 101-12; Warraq, p. 152.
465	Dungan, pp. 60-1 (Celsus), 97 (Porphyry had similar comments).
466	Although it is not entirely clear, it appears that the problem here is a moral one. Cf. Dungan, p. 93.
467	Wilken, p. 143. Wilken notes that the criticism may or may not have actually come from Porphyry.
468	Ibid., pp. 137-8; Dungan, p. 95.
469	Dungan, p. 96.
470	See Porphyry, *Against the Christians (Fragments)*, *The Tertullian Project*, ed. David Braunsberg, modified Roger Pearse, 2006, no. 64, http://www.tertullian.org/fathers/porphyry_against_christians_02_fragments.htm (accessed 6 Mar. 2013). From Macarius, *Apocriticus* II:14. Unfortunately, the ravages of time and a common Christian practice of destroying unorthodox books has left Julian the Apostate's and Porphyry's works fragmented.
471	Ibid.
472	Porphyry, no. 35. From Macarius, *Apocriticus* IV: 2.
473	Wilken, p. 147.
474	This was Porphyry's contention (Wilken, p. 146). Celsus appears to have argued that Christians had more unity in the beginning but that this unity dissipated as the movement grew in numbers and spread geographically (Dungan, p. 60). I think both critiques have merit.
475	Dungan, p. 94. Porphyry sarcastically suggested that this could be a test for church membership or office.
476	Dungan, p. 97. For similar views from Celsus see pp. 63-4.
477	Wilken, pp. 182-4. For similar view from Porphyry, see Dungan, p. 96.

478   Wilken, p. 182 (Julian).
479   Wilken, p. 184. Of course, it is unlikely Julian held modern explanations for linguistic diversity.
480   Julian the Apostate, *Against the Galileans*, in *Early Church Fathers- Additional Texts*, trans. Wilmer Cave Wright, transcribed Roger Pearse, p. 345, http://www.tertullian.org/fathers/julian_apostate_galileans_1_text.htm. Pearse notes that *Against the Galileans* is the "remains of the 3 books, excerpted from Cyril of Alexandria, *Contra Julianum* (1923) pp. 319-433."
481   Wilken, pp. 191-2. The NRSV translation shows this very distinction. Jews have commonly pointed out Matthew's misunderstanding of this verse. (The word "virgin" in Matthew comes from an error in translation in the Greek Septuagint from the Hebrew word for "young woman.") Jerome mentions this Jewish rejection of Matthew's use of Isaiah in *The Perpetual Virginity of the Blessed Mary*, no. 4, http://www.newadvent.org/fathers/3007.htm.
482   Wilken, pp. 110, 182.
483   Ibid., pp. 191-2. Medieval Jewish scholar Maimonides noted that that it is "the foundation of our Law that no other will ever take place" (Maimonides, 2.39, p. 140).
484   Wilken, p. 182. Cf. Davis, p. 18: "Many came to see the gods as reflections of the power and perfections of one supreme deity and the beautifully expressed stories about them as allegories."
485   Murdoch, pp. 140-1.
486   González, vol. 1, p. 171.
487   Davis, p. 21.
488   *The Catholic Encyclopedia*, s.v. "Infanticide" http://www.newadvent.org/cathen/08001b.htm; Augustine to Boniface (Letter 98), *Letters of St. Augustine of Hippo*, no. 6, http://www.newadvent.org/fathers/1102098.htm.
489   Tertullian, *Apology*, in *After the New Testament*, 39.7, p. 350. Granted, this is Tertullian's claim as an insider—but the sentiment seems to have merit.
490   Huxley, "Agnosticism," in *Agnosticism and Christianity and Other Essays*, p. 164.
491   John Henry Newman, *Apologia Pro Vita Sua: Being a History of His Religious Opinions* (London: Longmans, Green and Co., 1888), p. 262. Avail. at https://archive.org/details/apologiaprovitas00newm_2/page/262.
492   The Catholic Encyclopedia, s.v. "Scruple" http://www.newadvent.org/cathen/13640a.htm (accessed 22 Mar. 2013).
493   See Wulff, pp. 126, 244.
494   Thomas Merton, *The Seven Storey Mountain* (San Diego: Harvest/Harcourt Brace Jovanovich, 1978), p. 205.

495 Idries Shah, *Tales of the Dervishes* (New York: Penguin, 1993), p. 83.
496 See Davis, p. 326; Ehrman, *Misquoting Jesus*, pp. 155-6; Eusebius, 3.27, p. 93.
497 Davis, p. 327.
498 Davis, p. 249.
499 Many Gnostic Christians held this view.
500 Davis, pp. 171, 176-177, 196; Bellitto, p. 25; *The Concise Oxford Dictionary of the Christian Church*, s.v. "Eutyches" and "Monophysitism."
501 See Ehrman, *Misquoting Jesus*, p. 152; cf. Pagels, p. 3; González, vol. 1, p. 59.
502 Pagels, pp. 49-59.
503 H. Chadwick, p. 39; Dungan, pp. 50-6.
504 As quoted in Davis, p. 186. This is the definition of the Council of Chalcedon (451).
505 Ibid., p. 251. González gives the term as "melchites" and states it means "imperial" (vol. 1, p. 262). See also *The Catholic Encyclopedia*, s.v. "Melchites" newadvent.org/cathen/10157b.htm (accessed 22 Jan. 2019). Monophysites are generally known for believing that Christ had one nature. See Desta, p. x. The Oriental Orthodox Churches who espouse this view generally prefer the term miaphysitism or henophysitism. See *OrthodoxWiki*, s.v. "Miaphysitism" http://orthodoxwiki.org/Miaphysitism (accessed 13 Sep. 2013).
506 Davis, pp. 155, 329. The Eastern Orthodox sometimes refer to modern-day Protestants as "Crypto-Nestorians" in part for their rejection of the title "God-bearer" for Mary. See *OrthodoxWiki*, s.v. "Nestorianism" http://orthodoxwiki.org/Nestorianism (accessed 10 Sep. 2013). It is probably more accurate to say that Nestorians emphasized the differences in the human and divine nature of Christ—rather than thinking Christ was two persons.
507 Origen, *On First Principles*, in *After the New Testament*, 1.3.15, p. 420. For more on Origen's theology of the Trinity, see *The Westminster Dictionary of Theologians*, s.v. "Origen."
508 This belief has also been called "Sabellianism" or "modalism" (H. Chadwick, p. 87). Oneness Pentecostals hold to a similar view today. See also *OrthodoxWiki*, s.v. "Sabellianism" http://orthodoxwiki.org/Sabellianism (accessed 13 Sep. 2013).
509 *The Concise Oxford Dictionary of the Christian Church*, s.v. "Pneumatomachi." Pneumatomachianism was a pejorative term for those who were thought to be "fighters against the Spirit." For further discussions on Chris-

510 tology and angels, see Charles H. Talbert, *What Is a Gospel? The Genre of the Canonical Gospels* (Philadelphia: Fortress Press, 1977), pp. 70-3.
510 Davis, p. 40; *The Catholic Encyclopedia*, s.v. "Melchisedechians" http://www.newadvent.org/cathen/10157a.htm (accessed 30 Aug. 2018). Cf. Heb. 7:1-4.
511 St. Mark the Ascetic, *On Those Who Think They Are Made Righteous by Works: Two Hundred and Twenty-Six Texts*, in *The Philokalia: The Complete Text*, vol. 1, ed. and trans. G.E.H. Palmer et al. (London: Faber and Faber, 1979), no. 91, p. 133.
512 Wulff, pp. 222-3.
513 Paul Boyer, "The Growth of Fundamentalist Apocalyptic in the United States," in *The Continuum History of Apocalypticism*, ed. Bernard McMinn, John J. Collins, and Stephen J. Stein (New York: Continuum, 2003), p. 542.
514 For an interesting literal take on 2 Pet. 3:5-8 and the Noahic Flood, see John Calvin, *Commentaries on the Catholic Epistles*, ed. and trans. John Owen (Grand Rapids, MI: Christian Classics Ethereal Library, orig. pub. 1855), pp. 377-9 http://www.ccel.org/ccel/calvin/calcom45.pdf: "The world no doubt had its origin from waters …."
515 In Reformation theology, the "analogy of faith" is the use of Scripture to interpret Scripture. Here one non-historical event in Scripture suggests that another is mythical as well.
516 Boyer, "The Growth of Fundamentalist Apocalyptic in the United States," in *The Continuum History of Apocalypticism*, p. 521.
517 Brian E. Daley, "Apocalypticism in Early Christian Theology," in *The Continuum History of Apocalypticism*, p. 223.
518 See Rudolf Bultmann, *Jesus Christ and Mythology* (Upper Saddle River, NJ: Prentice Hall, 1958), p. 14: "Christianity has always retained the hope that the Kingdom of God will come in the immediate future, although it has waited in vain. … The course of history has refuted mythology." 2 Pet., a later work which is commonly thought to be inauthentic, is typically understood by critical scholars to contain an attempt to explain away why Christ did not return soon as promised (2 Pet. 3:8-9). See also Loftus, *Why I Became an Atheist*, p. 172; NAB, p. 369. For further discussion on dubious NT prophecies, see Daniels, pp. 216-223; Luke 21:25-33.
519 Said Amir Arjomand, "Islamic Apocalypticism in the Classical Period," in *The Continuum History of Apocalypticism*, pp. 383, 403; J. Eugene Clay, "Apocalypticism in Eastern Europe," p. 628 in the same volume. See also *The Penguin Dictionary of Religions*, s.v. "Anti-Christ (in Islam)"; "Jesus in Islam"; "Mahdi".

520   Hatcher, "Baha'i Faith," in *How Different Religions View Death and Afterlife*, pp. 27-8. Muhammad is also described as a return of Jesus, but not the Manifestation that would usher in the "universal transformation of mankind." See also Hatcher and Martin, footnote 27, p. 118,

521   *Encyclopedia of Mormonism*, s.v. "New Jerusalem" https://eom.byu.edu/index.php/New_Jerusalem (accessed 11 Jan. 2019).

522   Nigosian, p. 97; Moshe Idel, "Jewish Apocalypticism, 670-1670," in *The Continuum History of Apocalypticism* p. 356.

523   Florentino Garcia Martinez, "Apocalypticism in the Dead Sea Scrolls," in *The Continuum History of Apocalypticism*, pp. 89, 101; cf. *Mercer Dictionary of the Bible*, s.v. "Dead Sea Scrolls"; *The Concise Oxford Dictionary of the Christian Church*, s.v. "Dead Sea Scrolls."

524   Ignatius of Antioch, The Epistle of Ignatius to the Ephesians, in *Ante-Nicene Fathers*, vol. 1, ed. Alexander Roberts et al., trans. Alexander Roberts and James Donaldson (Buffalo, NY: Christian Literature Publishing Co., 1885), ch. 11, http://www.newadvent.org/fathers/0104.htm: "The last times have come upon us."

525   Daley, "Apocalypticism in Early Christian Theology," in *The Continuum History of Apocalypticism*, p. 224.

526   Second Clement, in *Ante-Nicene Fathers*, vol. 9, ed. Allan Menzies, trans. John Keith (Buffalo, NY: Christian Literature Publishing Co., 1896), ch. 16, http://www.newadvent.org/fathers/1011.htm. Likely written in the 140's, Second Clement urges that "the day of judgment draws near like a burning oven." Ehrman translates the phrase as "the day of judgment is already coming" (*The Apostolic Fathers*, in *The Loeb Classical Library*, vol. 1, ed. and trans. Bart D. Ehrman (Cambridge, MA: Harvard Univ. Press, 2003), p. 191.

527   See Ehrman, *Lost Scriptures*, p. 251; *The Westminster Dictionary of Theologians*, s.v. "Hermas (2nd century)" which notes "the imminent end of the world" in Hermas. In Hermas, a vision of the tower represents the Church (11:3)—and not until the tower is finished will the end come. Hermas adds: "But it will be built quickly" (16:9).

528   Dana Netherton, "Taking the Long View," *Christian History* 18.1, issue 61 (1999): p. 11; Daley, "Apocalypticism in Early Christian Theology," in *The Continuum History of Apocalypticism*, p. 227; Jonathan Kirsch, *A History of the End of the World: How the Most Controversial Book of the Bible Changed the Course of Western Civilization* (San Francisco: HarperSanFrancisco, 2006), pp. 104-6.

529   Daley, "Apocalypticism in Early Christian Theology," in *The Continuum History of Apocalypticism*, p. 226.

530 Ibid., p. 229.
531 Ibid., p. 228.
532 Netherton, p. 12. See also Daley, "Apocalypticism in Early Christian Theology," in *The Continuum History of Apocalypticism*, p. 228 has Hippolytus projecting out 500 years from the birth of Christ for the end in *On Christ and Anti-Christ* (4.23ff.). See also Kirsch, p. 106.
533 Bonner, pp. 169-70.
534 Daley, "Apocalypticism in Early Christian Theology," in *The Continuum History of Apocalypticism*, pp. 232-3.
535 Athanasius, *Life of Antony*, in *Christian Lives*, no. 69, p. 52. For references to the Antichrist, see (1 John 2:18; 2 Thess. 2:1-12). In Christian theology, the Antichrist is considered to be an evil figure who will be connected to the end times.
536 Kirsch, p. 124; cf. p. 139. His disciple Sulpicius Severus (d.c.420) continued with these sorts of sentiments. See also Daley, "Apocalypticism in Early Christian Theology," in *The Continuum History of Apocalypticism*, p. 235; Sulpicius Severus, *Life of Martin of Tours*, in *Early Christian Lives*, no. XXIV, p. 156 for Severus' belief that "the Antichrist is imminent."
537 Sulpicius Severus, *Life of Martin of Tours* in *Early Christian Lives*, no. XXII, p. 154.
538 Kirsh, p. 125; Daley, "Apocalypticism in Early Christian Theology," in *The Continuum History of Apocalypticism*, p. 236.
539 Daley, "Apocalypticism in Early Christian Theology," in *The Continuum History of Apocalypticism*, pp. 236-7, 242, 246-7.
540 Ibid., p. 249; Bernard McMinn, "Apocalypticism and Church Reform: 1100-1500," in *The Continuum History of Apocalypticism*, p. 275.
541 As quoted in Kirsch, p. 101.
542 Ibid., pp. 125-6.
543 Arjomand, "Islamic Apocalypticism in the Classical Period," in *The Continuum History of Apocalypticism*, pp. 385-6; Swarup, p. 216.
544 Bukhari, bk. 34, no. 169 (3.34.425) http://sunnah.com/bukhari/34/169. Cf. bk. 60, no. 118 (4.55.657) http://sunnah.com/bukhari/60/118. See also Swarup, pp. 23-4. (Swarup appears to be using one of Muslim's hadith; see p. 7).
545 Kirsch, pp. 128-9; *The Westminster Dictionary of Theologians*, s.v. "Beatus of Liebana."
546 James Reston, Jr., *The Last Apocalypse: Europe at the Year 1000 A.D.* (New York: Anchor, 1998), pp. 114-5.
547 Ibid., p. 79.

548 "The End of the World Is Near," *The Blickling Homilies*, trans. R. Morris, (London: N. Trübner and Co., 1880), no. 10, http://www.apocalyptic-theories.com/literature/blicklingx/meblickx.html (accessed 23 Apr. 2014). See also Reston, p. 11.
549 Arjomand, "Islamic Apocalypticism in the Classical Period," in *The Continuum History of Apocalypticism*, p. 398. The Islamic calendar starts in the year 622.
550 Reston, p. 259; McMinn, "Apocalypticism and Church Reform: 1100-1500," in *The Continuum History of Apocalypticism*, p. 273.
551 Reston, pp. 166-8.
552 Ibid., p. 260.
553 Adam Nemeroff, Apocalypticism and the First Crusade," *Dartmouth University*, 24 Apr. 2016, https://sites.dartmouth.edu/crusadememory/2016/04/24/apocalypticism-and-the-first-crusade/ (accessed 23 Nov. 2017).
554 Geoffrey Hindley, *The Crusades: Islam and Christianity in the Struggle for World Supremacy* (New York: Carroll and Graf Publishers, 2005), p. 16.
555 Kirsch, p. 126.
556 McMinn, "Apocalypticism and Church Reform: 1100-1500," in *The Continuum History of Apocalypticism*, pp. 282-4; Kirsch, pp. 142-4. See also Kirsch, p. 142.
557 McMinn, "Apocalypticism and Church Reform: 1100-1500," in *The Continuum History of Apocalypticism*, p. 279.
558 Hindley, p. 180.
559 Idel, "Jewish Apocalypticism, 670-1670," in *The Continuum History of Apocalypticism*, pp. 358, 367-9. Roger Bacon saw the Mongol attacks of 1258 as a sign of the proximity of the Antichrist. See McMinn, "Apocalypticism and Church Reform: 1100-1500," in *The Continuum History of Apocalypticism*, p. 282.
560 Idel, "Jewish Apocalypticism, 670-1670," in *The Continuum History of Apocalypticism*, p. 368.
561 Ibid., pp. 370; 359-60.
562 Ibid., p. 361.
563 McMinn, "Apocalypticism and Church Reform: 1100-1500," in *The Continuum History of Apocalypticism*, pp. 283, 285.
564 Ibid., pp. 285-7. See also Bonaventure, *The Life of St. Francis*, in *Bonaventure: The Soul's Journey into God – The Tree of Life – The Life of St. Francis*, trans. Ewert Cousins (Mahwah, NJ: Paulist Press, 1978), Prologue, no. 1, p. 181.
565 González, vol. 1, p. 360.

566	Gian Luca Potesta, "Radical Apocalyptic Movements in the Late Middle Ages," in *The Continuum History of Apocalypticism*, p. 310.
567	Kirsch, p. 164.
568	Potesta, "Radical Apocalyptic Movements in the Late Middle Ages," in *The Continuum History of Apocalypticism*, p. 304.
569	Ibid., p. 306.
570	Ibid., p. 314.
571	Ibid., p. 312; González, vol. 1, p. 352.
572	McMinn, "Apocalypticism and Church Reform: 1100-1500," pp. 290-1; Bert Ghezzi, *Mystics and Miracles: True Stories of Lives Touched by God* (Chicago: Loyola Press, 2002), p. 110.
573	Potesta, "Radical Apocalyptic Movements in the Late Middle Ages," in *The Continuum History of Apocalypticism*, p. 317. Kirsch, pp. 17, 166-9; *The Catholic Encyclopedia*, s.v. "Girolamo Savonarola" http://www.newadvent.org/cathen/13490a.htm (accessed 6 May 2015).
574	Reginald Stackhouse, "Columbus' Millennial Voyage," *Christian History* 18.1, issue 61 (1999): p. 19; cf. McMinn, "Apocalypticism and Church Reform: 1100-1500," p. 293.
575	Clay, "Apocalypticism in Eastern Europe," in *The Continuum History of Apocalypticism*, p. 629. This old Orthodox calendar had its beginning date as the creation instead of the birth of Christ (p. 635).
576	Idel, "Jewish Apocalypticism, 670-1670," in *The Continuum History of Apocalypticism*, p. 371.
577	Kirsch, p. 126.
578	Oberman, pp. 46-7, 71-2, 218, 266 etc. Cf. Robin Barnes, "Images of Hope and Despair: Western Apocalypticism," in *The Continuum History of Apocalypticism*, pp. 329-30.
579	Kirsch, pp. 126, 161.
580	Estep, p. 266. See also Robert L. Wise, "Munster's Monster," *Christian History* 18.1, issue 61 (1999): pp. 23-5; Kirsch, p. 164-5; Barnes, "Images of Hope and Despair: Western Apocalypticism," in *The Continuum History of Apocalypticism*, p. 327-8. Estep suggests that Hans Hutt predicted in 1527 that the end would come in 1529 (pp. 114-15) among other dates (p. 119). For 1533 prediction of Melchior Hoffman, see Estep, p. 154; González, vol. 2, pp. 57-8.
581	Idel, "Jewish Apocalypticism, 670-1670," in *The Continuum History of Apocalypticism*, p. 359.
582	Barnes, "Images of Hope and Despair: Western Apocalypticism," in *The Continuum History of Apocalypticism*, p. 336.

583 Alain Milhou, "Apocalypticism in Central and South American Colonialism," in *The Continuum History of Apocalypticism*, p. 422.
584 Clay, "Apocalypticism in Eastern Europe," in *The Continuum History of Apocalypticism*, pp. 630-1.
585 John Richards, *The Mughal Empire* (Cambridge: Cambridge Univ. Press, 1995), p. 38.
586 Damian Thompson, *Waiting for Antichrist: Charisma and Apocalypse in a Pentecostal Church* (New York: Oxford Univ. Press, 2005), pp. 145-6.
587 Kirsch, p. 175.
588 Ibid., p. 165; González, vol. 2, p. 146.
589 Kirsch, p. 177; Barnes, "Images of Hope and Despair: Western Apocalypticism," in *The Continuum History of Apocalypticism*, p. 338.
590 Kirsch, p. 197; Barnes, "Images of Hope and Despair: Western Apocalypticism," in *The Continuum History of Apocalypticism*, p. 339; Karen Armstrong, *The Battle for God: A History of Fundamentalism* (New York: Alfred A. Knopf, 2000), pp. 27-30. Sevi apparently converted to Islam under duress.
591 Clay, "Apocalypticism in Eastern Europe," in *The Continuum History of Apocalypticism*, pp. 632-3.
592 Ibid., pp. 633.
593 Kathleen B. McMurphy, "John Wesley and the End of the World," *Ministry*, Apr. 1960, https://www.ministrymagazine.org/archive/1960/04/john-wesley-and-the-end-of-the-world (accessed 1 May 2015); Barnes, "Images of Hope and Despair: Western Apocalypticism," in *The Continuum History of Apocalypticism*, p. 346; John Wesley, *Wesley's Explanatory Notes*, n.d., Rev. 12:14-16, http://www.biblestudytools.com/commentaries/wesleys-explanatory-notes/revelation/revelation-12.html (accessed 1 May 2015).
594 Smolinski, "Apocalypticism in Colonial North America," in *The Continuum History of Apocalypticism*, p. 456.
595 Boyer, "The Growth of Fundamentalist Apocalyptic in the United States," in *The Continuum History of Apocalypticism*, p. 519.
596 Clay, "Apocalypticism in Eastern Europe," in *The Continuum History of Apocalypticism*, pp. 638-9.
597 Barnes, "Images of Hope and Despair: Western Apocalypticism," in *The Continuum History of Apocalypticism*, p. 348.
598 *Encyclopedia Britannica*, s.v. "Ann Lee" https://www.britannica.com/biography/Ann-Lee (accessed 26 Apr. 2019).
599 Eoin O'Carroll, "Judgment Day? Five Failed End-of-the World Predictions," *Christian Science Monitor*, 18 May 2011, http://www.csmonitor.com/

Science/2011/0518/Judgment-Day-Five-failed-end-of-the-world-predictions/1806 (accessed 31 Aug. 2018).

600 Clay, "Apocalypticism in Eastern Europe," in *The Continuum History of Apocalypticism*, p. 640.

601 Bruce Shelley, "The Great Disappointment," *Christian History* 18.1, issue 61 (1999): pp. 31-3. Cf. Kirsch, pp. 183-5. James H. Moorhead, "Apocalypticism in Mainstream Protestantism, 1800 to the Present," in *The Continuum History of Apocalypticism*, p. 474; Stephen J. Stein, "Apocalypticism Outside the Mainstream in the United States," in *The Continuum History of Apocalypticism*, pp. 498-500. Cf. Boyer, "The Growth of Fundamentalist Apocalyptic in the United States," in *The Continuum History of Apocalypticism*, p. 520. See also González, vol. 2, pp. 255-6.

602 See Hatcher and Martin, pp. 6-9, 14, 16, 25-26 (the Báb as forerunner), 37, 40; Hatcher, in *How Different Religions View Death and Afterlife*, pp. 27-8 (Baha'u'llah as Second Coming).

603 Robert M. Levine, "Apocalyptic Movements in Latin America in the Nineteenth and Twentieth Centuries, in *The Continuum History of Apocalypticism*, p. 549.

604 Stein, "Apocalypticism Outside the Mainstream in the United States," in *The Continuum History of Apocalypticism*, pp. 497-8.

605 Kirsch, p. 192.

606 Nolt, p. 125.

607 Vinson Synan, "The 'Second Comers,'" *Christian History* 18.1, issue 61 (1999): pp. 38-9. See Boyer, "The Growth of Fundamentalist Apocalyptic in the United States," in *The Continuum History of Apocalypticism*, p. 529 for a further discussion of nascent Pentecostalism and the imminent return of Jesus.

608 Stein, "Apocalypticism Outside the Mainstream in the United States," in *The Continuum History of Apocalypticism*, pp. 504, 508; Boyer, "The Growth of Fundamentalist Apocalyptic in the United States," in *The Continuum History of Apocalypticism*, p. 529; Kirsch, p. 202.

609 González, vol. 2, p. 35.

610 Ung Kyu Pak, *Millennialism in the Korean Protestant Church* (New York: Peter Lang Publishing, 2005), p. 4.

611 Boyer, "The Growth of Fundamentalist Apocalyptic in the United States," in *The Continuum History of Apocalypticism*, p. 534; Kirsch, pp. 218-9.

612 González, vol. 2, p. 382; *The New International Dictionary of the Christian Church*, s.v. "Divine, Major J. ('Father Divine')."

613 Boyer, "The Growth of Fundamentalist Apocalyptic in the United States," in *The Continuum History of Apocalypticism*, pp. 535-7; Kirsch, pp. 222-5. The "Rapture" would be in 1981.
614 Robert G. Clouse, "Late Great Predictions," *Christian History* 18.1, issue 61 (1999): pp. 40-1.
615 Boyer, "The Growth of Fundamentalist Apocalyptic in the United States," in *The Continuum History of Apocalypticism*, p. 533.
616 Ibid., pp. 540-1.
617 Associated Press, "Doomsday Minister Harold Camping Dead at 92," *USA Today*, 18 Dec. 2013, http://www.usatoday.com/story/news/nation/2013/12/18/harold-camping-dead-minister/4107749/ (accessed 30 Apr. 2015); Clouse, pp. 40-1.
618 Michael W. Chapman, "Billy Graham's Daughter: 'The Day of the Lord is Near,' God Is 'Warning America,' We're in the 'Last' Generation,'" *CNS News*, 20 May 2015, http://cnsnews.com/blog/michael-w-chapman/billy-grahams-daughter-day-lord-near-god-warning-america-were-last-generation (accessed 31 Aug. 2018).
619 "Gay 'Marriage' a 'Sign of the Apocalypse': Russian Patriarch," *lifesitenews.com*, 22 Jul., 2013, https://www.lifesitenews.com/news/gay-marriage-a-sign-of-the-apocalypse-russian-patriarch (accessed 9 Jan. 2019); Michael Shermer, *The Moral Arc: How Science Makes Us Better People* (New York: St. Martin's Griffin, 2015), p. 251. Anatasia Clark and Chris Bell, "Smartphone Users Warned to Be Careful of the Antichrist," *BBC.com*, 8 Jan. 2019, https://www.bbc.com/news/blogs-trending-46794556 (accessed 8 Jan. 2019); Associated Press, "Russian Church Head: Smartphones Could Precede AntiChrist," *msn.com*, 8 Jan.2019, https://www.msn.com/en-us/news/world/russian-church-head-smartphones-could-precede-antichrist/ar-BBRXANc (accessed 8 Jan. 2019).
620 "The Second Coming of Jesus," *Pew Research Center*, 21 Apr. 2009, http://www.pewresearch.org/daily-number/the-second-coming-of-jesus/ (accessed 1 May 2015).
621 "Jesus Christ's Return to Earth," *Pew Research Center*, 14 Jul. 2010, http://www.pewresearch.org/daily-number/jesus-christs-return-to-earth/ (accessed 1 May 2015).
622 Tahir Nasser, "What Has Jesus Got to Do with ISIS? A Lot," *Religion News Service*, 21 Oct. 2016, www.religionnews.com/2016/10/21/what-has-jesus-got-to-do-with-isis-a-lot/ (accessed 25 Oct. 2016). See "The World's Muslims: Unity and Diversity: Chapter 3: Articles of Faith," *Pew Research Center*, 9 Aug. 2012, www.pewforum.org/2012/08/09/the-worlds-muslims-unity-and-diversity-3-articles-of-faith/ (accessed 25 Oct. 2016); Ruth Sher-

lock, "What is the Islamic State Trying to Achieve?" *The Telegraph*, 10 Jun. 2015, www.telegraph.co.uk/news/worldnews/islamic-state/11665474/What-is-Islamic-State-trying-to-achieve.html (accessed 25 Oct. 2016): "While the jihadists' actions focus on territorial expansion, their philosophy is to bring about the end of the world."

623   Jonas Bendiksen, "Messiah Complex," *National Geographic* (Aug. 2017): pp. 82-93.

624   Mumon Ekai, *The Gateless Gate*, in *Zen Flesh, Zen Bones: A Collection of Zen and Pre-Zen Writings*, ed. and trans. Nyogen Senzaki and Paul Reps (Rutland, VT: Tuttle, 1985), no. 19, pp. 146-157, Kindle. © 1957, 1985, Charles E. Tuttle Co. Quoted with permission. For an alternative translation, see Mumon Ekai, *The Gateless Gate*, in *Two Zen Classics: The Gateless Gate and the Blue Cliff Records*, ed. A.V. Grimestone, trans. Katsuri Sekida (Boston: Shambhala, 2005), case 19, p. 73.

625   Nigosian, p. 97.

626   I.e., Judaism, Christianity, and Islam; Abraham is regarded as a patriarch in all three faiths.

627   Per Ehrman, *Jesus, Interrupted*, p. 12: "The authors of Job and Ecclesiastes explicitly state that there is no afterlife." There are differing opinions on this issue, but it appears undeniable that the concept of the afterlife developed significantly after increased Jewish contact with Persia. Bible verses that show a very different concept of the afterlife in the OT include Ps. 6:4-5, Ps. 115:17-18, Eccles. 9:10. *The New Oxford Annotated Bible* notes regarding Ps. 115:17: "In early Israel it was believed that the dead in Sheol (*silence*) were separated from God (88.5-6)" (p. 775). Ben Zion Bokser notes in his introduction to The Tractate Sanhedrin in *The Talmud: Selected Writings*, "There is no explicit reference in the Bible to the resurrection of the dead and there were interpretations of Judaism that did not accept it. … Through an ingenious interpretation of certain texts this teaching was read into the Bible" (p. 199).

628   The Babylonian Captivity of the Jews ended in 538 BCE by edict of the Persian conqueror Cyrus. See *Mercer Dictionary of the Bible*, s.v. "Cyrus." Traditionally, the Book of Daniel was said to be written in 530 BCE. Scholarly consensus now puts the book at 167-164 BCE. See NAB, introduction to the Book of Daniel, p. 1021. Cf. *NIV Study Bible* which disagrees with this admittedly "widely held view" (p. 1298). The archangel Gabriel is mentioned in Daniel for first time (Dan. 9:21). *Mercer Dictionary of the Bible*, s.v. "Angel" notes that "Except within the Book of Daniel, angels were never named in the OT."

629   Rose, pp. xxii, 87-95. See Rose for comments on Dan. 12:2 and Isaiah (p. 90).
630   Parrinder, ed., *World Religions*, p. 191. For similar perspectives, see Nigosian, p. 97; Boyce, ed., pp. 20-1, 35; Jamsheed Choksy, "Zoroastrianism," in *How Different Religions View Death and Afterlife*, p. 246; *The Penguin Dictionary of Religions*, s.v. "Zoroaster" and s.v. "Zoroastrianism." Cf. *The New International Dictionary of the Christian Church*, s.v. "Zoroastrianism."
631   Rose, p. 12. Parsis can also be spelled "Parsees."
632   In mid-1960's, Zoroastrians in Iran numbered 60,000; by 2004, numbers had dwindled down to 25,000 (Rose, pp. 185, 187). Cf. Parrinder, ed., *World Religions*, p. 191 which notes just over 125,000 in India and 25,000 in Iran (by 1976 census).
633   Choksy describes a growing dominance of Zoroastrianism which culminated as a state religion in the Sasanian Empire ("Zoroastrianism," *How Different Religions View Death and Afterlife*, p. 251). Boyce, ed. describes a dominance in the earlier empires as well (p. 7); *The Penguin Dictionary of Religions*, s.v. "Zoroastrianism," p. 575 notes that "for over 1,000 years Zoroastrianism was the official religion of three major world empires, making it, perhaps, the most powerful religion of the time."
634   Boyce, ed., pp. 7, 23; Rose, p. xxii.
635   *Mercer Dictionary of the Bible*, s.v. "Cyrus."
636   Rose, pp. 51, 57; Choksy, "Zoroastrianism," in *How Different Religions View Death and Afterlife*, p. 247. Zoroastrian priests were commonly thought to have powers of dream interpretation. Cf. Parrinder, ed., *World Religions* which also calls the Magi Zoroastrian priests (pp. 188-90). The NRSV translates the Greek *magi* as "wise men."
637   *The Koran*, trans. Dawood, Sura 22:17, pp. 402-3. My italics.
638   Choksy, "Zoroastrianism," *How Different Religions View Death and Afterlife*, p. 257. I believe the answer to the question posed was penned by Choksy as well (pp. 284-6).
639   Ibid., p. 259: "The reduction of Zoroastrianism to the status of a minor religious community was incorporated into the faith's sacred history and explained in terms of a steady increase in evil and pollution that heralds the advent of the final days." Cf. 1 Tim 3:1-9. As Bonner describes, the Donatist sect of North Africa thought that "the Lord had preserved a very small remnant" in their own sect (pp. 251, 284).
640   Nigosian, pp. 96-7
641   Ibid., pp. 11-12, 18, 46. See also Rose, p. xix: "Zoroastrians regard the *Gathas* as the authoritative, original teachings of Zarathustra." The Gathas were given "from Ahura Mazda to humanity" and are thought to

have originated around the 2nd millennium BCE. (ibid., p. 9). Cf. Boyce, ed., p. 1.

642 Nigosian, p. 21.

643 Rose, p. 17. Modi, pp. 3, 9, etc.

644 From *Selected Precepts of the Ancient Sages*, in Boyce, ed., p. 100.

645 See Nigosian, pp. 34, 36, 38; Boyce, ed., pp. 62, 89, 110, 112-113; Rose pp. 115-6; Bonner, pp. 159-60 describes the death of Mani himself.

646 *The Penguin Dictionary of Religions*, s.v. "Zoroastrianism"; Nigosian, pp. 42-4. Nigosian suggests that while traditional accounts confirm that persecution was the reason for the migration to India, the intensity of that persecution is a matter of debate (p. 43).

647 Rose, pp. 83, 175, 179. *The Penguin Dictionary of Religions*, s.v. "Zoroastrianism"; Jamsheed K. Choksy, "How Iran persecutes its oldest religion," *CNN*, 14 Nov. 2011, http://www.cnn.com/2011/11/14/opinion/choksy-iran-zoroastrian/ (accessed 31 Aug. 2018).

648 Jivanji Jamshedji Modi, *A Catechism of the Zoroastrian Religion* (Bombay: J.N. Petit Parsi Orphange Captin Printing Works, 1911), p. 42, https://archive.org/details/catechismofzoroa00modirich. Cf. p. 41.

649 Nigosian, p. 38. Mihr Narseh drafted an edict in 449 CE advising that anyone who was not Zoroastrian was "deaf, blind and deceived by the *dev* of Ahriman" (Rose, p. 108).

650 Nigosian, pp. 36, 39-40, 69, 89; Rose, pp. p. xviii, 1, 7-8, 32, 101, 105, 131, 142-3, 223ff; Boyce, ed., p. 96. Rose, See also *The Penguin Dictionary of Religions*, s.v. "Zurvanism."

651 Rose, p. 21.

652 Boyce, p. 12.

653 Nigosian, pp. 102-3; Rose, pp. 57-8; Boyce, ed., pp. 106-7. At least some Zoroastrians have apparently been practicing a kind of exposure of the dead since the time of Herodotus (5th c. BCE). See Herodotus, *The Histories*, trans. Robin Waterfield (Oxford: Oxford Univ. Press, 1998), 1.140, p. 63: "It is said that the body of a Persian man is not buried until it has been mauled by a bird or dog." While I do not quote from this translation, a quick reference to all citations can be found on-line at: Herodotus, *The Histories*, ed. and trans. A.D. Godley (Cambridge: Harvard Univ. Press, 1920), from *Perseus Digital Library*, Tufts University, http://www.perseus.tufts.edu/hopper/text?doc=Perseus%3atext%3a1999.01.0126.

654 Rose, p. 192. Nigosian, pp. 36, 102-3.

655 Rose, p. 26.

656 Rose, pp. 26, 160, 167; Boyce, ed., p. 144.

657 Boyce, ed., pp. 43, 50, 97, 125; Rose, pp. 25, 27, 75-6, 177.

658	See Boyce, ed., p. 146. For a Muslim parallel with sneezing and yawning, see Swarup, pp. 149, 191.
659	Parrinder, ed., *World Religions*, p. 180. Boyce, ed., pp. 69, 140, 146; Modi, p. 36.
660	Nigosian, p. 113.
661	Ibid., p .23.
662	Rose, pp. 23, 89; Boyce, ed., pp. 12-15; Choksy, "Zoroastrianism," in *How Different Religions View Death and Afterlife*, p. 249; Nigosian, p. 116.
663	Choksy, "Zoroastrianism," in *How Different Religions View Death and Afterlife*, p. 251; Nigosian, p. 116.
664	Parrinder, ed., *World Religions*, p. 181; Nigosian, p. 73; Boyce, ed., p. 134.
665	Choksy, "Zoroastrianism," in *How Different Religions View Death and Afterlife*, p. 252.
666	Rose, pp. 63-5; Boyce, ed., p. 7. Alexander is known as "the accursed" rather than "the Great" by Zoroastrians. The Macedonian's conquest of the Persian Empire in the 4th c. BCE is remembered as a time of the horrific tragedy, the slaughter of priests, and the burning of religious texts.
667	See Boyce, ed., p. 1; Nigosian, p. 3; Rose, p. 104.
668	Choksy, "Zoroastrianism," in *How Different Religions View Death and Afterlife*, p. 248.
669	Parrinder, ed., *World Religions*, p. 177.
670	Boyce, ed., p. 11.
671	Choksy, "Zoroastrianism,"in *How Different Religions View Death and Afterlife*, p. 247.
672	Nigosian, pp. 14-17. Nigosian gives a wide range of opinions from antiquity and from the present ranging from earlier than 6,000 BCE to the 6th c. BCE.
673	Boyce, ed., from forward (before p. 1).
674	Paine, *The Age of Reason*, in *Works of Thomas Paine*, pt. 1, ch. 12, loc. 924.
675	Sam Harris, *Letter to a Christian Nation* (New York: Vintage Books, 2006) pp. 57, 60-1. Harris inspired my general theme about the God of the Bible knowing nothing about the modern age.
676	The term "prophecy" is used in different ways in biblical studies. Many times, prophets are thought to be communicating a true message from the Lord which does not necessarily have any predictive content. Here, however, I am using the common meaning of a supernatural ability to foresee the future.
677	For a somewhat classic traditionalist view of predictive prophecy, see Josh McDowell, *Evidence That Demands a Verdict: Historical Evidences for the Christian Faith*, vol. 1 (San Bernadino: Here's Life Publishers, 1979),

pp. 267-320. See also Josh McDowell, *More Than a Carpenter*, 5th printing (Wheaton, IL: Living Books, 1982), pp. 101-10.

678 Justin Martyr, *First Apology*, ch. 30, http://www.newadvent.org/fathers/0126.htm. See also no. 52.

679 *The Baltimore Catechism of 1891*, in *The Catholic Primer*, 2005, Catechism no. 3, Lesson Seventh, Q.350, p. 119, https://www.pcpbooks.net/docs/baltimore_catechism.pdf (accessed 28 Oct. 2013).

680 R.C. Sproul, "How Do You Know the Bible Is True," *Ligonier Ministries*, 23 Jul. 2010, www.ligonier.org/blog/how-do-you-know-bible-true/ (accessed 31 Mar. 2017).

681 Bruce Wilkinson and Kenneth Boa, *Talk Thru the Bible* (Nashville: Thomas Nelson, 1980), p.222. The *NIV Study Bible* has a similar conclusions: "The widely held view that the book of Daniel is largely fictional rests mainly on the philosophical assumption that long-range predictive prophecy is impossible" (p. 1298).

682 Perhaps it is even some sort of ego defense mechanism. Since prophetic fulfillments often seem so forced, it may be an expression of something akin to "reaction formation"—i.e., recognizing that it is dubious on one level and so proclaiming it is completely convincing to deal with the tension. For a short article on this general issue, see Neel Burton, "Why People Are Often the Opposite of What They Appear," *Psychology Today*, 23 Mar. 2012, https://www.psychologytoday.com/us/blog/hide-and-seek/201203/why-people-are-so-often-the-opposite-what-they-appear (accessed 7 Apr. 2017). Cf. Shermer, *The Moral Arc*, p. 199 for a similar dynamic in a discussion of cognitive dissonance.

683 E.g., Loftus, *Why I Became an Atheist*, pp. 352-63; Daniels, *Why I Believed*, pp. 199-223. Ken Daniels provided a very helpful critique and some great suggestions for this meditation in general, esp. on Hosea 11 and Isa. 53.

684 Loftus shows a similar list from Robert Miller (*Why I Became an Atheist*, p. 358). For an example of #6 (sometimes called "prophecy after the fact"), Matthew gives Jesus' prediction of his own death after it had of course transpired (e.g., Matt. 20:17-19). The Book of Daniel is also commonly believed to contain prophecy after the fact.

685 Matthew appears to have seized on the passage due to a translation of the name "Immanuel" as "God is with us" (or "God with us"), a tenuous connection to the Incarnation that could seemingly also be made if the child here was to be given numerous other religious names—like Abijah ("the Lord is my father"), Isaiah ("the salvation of the Lord"), Hosea ("salvation"), or of course Joshua/Jesus itself ("savior"). For an extensive list of the meaning of biblical names, see *Hitchcock's Bible Names Dictionary*, n.d.,

https://www.biblestudytools.com/dictionaries/hitchcocks-bible-names/ (accessed 28 Oct. 2019). Giving children such religious names was not just an Israelite practice. For instance, Carthaginians commonly gave their children names referencing Baal. E.g., Hannibal means "grace of Baal" (Matyszak, p. 26).

686   As has been commonly asserted by Jews and conceded by more moderate scholars today, the word "virgin" in Matthew appears to come from an error in translation in the Greek Septuagint from the Hebrew word for "young woman." The NRSV translation shows this distinction. Jerome mentions the Jewish rejection of Matthew's use of Isaiah in *The Perpetual Virginity of the Blessed Mary*, no. 4, http://www.newadvent.org/fathers/3007.htm: "For at the present day, now that the whole world has embraced the faith, the Jews argue that when Isaiah says, 'Behold, a virgin shall conceive and bear a son,' the Hebrew word denotes a young woman, not a virgin, that is to say, the word is Almah, not Bethulah…"

687   *The NIV Study Bible* itself notes of a fulfillment in Isaiah's time. See note on Isa. 7:16: "This happened in 732 B.C., when the boy was about two years old" (p. 1027).

688   Ibid., p. 1027, note on Isa 7:14. NAB, p. 832, note on Isa. 7:14 has similar reasoning: "The church has always followed St. Matthew in seeing the transcendent fulfillment of this verse in Christ and his Virgin Mother. The prophet need not have known the full force latent in his own words; and some Catholic writers have sought a preliminary and partial fulfillment in the conception and birth of the future King Hezekiah, whose mother, at the time Isaiah spoke, would have been a young, unmarried woman (Hebrew, *almah*)."

689   See note on NAB, p. 13: "The town of Nazareth is not mentioned in the Old Testament, and no such prophecy can be found there." NIV: "These exact words are not found in the OT …" (p. 1444). Calvin finds the question difficult, noting "there is no passage to be found that answers to the quotation." However, he attempts to resolve the issue by typological considerations. See Calvin, *Commentary on Matthew, Mark, Luke*, no. 23, pp. 151-2. See also Loftus, *Why I Became an Atheist*, pp. 357-8. According to the *Mercer Dictionary of the Bible*, s.v. "Nazareth," Nazareth's origins are unclear but pre-NT texts "make no mention of Nazareth."

690   *The New Oxford Annotated Bible*, p. 4, NT. The NAB (p. 13, note on Matt. 2:23) gives both this tenuous resolution and another based on the term "nazirite" (Judges 13:5-7).

691   NIV Study Bible, p.1442, note on Mt 1:22.

692 I'm leaving out the passages here for the sake of brevity. The story of the Massacre is not described in the gospels of Mark, Luke, or John. Ehrman explains, "there is no account in any ancient source whatsoever about King Herod slaughtering children in or around Bethlehem, or anyplace else" (Ehrman, *Jesus, Interrupted*, p. 32). See also *Mercer Dictionary of the Bible*, s.v. "Herod"; *Synopsis of the Four Gospels*, p. 10; Loftus, *Why I Became an Atheist*, p. 357. See also Calvin, *Commentary on Matthew, Mark, Luke*, vol. 1, no. 18, p. 148: "The prediction of Jeremiah having been accomplished at that time, Matthew does not mean that it foretold what Herod would do, but that the coming of Christ occasioned a renewal of that mourning, which had been experienced, many centuries before, by the tribe of Benjamin."

693 Ehrman, *Jesus, Interrupted*, p. 228-9; Helms, pp. 95-6; Loftus, *Why I Became an Atheist*, p. 356; Tovia Singer, "Who Is God's Suffering Servant? The Rabbinic Interpretation of Isaiah 53," *Outreach Judaism*, n.d., https://outreachjudaism.org/gods-suffering-servant-isaiah-53/ (accessed 17 Oct. 2019); Origen, *Against Celsus (Contra Celsum)*, in *Ante-Nicene Fathers*, vol. 4, ed. Alexander Roberts, et al., trans. Frederick Crombie (Buffalo, NY: Christian Literature Publishing Co., 1885), 1.54-5, http://newadvent.org/fathers/04161.htm (accessed 11 Jan. 2019). Bernard W. Anderson, *Understanding the Old Testament*, 4th ed., (Englewood Cliffs, NJ: Prentice-Hall, 1986), pp. 488-506 was also consulted for this section. Anderson finds reasons to see both Israel and the messiah in the Suffering Servant passage.

694 Michael Scott, *Delphi: A History of the Center of the Ancient World*, (Princeton: Princeton Univ. Press, 2014), pp. 28-9, Kindle.

695 While some find a prediction of the crucifixion in the NIV rendering of Isa. 5:5 that the servant was "pierced," (the NRSV renders it as the more generic "wounded"), this would still be a non-specific way to refer to many common forms of ancient execution (i.e., piercing with swords, spears, arrows, spikes, etc.). Furthermore, in order to match it to Jesus' crucifixion story, the "piercing" in v. 5a would (inconsistently it seems) have to be literal while the "crushed" in 5b would have to be figurative—for Jesus was not crushed to death but of course crucified. English translations are generally divided on whether מְחֹלָל should be rendered as "pierced" or "wounded." William L. Holladay, *A Concise Hebrew and Aramaic Lexicon of the Old Testament* (Grand Rapids, MI: William B. Eerdmans, 1988), p. 106 specifically renders it in this context as "wounded." Regardless, prediction of crucifixion on a Roman cross would certainly be more specific and striking.

696 The NAB gives this as a possible allusion. See p. 146, note on John 1:29.

697 Matthew states that Joseph is rich while John does not indicate whether or not he was wealthy (or if he owned the tomb). Cf. Mark 15:43; Luke 23:50.

698 See NAB, p. 65, note on Matt. 27:57-61 which suggests that Matthew may be providing an "allusion to Is 53,9 (the Hebrew reading of the text is disputed and the one followed in the NAB OT has nothing about the rich, but they are mentioned in the LXX version)." See also Loftus, *Why I Became an Atheist*, pp. 435-6.

699 See Warraq, p. 152 who cites R. Joseph Hoffman, *The Origins of Christianity* (Amherst, NY: 1985), p. 184: "Events may have been described based on 'deduction from Old Testament prophecy about what 'must have' happened when the Messiah came.'" Loftus notes in *Why I Became an Atheist* that the Gospel writers "shaped their stories about Jesus by making his life fit some of the details" (p. 356, cf. p. 419). In one example, the NAB notes that "It was a common ancient belief that a new star appeared at the time of a ruler's birth" (p. 12, footnote on Matt. 2:9); this may be a reason for a perceived need for Jesus to have a star announce his birth. See also Ehrman, *Jesus, Interrupted*, p. 32; *The Concise Oxford Dictionary of the Christian Church*, s.v. "Star of Bethlehem"; *Mercer Dictionary of the Bible*, s.v. "Star of Bethlehem"; *The NIV Study Bible*, p. 1422, footnote; T. Michael Davis, "The Star of Bethlehem," *Christian Research Institute*, 1 Jun. 2014, http://www.equip.org/article/the-star-of-bethlehem/ (accessed 24 May 2017); Calvin, *Commentary on Matthew, Mark, Luke*, vol. 1, no. 1, p. 125.

700 See Loftus, *Why I Became an Atheist*, p. 418. There are other general examples of Christians receiving "knowledge" of various types from God. See 1 Cor. 12:8, 2 Cor. 12:1-4, etc. There is also of course the belief that God revealed the nature of future events—so supposed knowledge of the past by divine revelation could work by the same general dynamics.

701 Even within the Christian tradition (derivatively anyway). E.g., in Roman Catholic theology, the suffering of every individual believer can become "a participation in the saving work of Jesus" (*Catechism of the Catholic Church*, no. 1521, p. 423). See also no. 1508, p. 419 with reference to Col. 1:24 ("completing what is lacking in Christ's afflictions"); Mary as co-sufferer and even "Mediatrix," nos. 964-969, pp. 273-4.

702 Harris, *Letter to a Christian Nation*, pp. 57, 60; cf. Loftus, *Why I Became an Atheist*, pp. 166, 332.

703 Archbishop James Ussher (1581-1656), famous for dating the world as being created in 4004 BC, predicted the Second Coming in 1996 (Thompson, p. 145). Interestingly, the Eastern Orthodox tradition dated the creation

at Sept. 1, 5508 BCE (Clay, "Apocalypticism in Eastern Europe," in *The Continuum History of Apocalypticism*, p. 629).

704 This section is indented for emphasis.

705 Thich Nhat Hanh, *The Miracle of Mindfulness: A Manual on Meditation*, trans. Mobi Ho, rev. ed. (Boston: Beacon Press, 1975), p. 58.

706 Justin Martyr, *First Apology*, ch. 21, http://www.newadvent.org/fathers/0126.htm.

707 Neill and Wright, p. 168.

708 Justin Martyr, *First Apology*, ch. 54, http://www.newadvent.org/fathers/0126.htm.

709 See ibid., ch. 59, etc.

710 Of course, this line of argumentation would also tend to undermine much of the basis for a Christian critique towards pagan thought–which is perhaps why this particular apologetic was not continued by later defenders of the faith. See Dungan, pp. 420-1, footnote no. 1. Of course, the persecution of Christians by Roman authorities was a terrible tragedy—regardless of the implications of religious parallels.

711 Justin, ch. 66, http://www.newadvent.org/fathers/0126.htm. While Christian eucharistic ceremonies may seem exotic at first glance, Herodotus demonstrates that suffering gods were associated with mystery rites BCE (2.171, p. 164; cf. Mark 14:22-24, 1 Cor. 11:23-26). Ehrman notes that "the celebration of the Lord's supper does share numerous similarities with cultic meals celebrated widely in pagan associations" (*After the New Testament*, p. 343). The ingesting of a god is somewhat commonplace in ancient religions, being present in both Zoroastrian and Vedic Indian traditions. See Wulff, p. 90; Parrinder, ed., *World Religions*, p. 181, 187, 201; Neill and Wright, p. 171. Mystery religions pre-dated and were concurrent with early Christianity. The oldest "mysteries" were the Eleusinian Mysteries," which dated to the 15th c. BCE.

712 Justin claims these types of similarities among paganism are also due to demonic imitation (*First Apology*, ch. 62, http://www.newadvent.org/fathers/0126.htm). Anointing and washing rituals, emphasized in the OT and NT, have parallels in Herodotus (e.g. 4.73, p. 259; 2.64, p. 120; cf. Exod. 29:6-7, Lev. 15:18, 1 Sam. 16:13, James 5:14; etc.). Mithraism provides another example of baptism in the ancient world (Parrinder, ed., *World Religions*, p. 187). The Eleusinian Mysteries of Greek paganism could include a baptism of regeneration (ibid., p. 150). See also *Mercer Dictionary of the Bible*, s.v. "Mystery Religions" and *The New International Dictionary of the Christian Church*, s.v. "Mystery Religions."

713　Justin, ch. 21, http://www.newadvent.org/fathers/0126.htm. Davis, p. 19 notes that the death and resurrection of Serapis were celebrated annually. Dionysus/Bacchus is another example of a popular dying and rising god (Hamilton, p. 62). The Egyptian god Osiris was thought to have died and been buried but to rise again; the Great Mother Goddess was often thought to have a consort who would die and then rise again. He was given names like Dumuzi, Tammuz, and Adonis (Parrinder, ed., *World Religions*, pp. 143, 146).

714　Justin includes Mercury, Aesculapius, Bacchus, Hercules, Castor and Pollux (the Dioscuri), Perseus, Bellerophon, and Ariadne (*First Apology*, ch. 21, http://www.newadvent.org/fathers/0126.htm). While the Ascension of Jesus immediately comes to mind, Elijah was clearly thought to have ascended into heaven in the OT (2 Kings 2:11).

715　Justin notes that "the poets and philosophers" of paganism likewise taught that the wicked were punished after death while the good went into a "blessed existence." See ch. 20, http://www.newadvent.org/fathers/0126.htm. See also Herodotus 4.94-95, p. 266; 5.4; p. 305. See Davis for brief discussion of mystery religions and the promise of a blissful afterlife (p. 19).

716　Justin specifically mentions that Perseus was born of a virgin in *First Apology*, ch. 22, http://www.newadvent.org/fathers/0126.htm. See also Warraq, pp. 144-5. Also note that Zoroaster has been said to have been born of a virgin (Nigosian, p. 11) as has Lao Tzu (*Seven Taoist Masters: A Folk Novel of China*, trans. Eva Wong [Boston: Shambhala, 1990], p. 108). See Loftus, *Why I Became an Atheist*, p. 379 for examples of Alexander the Great, Augustus Caesar, Plato, Apollonius of Tyana, Pythagorus, Krishna, Osiris, Dionysius, and Tammuz.

717　Justin notes that "while we say that there will be a burning up of all, we shall seem to utter the doctrine of the Stoics" (ch. 20, http://www.newadvent.org/fathers/0126.htm).

718　Justin notes that Aesculapius did these sort of things (*First Apology*, ch. 22, http://www.newadvent.org/fathers/0126.htm). Herdotus notes that these powers were also attributed to the pagan gods. For example, a mute person speaks after after a prophecy from Delphi (1.85, cf. Luke 1:62-66) and a blind person sees by a miraculous application of a bodily fluid (2.111, p. 136; cf. Mark 8:22-25, John 9:6-7).

719　Talbert, pp. 26-43, etc. Talbert explores the mythology of "the immortals" of Greco-Roman literature and notes how supernatural conception, announcements from the heavens, prophetic statements and predictions, miracles, great virtue, ascension into the heavens, post-ascension appearances to followers, and disappearance of the body were all common themes (pp. 26-9). Talbert discusses Justin Martyr on pp. 38-9. Talbert also notes that "myths of descending-ascending redeemers are found elsewhere in the Mediterranean world prior to and parallel with the origins of Christianity" (p. 54; Acts 14:8-18) as well as in non-canonical Jewish texts (pp. 53-66). Cf. Bultmann, p. 17.

720 See the meditation "Another Wise Lord" for sources pertaining to Zoroastrianism. For religions of the Ancient Near East, see Parrinder, ed., *World Religions*, pp. 10, 16, 118-23; *Mercer Dictionary of the Bible*, s.v. "Hammurabi." Like the later Mosaic Law, the Babylonian Code of Hammurabi (c.1750 BCE) was said to be given by a god. Babylonian myths contain the creation of humanity from clay by divine word, a paradise myth, and a flood myth. For numerous parallels pertaining to the OT, see Victor H. Matthews and Don C. Benjamin, *Old Testament Parallels: Laws and Stories from the Ancient Near East* (New York: Paulist Press, 1991). Matthews and Benjamin urge though: "Establishing the correct connection between biblical and non-biblical texts is never easy. Simple solutions are generally misleading solutions" (p. 1).

721 Herodotus, 7.152, p. 457. See Robin Waterfield, introduction to *The Histories*, by Herodotus, pp. xxvii-xxxv for a discussion of this quotation in particular and Herodotus' value as an historian in general. Waterfield appears to present a well-balanced approach noting that "Herodotus himself does not expect us to believe everything we read"—but also that we should not expect him to have a modern approach to historiography (p. xxvii).

722 Herodotus, 2.45 (cf. Judges 15:14-16, 1 Sam. 18:7).

723 Ibid., 2.37, 2.47, 4.186 (cf. Lev. 11, Deut. 14).

724 Ibid., 2.104 (cf. Gen. 17:10).

725 Ibid., 1.182 (cf. Exod. 33:9-11, 2 Chron. 5:14, 2 Chron. 7:1-3, etc.).

726 Ibid., 1.132, 2.52, 3.76, 4.76, 6.61, 9.62 (cf. 1 Kings 18:36-37, 1 Thess. 5:17, etc.). Intercessory prayer and adoration could be mentioned as well.

727 Ibid., 1.53, 1.62, 1.158, 2.139, 8.77, 9.93 (cf. Acts 21:10-11,1 Cor. 14:29-33).

728 Ibid., 1.120, 1.128, 1.34, 1.38, 1.43, 1.107-108, 2.141, 3.65, 3.124, 4.172, 5.55-56, 6.131 (cf. Gen. 40:8, Matt. 2:13, Matt. 2:19-20, etc.). Justin Martyr notes that demons appear in the dreams of pagans (*First Apology*, ch. 14, http://www.newadvent.org/fathers/0126.htm).

729 Herodotus notes that the voice of a god speaks to people and is confirmed by witnesses: 1.159 (witness name given), 8.38; cf. Matt. 3:17; and a god speaks from a cloud: 8.65; cf. Exod. 19:9, Matt. 17:5.

730 Ibid., 2.39, 4.7, 5.47, 7.43, etc. (cf. Exod. 29:36-37, Lev. 6:6-7, Lev. 16, 1 Kings 8:5, etc.); 4.62, 4.103, 7.197, 9.119 (cf. Rom. 3:21-26, Heb. 10:10). In the NT, Jesus is a presented as a perfect human sacrifice. In the OT, God is

portrayed as both hating human sacrifice (Deut. 12:31, Jer. 7:31)—but also calling murder an "atonement" (Num. 25:7-13) and asking that people be "devoted to destruction" (Lev. 27:28-29, Josh. 6:15-21).

731 Ibid., 2.144, 7.204, 8.131 (cf. Matt. 1:1-17, Luke 3:23-38.).

732 Ibid., 1.109, 1.126, 3.108, 9.16, 9.65, 9.100 (cf. Gal. 2:8, Gal. 4:4, Acts 6, etc.).

733 Ibid., 1.105, 6.91, 7.10, 8.106 (cf. Gen. 3:14-19, Gen. 12:3, etc.); 1.87, 7.129, 8.13, 8.37 (cf. Matt. 27:45,51, Luke 8:22-25, etc.); 1.60, 2.43-44, 5.114 (cf. OT needed here, Acts, etc.); 4.79 (cf. 1 Sam. 11:6, 1 Sam. 16:14, 1 Sam. 16:23, Mark 5:1-20, etc.).

734 Ibid., 7.192 (cf. 2 Sam. 22:3, Isa. 43:3, Tit. 3:6, etc.). See also Parrinder, ed., *World Religions*, pp. 148, 159, 167, 176 where "savior" is noted as one of qualities/attributes of Zeus, Osiris, the deified emperor Titus, Isis, and Mithras. Prometheus was called the "savior of mankind" in Greek myth—he had both a creator and redeemer role (Hamilton, pp. 25, 68).

735 Herodotus, 8.135; Acts 2:7-8.

736 Ibid., 4.205; cf. Acts 12:23.

737 Adolf Harnack, *What is Christianity?*, trans. Thomas Bailey Saunders (Philadelphia: Fortress, 1986), p. 18.

738 Justin Martyr, *First* Apology, ch. 2, http://www.newadvent.org/fathers/0126.htm.

739 Robert Green Ingersoll, *The Christian Religion*, in *The Works of Robert G. Ingersoll (Complete 12 Volumes)*, vol. VI (USA: Library of Alexandria, 1881), pt. 3, loc. 22602, Kindle. Some of Ingersoll's intended references will be found in the meditation below. I have omitted this phrase from the quotation: "never told a mother to sell her babe, never established polygamy." The first phrase here appears to be a is a slightly mistaken reference to Exod. 21:7-11—which in part gives instructions on how a father (not a mother) may (not a command) sell a child as a slave. For his reference on polygamy, see the marriage and divorce section in the "What Does the Scripture Say?" meditation. It may be more accurate to say that God "permitted" instead of "established" polygamy. A common prooftext for the acceptability of polygamy is 2 Sam. 12:7-8.

740 Bernard of Clairvaux, *On the Steps of Humility and Pride*, in *Bernard of Clairvaux: Selected Works*, IV.14, p. 112.

741 C.S. Lewis, *Mere Christianity*, rev. ed. (New York: Collier Books, 1952), p. 17.

742 While spiritualized readings avoid the general problem, it is a fair question to ask whether the authors had any such deeper meanings in mind.

743 Cf. Harris, *Letter to a Christian Nation*, p. 49.

744 These terms both refer to the first five books of the Bible: Genesis, Exodus, Leviticus, and Deuteronomy.

745 Cf. Parrinder, ed., *World Religions*, p. 402. For the Talmud's emphasis on some of these more positive elements, see Bokser and Bokser, introduction to *The Talmud: Selected Writings*, pp. 43-4.

746 See *The Catholic Encyclopedia*, c.v. "Inquisition" http://www.newadvent.org/cathen/08026a.htm (accessed 25 Aug. 2013) which cites Optatus, *De Schismate Donatistarum*, III, cc. 6-7.

747 Under the King James wording of Cotton Mather's day, "Thou shalt not suffer a witch to live" (Exod. 22:18). See John R. Mabry, *The Monster God: Coming to Terms with the Dark Side of Divinity* (Berkeley, CA: Apocryphile Press, 2015), loc. 1580, Kindle.

748 Nemeroff, Apocalypticism and the First Crusade," https://sites.dartmouth.edu/crusadememory/2016/04/24/apocalypticism-and-the-first-crusade/ (accessed November 23, 2017). For other examples of the biblical justification for wars, see Noonan, pp. 74-5; Hindley, p. 163; and Henry Wace, "Ulfilas," *A Dictionary of Christian Biography and Literature to the End of the Sixth Century A.D., with an Account of the Principal Sects and Heresies*, s.v. "Ulfilas" http://www.ccel.org/ccel/wace/biodict.html?term=ulfilas; Enns, "Inerrancy, However Defined, Does Not Describe What the Bible Does," in *Five Views on Biblical Inerrancy*, pp. 104-5.

749 Maimonides, *The Guide of the* Perplexed, 1.54, p. 75. These Bible verses do not recommend burning someone alive; however, Maimonides cited them as they were similar in levels of severity. Cf. 3.17-8, p. 170; 3.51, p. 185. See Lev. 21:9 for an example of death by burning in the Law.

750 Cecil Roth, *The Spanish Inquisition* (New York, W.W. Norton and Co., 1964), pp. 81-2; *The Catholic Encyclopedia*, s.v. "Inquisition" http://www.newadvent.org/cathen/08026a.htm. Pérez notes that while estimates of total deaths in the Spanish Inquisition have been as high as 31,912, he thinks that there were likely "fewer than 10,000 death sentences followed by execution" from 1480-1820 (p. 173)—although noting that the total damage of the Inquisition is measured in total bureaucratic cruelty and not just killings (pp. 174-5). Cf. Roth, pp. 123-4.

751 John Calvin, *Harmony of the Law*, vol. 2, trans. Charles William Bingham (Grand Rapids, MI: Christian Classics Ethereal Library, orig. pub. 1852), Deut. 13:5, p. 83, http://www.ccel.org/ccel/calvin/calcom04.pdf. Cf. Schaff, *History of the Christian Church*, vol. 8, pp. 436-7 http://www.ccel.org/ccel/schaff/hcc3.pdf.

752 Schaff, *History of the Christian Church*, vol. 8, p. 437, http://www.ccel.org/ccel/schaff/hcc3.pdf. Schaff notes that she was beheaded to "vindicate the

dignity of the 5th commandment." However, verses cited in the text have a derivative but even clearer Scriptural connection.

753 As noted above, some historical versions of Christianity were more willing to implement the brutality of OT laws in their penal systems—and so were not attempting to explain it away.

754 Ingersoll, *The Christian Religion*, in *The Works of Robert G. Ingersoll*, vol. VI, loc. 22351. See also Ezek. 20:25-26.

755 Martin Luther King, Jr., "Letter from a Birmingham Jail," Univ. of Penn. African Studies Center, 16 Apr. 1963, http://www.africa.upenn.edu/Articles_Gen/Letter_Birmingham.html (accessed 21 Apr. 2016). This may well be unwittingly on King's part—I have never read his direct thoughts on the OT Law. Cf. Augustine of Hippo, *On the Free Choice Of The Will*, in *On the Free Choice of the Will, On Grace and Free Choice, and Other Writings*, ed. and trans. Peter King (Cambridge: Cambridge Univ. Press, 2010), 1.5.11.33, p. 10. For a moral philosopher's discussion on the difficulties with using the Bible as a source of morality, see James Rachels, *The Elements of Moral Philosophy*, 3rd ed. (Boston: McGraw-Hill College, 1999), pp. 53-69.

756 See Bokser and Bokser, eds., introduction to *The Talmud: Selected Writings*, pp. 30-2; The Tractate Sotah, 14a, p. 159; The Tractate Makkot, Mishnah 1:10, pp. 213-14.

757 For a quotation of Frankl's on this section of the Talmud, see "Review: From Death Camp to Existentialism," *Manas Journal*, 12:46 (18 Nov. 1959): p. 6: http://www.manasjournal.org/pdf_library/VolumeXII_1959/XII-46.pdf (accessed 26 May 2018). Author's name not given. See also Viktor E. Frankl, *From death-camp to existentialism: A Psychiatrist's Path to a New Therapy*, trans. Ilse Lasch (Boston, MA: Beacon, 1959), p. 111.

758 Bokser and Bokser, eds., The Tractate Sanhedrin, *The Talmud: Selected Writings*, Mishnah 4:9, p. 207.

759 Denis Diderot, *Thoughts on Religion*, in *Faith in Faithlessness: An Anthology of Atheism*, ed. Demetrios Roussopoulos (Montreal: Black Rose Books, 2008), no. XX. For an on-line version of these thoughtful reflections, see Denis Diderot, *Thoughts on Religion, Oeuvres Complètes*, vol. 1, trans. Mitchell Abidor (Paris, Garnier Fréres, 1875). Avail. at http://www.marxists.org/reference/archive/diderot/1770/religion.htm. Cf. Paine, *The Age of Reason*, in *Works of Thomas Paine*, pt. 2, ch.1, loc. 1034.

760 Michael Edwardes, introduction to *The Life of Muhammad: Apostle of Allah* by Ibn Ishaq, p. 5.

761 "Carl Sagan on Alien Abduction," *NOVA*, 1996 interview, posted 27 Feb. 1996, http://www.pbs.org/wgbh/nova/space/sagan-alien-abduction.html

(accessed 1 Jan. 2017). For a similar dictum, see Michael Shermer, *Why People Believe Weird Things: Pseudoscience, Superstition, and Other Confusions of Our Time*, revised and expanded ed. (New York: Henry Holt & Co., 2002), p. 49.

762 For a common opinion of scholarship, see *Handbook of Biblical Criticism*, s.v. "Form Criticism": "The OT, in many instances, has hundreds of years of oral tradition behind it; the Synoptic Gospels, with which form criticism began, have 30-60 years at most, the Letters of Paul even less."

763 Thomas Paine, *The Age of Reason*, in *Works of Thomas Paine*, pt. 1, ch. 2, loc. 83.

764 This point is similar to one Christopher Hitchens made, perhaps mistakenly referencing David Hume: "which is more likely, that the whole natural order is suspended or that a Jewish minx should tell a lie?" See Christopher Hitchens vs. Al Sharpton: Is God Great?, *Hitchens Debate Transcripts*, 7 May 2007, http://hitchensdebates.blogspot.com/2010/11/hitchens-vs-sharpton-new-york-public.html (accessed 20 Jan. 2018). Cf. Paine, *The Age of Reason*, in *Works of Thomas Paine*, part 1, ch. 17, loc. 890.

765 John Loftus, "The Outsider Test for Faith," *Debunking Christianity* (blog), 20 Mar. 2009, http://debunkingchristianity.blogspot.com/2009/03/outsider-test-for-faith_20.html (accessed 26 Jan. 2013).

766 Ibid.

767 Al-Ghazali writes of dreams as being a proof of prophecy (p. 60) and visions being a manifestation of Sufi practice (p. 57); he also indicated that miracles were proof of the divine (p. 48).

768 Zoroaster said to be born of a virgin (Nigosian, p. 11) as has Lao Tzu (*Seven Taoist Masters*, p. 108). For a variety of other Taoist miracles, see *Seven Taoist Masters*, pp. 5, 15, 17, 23, 25, 108, 121, 166 and Eva Wong, *Tales of the Taoist Immortals* (Boston: Shambhala Publications, 2001). For Buddhist miracles, see *Buddhist Folk Tales from Ancient Ceylon*, trans. Dick de Ruiter (Havelte/Holland: Binkey Kok Publications, 2005), pp. 83-4, etc. For Sufi miracles in the Islamic tradition, see Jonathan Bloom and Sheila Blair, *Islam: A Thousand Years of Faith and Power* (New Haven, CT: Yale Univ. Press: 2002), p. 61; Carl W. Ernst, *Sufism: An Introduction to the Mystical Tradition of Islam* (Boston: Shambhala, 2011), pp. 68-9. For Hinduism, see Kim Knott, *Hinduism: A Very Short Introduction* (New York: Oxford Univ. Press, 1998), pp. 37, 43, 45. See also Loftus, *Why I Became an Atheist*, p. 379. See Pondering Parallels meditation for parallels between Christianity and other Mediterranean religions.

769 Bede's *Ecclesiastical History*, for instance, is full of miracles stories. Miracles were thought to confirm the truth of Catholic Christianity (1.26, p. 77).

770 See C. Bernard Ruffin, *Padre Pio: The True Story*, revised and expanded ed. (Huntingdon, IN: Our Sunday Visitor, 1991). In a book published just 23 years after his death, Pio (1887-1968) is described as bearing the miraculous wounds of Christ (*stigmata*), knowing people's thoughts, translating foreign letters with the help of angels, healing injuries and diseases, being beaten by literal demons, exorcising devils, bilocating (i.e., being in two places at once), and uttering prophecies. Ruffin notes that he "is reputed by rational people to have worked miracles similar to those performed by the prophets of the Old Testament and the apostles of the New" (p. 16). See also Ghezzi, pp. 58, 73; "Saint Pio of Pietrelcina," *BBC*, updated 11 Sep. 2011, http://www.bbc.co.uk/religion/religions/christianity/saints/pio.shtml (accessed 18 Jan. 2019). Some Protestants in fact advocate for a "cessationist" view wherein NT-type miracles ended with "the Apostolic age." See R.C. Sproul, "Does R.C. Sproul Believe in Miracles," *Ligonier Ministries*, 20 May 2015, https://www.ligonier.org/blog/does-rcsproul-believe-miracles/ (accessed 31 Jan. 2019); Armstrong, *The Battle for God*, p. 182.

771 For an interesting discussion of the placebo effect, healing, and religious belief, see Erik Vance, "Mind Over Matter," *National Geographic* (Dec. 2016): pp. 30-55.

772 For an interesting discussion of this issue, see Marshall Brain, *Why Won't God Heal Amputees?* 2006-2015, http://whywontgodhealamputees.com/god5.htm (accessed 9 Oct. 2015).

773 Anatole France, "Miracle," in *The Portable Atheist*, p. 112.

774 *The Penguin Dictionary of Religions*, s.v. "Sai Baba"; Tanya Datta, "Sai Baba: God man or Con man?" *BBC News*, 17 Jun. 2014, http://news.bbc.co.uk/2/hi/programmes/this_world/3813469.stm (accessed 4 Feb. 2017); *Secret Swami: Satya Sai Baba*, dir./prod. Eamon Hardy (11 Jun. 2004; BBC News, video). See http://news.bbc.co.uk/2/hi/programmes/this_world/3791921.stm for more info on this video. For a sympathetic and detailed accounting of his claimed miracles, see "Sri Sathya Sai Baba Miracles," *SaiBaba.ws*, n.d., www.saibaba.ws/miracles.htm (accessed 4 Feb. 2017). Magician and skeptic James Randi called Sai Baba a "fumbling sleight-of-hand artist," noting that each watch that Baba materialized came "strangely bearing a factory-imprinted serial number." See James Randi, "Another Baba Leaves the Scene," *James Randi Educational Foundation*, 24 Apr. 2011, archive.randi.org/site/index.php/swift-blog/1290-another-baba-leaves-the-scene.

html (accessed 1 Feb. 2017). Randi also notes that "His mother claimed that her son was born via virginal conception." Baba has also been accused of the sexual abuse of boys. See also *Encyclopedia Britannica*, s.v. "Sathya Sai Baba" http://www.britannica.com/biography/Sathya-Sai-Baba (accessed 22 Jan. 2016); Paul Lewis, "The Indian Living God, the Paedophilia Claims and the Duke of Edinburgh Awards," *The Guardian*, 4 Nov. 2006, http://www.theguardian.com/uk/2006/nov/04/voluntarysector.india (accessed 22 Jan. 2016); Tanya Datta, "Obituary: Indian Guru Sai Baba," *BBC News*, 24 Apr. 2011, http://www.bbc.co.uk/news/world-south-asia-13153536 (accessed 4 Feb. 2017).

775   Sam Harris, "Believing the Unbelievable: The Clash between Faith and Reason in the Modern World," 4 Jul. 2007 (speech, Aspen Ideas Festival, Aspen, CO), p. 10 of transcript, https://www.aspenideas.org/sites/default/files/transcripts/believingtheunbelievable.pdf (accessed 18 Sep. 2018).
776   Loftus, *Why I Became an Atheist*, p. 62.
777   Ibid., pp. 155-6.
778   Huxley, "Agnosticism and Christianity," in *Agnosticism and Christianity and Other Essays*, p. 193.
779   Jim Wilson, ed., "Space Shuttle: Shuttle Basics," *NASA*, 5 Mar. 2006, https://www.nasa.gov/returntoflight/system/system_STS.html (accessed 14 Apr. 2018).
780   See astronaut meme "So, Jesus Walked on Water? That's cool" at https://me.me/i/9859894 (accessed 10 May 2017). According to one interesting article, people would actually be able to run on water on the moon. See Seriously Science, "Study Shows That You Can Run on Water … on the Moon," *Discover*, 26 Oct. 2015, blogs.discovermagazine.com/seriouslyscience/2015/10/26/study-shows-that-you-can-run-on-water-on-the-moon/#.W5LBc_ZFyUl (accessed 10 May 2017).
781   Paine, *The Age of Reason*, in *Works of Thomas Paine*, pt. 1, ch. 17, loc. 856.
782   As quoted in Ehrman, *Lost Scriptures*, p. 37. See also Karen King, *The Gospel of Mary of Magdala: Jesus and the First Woman Disciple* (Santa Rosa, CA: Polebridge Press, 2003), p. 17. King presents translations of two different texts of the passage.
783   Cameron Jenkins and Lulu Garcia-Navarro, "The American Academy of Pediatrics on Spanking Children: Don't Do It, Ever," *NPR*, 11 Nov. 2018, https://www.npr.org/2018/11/11/666646403/the-american-academy-of-pediatrics-on-spanking-children-dont-do-it-ever (accessed 14 Nov. 2018).
784   For beating as a way that "good fathers" correct their children, see Bede quoting Pope Gregory, 1.27, p. 79.

Endnotes

785 According to the *Handbook of Biblical Criticism*, s.v. "Idiom", the phrase "heap burning coals upon his head" means "to make him ashamed." So, this expression may be figurative rather than literal.

786 Loftus, *Why I Became an Atheist*, p. 271; *Mercer Dictionary of the Bible*, s.v. "Urim and Thummim." The practice appears to be a form of divination. The *NIV Study Bible* gives the following explanation on Acts 1:26: "By casting lots they were able to allow God the right of choice" (p. 1645, footnote).

787 Charles Darwin to Joseph Hooker, 11 Jan. 1844, *Darwin Correspondence Project*, University of Cambridge, https://www.darwinproject.ac.uk/letter/?docId=letters/DCP-LETT-729.xml;query=darwin;brand=default (accessed 18 Oct. 2019). For a discussion of Darwin's developing doubt in the Bible (along with this letter), see *Questioning Darwin*, dir. Antony Thomas (2014, HBO, video). http://news.bbc.co.uk/2/hi/programmes/this_world/3791921.stm for more info on this video.

788 Ingersoll, *Why I Am an Agnostic*, in in *The Works of Robert G. Ingersoll*, vol. IV, no. IV, loc. 13427, Kindle.

789 Richard Fuller and Francis Wayland, *Domestic Slavery Considered as a Scriptural Institution: In a Correspondence Between the Rev. Richard Fuller and the Rev. Francis Wayland* (New York: Lewis Colby, 1845), p. 170 http://archive.org/details/domesticslaveryc00full (accessed 3 Jul. 2013). For a summary of Fuller's life, see "Richard Fuller," *Baptist Convention of Maryland/Delaware*, 7 Sep. 2016, http://bcmd.org/richard-fuller (accessed 11 Sep. 2018).

790 Noonan, pp. 74-5. Noonan, a practicing Catholic, provides extremely strong evidence for the Roman Catholic reversals of moral positions on slavery, freedom of conscience/torture, and usury. My readings have affirmed Noonan's general position that the Catholic Church has flatly contradicted itself—of course, my sensibilities regarding the implications of this conclusion are different from Noonan's.

791 Ibid., pp. 54-5. In fact, one 4th-c. master declared that he freed his slaves because of his "exceptional Christianity" (Glancy, p. 92).

792 See Glancy, pp. 90-1. Although very positive about Christianity's role in abolition in modern times, Stark is quite clear on this point: "This is not to deny that early Christians condoned slavery" (p. 291).

793 Milton Meltzer, *Slavery: A World History*, vols. 1 & 2 combined, updated ed. (New York: Da Capo Press, 1993), vol. 1, pp. 44-5, 93 (Aristotle); Stark, pp. 328-9; Lim, p. 149. For Essenes, see Philo, *Every Good Man is Free (A Treatise to Prove that Every Man who is Virtuous is Also Free)*, in *The Works of Philo Judaeus*, vol. III, trans. C. D. Yonge (London: Henry G. Bohn,

1855), no. XII, pp. 523-4. Avail. at https://archive.org/details/worksofphilojuda03phil/page/522. For the Therapeutae, see Philo, *On the Contemplative Life* (*A Treatise on a Contemplative Life or on the Virtues of Suppliants*), in *The Works of Philo Judaeus*, vol. IV, trans. C. D. Yonge (London: Henry G. Bohn, 1855), no. IX, p. 16. Avail. at https://archive.org/details/worksofphilojuda04phil/page/16. There appears to be some debate as to whether Philo actually wrote this work. Mainstream rabbinic Judaism seems to have mainly regulated slavery and attempted to soften its conditions. For the treatment of Jewish slaves, see Bokser and Bokser, eds., The Tractate Kiddushin, *The Talmud: Selected Writings*, 22a-22b, pp. 171-2; The Tractate Baba Batra, 13a, p. 193. See also Aristotle, *Politics of Aristotle*, vol. 1, trans. B. Jowett (Oxford: Clarendon Press, 1885), 1.3, p. 6. Avail. at: https://archive.org/details/politicsaristot08arisgoog/page/n164 (accessed 16 Oct. 2019). Aristotle accepted slavery but acknowledged that some of his opponents did not.

794 *The Catholic Encyclopedia*, s.v. "Ethical Aspect of Slavery" http://www.newadvent.org/cathen/14039a.htm (accessed 31 Dec. 2018) notes that it was commonplace until the end of the 18th c. for Christians—with certain qualifications—to "implicitly accept slavery as not in itself incompatible with the Christian Law."

795 Fuller, p. 179; "The Southern Argument for Slavery," *U.S. History Online Textbook*, 2013, http://www.ushistory.org/us/27f.asp (accessed 8 Jul. 2013); Noonan, p. 17; Jeremy Black, *A Brief History of Slavery* (Philadelphia: Running Press, 2011), pp. 14, 16, 160.

796 The NRSV of Prov. 29:19 makes the force of the passage even more clear: "By mere words servants are not disciplined, for though they understand, they will not give heed." St. Augustine cites this verse when writing of the value of fear and coercion in salvation; see Augustine of Hippo to Boniface (Letter 185), *Letters of St. Augustine of Hippo*, 6.21, http://www.newadvent.org/fathers/1102185.htm. Augustine also refers to Prov. 13:24 and Prov. 23:14 in his discussion. For more discussion of the pro-slavery sense of divine justification for slaveholding, see John Blassingame, *The Slave Community: Plantation Life in the Antebellum South*, rev. ed. (New York: Oxford Univ. Press, 1979), pp. 67, 84-88; cf. Black, p. 205; González, vol. 2, p. 251.

797 For one utilization of this passage, see Thomas Aquinas, *Summa Theologica*, 2nd and rev. ed., trans. Fathers of the English Dominican Province, II-II.Q65.A2, http://www.newadvent.org/summa/3065.htm. While there is more leniency in Sirach for masters with one slave (Sir. 33:31-33), other verses are very brutal (Sir. 33:27, 30b).

798 Assuming that all these actions are in fact immoral—I personally would doubt or even deny that some are.
799 See Linda Brent, *Incidents in the Life of a Slave Girl*, in *The Classic Slave Narratives*, ed. Henry Louis Gates, Jr., (New York: Mentor, 1987), ch. 13, pp. 397-8. Eph. 6:5 is quoted. John Calvin interpreted 1 Tim. 6:1-2 to mean that the gospel did not require emancipation. See John Calvin, *Commentary on Timothy, Titus, Philemon*, trans. William Pringle (Grand Rapids, MI: Christian Classics Ethereal Library, orig. pub. 1856), 1 Tim. 6:1-2, p. 122, http://www.ccel.org/ccel/calvin/calcom43.pdf. Cf. John Calvin, *Commentary on Galatians and Ephesians*, trans. William Pringle (Grand Rapids, MI: Christian Classics Ethereal Library, orig. pub. 1854), Eph. 6:5, p. 281; Eph. 6:7, p. 282 http://www.ccel.org/ccel/calvin/calcom41.pdf where God is said to have intentionally put slaves "in the power of your masters" (also Tit. 2:10, p. 262). Bouwsma notes that Calvin "loathed slavery" but acknowledged that the Bible permitted it (pp. 194-5). Martin Luther noted regarding Onesimus: "Nor does Paul release him from his servitude or ask him to do so. Indeed he confirms the servitude." See Martin Luther, *Lectures on Titus, Philemon, and Hebrews*, in *Luther's Works*, vol. 29, ed. and trans. Jaroslav Pelikan (St. Louis: Concordia Publishing House, 1968), loc. 2080, Kindle. See also Noonan, p. 68.
800 Glancy, p. 149.
801 Ibid., p. 148.
802 Noonan, p. 35.
803 Glancy, p. 103: "In the parables of Jesus, the bodies of slaves are vulnerable to abuse. Beaten, stoned, and executed, the figure of the parabolic slave is repeatedly the locus of corporal discipline and other bodily violations." Cf. Noonan, pp. 24-5 and Luke 7:2-10.
804 Glancy, p. 120.
805 Frederick Douglass, *Narrative of the Life of Frederick Douglass, an American Slave* (New York: Signet/Penguin, 1968), ch. 9, p. 68.
806 Cf. Matt. 25:14-36.
807 Some scholars think that Roman slavery could be harsher than slavery in the American South (see discussion in Glancy, p. 84; Noonan, p. 22). Meltzer describes the "brandings, burnings, floggings, and maimings" of Roman slaves (p. 176). Black describes great variance in conditions, describing Greco-Roman slaves in mines as having the worst existence (pp. 19-21). Stark also describes the brutality of Roman slavery, esp. on plantations (pp. 295-9).
808 Ignatius of Antioch, The Epsitle of Ignatius to Polycarp, in *Ante-Nicene Fathers*, vol. 1, ed. Alexander Roberts et al., trans. Alexander Roberts

and James Donaldson (Buffalo, NY: Christian Literature Publishing Co., 1885), ch. 4, http://www.newadvent.org/fathers/0110.htm. See also Hippolytus, *The Apostolic Tradition*, in *After the New Testament*, ch. 16.4-5, p. 353; Council of Elvira, can. 1 and 80, http://faculty.cua.edu/pennington/Canon%20Law/ElviraCanons.htm.

809   Acts of Thomas, in *Lost Scriptures*, ch.2, p. 123.

810   The Didache, in *After the New Testament*, 4.10-11, p. 386. See chs. 2-5 for numerous instructions on conduct and belief.

811   Apocalypse of Peter, in *After the New Testament*, ch. 11, p. 300; see Ehrman's introductory notes, p. 296.

812   Athenagoras, A *Plea for the Christians*, in *Ante-Nicene Fathers*, vol. 2, ed. Alexander Roberts, et al. (Buffalo, NY: Christian Literature Publishing Co., 1885), ch. 35, http://newadvent.org/fathers/0205.htm; Glancy, p. 131.

813   The Canons of the Blessed Peter, Archbishop of Alexandria, and Martyr, which are found in his Sermon on Penitence, *The Seven Ecumenical Councils of the Undivided Church*, can. VI-VII, p. 854.

814   Noonan, pp. 40-1.

815   Jerome was the child of slaveholding Catholic parents. See "Prolegomena to Jerome," *The Principal Works of St. Jerome*, in *Nicene and Post-Nicene Fathers, Series 2* (Grand Rapids, MI: Christian Classics Ethereal Library, n.d.), no. III (Life of Jerome), p. 12, http://www.ccel.org/ccel/schaff/npnf206.pdf; Noonan, pp. 40-1. See also Jerome, Letter LIV to Furia, no. 15, p. 280 where remarriage is critiqued but not slaveholding. See Jerome, Letter CVII to Laeta, no. 11, p. 477 where going to a wedding of a slave is bad for a young girl; owning those slaves is apparently not.

816   Noonan, pp. 36-40; Meltzer, vol. 1, p. 239.

817   St. Hesychios the Priest, *On Watchfulness and Holiness*, in *The Philokalia*, vol. 1, no. 65, p. 174. Hesychios also remarks that "When it offends, the body should be whipped mercilessly like a drunken runaway slave; it should taste the Lord's scourge" (no. 33, p. 168).

818   Basil of Caesarea, Letter 37, *Nicene and Post-Nicene Fathers, Second Series*, vol. 8, ed. Philip Schaff and Henry Wace, trans. Blomfield Jackson (Buffalo, NY: Christian Literature Publishing Co., 1895), http://www.newadvent.org/fathers/3202037.htm (accessed 17 Sep. 2018). Basil also taught that slaves marrying without the consent of their masters were guilty of fornication (letter 199, no. XLII, http://www.newadvent.org/fathers/3202199.htm).

819   Ware says of Chrysostom: "Of all the Fathers, perhaps the best loved in the Orthodox Church, and the ones whose works are most widely read" (p. 24).

820 John Chrysostom, Homily 19 on First Corinthians, *Nicene and Post-Nicene Fathers, First Series*, vol. 12, ed. Philip Schaff, trans. Talbot W. Chambers (Buffalo, NY: Christian Literature Publishing Co., 1889), no. 5, 1 Cor. 7:17-22, http://www.newadvent.org/fathers/220119.htm (accessed 17 Sep. 2018). Fuller refers to this homily pp. 140, 190. The avoidance of "spiritual slavery" is a common theme in the NT and in the early Church in general.

821 Augustine, *The City of God*, 19.15, http://www.newadvent.org/fathers/120119.htm. Glancy concurs that Augustine did not object to slavery (pp. 71-2) or the corporal punishment of slaves (pp. 9, 88). See also Augustine, *St. Augustine: Letters*, vol. 6 (1*-29*), in *The Fathers of the Church*, vol. 81, trans. Robert B. Eno (Washington, DC: The Catholic Univ. of America Press, 1989). Eno notes in the intro. to Letter 10* that "there was no abolitionist movement among the fathers of the church" (p. 75). As Letter 10* itself shows, Augustine objects to the kidnapping and enslavement of free persons but not slavery within the bounds of Roman law.

822 Synod of Gangra, *Nicene and Post-Nicene Fathers, Second Series*, vol. 14, ed. Philip Schaff and Henry Wace, trans. Henry Percival (Buffalo, NY: Christian Literature Publishing Co., 1900), can. 3 http://www.newadvent.org/fathers/3804.htm (accessed 17 Sep. 2018); Glancy, p. 90.

823 The Canons of the CCXVII Blessed Fathers who Assembled at Carthage, *The Seven Ecumenical Councils of the Undivided Church*, can. 129, pp. 731-2.

824 The Council of Chalcedon, can. IV, p. 398. Cf. Noonan, p. 38.

825 The Seventh Ecumenical Council: The Second Council of Nice, *The Seven Ecumenical Councils of the Undivided Church*, can. 8, 18, pp. 709, 808.

826 For other examples of manumission in the early church not described here, see *The Catholic Encyclopedia*, s.v. "Slavery and Christianity" http://www.newadvent.org/cathen/14036a.htm (accessed 6 May 2018).

827 Bede, 3.5, p. 150.

828 Ibid., 4.13, p. 227.

829 Theodore of Studium, *Reform Rules*, in *Internet Medieval Sourcebook*, ed. Paul Halsall, Fordham University, Mar. 1996, http://www.fordham.edu/halsall/source/theostud-rules.html (accessed 8 Jul. 2013). From *Theodore of Studium: His Life and Times*, trans. A. Gardner (London: Edward Arnold, 1905), pp. 71-4.

830 Noonan, pp. 43-5.

831 Gregory of Nyssa, "The Fourth Homily," *Commentary on Ecclesiastes*, trans. Richard McCambly, The Gregory of Nyssa Home Page, http://www.

sage.edu/faculty/salomd/nyssa/eccl.html (accessed 3 Jul. 2013). Site was maintained by David A. Salomon; link is now broken. See also Noonan, pp. 40-1, 235 (footnote). For Gregory's character, see González, vol. 1, p. 186.

832   Black, p. 27.
833   Noonan, pp. 52-4, 60; Black, p. 35.
834   Noonan, pp. 52-5; Black, p. 38. Unfortunately, serfdom typically took its place. See Meltzer, vol. 1, pp. 205-7; 209-25. Meltzer notes in vol. 1, p. 222 that there were "papal threats to excommunicate sellers of Christian slaves." The owning of Christians by Jews (pp. 223-4) or other infidels was also condemned (p. 211). However, Noonan notes that there was no directive against owning Catholic slaves if they were baptized after enslavement or if they were captured in war (p. 52-3). See also Black, p. 35.
835   Meltzer, vol. 1, pp. 209, 212; Noonan, pp. 46-7; Black, pp. 35-7. By a decree in 1009 CE, King Ethelred gave slaves three days off work to participate in the penance of his kingdom. If they did not, they were whipped (Reston, pp. 93-4).
836   Roth, pp. 152, 240; Black, pp. 39-41. See also Norwich, p. 259 which describes the "retinues of slaves and eunuchs" of nobles in Constantinople during the days of the Crusades. For another example, see St. Symeon the New Theologian, *On Faith*, in *The Philokalia: The Complete Text*, vol. 4, ed. and trans. G.E.H. Palmer et al. (London: Faber and Faber, 1995), p. 20.
837   Noonan, pp. 57-8: "in his day, slaves could be seen in Sicily, Sardinia, the kingdom of Naples, and, in numbers, in Bologna." Stark, however, states that "in Aquinas's day, slavery was a thing of the past or of distant lands" (p. 329). My research generally confirms that there was slavery around the Mediterranean at this time—but regardless, it does not appear that Aquinas was an abolitionist. See, for example, Aquinas, *Summa Theologica*, II-II.Q57.A3-A4 http://www.newadvent.org/summa/3057.htm; II-II.Q65.A2 http://www.newadvent.org/summa/3065.htm; Suppl.Q39.A3 http://www.newadvent.org/summa/5039.htm. Stark suggests the seemingly unwarranted conclusion that Aquinas condemned slavery in plain terms (pp. 329-31); this is not the conclusion of other historians (Meltzer, vol. 1, p. 211; Noonan, pp. 56-8, etc.; David T. Curp, "A Necessary Bondage? When the Church Endorsed Slavery," *Crisis*, 23:8 (Sept. 2005) https://www.catholiceducation.org/en/controversy/common-misconceptions/a-necessary-bondage-when-the-church-endorsed-slavery.html (accessed 12 Nov. 2017). See also Thomas Aquinas, *Summa Theologiae: A Concise Translation*, ed. Timothy McDermott (Notre Dame, IN: Christian Classics, 1991), pp. 147, 288, 341, 383. As this meditation attempts to

show, the Catholic Church's treatment of slavery is a complex and developing phenomenon.

838   Halsall, ed., *Twelfth Ecumenical Council: Lateran IV 1215*, in *Internet Medieval Sourcebook*, sec. "Holy Land Decrees," http://www.fordham.edu/halsall/basis/lateran4.asp. Bellitto notes this same general punishment in the Lateran III Council in 1179 (p. 51).

839   Roth, pp. 112-3, 157, 211-2, 291 (Portuguese Inquisition), 296-7 (Portuguese Inquisition); Pérez, p. 151. Penal slave labor is somewhat of a different category; however, this appeared worth mentioning. See also Black, p. 39.

840   Pope Nicholas V, *Romanus Pontifex*, http://www.papalencyclicals.net/nichol05/romanus-pontifex.htm (accessed 5 Sep. 2018). From Frances Gardiner Davenport, ed., *European Treaties bearing on the History of the United States and its Dependencies to 1648* (Washington, DC: Carnegie Institution of Washington, 1917), pp. 20-6. These rights were granted to Spain and Portugal by successive popes as well (Noonan, pp. 62-4). Shrady notes that "Nothing spurred the slave trade quite so effectively as Pope Nicholas V's papal bull *Romanus Pontifex* of 1455" (p. 77).

841   Thomas More, *Utopia*, ed. Henry Morley (1901; Project Gutenberg eBook: 22 Apr. 2005), sec.: Of Their Slaves, and of Their Marriages, http://www.gutenberg.org/files/2130/2130-h/2130-h.htm (accessed 5 Sep. 2018); Transcribed from the 1901 Cassell and Company ed. by David Price. Cf. Noonan, p. 69. Per Noonan, Dante does not recognize slavery as a sin (p. 212).

842   See Bartolomé de las Casas, *A Short Account of the Destruction of the West Indies*, ed. Nigel Griffin (London: Penguin, 1992). Although apparently exaggerated at points, the litany of murders of even children and infants, the ghastly tortures and dismemberments, and the barbaric cruelty is not for the faint of heart. Anthony Pagden notes in the intro. that despite some inaccuracies, "the numbing round of killings, beatings, rapes, and enslavements" did occur (p. xxxi). As time progressed, Las Casas also came to the defense of black slaves as well. As historian Justo González notes, his stand on this point was not commonplace: "It is significant that the few theologians who objected [to importing African slaves] did so, not on the basis of opposition to slavery, but rather because they had doubts on how profits should be distributed" González, vol. 1, p. 384).

843   For an exception that shows the rule, see Sam J. Steiner, "Mennonites, Slavery, and Black Immigrants to Canada," *In Search of Promised Lands: A Religious History of Mennonites in Ontario*, 20 Apr. 2015, https://ontariomennonitehistory.org/2015/04/20/mennonites-slavery-and-black-immigrants-to-canada/ (accessed 4 May 2018).

844 Nolt, p. 83; Estep, p. 268.
845 Meltzer, vol. 2, p. 141.
846 González, vol. 2, p. 250. See also *The New International Dictionary of the Christian Church*, s.v. "Friends, Society of (Quakers)."
847 Blassingame, pp. 75-83, 95. Noonan refers to Congregationalist (p. 92) and early Quaker and other non-conformist influence on abolition (pp. 94, 100-101). See also Black, p. 157; Meltzer, vol. 2, p. 132; *The Westminster Dictionary of Theologians*, s.v. "Finney, Charles Grandison." Methodist and Baptist revivals in the antebellum United States often led to manumission.
848 John Wesley, "Thoughts Upon Slavery," *Global Ministries: The United Methodist Church*, n.d., http://www.umcmission.org/Find-Resources/John-Wesley-Sermons/The-Wesleys-and-Their-Times/Thoughts-Upon-Slavery (accessed 3 Jul. 2013). González describes Wesley's relationship to Methodism in vol. 2, pp. 212-14. He notes that Wesley "had no interest in founding a new denomination. ... [H]e was an Anglican minister, and throughout his life he remained such."
849 *The Westminster Dictionary of Theologians*, s.v. "Finney, Charles Grandison."
850 Meltzer, vol. 2, p. 245; Noonan, pp. 100-1; Black, pp. 159, 165.
851 Paul III, *Sublimus Dei*, in *Papal Encyclicals Online*, orig. pub. 29 May 1537, http://www.papalencyclicals.net/Paul03/p3subli.htm (accessed 26 Jun. 2013).
852 As quoted in *Rome Has Spoken: A Guide to Forgotten Papal Statements, and How They Have Changed Through the Centuries*, ed. Maureen Fielder and Linda Rabben (New York: Crossroad Publishing, 1998), p. 83. The quotation is from the text of a *mantu propri* that he issued in 1548. Cf. Noonan, pp. 72, 79.
853 Meltzer, vol. 1, p. 230.
854 Noonan, p. 78.
855 Meltzer, vol. 2, p. 51.
856 Beardsley, John, ed., "Liberties of New Englishmen," *The Winthrop Society*, 2015, http://www.winthropsociety.com/liberties.php (accessed 3 Jul. 2013). *The Massachusetts Body of Liberties* are entirely reproduced in this article. See no. 91 for the quotation. Also noted therein is: "This exempts none from servitude who shall be judged thereto by Authority."
857 Meltzer, vol. 2, p. 44. Cf. Black, p. 120. Anglicans were at one time perhaps the worst slavers. See Stark, pp. 312-318; Frank Tannenbaum, "Slave and Citizen," in *Slavery in American Society*, ed. Richard D. Brown and

858 Stephen G. Rabe, 2nd ed. (Lexington, MA: DC Heath and Co., 1976), pp. 135-6; González, vol. 2, pp. 219-20.
858 *Encyclopedia Virginia*, 2012, s.v. "Letter to the Inhabitants of Maryland, Virginia, North and South Carolina," http://www.encyclopediavirginia.org/_Letter_to_the_Inhabitants_of_Maryland_Virginia_North_and_South_Carolina_1740#start_entry (accessed 22 Jul. 2013); "Jonathan Edwards College," *Yale, Slavery & Abolition*, n.d., http://www.yaleslavery.org/WhoYaleHonors/je.html (accessed 22 Jul. 2013).
859 Noonan, p. 102.
860 Charles Hodge, "Slavery," in *Essays and Reviews: Selected from the Princeton Review* (New York: Robert Carters and Brothers, 1857), ch. XIV, p. 481 https://archive.org/stream/essaysreviews00hodg#page/480/mode/2up (accessed 7 Sep. 2018). See also Loftus, *Why I Became an Atheist*, p. 217.
861 Black, p. 201.
862 See Noonan, p. 112; Leo XIII, *In Plurimus*, in *Papal Encyclicals Online*, orig. pub. 5 May 1888, http://www.papalencyclicals.net/leo13/l13abl.htm (accessed 17 Jul. 2013).
863 Fuller, pp. 4, 6, 11-12, 164-5, 188, 202.
864 Ibid., p. 12.
865 Black, p. 26.
866 Ibid., pp. 89-97, 128, 132-3; Stark, pp. 304-5. While the fact of course does nothing to lessen European sins, Africans were also complicit in the transatlantic slave trade of Africans.
867 Black, pp. 7, 11-12, 25, 47-9, 71, 218, 226, 228.
868 Ibid., p. 41; David Morgan, *The Mongols* (Malden, MA: Blackwell Publishers, 2000), p. 89.
869 N.J. Dawood, introduction to *The Koran*, pp. 13-14 and Sura 33:50, p. 294. See also Black, p. 28.
870 Black, pp. 11, 33, 52, 54-55, 71, 73-4; Ruthven, p. 91. See also Christopher Hitchens, *Thomas Jefferson: Author of America* (New York: HarperCollins, 2005), pp. 126-8 and Stark, pp. 301-4. Bloom and Blair, pp. 47-8 notes that the Qu'ran did not teach abolition and that Muslims took slaves from Africa, Asia, and Europe.
871 Meltzer, vol. 2, pp. 61-73; Black, pp. 11, 178, 215.
872 Ibid., p. 109; Tindall and Shi, p. 360.
873 While Aristotle (384-322 BCE) thought slavery was permissible, he acknowledged that he had contemporaries that found it to be inherently unjust. See Aristotle, *Politics*, The Internet Classics Archive, *MIT*, n.d., 1.3 http://classics.mit.edu/Aristotle/politics.1.one.html (accessed 26 Jun. 2013). See also Meltzer, vol. 1, p. 93.

874 Black, pp. 13-15.
875 Ibid., p. 25.
876 Reston, pp. 62-3, 66-8, 87; Black, p. 36.
877 Meltzer, vol. 1, pp. 213, 219, 221; Reston, p. 223; Roth, pp. 152, 240; Black, pp. 39-41. See also Norwich, p. 259 which describes the "retinues of slaves and eunuchs" belonging to nobles in Constantinople during the days of the Crusades. See also Philip Mansel, *Constantinople: City of the World's Desire 1453-1924* (St. Martin's Press, 1995), ch. 1, http://www.washingtonpost.com/wp-srv/style/longterm/books/chap1/constantinople.htm (accessed 28 Jul. 2013).
878 Black, pp. 57, 146-7, 199, 213-4, 227. See also *The Sudebnik*, ed. and trans. H.W. Dewey, *Bucknell Univ.*, 1996, articles 17-18, 42-3, and 66, http://www.departments.bucknell.edu/russian/const/sudebnik.html (accessed 17 Jul. 2013) from *Muscovite Judicial Texts, 1488-1556* (Ann Arbor: Dept. of Slavic Languages and Literatures, University of Michigan, 1966), pp. 7-21. See also *Sobornoe Ulozhenie [Law Code of the Assembly of the Land]*, *Univ. of Oregon*, ch. 20, http://pages.uoregon.edu/kimball/1649-Ulj.htm#ch1 (accessed 17 Jul. 2013).
879 For an interesting account dealing with Washington and slavery, see Erica Armstrong Dunbar, *Never Caught: The Washingtons' Relentless Pursuit of Their Runaway Slave, Ona Judge* (New York: 37Ink/Atria, 2017).
880 *Dictionary of Unitarian & Universalist Biography*, s.v. "John C. Calhoun" http://www25.uua.org/uuhs/duub/articles/johnccalhoun.html (accessed 26 Jul. 2013).
881 Black, p. 228.
882 Ibid., p. 240.
883 Black, p. 240ff; Shermer, *The Moral Arc*, pp. 210-12.
884 See Blassingame, pp. 76-7, 80; Rhys Isaac, *The Transformation of Virginia: 1740-1790* (New York: Norton, 1988), pp. 309-10; Black, pp. 154, 156. See also de las Casas, pp. 93-4 for treatment of golden rule. Anthony Pagden, introduction in *A Short Account of the Destruction of the West Indies*, by Bartolomé de las Casas, p. xxi discusses the primacy of the golden rule in de las Casas' thought.
885 Noonan, p. 99.
886 Baron d'Holbach, *On Religious Cruelty*, *Marxists.org*, trans. Mitchell Abidor, 2005, introduction, https://www.marxists.org/reference/archive/holbach/1769/religious-cruelty.htm (accessed 15 Nov. 2018). Orig. source: *De la Cruauté Réligieuse* (London: 1769).

887 As quoted in Norman L. Torrey, ed., *Les Philosophes: The Philosophers of the Enlightenment and Modern Democracy* (New York: Capricorn Books, 1960), pp. 277-8.

888 Or more precisely, "Without God and immortal life? All things are lawful then, they can do what they like?" Fyodor Dostoevsky, *The Brothers Karamazov* (New York: Barnes and Noble, 1995), p. 554. "Mitya" Karamazov is the character who speaks the line.

889 See particularly The Whole Counsel of God, No Law at All, and The Unknown Sin.

890 Aquinas, *Summa Theologica*, II-II.Q64.A6, http://www.newadvent.org/summa/3064.htm#article6. For a similar sentiment from Aquinas regarding murder, adultery, and theft, see I-II.Q94.A5, http://www.newadvent.org/summa/2094.htm. For a similar argument for the slaughter of children at God's command, see John Calvin, *Commentary on Joshua*, trans. Henry Beveridge (Grand Rapids, MI: Christian Classics Ethereal Library, orig. pub. 1854), 10:40, p. 144, http://www.ccel.org/ccel/calvin/calcom07.pdf.

891 Christopher Hitchens made similar points in his debates and speeches. See also Elizabeth Anderson, "If God is Dead, Is Everything Permitted?" in *The Portable Atheist*, pp. 333-48 for one exploration of the weakness of the moral argument for God when the basis of God's character is a literalistic reading of Judeo-Christian Scriptures.

892 Philip Schaff, *History of the Christian Church, Vol. VIII, Modern Christianity, The Swiss Reformation*, 3rd rev. ed., (Grand Rapids, MI: Christian Classics Ethereal Library, n.d.), p. 594, http://www.ccel.org/ccel/schaff/hcc8.pdf. Understandably, many also renounced the faith during persecution could be "great" (González, vol. 1, p. 151).

893 Tertullian, *To Scapula*, in *Ante-Nicene Fathers*, vol. 3, ed. Alexander Roberts, et al., trans. S. Thelwall (Buffalo, NY: Christian Literature Publishing Co., 1885), ch. 2 http://www.newadvent.org/fathers/0305.htm (accessed 14 Sep. 2018); Schaff, *History of the Christian Church*, vol. 8, p. 594, http://www.ccel.org/ccel/schaff/hcc3.pdf.

894 Lactantius, *Divine Institutes*, in *Ante-Nicene Fathers*, vol. 7, ed. Alexander Roberts, et al., trans. William Fletcher (Buffalo, NY: Christian Literature Publishing Co., 1886), 5.20, http://www.newadvent.org/fathers/07015.htm (accessed 14 Sep. 2018); Noonan, pp. 150, 157; *The Catholic Encyclopedia*, s.v. "Inquisition" http://www.newadvent.org/cathen/08026a.htm. See also Schaff, *History of the Christian Church*, vol. 8, p. 594. Cf. Paul J. Alexander, "Religious Persecution and Resistance in the Byzantine Empire of the Eighth and Ninth Centuries: Methods and Justifications," *Speculum* 52:2 (Apr. 1977): p. 254.

895   González, vol. 1, p. 36.

896   Athenagoras, *Plea Regarding the Christians*, in *After the New Testament*, ch. 4, p. 67. Diagoras of Melos was a 5th-c. BCE poet commonly accused of atheism.

897   Cyprian of Carthage, Epistle 61: To Pomponius, Concerning Some Virgins, in *Ante-Nicene Fathers*, vol. 5, ed. Alexander Roberts, et al., trans. Robert Ernest Wallis (Buffalo, NY: Christian Literature Publishing Co., 1886), no. 4 http://www.newadvent.org/fathers/050661.htm (accessed 14 Sep. 2018). Sullivan believes that Cyprian was only addressing lapsed Catholics here (pp. 20-4); I personally find this argument unconvincing.

898   Athanasius, *Life of Antony*, in *Early Christian Lives*, no. 68, pp. 51-2.

899   Ibid., no.91, p. 67.

900   Cf. Matt. 10:22-32, 2 Tim. 2:12.

901   Martyrdom of Polycarp, in *After the New Testament*, 11.2, p. 33. See also 2.3, p. 31.

902   The Letter of the Churches of Vienne and Lyons, in *After the New Testament*, p. 38. Likewise, an early Christian apologetical work has this pagan critique of Christianity: "They despise present torments, although they fear those which are uncertain and future ...." See Minucius Felix, *Octavius*, in *Ante-Nicene Fathers*, vol. 4, ed. Alexander Roberts, et al., trans. Robert Ernest Wallis (Buffalo, NY: Christian Literature Publishing Co., 1885), ch. 8, http://www.newadvent.org/fathers/0410.htm.

903   Tertullian, *The Shows (De Spectaculis)*, in Ante-Nicene Fathers, vol. 3, ed. Alexander Roberts, et al., trans. S. Thelwall (Buffalo, NY: Christian Literature Publishing Co., 1885), ch. 30 http://www.newadvent.org/fathers/0303.htm (accessed 14 Sep. 2018).

904   Second Clement, ch. 17, http://www.newadvent.org/fathers/1011.htm.

905   "St. Constantine the Great," *Catholic Online*, n.d., www.catholic.org/saints/saint.php?saint_id=2731 (accessed 1 Sep. 2017); "Equal of the Apostles and Emporer Constantine with His Mother Helen," *Orthodox Church in America*, n.d., https://oca.org/saints/lives/2012/05/21/101452-equalof-the-apostles-and-emporer-constantine-with-his-mother-he (accessed 1 Sep. 2017).

906   Williams, p. 78; Norwich, pp. 9, 15.

907   Schaff, *History of the Christian Church*, vol. 8, p. 595. See also H. Chadwick, pp. 145, 153-5, 160, 171, 179; Ware, p. 35; Murdoch, pp. 97, 136-7, 140. Bonner also mentions Arian persecution of Catholics (pp. 96, 122) and notes that the "use of violence was an all too frequent feature in the history of the Church in the fourth and fifth centuries" (p. 339; see also pp. 96, 122, 137-8, 344). See Williams for exile of Arius and others

after Nicaea (p. 71) and a riot in Alexandria after Arius arrives (p. 79). González talks of Constantine's banishment of the deposed Arian bishops after Nicaea and references how Athanasius and other Nicene leaders were banished (vol.1, p. 166).

908   Ammianus Marcellinus, *Roman History*, trans. C. D. Yonge (London: Henry G. Bohn, 1862), 22.5.4 https://archive.org/details/romanhistoryamm-m01marcgoog/page/n308 (accessed 21 Dec. 2018). See also Murdoch, pp. 135-6. Murdoch discusses some of Julian's aversions to persecution on more noble grounds—although this was not entirely consistent (p. 126). See also H. Chadwick, p. 145.

909   *The Catholic Encyclopedia*, s.v. "Inquisition" http://www.newadvent.org/cathen/08026a.htm and s.v. "Theodosius I" http://www.newadvent.org/cathen/14577d.htm (accessed 14 Dec. 2017). Schaff, *History of the Christian Church*, vol. 8, p. 595. See Parrinder, ed., *World Religions*, p. 430 for "Edict of Theodosius;" also p. 437. Torture was enacted against the heretical Priscillianists under Maximus, a "rival and colleague" of Theodosius.

910   Augustine of Hippo to Donatus (Letter 100), *Letters of St. Augustine of Hippo*, no. 1, http://www.newadvent.org/fathers/1102100.htm. Cf. Noonan, p. 151; Walsh, ed., *Butler's Lives of the Saints*, p. 268; *The Catholic Encyclopedia*, s.v. "Inquisition." St. Martin of Tours (c.316-397) and St. Ambrose (c.333-397) did as well; they both denounced the killing of the heresiarch Priscillian in 385.

911   Augustine of Hippo to Boniface (Letter 185), *Letters of St. Augustine of Hippo*, 6.23, http://www.newadvent.org/fathers/1102185.htm. See also Augustine of Hippo to Vincentius (Letter 93), no. 17, http://www.newadvent.org/fathers/1102093.htm; Bonner, pp. 237-8, 273; O. Chadwick, p. 326.

912   Augustine to to Boniface (Letter 185), *Letters of St. Augustine of Hippo*, 6.22, http://www.newadvent.org/fathers/1102185.htm.

913   Ibid., 6.21.

914   This is not to suggest that Augustine would have supported the extremes of the Inquisition. While he argued for corporal punishment and the appropriateness of beating with rods, he did not espouse more insidious instruments of torture. See Augustine of Hippo to Marcellinus (Letter 133), *Letters of St. Augustine of Hippo*, no. 2, http://www.newadvent.org/fathers/1102133.htm. Augustine shows support for schoolmasters, parents, magistrates, and bishops using the rod as punishment. Bonner thinks it is unfair to call him a "forerunner of the Inquisition" (pp. 233, 295)—however, beating with rods and compelling religious conversion by force and fear suggests that it is fair to call this a transitional period. Furthermore,

it is clear that an Augustinian sort of interpretation of Luke 14:22-23 was used by Inquisitors (see footnote, Bonner, p. 295). Lastly, it seems that history could well have taken a different turn if Augustine's considerable prestige had been fully against coercion. See also Bede's account of Pope Gregory noting that beatings of various severity can be a way to "save the wicked from hell-fire" (1.27, p. 79).

915   The Middle Ages has some of the most notorious examples of Catholic religious persecution. In the 13th c., the Church used the Inquisition to further persecute the stubborn yet peaceful group (Hindley, p. 172 and O'Shea, pp. 2, 7). In his 1184 bull *Ad Abolendam*, Lucius III advocated punishments of exile, confiscation of property, destruction of home, etc. Pope Innocent IV issued a bull in 1252 that authorized the use of torture; several successors approved of the practice as well. Other popes like Alexander IV (1254-1261), Clement IV (1265-1268), Nicholas IV (1288-1302), Boniface VIII (1294-1303) did similarly. See *The Catholic Encyclopedia*, s.v. "Inquisition" http://www.newadvent.org/cathen/08026a.htm. Pope Clement VII established the Inquisition in Portugal in 1531 by papal bull (Roth, p. 136); Pope Paul IV enthusiastically utilized the Inquisition (Roth, pp. 167-8; González, vol. 2, p. 119). See also R.R. Palmer and Joel Colton, *A History of the Modern World to 1815*, 6th ed. (New York: Alfred A. Knopf, 1984), p. 90. Pope Paul IV also promulgated his infamous *Index of Forbidden Books*. Popes Paul III, Pius IV, Pius V, and Sixtus V all utilized the Roman Inquisition in the 16th c. (*The Catholic Encyclopedia*, s.v. "Inquisition"). The Roman Inquisition handed heretics over to the executioners of the Papal States (Noonan, p. 202). Torture was also used by the Papal States (Palmer and Colton, p. 91).

916   See Augustine to Boniface (Letter 185), *Letters of St. Augustine of Hippo*, 6.23, http://www.newadvent.org/fathers/1102185.htm; Bonner, pp. 307-8; Sullivan, *Salvation Outside the Church?*, pp. 31-8. This line of reasoning is a clear corollary of Augustine's belief that there was "no salvation outside the Church." Spanish Inquisitors also had the salvation of souls as a prime goal and made great efforts to bring about repentance before executions (Pérez, p. 163; Roth, pp. 94, 106).

917   John Chrysostom, Homily 46 (on Matt. 13:24-30), *Nicene and Post-Nicene Fathers, First Series*, vol. 10, ed. Philip Schaff, trans. George Prevost, rev. M.B. Riddle (Buffalo, NY: Christian Literature Publishing Co., 1888), no. 1, http://www.newadvent.org/fathers/200146.htm. Cf. *The Catholic Encyclopedia*, s.v. "Inquisition" http://www.newadvent.org/cathen/08026a.htm. Chrysostom also had some anti-Jewish discourses per H. Chadwick, p. 171.

918   Ware, p. 36. Norwich affirms this position (p. 46). St. Cyril of Alexandria lived from c. 376-444.
919   Walsh, ed., *Butler's Lives of the Saints*, p. 195. Also note that the Byzantine emperor Phocas attempted to forcibly convert Jews to Christianity in the early 7th c. (Norwich, p. 89).
920   For apostasy, see *The Catholic Encyclopedia*, s.v. "Justinian I" http://www.newadvent.org/cathen/08578b.htm. Schaff, *History of the Christian Church*, vol. 8, pp. 595-6 notes the Justinian Code condemned heretics to death by fire. Justinian I (483-565) forced pagans to convert and persecuted Montanists. See *The New International Dictionary of the Christian Church*, s.v. "Justinian I."
921   Davis, pp. 304-5, 318; Norwich, p. 114. Walsh, ed., *Butler's Lives of the Saints*, pp. 429-30. See also the case of the icon-painter Lazarus who was whipped and then branded on his palms (Norwich, p. 138).
922   Alexander, "Religious Persecution and Resistance in the Byzantine Empire," pp. 238-64.
923   Bradley Nassif, "Kissers and Smashers: Why the Orthodox Killed One Another over Icons," *Christian History* 16.2, issue 54 (1997): p. 20.
924   *The Concise Oxford Dictionary of the Christian Church*, s.v. "Jews, Christian Attitudes to" notes that "From the time of the First Crusade there were violent attacks on Jews and in some places whole communities were massacred." See Roth for medieval massacres in England in 1189, Spain in 1390, and in German territories (pp. 19- 23). Jews were goaded into conversion or expelled from Spain in 1492 and in Portugal in 1496. For Portugal, see also Shrady, pp. 86ff; Palmer and Colton, p. 72; Roth, pp. 57-8, 134; Pérez, pp. 7-12, etc. Pérez notes the severity of the persecution but also warns against exaggeration (p. 34). *Encyclopedia Britannica*, s.v. "Pogrom" https://www.britannica.com/topic/pogrom (accessed 3 Oct. 2018); *Jewish Virtual Library*, s.v. "Modern Jewish History: Pogroms," https://www.jewishvirtuallibrary.org/pogroms-2 (accessed 3 Oct. 2018); *The New International Dictionary of the Christian Church*, s.v. "Anti-Semitism." Parrinder, ed., *World Religions*, p. 414 notes the Crusades, the Spanish Inquisition, and the Chmielnicki massacres (1648-9) as the greatest instances of the Christian persecution of Jews.
925   Leo XIII, *Aeterni Patris*, in *Papal Encyclicals Online*, orig. pub. 4 Aug. 1879, no. 22 http://www.papalencyclicals.net/Leo13/l13cph.htm (accessed 20 May 2013).
926   Aquinas, *Summa Theologica*, II-II.Q11.A3, http://www.newadvent.org/summa/3011.htm. Thomas advocates a "three strike rule" based on Tit.

3:10 (cf. Noonan, p. 151). See also II-II.Q11.A4. See Aquinas, *Summa Theologiae: A Concise Translation*, pp. 342-3 for a succinct summary.

927 Aquinas, *Summa Theologica*, Suppl.Q94.A1, http://www.newadvent.org/summa/5094.htm#article1. See A2-A3 in this same Question for further explanation.

928 "Council of Vienne 1311-1312 A.D.," in *Papal Encyclicals Online*, decrees 26-28, http://www.papalencyclicals.net/councils/ecum15.htm (accessed 10 Aug. 2018); Bellitto, p. 63.

929 *The Catholic Encyclopedia*, s.v. "Inquisition" http://www.newadvent.org/cathen/08026a.htm.

930 Walsh, ed., *Butler's Lives of the Saints*, p. 7.

931 Ibid., p. 352.

932 *The Catholic Encyclopedia*, s.v. "St. Toribio Alfonso Mogrovejo" http://www.newadvent.org/cathen/14781a.htm (accessed 7 Feb. 2016); Walsh, ed., *Butler's Lives of the Saints*, p. 90.

933 Allitt, p. 39; cf. Pérez, p. 33.

934 Roth, p. 221; *The New International Dictionary of the Christian Church*, s.v "Francis Xavier." See also O. Chadwick, p. 335.

935 O. Chadwick, pp. 281-2; Oberman, p. 10; *The New International Dictionary of the Christian Church*, s.v. "Pius V." See also Walsh, ed., *Butler's Lives of the Saints*, p. 128; *The Catholic Encyclopedia*, s.v. "Pope St. Pius V" http://www.newadvent.org/cathen/12130a.htm (accessed 25 Aug. 2013).

936 Pope John Paul II, "Saint Thomas More Patron Saint of Statesmen and Politician," *EWTN*, 31 Oct. 2000, https://www.ewtn.com/library/papaldoc/jp2more.htm (accessed 12 Dec. 2017).

937 *The Catholic Encyclopdedia*, s.v. "St. Thomas More" http://www.newadvent.org/cathen/14689c.htm (accessed 21 Sep. 2018) notes that "He agreed with the principle of the anti-heresy laws and had no hesitation in enforcing them" and that "only" four people "suffered the supreme penalty for heresy during his whole term of office." *The Stanford Encyclopedia of Philosophy*, s.v. "Thomas More" https://plato.stanford.edu/entries/thomas-more/ (accessed 7 Oct. 2018) notes rather that "Six heretics were executed during his tenure of office, three with his personal involvement." *The Encyclopedia Britannica*, s.v. "Sir Thomas More" https://www.britannica.com/biography/Thomas-More-English-humanist-and-statesman (accessed 7 Oct. 2018) only notes that he was known for "defending England's antiheresy laws and his own handling of heretics, both as magistrate and as writer, in two books of 1533: the Apology and the Debellacyon." For More's own defense of religious persecution, see Thomas More, *The Apology of Sir Thomas More, Knight*, ed. Mary Gottschalk (Center for Thomas Moore

Studies, 2014), chs. 25, 35, 47,49, etc., file:///E:/Sources%20and%20articles/Thomas%20More,%20Apology.pdf (accessed 7 Oct. 2018).

938 O. Chadwick, p. 398 (cf. p. 400). See also W. R. McGrath, loc. 252-366 and Shrady who notes "in Protestant societies of the sixteenth century heretics too could be imprisoned, exiled, stripped of their property, tortured, hanged, decapitated, or burned at the stake. Luther explicitly condoned capital punishment for unrepentant heretics; so too did Melanchthon, not to speak of Calvin" (p. 94). *The Westminster Dictionary of Theologians*, s.v. "Luther, Martin" however notes that despite Luther's stance on the 1525 Peasants' Revolt and his attitude toward Jews, he "did not instigate or participate in the execution of heretics, as Zwingli and Calvin would do." Armstrong echoes this sentiment that Calvin and Zwingli "were prepared to kill dissidents" but that Luther was just into burning heretical books (*The Battle for God*, p. 65).

939 Schaff, *History of the Christian Church*, Vol. V, p. 524, http://www.ccel.org/ccel/schaff/hcc5.pdf.

940 Schaff, *History of the Christian Church*, Vol. VII, pp.318-19, 436-8, http://www.ccel.org/ccel/schaff/hcc8.pdf; Shrady, pp. 94-5; *The Second Helvetic Confession* (Grand Rapids, MI: Christian Classics Ethereal Library, orig. pub. 1566), ch. XXX, http://www.ccel.org/creeds/helvetic.htm. O. Chadwick also notes Calvin's severity and strictness, pp. 87-90.

941 As quoted in Schaff, *History of the Christian Church*, vol. 8, p. 590 (also p. 437). For a description of this incident, see also González, vol. 2, pp. 67-8; O. Chadwick, p. 90. Cf. Bouwsma, p. 101.

942 Calvin, *Commentaries on the Four Last Books of Moses*, vol. 2, Deut 13:5, pp. 82-3, http://www.ccel.org/ccel/calvin/calcom04.pdf.

943 See Oberman, pp. 290-2; Eric W. Gritsch, "Was Luther Anti-Semitic," *Christian History* 12.3, issue 3 (1993) : pp. 38-9. Avail. at https://christianhistoryinstitute.org/magazine/article/was-luther-anti-semitic. *The Jewish Encyclopedia*, s.v. "Luther, Martin" http://www.jewishencyclopedia.com/articles/10196-luther-martin (accessed 21 Sep. 2018). For an online text, see Martin Luther, *On the Jews and Their Lies*, Christianity Revealed, n.d., http://jdstone.org/cr/pages/sss_mluther.html (accessed 21 Sep. 2018). See esp. sec. XII. For an academic source with a helpful intro., see Martin Luther, *On the Jews and Their Lies, 1543*, in *Internet Medieval Sourcebook*, trans. Martin H. Bertram, ed. Paul Halsall, Fordham University, 21 Feb. 2001, https://archive.org/details/MartinLuther14831546OnTheJewsAndTheirLies (accessed 15 Nov. 2018). For Luther's harsh comments on the Peasant's Revolt, see O. Chadwick, p. 60; Oberman, p. 289.

944 Estep, pp. 93, 97.

945 Schaff, *History of the Christian Church*, Vol. VIII, pp. 85-6, 437, http://www.ccel.org/ccel/schaff/hcc8.pdf. See also John S. Oyer, "Sticks and Stones Broke Their Bones, and Vicious Names Did Hurt Them!: 16th-Century Responses to the Anabaptists," *Christian History* 4.1, issue 5 (1985): pp. 17-19.

946 González, vol. 2, p. 56. For some estimates on numbers, Estep, pp. 30 (footnote 2), 74-5, 164; Nolt, p. 11-12.

947 Ware, pp. 111-12. Cf. *Sobornoe Ulozhenie*, ch. 1.1 "Blasphemers and Church Troublemakers," http://pages.uoregon.edu/kimball/1649-Ulj.htm#ch1. This 1649 Russian law code provided for execution by burning for blasphemy against God and saints of the Church.

948 Ware, pp. 111-12.

949 *The Concise Oxford Dictionary of the Christian Church*, s.v. "Witchcraft" estimates the total dead at about 500,000—other sources suggest this is high. Paul F. Boller and Ronald Story, eds., *A More Perfect Union: Documents in U.S. History*, vol. 1: to 1877, 2nd ed. (Houghton Mifflin: Boston, 1988), p. 27 estimates of "tens of thousands" for Europe in the 16th and 17th centuries. Stark gives a more conservative estimate of 60,000 deaths between 1450-1750 noting that "it is very unlikely that [there were] more than 100,000" (p. 203); he further notes that "Protestants proved to be as avid witch-hunters as their Catholic opponents" (p. 221). Pérez notes that "hundreds or even thousands" of witches were burned to death in Europe in the 16th and 17th centuries (p. 79). See also Palmer and Colton (pp. 278, 291); *The New International Dictionary of the Christian Church*, s.v. 'Witchcraft." Armstrong just notes "thousands" in the 16th and 17th c. (*The Battle for God*, p. 75). Cf. the "witch" of Endor (1 Sam. 28:3–25).

950 *The Catholic Encyclopedia*, s.v. "Witchcraft," http://www.newadvent.org/cathen/15674a.htm (accessed 8 Jan. 2019). See also Paul Halsall, ed., "Witchcraft Documents [15th Century]," *Internet Medieval Sourcebook*, Fordham University, Mar. 1996, https://sourcebooks.fordham.edu/source/witches1.asp (accessed 8 Jan. 2019). The bull is *Summis Desiderantes Affectibus*.

951 Beardsley, ed., "Liberties of New Englishmen," http://www.winthropsociety.com/liberties.php. *The Massachusetts Body of Liberties* are entirely reproduced in this article. See nos. 1, 43, 45, and 94. Puritans killed four Quakers in Boston Common (Mead and Hill, p. 293).

952 González, vol. 2, p. 202.

953 Jonathan Edwards, "The Eternity of Hell Torments," *Jonathan-edwards.org*, orig. pub. Apr. 1739, http://www.jonathan-edwards.org/Eternity.html (accessed 15 May 2013).

954 Gregory XVI, *Mirari Vos*, in *Papal Encyclicals Online*, orig. pub. 15 Aug. 1832, nos. 14-16, 20 http://www.papalencyclicals.net/Greg16/g16mirar.htm (accessed 29 Aug. 2013). Cf. O. Chadwick, p. 403; Leo XII, *Ubi Primum*, no. 12, http://www.papalencyclicals.net/Leo12/l12ubipr.htm; Noonan, pp. 145-9; Pius IX, *Quanta Cura*, in *Papal Encyclicals Online*, orig. pub. 8 Dec. 1864, nos. 3-5, http://www.papalencyclicals.net/pius09/p9quanta.htm (accessed 21 Sep. 2018); Leo XIII, *Immortale Dei*, 1 Nov. 1885, http://www.papalencyclicals.net/leo13/l13sta.htm (accessed 21 Sep. 2018).

955 González, vol. 2, p. 266. The French Revolution appears to have had more deistic than atheistic leanings. See P. N. Furbank, *Diderot: A Critical Biography* (New York: Alfred A. Knopf, 1992), p. 454 for Robespierre's denunciation of atheism.

956 Noonan, p. 152. *Encyclopedia Britannica*, s.v. "Joseph Stalin" https://www.britannica.com/biography/Joseph-Stalin notes, for instance, that his "political victims were numbered in tens of millions." See also ibid, s.v. "Pol Pot" https://www.britannica.com/biography/Pol-Pot which notes that "His radical communist government forced the mass evacuations of cities, killed or displaced millions of people, and left a legacy of brutality and impoverishment." Se also Mao Zedong," BBC, 2013, http://www.bbc.co.uk/history/historic_figures/mao_zedong.shtml (accessed 24 May 2013). Allitt notes that some have considered fascism and communism to be "political parody religions" which exploit the totalitarian principles of religions (p. 240; cf. pp. 250-1 and nationalism). Christopher Hitchens made this claim as well. Needless to say, these particular militant atheistic political philosophies are totally incompatible with the nobler aspirations of secular humanism and secular democracy which advocate freedom of religion in addition to many other rights.

957 Ware, pp. 148-9. Hitler does not appear to have been an atheist.

958 Reston, p. 260.

959 *The Concise Oxford Dictionary of the Christian Church*, s.v. "Bernard, St."

960 Not all though. For violent exceptions, see Nolt, p. 15; *Global Anabaptist Mennonite Encyclopedia Online*, s.v. "Beukelszoon, Jan" http://gameo.org/index.php?title=Beukelszoon,_Jan_(ca._1509-1536)&oldid=103529. (accessed 6 Dec. 2013) and s.v. "Batenburg, Jan van" http://gameo.org/index.php?title=Batenburg,_Jan_van_(1495-1538)&oldid=111688 (accessed 23 Jan. 2014); Walter Klaassen, "A Fire that Spread Anabaptist Beginnings," *Christian History* 4.1, issue 5 (1985): p. 9; *The Catholic Encyclopedia*, s.v. "Anabaptists" http://www.newadvent.org/cathen/01445b.htm (accessed 12 Dec. 2013); Robert L. Wise, "Munster's Monster," *Christian History* 18.1, issue 61 (1999): pp. 23-5; O. Chadwick, pp. 190-1.

961 Noonan, p. 157; Estep, p. 86; *The Schleitheim Confession of Faith*, sec. "Sixth. concerning the sword" http://courses.washington.edu/hist112/SCHLEITHEIM%20CONFESSION%20OF%20FAITH.htm.

962 Noonan, p. 153; *Handbook of Biblical Criticism*, s.v. "Erasmus, Desiderius, von Rotterdam"; *The Catholic Encyclopedia*, s.v. "Desiderius Erasmus" http://www.newadvent.org/cathen/05510b.htm (accessed 4 Sep. 2013).

963 Roger Williams, "The Bloody Tenent of Persecution" (excerpted "Twelve Conclusions"), in *A More Perfect Union: Documents in U.S. History*, p. 26; George B. Tindall and David E. Shi, *America: A Narrative History*, brief 2nd ed. (New York: W. W. Norton and Co., 1989), p. 25. *The New International Dictionary of the Christian Church*, s.v. "Roger Williams." See also Noonan, p. 157.

964 Ware, pp. 104-8. Quotation is on p. 105. See also *OrthodoxWiki*, s.v. "Nilus of Sora" http://orthodoxwiki.org/Nilus_of_Sora (accessed 6 Sep. 2013).

965 As quoted in David Wolpe, "Is Richard Dawkins Really the World's Leading Intellectual," *The Huffington Post*, 7 May 2013 (updated 7 Jul. 2013), http://www.huffingtonpost.com/rabbi-david-wolpe/is-richard-dawkins-really-the-worlds-leading-intellectual_b_3226638.html?utm_hp_ref=religion (accessed 1 Jan. 2018). For similar sentiments elsewhere, see Shermer, *The Moral Arc*, p. 150.

966 See Jon Meacham, "Pastor Rob Bell: What if Hell Doesn't Exist?" *Time*, 14 Apr. 2011, http://content.time.com/time/magazine/article/0,9171,2065289-1,00.html (accessed 7 Feb. 2019). For a distancing from the traditional idea of eternal conscious torment and literal hellfire, see Lewis, *The Great Divorce* and Keller, pp. 81-3.

967 Bloom and Blair, pp. 31, 147. For an example of the use of this phrase, see Bukhari, bk. 85, no. 30 (8.80.745) http://sunnah.com/bukhari/85/30; cf. bk. 23, no. 52 (2.23.382) http://sunnah.com/bukhari/23/53.

968 David Hume, *Of Miracles*, in *The Portable Atheist*, 1.13, pp. 35-6. Hume seems to have been very fond of commas—I have removed some here to make the sentence more readable.

969 Paine, *The Age of Reason*, in *Works of Thomas Paine*, part 1, ch. 3, loc. 117.

970 For a helpful tool to look at accounts side by side, see *Synopsis of the Four Gospels*, pp. 325-33.

971 A commonly noted reality. See Neill and Wright, p. 41; Ehrman, *Jesus, Interrupted*, pp. 102-12; Warraq, p. 15; Pagels, p. 17; *Mercer Dictionary of the Bible*, "Matthew, Gospel of."

972 Cf. Loftus, *Why I Became an Atheist*, pp. 155, 410. Assigning dates of composition is therefore educated guesswork, with traditional believers often arguing for earlier dates and more skeptical analyses for later ones. All,

however, tend to date them in the second half of the first century. (Jesus is typically thought to have died c. 30). While dates for the Gospels are therefore imprecise and often vary, Roman Catholic scholars of the *New American Bible* provide these common critical dates: Matthew (80?), Mark (after 70), Luke (80-90), and John (90-100). See NAB, pp. 10, 69, 96, 144. For a conservative evangelical example, see Wilkinson and Boa who give the following: Matthew (58-60), Mark (55-65), Luke (early 60's), John (60-90). See pp. 309, 319, 328, and 336. Cf. *The NIV and Study Bible*, pp. 1437-9, 1490, and 1532, and 1591.

973 Eusebius, 3.39.15-16, pp. 105-6. See also discussions in Dungan, pp. 18-27; Ehrman, *Misquoting Jesus*, p. 199; Ehrman, *Jesus, Interrupted*, pp. 101-12; Neill and Wright, pp. 116, 127. *The Westminster Dictionary of Theologians*, s.v. "Papias" notes that current scholars "attribute little value to the testimony" of Papias because the Gospels are commonly believed to be based on oral traditions of a "communal origin." See also *Handbook of Biblical Criticism*, s.v. "Synoptic Problem (The)" and also s.v. "Agrapha (sg. Agraphon)" which notes that "it is known that Jesus' teachings were first passed down orally." For an example of problematic apologetical claims that the Gospels are "eyewitnesses," see Lee Strobel, *The Case for Christ: A Journalist's Personal Investigation into the Evidence for Jesus*, updated & expanded ed. (Grand Rapids, MI: Zondervan, 2016), pp. 19-37. Strobel must still concede that Mark and Luke would be deemed "indirect eyewitnesses" (p. 25)—which are not eyewitnesses. Strobel is a gifted writer but his claims that his book was a product of a skeptical search don't come across as genuine—especially as he has the habit of interviewing almost exclusively conservative Protestant evangelicals—and then just giving traditional Protestant works as "further reading" at the end of each section. Sparse interaction with critical scholars and non-Protestant Christians leaves the impression that he is more interested in saving his readers' souls via traditional Protestant gospel then in finding out what is probably true.

974 See Eusebius, 3.39.15-16, pp. 105-6. See esp. Dungan's discussion of John's Gospel, pp. 23-5.

975 Irenaeus, *Against the Heresies*, 3.1.1, http://www.newadvent.org/fathers/0103301.htm. For discussion, see *Mercer Dictionary of the Bible*, s.v. "John, Gospels and Letter of" and s.v. "Luke, Gospel of."

976 See Dungan, pp. 23-5.

977 NAB, p. 144; Ehrman, *Jesus, Interrupted*, pp. 102-112 (all Gospels discussed); *Mercer Dictionary of the Bible*, s.v. "John, Gospel and Letters of."

978 See thoughts of Albert Schweitzer in Neill and Wright, p. 209. See also Neill and Wright's comments re: David Friedrich Strauss (1808-1874): "When we consider the differences in order between the several Gospels, the way in which sayings are reported in different contexts, the inner contradictions, we become aware that what we have are no more than isolated fragments, on which some kind of order has been imposed by the evangelists. The facts and sayings are like a necklace of pearls, of which the string has broken" (pp. 16-17).

979 See Neill and Wright, p. 310 where H. F. von Campenhausen is noted as stating that "we have to reckon with the possibility of later reburial; or alteration of the sight of the grave; of the theft of the body (not necessarily only by the disciples); of malicious activity on the part of the enemies of Jesus; of one or other of many accidents that could have happened …."

980 Marcus J. Borg and N.T. Wright, *The Meaning of Jesus: Two Visions* (New York: HarperCollins, 1999), p. 130. This general idea of a metaphorical resurrection was held to by early Gnostic Christians who found the claims about a literal resurrection to be "extremely revolting, repugnant, and impossible" (Pagels, pp. 5, 12).

981 A common apologetical approach is to claim that the apostles would not have "died for a lie" and therefore a literal Resurrection is likely (e.g., Josh McDowell, *More Than a Carpenter*, pp. 60-70). However, the fates of most of the apostles seem uncertain; furthermore, there appears to be no record of any apostle dying for a specific belief in the Resurrection. See Bart D. Ehrman, "Is There Historical Evidence for the Resurrection of Jesus?" 28 Mar. 2006, (debate with William Lane Craig, College of the Holy Cross, Worcester, MA), Dr. Ehrman's conclusion, http://www.philvaz.com/apologetics/p96.htm (accessed 21 Jul. 2018). Josh McDowell's son gives a less "optimistic" assessment of how many apostles were actually martyred. See Sean McDowell, "Did the Apostles Really Die as Martyrs for Their Faith?" *Biola Magazine*, Fall 2013, http://magazine.biola.edu/article/13-fall/did-the-apostles-really-die-as-martyrs-for-their-f/ (accessed 21 Jul. 2018). Evangelical scholar McBirnie tends to be more hopeful about martyrdoms. However, his historical analysis often seems lacking and his conclusions are still often tenuous anyway. (See McBirnie, *The Search for the Twelve* Apostles, pp. 21-2, 80, 131-3, 175-82, etc.). James the brother of John is killed by Herod in Acts 12:1-2; Herod's specific reasons are not mentioned. St. Paul, though likely martyred, was not a witness to the historical Jesus. Peter's martyrdom in Rome is likely the most credible tradition outside the Bible for the so-called Twelve (*Mercer Dictionary of the Bible*, s.v. "Peter"). According to *Mercer*, the fates of other apos-

tles are uncertain, s.v. "Thomas"; s.v. "Andrew"; s.v. "Matthew"; s.v. "Bartholomew"; s.v. "Philip"; and s.v. "Thaddaeus" for examples. Cf. Hippolytus (pseudonymous), *On the Apostles and Disciples*, in Ante-Nicene Fathers, vol. 5, ed. Alexander Roberts et al., trans. J.H. MacMahon (Buffalo, NY: Christian Literature Publishing Co., 1886), http://www.newadvent.org/fathers/0524.htm. John is deemed by tradition to have lived to old age and has never been claimed as a martyr. Christian historian Justo González appears accurate when he more generally notes that besides the cases of Peter, John, Paul and "Perhaps other apostles, such as Thomas … most of the traditions regarding apostolic travels date from a later period, when it was believed that the apostles divided the world among themselves, and when the church in each country or city sought to claims apostolic origins. In truth, most of the missionary work was not carried out by the apostles, but rather by the countless and nameless Christians …" (vol. 1, p. 30). Further, it was possible to be a Christian martyr in the ancient world without believing in a literal Resurrection. Eusebius, *Ecclesiastical History*, ch. 8, The Book of the Martyrs, no. 10, p. 322 mentions a Marcionite martyr bishop named Asclepius. (Marcionites generally believed that Christ just appeared to have suffered.) See also Pagels, pp. 89-90. For dubious early papal martyr traditions which highlight the romantic reasons why martyrdom was ascribed to prominent forebears, see Richard P. McBrien, *Lives of the Popes: The Pontiffs from St. Peter to John Paul II* (New York: HarperCollins, 2000), pp. 34-55.

982 Lewis, *The Joyful Christian*, pp. 110-12; Dennis Bratcher, "C.S. Lewis and the Inerrancy, Inspiration, and Historicity of Scripture," *The Voice*, 2013, http://www.crivoice.org/lewisbib.html (accessed 11 Sep. 2016).

983 Schulz, pp. 222ff. For an interesting TED Talk on the issue of memory, see Elizabeth Loftus, "How Reliable Is Your Memory?" *TED Global 2013*, Jun. 2013, https://www.ted.com/talks/elizabeth_loftus_the_fiction_of_memory#t-10018 (accessed 27 Sep. 2018). For a discussion of false memories as related to sexual abuse, see Shermer, *Why People Believe Weird Things*, pp. 108-13. For false memories and alien abduction, see p. 312.

984 Tohru Ohnuma and Heii Arai, "Genetic or Psychogenic? A Case Study of (Folie à Quatre) Including Twins," *Case Reports in Psychiatry*, (2015): pp. 1-3 which notes that "Shared psychotic disorder, characterized by shared delusion among two or more subjects (termed "Folie `a deux," "trois," etc.), is often associated with strong religious beliefs or social isolation, factors creating strong psychological sympathy." See also V.K. Aravind, V.D. Krishnaram, and Rupavathy A. Vimala, "Folie a Trois: Atypical Presentation as Shared Transient Psychotic Episode," *Indian Journal of*

Psychological Medicine 36.2 (Apr.-Jun. 2014): pp. 211-14; Richard A. Bryant, "Folie à Familie: A Cognitive Study of Delusional Beliefs," *Psychiatry* 60.1 (Spring 1997): pp. 44-50; Neena Sawant and Chetan Vispute, "Delusional Parasitosis with Folie a Deaux: A Case Series," *Industrial Psychiatry Journal*, 24.1 (Jan.-Jun. 2015): pp. 97-8. See also this entry from the DSM-V: "It was previously difficult to diagnose delusional beliefs in more than one person if the belief in question might ordinarily be widely shared in the patients' culture, such as demonic possession at certain times in history or the existence of elves in certain countries. The revised criteria simply propose that if two patients strongly espouse an erroneous belief and have the other symptoms described above, then both patients have delusional disorder." See "Delusional Disorder DSM-5 297.1 (F22)," *theravive.com*, n.d., https://www.theravive.com/therapedia/delusional-disorder-dsm--5-297.1-(f22) (accessed 13 Jan. 2019). For comments on "group delusions" in reference to solar phenomena and Marian visions, see Hector Avalos, "Mary at Medjugorje: A Critical Inquiry," *Free Inquiry*, 14.2 (Spring 1994): pp. 48ff.

985   Tertullian, *The Shows (De Spectaculis)*, ch. 30, http://www.newadvent.org/fathers/0303.htm. For a brief discussion by one skeptic, see Robert M. Price, "Jesus' Burial in a Garden: The Strange Growth of the Tradition," *Religious Traditions* 12, (1989): http://www.robertmprice.mindvendor.com/burial.htm (accessed 4 Nov. 2015). Cf. John 20:15 where Mary Magdalene thinks the risen Christ is the gardener.

986   From William Lane Craig and Bart Ehrman, "Is There Historical Evidence for the Resurrection of Jesus?" Dr. Ehrman's opening statement, 4th para. From the bottom, http://www.philvaz.com/apologetics/p96.htm.

987   Robert B. Stewart, ed., *The Resurrection of Jesus: John Dominic Crossan and N.T. Wright in Dialogue* (Minneapolis: Fortress Press, 2006), p. 74.

988   *Encyclopedia of Mormonism*, s.v. "Revelation" https://eom.byu.edu/index.php/Revelation (accessed 11 Jan. 2019). See no. 9 in "Types of Revelation" section.

989   See Richard Carrier, "Why I Don't Buy the Resurrection Story," 6th ed. (Richard Carrier and Internet Infidels, 2006), Main Argument, http://infidels.org/library/modern/richard_carrier/resurrection/lecture.html#41 (accessed 30 Oct. 2015).

990   Wulff, pp. 49, 75-6, 85-9, 93, 151-2.

991   Shermer, *Why People Believe Weird Things*, p. 77 notes the link between hallucinations and "extreme stress, drugs, or sleep deprivation." See also pp. 88-98 for hallucinations, dreams, and alien abduction stories. In an interesting potential parallel, Shermer notes of alien abductions that

"Since there is no physical evidence to confirm the validity ..., the logical conclusion to draw, knowing that we do about he fantastic imagery the brain is capable of producing, is that the experiencer's experiences are nothing more than mental representations of strictly internal brain phenomena" (p. 310).

992 Per Ehrman, *Jesus, Interrupted*, p. 178; Vaughan Bell, "Ghost Stories: Visits from the Deceased," *Scientific American*, 2 Dec. 2008, https://www.scientificamerican.com/article/ghost-stories-visits-from-the-deceased/ (accessed 10 Oct. 2018).

993 See Danilo Arnone, Anish Patel, and Giles Ming-Yee Ta, "The Nosological Significance of Folie à Deux: A Review of the Literature," *Annals of General Psychiatry*, 5.11 (2006). Avail. at https://www.ncbi.nlm.nih.gov/pmc/articles/PMC1559622/ (accessed 13 Jan. 2019). This article concludes that there can be "shared delusions and hallucinations." See also Ohnuma and Arai, "Genetic or Psychogenic? A Case Study of (Folie à Quatre) Including Twins," which notes that "strong familial connection appeared to be the most important factor for the common delusion and hallucination."

994 Gary J. Whittenberger, "On Visions and Resurrections," *eSkeptic*, 1 Feb. 2012, https://www.skeptic.com/eskeptic/12-02-01/ (accessed 14 Jan. 2019).

995 Avalos, "Mary at Medjugorje: A Critical Inquiry," pp. 48ff.

996 Hector Avalos, "Jesus' Resurrection and Marian Apparitions: Medjugorge as a Living Laboratory," *Debunking Christianity* (blog), 29 Apr. 2013, www.debunking-christianity.com/2013/04/jesus-resurrection-and-marian.html (accessed 14 Jan. 2019).

997 See *Mercer Dictionary of the Bible*, s.v. "Visions": "A revelation, often at night, in the form of things heard as well as things seen. Visions are akin to dreams, but usually come while the recipient is conscious, and often under great stress. ... Visions are sometimes induced by music, dancing, or the drinking of particular potions, or especially by extended fasting." See also Loftus, *Why I Became an Atheist*, pp. 283-4. (Loftus quotes at length from the *New Bible Dictionary*.) Ibn Ishaq notes regarding Muhammad's revelations: "The apostle of Allah was in the habit of saying: 'My eye sleeps, while my heart is awake,' but Allah knows best whether what was revealed to him took place in a waking or sleeping state" (p. 59). Ibn Ishaq also relates that Muhammad always "lost consciousness ... before a revelation" (p. 118).

998 Herodotus, 7.194, p. 473.

999 Josephus, *The Life of Flavius Josephus*, in *The Works of Flavius Josephus*, trans. William Whiston (Grand Rapids, MI: Christian Classics Ethereal

Library, n.d.), no. 75, http://www.ccel.org/j/josephus/works/autobiog.htm. See also Matyszak, p. 211. (Matzyak states that two survived but that appears incorrect based on Josephus.)

1000 Furbank, p. 210 notes one nun was nailed to a cross for three hours. B. Robert Kreiser, "Religious Enthusiasm in Early Eighteenth-Century Paris: The Convulsionaries of Saint-Médard," *The Catholic Historical Review* 61.3 (Jul. 1975): p. 371 for a mention of crucifixion and other torments. Richard F. Costigan, review of *Suffering Saints: Jansenists and Convulsionnaires in France, 1640–1799*, by Brian E. Strayer, *Church History* 79.1 (Mar. 2010): p. 213. Costigan notes the descent into "convulsions, wild dances, and finally gruesome tortures of each other."

1001 Aaron Favila, "In The Philippines, Observers Perform Crucifixion Reenactment In Good Friday Ritual (PHOTOS)" *The Huffington Post*," 18 Apr. 2014, http://www.huffingtonpost.com/2014/04/18/philippines-crucifixion-reenactment_n_5173257.html (accessed 30 Oct. 2015).

1002 Harriet Alexander, "Isis Crucifies Nine People in Syrian Villages," *The Telegraph*, 29 Jun. 2014, http://www.telegraph.co.uk/news/worldnews/middleeast/syria/10933851/Isis-crucifies-nine-people-in-Syrian-villages.html (accessed 24 Sep. 2018).

1003 Often called the "swoon hypothesis."

1004 The mythicist perspective that Jesus of Nazareth was not a historical person is rejected by most critical scholars. For instance, see Bart D. Ehrman, "Did Jesus Exist?" *The Huffington Post*, 20 Mar. 2012, http://www.huffingtonpost.com/bart-d-ehrman/did-jesus-exist_b_1349544.html (accessed 21 Feb. 2013). Ehrman even states the following: "These views are so extreme and so unconvincing to 99.99 percent of the real experts that anyone holding them is as likely to get a teaching job in an established department of religion as a six-day creationist is likely to land on in a bona fide department of biology."

1005 See Richard Carrier, "Why We Might Have Reason for Doubt: Should We Still Be Looking for a Historical Jesus?" *The Bible and* Interpretation, Aug. 2014, http://www.bibleinterp.com/articles/2014/08/car388028.shtml (accessed 8 Oct. 2018); Earl Doherty, "Was There No Historical Jesus?" *Internet Infidels Newsletter*, Apr. 1999, https://infidels.org/infidels/newsletter/1999/april.html (accessed 9 Oct. 2018); Bertrand Russell, "Why I Am Not a Christian" in *Why I Am Not a Christian and Other Essays on Religion and Related Subjects*, ed. Paul Edwards (New York: Touchstone/Simon and Schuster, 1957), p. 16. I personally hold that it is more likely that myths and legends grew around a historical Jesus of Nazareth.

1006 Bonner, p. 167.

1007   Pagels, pp. 5, 12.
1008   Ehrman, *Jesus, Interrupted*, p. 177; Loftus, *Why I Became an Atheist*, p. 160.
1009   Carl Sagan, "The God Hypothesis," in *The Portable Atheist*, p. 228.
1010   Origen, *On First Principles*, in *After the New Testament*, 1.2, p. 414.
1011   "How Can I Be Led by the Holy Spirit?" Kenneth Copeland Ministries, n.d., http://www.kcm.org/real-help/spiritual-growth/learn/how-can-i-be-led-the-holy-spirit (accessed 26 Sep. 2018).
1012   Pagels, p. xxii. Pagels further asserts that "Hundreds of rival teachers all claimed to teach the 'true doctrine of Christ' and denounced on another as frauds" (p. 7).
1013   Irenaeus of Lyons, *Against the Heresies, Book I*, ed. Walter J. Burghardt et al., trans. Dominic J. Unger, *Ancient Christian Writers: The Works of the Fathers in Translation*, vol. 55 (New York: Paulist, 1992), 28.2, p. 93. For an online translation, see http://www.newadvent.org/fathers/0103128.htm. Stark notes that Irenaeus describes "nearly two dozen groups" and Hippolytus "nearly fifty" (p. 27).
1014   For another example of this phenomenon, see James Milton Carroll, "The Trail of Blood" ... *Following the Christians Down Through the Centuries ... Or the History of the Baptist Churches From the Time of Christ, Their Founder, to the Present Day*," orig. pub. 1931, https://archive.org/details/TheTrailOfBlood/page/n0 (accessed 8 Oct. 2018). Carroll's idea is rather unconvincing when comparisons are made with the groups that he equates with 20th-c. Baptists (i.e., ""Montanists, Novationists, Donatists, Paulicians, Albigenses, Waldenses, etc." See p. 7).
1015   Williams, p. 238.
1016   The Infancy Gospel of Thomas, in *After the New Testament*, chs. 3-5, 8, 14; pp. 256-8.
1017   Ibid., chs. 3-5, 8, 14; pp. 256-8.
1018   See, for example, The Secret Book of John, in *After the New Testament*, pp. 146ff and *On the Origin of the World*, in *After the New Testament*, p. 173-6. Cf. Irenaeus, 1.27.2, http://newadvent.org/fathers/0103127.htm.
1019   Marshall, pp. 81, 219. See also Bruce, p. 432.
1020   For an example see Ignatius of Antioch to the Smyrneans, *The Apostolic Fathers*, ed. and trans. Bart D. Ehrman, vol. 1 (Cambridge, MA: Harvard Univ. Press, 2003), 8.1-2, pp. 303-5. For further description of this "early catholic" phenomenon, see *Handbook of Biblical Criticism*, 3rd ed., s.v. "Catholicizing Tendency."
1021   The Acts of Thecla, in *After the New Testament*, Ehrman, ed., chs.5-8, 22, 28; pp. 279-82. The Acts of John, *After the New Testament* describes abstention from any marital relations in pious terms (ch. 63, p. 285). Early

church father Hippolytus (160-235 CE) also talks about "signing yourself" in his *Apostolic Tradition* (36.11 and 37.1, p. 332); Tertullian does as well (*On the Crown*, p. 352); cf. Carolinne White, Introduction to *Early Christian Lives*, p. xxxiv.

1022   The Martyrdom of Polycarp, *After the New Testament*, ch. 17, p. 34. *The New International Dictionary of the Christian Church*, s.v. "Relics" dates this work to 156 and describes it as the "earliest classical instance of the veneration of relics." Acts 19:12, 2 Kings 2:14, and 2 Kings 13:21 are classic prooftexts for the efficacy of relics. Eusebius notes that martyred bodies were considered "sacred and holy" (ch. 8, The Book of the Martyrs, no. 11, p. 326; see also no. 12, p. 328). Patrick J. Geary, *Furta Sacra: Thefts of Relics in the Central Middle Ages* (Princeton, NJ: Princeton Univ. Press, 1990), p. 32 notes that Claudius of Turin (d. 827) himself admitted that he was the sole opposition to the cult of relics in his day.

1023   The Didascalia, in *After the New Testament*, ch.14, pp. 338-9. Cf. the Russian Orthodox *Stoglav* Council (Troyat, pp. 179-80). This was a continuing issue in the Byzantine Church where even second marriages were sometimes condemned for widowed spouses. See Norwich, pp. 135, 161-2, 191 (penance for a second marriage), 226.

1024   Sulpicius Severus, *Life of Martin of Tours*, in *Early Christian Lives,* nos. XIII-XV, pp. 146-8. God sometimes assisted Martin in his destructive deeds. For similar behavior, see Gregory the Great, *Life of Benedict*, in *Early Christian Lives,* no. VIII.11, p. 178; Bede, 1.30, p. 92; 1.32, p. 94; 3.8, p. 155.

1025   Steven Bigham, *Early Christian Attitudes toward Images* (Rollinsford, NH: Orthodox Research Institute, 2004), p. 90. Bigham notes that the tradition is first found in Theodore the Reader in 530.

1026   Norwich, p. 316.

1027   While the use of symbols started very early and there are famous paintings with religious motifs from the Roman catacombs that likely emerged in the late 2nd c., early church fathers often speak negatively about images and statues and there was likely a gradual borrowing from pagan influences. See H. Chadwick, pp. 277-84; Davis, pp. 291-3; Eduard Syndicus, *Early Christian Art*, trans. J. R. Foster (New York: Hawthorn Books, 1962), pp. 7-10; David W. Bercot, *A Dictionary of Early Christian Beliefs* (Peabody, MA: Hendrickson Publishers, 1998), pp. 350-1. Eastern Orthodox theologian Steven Bigham has a traditional Eastern Orthodox view, but still notes that "Christian images developed ... from indirect symbols to direct images of persons and events" (p. 179). For discussions in the fathers that seem quite contrary to medieval Catholic uses of statues and images, see Clement of Alexandria, *The Stromata, or Miscellanies*, in *Ante-Nicene Fathers*, vol. 2, ed. Alexander Roberts et al., trans. William Wilson (Buffalo, NY: Christian Literature Publishing Co., 1885), 7.5, http://www.newadvent.org/fathers/02107.htm (accessed 26 Sep. 2018); Irenaeus, 1.25.6, http://www.newadvent.org/fathers/0103125.htm (accessed 26 Sep. 2018); Origen, *Against Celsus*, 7.64, http://www.newadvent.org/fathers/04167.htm; Eusebius, 7.18, pp. 253-4; Minucius Felix, *Octavius*, ch. 27, http://www.newadvent.org/fathers/0410.htm; Tertullian, *On Idolatry*, in *Ante-Nicene Fathers*, vol. 3, ed. Alexander Roberts et al., trans. S. Thelwall (Buffalo, NY: Christian Literature Publishing Co., 1885), ch. 3, http://www.newadvent.org/fathers/0302.htm; "The Council of Elvira," can. 36, https://www.webcitation.org/6AS7rgB7f?url=http://faculty.cua.edu/pennington/canon%20Law/ElviraCanons.htm. *The Catholic Encyclopedia*, s.v. "The Veneration of Images" http://www.newadvent.org/cathen/07664a.htm (accessed 25 Sep. 2018) confirms that Eusebius "the Father of Church History, must be counted among the enemies of icons." It is difficult to find any explicit and clear references supporting icons in the Fathers as late as the 4th c. An example of this reality is John of Damascus (d. 749), a classic defender of icons, who cites 4th-c. St. Basil's remark that "the honor paid to the image passes on to the prototype." See John of Damascus, 4.16, http://www.newadvent.org/fathers/33044.htm. In context, however, Basil does not appear to be discussing icons at all but just giving an illustration about a king and his image while defending another theological position. See Basil of Caesarea, *De Spiritu Sancto (On the Holy Spirit)*, 18.45, http://www.newadvent.org/fathers/3203.htm. Cf. Davis, p. 310 and his discussion of Council of Nicaea II. *Mercer Dictionary of the Bible*, s.v. "Idolatry" notes that this basic dynamic was found in pagan religions: "Ancient Near Eastern writings indicate an awareness of the difference between gods themselves and the images that represented the gods or that the gods temporarily inhabited." Celsus also shows that this general notion was a pre-Christian, pagan opinion (Syndicus, p. 9; Wilken, pp. 118-9).

1028 Augustine, *City of God*, 4.31, http://www.newadvent.org/fathers/120104.htm.

1029 See Origen, *On First Principles*, 4.3.4-5, p. 429. See discussion in Dungan, p. 81. For a short review of Origen's exegetical approach, see Froehlich, pp. 16-18. Philo had a similar approach (but from a Jewish perspective). See Froehlich, p. 7.

1030 Bonner, pp. 25, 278-9.

1031 Davis, p. 66.

1032 "The Council of Elvira," can. 71, https://www.webcitation.org/6AS7rgB-7f?url=http://faculty.cua.edu/pennington/canon%20Law/ElviraCanons.htm. Pennington notes that the origins of many of the canons are disputed and may have been appended from other Iberian councils.

1033 *The Concise Oxford Dictionary of the Christian Church*, s.v. "Simeon Stylites, St." See also *The New International Dictionary of the Christian Church*, s.v. "Simeon the Stylite."

1034 *The Concise Oxford Dictionary of the Christian Church*, s.v. "Daniel, St."; Norwich, p. 53.

1035 Ehrman, *Lost Christianities*, pp. 99-103; *The Catholic Encyclopedia*, s.v. "Ebionites" http://www.newadvent.org/cathen/05242c.htm (accessed 15 Jan. 2019); *Mercer Dictionary of the Bible*, s.v. "Ebionites, Gospel of."

1036 As quoted in *The Catholic Encyclopedia*, s.v. "Arianism" http://www.newadvent.org/cathen/01707c.htm (accessed 26 Mar. 2017). See also Bellitto, p. 20.

1037 *The Penguin Dictonary of Religions*, s.v. "Manichaeism, History of." See also *The New International Dictionary of the Christian Church*, s.v. "Manichaeism." Bonner states that it lasted for twelve centuries (p. 157). It became the state religion of the Uighur Turkish kingdom in 762 (Morgan, p. 45).

1038 Bonner, pp. 167-70. (See Bonner, pp. 58, 159, 161 for Manichaean adoption of Christian language, etc.) *The Catholic Encyclopedia*, s.v. "Manichaeism" http://www.newadvent.org/cathen/0951a.htm (accessed 2 May 2017) confirms that Mani called himself the promised Paraclete as well as the "Apostle of Jesus Christ by the providence of God the Father."

1039 Bonner, pp. 137, 240-3, 252-3; González, vol. 1, p. 156. Islamic terrorists are known for shouting "Allahu Akbar" or "God is greater!"

1040 Davis, pp. 249-50.

1041 Augustine, *On Christian Doctrine*, Preface, no. 4, http://www.newadvent.org/fathers/12020.htm.

1042 Jerome, *Life of Hilarion*, in *Early Christian Lives*, no. 15, p. 96.

1043 James Reston, Jr., "Be Christian or Die," *Christian History* 18.3, issue 63 (1999): pp. 13-17.

1044 González, vol. 1, pp. 266-8.

1045 Ibid., p. 274.

1046 *The Concise Oxford Dictionary of the Christian Church*, s.v. "Vladimir, St"; "Did You Know …?" *Christian History* 7.2, issue 18 (1988): p. 4. (See also p. 9.) For an assertion that his subjects were "urged" but otherwise "willingly baptized," see *The Catholic Encyclopedia*, s.v. "St. Vladimir the Great" http://www.newadvent.org/cathen/15497a.htm.

1047 *The New International Dictionary of the Christian Church*, s.v. "Paulicians"; Norwich, p. 140.
1048 Both Cathars and others in battle, executions, and other circumstances of the general conflict.
1049 Hindley, p. 172 and O'Shea, pp. 2, 7. More than 200 Cathars were burned alive after the siege of Montségur in 1244. The Waldensians, also called the Poor of Lyons, were another pacifist sect that were the subject of Inquisition and Crusade. Pope Innocent VIII ordered a crusade against them in 1488 to try to eradicate them. See *The Catholic Encyclopedia*, s.v. "Waldenses" http://www.newadvent.org/cathen/15527b.htm (accessed 23 Sep. 2013). In perhaps the worst single event of this calamity, perhaps 15,000 people in the town of Béziers were slaughtered—including women and children. See Hindley, pp. 166-73; O'Shea, pp. 5, 84-7. In his 1184 bull *Ad Abolendam*, Lucius III advocated punishments of exile, confiscation of property, destruction of home, etc. Pope Innocent IV issued a bull in 1252 that authorized the use of torture; several successors approved of the practice as well. Other popes like Alexander IV (1254-1261), Clement IV (1265-1268), Nicholas IV (1288-1302), Boniface VIII (1294-1303) did similarly. See *The Catholic Encyclopedia*, s.v. "Inquisition" http://www.newadvent.org/cathen/08026a.htm. The Lateran III Council (1179) had previously forbade Catholics to give any food or shelter to Cathars or to have any business transactions with them (Bellitto, p. 53). Cf. Halsall, ed., *Twelfth Ecumenical Council: Lateran IV 1215, Internet Medieval Sourcebook*, can. 3, http://www.fordham.edu/halsall/basis/lateran4.asp which, under certain conditions, encourages the persecution and "extermination of the heretics" as well as the confiscation of their property.
1050 Bonner, p. 171.
1051 González, vol 1, p. 293ff.
1052 A "crusade" is generally defined as being at the direction of a pope or papal representative. Councils also participated in the crusading spirit; the Fourth Lateran Council even developed a plan for the capture of Jerusalem (see Hindley, pp. 1, 180. For a link to the Council's decrees, see "Canons of the Fourth Lateran Council," http://www.fordham.edu/halsall/basis/lateran4.asp). A traditional rendering yields nine main crusades as well as frequent other minor crusades and crusading activities. Hindley notes over thirty from 1095 to 1588 (pp. xvi-xx, 2, 250, etc.). See also Palmer and Colton, pp. 125-30. 350.
1053 See Walsh, ed., *Butler's Lives of the Saints*, p. 257; *The Westminster Dictionary of Theologians*, s.v. "Bernard of Clairvaux"; *The New International Dictionary of the Christian Church*, s.v. "Bernard of Clairvaux." Bernard

also wrote the Rule of the Knights Templar (Hindley, p. 59). Although known for his peaceful preaching, St. Francis of Assisi joined the Crusaders in Egypt in 1219 and preached to the Sultan (Brown, p. 15; Hindley, p. 188). See also Norwich, p. 276.

1054   Walsh, ed., *Butler's Lives of the Saints*, p. 126.

1055   Ibid., pp. 380-1.

1056   It is clear that the vast majority of Catholics supported the Crusades and regarded them as the will of Christ (Hindley, pp. 1-2, 223, etc). However, Hindley does note that St. Anselm (c. 1033-1109) advocated the monastic way of life as a more appropriate alternative (p. 19). Anselm, however, lived at the genesis of the Crusades before the notion became fully part of an established Catholic tradition. Ralph Niger wondered if killing was a proper way to atone for sin (Hindley, p. 164). Of course, there is no doctrine of the Catholic faith that has complete unanimity or was forged without any dissent. (Even in expounding his canon of "everywhere, always, by all," Vincent meant a vast majority or "at the least of almost all"—see *The Comminitory*, 2.6, http://www.newadvent.org/fathers/3506.htm). Cf. the military aggression of the Papal States (Oberman, p. 72). The missionary Ramon Lull (1213-1315) was another rare figure who came to regard holy war as entirely misguided. See Steven Gertz, "Spiritual Warriors," *Christian History* 21.1, issue 74 (2002): pp. 28-30.

1057   González, vol. 1, pp. 343-4; *The Concise Oxford Dictionary of the Christian Church*, s.v. "Great Schism."

1058   Ferrara and Woods, loc. 2413-2421, Kindle. While the Great Schism was an unusual event in some ways, it is perhaps germane to mention that there were been as many as 37 papal pretenders or "antipopes" between 217 and 1439. *The Catholic Encyclopedia*, s.v. "Antipope" http://www.newadvent.org/cathen/01582a.htm (accessed 13 Nov. 2015) notes 29 anti-popes; *Encyclopedia Britannica*, s.v. "Antipope" http://www.britannica.com/topic/antipope (accessed 13 Nov. 2015) notes at least 37 from 217 to 1439.

1059   *The Westminster Dictionary of Theologians*, s.v. "Bernard of Clairvaux."

1060   Wood, p. 113; *The Catholic Encyclopedia*, s.v. "John Wyclif" http://www.newadvent.org/cathen/15722a.htm. Likewise, the Council of Constance condemned both Wycliffe and Hus but a doctrine of justification by faith alone was not among their criticisms. See "Council of Constance 1414-1418," http://www.papalencyclicals.net/Councils/ecum16.htm; A. McGrath, *Iustitia Dei*, p. 216.

1061   Galli and Olsen, eds., *131 Christians*, p. 211.

1062   George, "The Reformation Connection,"p. 35; *The Catholic Encyclopedia.*, s.v. "Hussites" http://www.newadvent.org/cathen/07585a.htm. The Hussite

Four Articles, which summarized their chief complaints with Catholicism, did not mention justification by faith alone.

1063   González, vol. 1, pp. 346-53. González makes no reference to justification by faith alone in his discussion. A. C. Spearing, Introduction to *Revelations of Divine Love*, by Julian of Norwich, p. xiii also notes that the Lollards disapproved of images. Simony is the buying or selling of church offices.

1064   See "Council of Constance 1414-1418," http://www.papalencyclicals.net/councils/ecum16.htm. Quote is from Sess. 5 of the Council, 6 Apr. 1415. See also Hindley, p. 242; Oberman, p. 54.

1065   Bellitto, pp. 81-95; 119-24.

1066   Walsh, ed., *Butler's Lives of the Saints*, pp. 223, 293. Cf. St. Teresa of Ávila and St. Joan of Arc (Ghezzi, pp. 126, 153).

1067   Leo XIII, *Aeterni Patris*, nos. 14, 21, 26, etc. http://www.papalencyclicals.net/Leo13/l13cph.htm.

1068   Dan Graves, "Article #29: 'I Can Write No More. All That I Have Written Seems Like Straw,'" *Christian History Institute*, n.d., https://christianhistoryinstitute.org/incontext/article/aquinas/ (accessed 24 Feb. 2019); "1272 Thomas Aquinas Concludes His Word on *Summa Theologiae*," *Christian History* 9.4, issue 28 (1990): p. 23; *The Catholic Encyclopedia*, s.v. "St. Thomas Aquinas" http://www.newadvent.org/cathen/14663b.htm (accessed 14 Jul. 2016) for a slightly different translation.

1069   Norwich, pp. 187, 204.

1070   Geary, pp. 3, 114, 152. For more on the importance of relics in Catholicism, see Bede, 1.18, p. 67; 1.30, p. 92; 3.6, p. 152; 3.13, p. 163; 3.29, p. 198; 4.32, p. 265; 5.11, p. 282; 4.10, p. 221; etc. The Shroud of Turin, purported to be the burial cloth of Christ, is certainly a more impressive relic. However, even believers have often been skeptical. See *The Catholic Encyclopedia*, s.v. "The Holy Shroud (of Turin)" http://newadvent.org/cathen/13762a.htm (accessed 11 Nov. 2018). Though a dated article, it notes various problems identified in the early 20th c. *The Concise Oxford Dictionary of the Christian Church*, s.v. "Holy Shroud" notes that "Carbon testing in 1988 indicated a date between 1260 and 1390 for harvesting the flax from which it is woven." *Encyclopedia Britannica*, s.v. "Shroud of Turin" suggests that the controversy about authenticity is ongoing despite the results of the carbon dating; there are a wide range of tests that have been done on the Shroud. For a short skeptical review, see Daniel Loxton, "Shroud of Turin: Redux," *eSkeptic*, 28 Dec. 2011, https://www.skeptic.com/eskeptic/11-12-28/ (accessed 16 Nov. 2018). John Calvin pointed out that John 20:6-7 describes Christ's burial cloth as having a separate piece for the head. The Shroud is one piece—putting its authenticity at apparent odds with the Gospel. See John Calvin, *Treatise on Relics* (Edinburgh: Johnstone and Hunter, 1854), p.239. Avail. at https://archive.org/details/atreatiseonreli00krasgoog/page/n262.

1071 There are apparently close to 100 extant accounts of the thefts of Christian relics from the 9th to 11th centuries (Geary, p. xii. For reasons for relic thefts, see pp. 129-30). For an example of the desire to obtain apostolic relics, see Bede, 5.11, p. 282; 5.20, p. 307.

1072 Geary, p. 94ff.

1073 Gregory the Great, *Life of Benedict*, in *Early Christian Lives*, no. 2, p. 168.

1074 Bede, 5.12, p. 289.

1075 St. Symeon the New Theologian, *One Hundred and Fifty-Three Practical and Theological Texts*, in *The Philokalia*, vol. 4, p. 27. Symeon did allow for the practice only if "your spiritual father insists." See also "One Hundred and Fifty-Three Practical and Theological Texts" no. 135, p. 55 in the same volume. Cf. González, vol. 1, p. 202 on St. Jerome; Athanasius, *Life of Antony*, in *Christian Lives*, no. 47, p. 38 which notes that Antony "never washed his body."

1076 Bonaventure, *The Life of St. Francis*, 11.2, p. 281.

1077 Ibid., 5.1-4, pp. 218-21; 13. 1, p. 304; 12.3-4, pp. 294-5.

1078 *The Catholic Encyclopedia*, s.v. "Witchcraft" http://www.newadvent.org/cathen/15674a.htm.

1079 Ware, p. 66.

1080 Wulff, p. 75.

1081 Reston, p. 159.

1082 O. Chadwick, p. 295; Bede, 3.6, p. 152; 3.19, p. 176; 4.19, p. 236. St. Eustochia Calafato (1434-1491), St. Rita of Sacia (1381-1457), St. Germaine of Pibrac (1579-1601), and St. Withburga (d.c. 743) are but four examples of incorrupt bodies of saints. See Walsh, ed., *Butler's Lives of the Saints*, pp. 17-18; 151-2; 181-2; 208. See Geary, p. 69 for other examples of incorrupt corpses. For examples of floating nuns see St. Magdalen of Canossa (1774-1835) and St. Teresa of **Ávila** (1515-1582) in Walsh, ed., *Butler's Lives of the Saints*, pp. 139, 336. Ghezzi claims that was said about St. Catherine of Siena and St. Lutgarde as well (pp. 31, 175). See also Geary, p. 125 for bleeding relics, incorrupt bodies, and fragrant odors of corpses. St. Jerome claimed that St. Hilarion was incorrupt and had a sweet smell (Jerome, *Life of Hilarion* in *Early Christian Lives*, no. 46, p. 115). See also Ghezzi, p. 12 for St. Theresa Margaret (1747-1770). For St. Francis levitating in prayer, see Bonaventure, *The Life of St. Francis*, 10.4, p. 275.

1083 Leo X, *Exsurge Domine*, in *Papal Encyclicals Online*, orig. pub. 1520, no. 33, http://www.papalencyclicals.net/Leo10/l10exdom.htm (accessed 28 Feb. 2017). Martin Luther, the main subject of the bull, would have no doubt met this fate if he had not obtained secular protection (Oberman, p. 23). Jan Huss is an example burning of a heretic (Hindley, p. 242; Oberman, p. 54); Savonarola (1452-98) was hung and then burned (González, vol. 1, p. 356).

1084 Oberman, p. 62.

1085 O. Chadwick, pp. 435, 438-9; Bouwsma, p. 225; John Calvin, *Commentary on Psalms*, vol. 1, trans. James Anderson (Grand Rapids, MI: Christian Classics Ethereal Library, orig. pub. 1845), 33:2, p. 513. http://www.ccel.org/ccel/calvin/calcom08.pdf; "We Used to Sing Only Psalms—What Happened?" *Reformed Worship*, Mar. 1987, http://www.reformedworship.org/article/march-1987/we-used-sing-only-psalms-what-happened (accessed 12 Mar. 2019). retrieved 12/28/14, Ps 33:2, p.513

1086 Robert L. Wise, "Munster's Monster," *Christian History* 18.1, issue 61 (1999): pp. 23-5.

1087 Galli and Olsen, pp. 172-3.

1088 O. Chadwick, p. 300.

1089 Rachel Schnepper, "Yuletide's Outlaws," *The New York Times*, 14 Dec. 2012, http://www.nytimes.com/2012/12/15/opinion/the-puritan-war-on-christmas.html?_r=0 (accessed 22 Jan. 2016); Hector Avalos, "The Puritan War on Christmas," *The Ames Tribune*, 7 Dec. 2013, http://amestrib.com/opinion/hector-avalos-puritan-war-christmas (accessed 22 Jan. 2016).

1090 González, vol. 2, pp. 159-60.

1091 Palmer and Colton, pp. 169-70.

1092 Pascal, no. 881, p. 274.

1093 Walsh, ed., *Butler's Lives of the Saints*, pp. 236-9.

1094 *The Catholic Encyclopedia*, s.v. "St. Rose of Lima" http://newadvent.org/cathen/13192c.htm (accessed 3 Nov. 2018); Walsh, ed., *Butler's Lives of the Saints*, p. 260.

1095 Kreiser, pp. 367-78.

1096 Alfred Loisy, *My Duel with the Vatican: The Autobiography of a Catholic Modernist*, trans. Richard Wilson Boynton (New York: Greenwood Press, 1968), pp. 62, 67.

1097 Hindley, p. 255. See also Rory Carroll, "Pope Says Sorry for Sins of Church," *The Guardian*, 13 Mar. 2000, http://www.guardian.co.uk/world/2000/mar/13/catholicism.religion (accessed 7 Jun. 2013).

1098 See *Catechism of the Catholic Church*, secs. 2307-2317, pp. 614-17. Cf. Merton, p. 312: "Self-defense is good, and a necessary war is licit: but methods that descend to wholesale barbarism and ruthless, indiscriminate slaughter of non-combatants practically without defense are hard to see as anything else but mortal sins."

1099 For an interesting juxtaposition, see *The Catholic Encyclopedia*, s.v. "Limbo" http://newadvent.org/cathen/09256a.htm and Philip Pullella, "Catholic Church Buries Limbo after Centuries," *Reuters*, 20 Apr. 2007 https://www.reuters.com/article/us-pope-limbo-idUSL2028721620070420 (accessed 1 Oct. 2018). See also International Theological Commission, *The Hope of Salvation for Infants who Die without Being Baptised*, 22 Apr. 2007, http://www.vatican.va/roman_curia/congregations/cfaith/cti_documents/rc_con_cfaith_doc_20070419_un-baptised-infants_en.html (accessed 1 Oct. 2018) where Limbo still remains "a possible theological hypothesis" but nonetheless notes a favored conclusion that "there are theological and liturgical reasons to hope that infants who die without baptism may be saved and brought into eternal happiness."

1100 Ferrara and Woods, loc. 3707ff. See also Pérez, pp. 3-4; Bellitto, p. 71.

1101 Ferrara and Woods, loc. 606. See also the assertion of the authors that "the creation of Eve ex Adamo is an infallible teaching of the universal ordinary Magisterium, a doctrine the Church has always held" (loc. 11357). See also *Handbook of Biblical Criticism*, s.v. "Divino Afflante Spiritu" which notes that the 1943 papal encyclical changed the Catholic Church's historical stance on biblical criticism. For a text of this papal bull (with its acceptance of certain aspects of modern textual criticism), see Pius XII, *Divino Afflante Spiritu*, in *Papal Encyclicals Online*, orig. pub. 30 Sep. 1943, nos. 11, 18, 19 etc., http://www.papalencyclicals.net/pius12/p12divin.htm (accessed 2 Oct. 2018). Roman Catholic sensibilities here seem to have developed even further since Vatican II.

1102 For a brief description of sedevacantism, see Ferrara and Woods, locs. 697, 955. See also "Why Sedevacantism? A Conversation with a Sedevacantist Priest," *Novus Ordo Watch: Unmasking the Modernist Vatican II Church*, 5 Sep. 2013, https://novusordowatch.org/2013/09/why-sedevacantism-cekada/ (accessed 3 Mar. 2017). For biblical literalism and Genesis, see Loisy, pp. 125-6, etc.

1103 Magnus Lundberg, "Holy Apostolic Palmarian Catholic Church," *World Religions and Spirituality*, 28 Sep. 2015, https://wrldrels.org/2016/10/08/palmarian-catholic-church/ (accessed 16 Mar. 2018).

1104 Plummer, pp. 2ff. Many other examples are found in this book as well.

1105 Tindall and Shi, p. 306; Vidler, p. 238, Wulff, pp. 84-5; González, vol. 2, p. 246.

1106 Nolt, pp. 204-5.

1107 Edmund Massey, "A sermon against the dangerous and sinful practice of inoculation," (Boston: Benjamin Indicott, 1730), pp. 31-2. Avail. at http://quod.lib.umich.edu/e/evans/n02782.0001.001?rgn=main;view=fulltext.

1108 Hitchens, *Thomas Jefferson: Author of America*, p. 44; cf. Loftus, *Why I Became an Atheist*, p. 131; Jacoby, p. 78.

1109 Armstrong, *The Battle for God*, p. 180.

1110 Wulff, p. 68.

1111 Nolt, p. 177.

1112 *The Penguin Dictionary of Religions*, "Family, The." See also Gustav Niebuhr, "'The Family' and the Final Harvest,'" *The Washington Post*, 2 Jun. 1993, http://www.washingtonpost.com/wp-srv/national/longterm/cult/children_of_god/child1.htm, (accessed 23 Jan. 2016).

1113 Erin Blakemore, "There Are Only Two Shakers Left in the World: One of America's oldest religious sects still survives," *Smithsonian.com*, 6 Jan. 2017, https://www.smithsonianmag.com/smart-news/there-are-only-two-shakers-left-world-180961701/ (accessed 7 Jan. 2017); *The Concise Oxford Dictionary of the Christian Church*, s.v. "Shakers."

1114 See, for example, Mim Bizic, "Orthodox Baptism," *American Serb History 101*, 2009, http://www.babamim.com/orthodox_baptism (accessed 9 Dec. 2013). A description of the baptism ritual notes that believers are "asked to reject Satan three times and to breathe and spit upon Satan." Cf. "Understanding the Holy Baptism," *St. George Orthodox Cathedral*, n.d., http://www.stgeorgerossford.org/parish-life-and-ministries/reflections/understanding-the-mystery-of-repentance/16-understanding-the-holy-baptism (accessed 28 Sep. 2018).

1115 *The New International Dictionary of the Christian Church*, s.v. "Ethiopia."

1116 Wulff, pp. 70-1.

1117 Paul Raffaele, "Keepers of the Lost Ark?" *Smithsonian.com*, Dec. 2007, https://www.smithsonianmag.com/travel/keepers-of-the-lost-ark-179998820/ (accessed 10 Mar. 2018).

1118 *Handbook of Biblical Criticism*, s.v. "Aquila." Presumably this was early catholic Christianity.

1119 Bellitto, p. 93. This in the context of the Council of Florence (or Basel-Ferrara-Florence-Rome).

1120 *The Catholic Encyclopedia*, s.v. "Chaldean Christians" http://newadvent.org/cathen/03559a.htm.

1121 See Newman, *Apologia Pro Vita Sua*. For another work on why he found Roman Catholicism more tenable then Protestantism, see John Henry Newman, *An Essay on the Development of Christian Doctrine* (London: James Toovey, 1845). Avail. at https://archive.org/details/OnTheDevelopmentOfChristianDoctrine1845/page/n3. This work was very influential in my re-consideration of Roman Catholicism.

1122   Allitt, pp. ix, etc.
1123   Plummer, pp. 26-7.
1124   See "Conversion Stories," *The Coming Home Network International*, n.d., https://chnetwork.org/converts/other/ (accessed 28 Dec. 2018).
1125   "Other Christians," *Journey to Orthodoxy*, n.d., https://journeytoorthodoxy.com/category/latest-stories/non-orthodox-christians/ (accessed 28 Dec. 2018).
1126   Peter E. Gillquist, *Becoming Orthodox: A Journey to the Ancient Christian Faith*, rev. ed. (Ben Lomond, CA: Conciliar Press: 1992); Sarah Eekhoff Zylstra, "'Bible Answer Man' Converts to Orthodoxy," *Christianity Today*, 12 Apr. 2017, https://www.christianitytoday.com/news/2017/april/bible-answer-man-hank-hanegraaff-orthodoxy-cri-watchman-nee.html (accessed 27 Dec. 2018).
1127   William Webster, "Did I Really Leave the Holy Catholic Church?: The Journey into Evangelical Faith and Church Experience," in *Roman Catholicism: Evangelical Protestants Analyze What Divides and Unites Us*, ed. John Armstrong (Chicago: Moody Bible Institute, 1994), pp. 269-93.
1128   Richard Bennett, *Far from Rome, Near to God: Testimonies of 50 Converted Roman Catholic Priests* (Carlisle, PA: The Banner of Truth Trust, 1997). I read this book years ago after converting to Protestantism. For a summary by an evangelical Protestant, see Matt Slick, "Testimonies from ex-Roman Catholic Priests," *Christian Apologetics and Research Ministry*, n.d., https://carm.org/testimonies-ex-roman-catholic-priests (accessed 8 Nov. 2017).
1129   "Religion in Latin America: Chapter 1: Religious Switching," *Pew Research Center: Religion and Public Life*, 13 Nov. 2014, http://www.pewforum.org/2014/11/13/chapter-1-religious-switching/ (accessed 11 Mar. 2018).
1130   Galli and Olsen, p. 77.
1131   *OrthodoxWiki*, s.v. "Frank Schaeffer" https://orthodoxwiki.org/Frank_Schaeffer (accessed 27 Dec. 2018); Religion News Service, "Frank Schaeffer, Former Evangelical Leader, Is a Self-Declared Atheist who Believes in God," *The Huffington Post*, 13 Jun. 2014, https://www.huffingtonpost.com/2014/06/12/frank-schaeffer-atheist_n_5489696.html?ec_carp=5826479811394687015 (accessed 27 Dec. 2018).
1132   Lyudmila Alexandrova, "Why Orthodox Believers Are Converting to Other Christian Denominations," *Itar-Tass (Russia Beyond)*, 5 May 2013, https://www.rbth.com/society/2013/05/05/why_orthodox_believers_are_converting_to_other_christian_denomination_24509 (accessed 28 Dec. 2018).

1133 Ryan P. Burge, "Where Protestants and Catholics Go When They Leave Their Churches," Christianity Today, 20 Feb. 2018, https://www.christianitytoday.com/news/2018/february/how-protestants-catholics-leave-church-change-religion-cces.html (accessed 11 Mar. 2018). This article describes current trends in American Christianity.
1134 Roger Christan Schriner, Bridging the God Gap: Finding Common Ground Among Believers, Atheists and Agnostics, 2nd ed. (Fremont, CA: Living Arts Publications, 2011), p. 138.
1135 Pascal, no. 423, p. 127.
1136 As quoted in www.twainquotes.com, s.v. "Religion" http://www.twainquotes.com/Religion.html (accessed 17 Feb. 2017); source is given as Mark Twain, a Biography. John Loftus also quotes this sentence—and provides further reflections on viewing religious systems as an outsider; see "The Outsider Test for Faith."
1137 Wulff, p. 633.
1138 Parrinder, ed., World Religions, pp. 16, 22-23. See also Barbara J. King and Michel Martin, "Discoveries Give New Clues to Possible Neanderthal Religious Practices," NPR, 11 Dec. 2016, http://www.npr.org/2016/12/11/505187953/discoveries-give-new-clues-to-possible-neanderthal-religious-practices (accessed 1 Jan. 2017).
1139 Charles C. Mann, "The Birth of Religion," National Geographic (Jun. 2011) pp. 39-59.
1140 Parrinder, ed., World Religions, pp. 10, 16; Mercer Dictionary of the Bible, s.v. "Hammurabi." For a discussion of the similarities of laws of the Ancient Near East and the Pentateuch, see Handbook of Biblical Criticism, s.v. "Law."
1141 Parrinder, ed., World Religions, pp. 118-23.
1142 Scott, p. 24.
1143 Wilken, p. 167.
1144 Parrinder, ed., World Religions, p. 146.
1145 For one example, see Herodotus, 8.77, p. 513.
1146 H. Chadwick, pp. 79, 121.
1147 Parrinder, ed., World Religions, p. 176.
1148 Davis, p. 18.
1149 Parrinder, ed., World Religions, p. 175; Bonner, p. 19.
1150 Norwich, pp. 7, 10.
1151 Parrinder, ed., World Religions, p. 111.
1152 Ibid., pp. 102, 107.

1153 Ibid., p. 513. See also Patricia Ward Beiderman, "Cao Dai Fuses Great Faiths of the World," *Los Angeles Times*, 7 Jan. 2006, http://articles.latimes.com/2006/jan/07/local/me-beliefs7 (accessed 2 Oct. 2018).
1154 Knott, pp. 50-1.
1155 Parrinder, ed., *World Religions*, pp.251, 256.
1156 McLeod, pp. xv, 127.
1157 Morgan, p. 43.
1158 Anne Klein, "Buddhism," in *How Different Religions View Death and Afterlife*, p. 55.
1159 Sushmita Pathak, "Cow Dung Soap is Cleaning Up in India," *NPR*, 3 Oct. 2018, https://www.npr.org/sections/goatsandsoda/2018/10/03/653739760/cow-dung-soap-is-cleaning-up-in-india (accessed 3 Oct. 2013).
1160 Isabella Tree, "Living Goddesses of Nepal," *National Geographic* (Jun. 2015): pp. 86-8.
1161 James Miller, pp. 50, 69, 72, 81, 92, 96, 107-118, etc.
1162 Ibid., p. 83; cf. return of Lao Tzu, p. 86.
1163 Mumon Ekai, *The Gateless Gate*, in *Two Zen Classics*, case 21, p. 77.
1164 The Dalai Lama, *An Open Heart: Practicing Compassion in Everyday Life*, ed. Nicholas Vreeland (Boston: Little, Brown and Co., 2001), p. 120.
1165 Parrinder, ed., *World Religions*, p. 369.
1166 Ibid., p. 377. See also "Frequently Asked Questions about Oomoto," *Oomoto.or.jp*, 2010, http://www.oomoto.or.jp/English/enFaq/indexfaq.html (accessed 27 Nov. 2013).
1167 Parrinder, ed., *World Religions*, pp. 240-2.
1168 Ibid., pp. 246-7.
1169 *Sûtrakritâṅga*, in *Jaina Sutras: Part II*, bk. 1, lect. 11: The Path, nos. 9-10 www.sacred-texts.com/jai/sbe45/sbe4559.htm.
1170 Parrinder, ed., *World Religions*, pp. 240, 248; "Jainism: Morals and Values," *Jainism*, n.d., http://jainismonline.weebly.com/morals--values.html (accessed 10 Nov. 2018).
1171 Wulff, p. 71.
1172 Mead and Hill, p. 213; *The Penguin Dictionary of Religions*, s.v. "Nation of Islam"; Steven Fink, *Dribbling for Dawah: Sports Among Muslim Americans* (Macon, GA: Mercer Univ. Press, 2016), p. 132.
1173 Warraq, p. 326.
1174 Parrinder, ed., *World Religions*, p. 503; Armstrong, *The Battle for God*, p. 54.
1175 *Encyclopedia Britannica*, s.v. "Alawite" https://www.britannica.com/topic/Alawite (accessed 9 Feb. 2019); Armstrong, *The Battle for God*, pp. 47, 53.
1176 Safi, pp. 32, 34-5, 171, etc. Cf. Bloom and Blair, p. 71.

1177 Ernst, p. 170.
1178 Ibid., pp. 129-30.
1179 Bloom and Blair, p. 61.
1180 Al-Ghazali, pp. 56-7.
1181 Bukhari, bk. 4, no. 3 (1.4.139) http://sunnah.com/bukhari/4/3. See bk. 4, no. 1 (1.4.137) http://sunnah.com/bukhari/4/1 and bk. 4, no. 42 (1.4.176) http://sunnah.com/bukhari/4/42 for further discussion.
1182 Ibid., bk. 10, no. 6 (1.11.582) http://sunnah.com/bukhari/10/6.
1183 Ibid., bk. 19, no. 25 (2.21.245) http://sunnah.com/bukhari/19/25; bk. 59, no. 80 (4.54.492) http://sunnah.com/bukhari/59/80.
1184 Ibid., bk. 59, no. 98 (4.54.509) http://sunnah.com/bukhari/59/98; bk. 59, no. 101 (4.54.512) http://sunnah.com/bukhari/59/101; bk. 59, no. 104 (4.54.516) http://sunnah.com/bukhari/59/104; Swarup, p. 26.
1185 Bukhari, bk. 60, no. 102 (4.55.641) http://sunnah.com/bukhari/60/102.
1186 *The Koran*, Sura 6:112, p. 436; Sura 18:50, p. 95. "Jinn" has come into English as the word "genie."
1187 Ibid., Sura 7:178-179, p. 261. Cf. Ibn Ishaq, p. 75; Swarup, pp. 196-7.
1188 *The Koran*, footnote on p. 294 notes: "At this time Muhammed had nine wives, apart from slave girls." See Sura 33:50, p. 294; cf. Sura 4:3, p. 366. Parrinder, ed., *World Religions*, p. 466 just notes that he had "a number of marriages." Swarup notes in the footnote on p. 178 that Muhammad had eleven wives and four concubines—although not all the marriages were consummated. Bloom and Blair, p. 47 also notes eleven wives.
1189 Bukhari, bk. 67, no. 69 (7.62.64) http://sunnah.com/bukhari/67/69. See also bk. 63, no. 122 (5.58.236) http://sunnah.com/bukhari/63/122 and bk. 67, no. 70 (7.62.65) http://sunnah.com/bukhari/67/70. See also Swarup, p. 169. Without giving ages, Safi notes that A'isha "was betrothed to Muhammad at a young age," that there are "conflicting reports about her exact age when the marriage was consummated," and that it is a point of "great controversy" among both Muslims and "polemicists against Islam" (p. 148).
1190 *The Koran*, Sura 4:34, p. 370: "Men have authority over women because Allah made the one superior to the other, and because they spend their wealth to maintain them. … As for those from whom you fear disobedience, admonish them and send them to beds apart and beat them." Cf. Bukhari, bk. 52, no. 22 (3.48.826) http://sunnah.com/bukhari/52/22 which speaks of "the deficiency of a woman's mind."
1191 Bukhari, bk. 56, no. 226 (4.52.260) http://sunnah.com/bukhari/56/226: "If somebody (a Muslim) discards his religion, kill him." Cf. Swarup, pp. 94, 96. Mohammad Hashim Kamali, *Shari'ah Law: An Introduction* (Oxford:

Oneworld Publications, 2008) argues that although "many of the modern works" take this traditional view, it should be discontinued as (1) it is not commanded in the Qur'an, (2) it is only mentioned in one hadith, and (3) it is best viewed as "temporary legislation" in a particular historical context (pp. 220, 173).

1192 Swarup, pp. 70-1, 75, 77, 83-4, 110, 117, 182.
1193 Ibn Ishaq, p. 139; Bukhari, bk. 56, no. 227 (4.52.261) http://sunnah.com/bukhari/56/227. Cf. Swarup, p. 96.
1194 Ibn Ishaq, pp. 65-6, 92, 104-5, 163-4; cf. Swarup, pp. 10, 39 (footnote), 130-4.
1195 Ibn Ishaq, p. 87; cf. Swarup, pp. 94, 98, 100-1. However, Kamali makes it clear that the Qur'anic punishment for adultery is rather whipping (*Shari'ah Law*, pp. 131, 192; but cf. p. 183).
1196 Ibn Ishaq, p. 139; Swarup, p. 74.
1197 Sasha Ingber, "70 Muslim Clerics Issue Fatwa Against Violence and Terrorism," *NPR*, 11 May 2018, https://www.npr.org/sections/thetwo-way/2018/05/11/610420149/70-muslim-clerics-issue-fatwa-against-violence-and-terrorism (accessed 13 May 2018).
1198 James A. Maxwell, ed., *America's Fascinating Indian Heritage* (Pleasantville, NY: Reader's Digest Association, 1978), pp. 189-91.
1199 *Aztecs: Reign of Blood and Splendor* (Alexandria, VA: Time-Life Books, 1992), pp. 140-1; Parrinder, ed., *World Religions*, p. 75.
1200 *Aztecs: Reign of Blood and Splendor*, pp. 104-5; Parrinder, ed., *World Religions*, p. 75; Birgit Katz, "Archeologists Find First-Known Temple of 'Flayed Lord' in Mexico," *Smithsonian*.com, 3 Jan. 2019, https://www.smithsonianmag.com/smart-news/temple-flayed-lord-found-mexico-180971165/ (accessed 7 Jan. 2019).
1201 Parrinder, ed., *World Religions*, pp. 187-8. See also Nathaniel Deutsch, "Save the Gnostics," *The New York Times*, 7 Oct. 2007, http://www.nytimes.com/2007/10/07/opinion/07iht-edeutsch.1.7783203.html?_r=0 (accessed 25 Nov. 2013); Tarmida Yuhana Nashmi, "Contemporary Issues for the Mandaean Faith," *Mandaean Associations Union*, 28 Mar. 2013, http://www.mandaeanunion.com/culture/item/172-mandaean-faith (accessed 11 Sep. 2016).
1202 Martin and Hatcher, pp. 157-161, 174, 180, 194.
1203 Bloom and Blair, pp. 214-18; Richards, pp. 34-40; 45-9.
1204 Wulff, pp. 83-4.
1205 Parrinder, ed., *World Religions*, p. 513.

1206 Wulff, p. 145. See also Marlene Winell, *Leaving the Fold: A Guide for Former Fundamentalists and Others Leaving Their Religion* (Oakland, CA: New Harbinger Publications, 1993), p. 98.
1207 Parrinder, ed., *World Religions*, p. 161. Cf. p. 126.
1208 Ibid., pp. 233-4, 254, 494-5, 400. See also John Baldock, *The Essence of Rumi* (Edison, NJ: Chartwell Books, 2005), pp. 69, 140; Knott, pp. 24-31.
1209 Parrinder, ed., *World Religions*, pp. 20, 72, 81, 82, 88, 94, 97, 103, 111, 106, 217, 308; Herodotus, 4.62, p. 255; 4.103, p. 269; 7.197, p. 474; 9.119, p. 588; Matyszak, pp. 26-7, 173, 181, 222; Reston, pp. 20, 62. For Berbers, see Bonner, p. 22. For Chimú, see Kristin Romey "What Made This Ancient Society Sacrifice Its Own Children?" *National Geographic*, Feb. 2019, https://www.nationalgeographic.com/magazine/2019/02/chimu-people-sacrificed-children-llamas-peru-mystery/ (accessed 7 Feb. 2019).
1210 Parrinder, ed., *World Religions*, p. 57.
1211 Ibid., p. 59.
1212 Bloom and Blair, p. 133.
1213 Knott, p. 9.
1214 James Miller, pp. 48, 122-4, 130.
1215 McLeod, p. 263.
1216 Robert E. Van Voorst, *Anthology of World Scriptures*, 6th ed. (Belmont, CA: Wadsworth Cengage Learning, 2008), pp. 122-4; Parrinder, ed., *World Religions*, pp. 259-60. See also McLeod, p. xxix.
1217 Schriner, p. 30.
1218 Nicholas Wade, *Before the Dawn: Recovering the Lost History of Our Ancestors* (New York: Penguin Books, 2007), p. 164. I generally have not waded into the subject of evolution in this book. However, I note that (1) many Christians accept evolution and (2) those who favor intelligent design are still often forced to admit common descent. For a Christian biologist who accepts evolution, see Kenneth R. Miller, *Finding Darwin's God: A Scientist's Search for Common Ground Between God and Evolution* (New York: Harper Perennial, 2002). For an acceptance of the common descent of species in the intelligent design community, see Michael J. Behe, *Darwin's Black Box: The Biochemical Challenge to Evolution* (New York: Touchstone/Simon and Schuster, 1998), p. 176 who notes that "the evidence strongly supports common descent."
1219 For an interesting article in this regard, see Elizabeth Kolbert, "Why Facts Don't Change Our Minds: New Discoveries about the Human Mind Show the Limitations of Reason," *The New Yorker*, 27 Feb. 2017, http://www.newyorker.com/magazine/2017/02/27/why-facts-dont-change-our-minds (accessed 23 Feb. 2017). See also Shermer, *The Moral Arc*, pp. 325-6.

1220 Loftus, *Why I Became an Atheist*, pp. 70-1; Robert Kurzbahn, *Why Everyone (Else) Is a Hypocrite* (Princeton, NJ: Princeton Univ. Press, 2010), p. 96.

1221 Mark Twain, *The Wit and Wisdom of Mark Twain: A Book of Quotations* (Mineola, NY: Dover Publications, 1999), p. 24.

1222 Marcus Tullius Cicero, *The Nature of the Gods*, trans. Horace C.P. McGregor (New York: Penguin Books, 1972), 1.~4-6, p. 71. It is perhaps more accurate to say that "it is impossible that more than one of them is *completely* true." I.e., individual religious expressions could be partially right and partially wrong in a variety of ways.

1223 See ibid., 1.~13-16, p. 75: "Surely even those who believe that they have attained certainty in these matters must feel some doubts when they see how widely wise men have different about so crucial a question."

1224 Cf. Loftus, *Why I Became an Atheist*, p. 64: "It is highly likely that any given adopted religious faith is false."

1225 *The Catholic Encyclopedia*, s.v. "Messalians" http://www.newadvent.org/cathen/10212a.htm (accessed 4 Feb. 2018). See also *New International Dictionary of the Christian Church*, s.v. "Messalians" which states it survived to only the 7th c. as does *The Concise Oxford Dictionary of the Christian Church*, s.v. "Messalians."

1226 *The Concise Oxford Dictionary of the Christian Church*, s.v. "Muggletonians."

1227 Parrinder, ed., *World Religions*, p. 243. See also "Jain Sects," BBC, 11 Sep. 2009, http://www.bbc.co.uk/religion/religions/jainism/subdivisions/subdivisions.shtml (accessed 14 Nov. 2015).

1228 Nigosian, pp. 36, 39-40, 69, 89; Rose, pp. p. xviii, 1, 7-8, 32, 101, 105, 131, 142-3, 223ff; Boyce, ed., p. 96. Rose, See also *The Penguin Dictionary of Religions*, s.v. "Zurvanism."

1229 Bonner, pp. 247-8, 252.

1230 "History of Jain Sects," *jainworld.com*, 2011, http://www.jainworld.com/societies/jainsects.asp (accessed 14 Nov. 2015).

1231 Carl Roebuck, *The World of Ancient Times* (New York: Charles Scribner's Sons, 1966), pp. 36-7.

1232 Boyce, ed., pp. 12-13; Nigosian, pp. 20-1; Rose, pp. 19-20.

1233 Knott, p. 16.

1234 Roebuck, pp. 65-8.

1235 Hatcher and Martin, pp. 2-3, 81. See also "The Baha'i Faith," *Bahai.org*, n.d., http://www.bahai.org/ (accessed 3 Feb. 2017). Interestingly, Hatcher and Martin do not include Krishna in their list.

1236 John Renard, *The Handy Religion Answer Book*, 2nd ed. (Canton, MI: Visible Ink Press, 2012), p. 438.

1237 Ibid., pp. 437-8.
1238 Shannon M. Turner, "Conciliar Creeds of the Fourth Century," *Fourth Century Christianity*, Wisconsin Lutheran College, 17 Apr. 2011, http://www.fourthcentury.com/conciliar-creeds-of-the-fourth-century/ (accessed 2 Oct. 2018). González mentions the "Blasphemy of Sirmium" (vol. 1, p. 179). What is called the "Nicene Creed" in today's usage is actually a later creed technically known as the "Niceno-Constantinopolitan Creed." For discussion, see *The Concise Oxford Dictionary of the Christian Church*, s.v. "Nicene Creed" and *The New International Dictionary of the Christian Church*, s.v. "Nicene Creed."
1239 McLeod, pp. 183-204; *The Penguin Dictionary of Religions*, s.v. "Sikh Sects."
1240 Parrinder, ed., *World Religions*, p. 302; cf. Harvey, p. 2.
1241 Renard, pp. 270-1; *The Penguin Dictionary of Religions*, s.v. "Tantra (2)."
1242 Davis, pp. 249-50.
1243 *The Penguin Dictionary of Religions*, s.v. "Councils of the Church." Bellitto notes that the Eastern Orthodox often accept a council in 879 presided over by Archbishop Photius "as the true eighth ecumenical council or at least a synod of unity." Another council held in 869-70 in Constantinople (Constantinople IV in the West) is typically rejected in the East (pp. 33-4).
1244 Merle and Phyllis Good, *20 Most Asked Questions about the Amish and Mennonites*, rev. ed. (Intercourse, PA: Good Books, 1995), p. 80.
1245 Mead and Hill, p. 199.
1246 Stark, pp. 25-6.
1247 Renard, pp. 327-8; *The Penguin Dictionary of Religions*, s.v. "Tao Chiao"; cf. James Miller, pp. 8-13, etc.
1248 Mead and Hill, p. 49.
1249 William Hendricks, "A Baptist Perspective," in *How Different Religions View Death and Afterlife*, p. 31.
1250 For a list of links to these groups and more, see "Baptist Denominations in America," *Baylor Baptists Studies Center for Research*, n.d., https://www.baylor.edu/baptiststudies/index.php?id=93653 (accessed 19 Sep. 2018).
1251 Renard, p. 185.
1252 *The Penguin Dictionary of Religions*, s.v. "Veda."
1253 Knott, pp. 122, 58.
1254 Parrinder, ed., *World Religions*, p. 163.
1255 Ernst, pp. 112-13, 123, 192.
1256 Nolt, p. 334.
1257 Yu-hsiu Ku, *History of Zen* (Singapore: Springer, 2016), pp. 169-73. *Two Zen Classics*, ed. A.V. Grimestone, p. 62 notes five major Zen schools.

1258 See *The Penguin Dictionary of Religions*, s.v. "Cargo Cults" for numbers. Quotation from *New World Encyclopedia*, s.v. "Cargo Cult" http://www.newworldencyclopedia.org/p/index.php?title=Cargo_cult&oldid=1002614 (accessed 12 Feb. 2017). See also Paul Raffaele, "In John They Trust," *Smithsonian.com*, Feb. 2006, https://www.smithsonianmag.com/history/in-john-they-trust-109294882/ (accessed 29 May 2019).

1259 Al-Ghazali, p. 18.

1260 Ernst notes generally that Sufism has "permeated most Muslim societies" (p. 120). For his discussion of Shiites and Sufism, see esp. pp. 137-8. See also *The Penguin Dictionary of Religions*, s.v. "Sufi Orders."

1261 Bloom and Blair, p. 51. See also Warraq, p. 244; *The Penguin Dictionary of Religion*, s.v. "Kharijites." For the divisions of the Kharijites and others, see also Stark, pp. 29-31.

1262 *The Penguin Dictionary of* Religions, s.v. "Ahmadis"; Warraq, p. 175. See also Syed Raza Hassan, "Pakistan Mob Kills Woman and 2 Girls Over 'Blasphemous' Facebook Post, Police Say," *Huffington Post*, 28 Jul. 2014 (updated 26 Sep. 2014), http://www.huffingtonpost.com/2014/07/28/pakistan-mob-facebook-killings_n_5625838.html?utm_hp_ref=religion&ir=Religion (accessed 7 Oct. 2018): "A 1984 Pakistani law declared them non-Muslims and many Pakistanis consider them heretics."

1263 Warraq, p. 281.

1264 Ibid., pp. 245-6. According to Bloom and Blair, Mutazilities rejected the doctrine of the eternal and uncreated nature of the Qur'an (p. 133).

1265 Parrinder, ed., pp. 496-7; cf. Bloom and Blair, p. 238: "there are, as there have always been, many Islams." See also Ruthven, pp. 51-6 for discussion of sectarian groups.

1266 *The Catholic Encyclopedia*, s.v. "Epiphanius of Salamis" http://www.newadvent.org/cathen/13393b.htm (accessed 2 Oct. 2018). Twenty of these "heresies" predate Christianity; the other sixty are Christian ones. See also Ehrman, *Lost Christianities*, p. 102.

1267 Pius IX, *The Syllabus of Errors*, in *Papal Encyclicals Online*, orig. pub. 1864, http://www.papalencyclicals.net/Pius09/p9syll.htm (accessed 20 Feb. 2017). González notes that many Americans saw this as a "confirmation of their worst fears regarding the political goals of the Catholic Church" (vol. 2, p. 243). González also lists some of these "errors" on pp. 297-8.

1268 For one traditionalist assessment of the changes of the Vatican II Council, see Ferrara and Woods, *The Great Façade*. It is difficult to regard the council as anything less than a dramatic shift. See also Jordan G. Teicher, "Why Is Vatican II So Important?" *NPR*, 10 Oct. 2012, https://www.npr.

org/2012/10/10/162573716/why-is-vatican-ii-so-important (accessed 25 Aug. 2018).

1269 Harvey, p. 324. This also sites "Kangyur" and "Tengyur"—but note discrepancies in volume numbers. Appears different editions have different volume numbers.

1270 Hatcher and Martin, p. 84; "Writings of Bahá'u'lláh," *Bahá'í Reference Library*, n.d., https://www.bahai.org/library/authoritative-texts/bahaullah/ (accessed 29 Sep. 2019).

1271 Jaegeon Ha, "Unity and Catholicity in the Korean Presbyterian Church: An Ecumenical Reformed Assessment," *Verbum et Ecclesia*, 37:1 (19 Aug. 2016): pp. 1-8 https://repository.up.ac.za/bitstream/handle/2263/58100/Ha_Unity_2016.pdf?sequence=1&isAllowed=y (accessed 19 Sep. 2018). The abstract (p. 1) notes that there are "more than 100 denominations" but p. 2 notes that "it is said that the PCK has been divided into over 200 denominations." See also Chris Meehan, "Touched by Devotion in South Korea," *Christian Reformed Church*, 4 Oct. 2010, https://www.crcna.org/news-and-views/touched-devotion-south-korea (accessed 3 Mar. 2016). This earlier source notes that there are "about 100 Presbyterian denominations." For a list of many of these denominations, see "Presbyterianism in South Korea," *Wikipedia*, last ed. 2 Jul. 2018, https://en.wikipedia.org/wiki/Presbyterianism_in_South_Korea (accessed 19 Sep. 2018).

1272 Renard, p. 387.

1273 Juan Mascaro, introduction to *The Upanishads* (New York: Penguin Books, 1965), p. 7.

1274 Siegmar Dopp and Wilhelm Geerlings, *Dictionary of Early Christian Beliefs*, trans. Matthew O'Connell (New York, Crossroad, 2000), p. 236.

1275 Mead and Hill, pp. 7-18, 28, 108, 116. Other religious groups (Hindu, Jewish, Muslim, etc.) are mentioned but over 200 Christian denominations are given entries. See also *The Penguin Dictionary of Religions*, s.v. "American Christian Denominations" which notes "there are approximately 200 Protestant denominations in the *Yearbook of American and Canadian Churches*."

1276 David M. Cheney, "Religious Orders," *Catholic-Hierarchy.org*, n.d., http://www.catholic-hierarchy.org/country/xrel.html (accessed 29 Nov. 2015). See also Mead and Hill, p. 272 (source cited is the *Catholic Directory*).

1277 Plummer, pp. 2ff.

1278 *The Penguin Dictionary of Religions*, s.v. "African Religions."

1279 Parrinder, ed., *World Religions*, p. 103.

1280 Shields, foreword to *The Scattering of the Saints*, p. ix. Cf. Newell G. Bringhurst and John C. Hamer, introduction to *The Scattering of the Saints*, pp. 1-5; Mead and Hill, pp. 165-73; *The Penguin Dictionary of Religions*, s.v. "Mormons"; *Wikipedia*, s.v. "List of sects in the Latter Day Saint movement" https://en.wikipedia.org/wiki/List_of_denominations_in_the_Latter_Day_Saint_movement (accessed 14 Oct. 2018).

1281   Mabry, *The Monster God*, loc. 947.

1282   James Miller, pp. 3, 125-9; Renard, p. 303; *The Penguin Dictionary of Religions*, s.v. "Tao Tsang."

1283   Harvey, p. 4.

1284   See "Translation of the Mahayana Buddhist Canon: The BDK English Tripiṭaka Project" *BDK America*, 2018, http://www.bdkamerica.org/translation-mahayana-buddhist-canon (accessed 20 Jan 2018). More precisely it "contains 2,920 works (3,053 including variant versions), 11,970 fascicles and 80,645 pages." Harvey states rather that the Chinese canon contains "55 volumes containing 2,184 texts, with a supplement of 45 volumes" (p. 323) and also confirms that it is the *"largest and most definitive edition of the Chinese Canon"* (p. 234). *For general discussion of these canons, see* Harvey, pp. 3-4, 322-324. For more on the P li Canon, see Batchelor, *Confession of a Buddhist Atheist*, pp. 241-3. Renard notes that Tibetan or "Tantric" Buddhism has 108 volumes in their *Kanjur* collection of scriptures and 225 volumes in their *Tanjur* collection of scriptures (p. 272).

1285   *The Penguin Dictionary of Religions*, s.v. "Africa, New Religious Movements."

1286   David Barrett, George Kurian and Todd M. Johnson, *World Christian Encyclopedia*, vol. 2, 2nd ed. (New York: Oxford Univ. Press, 2001), p. 1.

1287   Van Over, ed., *Taoist Tales*, p. 1.

1288   See "Status of Global Mission, 2017, in the Context of AD 1900–2050," *Center for the Study of Global Christianity*, Gordon-Conwell Seminary, 2017, http://www.gordonconwell.edu/ockenga/research/documents/StatusofGlobalChristianity2017.pdf (accessed 14 Oct. 2018). Cf. "Global Christianity – A Report on the Size and Distribution of the World's Christian Population," *Pew Research Center: Religion and Public Life*, 19 Dec. 2011, http://www.pewforum.org/2011/12/19/global-christianity-exec/ (accessed 14 Oct. 2018).

1289   *The Penguin Dictionary of Religions*, s.v. "Kami."

1290   Harvey, pp. 129-33; *The Blue Cliff Records*, in *Two Zen Classics*, case 10, p. 173; Thich Nhat Hanh, *Interbeing: Fourteen Guidelines for Engaged Buddhism*, ed. Fred Eppsteiner, 3rd ed. (Berkeley, CA: Parallax Press, 1998), pp. 63-4.

1291   Parrinder, ed., *World Religions*, p. 211.

1292   Ibid., pp. 65, 68.

1293 *The Penguin Dictionary of Religions*, s.v. "Chinese Pantheon." Cf. James Miller, p. 13 who notes the "ever-expanding pantheon of Taoist deities."

1294 Voltaire to Frederick William, Prince of Prussia, 28 Nov 1770, in *Voltaire in His Letters: Being a Selection from His Correspondence*, ed. and trans. S.G. Tallentyre (New York: G.P. Putnam's Sons, 1919), letter LXXI, p. 232 https://archive.org/stream/cu31924026378335#page/n283/mode/2up, (accessed 20 Jan 2018).

1295 See John Vaughan, Preface to *Francis and Clare: The Complete Works*, p. xiii. For a similar conclusion, see Albert Haase, *Instruments of Christ: Reflections on the Peace Prayer of St. Francis* (Cincinnati: St. Anthony Messenger Press, 2004), p. 2.

1296 Thomas à Kempis, *The Imitation of Christ*, ed. Harold C. Gardiner (New York: Image Books, 1955), 1.5, p. 37.

1297 Christian Renoux, "The Origin of the Peace Prayer of St. Francis," n.d., *Franciscan Archive*, http://www.franciscan-archive.org/franciscana/peace.html (accessed 13 Jan. 2013); Haase, pp. 2-5 (p. 5 of Haase has the English version that I see most frequently). See also Jack Wintz, "Who Wrote the Peace Prayer of St. Francis?" *Friar Jack's E-spirations, American Catholic*, 30 Sep. 2009, http://www.americancatholic.org/e-News/FriarJack/fj093009.asp (accessed 1 May 2016); Scott Richert, "The Prayer of St. Francis of Assisi," *About.com*, http://catholicism.about.com/od/prayers/fl/The-Prayer-of-Saint-Francis.htm (accessed 1 May 2016). As an example of how widespread the mistaken attribution is, see Tim Dowley, ed., *Introduction to the History of Christianity* (Minneapolis: Fortress Press, 1995), p. 274 which includes a form of the prayer and attributes it to St. Francis.

1298 John Vaughan seems to state that it was first written in Italian. See Vaughan, preface to *Francis and Clare: The Complete Works*, p. xiii. Vaughan also holds that it was not written by St. Francis but is a 20th c. work.

1299 Renoux's article cited above clearly shows the two additional lines of French text. See also Garson O'Toole, "Prayer Credited to St. Francis of Assisi," *Quote Investigator: Tracing Quotations*, 22 Dec. 2011, http://quoteinvestigator.com/2011/12/22/prayer-assisi/ (accessed 2 May 2016). Here the translation includes the truth/error and the discord/union lines of the original French. See also "And I would just like to remember some words of St. Francis of Assisi ..." *Margaret Thatcher Foundation*, n.d., http://www.margaretthatcher.org/archive/StFrancis.asp (accessed 2 May 2016). This site also notes on occasion that the line about truth/error has been omitted. For another translation of the prayer, see "St. Francis 'Peace Prayer,'" *tralvex.com*, 25 Mar. 2005 (revised 27 Feb. 2014), http://tralvex.com/pub/spiritual/st-francis.htm (accessed 2 May 2016).

1300 For literature reviews see Alex H.S. Harris, Carl E. Thoreson, Michael E. McCullough and David B. Larson, "Spiritually and Religiously Oriented Health Interventions," *Journal of Health Psychology* no. 4 (1999): pp. 413-33; P. Scott Richards and Allen E. Bergin, *A Spiritual Strategy for Counseling and Psychotherapy* (Washington, DC: American Psychological Association, 1997). See also Clay Routledge, "Science Reveals the Benefits of Prayer," *Psychology Today*, 21 Mar. 2016, https://www.psychologytoday.com/blog/more-mortal/201603/science-reveals-the-benefits-prayer (accessed 23 Sep. 2016); Clay Routledge, "5 Scientifically Supported Benefits of Prayer," *Psychology Today*, 23 Jun. 2014, https://www.psychologytoday.com/blog/more-mortal/201406/5-scientifically-supported-benefits-prayer (accessed 23 Sep. 2016). Routledge asserts in these articles that prayer can aid self-control, kindness, trust, stress reduction, and forgiveness. For two popular articles, see also Barbara Bradley Hagerty, "Prayer May Reshape Your Brain ... And Your Reality," *NPR*, 20 May 2009 https://www.npr.org/templates/story/story.php?storyId=104310443 (accessed 28 Oct. 2018); Guy Winch, "Study Shows Prayer Reduces Anger and Aggression: Benevolent Prayer as an Effective Form of Emotional Regulation," *Psychology Today*, 20 May 2013, https://www.psychologytoday.com/us/blog/the-squeaky-wheel/201305/study-shows-prayer-reduces-anger-and-aggression (accessed 28 Oct. 2018). Winch notes that positive ruminations could be a "secular version of this exercise." For my prior consideration of this issue in the Catholic tradition, see Barrett A. Evans, "Ancient and Classic Pastoral Counsel: Approaches to Anxiety, Doubt and Guilt," *Journal of Psychology and Christianity* 24.1 (2005): pp. 81-2. For positive effects on anger, see Ryan H. Bremner, Sander L. Koole, Brad J. Bushman, "'Pray for Those Who Mistreat You': Effects of Prayer on Anger and Aggression," *Personality and Social Psychology Bulletin* 37.6 (2011): pp. 830-837. The authors hold these results are "consistent with recent evolutionary theories" (p. 830).

1301 For an informal exploration of humanist prayer, see Patricia Montley, "A Humanist's Guide to Prayer," *UU World*, 25 Feb. 2013, www.uuworld.org/articles/humanist-guide-prayer (accessed 23 Sep. 2016). Essentially, humanist prayer seeks to retain some of the contemplative and meditative aspects of prayer while rejecting its attachments to supernaturalism. Cf. Murray, pp. 46, 10.

1302 Text here is largely derived here from the translation in the 1912 original version given at *Wikipedia*, s.v. "Prayer of Saint Francis" https://en.wikipedia.org/wiki/Prayer_of_Saint_Francis (accessed 7 Jan. 2018). Most of the wording is directly taken from this article.

1303   Wulff, p. 604. Yao was the founder of Fundamentalists Anonymous in 1985. For a discussion of fundamentalism and these general themes, see Yao, *There Is a Way Out*.

1304   John of the Cross, *Dark Night*, in *John of the Cross: Selected Writings*, ed. Kiernan Kavanaugh (New York: Paulist Press, 1987), 2.9.1; p. 204.

1305   Wulff, p. 248: "the bulk of the evidence suggests that religion is associated with positive mental health." (See also pp. 244-7, 636.) Ronald J. Comer, *Abnormal Psychology*, 4th ed. (New York: Worth Publishers, 2001), p.71 suggests that those who conceive of God as "warm, caring, helpful, and dependable" derive mental health benefits. See also Patty Van Cappellen, Maria Toth-gauthier, Vassilis Saroglou, Barbara L. Fredrickson, "Religion and Well-Being: The Mediating Role of Positive Emotions," *Journal of Happiness Studies* 17.2 (Apr. 2016): pp. 485: "Research has consistently shown that endorsing a religion or spirituality is to some extent related to one's well-being." See also Amy B. Washoltz and Kenneth I. Pargament, "Is Spirituality a Critical Ingredient of Meditation? Comparing the Effects of Spiritual Meditation, Secular Meditation, and Relaxation of Spiritual, Psychological, Cardiac, and Pain Outcomes," *Journal of Behavioral Medicine* 28.4 (Aug. 2005): pp. 369-84. Authors note that several studies have shown correlations between religiosity and mental stability.

1306   Ibid.

1307   Winell notes: "Despite the negative aspects of dogmatic thinking and judgment, church groups often provide a social context that is difficult to match in the secular world" (p. 21). For a similar such list related to Buddhism, see Batchelor, *Confession of a Buddhist Atheist*, p. 73. For forgiveness: Neal Krause and Christopher G. Ellison, "Forgiveness by God, Forgiveness of Others, and Psychological Well-being in Late Life," *Journal for the Scientific Study of Religion*, 42.1 (Mar. 2003): pp. 77-94, https://www.ncbi.nlm.nih.gov/pmc/articles/PMC3046863/ (accessed 15 Dec. 2018). See also Alex H.S. Harris, Carl E. Thoreson, Michael E. McCullough and David B. Larson, "Spiritually and Religiously Oriented Health Interventions," *Journal of Health Psychology* no. 4 (1999): pp. 413-33; Richards and Bergin.

1308   Kieran Kavanaugh, introduction to *The Dark Night*, in *John of the Cross: Selected Writings*, p. 159.

1309   Winell, p. 15 (see also p. 18). For a further exploration of "Religious Trauma Syndrome" and similar ideas, see Valerie Tarico and Marlene Winell, "The Sad, Twisted Truth about Conservative Christianity's Effect on the Mind,"

Salon, 1 Nov. 2014, https://www.salon.com/2014/11/01/the_sad_twisted_truth_about_conservative_christianitys_effect_on_the_mind_partner/ (accessed 7 Feb. 2019); Jon Fortenbury, "The Health Effects of Leaving Religion," *The Atlantic*, 28 Sep. 2014, https://www.theatlantic.com/health/archive/2014/09/the-health-effects-of-leaving-religion/379651/ (accessed 7 Feb. 2019). For discussion of "ecclesiogenic neuroses," see Wulff, p. 244.

1310   As quoted in Murdoch, p. 211.

1311   Frederick Douglass, *The Autobiography of Frederick Douglass*, University of Groningen, http://www.let.rug.nl/usa/biographies/frederick-douglass/a-general-survey-of-the-slave-plantation.php (accessed 14 Oct. 2018).

1312   For a similar concept, see Yao, *Fundamentalists Anonymous*. It appears that FA is now defunct.

1313   Stephen Batchelor, *Buddhism Without Beliefs: A Contemporary Guide to Awakening* (New York: Rivenhead Books, 1997), pp. 40-1. Cf. Alan W. Watts, *The Wisdom of Insecurity: A Message for an Age of Anxiety* (New York: Vintage Books, 2011), pp. 78-9, etc.

1314   Eric Hoffer, *The True Believer: Thoughts on the Nature of Mass Movements* (New York: Perennial Library, 1966), p. 22.

1315   I.e., believe themselves to be saved but actually are not.

1316   Batchelor, *Buddhism Without Beliefs*, p. 38.

1317   Kenneth I. Pargament, *The Psychology of Religion and Coping*, (New York: Guilford Press, 1997), p. 321.

1318   For the original Alcoholics Anonymous steps, see "The Twelve Steps of Alcoholics Anonymous," A. A. World Services, 9 May 2002, http://www.aa.org/en_pdfs/smf-121_en.pdf (accessed 29 Oct. 2012). For a secular list of the Twelve Steps without a reference to a "Higher Power," see "Agnostic AA Twelve Steps," *AA Agnostics of the San Francisco Bay Area*, n.d., http://www.aaagnostics.org/agnostic12steps.html (accessed 16 Feb. 2013). I utilized concepts and some wording from both of these lists.

1319   See Michael Arnheim, "God without Religion," in *Pandeism: An Anthology*, ed. Knujon Mapson (Winchester, UK: iff Books, 2017), loc. 2700ff. pp. 168-9, Kindle. The rest of Arnheim's essay, along with the entirety of this anthology, further informed my definitions here.

1320   For a brief discussion of how someone can have a "firmly held belief" in atheism without succumbing to dogmatism, see Julian Baggini, *Atheism: A Very Short Introduction* (Oxford: Oxford Univ. Press, 2003), pp. 23-5. While holding to atheism with conviction, Baggini also notes that "I am as opposed to dogmatic atheism as anyone" and "dogmatic views of any kind are in general more dangerous than the views themselves."

1321 There is much dispute on whether agnosticism should be considered as either (1) a synonym for atheism or (2) a descriptor of what one "knows" instead of what one "believes." For an example of the latter view, see Neil Carter, "Agnostic or Atheist? What's the Difference," YouTube video, 2:13, posted 25 July 2015, https://www.youtube.com/watch?v=cUHOHzf5wX8 (accessed 27 Jan. 2019). My definition here is based on my experience of popular usage of "agnosticism" and "atheism" along with definitions like: *Merriam-Webster*, s.v. "agnostic" https://www.merriam-webster.com/dictionary/agnostic (accessed 8 Aug. 2018) which discusses both lack of knowledge and lack of commitment as components. I also find this definition from Anthony Kenny to be illustrative of usage of the term: "I do not myself know of any argument for the existence of God which I find convincing; in all of them I think I can find flaws. Equally, I do not know of any argument against the existence of God which is totally convincing; in the arguments I know against the existence of God I can equally find flaws. So that my own position on the existence of God is agnostic." As quoted in *Stanford Encyclopedia of Philosophy*, s.v. "Atheism and Agnosticism," 2 Aug. 2017, https://plato.stanford.edu/entries/atheism-agnosticism/#DefiAgno (accessed 8 Aug. 2018). For an example of a definition of atheism as simply a denial of the divine, see Julian Baggini, *Atheism: A Very Short Introduction* (Oxford: Oxford Univ. Press, 2003), p. 3: "Atheism … is the belief that there is no God or are no gods." Baggini also differentiates atheism from agnosticism—while still suggesting that atheism is best held without dogmatism (pp. 24-5). Jacoby rather notes that there is "both confusion and willful distortion in American discourse" on this point, concluding that atheism and agnosticism are in fact the same thing (pp. 17-8). While I understand this is a common position among atheists, I think it is clearer to both acknowledge that (1) rejecting God-beliefs has no necessary connection to dogmatism and (2) agnosticism can be fairly understood as the lack of commitment to either atheism or theism. Richard Dawkins, *The God Delusion* (Boston: Mariner Books, 2008) also differentiates between agnosticism and atheism while discussing "the poverty of agnosticism," pp. 69-77. In my estimation, Dawkins' discussion would be strengthened by noting that one can firmly deny traditional forms of theism while still being agnostic about deism or other more philosophical conceptions of divinity.

1322 See also Dave Gaddis, "One Deist's Concept of God (DeismTV#14)," *Reasoned Way*, YouTube video 8:06, posted 6 Jan. 2013, https://youtu.be/iSU-fRFp2S9Y (accessed 25 Oct. 2018).

1323 Murray, p. 17 (also pp. xvi, etc.). Unitarian Universalists often adopt this perspective.
1324 *The Concise Oxford Dictionary of the Christian Church*, s.v. "liberalism." Some types of theological liberalism retain certain supernatural beliefs. Some types of theological liberalism can tend towards dogmatism, especially in social issues.
1325 Batchelor, *Confession of a Buddhist Atheist*, p. 135.
1326 As quoted in Review of *Doubt: A History*, by Jennifer Michael Hecht, *Publisher's Weekly*, 29 Sep. 2003, https://www.publishersweekly.com/978-0-06-009772-1 (accessed 5 Apr. 2019). No author given. Cf. Batchelor, *Confession of a Buddhist Atheist*, p. 65.
1327 Batchelor, *Confession of a Buddhist Atheist*, p. 10.
1328 Ibid., p. 45.
1329 Ibid., p. 41.
1330 Ibid., p. 135.
1331 Ibid., p. 174.
1332 Ibid., p. 198.
1333 For discussion of the range of usage of the terms "agnosticism" and "atheism," see "True Believers Anonymous" meditation and corresponding footnotes. I am using Baggini's definition of atheism here: "the belief that there is no God or are no gods" (p. 3). If defining atheism differently, there would be no necessary tension.
1334 Ibid., p. 66; cf. Batchelor, *Buddhism Without Beliefs*, pp. 19, 97.
1335 Batchelor, *Confession of a Buddhist Atheist*, p. 7. Cf. Watts and the "craving for security" (p. 78).
1336 As quoted in Walter Isaacson, *Einstein: His Life and Universe* (New York: Simon and Schuster, 2007), pp. 388-9. Also quoted in Hitchens, *The Portable Atheist*, p. 157.
1337 As quoted in Roger Scruton, *Spinoza: A Very Short Introduction* (Oxford Press, 2002), p. 38. Proposition 14 from his *Ethics*. See also *The 100 Most Influential Philosophers*, s.v. "Benedict de Spinoza."
1338 Dawkins, p. 40.
1339 Hitchens, *The Portable Atheist*, p. 155. Hitchens perhaps was unfair in stating that Isaacson was trying to call Einstein a believer. Although Isaacson is perhaps slightly inaccurate in using the term "deistic" to describe Einstein (pp. 385, 389), he nevertheless is abundantly clear that Einstein does not believe in a personal god that is concerned with human affairs. Isaacson also brings out some of the tension in Einstein's comments about god, religion, atheism, and the like. See also Hitchens, *god Is Not Great*, pp. 271-2.

1340 As quoted in Hitchens, *The Portable Atheist*, p. 163. Most of this passage is also quoted in Isaacson, p. 390.
1341 Dungan, p. 210; Hitchens, p. 21.
1342 As quoted in Scruton, p. 38. Prop. 15 from his *Ethics*. See also *The 100 Most Influential Philosophers*, s.v. "Benedict de Spinoza." Similar language is found in Benedict de Spinoza, *Theological-Political Treatise*, ed. Jonathan Israel, trans. Michael Silverstone and Jonathan Israel (Cambridge Univ. Press, 2007), sec. 60, no. 4, p. 59.
1343 Scruton, p. 51. *The 100 Most Influential Philosophers*, s.v. "Benedict de Spinoza" states he held a "form of blessedness amounting to a kind of rational-mystical experience." Dungan notes he advocated a "unitive mysticism, the feeling of oneness with the All [which] can indeed lead to a life of serenity and service to all sentient beings" (p. 211). See also Rebecca Newberger Goldstein, "Why Spinoza is Back," *bigthink.com*, 2 Feb. 2010, https://bigthink.com/videos/why-spinoza-is-back (accessed 9 Jan. 2017); Armstrong, *The Battle for God*, p. 23: "there was spirituality in Spinoza's atheism, since he experienced the world as divine."
1344 *The New International Dictionary of the Christian Church*, s.v. "Spinoza, Benedict (or "Baruch") de." For some discussion of some differing interpretations, see *The Catholic Encyclopedia.*, s.v. "Benedict Spinoza" http://www.newadvent.org/cathen/14217a.htm (accessed 14 Jan. 2017).
1345 As quoted in Hitchens, *The Portable Atheist*, p. 156 and Isaacson, p. 536.
1346 Albert Einstein, "Science and Religion," in *Faith in Faithlessness*, p. 208.
1347 As quoted in Hitchens, *The Portable Atheist*, p. 157.
1348 As quoted in Isaacson, p. 20 and Hitchens, p. 156.
1349 As quoted in Hitchens, p. 159 and Isaacson, p. 388. From a response that Einstein had written to a child in 1936. Cf. Isaacson, p. 551.
1350 As quoted in Hitchens, *The Portable Atheist*, p. 158.
1351 Ibid., p. 158.
1352 Ibid., p. 156.
1353 Ibid., p. 157.
1354 Albert Einstein, "An Ideal of Service to Our Fellow Man," in *This I Believe*, ed. Jay Allison and Dan Gediman (New York: Henry Holt and Co., 2006), pp. 58-9. Cf. Isaacson, p. 390 and his "cosmic religious feeling."
1355 As quoted in Hitchens, *The Portable Atheist*, p. 163.
1356 As quoted in Isaacson, p. 389.
1357 As quoted in Hitchens, *The Portable Atheist*, p. 163. Also quoted in Isaacson, p. 389. According to testimony of Prince Hubertus of Lowenstein. See also George Sylvester Viereck, *Glimpses of the Great* (New York: The Macauley Co., 1930), pp. 447: "I am not an Atheist. I do not know if I

can define myself as a Pantheist. The problem involved is too vast for our limited minds. … We are in the position of a little child, entering a huge library, whose walls are covered to the ceiling with books in many different tongues. The child knows that someone must have written those books. It does not know who or how." Also "What Life Means to Einstein: An Interview by George Sylvester Viereck," *The Saturday Evening Post*, 26 Sep. 1929, http://www.saturdayeveningpost.com/wp-content/uploads/satevepost/what_life_means_to_einstein.pdf (accessed 13 Jan. 2017).

1358 As quoted in Isaacson, p. 390. Cf. Isaacson, p. 462 where Einstein is quoted as noting the "weakness of positivists and professional atheists." For further on Spinoza, see Viereck, *Glimpses of the Great*, pp. 447-8.

1359 Einstein, "An Ideal of Service to Our Fellow Man," in *This I Believe*, p. 59.

1360 Albert Einstein, "Einstein's Credo (My Credo)," in *Albert Einstein in the World Wide Web*, orig. pub. 1932, http://www.einstein-website.de/z_biography/credo.html (accessed 6 Jan. 2017).

1361 Dawkins, p. 40. Isaacson notes that some both religious and nonreligious people do not think that Einstein believed in God (pp. 388-9). Christopher Hitchens does not flatly claim that Spinoza was an atheist—rather nothing that his pantheism has great affinities with atheism and that perhaps he was communicating in a circumspect manner due to threats of persecution (Hitchens, *god Is Not Great*, pp. 262-4).

1362 Einstein, "My Credo." See also Isaacson, p. 550.

1363 As quoted in Steven Nadler, *A Book Forged in Hell: Spinoza's Scandalous Treatise and the Birth of the Secular Age* (Princeton Univ. Press, 2011), p. 186. For an alternate translation, see Spinoza, *Theological-Political Treatise*, sec. 180, no. 13, pp. 184-5. For a discussion of Spinoza's redefinition of religious terms, see Dungan, pp. 212-15.

1364 As quoted in Isaacson, p. 390.

1365 Lyof N. Tolstoi (Leo Tolstoy), *What Is Religion? And What Is Its Essence?*, in *What Is Religion? And Other New Articles and Letters*, trans. V. Tchertkoff and A.C. Fifield (New York: Thomas Y. Crowell and Co., 1902), ch. 6, p. 15. Avail. at https://archive.org/details/whatisreligionot00tols/page/n11.

1366 Lyof N. Tolstoi (Leo Tolstoy), *My Confession*, in *My Confession and The Spirit of Christ's Teaching* (New York: Thomas Y. Crowell and Co., 1887), no. 12, p. 107. Translator not given. Avail. at https://archive.org/details/myconfessionands00tolsrich/page/n9.

1367 See Hanh, *The Miracle of Mindfulness*, p. 76; Parrinder, ed., *World Religions*, p. 237; Paul Wood, "The Unbroken Chain: Tolstoy's Legacy of Nonviolence Influenced Many Great Leaders," *LAS News Magazine*, Spring 2009, www.las.illinois.edu/alumni/magazine/articles/2009/tolstoy/

(accessed 27 Oct. 2017); Mohandas Gandhi, *Autobiography: The Story of My Experiments with Truth*, trans. Mahadev Desai (New York: Dover Publications, 1983), p. 77; Louis Fischer, *Gandhi: His Life and Message for the World* (New York: Signet Classics, 2010), pp. 39-41.

1368 *The Concise Oxford Dictionary of the Christian Church*, s.v. "Tolstoy, Leo"; Ware, pp. 120-1, footnote no. 2.

1369 Jane Kentish, introduction to *A Confession and Other Religious Writings*, by Leo Tolstoy (London: Penguin, 1987), p. 11.

1370 Ibid., p. 8; *The Westminster Dictionary of Theologians*, s.v. "Tolstoy, Leo." Among other things, *The New International Dictionary of the Christian Church*, s.v. "Tolstoy, Leo" notes that Tolstoy's spirituality was "emphasizing as a central creed the non-resistance to evil."

1371 Tolstoi (Tolstoy), *What Is Religion? And What Is Its Essence?* in *What Is Religion? And Other New Articles and Letters*, no. 11, p. 32.

1372 As quoted in Hanh, *The Miracle of Mindfulness*, p. 75.

1373 Tolstoi (Tolstoy), *My Confession*, in *My Confession and The Spirit of Christ's Teaching*, no. 16, p. 137. Cf. Charles Darwin, *The Autobiography of Charles Darwin* (New York: W. W. Norton & Co., 2005), p. 78.

1374 Ibid. gives an exploration of this struggle. Tolstoy states both that "Without faith, there is no life (no. 9, p. 83) and that he could not accept a form of faith that was a "direct denial of reason" (no. 10, p. 88).

1375 Ibid., no. 14, p. 40.

1376 Tolstoi (Tolstoy), *What Is Religion? And What Is Its Essence?* in *What Is Religion? And Other New Articles and Letters*, no. 6, p. 14.

1377 Ibid., no. 7, p. 17. See also *The Westminster Dictionary of Theologians*, s.v. "Tolstoy, Leo"; *The Concise Oxford Dictionary of the Christian Church*, s.v. "Tolstoy, Leo".

1378 Tolstoi (Tolstoy), *What Is Religion? And What Is Its Essence?* in *What Is Religion? And Other New Articles and Letters*, no. 13, pp. 36-7.

1379 Ibid., no. 13, p. 37.

1380 Ibid.

1381 Some of his metaphysical beliefs are a bit vague. More concerning, his views on abstinence and sexuality appear extreme and at times even destructive. See Jacoby, pp. 164-6; William Grimes, "More than a Century Later, Sophia Tolstoy Has Her Say," *The New York Times*, 19 Aug. 2014, https://www.nytimes.com/2014/08/20/books/kreutzer-sonata-variations-has-a-scorned-wifes-rebuttal.html (accessed 6 Aug. 2018).

1382 For another example, see Paul Tillich, *The Courage to Be*, 2nd ed. (New Haven: Yale Nota Bene, 2000). While I find some value in Tillich's notion of God as "ground of being," of his call to find "the God above the God of theism," and of a renewed definition of faith as "ultimate concern," I also find his style of expression unclear.

1383 Tolstoi (Tolstoy), *My Confession*, in *My Confession and The Spirit of Christ's Teaching*, no. 9, p. 85.

1384 As quoted in Kentish, introduction to *A Confession and Other Religious Writings*, by Leo Tolstoy, p. 12.

1385 As quoted in Hitchens, *Thomas Jefferson: Author of America*, p. 175.

1386 Thomas Jefferson to Peter Carr, 10 Aug. 1787, in *The Portable Thomas Jefferson*, ed. Merrill Peterson (New York: Penguin, 1975), p. 425.

1387 Deism, usu. the belief in a "clockmaker" God who set the universe in motion but does not interfere in human affairs, still has some adherents today (including among Unitarian Universalists). For more on deism, see *World Union of Deists*, http://deism.com/ (accessed 5 Feb. 2017); *The Penguin Dictionary of Religions*, s.v. "Deism"; *The Concise Oxford Dictionary of the Christian Church*, s.v. "Deism." For Jefferson described as a deist, see *The New International Dictionary of the Christian Church*, s.v. "Jefferson, Thomas"; *Encyclopedia Britannica*, s.v. "Deism" https://www.britannica.com/topic/Deism (accessed 5 Feb. 2017); Schriner, p. 80; Hitchens, *Thomas Jefferson: Author of America*, p. 37. Merrill Peterson, Introduction to *The Portable Thomas Jefferson*, pp. xxxviii-xxxxix notes that his religion was "morally earnest but stripped of supernaturalism, of which he saw anticipations in Unitarianism." For low percentage of U.S. church members at the end of the 18th c., see Vidler, p. 237.

1388 See Hitchens, *Thomas Jefferson: Author of America*, p. 178. See also above footnote on deism. However, Jefferson was perhaps not entirely consistent on this point. See Thomas Jefferson, *Notes on the State of Virginia*, in *The Portable Thomas Jefferson*, XVIII, p. 215; Tindall and Shi, p. 144.

1389 Thomas Jefferson to John Adams, 11 Apr. 1823, *Founders Online*, National Archives, https://founders.archives.gov/?q=%20Author%3A%22Jefferson%2C%20Thomas%22&s=1111311111&sa=&r=18858&sr (accessed 29 Sep. 2018).

1390 Thomas Jefferson to Peter Carr, 10 Aug. 1787, in *The Portable Thomas Jefferson*, p. 425.

1391 Thomas Jefferson to Ezra Stiles Ely, 25 Jun. 1819, Papers of Thomas Jefferson, *Founders Online*, National Archives, last modified 29 Jun. 2017, https://founders.archives.gov/documents/Jefferson/98-01-02-0542 (accessed 5 Nov. 2017).

1392 See Rebecca Bowman, "Jefferson's Religious Beliefs," *Monticello.org*, 1997, http://www.monticello.org/site/research-and-collections/jeffersons-religious-beliefs, (accessed 3 Jul. 2013). This article suggests that Jefferson inclined toward Unitarianism. See also "Jefferson's Bible: The Life and Morals of Jesus of Nazareth," Smithsonian exhibit, http://www.si.edu/Exhibitions/Details/Jefferson's-Bible-The-Life-and-Morals-of-Jesus-of-Nazareth-4677 (accessed 3 Jul. 2013). Peterson, Introduction to *The Portable Thomas Jefferson* was also consulted as was Saul K. Padover, *Jefferson*, abridged (New York: Mentor, 1970), pp. 116-21, 166-9. Padover relates how Jefferson even called himself a "real Christian"—not in a traditional sense but rather as a follower of his true moral teachings (p. 167).

1393 Thomas Jefferson to Peter Carr, 10 Aug. 1787, in *The Portable Thomas Jefferson*, p. 426. The spelling in the quotation here is exact.

1394 Thomas Jefferson to Alexander Smyth, 17 Jan. 1825, *Founders Online*, National Archives, https://founders.archives.gov/?q=%20Author%3A%22Jefferson%2C%20Thomas%22&s=1111311111&r=19461 (accessed 29 Sep. 2018).

1395 Thomas Jefferson to John Adams, 11 Apr. 1823, *Founders Online*, National Archives, https://founders.archives.gov/?q=%20Author%3A%22Jefferson%2C%20Thomas%22&s=1111311111&sa=&r=18858&sr (accessed 29 Sep. 2018). I personally find it extremely difficult to propose a reliable method of determining what words Jesus actually may have said. Jefferson may have been overly eager to excise sayings based on philosophical grounds.

1396 Jefferson to William Short, 31 Oct. 1819, in *The Portable Thomas Jefferson*, p. 565.

1397 Thomas Jefferson to John Adams, 11 Apr. 1823, *Founders Online*, National Archives, https://founders.archives.gov/?q=%20Author%3A%22Jefferson%2C%20Thomas%22&s=1111311111&sa=&r=18858&sr (accessed 29 Sep. 2018). This quotation and others are evidence of how rules concerning grammar and spelling have changed over time. The Five Points of Calvinism generally refer to salvation and the Christian life being controlled by God's predestinating grace. They are often referred to through the acronym of TULIP: Total depravity, Unconditional election, Limited atonement, Irresistible grace, and Perseverance of the saints.

1398 Thomas Jefferson to Benjamin Rush, 23 Sep. 1800, *Founders Online*, National Archives, https://founders.archives.gov/documents/Jefferson/01-32-02-0102 (accessed 23 Mar. 2018). Also quoted in Hitchens, *Thomas Jefferson: Author of America*, p. 178.

1399 Thomas Jefferson, *Notes on the State of Virginia*, in *The Portable Thomas Jefferson*, XVII, p. 212.

1400 Thomas Jefferson to the Danbury Baptist Association, 1 Jan. 1802, *Founders Online*, National Archives, https://founders.archives.gov/?q=%20

Author%3A%22Jefferson%2C%20Thomas%22&s=1111311111&r=9170 (accessed 29 Sep. 2018).

1401 Thomas Jefferson, *Notes on the State of Virginia*, in *The Portable Thomas Jefferson*, XVII, p. 211.

1402 See Thomas Jefferson, "Declaration of Independence," in *The Portable Thomas Jefferson*, pp. 238-9. See also ibid., footnote no. 1, p. 236; Hitchens, *Thomas Jefferson: Author of America*, pp. 26-8.

1403 Tindall and Shi, p. 208.

1404 Christopher Hitchens, "Hitchens v. Hitchens," 3 Apr. 2008, (debate with Peter Hitchens, Hauenstein Center, Grand Rapids, MI), 32:43-47, https://www.youtube.com/watch?v=ngjQs_QjSwc (accessed 15 Oct. 2018). Pub. 15 Jun. 2011.

1405 Hitchens, *Thomas Jefferson: Author of America*, p. 188. For a discussion and differing opinions regarding Jefferson's relationship with his slave Sally Hemings, see "Thomas Jefferson and Sally Hemings: A Brief Account," *Monticello.org*, https://www.monticello.org/site/plantation-and-slavery/thomas-jefferson-and-sally-hemings-brief-account (accessed 29 Sep. 2018). Further implications for Jefferson's character are of course at stake.

1406 Helen Waddell, trans. and ed., *The Desert Fathers* (Ann Arbor, MI: Univ. of Michigan Press, 1957), 2.2, p. 63. Benedicta Ward gives a similar saying that mentions fornication instead (*The Sayings of the Desert Fathers*, Anthony the Great, no. 11, p. 3).

1407 *The Sayings of the Desert Fathers*, Xanthius, no. 3, p. 159.

1408 H. Chadwick notes that already in the 2nd c. there were "individual Christians in local communities that renounced marriage and all but the minimum of possessions" (p. 175). John the Baptist was commonly thought of as a model ascetic. The impetus for the life of renunciation is in many ways based on the example of Jesus himself in the Gospels—in addition to specific teachings on renunciation like in Luke 18:28-30 and 1 Cor. 7-8-9. There are also examples of female acscetics and "ammas"—however these were less common and influential.

1409 See Athanasius, *Life of Antony*, in *Early Christian Lives*, pp. 1-70; González, vol. 1, p. 147.

1410 H. Chadwick, p. 141; Walsh, ed., *Butler's Lives of the Saints*, p. 133.

1411 Davis, pp. 111-2; *The New International Dictionary of the Christian Church*, s.v. "Basil the Great"; Br. Gregory Augustine, "St. Basil of Caesarea and His Rule," *OPWest Novices*, 20 Oct. 2012, http://novices.opwest.org/wordpress/2012/10/st-basil-of-caesarea-and-his-rule/, (accessed 1 Dec. 2013); Parrinder, ed., *World Religions*, p. 429. González, vol. 1, p. 147 notes Basil's affinity with monasticism—but also notes that he had not intended to write a monastic rule per se but that his treatises were used as such.

1412 Blomfield Jackson, prolegomena to *Basil: Letters and Select Works*, in *Nicene and Post-Nicene Fathers, Series 2*, ed. Philip Schaff, vol. 8 (Grand Rapids, MI: Christian Classics Ethereal Library, n.d.), p. 18 http://www.ccel.org/ccel/schaff/npnf208.pdf.

1413 González, vol. 1, pp. 138-9, 147; Law, p. 154; Jerome, *Life of Paul of Thebes*, in *Early Christian Lives*, pp. 71-84.

1414 González, vol. 1, p. 204; Law, p. 156.

1415 Bonner, p. 330.

1416 Augustine, *The Confessions*, 8.6.15, http://www.newadvent.org/fathers/110108.htm; Augustine, *Of the Works of Monks*, in *Nicene and Post-Nicene Fathers, First Series*, vol. 3, ed. Philip Schaff, trans. H. Browne (Buffalo, NY: Christian Literature Publishing Co., 1887), no. 37, etc., http://www.newadvent.org/fathers/1314.htm; Bonner, pp. 4, 41, 94, 108-14, 128-32, 396-7. Augustine is also sometimes credited with writing *The Rule of St. Augustine* for monastic communities. See *The Rule of St. Augustine*, Fordham University, trans. Robert Russell, Brothers of the Order of Hermits of Saint Augustine, Inc., orig. pub. 1976, http://www.fordham.edu/halsall/source/ruleaug.html (accessed 24 Sep. 2013). Although some scholars think that he may not have written the Rule since he did not reference it in his Retractions, it is clear that he did live a monastic-like existence from 388-391 before he was ordained as a priest. See also *The Concise Oxford Dictionary of the Christian Church*, s.v. "St. Augustine of Hippo" and s.v. "Rule of St. Augustine of Hippo"; González, vol. 1, pp. 147, 211-12; Carolinne White, introduction to *Early Christian Lives*, p. xxxviii.

1417 Augustine, *On Christian Doctrine*, Preface, no. 4, http://www.newadvent.org/fathers/12020.htm.

1418 Benedicta Ward, foreword to *The Sayings of the Desert Fathers*, pp. xvii-xviii; H. Chadwick, pp. 181-3; *The New International Dictionary of the Christian Church*, s.v. "John Cassian."

1419 See *The Little Flowers of Saint Francis* which is replete with the glorification of poverty, chastity, obedience, and asceticism. The miracles of the desert have many similarities to these stories surrounding St. Francis as well. See also Bonaventure, *The Life of St. Francis*.

1420 *The Sayings of the Desert Fathers*, Abba Poemen, no. 38, p. 172.

1421 A story of the famed Symeon the Stylite is mentioned in ibid., Abba Gelasius, no. 2, pp. 46-7.

1422 *The Sayings of the Desert Fathers*, Zacharias, no. 1, p. 67.

1423 Ward, p. 40 (introductory note to Bessarion section); H. Chadwick, p. 179. González, vol. 1, p. 143 notes that "rioting monks would seek to impose by force and violence what they considered to be orthodox doctrine." See also Stark, p. 35. Cf. the Circumcellions of the Donatist Church (Bonner, pp. 240-2).

1424 Wulff, p. 70.

1425 Wulff, p. 75. Sleep deprivation is not uncommonly attributed to Catholic saints in hagiographic accounts. For example, St. Martin de Porres is said to have "slept only sporadically and as little as possible" (Ghezzi, p. 9). For another example of night prayer, see *The Sayings of the Desert Fathers*, Isidore the Priest, no. 4, p. 97. "Night vigils" is a common phrase used for forgoing sleep for prayer. Wulff also describes the potential neurotic or psychotic effects of fasting, pp. 70-4.

1426 *The Sayings of the Desert Fathers*. The source for these seven quotes can be found as follows: (1) Motius, no. 1, p. 148; (2) Sisoes, no. 38, p. 219; (3) Poemen, no. 35, p. 172; (4) Poemen, no. 80, p. 178; (5) Poemen, no. 126, p. 185; (6) Sisoes, no. 54, p. 222; (7) Poemen, no. 81, p. 178.

1427 Ibid., Abba Arsenius, no. 40, p. 18: "When his death drew near, the brethren saw him weeping and they said to him 'Truly, Father, why are you so afraid?' "Indeed,' he answered them, 'the fear which is mine at this hour has been with me ever since I became a monk.'"

1428 Safi, p. 29.

1429 Schriner, p. 169.

1430 Thomas Jefferson, *Notes on the State of Virginia*, in *The Portable Thomas Jefferson*, XVII, p. 211. As Norwich explains, "It has seemed worth describing the religious riots in some detail simply to emphasize that aspect of daily life in Byzantium the twentieth century finds hardest to comprehend: the involvement by all classes of society in what appear today to be impossibly abstruse doctrinal niceties" (p. 59).

1431 For one interesting discussion on the number of atheistic and non-believing scientists, see "Scientists and Belief," *Pew Research Center*, 5 Nov. 2009, www.pewforum/org/2009/11/05/scientists-and-belief/ (accessed 29 Mar. 2017). According to this article, a survey of members of the American Association for the Advancement of Science found that 33% of scientists believed in God, 18% in some sort of higher power, and 41% denied both. (7% don't know or refused to answer). See also Tom Miles, "Irreverent Atheists Crowdsource Charitable Giving," *Reuters*, 11 Dec. 2011, https://www.reuters.com/article/us-atheists-donations-idUS-TRE7B81SU20111209 (accessed 29 Mar. 2017). Atheists, like many other "heretics," have often had to be brave if they wanted to openly voice their opinions. See Benjamin Franklin, *The Autobiography and Other Writings*, ed. Kenneth Silverman (New York: Penguin, 1986), p. 259. From a Letter to Benjamin Vaughan, 24 Oct. 1788. Shri Goparaju Ramachandra Rao (1902-1975), Robert Ingersoll (1833-1899), Denis Diderot (1713-1784), Ayaan Hirsi Ali (b. 1969) are some other examples of exemplary atheists.

1432 Justin Martyr, *First Apology*, no.4, http://www.newadvent.org/fathers/0126.htm (accessed 27 Sep. 2014). Justin unfortunately goes somewhat against this principle here by lamenting that some philosophers of the past had taught atheism (cf. also ch. 58).

1433 Cf. Hitchens, *god is Not Great: How Religion Poisons Everything*, pp. 13, 22, etc. Unlike some more aggressive atheists, Robert Ingersoll found it much more effective and advantageous to work with moderate and liberal believers against fundamentalist excesses (Jacoby, p. 90, etc.). Shermer, *The Moral Arc*, pp. 173-4, mentioning this phrase, agrees that religion is a mixed bag.

1434 I regard religious fundamentalism as a general category of poisonous belief—although there are certainly particular types of fundamentalism that are much more destructive and dangerous than others. Dogmatic atheism, especially in its communist and Stalinist expressions, has been catastrophically harmful. It has been argued with some justification that atheism has no political content and cannot be blamed for Stalinism and the like (e.g., Dawkins, pp. 315-16). Although secular European democracies demonstrate that non-belief can be prevalent in some of the world's happiest societies (see Phil Zuckerman, "Secular Societies Fare Better Than Religious Societies," *Psychology Today*, 13 Oct. 2014, https://www.psychologytoday.com/blog/the-secular-life/201410/secular-societies-fare-better-religious-societies [accessed 29 Mar. 2017]), since oppressive communistic regimes were typically atheistic I think that it can be fairly maintained that atheism can be a component of aggressive and poisonous belief systems. Alternatively, one can have god-beliefs that stress harmony, compassion, and freedom and utterly reject persecution. Shermer, *The Moral Arc*, pp. 173-4 notes that religion, while varied, is not necessary for a better society.

1435 Tony Campolo and Bart Campolo, *Why I Left, Why I Stayed: Conversations on Christianity between an Evangelical Father and His Humanist Son* (New York: HarperOne, 2017), pp. 63, 68.

1436 Mohammad Hashim Kamali, *A Textbook of Hadith Studies: Authenticity, Compilation, Classification and Criticism of Hadith*, 3rd impression (Leicestershire, UK: The Islamic Foundation, 2004), pp. 1-2. Kamali thinks it is possible to overcome these difficulties. Cf. Parrinder, ed., *World Religions*,

p. 482: "When the Muslims looked for precedents and failed to find what was needed, they often fabricated traditions to satisfy their need."

1437 Abdul Malik Mujahid, ed. and trans., *200 Golden Hadiths* (Darussalam Publishers, 2013), no. 135, Kindle. Cf. Bukhari, bk. 46, no. 27 (3.43.646) http://sunnah.com/bukhari/46/27: "Yes, there is a reward for serving any animate (living being)."

1438 *The Penguin Dictionary of Religions*, s.v. "Hadith." By another reckoning, there was perhaps 700,000 (see Kamali, *A Textbook of Hadith Studies*, p. 27). Kamali states that al-Bukhari narrowed it from 600,000 to 9,082—but that both numbers can be reduced considerably when repetition is considered. He places the final number without repetitions at 2,602 (pp. 33-4). Likewise, he states that Muslim's collection is best numbered as 300,000 reduced down to 3,030 when repetitions are considered (p. 36). Kamali also confirms the six "sound collections" of hadith (p. 14). Swarup nots that there were over 1,000 collections that died away and also notes that there are six authoritative traditions (pp. 6-7). See also Safi, pp. 278-80.

1439 Ernst, pp. 49, 53, 64; Swarup, p. 5. These chains are called *isnads*. Bloom and Blair, p. 45 note that "These traditions were translated orally for several generations before being written down." Safi likewise notes they were "circulated for many decades orally"(p. 278).

1440 Regarding the hadith collection process, Ruthven notes: "Modern scholarship, however, is bound to question this methodology" (p. 29). See also pp. 40-1.

1441 Unless otherwise indicated, all the following hadith quotations are from Abdul Malik Mujahid, ed. and trans., *200 Golden Hadiths*. I read this little volume of hadith and the first four volumes of Bukhari for this meditation.

1442 Bukhari, bk. 51, no. 42 (3.47.780) http://sunnah.com/bukhari/51/42.

1443 John R. Mabry, "Responsibility," *Salvation of the True Rock: The Sufi Poetry of Najat Ozkaya* (Berkeley, CA: The Apocryphile Press, 2011), pp. 100-1. Quoted with permission.

1444 à Kempis, *The Imitation of Christ*, 1.9, p. 40.

1445 As quoted in Harold C. Gardiner, introduction to *The Imitation of Christ*, by Thomas à Kempis, p. 5.

1446 Like so many things in religion, this too is disputed. Gerard Groote and Jean de Gerson appear to be the usual suspects. Gardiner, introduction to *The Imitation of* Christ, pp. 10-11.

1447 Biographical information for this section was taken from Gardiner, introduction to *The Imitation of Christ*, by Thomas à Kempis, pp. 5-19; *The Westminster Dictionary of Theologians*, s.v. "Kempis, Thomas à."

1448 Cf. Ps. 22:6.

1449 "Thomas à Kempis: Author of the Most Popular Devotional Classic," *Christianity Today*, n.d., https://www.christianitytoday.com/history/people/innertravelers/thomas-kempis.html (accessed 8 Mar. 2019).
1450 *The Catholic Encyclopedia*, s.v. "Ignorance" http://www.newadvent.org/cathen/07648a.htm (accessed 15 Feb. 2013).
1451 Sam Harris, *Waking Up: A Guide to Spirituality Without Religion* (New York: Simon and Schuster, 2014), p. 89.
1452 "Fascinating Facts," *Library of Congress*, n.d., http://www.loc.gov/about/facts.html (accessed 7 Jan. 2013 and 6 Apr. 2019). The 830 miles statistic was found in my 2013 viewing.
1453 Mohandas Gandhi, *The Bhagavad Gita According to Gandhi*, trans. Mahadev Desai (Blacksburg, VA: Wilder Publications, 2011), p.13, introductory comment.
1454 Gandhi, *Autobiography*, p. viii.
1455 Fischer, pp. 18, 21; Gandhi, *Autobiography*, pp. 53-5. Bhiku Parekh, *Gandhi: A Very Short Introduction* (New York: Oxford Univ. Press, 2001), pp. 13, 15 notes his "massive self-confidence" and his considerable communication skills.
1456 Fischer, p. 16; Gandhi, *Autobiography*, pp. 70-2.
1457 Gandhi, *Autobiography*, p. 276; Fischer, pp. 138-9.
1458 Gandhi, *Autobiography*, pp. 230-3; Fischer, p. 30.
1459 Gandhi, *Autobiography*, pp. 193-4.
1460 Mahatma Gandhi, *The Essential Gandhi: An Anthology of His Writings on His Life, Work, and Ideas*, ed. Louis Fischer (New York: Vintage Books, 1983), pp. 9, 51, 57; Fischer, p. 29.
1461 Fischer, p. 88; Gandhi, *Autobiography*, p. viii. Cf. "Idol of Gandhi worshipped in Orissa temple," *The Indian Express*, 3 Apr. 2009, http://archive.indianexpress.com/news/idol-of-gandhi-worshipped-in-orissa-temple/442651/0 (accessed 31 May 2016); "Mahatma Gandhi Temple in Orissa," *Economic* Times, 3 Apr. 2009, https://economictimes.indiatimes.com/mahatma-gandhi-temple-in-orissa/articleshow/4353287.cms (accessed 19 Oct. 2018); *Mahatma Gandhi Temple*, www.mahatmagandhitemple.org.
1462 Gandhi, *Autobiography*, p. 3; cf. Gandhi, *The Essential Gandhi*, pp. 4, 119.
1463 Gandhi, *Autobiography*, pp. 35 (meat and wine), 43, 290, 235-236 (vegetarian), 51 (eggs), 219 (eggs and chicken broth), 239 ("nothing but sunbaked fruits and nuts"), 291 (tea), 292 (salt). 293 (milk), 294 (fruit only), 295 (no cereals), 308 (fruitarians), 318 (milk, cereals, and "pulses" or beans/lentils); Fischer, pp. 9 (wine), 43 (fruitarian), 75 and 108 (vegetarian but has goat's milk), 106 (alcohol and salt). Avoidance could be for ethical or political reasons.

1464 Gandhi, *Autobiography*, p. 208.
1465 As quoted in Gandhi, *The Essential Gandhi*, p. 301. A "fakir" is an ascetic. See also Fischer, pp. 111-12.
1466 Gandhi, *Autobiography*, p. 53; Fischer, p. 137.
1467 Fischer, p. 6.
1468 For the vow of *brahmacharya*, see Gandhi, *Autobiography*, p. 182. For sleeping naked with young women, see Parekh, pp. 28-9; Wulff, p. 412; Fischer, pp. 32-4.
1469 Parekh, pp. 1, 8; Fischer, p. 8.
1470 Gandhi, *Autobiography*, p. 191.
1471 Ibid., p. 140.
1472 Ibid., p. 60. See also Parekh, p. 3.
1473 Parekh, pp. 46, 68.
1474 Fischer, p. 143.
1475 As quoted in Gandhi, *The Essential Gandhi*, p. 202. See also Parekh, p. 57.
1476 Fischer, p. 133; Gandhi, *Autobiography*, p. 353, etc.; Parekh, p. 45.
1477 Gandhi, *Autobiography*, p. 233.
1478 As quoted in Fischer, pp. 11-12.
1479 Gandhi, *Autobiography*, p. 18; Parekh, p. 46. Jain avoidance of meat is particularly in view here, although Jainism regards ahimsa or non-violence as their chief ethical ideal.
1480 Parekh, p. 46.
1481 For a critique of his idealistic tendencies, see ibid., pp. 109-11; 119ff.
1482 Gandhi, *Autobiography*, pp. 223, 453, etc. See also Parekh, pp. 64-66 and esp. p. 69.
1483 Parekh, pp. 42-4.
1484 As quoted in ibid., p. 43.
1485 Gandhi, *Autobiography*, p. ix.
1486 Parekh, p. 35.
1487 Ibid., p. 101.
1488 Gandhi, *Autobiography*, p. 30 (cf. p. 61—he of course did not adopt atheism).
1489 Parekh, p. 36.
1490 As quoted in Goparaju Ramchandra Rao, *An Atheist with Gandhi*, in Mkgandhi.org, orig. pub. 1951, p. 34, http://www.mkgandhi.org/ebks/an_atheist.pdf (accessed 13 Feb. 2017). For an interesting short article on Rao, see "'Gora' Shri Goparaju Ramachandra Rao (aka Gora) (1902-1975)," *British Humanist Association*, 2018, https://humanism.org.uk/humanism/the-humanist-tradition/20th-century-humanism/gora/ (accessed 13 Feb. 2017).

1491   St. Maximos the Confessor, *Four Hundred Texts on Love*, in *The Philokalia*, vol. 2, no. 30 in Second Century, p. 70.

1492   From *The Poetic Edda*, trans. Henry Adams Bellows (New York: The American-Scandinavian Foundation, 1923), Hovamol, no. 22, p. 33. Avail. at https://archive.org/details/poeticedda00belluoft/page/32. Confirmed in the public domain. Cf. Hamilton, p. 314.

1493   The five "fundamentals" of 20th-c. American Protestantism are: (1) biblical inerrancy/sola scriptura, (2) virgin birth, (3) substitutionary atonement/justification by faith alone, (4) Christ's resurrection and deity, (5) the Second Coming of Christ. See *The New International Dictionary of the Christian Church*, s.v. "Fundamentalism"; Vidler, p. 241. Cf. Wulff, p. 653. "Scripture alone" and "faith alone" were generally not pre-Reformation distinctives. The exaggerated views of inerrancy put forth by some American fundamentalists would not necessarily have been fully advanced by Christians in centuries past.

1494   Neill and Wright, p. 33.

1495   *Westminster Confession of Faith*, https://reformed.org/documents/wcf_with_proofs/index.html; *Synod of Dort*, http://www.ccel.org/ccel/anonymous/canonsofdort.pdf; *Schleitheim Confession of Faith*, http://courses.washington.edu/hist112/SCHLEITHEIM%20CONFESSION%20OF%20FAITH.htm; *The Baltimore Catechism of 1891* https://www.pcpbooks.net/docs/baltimore_catechism.pdf; *The Seven Ecumenical Councils of the Undivided Church*, in *Nicene and Post-Nicene Fathers of the Christian Church*, etc. For further historic creeds with fundamentalist tendencies, see pre-20th c. creeds and confessions for a variety of perspectives in Leith, ed., *Creeds of the Churches*; Philip Schaff, *Creeds of Christendom,* vol. 1 (Grand Rapids, MI: Christian Classics Ethereal Library, orig. pub. 1876), http://www.ccel.org/ccel/schaff/creeds1.pdf. On this point I differ somewhat from Karen Armstrong, since it seems to me that modern "fundamentalist" groups, while certainly affected by modernity, are usu. attempting to hold on to older and more literal expressions of faith. While all religions develop and change with time, I believe our religious forebears would typically regard liberal religious expressions as much more alien. For Armstrong's perspective, see *The Battle for God*, pp. xv-xviii, etc.; Karen Armstrong, *The Spiral Staircase: My Climb out of Darkness* (New York: Anchor Books, 2005), pp. 253, 280, 299, etc.

1496   As quoted in Thomas E. Woods, *How the Catholic Church Built Western Civilization* (Washington, DC: Regnery Publishing, 2005), pp. 171-2.

1497   *The Concise Oxford Dictionary of the Christian Church*, s.v. "Kolbe, St. Maximilian."

1498 Mustafa Akyol, "Why the Middle East's Christians Are Under Attack," *The New York Times*, 26 May 2017, https://www.nytimes.com/2017/05/26/opinion/why-the-middle-easts-christians-are-under-attack.html (accessed 26 May 2018).

1499 Davis, p. 21.

1500 Galli and Olsen, p. 260. See also González, *The Westminster Dictionary of Theologians*, s.v. "Catherine of Siena."

1501 Galli and Olsen, pp. 326-7. However, St. Louis also commanded the branding all those who committed blasphemy (Walsh, ed., *Butler's Lives of the Saints*, p. 262).

1502 Walsh, ed., *Butler's Lives of the Saints*, pp. 360-1. He did apparently own at least one slave. See also *Encyclopedia of World Biography*, s.v. "Martin Porres Biography," notablebiographies.com, n.d., https://www.notablebiographies.com/supp/Supplement-Mi-So/Porres-Mart-n.html (accessed 29 Sep. 2018).

1503 See "Our Impact: Solving the Puzzle of Poverty," World Vision http://www.worldvision.org/our-impact (accessed 19 Dec. 2015); "Statement of Faith," https://www.worldvision.org/statement-of-faith (accessed 29 Sep. 2018); Celeste Gracey and Jeremy Weber, "World Vision Reverses Decision to Hire Christians in Same-Sex Marriages," *Christianity Today*, 26 Mar. 2014 http://www.christianitytoday.com/ct/2014/march-web-only/world-vision-reverses-decision-gay-same-sex-marriage.html (accessed 19 Dec. 2015).

1504 Walsh, ed., *Butler's Lives of the Saints*, pp. 314-20, 246-7.

1505 O. Chadwick, p. 383.

1506 Ware, p. 79.

1507 Ware, pp. 104-8. Quotation is from p. 105. See also *OrthodoxWiki*, s.v. "Nilus of Sora," http://orthodoxwiki.org/Nilus_of_Sora (accessed 6 Sep. 2013).

1508 González, vol. 1, pp. 392-4.

1509 Allitt, pp. 148-52. *The Concise Oxford Dictionary of the Christian Church*, s.v. "Day, Dorothy." While in many respects progressive, Day seems to have been a traditional Roman Catholic. See Cardinal John O'Conner, "Dorothy Days Sainthood Cause Begins," *Catholic New York*, 16 Mar. 2000, http://www.catholicworker.org/pages/o'connor-cause-begins.html, (accessed19 Dec. 2015).

1510 "St. Wulfstan", Worcester Cathedral, http://worcestercathedral.co.uk/Wulfstan.php (accessed 16 Jul. 2013). No author or pub. date given. See also Black, p. 37; Walsh, ed., *Butler's Lives of the Saints*, p. 17.

1511 Galli and Olsen, pp. 284-5; González, vol. 2, p. 272. Thomas Clarkson (1760-1846) was also a leading Christian figure in British abolitionism—

although Enlightenment ideals were certainly a powerful influence on the abolition movement.

1512 Galli and Olsen, p. 296.
1513 *The Westminster Dictionary of Theologians*, s.v. "Origen"; Galli and Olsen, pp. 332-4.
1514 "His writings," *Augnet*, n.d., http://www.augnet.org/?ipageid=223 (accessed 19 Dec. 2015); "Writings of Saint Augustine," *Augustinians*, 2013, http://www.osa.org.au/en/augustine/writings-of-st-augustine/ (accessed 19 Dec. 2015).
1515 "St. Augustine: Did You Know …" *Christian History Institute*, https://www.christianhistoryinstitute.org/magazine/article/augustine-did-you-know/ (accessed 19 Dec. 2015). Orig. pub. *Christian History* issue 15, (1987). Per Bonner, Victor of Vita numbered the books at 232 (p. 156).
1516 Bonner, p. 127.
1517 Walsh, ed., *Butler's Lives of the Saints*, p. 102; *The Concise Oxford Dictionary of the Christian Church*, s.v. "Isidor, St."
1518 Walsh, ed., *Butler's Lives of the Saints*, pp. 352-3.
1519 Galli and Olsen, pp. 121-3; *The Westminster Dictionary of Theologians*, "Dostoyevsky, Fyodor."
1520 Bradley Birzer, "Tolkein: Man Behind the Myth," *Christianity Today*, 13 Dec. 2012, http://www.christianitytoday.com/ct/2012/december-web-only/tolkien-man-behind-myth.html (accessed 27 Dec. 2015); "J.R.R. Tolkein," *EWTN*, https://www.ewtn.com/library/HOMELIBR/TOLKIEN.HTM (accessed 27 Dec. 2015); Joseph Pearce, "J.R.R. Tolkien: Truth and Myth," *CatholicAuthors.com*, n.d., http://www.catholicauthors.com/tolkien.html, (accessed 27 Dec. 2015); originally taken from *Lay Witness* magazine.
1521 Galli and Olsen, p. 61.
1522 *The Catholic Encyclopedia*, s.v. "Mendel, Mendelism" http://www.newadvent.org/cathen/10180b.htm (accessed 27 Dec. 2015).
1523 Kirsch, p. 176. See also discussions in Stark, pp. 167-72 and Barnes, "Images of Hope and Despair: Western Apocalypticism," in *The Continuum History of Apocalypticism*, p. 343. For his beliefs on the Trinity, see *The Concise Oxford Dictionary of the Christian Church*, s.v. "Newton, Isaac"; *The New International Dictionary of the Christian Church*, s.v. "Newton, Sir Isaac."
1524 Galli and Olsen, pp. 63-6, 83-7.
1525 Franklin, pp. 116-19.
1526 *The Concise Oxford Dictionary of the Christian Church*, s.v. "Michelangelo." *The Catholic Encyclopedia*, s.v. "Mchaelangelo Buonarroti" 27 Dec. 2015 http://www.newadvent.org/cathen/03059b.htm (accessed 27 Dec.

2015). Other sources describe the unmarried artist as devout but with homosexual inclinations.

1527 Galli and Olsen, pp. 110-11.
1528 Ibid., p. 316.
1529 *The Concise Oxford Dictionary of the Christian Church*, s.v. "Gregory I, St."; Walsh, ed., *Butler's Lives of the Saints*, pp. 273-5.
1530 Galli and Olsen, eds., *131 Christians*, pp. 348-349.
1531 Walsh, ed., *Butler's Lives of the Saints*, pp. 5, 221.
1532 González, vol. 2, p. 310.
1533 "Grace, Gold & Glory: My Leap of Faith by Gabrielle Douglas with Michelle Burford," Zondervan, YouTube video 2:38, posted 21 Nov. 2012, https://www.youtube.com/watch?time_continue=138&v=t_Spdtilkkg (accessed 3 Feb. 2019).
1534 From *The Poetic Edda*, Hovamol, no. 133, p. 58. Avail. at https://archive.org/details/poeticedda00belluoft/page/58. Confirmed in the public domain.
1535 Bernard of Clairvaux, Sermon 83, from *An Anthology of Christian Mysticism*, ed. Harvey Egan (Collegeville, MN: The Liturgical Press, 1991), II.4, pp. 176-7.
1536 Dietrich Bonhoeffer, *The Cost of Discipleship*, trans. R. H. Fuller, 2nd ed. (New York: The MacMillan Co., 1959), p. 165.
1537 Ignatius of Loyola, *The Spiritual Exercises of St. Ignatius*, p. 5.
1538 Ibid., "Rules for Thinking with the Church," no. 13, p.126.
1539 Avery Dulles, Preface to *The Spiritual Exercises of St. Ignatius*, pp. xvi-xxii. (The "Chronology of the Life of St. Ignatius of Loyola" was also utilized, pp. xxxi-xxxvi. See also *The Catholic Encyclopedia*, s.v. "St. Ignatius Loyola," http://www.newadvent.org/cathen/07639c.htm (accessed 1 Aug. 2013); *The New International Dictionary of the Christian Church*, s.v. "Ignatius of Loyola."
1540 Merton, p. 268. Highlighting this lack of mysticism, Merton even called them "very pedestrian."
1541 Ignatius of Loyola, p. 5.
1542 Ibid., no. 21, p. 12.
1543 cf. ibid., no. 179, p. 58.
1544 Ibid., "Rules for Thinking with the Church," no. 13, p. 126.
1545 Certain forms of Protestant biblicism provide a parallel.
1546 Ibid., no. 58.5, p. 25.
1547 Ibid., no. 353, p. 124; cf. no. 170, p. 56.
1548 Ibid., no. 361, p. 125.
1549 Ibid., no. 193, p. 63; no. 53, p. 23; no. 55, p. 24; etc.
1550 Ibid., no. 206, p. 66; no. 195, p. 64; no. 78, p. 30.

1551 Ibid., no. 50, p. 23; cf. no. 48, no. 50, p. 22.
1552 Ibid., no. 65-71, p. 27. My italics.
1553 Ibid., no. 82, p. 30.
1554 Ibid., no. 85, p. 31.
1555 This phrase is taken from Daniel Taylor, *The Myth of Certainty: The Reflective Christian and the Risk of Commitment* (Waco, TX: Word, 1986). Taylor still holds to a conservative Protestant faith but acknowledges that uncertainty is an inherent part of the human predicament.
1556 Ignatius of Loyola, no. 2, p. 5.
1557 Lao Tzu, *Tao Te Ching*, trans. Mabry , no. 67, loc. 746. Quoted with permission. All quotations from the *Tao Te Ching* are from this translation unless otherwise noted.
1558 *Seven Taoist Masters*, p. 108.
1559 Yi-Ping Ong, introductions to *Tao Te Ching*, trans. Charles Muller (New York: Barnes and Noble, 2005), pp. v, x, xiii-xxxi; Parrinder, ed., *World Religions*, pp. 328-33.
1560 James Miller, p. 82; cf. p. 8.
1561 I concede here that I may be misinterpreting the *Tao Te Ching* through modern, Western eyes—although the Taoist tradition itself is diverse and changing in nature. See James Miller, pp. 136-8.
1562 Van Over, ed., *Taoist Tales*, p. 120 notes that The Divine Panorama is "considered important enough to be circulated gratuitously all over China by those who wish to 'build up their store of good works.'"
1563 For example, the Qur'an describes chains, scalding water which melts the skin, garments of fire, lashing with rods of iron, etc. See Sura 13:5, p. 143; Sura 22:19-22, p. 403; Sura 40:70-76, p.168; etc. Zoroastrianism's *Arda Viraz Namag* provides graphic pictures of hell which include darkness, stench, beatings, torment, and flames (in Boyce, ed., 6.3.12-6.3.16, chs. 54-58, pp. 88-9). For gruesome Jain descriptions of hell, see *Sûtrakritâṅga*, in *Jaina Sutras: Part II*, bk. 1, lect. 5, ch. 1 http://www.sacred-texts.com/jai/sbe45/sbe4552.htm; and bk. 1, lect. 5, ch. 2 http://www.sacred-texts.com/jai/sbe45/sbe4553.htm.
1564 Van Over, ed., *The Divine Panorama*, in *Taoist Tales*, The Eighth Court, p. 138.
1565 Ibid., The Fifth Court, p. 132.
1566 Ibid., The Eighth Court, pp. 138-9. "His Infernal Majesty Tu Shih" is named here and it appears he is the "God" who is making the promises at the end of this section.
1567 For an interesting exploration of this idea, see Shermer, *The Moral Arc*. While scientific knowledge of course does not necessarily bring about

more ethical behavior, Shermer argues that science and reason applied to human flourishing have demonstrably made humanity more ethical. See pp. 2-7, etc. Cf. Sam Harris, "Science Can Answer Moral Questions," TED, YouTube video 23:34, posted 22 Mar. 2010, https://www.youtube.com/watch?v=Hj9oB4zpHww (accessed 25 Feb. 2019).

1568   Mother Teresa, *Mother Teresa: Come Be My Light*, ed. Brian Kolodiejchuk (New York: Doubleday, 2007). Quotation is given before the Table of Contents.

1569   Hitchens, *god Is Not Great*, p. 52.

1570   Brian Kolodiejchuk, introduction to *Mother Teresa: Come Be My Light*, p. 11. See p. 63 in same book. For a short biography of Mother Teresa's life, see "Mother Teresa Biography," *Biography.com*, 2 Apr. 2014, http://www.biography.com/people/mother-teresa-9504160 (accessed 1 May 2013).

1571   In his own words, Mother Teresa was "a religious fundamentalist, a political operative, a primitive sermonizer and an accomplice of worldly, secular powers." See Christopher Hitchens, *The Missionary Position: Mother Teresa in Theory and Practice* (New York: Twelve, 2012), p. 12.

1572   Christopher Hitchens, "Mommie Dearest: The Pope Beatifies Mother Teresa, a Fanatic, a Fundamentalist, and a Fraud," *Slate*, 20 Oct. 2003, http://www.slate.com/articles/news_and_politics/fighting_words/2003/10/mommie_dearest.html (accessed 7 Feb. 2013).

1573   See *Hell's Angel: Mother Teresa of Calcutta*, dir. by Jenny Morgan (1994; BBC Channel 4, video) https://archive.org/details/65JxnUW7Wk4 (accessed 15 Oct. 2018). Christopher Hitchens was a writer and narrator of this documentary.

1574   *Mother Teresa: Come Be My Light*, p. 149. Fr. Kolodiejchuk, "Postulator, Cause of Canonization of Blessed Teresa of Calcutta" and "Director, Mother Teresa Center" interprets such negative statements in a consistently positive light. Although there is much in Teresa to admire, he does not recognize the tragedy of her theological convictions for both herself and others. It appears that Teresa's "dark night of the soul" was all but continuous for decades, from the founding of her order until her death—almost fifty years (pp. 326, 336-7).

1575   A term associated with St. John of the Cross (1542-1591), the dark night of the soul is generally thought of as the path of purgation, instigated by God, in which the believer undergoes significant pain and anguish in order to purify the soul. See *The Catholic Encyclopedia*, s.v. "St. John of the Cross" http://www.newadvent.org/cathen/08480a.htm (accessed 5 May 2013).

1576   Mother Teresa, *Mother Teresa: Come Be My Light*. p .67; cf. p. 41.

1577 Ibid., p. 247. This notion is not at all foreign to the Catholic spiritual tradition's emphasis on martyrdom, asceticism, penance, mortification and the like. Julian of Norwich provides an interesting example, describing how she prayed for an experience of Christ's sufferings and bodily illness. See Julian of Norwich, *Revelations of Divine Love*, Short Text, no. 1, p. 3. Cf. no. 3, p. 6. Cf. A.C. Spearing, introduction in this same book, p. xiii.

1578 Mother Teresa, *Mother Teresa: Come Be My Light*, p. 281. Cf. p. 24 which notes that "Jesus has surely chosen her for something special, since He has given her so much suffering." Cf. also p. 155. Hitchens describes a dialogue on camera between Teresa and a dying person dying in pain. Teresa reportedly said: "You are suffering like Christ on the cross. So Jesus must be kissing you." The reply was simply: "Then please tell him to stop kissing me." See Hitchens, *The Missionary Position*, p. 44.

1579 Ibid., p. 49.

1580 Ibid., p. 41. Cf. Julian of Norwich, Long Text, no. 31, p. 83: "for this is the spiritual thirst of Christ, the love-longing that lasts and ever shall do until we see the revelation on Judgement Day."

1581 Mother Teresa, *Mother Teresa: Come Be My Light*, pp. 50, 331, 75, 111.

1582 Ibid., p. 20.

1583 Ibid., p. 214.

1584 See, for example, Deborah Mitchell, "Mother Teresa Less Than a Saint for the Sick," *EmaxHealth*, 3 Mar. 2013, http://www.emaxhealth.com/1275/mother-teresa-less-saint-sick (accessed 5 May 2013); Sanal Edamaruku, "India Has No Reason to Be Grateful to Mother Teresa," *mm-gold.azureedge.net*, 13 May 2010, https://mm-gold.azureedge.net/Articles/mother_teresa/sanal_ed.html (accessed 14 Oct. 2014).

1585 Mother Teresa, *Mother Teresa: Come Be My Light*, p. 187. Cf. pp. 238 and 207: "I deceive people with this weapon—even my sisters."

1586 Ibid, p. 15.

1587 Ibid., p. 163.

1588 "Christopher Hitchens Biography," *Biography.com*, 2 Apr. 2014, http://www.biography.com/people/christopher-hitchens-20845987 (accessed 1 May 2013).

1589 "Galloway and the Mother of All Invective," *The Guardian*, 18 May 2005, http://www.guardian.co.uk/uk/2005/may/18/usa.iraq (accessed 28 Apr. 2013).

1590 "Outspoken and outrageous: Christopher Hitchens," *60 Minutes*, 6 Mar. 2011, http://m.cbsnews.com/searchfullstory.rbml?catid=20038931&query=60%20minutes%20broad (accessed 5 May 2013). Quote attributed to Alexander Cockburn, a "former

	friend" of Hitchens. See also https://www.cbsnews.com/news/outspoken-and-outrageous-christopher-hitchens/4/.
1591	Kyle Butt, "On Death of Christopher Hitchens," *Apologetics Press*, 2012, http://www.apologeticspress.org/APContent.aspx?category=12&article=1617 (accessed 2 May 2013).
1592	Hitchens, *Thomas Jefferson: Author of America*, p. 5. I have heard Hitchens call Jefferson a "hero" in speeches.
1593	Christopher Hitchens, "Princess Di, Mother T., and Me," in *After Diana: Irreverent Elegies*, ed. Mandy Merck (London: Verso, 1998), Sep. 14 and 15, p. 59. He did acknowledge elsewhere that this was "I admit, an exercise in seeing how far I could go." See "Outspoken and Outrageous," CBS News.
1594	Mother Teresa, *No Greater Love*, ed. Becky Benenate and Joseph Durepos (Novato, CA: New World Library, 2001), p. 179.
1595	Hitchens, *god is not Great*, p. 8.
1596	Ibid., p. 87.
1597	Thomas Jefferson to Dr. Benjamin Rush, 21 Apr. 1803, in *The Portable Thomas Jefferson*, p. 490.
1598	As quoted in Hitchens, *The Portable Atheist*, p. 158. For further positive comments on Jesus, see Viereck, *Glimpses of the Great*, pp. 448-9.
1599	Dawkins, p. 283: "The Sermon on the Mount is way ahead of its time. His 'turn the other cheek' anticipated Gandhi and Martin Luther King by two thousand years."
1600	For Porphyry, see Augustine, *City of God*, 19.22-23, http://www.newadvent.org/fathers/120119.htm; Wilken, pp. 152-3, 158-60). See Jackson Browne, "The Rebel Jesus," Jackson Browne - Topic, 4:39, posted 24 Jul. 2017, https://www.youtube.com/watch?v=SKuCTgGDX5Y (accessed 23 Oct. 2018). As has been expressed in other meditations, Gandhi revered Jesus' teachings on non-violence and the Sermon on the Mount; Tolstoy rejected Christian traditionalism but called himself a follower of Jesus. Albert Einstein apparently felt drawn to the personality of Jesus (Isaacson, p. 386).
1601	From my perspective, the ethics of these passages are sometimes tainted by threats of divine punishment or reward in the afterlife. Other verses could certainly have been included.
1602	For an emphatically literal interpretation of this passage, see Jerome, *Life of Hilarion* in *Early Christian Lives*, no. 40, p. 112. In Jerome's narrative, the saint causes a tidal wave.
1603	For some an example of a straightforward interpretation of Matt. 7:7, Matt. 17:20, John 16:23-24, and Matt. 10:8 regarding miracles, see Athanasius, *Life of Antony* in *Christian Lives*, no. 48, p. 38; no. 83, p. 62; Marco Polo, *The Travels of Marco Polo*, ed. Manuel Komroff (New York: Modern

Library, 2001), 1.10, p. 31. For further exploration of the problem of these verses, see Brain, "Why Won't God Heal Amputees," http://whywontgodhealamputees.com/important.htm. While the interpretation of these kinds of verses are always open to discussion, straightforward readings suggest that they are misleading at best. I would say that more realistic believers have largely discounted them.

1604 Russell seems to make a fair criticism here that "It is a doctrine that put cruelty into the world and gave the world generations of cruel torture; and the Christ of the Gospels, if you take Him as His chroniclers represent Him, would certainly have to be considered partly responsible for that." See Russell, "Why I Am Not a Christian," in *Why I Am Not a Christian and Other Essays on Religion and Related Subjects*, p. 18. Russell also believed Christ's belief in his Second Coming was a defective teaching (p. 16).

1605 Darwin, p. 72. The term "gospel" literally means "good news."

1606 For instance, it was somewhat common in the Middle Ages for spouses to leave their mates to join monasteries. E.g., Jean LeClerq, introduction to *Bernard of Clairvaux: Selected Works*, p. 17. Many missionaries have left families to evangelize people groups in remote parts of the world. In the Roman Catholic tradition, cloistered nuns were sometimes permanently forbidden to see family members.

1607 Roman Catholic reluctance to give "annulments," particularly in generations passed, provides a primary example of this dynamic. This reality is often forgotten due to the much greater acceptance of divorce in our time.

1608 See the meditations "No Law at All" and "All Things Are Permissible" for further discussion.

1609 For two examples, see Simon Turpin, "Who Is Jesus and What Did He Believe about Creation?" *answersingenesis.org*, 24 Dec. 2015, https://answersingenesis.org/jesus-christ/what-did-jesus-believe-about-creation/ (accessed 8 Jan. 2019); Kyle Butt, "Believing What Jesus Believed," *Apologeticspress.org*, 2003, www.apologeticspress.org/APContent.aspx?category=13&article=1223 (accessed 8 Jan. 2019). Cf. Todd Wilson, "Ten Theses on Creation and Evolution that (Most) Evangelicals Can Support," *Christianity Today*, 4 Jan. 2019, https://www.christianitytoday.com/ct/2019/january-web-only/ten-theses-creation-evolution-evangelicals.html (accessed 8 Jan. 2019). While a historical Jesus would of course have historically-conditioned beliefs, a divine one would presumably know better (although some have said that he gave up his omniscience after becoming man).

1610 *Handbook of Biblical Criticism*, s.v. "Jesus Christ."

1611 Campolo and Campolo, pp. 91-2.

1612 Cf. Murray, p. 6 who notes that Ludwig Feuerbach forwarded "the idea of God as a projection of the best qualities, noblest values, and highest ideals humankind an imagine."
1613 In apparent opposition to some of the verses cited earlier.
1614 Harris, *Waking Up*, p. 79.
1615 As quoted in Parrinder, ed., *World Religions*, p. 156.
1616 Wulff, p. 534; *The Westminster Dictionary of Theologians*, s.v. "Otto, Rudolf."
1617 Some wording of the "lorica" below comes from John Healy, *The Ancient Irish Church* (London: The Religious Tract Society, 1892), pp. 34-7. Avail. at https://archive.org/details/ancientirishchur00healrich/page/34. For another version of St. Patrick's Lorica along with some background information, see Martin P. Harney, "The Lorica, or Breastplate, of St. Patrick," *The Legacy of St. Patrick* (Boston: The Daughters of St. Paul, 1979), pp. 139-43. "Lorica" is often translated as "breastplate."
1618 Gandhi, *The Essential Gandhi*, p. 180.
1619 Gandhi, *Autobiography*, p. 242.
1620 Ibid., p. 312.
1621 See Barrett Evans, "Why Compassion Is the Cornerstone of Ethics," *Claims Management* (Jun. 2012): pp. 16-17 http://theclm.claimsmanagement.epubxp.com/i/68571/16.
1622 Parekh, p. 69.
1623 Gandhi, *Autobiography*, p. 454.
1624 See also Corey, p. 472: "It is a foundation for building a trusting relationship, applicable to all therapies." For a discussion of empathic understanding in Rogerian counseling, see Corey, pp. 207, 468.
1625 Corey, p. 209.
1626 As quoted in Frederick Hadland Davis, *Jalálu'd-dín Rúmí: The Persian Mystics* (1920; Project Gutenberg 2014), loc. 638, Kindle.
1627 Hafiz of Shiraz, *The Divan*, no. XXXI, loc. 5850.
1628 See Kamali, *Sharia'ah Law*, pp. 5-6. This, however, is not necessarily the case. E.g., Al-Ghazali, p. 56.
1629 Ernst, pp. 23, 29-31. Breath control, visualization, and mantra-like repetitions/chanting appear to be among the practices (pp. 106-11).
1630 Shah, p. 38.
1631 Safi, p. 188.
1632 As quoted in Ernst, p. 23.
1633 Ernst, pp. 30, 42, 48 (40-day retreats), 66-7 (miraculous powers), 71-5 (shrines, pilgrimages, and miracles at shrines), 99-102, 129, 221 (asceti-

cism and fasting), 112-13 (Sufi orders), 126 (poverty), etc. Ernst reminds on p. 121 that these parallels "cannot be pressed too far."

1634 Ibid., pp. 205-6.
1635 Ernst, p. xv. See also pp. xiii-xiv, xvii.
1636 Parrinder, ed., *World Religions*, p. 496. See also Safi, p. 210; footnote no. 7, ch. 4, p. 323. For Sufism's "drastic decline," see Ruthven, pp. 16-17.
1637 Ernst, p. xxii.
1638 Mojdeh Bayat and Mohammad Ali Jamnia, *Tales from the Land of the Sufis* (Boston: Shambhala, 1994), pp. 48-9, 67-71. The wording of the story is my condensed paraphrase. I have made an alteration from the original story—wherein the ring was to make the king happy when sad and sad when happy.
1639 Murray, p. 18.
1640 *The Little Flowers of Saint Francis*, The Sayings of Brother Giles, no. 1, p. 262.
1641 *The Catholic Encyclopedia*, s.v. "Litany" http://www.newadvent.org/cathen/09286a.htm (accessed 18 Jan. 2013); *The Concise Oxford Dictionary of the Christian Church*, s.v. "Litany."
1642 See "Litanies," *EWTN*, n.d., http://ewtn.com/Devotionals/Litanies/index.htm (accessed 8 May 2016) for links to the texts of over 25 litanies. Some audio versions are also avail. on the site.
1643 For the text, see "Litany of Humility," *EWTN*, n.d., http://www.ewtn.com/devotionals/prayers/humility.htm#ixzz20KnAgVOc (accessed 18 Jan. 2013). Apparently the litany's authorship is uncertain. See *Wikipedia*, s.v. "Litany of Humility," last edited 5 Jan. 2018, https://en.wikipedia.org/wiki/Litany_of_humility (accessed 6 Jan. 2018).
1644 As quoted in Viereck, *Glimpses of the Great*, p. 447.
1645 Neil deGrasse Tyson, *Brainyquote*, n.d., https://brainyquote.com/quotes/neil_degrasse_tyson_615079 (accessed 1/29/18). I have not been able to verify this attribution—but it sounds like Tyson to me!
1646 Neil DeGrasse Tyson, *Astrophysics for People in a Hurry* (New York: W. W. Norton & Co., 2017), p. 166 (30 km/sec).
1647 Brian Dunbar, "Extreme Space Facts," *NASA*, 15 Jun. 2017, https://www.jpl.nasa.gov/edu/pdfs/ss_extreme_poster.pdf (accessed 7 Mar. 2018).
1648 Tyson, p. 118; *Ultimate Weird but True* (Washington, DC: National Geographic, 2011), p. 17. All temperatures and measurements here are approximate.
1649 Lara Maiklem, ed., *Ultimate Visual Dictionary of Science* (New York: Barnes and Noble, 2005), p. 312.

1650 Dunbar, "Extreme Space Facts," https://www.jpl.nasa.gov/edu/pdfs/ss_extreme_poster.pdf.
1651 Maiklem, ed., pp. 314-5; Jason Daley, "Mercury's Newly-Discovered 'Great Valley' Puts Earth's Grand Canyon to Shame," *Smithsonian.com*, 21 Nov. 2016, https://www.smithsonianmag.com/smart-news/valley-twice-big-grand-canyon-found-mercury-180961180/ NDU2ODc1S0 (accessed 14 Oct. 2018). See also Dunbar, "Extreme Space Facts," https://www.jpl.nasa.gov/edu/pdfs/ss_extreme_poster.pdf. For a photo of the Valles Marineris, see "Valles Marineris: The Grand Canyon of Mars," *NASA*, 23 Mar. 2008 (updated 31 Jul. 2015), https://www.nasa.gov/multimedia/imagegallery/image_feature_83.html (accessed 7 Jan. 2017).
1652 "Saturn: Moons," *NASA*, updated 6 Dec. 2017, http://solarsystem.nasa.gov/planets/saturn/moons (accessed 23 Oct. 2016); Bill Douthitt, "Beautiful Stranger: Saturn's Mysteries Come to Light," *National Geographic* (Dec. 2006): p. 52.
1653 Maiklem, ed., p. 318; Dunbar, "Extreme Space Facts," https://www.jpl.nasa.gov/edu/pdfs/ss_extreme_poster.pdf.
1654 "Jupiter: Moons," *NASA*, 17 Jul. 2018, http://solarsystem.nasa.gov/planets/jupiter/moons (accessed 14 Oct. 2018).
1655 Maiklem, ed., p. 316. Per Tyson, "at least 350 years" (p. 43).
1656 Dunbar, "Extreme Space Facts," https://www.jpl.nasa.gov/edu/pdfs/ss_extreme_poster.pdf.
1657 "Saffir-Simpson Hurricane Wind Scale," *National Hurricane Center*, NOAA, n.d., https://www.nhc.noaa.gov/aboutsshws.php (accessed 7 Mar. 2018).
1658 Dunbar, "Extreme Space Facts," https://www.jpl.nasa.gov/edu/pdfs/ss_extreme_poster.pdf.
1659 "10 Facts about Space!" *National Geographic Kids*, n.d., https://www.natgeokids.com/nz/discover/science/space/ten-facts-about-space/#!/register (accessed 7 Mar. 2018).
1660 Nola Taylor Redd, "What Is the Biggest Star?" *Space.com*, 25 Jul. 2018, https://www.space.com/41290-biggest-star.html (accessed 17 Sep. 2018); Jillian Scudder, "How Big Is the Biggest Star We Have Ever Found?" *The Conversation*, 9 Feb. 2015, https://theconversation.com/how-big-is-the-biggest-star-we-have-ever-found-37304 (accessed 17 Sep. 2018). UY Scuti, KY Cigni, or VY Canis Majoris may be the largest known star. See also "Star Sizes," *National Schools' Observatory*, n.d., https://www.schoolsobservatory.org/learn/astro/stars/class/starsize (accessed 16 Sep. 2018). Fraser Cain, 'What Is the Biggest Star in the Universe?" *Universe Today*, 12 May

Endnotes 491

        2016, https://www.universetoday.com/13507/what-is-the-biggest-star-in-the-universe/ (accessed 16 Sep. 2018).

1661 Colin Schultz, "You Can't Throw a Rock in the Milky Way Without Hitting an Earth-Like Planet," *Smithsonian.com*, 8 Jan. 2013, http://www.smithsonianmag.com/smart-news/you-cant-throw-a-rock-in-the-milky-way-without-hitting-an-earth-like-planet-562384/ (accessed 8 Jan. 2017). See also Associated Press, "Milky Way has at least 17 billion Earth-size planets," *cbc.ca*, 7 Jul. 2013, http://www.cbc.ca/news/technology/milky-way-has-at-least-17-billion-earth-size-planets-1.1373061 (accessed 8 Jan. 2017; Jason Palmer, "Kepler telescope: Earth-sized planets 'number 17bn,'" *BBC News*, 8 Jan. 2013, http://www.bbc.com/news/science-environment-20942440 (accessed 8 Jan. 2017).

1662 Jorge Cham and Daniel Whiteson, *We Have No Idea: A Guide to the Unknown Universe* (New York: Riverhead Books, 2017), pp. 77, 316; "7 Facts That Will Make You Feel Very Small," *NASA Tumblr*, 6 Jan. 2016, https://nasa.tumblr.com/post/136762377389/7-facts-that-will-make-you-feel-very-small (accessed 7 Mar. 2018).

1663 Rebecca Hersher, "The Universe Has Almost 10 Times More Galaxies than We Thought," 14 Oct. 2016, *NPR*, http://www.npr.org/sections/thetwo-way/2016/10/14/497965415/the-universe-has-almost-10-times-more-galaxies-than-we-thought (accessed 23 Oct. 2016).

1664 Robert Krulwich, "Which Is Greater, the Number of Sand Grains on the Earth or Stars in the Sky?" *NPR*, 17 Sep. 2012, http://www.npr.org/sections/krulwich/2012/09/17/161096233/which-is-greater-the-number-of-sand-grains-on-earth-or-stars-in-the-sky (accessed 23 Oct. 2016). See also "10 Facts about Space!" *National Geographic Kids*, https://www.natgeokids.com/nz/discover/science/space/ten-facts-about-space/#!/register. Cf. Tyson, p. 202.

1665 Ethan Siegel, "Space is Full of Planets, and Most of Them Don't Even Have Stars," *Forbes*, 13 Mar. 2018 https://www.forbes.com/sites/startswithabang/2018/03/13/space-is-full-of-planets-and-most-of-them-dont-even-have-stars/#24440a733b2a (accessed 17 Oct. 2018). Cf. Rebecca Boyle, "On Average, Every Star Has at Least One Planet, New Analysis Shows," *Popular Science*, 11 Jan. 2012, https://www.popsci.com/science/article/2012-01/new-exoplanet-analysis-determines-planets-are-more-common-stars-milky-way (accessed 17 Oct. 2018); Mike Wall, "Nearly Every Star Hosts at Least One Alien Planet," *Space.com*, 4 Mar. 2014 https://www.space.com/24894-exoplanets-habitable-zone-red-dwarfs.html (accessed 17 Oct. 2018). Cf. Tyson, p. 192.

1666 Tyson, pp. 124, 142.

1667	Clara Moskowitz, "What's 96 Percent of the Universe Made of? Astronomers Don't Know," *Space.com*, 12 May 2011, https://amp.space.com/11642-dark-matter-dark-energy-4-percent-universe-panek.html (accessed 7 Mar. 2018); "7 Facts That Will Make You Feel Very Small," https://nasa.tumblr.com/post/136762377389/7-facts-that-will-make-you-feel-very-small; Cham and Whiteson, pp. 13-42; Tyson, p. 107.
1668	Cham and Whiteson, pp. 55-6, 186; Tyson, pp. 91-2.
1669	Ibid., pp. 201, 280; cf. p. 91.
1670	Neil DeGrasse Tyson, *Astrophysics for People in a Hurry* (New York: W. W. Norton & Co., 2017), p. 32.
1671	Cham and Whiteson, pp. 248-50; Tyson, pp. 89, 145-6.
1672	"Extra Eyes Direct Light: Spookfish," AskNature, n.d., http://www.asknature.org/strategy/3323ce08f6737c5af53e56597abb68fd (accessed 24 Sep. 2016).
1673	*Ultimate Weird but True*, p. 132.
1674	Christine Dell'Amore, "The 10 Weirdest Animal Stories of 2016," *National Geographic*, 20 Dec. 2016, http://news.nationalgeographic.com/2016/12/weirdest-animal-stories-2016-sharks/ (accessed 20 Dec. 2016). See also Amy B Wang, "Watch: Mysterious Ghost Shark Captured on Camera for the First Time," *The Washington Post*, 17 Dec. 2016, https://www.washingtonpost.com/amphtml/news/speaking-of-science/wp/2016/12/17/watch-mysterious-ghost-shark-captured-on-camera-for-the-first-time/?noredirect=on (accessed 20 Dec. 2016).
1675	"The Top Ten Animal Superpowers," *Smithsonian.com*, 2 Dec. 2012, http://www.smithsonianmag.com/science-nature/The-Top-10-Animal-Superpowers-182396261.html?c=y&page=10&navigation=thumb#IMAGES (accessed 13 Dec. 2012); "Electric Eel," *National Geographic*, n.d., http://animals.nationalgeographic.com/animals/fish/electric-eel/ (accessed 24 Sep. 2016).
1676	Liz Langley, "7 Gender-Altering Animals," *National Geographic*, 22 Sep. 2013, http://voices.nationalgeographic.com/2013/09/22/7-gender-bending-animals/ (accessed 24 Sep. 2016).
1677	*Ultimate Weird but True*, pp. 135-6; Ocean Portal Team, "Bioluminescence," *Smithsonian National Museum of Natural History*, Apr. 2018, http://ocean.si.edu/bioluminescence (accessed 2 Oct. 2016).
1678	Sean B. Carroll, *The Making of the Fittest* (New York: W.W. Norton and Co, 2007), pp. 21-4.
1679	Alison Fromme, "Squid in Flight," *National Geographic* (Nov. 2014), p. 20.
1680	"The Top Ten Animal Superpowers," *Smithsonian.com*; John P. Clare, "Introduction," *Axolotls*, http://www.axolotl.org/ (accessed 24 Sep. 2016).

1681 Kevin Krajick, "Discoveries in the Dark," *National Geographic* (Sep. 2007): pp. 134-47.
1682 Dell'Amore, "The 10 Weirdest Animal Stories of 2016," http://news.nationalgeographic.com/2016/12/weirdest-animal-stories-2016-sharks/; Rebecca Morelle, "400-year-old Greenland Shark 'Longest-Living Vertebrate," *BBC News*, 12 Aug. 2016, https://www.bbc.com/news/science-environment-37047168 (accessed 14 Oct. 2018).
1683 Liz Langley, "Meet the Animal That Lives for 11,000 Years," *National Geographic*, 23 Jul. 2016, http://news.nationalgeographic.com/2016/07/animals-oldest-sponges-whales-fish/ (accessed 20 Dec. 2016); Elahe Izadi, "A Sea Sponge the Size of a Minivan Could Be One of the World's Oldest Animals," *The Washington Post*, 26 May 2016, https://www.washingtonpost.com/news/speaking-of-science/wp/2016/05/26/a-sea-sponge-the-size-of-a-minivan-could-be-one-of-the-worlds-oldest-living-animals/?noredirect=on&utm_term=.c77b84ef948d (accessed 20 Dec. 2016).
1684 Mindy Weisberger, "Worms Frozen for 42,000 Years in Siberian Permafrost Wriggle to Life," *LiveScience*, 27 July 2018, https://www.livescience.com/63187-siberian-permafrost-worms-revive.html (accessed 11 Feb. 2019).
1685 Patricia Edmonds, "All Moms, No Dads," *National Geographic* (Nov. 2016): p. 29.
1686 John Roach, "How "Jesus Lizards' Walk on Water," *National Geographic*, 16 Nov. 2004, http://news.nationalgeographic.com/news/2004/11/1116_041116_jesus_lizard.html (accessed 20 Dec. 2016).
1687 Birgit Katz, "Turtle That Breathes Through Its Genitals Lands on Endangered Reptiles List," *Smithsonian.com*, 13 Apr. 2018, https://www.smithsonianmag.com/smart-news/green-haired-turtle-breathes-through-its-genitals-lands-endangered-reptiles-list-180968788/ (accessed 14 Apr. 2018).
1688 Mason Inman, "World's Longest Migration Found—2x Longer Than Thought," *National Geographic*, 12 Jan. 2010, https://news.nationalgeographic.com/news/2010/01/100111-worlds-longest-migration-arctic-tern-bird/ (accessed 14 Oct. 2018).
1689 Patricia Edmonds, "One Part He, One Part She," *National Geographic* (Jan. 2017): p. 26.
1690 Jennifer Billock, Where to See the World's Biggest Spiders, *Smithsonian.com*, 31 Oct. 2016, https://www.smithsonianmag.com/travel/where-see-worlds-biggest-spiders-180960938/ (accessed 7 Jan. 2017); Tanya Lewis, "Goliath Encounter: Puppy-Sized Spider Surprises Scientist in Rainforest," *Livescience*, 17 Oct. 2014, http://www.livescience.com/48340-goliath-birdeater-surprises-scientist.html (accessed 7 Jan. 2017).

1691   David Quammen, "Forest Giant," *National Geographic* (Dec. 2012): pp. 34-7.
1692   Jason Daley, "This Humongous Fungus Is as Massive as Three Blue Whales," *Smithsonian.com*, 15 Oct. 2018, https://www.smithsonianmag.com/smart-news/mushroom-massive-three-blue-whales-180970549/ (accessed 16 Oct. 2018).
1693   Carl Zimmer, "Meet Nature's Mindsuckers," *National Geographic* (Nov. 2014): pp. 36-55. See also Jason Daley, "These Wasps Hijack Spiders' Brains And Make Them Do Their Bidding," *Smithsonian.com*, 29 Nov. 2018, https://www.smithsonianmag.com/smart-news/wasp-turns-social-spiders-zombies-build-their-cocoons-real-life-horror-story-180970919/ (accessed 22 Dec. 2018).
1694   Birgit Katz, "A Dracula Ant's Snapping Jaw Is the Fastest Known Appendage in the Animal Kingdom," *Smithsonian.com*, 18 Dec. 2018, https://www.smithsonianmag.com/smart-news/dracula-ants-snapping-jaws-are-fastest-known-appendage-any-animal-180971061/ (accessed 22 Dec. 2018).
1695   Paul Raffaele, *Among the Great Apes: Adventures on the Trail of Our Closest Relatives* (New York: HarperCollins, 2010), pp. 133, 72, 76. Further transfusions are not possible as antibodies prevent it.
1696   Wade, p. 90.
1697   Nathan Wolfe, "Small, Small World," *National Geographic* (Jan. 2013): pp. 138, 145.
1698   Russ Rymer, "Vanishing Voices," *National Geographic* (Jul. 2012): pp. 60, 92-3. Wade puts the number at closer to 6,000 (p. 202).
1699   Wade, pp. 3-5.
1700   David Dobbs, "A Cure in Sight," *National Geographic* (Sep. 2016): p. 40.
1701   Catherine Zuckerman, "Living It Up," *National Geographic* (Jun. 2011): p. 33.
1702   "FAQ: What is the Catalogue of Life?" *Catalogue of Life*, n.d., http://www.catalogueoflife.org (accessed 10 Oct. 2018). Over 1.8 million species are described as being in the Catalogue. See also Geoffrey Giller, "Are We Any Closer to Knowing How Many Species There Are on Earth?" *Scientific American*, 8 Apr. 2014, https://www.scientificamerican.com/article/are-we-any-closer-to-knowing-how-many-species-there-are-on-earth/ (accessed 7 Mar. 2018).
1703   Carroll, p. 133.
1704   John Updike, "Extreme Dinosaurs," *National Geographic* (Dec. 2007): pp. 38-9.

1705 George Olshevsky, "Dinosaur Genera List," *polychora.com*, 21 Nov. 2018 update, http://polychora.com/dinolist.html (accessed 28 Nov. 2018). Genera is the plural of genus.
1706 Nic Fleming, "Ten Giant Animals that Are Long Since Dead," *BBC Earth*, 7 May 2015, http://www.bbc.com/earth/story/20150507-ten-lost-giants-from-earths-past (accessed 2 Oct. 2016).
1707 John Pickrell, "Ancient Winged Terror Was One of the Largest Animals to Fly," *National Geographic*, 31 Oct. 2017, https://news.nationalgeographic.com/2017/10/new-pterosaur-found-mongolia-largest-fossils-science/ (accessed 7 Mar. 2018).
1708 Fleming, "Ten Giant Animals that Are Long Since Dead," http://www.bbc.com/earth/story/20150507-ten-lost-giants-from-earths-past.
1709 Ibid.
1710 "Argentinosaurus," BBC Earth, n.d., http://www.bbcearth.com/walking-with-dinosaurs/modal/argentinosaurus/, (accessed 20 Nov. 2016); Dougal Dixon, *Dinosaurs* (San Diego, CA: Thunder Bay Press, 2005), p. 97.
1711 *The 100 Most Influential Philosophers*, s.v. "Sextus Empiricus"; Sextus Empiricus, *Outlines of Pyrrhonism*, trans. R. G. Bury (Amherst, NY: Prometheus Books, 1990), 1.6-12, pp. 18-25.
1712 Empiricus, 1.12, pp. 23-4.
1713 As quoted in Barbara Stoler Miller, afterword to *The Bhagavad-Gita: Krishna's Counsel in Time of War*, p. 147.
1714 Gandhi, *The Bhagavad Gita According to Gandhi*, no. 18, p. 9.
1715 Ibid., no. 5:22, p. 34. Gandhi apparently described the essence of the spiritual life in one word: "Desirelessness" (Fischer, p. 15).
1716 A. C. Bhakivedanta Swami Prabhupada, *Bhagavad-gita As It Is* (Los Angeles: Bhaktivedanta Trust International, 1998?), 2.55. Avail. at: http://www.bhagavatgita.ru/files/Bhagavad-gita_As_It_Is.pdf (accessed 12 Jun. 2019).
1717 Ibid., 2.70.
1718 Gandhi, *The Bhagavad Gita According to Gandhi*, p. 16. Cf. Knott, p. 37.
1719 Ibid.: "In other words, if the means and the end are not identical, they are almost so." However, a well-ordered and healthy sense of desire (like curiosity, love, and responsibility) seem indispensable for human flourishing. See Karen Armstrong discusses the "poverty of desire" among modern Britain's youth (*The Spiral Staircase*, p. 175). Armstrong's memoir in fact seems to highlight her struggle to find desires that are life-affirming and non-destructive.

1720 St. Hesychios the Priest, *On Watchfulness and Holiness*, in *The Philokalia*, vol. 1, no. 155, pp. 189-90. Cf. St. Philotheos of Sinai, *Forty Texts on Watchfulness*, in *The Philokalia*, vol. 3, no. 38, p. 30.

1721 *Maranassati Sutta: Mindfulness of Death (1)*, trans. Thanissaro Bhikkhu, 1997, AN 6.19, www.accesstoinsight.org/tipitaka/an/an06/an06.019.than.html (accessed 15 Jun. 2017).

1722 "World Birth and Death Rates," *Ecology Global Network*, n.d., http://www.ecology.com/birth-death-rates/ (accessed 8 Feb. 2013). Based on 2011 statistics. See also David Bleja, *Breathing Earth*, 2015 http://www.breathingearth.net/ (accessed 16 Oct. 2018) which attempts a live display of births, deaths, and CO_2 emissions.

1723 For a short description, see "Memento Mori," in *Final Farewell: The Culture of Death and the Afterlife*, Museum of Art and Archaeology, University of Missouri, 2007, http://maa.missouri.edu/exhibitions/finalfarewell/mementointro.html (accessed 17 Oct. 2018); Dean Rolston, "Memento Mori: Notes on Buddhism and AIDS," *Tricycle: The Buddhist Review* (Fall 1991): https://tricycle.org/magazine/memento-mori-notes-buddhism-and-aids/ (accessed 17 Oct. 2018).

1724 As quoted in John S. Strong, ed., *The Experience of Buddhism: Sources and Interpretations*, 2nd ed. (Belmont, CA: Wadsworth, 2002), p. 120. Source noted as a translation from "Satipaṭṭhānasutta," in *The Majjhima-Nikāya*, ed. V. Treckner (London: Pali Text Society, 1888), 1:55-63.

1725 Not entirely though. The epilogue of the book (Eccl. 12:13-14) contains the more traditional religious notions that one should fear God, keep his laws, and prepare for a judgment based on deeds. Some hold that the epilogue is an interpolation as the rest of the book appears to regard God as a mystery (see *Mercer Dictionary of the Bible*, s.v. "Ecclesiastes, Book of"). *Mercer* also notes the reality that "in many respects the book reflects a form of early existentialism that is without parallel elsewhere in the Bible."

1726 Holder, ed., *Early Buddhist Discourses*, p. xx; cf. p. xvii.

1727 *The Dhammapada: A Collection of Verses*, trans. F. Max Muller, 2nd ed. (Oxford: The Clarendon Press, 1898), I.3-I.5, pp. 3-5. Avail. at: https://archive.org/details/in.ernet.dli.2015.223782/page/n61 (accessed 4 Jul. 2019). All quotations from *The Dhammapada* come from this source. Periods have been added for clarity. For a beautiful modern translation, see *The Dhammapada: The Path of Perfection*, trans. Juan Mascaró (New York: Penguin, 1973).

1728 Holder, ed., *Early Buddhist Discourses*, pp. xvii, 59. See also p. xx.

1729 Cf. ibid., p. xviii; Batchelor, *Confession of a Buddhist Atheist*, pp. 160-1; Batchelor, *Buddhism Without Beliefs*, p. 11; Chade-Meng Tan, *Joy on Demand: The Art of Discovering the Happiness Within* (New York: HarperCollins, 2016), p. 23.
1730 Buddhism generally ascribes to supernatural ideas like the karmic cycle and nirvana as integral doctrines. However, in addition to Holder, other scholars and secularists have found significant stimulation from a non-supernatural appropriation of many Buddhist ideas and practices. See Batchelor, *Buddhism Without Beliefs* and Sam Harris, "Killing the Buddha," *Shambhala Sun*, Mar. 2006, http://www.shambhalasun.com/index.php?option=com_content&task=view&id=2903&Itemid=244 (accessed 15 Nov. 2013).
1731 See Holder, ed., *Early Buddhist Discourses*, pp. xvii-xviii; *The Greater Discourse on the Foundations of Mindfulness* (*Mahāsatipaṭṭhāna Sutta*), pp. 56-7.
1732 Cf. Batchelor, *Buddhism Without Beliefs*, p. 237; Holder, pp. xiii-xx.
1733 For non-attachment to speculative views, see *Discourse to Vacchagotta on Fire* (*Aggivacchagotta Sutta*), in *Early Buddhist Discourses*, no. 4, pp. 119-20; and esp. the Parable of the Arrow in *The Shorter Discourse to Mālunkaputta* (*Cūla-mālunkya Sutta*), in ibid., p. 96. Zen master Thich Nhat Hanh calls non-attachment to views "the most important teaching of Buddhism" (Hanh, *Interbeing*, p. 8; cf. p. 76.) Traditional Buddhist ties to the doctrine of karma suggest that this teaching is inconsistently applied. I like Holder's perspective here: "Similarly, the sufferings of this life pose an urgent need for treatment, and thus these should be the focus of living the religious life, not the vague, unfathomable, and irrelevant issues of speculative metaphysics" (*Early Buddhist Discourses*, pp. 95-6).
1734 See "A Simple, Fast Way to Reduce Stress," *Mayo Clinic*, 17 Oct. 2017, http://www.mayoclinic.com/health/meditation/HQ01070 (accessed 19 Oct. 2018).
1735 *Discourse to the Kālāmas* (*Kālāma Sutta*), in *Early Buddhist Discourses*, no. 3, p. 21.
1736 Just as a raft becomes an impediment to travel after a river is crossed, so too a rigid or dogmatic fixation on even sound ideas can become destructive. See *Discourse on the Parable of the Water Snake* (*Alagaddūpama Sutta*), in *Early Buddhist Discourses*, no. 7, pp. 107-8. See also Holder's introductory remarks, pp. 101-2; Hanh, *Interbeing*, p. 23.
1737 Batchelor, *Buddhism Without Beliefs*, pp. 104-5.
1738 Amen-em-ope, "The Teachings of Amen-em-ope," in Matthews and Benjamin, ch. 1, no. iii, p. 190.

1739   See Matthews and Benjamin, pp.179-98.
1740   *The 100 Most Influential Philosophers*, s.v. "Plato."
1741   *Mercer Dictionary of the Bible*, s.v. "Proverbs, Book of"; New American Bible, p. 723 (footnote on Prov. 22:19f); *The New Oxford Annotated Bible*, p. 828 OT (footnote on Prov. 22:17-24:34); Matthews and Benjamin, p. 190.
1742   Amen-em-ope, "The Teachings of Amen-em-ope," in Matthews and Benjamin, ch. 30, p. 198.
1743   Ibid., ch. 18, no. xx, p. 196.
1744   Ibid., ch. 13, no. xvi, p. 196.
1745   As quoted in D.C. Lau, introduction to *The Analects*, by Confucius (London: Penguin, 1979), p. 53.
1746   Confucius, *The Analects*, trans. Lau, 7.2, p. 86.
1747   Parrinder, ed., *World Religions*, p. 319.
1748   Introduction to *The Sayings of Confucius* (USA: Barnes and Noble Books, 1994), p. viii.
1749   Van Voorst, p. 139. Of course, Buddhism, Taoism, and folk religions have had a tremendous impact as well.
1750   Parrinder, ed., *World Religions*, p. 142. *The Penguin Dictionary of Religions*, s.v. "Confucius" notes that Confucius "was not, as some have supposed, an agnostic or skeptic." Introduction to *The Sayings of Confucius*, p. vii: "He dealt with neither theology or metaphysics, but with moral and political conduct." Lau, introduction to *The Analects*, p. 12 notes: "Unlike religious teachers, Confucius could hold out no hope of rewards either in this world or in the next. As far as survival after death is concerned, Confucius' attitude can, at best, be described as agnostic." Cf. Parrinder, ed., *World Religions*, p. 320: "In short, service to god becomes meaningless if service to other people is neglected."
1751   Lau, p. 13.
1752   *The Penguin Dictionary of Religions*, s.v. "Confucius"; Van Voorst, p. 141. All sayings below are taken from

Confucius, *Confucian Analects*, in *Chinese Classics: Part I, Confucius*, trans. James Legge (New York: John B. Alden, 1883). Avail. in public domain at: https://archive.org/details/chineseclassics00confiala/page/n19 (accessed 24 Oct. 2018).

1753   Wikipedia, s.v. "Teresa of **Ávila**" https://en.wikipedia.org/wiki/Teresa_of_%C3%81vila (accessed 7 Jan. 2018). This states that the prayer is often attributed to her but is not found in her writings. See also Teresa of **Ávila**, "Christ Has No Body," *The Journey with Jesus: Poems and Prayers*, ed. Dan Clendenin, http://www.journeywithjesus.net/PoemsAndPrayers/Teresa_Of_Avila_Christ_Has_No_Body.shtml (accessed 7 Jan. 2018).

1754 Robert G. Ingersoll, *The Gods: An Honest God Is the Noblest Work of Man*, in *The Works of Robert G. Ingersoll*, vol. I, loc. 473.

1755 For a fascinating analysis of the array of problematic variables inherent in the process, see Chittaranjan Andrade and Rajiv Radhakrishnan, "Prayer and Healing: A Medical and Scientific Perspective on Randomized Controlled Trials," *Indian Journal of Psychiatry* 51.4 (Oct. 2009): pp. 247-253 https://www.ncbi.nlm.nih.gov/pmc/articles/PMC2802370/ (accessed 28 Oct. 2018). See also Wulff, pp. 175; 206ff; Benedict Carey, "Long-awaited Medical Study Questions the Power of Prayer," *The New York Times*, 31 Mar. 2006, https://www.nytimes.com/2006/03/31/health/31pray.html (accessed 28 Oct. 2018). Kevin S. Masters and Glen I. Spielmans, "Prayer and Health: Review, Meta-Analysis, and Research Agenda," *Journal of Behavioral Medicine* 30.4 (2007): pp. 329-38 notes that "no discernable effects can be found." Candy Gunther Brown, "How Should Prayer Be Studied?: Study Methods May Predetermine Study Results," *Psychology Today*, 1 Mar. 2012, https://www.psychologytoday.com/us/blog/testing-prayer/201203/how-should-prayer-be-studied (accessed 28 Oct. 2018) notes that intercessory prayer has "mixed results." Bremner et al. conclude that intercessory prayer has "predictably yielded very meager results" but that "prayer was found to have pervasive effects on the emotional experience, social behavior, and cognitive appraisals of praying individuals" (p. 835). There are presumably results that are medically impossible and would make the power of intercessory prayer undeniable (restoration of a rotten corpse, regrowth of head after decapitation, etc.). E.g., it appears that prayer for amputees fails every time (Brain, "Why Won't God Heal Amputees," http://whywontgodhealamputees.com/important.htm). See also Loftus, *Why I Became an Atheist*, pp. 200-13; Harold S. Kushner, *When Bad Things Happen to Good People* (New York, Avon Books, 1981), pp. 113-14.

1756 See citations in "The Prayer of St. Spurious" meditation.

1757 *Shadowlands*, dir. by Richard Attenborough (1993; video) http://www.imdb.com/title/tt0108101/quotes (accessed 20 Nov. 2012). Cf. Oswald Chambers, *My Utmost for His Highest*, 1934, http://utmost.org/the-purpose-of-prayer/ (accessed 23 Sep. 2014): "Prayer changes *me* and then I change things."

1758 For a brief description of the practice, see *The Catholic Encyclopedia*, s.v. "The Way of the Cross" http://www.newadvent.org/cathen/15569a.htm (accessed 2 Dec. 2013).

1759 E.g., St. Gregory of Sinai, *On Prayer: Seven Texts*, in *The Philokalia*, vol. 4, no. 6, p. 280 where the stomach is the "queen of the passions." Cf. St. Neilos the Ascetic, *Ascetic Discourse*, in *The Philokalia*, vol. 1, pp. 237-39.

1760 See Hanh, *Interbeing*, p. 71 who describes "certain TV programs, magazines, books, films, and conversations" as "toxins" to spiritual practice.

1761 See Leo Tolstoy quotation in Hanh, *The Miracle of Mindfulness*, p. 75.

1762 For sources on humor on cognitive states, see Attila Szabo, "The Acute Effects of Humor and Exercise on Mood and Anxiety," *Journal of Leisure Research*, 35.2 (2nd Q. 2003): pp. 152-62; Roberta H. Mawdsley, Elizabeth J. Verazin, Eric S. Bersch, et al., "The Relationship between Humor and Physical Therapist Students' Anxiety," *Journal of Physical Therapy Education*, 21.1 (Spring 2007): pp. 70-5; F.N. Gonot-Schoupinsky, G. Garip, "Laughter and Humour Interventions for Well-being in Older Adults: A Systematic Review and Intervention Classification," *Complementary Therapies in Medicine* 38 (2018): pp. 85-91; William E. Kelly, "An Investigation of Worry and Sense of Humor," *The Journal of Psychology*, 136.6 (Nov. 2002): pp. 657-66.

1763 Henri Nouwen, *The Wounded Healer*, in *Ministry and Spirituality* (New York: Continuum, 1996), p. 137.

1764 "Anima Foci" here would mean "Soul of Focus." "Focus" in Latin actually means altar or hearth; I use principally the English meaning here.

1765 Pascal, no. 136, p. 37.

1766 Kurt Vonnegut, *Slaughterhouse-Five* (New York: RosettaBooks, 2010), loc. 234, p. 23, Kindle.

1767 *The Catholic Encyclopedia*, s.v. "Anima Christi" http://www.newadvent.org/cathen/01515a.htm (accessed 29 Jul. 2013). See also "The Anima Christi," *EWTN*, n.d., https://www.ewtn.com/devotionals/prayers/anima2.htm (accessed 26 Dec. 2016).

1768 *Seven Taoist Masters*, p. 111.

1769 Van Over, ed., *Taoist Tales*, p. 160.

1770 Parrinder, ed., *World Religions*, p. 328.

1771 Eva Wong, introduction to *Seven Taoist Masters*, pp. xvi-xxiii.

1772 *Seven Taoist Masters*, p. 45. Cf. Wong, p. xviii in same book.

1773 I think *Seven Taoist Masters* displays too much severity on especially sexual issues at times—an expression of the frequent religious error of believing sexuality itself to be immoral. In my view, sexuality is just another area of human behavior that should be guided by general ethical principles—like compassion, justice, honesty, prudence, and respectfulness.

1774 Ibid., p. xx.

1775 Cf. Van Over, ed., *The Divine Panorama*, in *Taoist Tales*, pp. 122, 133. Those who disbelieve "the doctrine of Cause and Effect" are deemed to be destined for "the everlasting tortures of hell."
1776 *Seven Taoist Masters*, pp. 5, 15, 17, 23, 25, 108, 121, 166.
1777 Ibid., p. 2.
1778 Ibid., pp. 48-9.
1779 Ibid., p. 54.
1780 As quoted in Herbert A. Giles, *A History of Chinese Literature* (New York: D. Appleton and Co., 1901), p. 233. Avail. at: https://archive.org/details/cu31924086054776/page/n247 (accessed 25 Oct. 2018). See also Van Over, ed., *Taoist Tales*, pp. 241-2.
1781 Batchelor, *Buddhism Without Beliefs*, p. 58.
1782 Achaan Chah, *A Still Forest Pool: The Insight Meditation of Achaan Chah*, ed. Jack Kornfield and Paul Breiter (Wheaton, IL: The Theosophical Publishing House, 1985), p. 157.
1783 Chah, p. 72. See also pp. 5, 115, 119.
1784 Hanh, *Interbeing*, pp. 30-1.
1785 Pope Pius IX, *Dives in Misercordia Deus*, The Salesian Center for Faith and Culture: Papal Documents about Salesian Spirituality, trans. Daniel G. Gambet, orig. pub. 16 Nov. 1877, http://www.desales.edu/_fileserver/salesian/PDF/PiusIX-Dives.pdf (accessed 2 Feb 2018).
1786 Jean Pierre Camus, *The Spirit of S. Francis de Sales: Bishop and Prince of Geneva* (London: Rivingtons, 1880), p. 3. Avail. at https://archive.org/details/spiritsfrancisd00camugoog/page/n26.
1787 As quoted in Glen G. Scorgie, *A Little Guide to Christian Spirituality: Three Dimensions of Life with God* (Grand Rapids, MI: Zondervan, 2007), p. 40. See also *The New International Dictionary of the Christian Church*, s.v. "Francis of Sales." There is unfortunately some apparent exception to his pacifist tendencies pertaining to the civil punishment for heresy (O. Chadwick, p. 398).
1788 As quoted in Thomas F. Dailey, "The 'Real Story' on St. Francis de Sales," *Theological Review of the Episcopal Academy*, Dec. 2005, http://ws-prod-web01.desales.edu/docs/default-source/salesian/daileyrealstory.pdf?sfvrsn=0 (accessed 17 Oct. 2018).
1789 All quotations below are taken from St. Francis de Sales, *Introduction to the Devout Life* (London: Longmans, Green, and Co., 1891). Trans. not given. Avail. in public domain at: https://archive.org/details/IntroductionToTheDevoutLife/page/n7 (accessed 24 Oct. 2018). See pp. 95, 112, 115-116, 118-119, 165, 222, 177-8.

1790 Cf. Edward M. Egan, preface to *Introduction to the Devout Life*, by Francis de Sales (New York: Random House, 2002), p. xviii.

1791 St. Teresa of Ávila is often said to have remarked: "Lord, save us from gloomy saints." Michael Sean Winters, "Save Us from Gloomy Saints," *National Catholic Reporter*, 16 Oct. 2013, https://www.ncronline.org/blogs/distinctly-catholic/save-us-gloomy-saints (accessed 30 Nov. 2018).

1792 G.E.H. Palmer, Philip Sherrard, Kallistos Ware, ed. and trans., introduction to *The Philokalia: The Complete Text*, vol. 1, pp. 13-14.

1793 Ware, p. 100; G.E.H. Palmer, Philip Sherrard, Kallistos Ware, introduction to *The Philokalia*, vol. 1, pp. 11ff.

1794 *The Way of the Pilgrim*, p. 19.

1795 Anthony M. Coniaris, *Introducing the Orthodox Church: Its Faith and Life*, 13th printing (Minneapolis, MN: Light and Life Publishing Co., 1982), p. 67; G.E.H. Palmer, et al., introduction to *The Philokalia*, vol. 1, pp. 15, 363. In vol. 4 of *The Philokalia*, the editors note that "Modern Western writers have compared the psychosomatic technique with certain methods used in Yoga and Sufism, but the parallels should not be exaggerated" (p. 64). See also Ware, p. 100; *The Way of a Pilgrim and The Pilgrim Continues His Way*, trans. Helev Bacovcin, 1992 ed. (New York: Image/Doubleday, 1978), p. 54.

1796 For a brief explanation see "What is a Prayer Rope," *Orthodox Prayer*, n.d., http://www.orthodoxprayer.org/Prayer%20Rope.html, (accessed 27 Mar. 2015).

1797 As quoted in *The Way of the Pilgrim*, p. 19.

1798 See Sam Harris, "How to Meditate," *Samharris.org*, 10 May 2011, http://www.samharris.org/blog/item/how-to-meditate (accessed 15 Nov. 2013).

1799 See Kurzbahn, *Why Everyone (Else) Is a Hypocrite*.

1800 This generally involves the concept of neuroplasticity. See Hagerty, "Prayer May Reshape Your Brain … And Your Reality," https://www.npr.org/templates/story/story.php?storyId=104310443. For an analogous notion pertaining to meditation, see Sara W. Lazar et al., "Meditation Experience Is Associated with Increased Cortical Thickness," *NeuroReport* 16.17 (2005): pp. 1893-7 https://www.ncbi.nlm.nih.gov/pmc/articles/PMC1361002/ (accessed 1 Nov. 2018). For a study involving the positive effects on mood due to praying the Jesus Prayer, see Marta Rubinart, Albert Fornieles, and Joan Deus, "The Psychological Impact of the Jesus Prayer among Non-Conventional Catholics," *Pastoral Psychology* 66.4 (2017): pp.487-504. For general information on the positive effects of non-intercessory prayer, see citations in "The Prayer of St. Spurious"

	meditation. For prayer as building self-discipline, see Shermer, *The Moral Arc*, p. 175.
1801	See *The Way of a Pilgrim*, p. 180.
1802	Ibid., p. 179. Cf. Dan Harris, "The Long Journey to Becoming '10% Happier,'" ABC News, YouTube video 13:23, posted 12 Mar. 2014, https://www.youtube.com/watch?v=4sXBEfIXUno (accessed 26 Feb. 2016).
1803	Paul Raffaele, "Sleeping with Cannibals," Smithsonian.com, Sep. 2006, https://www.smithsonianmag.com/travel/sleeping-with-cannibals-128958913/ (accessed 30 Nov. 2018).
1804	*A Discourse on Abba Philimon*, in *The Philokalia*, vol. 2, p. 345. (This is an anonymous work.)
1805	St. Peter of Damaskos, *A Treasury of Divine Knowledge*, in *The Philokalia*, vol. 3, p. 137.
1806	St. Hesychios the Priest, *On Watchfulness and Holiness*, in *The Philokalia*, vol. 1, no. 5, p. 163.
1807	Evagrios the Solitary, *Outline Teaching on Asceticism and Stillness in the Solitary Life*, in *The Philokalia*, vol. 1, p. p. 33.
1808	St. Symeon the New Theologian, *The Three Methods of Prayer*, in *The Philokalia*, vol. 4, p. 72.
1809	St. Peter of Damaskos, *A Treasury of Divine Knowledge*, in The *Philokalia*, vol. 3, p. 162.
1810	St. Theodoros the Ascetic, *A Century of Spiritual Texts*, in *The Philokalia*, vol. 2, no. 27, p. 19.
1811	St. Mark the Ascetic, *On Those Who Think They Are Made Righteous by Works*, in *The Philokalia*, vol. 1, no. 107, p. 134.
1812	Ilias the Presbyter, *A Gnomic Anthology* (part 1), in *The Philokalia*, vol. 3, nos. 40 and 46, pp. 38-9.
1813	St. Peter of Damaskos, *A Treasury of Divine Knowledge*, in *The Philokalia*, vol. 3, p. 162.
1814	Jeremiah Burroughs, *The Rare Jewel of Christian Contentment* (Pensacola, FL: Chapel Library, 2010), p. 7 http://www.chapellibrary.org/files/1113/7658/4062/rjoc.pdf (accessed 2 Jan. 2014).
1815	Johnson Oatman, "Count Your Blessings," *Hymnary.org*, 1897, http://www.hymnary.org/text/when_upon_lifes_billows_you_are_tempest (accessed 20 Feb. 2016).
1816	Harris, *Waking Up*, p. 96.
1817	Epictetus, *The Enchiridion*, in *The Works of Epictetus*, trans. Thomas Wentworth Higginson (Boston: Little, Brown, and Co., 1866), no. 5, p. 377. Avail. in public domain at: https://archive.org/details/cu31924029001606/page/376 (accessed 19 Oct. 2018).

1818 Harris, *Waking Up*, p. 96. See also Robert A. Emmons and Michael E. McCullough, "Counting Blessings Versus Burdens: An Experimental Investigation of Gratitude and Subjective Well-Being in Daily Life," *Journal of Personality and Social Psychology* 84.2 (2003): pp. 377-89: "Results suggest that a conscious focus on blessings may have emotional and interpersonal benefits"—although the article itself concedes that "Contemporary research on gratitude is still in a fledgling state" (p. 377). Harris cites this article. See also Robert Emmons, "Why Gratitude is Good," *Greater Good Magazine*, 16 Nov. 2010, https://greatergood.berkeley.edu/article/item/why_gratitude_is_good (accessed 19 Oct. 2018).

1819 See *NIV Study Bible*, p. 1801; *The Concise Oxford Dictionary of the Christian Church*, s.v. "Philippians, Epistle to the"; *Mercer Dictionary of the Bible*, s.v. Philipppians, Letter to the." The NAB notes that some scholars see Philippians as a compilation of three of Paul's letters (p. 301).

1820 Herodotus, 7.152, p. 457. Cf. Kushner, p. 112: "If we knew the facts, we would very rarely find someone whose life was to be envied."

1821 As quoted in Matt, p. 7. From *Guide to the Perplexed*, 1:58-59. This is an example of "negative" theology from the Jewish tradition.

1822 *The Cloud of Unknowing*, in *The Cloud of Unknowing and Other Works*, trans. Clifton Walters (New York: Penguin Books, 1961), no. 6, p. 67.

1823 Ibid., no. 4, p. 66; *The Concise Oxford Dictionary of the Christian Church*, s.v. "Cloud of Unknowing, The."

1824 As quoted in Ware, p. 63. For more on negative or apophatic theology, see Ware, pp. 63-4; John of Damascus, *An Exposition of the Orthodox Faith*, 1.4 http://www.newadvent.org/fathers/3304.htm: "God then is infinite and incomprehensible and all that is comprehensible about Him is His infinity and incomprehensibility." Cf. the Sikh Scriptures which say: "If God can be described by writing, then describe Him; but such description is impossible" (Van Voorst, p. 127- from the *Japji* of the *Adi Granth*).

1825 *The Cloud of Unknowing*, no. 13, p. 78.

1826 Ibid., no. 12, p. 77.

1827 Ibid., no. 31, pp. 97-8.

1828 Steven C. Hayes with Spencer Smith, *Get Out of Your Mind and into Your Life: The New Acceptance and Commitment Therapy* (Oakland, CA: New Harbinger Publications, 2005), p. 3. On p. 7: "The 'acceptance' in Acceptance and Commitment Therapy is based on the notion that, as a rule, trying to get rid of your pain only amplifies it, entangles you further in it, and transforms it into something traumatic."

1829 *The Cloud of Unknowing*, no. 32, p. 98. Not surprisingly, both "dodges" have the Catholic God interwoven into the approach. As noted, it is my

contention that both techniques have validity regardless of one's religious beliefs.
1830   Ibid., no. 32, p. 98.
1831   Ibid., no. 12, p. 77.
1832   Huxley, "Naturalism and Supernaturalism," in *Agnosticism and Christianity and Other Essays*, p. 118. Cf. Shermer, *The Moral Arc*, pp. 2-7, etc.—which seems to give some credence to the idea that Huxley was in fact on the right track here.
1833   Harris, *Waking Up*, pp. 8, 122, etc. For general comments on the efficacy of different types of meditation, see Charles G. Morris, *Psychology: An Introduction* (Englewood Cliffs, NJ: Prentice Hall, 1988), pp. 148-9.
1834   Candace L. Hogan, Jutta Matta, Laura L. Carstensen, "Exercise Holds Immediate Benefits for Affect and Cognition in Younger and Older Adults," *Psychology and Aging* 28.2 (2013): pp. 587-94 http://psycnet.apa.org/record/2013-21685-007 (accessed 28 Oct. 2018).
1835   See, for instance, Francis de Sales, *Introduction to the Devout Life*, p. 56 https://archive.org/details/IntroductionToTheDevoutLife/page/n91.
1836   For meditation, see Wulff, pp. 176-88. Corey notes that "spirituality is a significant force" for many which can affect the efficacy of counseling in general terms (pp. 451-3). Charles R. Carlson, Panayiota E. Bacaseta, Dexter A. Simanton, "A Controlled Evaluation of Devotional Meditation and Progressive Muscle Relaxation," *Journal of Psychology and Theology* 16.4 (1988): pp. 362-368 found that "Devotional Meditation" (prayer and meditation on Scripture readings) could have effects similar and perhaps even greater than Progressive Muscle Relaxation (whose efficacy was also affirmed). See further below.
1837   Matthew MacKinnon, "The Science of Slow Deep Breathing," *Psychology Today*, 7 Feb. 2016, https://www.psychologytoday.com/us/blog/neuraptitude/201602/the-science-slow-deep-breathing (accessed 1 Nov. 2018) notes that there is "robust scientific evidence for the benefits of mindful breathing." See also Alice Boyes, "Breathing Techniques for Anxiety: Ways to Relieve Anxiety Using Breathing Exercises," *Psychology Today*, 12 Jul. 2016, https://www.psychologytoday.com/us/blog/in-practice/201607/breathing-techniques-anxiety (accessed 1 Nov. 2018); Corey, p. 291; Valentina Perciavalle et al., "The Role of Deep Breathing on Stress," *Neurological Sciences* 38.3 (2017): pp. 451-8. Ravinder Jerath, Molly W. Crawford, Vernon A. Barnes, Kyler Harden, "Self-Regulation of Breathing as a Primary Treatment for Anxiety," *Applied Psychophysiology and Biofeedback* 40.2 (Jun. 2015): pp. 107-115 notes: "Meditation and breathing techniques reduce stress, anxiety, depression, and other negative emotional states.

... Breathing and meditation techniques are simple, easy, and cost-effective yet they are not widely used as treatments." For an interesting survey of the use of breath control in traditional spiritual practices (including rhythmic breathing, hyperventilation, and holding the breath), see Wulff, pp. 77-9.

1838   For information, see "How to Use Paced Breathing," 3 Apr. 2015, pacedbreathing.blogspot.com (accessed 2 Nov. 2018). I have used this app for a few years now.

1839   Hamilton Cline, eXHALeR breathing application, 2016, http://www.xhalr.com/about.php (accessed 2 Dec. 2018). For the application itself, see http://www.xhalr.com/.

1840   Lori Granger, "Sitting with Breath—A Guided Meditation with Lori Granger, LMFT," Lori Granger, LMFT, YouTube video 15:02, posted 12 Dec. 2010, https://www.youtube.com/watch?v=qBbf8SvM2Bw (accessed 2 Nov. 2018). A search of "deep breathing" on YouTube yields many similar options.

1841   For more information specifically on Progressive Muscle Relaxation, see Murali Sundram, Maznah Dahlui, and Karuthan Chinna, "Effectiveness of Progressive Muscle Relaxation Therapy as a Worksite Health Promotion Program in the Automobile Assembly Line," *Industrial Health*, 54.3 (May 2016): pp. 204-14, https://www.ncbi.nlm.nih.gov/pmc/articles/PMC4939865/ (accessed 25 Mar. 2018). For a short general article on relaxation techniques, see "Types of Relaxation Techniques," *Mayo Clinic*, 19 Apr. 2017, https://www.mayoclinic.org/healthy-lifestyle/stress-management/in-depth/relaxation-technique/art-20045368?pg=2 (accessed 25 Mar. 2018). No author given. For a more in-depth review, see "Progressive Muscle Relaxation (PMR): A Positive Psychology Guide," *Positive Psychology Program*, 26 Jan. 2018, https://positivepsychologyprogram.com/progressive-muscle-relaxation-pmr/ (accessed 25 Mar. 2018). This article also contains links to on-line video samples of Progressive Muscle Relaxation. See also Corey, pp. 290-1.

1842   Beth Salsedo, *Progressive Muscle Relaxation: 20 Minutes to Total Relaxation*, Beth Salsedo, digital, 2007.

1843   Mark Connelly, "Progressive Muscle Relaxation," Children's Percy Hospital and Bazillion Pictures, YouTube video 14:55, posted 23 Jul. 2015, https://www.youtube.com/watch?v=ihO02wUzgkc (accessed 25 Mar. 2018).

1844   Dr. Jaan Reitav, "Progressive Muscle Relaxation," Cardiac Rehab Alumni Channel, YouTube video 24:12, posted 25 Jun. 2013, https://www.youtube.com/watch?v=f7I2Upk5jqI (accessed 4 Nov. 2018).

1845 Beth Freschi, A *Time for Relaxation: Guided Relaxation, Techniques for Wellness*, vol. 1, no label, CD, 2010.
1846 See Corey, pp. 290-1; Wulff, pp. 77-8; 177-8; Sam Harris, *Waking Up*, pp. 8, 122, etc.; Mayo Clinic Staff, "Meditation: A Simple, Fast Way to Reduce Stress," *Mayo Clinic*, n.d., https://www.mayoclinic.org/tests-procedures/meditation/in-depth/meditation/art-20045858 (accessed 4 Nov. 2018); Daphne Davis and Jeffrey Hayes, "What Are the Benefits of Mindfulness?," *American Psychological Association*, 43.7 (Jul./Aug. 2012) http://www.apa.org/monitor/2012/07-08/ce-corner.aspx (accessed 27 Apr. 2018): "Many studies show that practicing mindfulness reduces stress. In 2010, Hoffman et al. conducted a meta-analysis of 39 studies that explored the use of mindfulness-based stress reduction and mindfulness-based cognitive therapy. The researchers concluded that mindfulness-based therapy may be useful in altering affective and cognitive processes that underlie multiple clinical issues." Some have become concerned, however, that the effects have been exaggerated. See Bret Stetka, "Where's the Proof That Mindfulness Meditation Works?," *Scientific American*, 11 Oct. 2017, https://www.scientificamerican.com/article/wheres-the-proof-that-mindfulness-meditation-works1/ (accessed 27 Apr. 2018). See also Dilwar Hussain and Braj Bjushan, "Psychology Meditation and Health: Present Status and Future Directions, *International Journal of Psychology and Psychological Therapy* 10.3 (2010): pp. 447 which points to the lack of quality studies in meditation generally and the potential for bias. My overall impression is that the benefits are likely real but that one should be cognizant of potential exaggeration.
1847 For information, see http://awaremeditationapp.com/ (accessed 4 Nov. 2018).
1848 Dan Harris, "The Long Journey to Becoming '10% Happier,'" https://www.youtube.com/watch?v=4sXBEfIXUno.
1849 Dan Harris and Joseph Goldstein, "The Basics (retired longer version)," *10% Happier: Meditation for Fidgety Skeptics*, https://api.changecollective.com/courses/10%25-happier
(accessed 1 Feb. 2017). Pub. date not given. For further explanation, see www.10percenthappier.com/mindfulness-meditation-the-basics.
1850 Sam Harris, "The Mirror of Mindfulness: Two Guided Meditations," *Samharris.org*, 26 Sep. 2013, http://www.samharris.org/blog/item/mindfulness-meditation (accessed 10 Oct. 2013).
1851 For an interesting review of the psychological literature, see Carolyn J. Murrock and Abir K. Bekhet, "Concept Analysis: Music Therapy," *Research and Theory for Nursing Practice: An International Journal* 30.1

(2016); pp. 44-59. There are claims that music can help alleviate the severity of pain as well. See Lucanne Magill, "The Use of Music Therapy to Address the Suffering in Advanced Cancer Pain," *Journal of Palliative Care* 17.3 (Fall 2001): pp. 167-72. See also Meilan Solly, "British Doctors May Soon Prescribe Art, Music, Dance, Singing Lessons," *Smithsonian. com*, 8 Nov. 2018, https://www.smithsonianmag.com/smart-news/british-doctors-may-soon-prescribe-art-music-dance-singing-lessons-180970750/ (accessed 28 Nov. 2018).

1852 "Chant: A Healing Art?," *The Washington Times*, 25 Jun. 2008, https://www.washingtontimes.com/news/2008/jun/25/chant-a-healing-art/ (accessed 27 Apr. 2018). Author not given. "Gregorian Chanting 'Can Reduce Blood Pressure and Stress'," *Daily Mail*, 2 May 2008, http://www.dailymail.co.uk/sciencetech/article-563533/Gregorian-chanting-reduce-blood-pressure-stress.html (accessed 27 Apr. 2018). Chanting has been used a means to alter consciousness. See Carol R. Ember and Christina Carolus, "Altered States of Consciousness," *Human Relations Area Files at Yale University*, 10 Jan. 2017, http://hraf.yale.edu/ehc/summaries/altered-states-of-consciousness (accessed 27 Apr. 2018). See also Alpna Agarwal and Anshu Agarwal, "Impact of Mantra Chanting on Stress Coping," *Indian Journal of Positive Psychology* 4.1 (2013): pp. 96-8; David B. Wolf and Neil Abell, "Examining the Effects of Meditation Techniques on Psychosocial Functioning," *Research on Social Work Practice* 13.1 (Jan. 2003): pp. 27-42. Chanting is an interesting topic and seems to support the general notion that traditional spiritual practices can have psychological effects. I am skeptical, however, of when researchers claim that these practices have supernatural benefits or are somehow supportive of traditional religious metaphysics. While noting some marked claimed benefits of Transcendental Meditation (TM), Wulff also expresses concerns about the methodology of certain studies on chanting and the possible influence of placebo effects (pp. 184-6). This area of research is intriguing but appears underdeveloped.

1853 *33 Bowls: Tibetan Singing Bowls*, 33 Bowls, digital, 2009. For information see http://33bowls.com/.

1854 *The 99 Most Essential Gregorian Chants*, performed by various artists, X5 Music Group, digital, 2011.

1855 Surinder Dhupar, ed., "Wahe Guru WaheGuru simran - Bhai Rai Singh Dehradun wale, India," YouTube video 10:12, posted 28 Dec. 2018, https://www.youtube.com/watch?v=VOVbRVImbhI&list=PL83E34D639EF-31DE4&index=4 (accessed 30 Dec. 2017).

1856　Sheikh Abdur Rahman Al Ossi, "Best Quran Recitation in the World 2017," AWAZ, YouTube video 22:27, posted 18 Feb. 2017, https://www.youtube.com/watch?v=B01Cwq_cpqs (accessed 30 Dec. 2017). "The Qur'an" actually means "The Recitation." There are numerous examples of Qur'anic recitations on YouTube.

1857　*Divine Liturgy of St. John Chrysostom*, conducted by Lycourgos Angelopolous, performed by The Greek Byzantine Choir, Opus 111, CD, 1994. See esp. track 2, Ps. 102 (103).

1858　Kristen Weir, "The Exercise Effect," *American Psychological Association*, 42.1 (Dec. 2011): p. 48 (print version) https://www.apa.org/monitor/2011//12/exercise.aspx (accessed 28 Oct. 2018); Christopher Bergland, "25 Studies Confirm: Exercise Prevents Depression," *Psychology Today*, 29 Oct. 2013 https://www.psychologytoday.com/us/blog/the-athletes-way/201310/25-studies-confirm-exercise-prevents-depression (accessed 28 Oct. 2018); "Depression and Anxiety: Exercise Eases Symptoms," *Mayo Clinic*, 27 Sep. 2017, http://www.mayoclinic.org/diseases-conditions/depression/in-depth/depression-and-exercise/art-20046495 (accessed 25 Jun. 2017). No author given.

1859　Hogan et al., "Exercise Holds Immediate Benefits for Affect and Cognition in Younger and Older Adults," http://psycnet.apa.org/record/2013-21685-007. In addition to implications of this particular study, authors note that "A growing literature demonstrates that exercise benefits both affective experience and cognitive performance." See also Julia C. Basso and Wendy A. Suzuki, "The Effects of Acute Exercise on Mood, Cognition, Neurophysiology, and Neurochemical Pathways: A Review," *Brain Plasticity* 2.2 (2017): pp. 127-52 https://www.ncbi.nlm.nih.gov/pmc/articles/PMC5928534/ (accessed 30 Oct. 2018); Yue Liao, Eleanor T. Shonkoff, Genevieve F. Dunton, "The Acute Relationships between Affect, Physical Feeling States, and Physical Activity in Daily Life: A Review of Current Evidence," *Frontiers in Psychology* 6.1975 (Dec. 2015): pp. 1-7 http://citeseerx.ist.psu.edu/viewdoc/download?doi=10.1.1.791.5099&rep=rep1&type=pdf (accessed 30 Oct. 2018).

1860　See Mary and Richard Maddux, *Meditation Oasis*, www.meditationoasis.com (accessed 19 Oct. 2018) for a bunch of resources including apps, written meditations, and a meditation blog.

1861　While I personally have little experience with yoga and tai chi, psychological literature suggests that there may be benefits to the practices. For yoga, see Wulff, pp. 178-9, 187-8; "Yoga: In Depth," *U.S. Dept. of Health and Human Services*, National Institutes of Health, National Center for Complementary and Integrative Health, Jun. 2013, https://nccih.nih.gov/

health/yoga/introduction.htm (accessed 30 Dec. 2017); Nicole Butterfield, Tim Schulz, Philippa Rasmussen, and Michael Proeve, "Yoga and Mindfulness for Anxiety and Depression and the Role of Mental Health Professionals: A Review," *The Journal of Mental Health Training, Education, and Practice* 12.1 (2017); pp. 44-54; Tanya Sharma, Paul Kumari, and Vikas Kumar, "Yoga and Mental Health: A Review," *Journal of the Indian Academy of Applied Psychology* 43.1 (Jan. 2017): pp. 128-133; Holger Cramer, Romy Lauche, Jost Langhorst, Gustav Dobos, "Is One Yoga Style Better Than Another? A Systematic Review of Associations of Yoga Style and Conclusions in Randomized Yoga Trials, *Complementary Therapies in Medicine* 25 (2016): pp. 178-87. While yoga seems to yield positive psychological benefits, there are many types of yoga and scientific study appears to be in its early stages. This web resource mentions both tai chi and yoga: Mayo Clinic Staff, "Meditation: A Simple, Fast Way to Reduce Stress," https://www.mayoclinic.org/tests-procedures/meditation/in-depth/meditation/art-20045858. For more on tai chi, see "The Health Benefits of Tai Chi," Harvard Health Publishing, Harvard Medical School, May 2009 (updated 4 Dec. 2015), https://www.health.harvard.edu/staying-healthy/the-health-benefits-of-tai-chi (accessed 30 Dec. 2017); "Tai Chi and Qi Gong: In Depth," U.S. Dept. of Health and Human Services, National Institutes of Health, National Center for Complementary and Integrative Health, Oct. 2016, https://nccih.nih.gov/health/taichi/introduction.htm (accessed 30 Dec. 2017). I have also tried David-Dorian Ross, *Tai Chi Fitness Workouts*, The Great Courses/YMAA Publication Center, DVD, 2018.

1862   Anastasia Ejova, "Awe: A Direct Pathway from Extravagant Displays to Prosociality," *Behavioral and Brain Sciences* 39 (2016): p. 28. See Van Cappellen et al., pp. 487-9 (etc.) for the association of awe with well-being (p. 500). See also Kirk J. Schneider, "Rediscovering Awe: A New Front in Humanistic Psychology, Psychotherapy, and Society" *Canadian Journal of Counselling* 42.1 (Jan. 2008): pp. 67-74 which attempts to chart a healthy path between "dogmatic fundamentalism and postmodern nihilism" by focusing on "a rediscovery of our native capacity for *awe*." For a further exploration of the topic, see Dacher Keltner and Jonathan Haidt, "Approaching Awe, a Moral, Spiritual, and Aesthetic Emotion, *Cognition and Emotion* 17.2 (2003): pp. 297–314. For a popular review of the benefits and potential pitfalls of awe, see Michelle Nijhuis, "Awe Isn't Necessarily Good for You," *The Atlantic*, 22 Sep. 2016, https://www.theatlantic.com/health/archive/2016/09/is-awe-really-good-for-you/501086/ (accessed 4 Nov. 2018).

1863 *Cosmos: A Spacetime Odyssey*, exec. prod. Seth MacFarlane, Ann Druyan, et al. (2014; Fox Broadcasting Company and National Geographic Channel, video). Hosted by Neil DeGrasse Tyson.
1864 Morn1415, "Star Comparison 2," YouTube video 6:50, posted 1 Aug. 2016, https://www.youtube.com/watch?v=GoW8Tf7hTGA (accessed 25 Aug. 2018).
1865 Carykh, "The Scale of the Universe 2," YouTube 3:23, posted 1 Feb. 2012, https://www.youtube.com/watch?v=uaGEjrADGPA (accessed 4 Nov. 2018).
1866 Richard J. Foster, *Celebration of Discipline: The Path to Spiritual Growth*, rev. ed (San Francisco: HarperSanFrancisco, 1988), p. 186.
1867 Robert H. King, *Thomas Merton and Thich Nhat Hanh: Engaged Spirituality in an Age of Globalization* (New York: Continuum, 2003), p. 119.
1868 As quoted in *The 100 Most Influential Philosophers*, s.v. "Hypatia." Hypatia, a Neoplatonist philosopher, is well known for having been killed by a Christian mob. See Sarah Zielinski, "Hypatia, Ancient Alexandria's Great Female Scholar," *Smithsonian.com*, 14 Mar. 2010, https://www.smithsonianmag.com/history/hypatia-ancient-alexandrias-great-female-scholar-10942888/ (accessed 5 Dec. 2018).
1869 Although surely more apparent at some moments than others …
1870 As quoted in Foster, p. 2.
1871 Batchelor, *Confession of a Buddhist Atheist*, p. 128.
1872 Bernard of Clairvaux, *On Consideration* in *Bernard of Clairvaux: Selected Works*, p. 172. Cf. Merton, p. 423.

Select Bibliography

The 100 Most Influential Philosophers. Edited by Encyclopedia Britannica. New York: Fall River Press, 2011.

131 Christians Everyone Should Know. Nashville, TN: Broadman and Holman, 2000.

Abelard, Peter. *Yes and No: The Complete Translation of Peter Abelard's Sic Et Non*, 2nd ed. Translated by Priscilla Throop. Charlotte, VT: Medieval MS, 2008.

Agarwal, Alpna and Anshu Agarwal. "Impact of Mantra Chanting on Stress Coping." *Indian Journal of Positive Psychology* 4.1 (2013): pp. 96-98.

"Agnostic AA Twelve Steps." AA Agnostics of the San Francisco Bay Area, n.d., http://www.aaagnostics.org/agnostic12steps.html (accessed 16 Feb. 2013).

Aland, Barbara, Kurt Aland, et al., eds. *Nestle-Aland Novum Testamentum Graece*, 27th ed. Stuttgart, Germany: Deutsche Bibelgesellschaft, 1993.

Aland, Kurt, ed. *Synopsis of the Four Gospels*. Rev. English ed. New York?: United Bible Societies, 1985.

Al-Bukhari, Muhammad. *Sahih al-Bukhari*. Sunnah.com. Translated by M. Muhsin Khan. N.d. https://sunnah.com/bukhari.

Alexander, Paul J. "Religious Persecution and Resistance in the Byzantine Empire of the Eighth and Ninth Centuries: Methods and Justifications." *Speculum* 52:2 (Apr. 1977): p. 238-64.

Al-Ghazali. *Path to Sufism, His Deliverance from Error (Al-Munqidh min al-Dalal)*, 3rd ed. Translated by R.J. McCarthy. Louisville, KY: Fons Vitae, 2006.

Allison, Jay and Dan Gediman, eds. *This I Believe*. New York: Henry Holt and Co., 2006.

Allitt, Patrick. *Catholic Converts: British and American Intellectuals Return to Rome*. Ithaca, NY: Cornell Univ. Press, 1997.

Alston, William P., ed. *Religious Belief and Philosophical Thought*. New York: Harcourt, Brace, and World, 1963.

Andrade, Chittaranjan and Rajiv Radhakrishnan. "Prayer and Healing: A Medical and Scientific Perspective on Randomized Controlled Trials." *Indian Journal of Psychiatry* 51.4 (Oct. 2009): pp. 247-253, https://www.ncbi.nlm.nih.gov/pmc/articles/PMC2802370/ (accessed 28 Oct. 2018).

"The Anima Christi." *EWTN*, n.d., https://www.ewtn.com/devotionals/prayers/anima2.htm (accessed 26 Dec. 2016).

Aquinas, Thomas. *The Catechetical Instructions of Thomas Aquinas*. Translated by J. Collins. New York: Joseph F. Wagner, 1939.

———. *Summa Theologica*, 2nd ed. Translated by Fathers of the English Dominican Province. 1920. Revised and edited for New Advent by Kevin Knight. http://www.newadvent.org/summa/index.html.

———. *Summa Theologiae: A Concise Translation*. Edited by Timothy McDermott. Notre Dame, IN: Christian Classics, 1991.

Aravind, V.K., V.D. Krishnaram, and Rupavathy A. Vimala. "Folie a Trois: Atypical Presentation as Shared Transient Psychotic Episode." *Indian Journal of Psychological Medicine* 36.2 (Apr.-Jun. 2014): pp. 211-14.

Armstrong, John, ed. *Roman Catholicism: Evangelical Protestants Analyze What Divides and Unites Us*. Chicago: Moody Bible Institute, 1994.

Armstrong, Karen. *The Battle for God: A History of Fundamentalism*. New York: Alfred A. Knopf, 2000.

———. *The Spiral Staircase: My Climb out of Darkness*. New York: Anchor Books, 2005.

Arnone, Danilo, Anish Patel, and Giles Ming-Yee Ta. "The Nosological Significance of Folie à Deux: A Review of the Literature." *Annals of General Psychiatry*, 5.11 (2006). Available at https://www.ncbi.nlm.nih.gov/pmc/articles/PMC1559622/ (accessed 13 Jan. 2019).

Athanasius. *Letters*. In *Nicene and Post-Nicene Fathers*, Second Series. Vol. 4. Edited by Philip Schaff. Translated by R. Payne-Smith. Buffalo, NY: Christian Literature Publishing Co., 1892. Revised and edited for New Advent by Kevin Knight. http://www.newadvent.org/fathers/2806.htm.

———. *Life of St. Anthony*. In *Nicene and Post-Nicene Fathers, Second Series*. Vol. 4. Edited by Philip Schaff and Henry Wace. Translated by H. Ellershaw. Buffalo, NY: Christian Literature Publishing Co., 1892.

Revised and edited for New Advent by Kevin Knight. http://www.newadvent.org/fathers/2811.htm.

Athenagoras. *A Plea for the Christians*. In *Ante-Nicene Fathers*. Vol. 2. Edited by Alexander Roberts, et al. Translated by B. P. Pratten. Buffalo, NY: Christian Literature Publishing Co., 1885. Revised and edited for New Advent by Kevin Knight. http://newadvent.org/fathers/0205.htm.

Augustine of Hippo. *The City of God*. In *Nicene and Post-Nicene Fathers, First Series*. Vol. 2. Edited by Philip Schaff. Translated by Marcus Dods. Buffalo, NY: Christian Literature Publishing Co., 1887. Revised and edited for New Advent by Kevin Knight. http://www.newadvent.org/fathers/1201.htm.

———. *The Confessions*. In *Nicene and Post-Nicene Fathers, First Series*. Vol. 1. Edited by Philip Schaff. Translated by J. G. Pilkington. Buffalo, NY: Christian Literature Publishing Co., 1887. Revised and edited for New Advent by Kevin Knight. http://www.newadvent.org/fathers/1101.htm.

———. *Homilies on the First Epistle of John*. In *Nicene and Post-Nicene Fathers, First Series*. Vol. 7. Edited by Philip Schaff. Translated by H. Browne. Buffalo, NY: Christian Literature Publishing Co., 1888. Revised and edited for New Advent by Kevin Knight. http://www.newadvent.org/fathers/1702.htm.

———. *Later Works*. Edited by John Burnaby. Philadelphia: Westminster Press, 1955.

———. *Letters of St. Augustine of Hippo*. In *Nicene and Post-Nicene Fathers, First Series*. Vol. 1. Edited by Philip Schaff. Translated by J.G. Cunningham. Buffalo, NY: Christian Literature Publishing Co., 1887. Revised and edited for New Advent by Kevin Knight. http://www.newadvent.org/fathers/1102.htm.

———. *Of the Works of Monks*. In *Nicene and Post-Nicene Fathers, First Series*. Vol. 3. Edited by Philip Schaff. Translated by H. Browne. Buffalo, NY: Christian Literature Publishing Co., 1887. Revised and edited for New Advent by Kevin Knight. http://www.newadvent.org/fathers/1314.htm.

———. *On Baptism, Against the Donatists*. In *Nicene and Post-Nicene Fathers, First Series*. Vol. 4. Edited by Philip Schaff. Translated by J.R. King. Revised by Chester D. Hartranft. Buffalo, NY: Christian Literature Publishing Co., 1887. Revised and edited for New Advent by Kevin Knight. http://www.newadvent.org/fathers/14084.htm.

———. *On Christian Doctrine*. In *Nicene and Post-Nicene Fathers, First Series*. Vol. 2. Edited by Philip Schaff. Translated by James Shaw. Buffalo, NY: Christian Literature Publishing Co., 1887. Revised and edited for New Advent by Kevin Knight. http://www.newadvent.org/fathers/1202.htm.

———. *On the Free Choice of the Will, On Grace and Free Choice, and Other Writings*. Edited and translated by Peter King. Cambridge: Cambridge Univ. Press, 2010.

———. *On Nature and Grace*. In *Nicene and Post-Nicene Fathers, First Series*. Vol. 5. Edited by Phillip Schaff. Translated by Peter Holmes and Robert Ernest Wallis. Revised by Benjamin B. Warfield. Buffalo, NY: Christian Literature Publishing Co., 1887. Revised and edited for New Advent by Kevin Knight. http://www.newadvent.org/fathers/1503.htm.

———. *Reply to Faustus the Manichaean (Contra Faustum)*. In *Nicene and Post-Nicene Fathers, First Series*. Vol. 4. Edited by Philip Schaff. Translated by Richard Stothert. Buffalo, NY: Christian Literature Publishing Co., 1887. Revised and edited for New Advent by Kevin Knight. http://www.newadvent.org/fathers/1406.htm.

———. *St. Augustine: Letters, vol. 6 (1*-29*)*. Vol. 81. *The Fathers of the Church*. Translated by Robert B. Eno. Washington, DC: The Catholic Univ. of America Press, 1989.

———. *St. Augustine: Treatises on Marriage and Other Subjects*. Edited by Roy J. Deferrari. Translated by John A. Lacy. Washington, DC: The Catholic Univ. of America Press, 1969.

Avalos, Hector. "Jesus' Resurrection and Marian Apparitions: Medjugorje as a Living Laboratory." *Debunking Christianity* (blog), 29 Apr. 2013, www.debunking-christianity.com/2013/04/jesus-resurrection-and-marian.html (accessed 14 Jan. 2019).

———. "Mary at Medjugorje: A Critical Inquiry." *Free Inquiry* 14.2 (Spring 1994): pp. 48ff.

———. "The Puritan War on Christmas." *The Ames Tribune*, 7 Dec. 2013, http://amestrib.com/opinion/hector-avalos-puritan-war-christmas (accessed 22 Jan. 2016).

Aztecs: Reign of Blood and Splendor. Alexandria, VA: Time-Life Books, 1992.

Badger, George Percy. *The Nestorians and Their Rituals.* Vol. 2. London: Joseph Masters, 1852. Available at https://archive.org/details/TheNestoriansAndTheirRituals/page/n11.

"The Baha'i Faith." *Bahai.org*, n.d., http://www.bahai.org/ (accessed 3 Feb. 2017).

Baggini, Julian. *Atheism: A Very Short Introduction.* Oxford: Oxford Univ. Press, 2003.

Baldock, John. *The Essence of Rumi.* Edison, NJ: Chartwell Books, 2005.

The Baltimore Catechism of 1891. The Catholic Primer, 2005, https://www.pcpbooks.net/docs/baltimore_catechism.pdf (accessed 28 Oct. 2013).

"Baptist Denominations in America." *Baylor Baptists Studies Center for Research*, n.d., https://www.baylor.edu/baptiststudies/index.php?id=93653 (accessed 19 Sep. 2018).

Barker, Kenneth, ed. *The NIV Study Bible: New International Version.* Grand Rapids, MI: Zondervan, 1985.

Barnstone, Willis, ed. *The Other Bible.* San Francisco: HarperSanFrancisco, 1984.

Barrett, David and George Kurian and Todd M. Johnson. *World Christian Encyclopedia*, 2nd ed. Vol. 2. New York: Oxford Univ. Press, 2001.

Barth, Karl. *Church Dogmatics: The Doctrine pf the Word of God.* Edited by G.W. Bromley and T.F. Torrance. Translated by G.T. Thomson and Harold Knight. London: T&T Clark, 2004.

Basil of Caesarea. *De Spiritu Sancto (On the Holy Spirit).* In *Nicene and Post-Nicene Fathers, Second Series.* Vol. 8. Edited by Philip Schaff and Henry Wace. Translated by Blomfield Jackson. Buffalo, NY: Christian Literature Publishing Co., 1895. Revised and edited for New Advent by Kevin Knight. http://www.newadvent.org/fathers/3203.htm.

Basso, Julia C. and Wendy A. Suzuki. "The Effects of Acute Exercise on Mood, Cognition, Neurophysiology, and Neurochemical Pathways: A Review." *Brain Plasticity* 2.2 (2017): pp. 127-52, https://www.ncbi.nlm.nih.gov/pmc/articles/PMC5928534/ (accessed 30 Oct. 2018).

Batchelor, Stephen. *Buddhism Without Beliefs: A Contemporary Guide to Awakening.* New York: Rivenhead Books, 1997.

———. *Confession of a Buddhist Atheist*. New York: Spiegel and Grau, 2011.

Bayat, Mojdeh and Mohammad Ali Jamnia. *Tales from the Land of the Sufis*. Boston: Shambhala, 1994.

Baytsar, Taras. "Eastern Orthodoxy and Contraception." *Orthodox Evangelical*, 2 Feb. 2014, http://www.orthodoxevangelical.com/2014/02/04/eastern-orthodoxy-and-contraception/ (accessed July 4, 2016).

Beardsley, John, ed. "Liberties of New Englishmen." *The Winthrop Society*, 2015, http://www.winthropsociety.com/liberties.php (accessed 3 Jul. 2013).

Bede. *Ecclesiastical History of the English People*. Rev. ed. Edited by R. E. Latham. Translated by Leo Sherley-Price. New York: Penguin, 1990.

Behe, Michael J. *Darwin's Black Box: The Biochemical Challenge to Evolution*. New York: Touchstone/Simon and Schuster, 1998.

Beiderman, Patricia Ward. "Cao Dai Fuses Great Faiths of the World." *The Los Angeles Times*, 7 Jan. 2006, http://articles.latimes.com/2006/jan/07/local/me-beliefs7 (accessed 2 Oct. 2018).

Bell, Vaughan. "Ghost Stories: Visits from the Deceased." *Scientific American*, 2 Dec. 2008, https://www.scientificamerican.com/article/ghost-stories-visits-from-the-deceased/ (accessed 10 Oct. 2018).

Bellitto, Christopher. *The General Counsels: A History of Twenty-One Church Councils from Nicaea to Vatican II*. New York: Paulist Press, 2002.

Belt, Don, ed. *The World of Islam*. Washington, DC: National Geographic, 2001.

Bendiksen, Jonas. "Messiah Complex." *National Geographic* (Aug. 2017): pp. 82-93.

Bennett, Richard. *Far from Rome, Near to God: Testimonies of 50 Converted Roman Catholic Priests*. Carlisle, PA: The Banner of Truth Trust, 1997.

Bercot, David W. *A Dictionary of Early Christian Beliefs*. Peabody, MA: Hendrickson Publishers, 1998.

Bergland, Christopher. "25 Studies Confirm: Exercise Prevents Depression." *Psychology Today*, 29 Oct. 2013, https://www.psychologytoday.com/us/blog/the-athletes-way/201310/25-studies-confirm-exercise-prevents-depression (accessed 28 Oct. 2018).

Bernard of Clairvaux. *Bernard of Clairvaux: Selected Works*. New York: Paulist Press, 1987.
The Bhagavad-Gita: Krishna's Counsel in Time of War. Translated by Barbara Stoler Miller. New York: Bantam Dell, 2004.
"The Bible." *The Ethiopian Orthodox Tewahedo Church Faith and Order*, n.d., http://www.ethiopianorthodox.org/english/canonical/books.html (accessed 17 Jul. 2018).
Bigham, Steven. *Early Christian Attitudes toward Images*. Rollinsford, NH: Orthodox Research Institute, 2004.
Billock, Jennifer. "Where to See the World's Biggest Spiders." *Smithsonian.com*, 31 Oct. 2016, https://www.smithsonianmag.com/travel/where-see-worlds-biggest-spiders-180960938/ (accessed 7 Jan. 2017).
Black, Jeremy. *A Brief History of Slavery*. Philadelphia: Running Press, 2011.
Blakemore, Erin. "There Are Only Two Shakers Left in the World: One of America's Oldest Religious Sects Still Survives." *Smithsonian.com*, 6 Jan. 2017, http://www.smithsonianmag.com/smart-news/there-are-only-two-shakers-left-world-180961701/#wSqhoYkFfUCAibdK.99 (accessed 7 Jan. 2017).
———. "The Vatican Just Banned Scattering Ashes." *Smithsonian.com*, 25 Oct. 2016, https://www.smithsonianmag.com/smart-news/vatican-just-banned-scattering-ashes-180960907/ (accessed 30 Dec. 2018).
Blassingame, John. *The Slave Community: Plantation Life in the Antebellum South*. Rev. ed. New York: Oxford Univ. Press, 1979.
Bloom, Jonathan and Sheila Blair. *Islam: A Thousand Years of Faith and Power*. New Haven, CT: Yale Univ. Press: 2002.
Bokser, Ben Zion and Baruch M. Bokser, eds. *The Talmud: Selected Writings*. New York: Paulist Press, 1989.
Boller, Paul F. and Ronald Story, eds. *A More Perfect Union: Documents in U.S. History, vol. 1: to 1877*. 2nd ed. Houghton Mifflin: Boston, 1988.
Bonaventure. *Bonaventure: The Soul's Journey into God – The Tree of Life – The Life of St. Francis*. Translated by Ewert Cousins. Mahwah, NJ: Paulist Press, 1978.
Bonhoeffer, Dietrich. *The Cost of Discipleship*, 2nd ed. Translated by R. H. Fuller. New York: The MacMillan Co., 1959.
Bonner, Gerald. *St. Augustine of Hippo: Life and Controversies*. Norwich: The Canterbury Press, 1986.

The Book of Mormon. Salt Lake City, UT: The Church of Jesus Christ of Latter-Day Saints, 1989.

Borg, Marcus J. *The Heart of Christianity: Rediscovering a Life of Faith*. New York: HarperCollins, 2003.

Borg, Marcus J. and N.T. Wright. *The Meaning of Jesus: Two Visions*. New York: HarperCollins, 1999.

Bouwsma, William J. *John Calvin: A Sixteenth Century Portrait*. New York: Oxford University Press, 1988.

Bowman, Rebecca. "Jefferson's Religious Beliefs." *Monticello.org*, 1997, http://www.monticello.org/site/research-and-collections/jeffersons-religious-beliefs (accessed 3 Jul. 2013).

Boyce, Mary. *Textual Sources for the Study of Zoroastrianism*. Chicago: Univ. of Chicago Press, 1990.

Boyes, Alice. "Breathing Techniques for Anxiety: Ways to Relieve Anxiety Using Breathing Exercises." *Psychology Today*, 12 Jul. 2016, https://www.psychologytoday.com/us/blog/in-practice/201607/breathing-techniques-anxiety (accessed 1 Nov. 2018).

Boyle, Rebecca. "On Average, Every Star Has at Least One Planet, New Analysis Shows." *Popular Science*, 11 Jan. 2012, https://www.popsci.com/science/article/2012-01/new-exoplanet-analysis-determines-planets-are-more-common-stars-milky-way (accessed 17 Oct. 2018).

Brain, Marshall. *Why Won't God Heal Amputees?* 2006-2015, http://whywontgodhealamputees.com/ (accessed 9 Oct. 2015).

Bray, Gerald, ed. *Ancient Christian Commentary on Scripture: James, 1-2 Peter, 1-3 John. Jude*. Vol. XI. Downers Grove, IL: InterVarsity Press, 2000.

Brayford, Susan. "Reading Glasses: Feminist Criticism." *Teaching the Bible* (e-newsletter), *The Society of Biblical Literature*, n.d., https://www.sbl-site.org/assets/pdfs/TB7_FeministCriticism_SB.pdf (accessed 8 Jul. 2017).

Bremner, Ryan H., Sander L. Koole, and Brad J. Bushman. "'Pray for Those Who Mistreat You': Effects of Prayer on Anger and Aggression." *Personality and Social Psychology Bulletin* 37.6 (2011): pp. 830-37.

Bringhurst, Newell G. and John C. Hamer. *The Scattering of the Saints: Schism within Mormonism*. Independence, MO: John Whitmore Books, 2007.

Brown, Candy Gunther. "How Should Prayer Be Studied?: Study Methods May Predetermine Study Results." *Psychology Today*, 1 Mar. 2012, https://www.psychologytoday.com/us/blog/testing-prayer/201203/how-should-prayer-be-studied (accessed 28 Oct. 2018).

Brown, Richard D. and Stephen G. Rabe, eds. *Slavery in American Society*, 2nd ed. Lexington, MA: DC Heath and Co., 1976.

Bruce, F. F. *Paul: Apostle of the Heart Set Free*, 2nd ed. Grand Rapids, MI: Wm. B. Eerdmans, 1998.

Bryant, Richard A. "Folie à Familie: A Cognitive Study of Delusional Beliefs." *Psychiatry* 60.1 (Spring 1997): pp. 44-50.

Buddhist Folk Tales from Ancient Ceylon. Translated by Dick de Ruiter. Havelte/Holland: Binkey Kok Publications, 2005.

Bultmann, Rudolf. *Jesus Christ and Mythology*. Upper Saddle River, NJ: Prentice Hall, 1958.

Burge, Ryan P. "Where Protestants and Catholics Go When They Leave Their Churches." *Christianity Today*, 20 Feb. 2018, https://www.christianitytoday.com/news/2018/february/how-protestants-catholics-leave-church-change-religion-cces.html (accessed 11 Mar. 2018).

Burroughs, Jeremiah. *The Rare Jewel of Christian Contentment*. Pensacola, FL: Chapel Library, 2010. Available at http://www.chapellibrary.org/files/1113/7658/4062/rjoc.pdf (accessed 2 Jan. 2014).

Burton, Robert. "The Certainty Epidemic." *Salon*, 29 Feb. 2008, https://www.salon.com/2008/02/29/certainty/ (accessed 24 Jun. 2018).

Butt, Kyle. "On Death of Christopher Hitchens." *Apologetics Press*, 2012, http://www.apologeticspress.org/APContent.aspx?category=12&article=1617 (accessed 2 May 2013).

Camus, Jean Pierre. *The Spirit of S. Francis de Sales: Bishop and Prince of Geneva*. London: Rivingtons, 1880. Available at https://archive.org/details/spiritsfrancisd00camugoog/page/n4.

Carey, Benedict. "Long-awaited Medical Study Questions the Power of Prayer." *The New York Times*, 31 Mar. 2006, https://www.nytimes.com/2006/03/31/health/31pray.html (accessed 28 Oct. 2018).

Carroll, James Milton. *"The Trail of Blood" ... Following the Christians Down Through the Centuries ... Or the History of the Baptist Churches from the Time of Christ, Their Founder, to the Present Day*. 1931, https://archive.org/details/TheTrailOfBlood/page/n0 (accessed 8 Oct. 2018).

Calvin, John. *Commentaries on the Catholic Epistles*. Edited and Translated by John Owen. Grand Rapids, MI: Christian Classics Ethereal Library, orig. pub. 1855. http://www.ccel.org/ccel/calvin/calcom45.pdf.

———. *Commentary on Galatians and Ephesians*. Translated by William Pringle. Grand Rapids, MI: Christian Classics Ethereal Library, orig. pub. 1854. http://www.ccel.org/ccel/calvin/calcom41.pdf.

———. *Commentary on Genesis*. Vols 1-2. Translated by John King. Grand Rapids, MI: Christian Classics Ethereal Library, orig. pub. 1847. https://www.ccel.org/ccel/calvin/calcom01.pdf and http://www.ccel.org/ccel/calvin/calcom02.pdf.

———. *Commentary on John*. Vol. 1. Translated by William Pringle. Grand Rapids, MI: Christian Classics Ethereal Library, orig. pub. 1847. http://www.ccel.org/ccel/calvin/calcom34.pdf.

———. *Commentary on Joshua*. Translated by Henry Beveridge. Grand Rapids, MI: Christian Classics Ethereal Library, orig. pub. 1854. http://www.ccel.org/ccel/calvin/calcom07.pdf.

———. *Commentary on Matthew, Mark, Luke*. Vol. 1. Translated by William Pringle. Grand Rapids, MI: Christian Classics Ethereal Library, orig. pub. 1845. http://www.ccel.org/ccel/calvin/calcom31.pdf.

———. *Commentary on Psalms*. Vol. 1. Translated by James Anderson. Grand Rapids, MI: Christian Classics Ethereal Library, orig. pub. 1845. http://www.ccel.org/ccel/calvin/calcom08.pdf.

———. *Commentary on Timothy, Titus, Philemon*. Translated by William Pringle. Grand Rapids, MI: Christian Classics Ethereal Library, orig. pub. 1856. http://www.ccel.org/ccel/calvin/calcom43.pdf.

———. *Harmony of the Law*. Vol. 2. Translated by Charles William Bingham. Grand Rapids, MI: Christian Classics Ethereal Library, orig. pub. 1852. http://www.ccel.org/ccel/calvin/calcom04.pdf.

———. *Institutes of the Christian Religion*. Translated by Henry Beveridge. Grand Rapids, MI: Christian Classics Ethereal Library, orig. pub. 1845. http://www.ccel.org/ccel/calvin/institutes.pdf.

———. *Treatises against the Anabaptists and against the Libertines*. Edited and translated by Benjamin Wirt Farley. Grand Rapids, MI: Baker, 1982.

Campolo, Tony and Bart Campolo. *Why I Left, Why I Stayed: Conversations on Christianity between an Evangelical Father and His Humanist Son.* New York: HarperOne, 2017.

The Canons and Decrees of the Council of Trent. Translated by H. J. Schroeder. Rockford, IL: Tan Books and Publishers, 1978.

Schroeder, H. J. *Disciplinary Decrees of the General Councils: Text, Translation and Commentary.* St. Louis: B. Herder, 1937.

Carlson, Charles R., Panayiota E. Bacaseta, Dexter A. Simanton. "A Controlled Evaluation of Devotional Meditation and Progressive Muscle Relaxation." *Journal of Psychology and Theology* 16.4 (1988): pp. 362-68.

Carrier, Richard. "Why I Don't Buy the Resurrection Story," 6th ed. *The Secular Web (Internet Infidels)*, 2006, http://infidels.org/library/modern/richard_carrier/resurrection/lecture.html#41 (accessed 30 Oct. 2015).

———. "Why We Might Have Reason for Doubt: Should We Still Be Looking for a Historical Jesus?" *The Bible and Interpretation*, Aug. 2014, http://www.bibleinterp.com/articles/2014/08/car388028.shtml (accessed 8 Oct. 2018)

Carroll, Rory. "Pope Says Sorry for Sins of Church." *The Guardian*, 13 Mar. 2000, http://www.guardian.co.uk/world/2000/mar/13/catholicism.religion (accessed 7 Jun. 2013).

Carroll, Sean B. *The Making of the Fittest.* New York: W.W. Norton and Co., 2007.

Carson, D. A. *Exegetical Fallacies*, 2nd ed. Grand Rapids, MI: Baker Books, 1996.

Catechism of the Catholic Church. New York: Image/Doubleday, 1995.

The Catholic Encyclopedia. New York: Robert Appleton Company, 1917. http://www.newadvent.org/cathen/.

Chadwick, Henry. *The Early Church.* Rev. ed. New York: Penguin, 1993.

Chadwick, Owen. *The Reformation.* New York: Penguin, 1990.

Chah, Achaan. *A Still Forest Pool: The Insight Meditation of Achaan Chah.* Edited by Jack Kornfield and Paul Breiter. Wheaton, IL: The Theosophical Publishing House, 1985.

Cham, Jorge and Daniel Whiteson. *We Have No Idea: A Guide to the Unknown Universe.* New York: Riverhead Books, 2017.

Choksy, Jamsheed K. "How Iran Persecutes Its Oldest Religion." *CNN*, 14 Nov. 2011, http://www.cnn.com/2011/11/14/opinion/choksy-iran-zoroastrian/ (accessed 31 Aug. 2018).

Chrysostom, John. *Homilies on the Epistles of Paul to the Corinthians*. In *Nicene and Post-Nicene Fathers*, Series 1. Vol. 12. Edited by Philip Schaff. Translated by Talbot W. Chambers. Grand Rapids, MI: Christian Classics Ethereal Library, orig. pub. 1889. http://www.ccel.org/ccel/schaff/npnf112.pdf.

———. *Homilies on the Gospel of Saint Matthew*. In *Nicene and Post-Nicene Fathers*, Series 1. Vol. 10. Edited by Philip Schaff. Grand Rapids, MI: Christian Classics Ethereal Library, orig. pub. 1888. http://www.ccel.org/ccel/schaff/npnf110.pdf.

Cicero, Marcus Tullius. *The Nature of the Gods*. Translated by Horace C. P. McGregor. New York: Penguin, 1972.

Clement of Alexandria. *The Stromata, or Miscellanies*. In *Ante-Nicene Fathers*. Vol. 2. Edited by Alexander Roberts et al. Translated by William Wilson. Buffalo, NY: Christian Literature Publishing Co., 1885. Revised and edited for New Advent by Kevin Knight. http://www.newadvent.org/fathers/02107.htm.

Clendenin, Daniel B. "Why I'm Not Orthodox: An Evangelical Explores the Ancient and Alien World of the Eastern Church." *Christianity Today*, 6 Jan. 1997, http://www.christianitytoday.com/ct/1997/january6/7t1032.html?paging=off (accessed 9 Oct. 2013).

———. "What the Orthodox Believe." *Christian History* 16.2, issue 54 (1997): p. 35.

The Cloud of Unknowing and Other Works. Translated by Clifton Walters. New York: Penguin, 1961.

Clouse, Robert G. "Late Great Predictions." *Christian History* 18.1, issue 61 (1999): pp. 40-1.

Comer, Ronald J. *Abnormal Psychology*, 4th ed. New York: Worth Publishers, 2001.

Confucius. *The Analects*. Translated by D. C. Rau. London: Penguin, 1979.

———. *Chinese Classics: Part I, Confucius*. Translated James Legge. New York: John B. Alden, 1883. Available at https://archive.org/details/chineseclassics00confiala/page/n7.

Coniaris, Anthony M. *Introducing the Orthodox Church: Its Faith and Life*, 13th printing. Minneapolis: Light and Life Publishing Co., 1982.

———. "The Rapture: Indisputable Christian Heresy." *Mystagogy Resource Center*, 22 Apr. 2010, http://www.johnsanidopoulos.com/2010/04/rapture-indisputable-christian-heresy.html?m=1 (accessed 20 Nov. 2016).

Corey, Gerald. *Theory and Practice of Counseling and Psychotherapy*, 5th ed. Pacific Grove, CA: Brooks/Cole Publishing Co., 1996.

Craig, William Lane. "#75 Monotheletism." *Reasonable Faith with William Lane Craig*, 22 Sep. 2008, http://reasonablefaith.org/monotheletism.

Curp, David T. "A Necessary Bondage? When the Church Endorsed Slavery." *Crisis*, 23:8 (Sept. 2005), https://www.catholiceducation.org/en/controversy/common-misconceptions/a-necessary-bondage-when-the-church-endorsed-slavery.html (accessed 12 Nov. 2017).

Cyprian of Carthage. *Epistles of Cyprian of Carthage*. In *Ante-Nicene Fathers*. Vol. 5. Edited by Alexander Roberts, et al. Translated by Robert Ernest Wallis. Buffalo, NY: Christian Literature Publishing Co., 1886. Revised and edited for New Advent by Kevin Knight. http://www.newadvent.org/fathers/0506.htm.

———. *On the Lapsed*. In *Ante-Nicene Fathers*. Vol. 5. Edited by Alexander Roberts et al. Translated by Robert Ernest Wallis. Buffalo, NY: Christian Literature Publishing Co., 1886. Revised and edited for New Advent by Kevin Knight. http://www.newadvent.org/fathers/050703.htm.

———. *On the Unity of the Church*. In *Ante-Nicene Fathers*. Vol. 5. Edited by Alexander Roberts et al. Translated by Robert Ernest Wallis. Buffalo, NY: Christian Literature Publishing Co., 1886. Revised and edited for New Advent by Kevin Knight. http://www.newadvent.org/fathers/050701.htm.

Cyril of Jerusalem. *The Works of St. Cyril of Jerusalem: Lenten Lectures (Catecheses)*. In *The Fathers of the Church: A New Translation*. Vol. 61. Edited by Bernard Peebles et al. Translated by L. P. McCauley and A. A. Stephenson. Washington, DC: Catholic Univ. of America: 1969.

The Dalai Lama. *An Open Heart: Practicing Compassion in Everyday Life*. Edited by Nicholas Vreeland. Boston: Little, Brown and Co., 2001.

Daley, Jason. "These Wasps Hijack Spiders' Brains and Make Them Do Their Bidding." *Smithsonian.com*, 29 Nov. 2018, https://www.smithsonianmag.com/smart-news/wasp-turns-social-spiders-zombies-build-their-cocoons-real-life-horror-story-180970919/ (accessed 22 Dec. 2018).

Daniels, Kenneth. *Why I Believed: Reflections of a Former Missionary*. Duncanville, TX: self-published, 2009.

Darwin, Charles. *The Autobiography of Charles Darwin*. New York: W. W. Norton & Co., 2005.

Datta, Tanya. "Sai Baba: God Man or Con Man?" *BBC News*, 17 Jun. 2014, http://news.bbc.co.uk/2/hi/programmes/this_world/3813469.stm (accessed 4 Feb. 2017).

Davis, Daphne and Jeffrey Hayes. "What Are the Benefits of Mindfulness?" *American Psychological Association* 43.7 (Jul./Aug. 2012): p. 64, http://www.apa.org/monitor/2012/07-08/ce-corner.aspx (accessed 27 Apr. 2018).

Davis, Leo Donald. *The First Seven Ecumenical Councils (325-787): Their History and Theology*. Collegeville, MN: Liturgical Press, 1990.

Dawkins, Richard. *The God Delusion*. Boston: Mariner Books, 2008.

De las Casas, Bartolomé. *A Short Account of the Destruction of the Indies*. Edited and translated by Nigel Griffin. London: Penguin, 1992.

De Sales, Francis. *Introduction to the Devout Life*. London: Longmans, Green, and Co., 1891. Available at https://archive.org/details/IntroductionToTheDevoutLife/page/n7

———. *Introduction to the Devout Life*. New York: Vintage, 2002.

Dell'Amore, Christine. "The 10 Weirdest Animal Stories of 2016." *National Geographic*, 20 Dec. 2016, http://news.nationalgeographic.com/2016/12/weirdest-animal-stories-2016-sharks/ (accessed 20 Dec. 2016).

Dennett, Daniel C. *Breaking the Spell: Religion as a Natural Phenomenon*. New York: Viking/Penguin, 2006.

Desta, Alemayehu. *Introduction to the Ethiopian Orthodox Tewahedo Faith*. Bloomington, IN: AuthorHouse, 2012.

Deutsch, Nathaniel. "Save the Gnostics." *The New York Times*, 7 Oct. 2007, http://www.nytimes.com/2007/10/07/opinion/07iht-edeutsch.1.7783203.html?_r=0 (accessed 25 Nov. 2013).

The Dhammapada: A Collection of Verses, 2nd ed. Translated by F. Max Muller. Oxford: The Clarendon Press, 1898. Available at https://archive.org/details/in.ernet.dli.2015.223782.

Diderot, Denis. *Early Philosophical Works*. Edited and translated by Marget Jourdain. Chicago: The Open Court Publishing Co., 1916. Available at https://archive.org/details/diderotsearlyph00jourgoog/page/n8.

Dixon, Dougal. *Dinosaurs*. San Diego, CA: Thunder Bay Press, 2005.

Dobbs, David. "A Cure in Sight." *National Geographic* (Sep. 2016): pp. 30-53.

Doherty, Earl. "Was There No Historical Jesus?" *Internet Infidels Newsletter*, Apr. 1999, https://infidels.org/infidels/newsletter/1999/april.html (accessed 9 Oct. 2018).

Dollar, Creflo. "Unlocking the Door to Financial Blessings." *Creflo Dollar Ministries*, 29 Aug. 2016, http://www.creflodollarministries.org/Bible-Study/Articles/Unlocking%20the%20Door%20to%20Financial%20Blessings (accessed 24 Feb. 2017)

Dopp, Siegmar and Wilhelm Geerlings. *Dictionary of Early Christian Beliefs*. Translated by Matthew O'Connell. New York, Crossroad, 2000.

The Dordrecht Confession of Faith, 1632. The Beachy Amish-Mennonites, n.d., http://www.beachyam.org/dortrecht.htm (accessed 2 Sep. 2016).

Dostoevsky, Fyodor. *The Brothers Karamazov*. New York: Barnes and Noble, 1995.

———. *Letters of Fyodor Michailovitch Dostoevsky to His Family and Friends*, 2nd ed. Translated by Ethel Colburn Mayne. New York: The MacMillan Co., 1917. Available at https://archive.org/details/lettersfyodormi00eliagoog/page/n10.

Douglas, J. D., ed. *The New International Dictionary of the Christian Church*. Rev. ed. Grand Rapids, MI: Zondervan, 1978.

Douglass, Frederick. *Narrative of the Life of Frederick Douglass, an American Slave*. New York: Signet/Penguin, 1968.

Douthitt, Bill. "Beautiful Stranger: Saturn's Mysteries Come to Light." *National Geographic* (Dec. 2006): pp. 38-57.

Dowley, Tim, ed. *Introduction to the History of Christianity*. Minneapolis: Fortress Press, 1995.

Dunbar, Brian. "Extreme Space Facts." NASA, 15 Jun. 2017, https://www.jpl.nasa.gov/edu/pdfs/ss_extreme_poster.pdf (accessed 7 Mar. 2018).

Dungan, David Laird. *A History of the Synoptic Problem: The Canon, the Text, the Composition, and the Interpretation of the Gospels.* New York: Doubleday, 1999.

Edamaruku, Sanal. "India Has No Reason to Be Grateful to Mother Teresa." *mm-gold.azureedge.net*, 13 May 2010, https://mm-gold.azureedge.net/Articles/mother_teresa/sanal_ed.html (accessed 14 Oct. 2014).

Edmonds, Patricia. "All Moms, No Dads." *National Geographic* (Nov. 2016): p. 29.

———. "One Part He, One Part She." *National Geographic* (Jan. 2017): p. 26.

Edwards, Jonathan. "The Eternity of Hell Torments." *Jonathan-edwards.org*, n.d., http://www.jonathan-edwards.org/Eternity.html (accessed 15 May 2013).

Edwards, Paul and Arthur Pap, eds. *A Modern Introduction to Philosophy.* Rev. ed. New York: Free Press, 1965.

Egan, Harvey, ed. *An Anthology of Christian Mysticism.* Collegeville, MN: The Liturgical Press, 1991.

Ehrman, Bart D., ed. and trans. *The Apostolic Fathers*, Vol. 1. Loeb Classical Library. Cambridge, MA: Harvard Univ. Press, 2003.

———, ed. *After the New Testament: A Reader in Early Christianity.* New York: Oxford Univ. Press, 1999.

———. "Did Jesus Exist?" *The Huffington Post*, 20 Mar. 2012, http://www.huffingtonpost.com/bart-d-ehrman/did-jesus-exist_b_1349544.html (accessed 21 Feb. 2013).

———. *Jesus, Interrupted: Revealing the Hidden Contradictions in the Bible (and Why We Don't Know about Them).* New York: HarperOne, 2009.

———. *Lost Christianities: The Battle for Scripture and the Faiths We Never Knew.* Oxford: Oxford Univ. Press, 2003.

———. *Lost Scriptures: Books That Did Not Make It into The New Testament.* New York: Oxford Univ. Press, 2003.

———. *Misquoting Jesus: The Story Behind Who Changed the Bible and Why.* San Francisco: HarperSanFrancisco, 2005.

Ehrman, Bart D. and William Lane Craig. "Is There Historical Evidence for the Resurrection of Jesus?" Debate, College of the Holy Cross, Worcester, MA, 28 Mar. 2006. http://www.philvaz.com/apologetics/p96.htm.

Einstein, Albert. "Einstein's Credo (My Credo)." *Albert Einstein in the World Wide Web*, orig. pub. 1932, http://www.einstein-website.de/z_biography/credo.html (accessed 6 Jan. 2017).

Ejova, Anastasia. "Awe: A Direct Pathway from Extravagant Displays to Prosociality." *Behavioral and Brain Sciences* 39 (2016): pp. 28-9.

Emmons, Robert A. and Michael E. McCullough. "Counting Blessings Versus Burdens: An Experimental Investigation of Gratitude and Subjective Well-Being in Daily Life." *Journal of Personality and Social Psychology* 84.2 (2003): pp. 377-89.

Empiricus, Sextus. *Outlines of Pyrrhonism*. Translated by R. G. Bury. Amherst, NY: Prometheus Books, 1990.

Encyclopedia Britannica, (online version). http://www.britannica.com.

Encyclopedia of Mormonism. Brigham Young University, 2007. Available at https://eom.byu.edu/index.php/.

Epictetus. *The Works of Epictetus*. Translated by Thomas Wentworth Higginson. Boston: Little, Brown, and Co., 1866. Available at https://archive.org/details/cu31924029001606/page/n3.

Epiphanius. *The Panarion of Epiphanius, Books II & III (Sects 47-80, De Fide)*. Translated by Frank Williams. New York: E. J. Brill, 1994.

Ernst, Carl W. *Sufism: An Introduction to the Mystical Tradition of Islam*. Boston: Shambhala, 2011.

Estep, William. *The Anabaptist Story: An Introduction to Sixteenth-Century Anabaptism*, 3rd ed. Grand Rapids, MI: Wm. B. Eerdmans, 1996.

Eusebius of Caesarea. *Ecclesiastical History*. Translated by C. F. Cruse. Peabody, MA: Hendrickson, 1998.

Evans, Barrett A. "Ancient and Classic Pastoral Counsel: Approaches to Anxiety, Doubt and Guilt." *Journal of Psychology and Christianity* 24.1 (2005): pp. 80-88.

Evans, Craig. "Directions: Doubting Thomas's Gospel." *Christianity Today*, 15 Jun. 1998 https://www.christianitytoday.com/ct/1998/june15/8t7053.html (accessed 11 May 2016).

"Fascinating Facts." *Library of Congress*, n.d., http://www.loc.gov/about/facts.html (accessed 7 Jan. 2013).

Favila, Aaron. "In The Philippines, Observers Perform Crucifixion Reenactment In Good Friday Ritual (PHOTOS)." *The Huffington Post*, 18

Apr. 2014, http://www.huffingtonpost.com/2014/04/18/philippines-crucifixion-reenactment_n_5173257.html (accessed 30 Oct. 2015).
Felix, Minucius. *Octavius*. In *Ante-Nicene Fathers*. Vol. 4. Edited by Alexander Roberts et al. Translated by Robert Ernest Wallis. Buffalo, NY: Christian Literature Publishing Co., 1885. Revised and edited for New Advent by Kevin Knight. http://www.newadvent.org/fathers/0410.htm.
Ferrara, Christopher A. and Thomas E. Woods, Jr. *The Great Façade: The Regime of Novelty in the Catholic Church from Vatican II to the Francis Revolution*, 2nd ed. Kettering, OH: Angelico Press, 2015.
Fielder, Maureen and Linda Rabben, eds. *Rome Has Spoken: A Guide to Forgotten Papal Statements, and How They Have Changed Through the Centuries*. New York: Crossroad Publishing, 1998.
Fink, Steven. *Dribbling for Dawah: Sports Among Muslim Americans*. Macon, GA: Mercer Univ. Press, 2016.
Fischer, Louis. *Gandhi: His Life and Message for the World*. New York: Signet Classics, 2010.
Fleming, Nic. "Ten Giant Animals that Are Long Since Dead." *BBC Earth*, 7 May 2015, http://www.bbc.com/earth/story/20150507-ten-lost-giants-from-earths-past (accessed 2 Oct. 2016).
Fortenbury, Jon. "The Health Effects of Leaving Religion." *The Atlantic*, 28 Sep. 2014, https://www.theatlantic.com/health/archive/2014/09/the-health-effects-of-leaving-religion/379651/ (accessed 7 Feb. 2019).
Foster, Richard J. *Celebration of Discipline: The Path to Spiritual Growth*. Rev. ed. San Francisco: HarperSanFrancisco, 1988.
Francis of Assisi and Clare of Assisi. *Francis and Clare: The Complete Works*. Translated by Regis J. Armstrong and Ignatius C. Brady. New York: Paulist Press, 1982.
Franklin, Benjamin. *The Autobiography and Other Writings*. Edited by Kenneth Silverman. New York: Penguin, 1986.
"Frequently Asked Questions about Oomoto." *Oomoto.or.jp*, 2010, http://www.oomoto.or.jp/English/enFaq/indexfaq.html (accessed 27 Nov. 2013).
Froehlich, Karlfield. *Biblical Interpretation in the Early Church*. Philadelphia: Fortress Press, 1984.
Fromme, Alison. "Squid in Flight." *National Geographic* (Nov. 2014): p. 20.

Fuller, Richard and Francis Wayland. *Domestic Slavery Considered as a Scriptural Institution: In a Correspondence between the Rev. Richard Fuller and the Rev. Francis Wayland*. New York: Lewis Colby, 1845. Available at http://archive.org/details/domesticslaveryc00full.

Furbank, P. N. *Diderot: A Critical Biography*. New York: Alfred A. Knopf, 1992.

Gambero, Luigi. *Mary and the Fathers of the Church: The Blessed Virgin Mary in Patristic Thought*. Translated by Thomas Buffer. San Francisco: Ignatius Press, 1991.

Gandhi, Mohandas. *Autobiography: The Story of My Experiments with Truth*. Translated by Mahadev Desai. New York: Dover Publications, 1983.

———. *The Bhagavad Gita According to Gandhi*. Translated by Mahadev Desai. Blacksburg, VA: Wilder Publications, 2011.

———. *The Essential Gandhi: An Anthology of His Writings on His Life, Work, and Ideas*. Edited by Louis Fischer. New York: Vintage Books, 1983.

The Garuda Purana. Translated by Ernest Wood and S.V. Subrahmanyam. 1911. Available at *Internet Sacred Text Archive*, http://www.sacred-texts.com/hin/gpu/gpu03.htm. Also available at https://archive.org/details/in.ernet.dli.2015.45762/page/n5.

Gates, Henry Louis, Jr., ed. *The Classic Slave Narratives*. New York: Mentor, 1987.

Geary, Patrick J. *Furta Sacra: Thefts of Relics in the Central Middle Ages*. Princeton, NJ: Princeton Univ. Press, 1990.

Geisler, Norman. "A Note on the Percent of Accuracy in the New Testament Text." *Normangeisler.com*, 2014, http://www.normgeisler.com/articles/Bible/Reliability/NoteOnPercentAccuracyOfNT.htm, (accessed 14 Dec. 2014).

Geisler, Norman and Thomas Howe. *When Critics Ask: A Popular Handbook on Bible Difficulties*. Grand Rapids, MI: Baker Books, 1997.

George, Timothy. "The Reformation Connection." *Christian History* 19.4, issue 68 (2000): pp. 35-38.

Gertz, Steven. "Spiritual Warriors." *Christian History* 21.1, issue 74 (2002): pp. 28-30.

Ghezzi, Bert. *Mystics and Miracles: True Stories of Lives Touched by God.* Chicago: Loyola Press, 2002.

Giles, Herbert A. *A History of Chinese Literature.* New York: D. Appleton and Co., 1901. Available at https://archive.org/details/cu31924086054776/page/n9.

Giller, Geoffrey. "Are We Any Closer to Knowing How Many Species There Are on Earth?" *Scientific American*, 8 Apr. 2014, https://www.scientificamerican.com/article/are-we-any-closer-to-knowing-how-many-species-there-are-on-earth/ (accessed 7 Mar. 2018).

Gillquist, Peter E. *Becoming Orthodox: A Journey to the Ancient Christian Faith*, rev. ed. Ben Lomond, CA: Conciliar Press: 1992.

Gingrich, F. Wilbur. *Lexicon of the Greek New Testament*, 2nd ed. Revised by Frederick Danker. Chicago: Univ. of Chicago Press, 1983.

Glancy, Jennifer A. *Slavery in Early Christianity.* Minneapolis: Fortress Press, 2006.

Global Anabaptist Mennonite Encyclopedia Online. https://gameo.org/index.php?title=Welcome_to_GAMEO.

"God as One vs. The Trinity." *Jews for Judaism*, n.d., http://jewsforjudaism.org/knowledge/articles/god-as-one-vs-the-trinity/ (accessed 19 Mar. 2018).

Gonot-Schoupinsky, F.N. and G. Garip. "Laughter and Humour Interventions for Well-being in Older Adults: A Systematic Review and Intervention Classification." *Complementary Therapies in Medicine* 38 (2018): pp. 85-91.

González, Justo L. *The Story of Christianity: The Early Church to the Dawn of the Reformation.* Vol. 1. San Francisco: HarperSanFrancisco, 1985.

———. *The Story of Christianity: The Reformation to the Present Day.* Vol. 2. San Francisco: HarperSanFrancisco, 1985.

———, ed. *The Westminster Dictionary of Theologians.* Translated by Suzanne E. Hoeferkamp Segovia. Louisville, KY: Westminster John Knox Press, 2006.

Good, Merle and Phyllis. *20 Most Asked Questions about the Amish and Mennonites.* Rev. ed. Intercourse, PA: Good Books, 1995.

Goold, G. P., ed. *The Apostolic Fathers.* Vol. 2. Translated by Kirsopp Lake. Loeb Classical Library. Cambridge, MA: Harvard Univ. Press, 1948.

"'Gora' Shri Goparaju Ramachandra Rao (aka Gora) (1902-1975)." *British Humanist Association*, 2018, https://humanism.org.uk/humanism/the-humanist-tradition/20th-century-humanism/gora/ (accessed 13 Feb. 2017).

Grabar, Andre. *Christian Iconography: A Study of Its Origins*. Princeton, NJ: Princeton Univ. Press, 1968.

Gregory of Nyssa. *Commentary on Ecclesiastes*. The Gregory of Nyssa Home Page, The Sage Colleges. Translated by Richard McCambly. http://www.sage.edu/faculty/salomd/nyssa/eccl.html (accessed 3 Jul. 2013). Site was maintained by David A. Salomon; link is now broken.

Grimestone, A. V., ed. *Two Zen Classics: The Gateless Gate and the Blue Cliff Record*. Translated by Katsuri Sekida. Boston: Shambhala, 2005.

Gritsch, Eric W. "Was Luther Anti-Semitic?" *Christian History* 12.3, issue 3 (1993): pp. 38-9. Available at https://christianhistoryinstitute.org/magazine/article/was-luther-anti-semitic.

Ha, Jaegeon. "Unity and Catholicity in the Korean Presbyterian Church: An Ecumenical Reformed Assessment." *Verbum et Ecclesia*, 37:1 (19 Aug. 2016): pp. 1-8. https://repository.up.ac.za/bitstream/handle/2263/58100/Ha_Unity_2016.pdf?sequence=1&isAllowed=y (accessed 19 Sep. 2018).

Halsall, Paul, ed. *Internet Medieval Sourcebook*. Fordham University, 1996, https://sourcebooks.fordham.edu/sbook.asp (accessed 2013-2019).

Haase, Albert. *Instruments of Christ: Reflections on the Peace Prayer of St. Francis*. Cincinnati: St. Anthony Messenger Press, 2004.

Hafiz of Shiraz. *The Divan*. In *Persian Literature, Volume 1, Comprising The Shah Nameh, The Rubaiyat, The Divan, and The Gulistan*. Project Gutenberg, 26 Nov. 2003. Kindle.

———. *The Tangled Braid: Ninety-Nine Poems by Hafiz of Shiraz*. Translated by Jeffrey Einboden and John Slater. Louisville, KY: Fons Vitae, 2009.

Hagerty, Barbara Bradley. "Prayer May Reshape Your Brain … And Your Reality." *NPR*, 20 May 2009 https://www.npr.org/templates/story/story.php?storyId=104310443 (accessed 28 Oct. 2018).

Hamel, John. "The 'Jesus Drank Wine' Lie," *John Hamel Ministries*, n.d., http://www.johnhamelministries.org/wine_lie_Jesus.htm (accessed 28 Dec. 2014).

Hamilton, Edith. *Mythology: Timeless Tales of Gods and Heroes*. New York: Mentor, 1969.

Hanh, Thich Nhat. *Interbeing: Fourteen Guidelines for Engaged Buddhism.*, 3rd ed. Edited by Fred Eppsteiner. Berkeley, CA: Parallax Press, 1998.

———. *The Miracle of Mindfulness: A Manual on Meditation*. Rev. ed. Translated by Mobi Ho. Boston: Beacon Press, 1975.

Hardy, Edward R. ed. *Christology of the Later Fathers*. Louisville, KY: Westminster John Knox Press, 1954.

Harnack, Adolf. *What is Christianity?* Translated by Thomas Bailey Saunders. Philadelphia: Fortress, 1986.

Harney, Martin P. *The Legacy of St. Patrick*. Boston: The Daughters of St. Paul, 1979.

Harris, Alex H.S., Carl E. Thoreson, Michael E. McCullough, and David B. Larson. "Spiritually and Religiously Oriented Health Interventions." *Journal of Health Psychology* no. 4 (1999): pp. 413-33.

Harris, Dan. "The Long Journey to Becoming '10% Happier.'" ABC News. YouTube video, 13:23. Posted 12 Mar. 2014. https://www.youtube.com/watch?v=4sXBEfIXUno.

Harris, Sam. *The End of Faith: Religion, Terror, and the Future of Reason*. New York: W.W. Norton and Co., 2004.

———. "How to Meditate." *Samharris.org*, 10 May 2011, http://www.samharris.org/blog/item/how-to-meditate (accessed 15 Nov. 2013).

———. "Killing the Buddha," *Shambhala Sun*, Mar. 2006, http://www.shambhalasun.com/index.php?option=com_content&task=view&id=2903&Itemid=244 (accessed 15 Nov. 2013).

———. *Letter to a Christian Nation*. New York: Vintage Books, 2006.

———. "Science Can Answer Moral Questions." TED. YouTube video 23:34. Posted 22 Mar. 2010. https://www.youtube.com/watch?v=Hj9oB4zpHww.

———. *Waking Up: A Guide to Spirituality Without Religion*. New York: Simon and Schuster, 2014.

Harvey, Peter. *An Introduction to Buddhism: Teachings, History and Practices*. New York: Cambridge Univ. Press, 1990.

Hatcher, William S. and J. Douglas Martin. *The Baha'i Faith: The Emerging Global Religion*. New York: Harper and Row, 1989.

Hayes, Steven C. with Spencer Smith. *Get Out of Your Mind and into Your Life: The New Acceptance and Commitment Therapy.* Oakland, CA: New Harbinger Publications, 2005.

Healy, John. *The Ancient Irish Church.* London: The Religious Tract Society, 1892. Available at https://archive.org/details/ancientirishchur00healrich/page/n5.

Helms, Randall McCraw. *The Bible Against Itself: Why the Bible Seems to Contradict Itself.* Altadena, CA: Millennium Press, 2006.

Herodotus. *The Histories.* Translated by Robin Waterfield. Oxford: Oxford Univ. Press, 1998.

Hersher, Rebecca. "The Universe Has Almost 10 Times More Galaxies than We Thought." *NPR,* 14 Oct. 2016, http://www.npr.org/sections/thetwo-way/2016/10/14/497965415/the-universe-has-almost-10-times-more-galaxies-than-we-thought (accessed 23 Oct. 2016).

Hindley, Geoffrey. *The Crusades: Islam and Christianity in the Struggle for World Supremacy.* New York: Carroll and Graf Publishers, 2005.

Hippolytus of Rome. *The Apostolic Tradition of Hippolytus.* Translated by Burton Scott Easton. Ann Arbor, MI: Archon Books, 1962.

Hippolytus (pseudonymous). *On the Apostles and Disciples.* In *Ante-Nicene Fathers.* Vol. 5. Edited by Alexander Roberts et al. Translated by J. H. MacMahon. Buffalo, NY: Christian Literature Publishing Co., 1886. Revised and edited for New Advent by Kevin Knight. http://www.newadvent.org/fathers/0524.htm.

Hitchens, Christopher. *god is not Great: How Religion Poisons Everything.* New York: Twelve, 2007.

———. *The Missionary Position: Mother Teresa in Theory and Practice.* New York: Twelve, 2012.

———. "Mommie Dearest: The Pope Beatifies Mother Teresa, a Fanatic, a Fundamentalist, and a Fraud." *Slate,* 20 Oct. 2003, http://www.slate.com/articles/news_and_politics/fighting_words/2003/10/mommie_dearest.html (accessed 7 Feb. 2013).

———, ed. *The Portable Atheist: Essential Readings for the Non-Believer.* Philadelphia: Da Capo Press, 2007.

———. *Thomas Jefferson: Author of America.* New York: HarperCollins, 2005.

Hinnells, John R., ed. *The Penguin Dictionary of Religions.* New York: Penguin Books, 1997.

"History of Jain Sects." *Jainworld.com,* 2011, http://www.jainworld.com/societies/jainsects.asp (accessed 14 Nov. 2015).

Hodge, Charles. *Essays and Reviews: Selected from the Princeton Review.* New York: Robert Carters and Brothers, 1857. Available at https://archive.org/stream/essaysreviews00hodg#page/n5/mode/2up.

Hoffer, Eric. *The True Believer: Thoughts on the Nature of Mass Movements.* New York: Perennial Library, 1966.

Hogan, Candace L., Jutta Matta, and Laura L. Carstensen. "Exercise Holds Immediate Benefits for Affect and Cognition in Younger and Older Adults." *Psychology and Aging* 28.2 (2013): pp. 587-94, http://psycnet.apa.org/record/2013-21685-007 (accessed 28 Oct. 2018).

Holder, John J., ed. and trans. *Early Buddhist Discourses.* Indianapolis: Hackett Publishing Co., 2006.

The Holy Bible: Authorized King James Version. Iowa Falls, IA: Word Publishing, 1989.

Holy Bible: Revised Standard Version. Nashville, TN: Thomas Nelson, 1972.

Hussain, Dilwar and Braj Bjushan. "Psychology Meditation and Health: Present Status and Future Directions." *International Journal of Psychology and Psychological Therapy* 10.3 (2010): pp. 439-51.

Huxley, Thomas. *Agnosticism and Christianity and other Essays.* Buffalo, NY: Prometheus Books, 1992.

Ignatius of Antioch. The Epistle of Ignatius to the Ephesians. In *Ante-Nicene Fathers.* Vol. 1. Edited by Alexander Roberts et al. Translated by Alexander Roberts and James Donaldson. Buffalo, NY: Christian Literature Publishing Co., 1885. Revised and edited for New Advent by Kevin Knight. http://www.newadvent.org/fathers/0104.htm.

———. The Epistle of Ignatius to Polycarp. In *Ante-Nicene Fathers.* Vol. 1. Edited by Alexander Roberts et al. Translated by Alexander Roberts and James Donaldson. Buffalo, NY: Christian Literature Publishing Co., 1885. Revised and edited for New Advent by Kevin Knight. http://www.newadvent.org/fathers/0110.htm.

Ignatius of Loyola. *The Spiritual Exercises of St. Ignatius.* Translated by Louis J. Puhl. New York: Random House, 2000.

Ingber, Sasha. "70 Muslim Clerics Issue Fatwa Against Violence and Terrorism." *NPR*, 11 May 2018, https://www.npr.org/sections/thetwo-way/2018/05/11/610420149/70-muslim-clerics-issue-fatwa-against-violence-and-terrorism (accessed 13 May 2018).

Ingersoll, Robert Green. *The Works of Robert G. Ingersoll (Complete 12 Volumes)*. USA: Library of Alexandria, 1881. Kindle.

International Theological Commission. *The Hope of Salvation for Infants who Die without Being Baptised*, 22 Apr. 2007, http://www.vatican.va/roman_curia/congregations/cfaith/cti_documents/rc_con_cfaith_doc_20070419_un-baptised-infants_en.html (accessed 1 Oct. 2018).

Irenaeus. *Against Heresies*. In *Ante-Nicene Fathers*. Vol. 1. Edited by Alexander Roberts, et al. Translated by Alexander Roberts and William Rambaut. Buffalo, NY: Christian Literature Publishing Co., 1885. Revised and edited for New Advent by Kevin Knight. http://newadvent.org/fathers/0103.htm.

Isaac, Rhys. *The Transformation of Virginia: 1740-1790*. New York: Norton, 1988.

Isaacson, Walter. *Einstein: His Life and Universe*. New York: Simon and Schuster, 2007.

Ishaq, Ibn. *The Life of Muhammad: Apostle of Allah*. Edited by Michael Edwardes. London: The Folio Society, 2003.

Jacoby, Susan. *The Great Agnostic: Robert Ingersoll and American Freethought*. New Haven: Yale Univ. Press, 2013.

"Jain Sects." *BBC*, 11 Sep. 2009, http://www.bbc.co.uk/religion/religions/jainism/subdivisions/subdivisions.shtml (accessed 14 Nov. 2015).

Jefferson, Thomas. Letters. In *Founders Online*. Available at National Archives, https://founders.archives.gov/?q=%20Author%3A%22Jefferson%2C%20Thomas%22&s=1111211111&r=1.

———. *The Portable Thomas Jefferson*. Edited by Merrill Peterson. New York: Penguin, 1975.

Jensen, David H. *1 & 2 Samuel: A Theological Commentary on the Bible*. Louisville, KY: Westminster John Knox Press, 2015.

Jerath, Ravinder, Molly W. Crawford, Vernon A. Barnes, and Kyler Harden. "Self-Regulation of Breathing as a Primary Treatment for Anxiety." *Applied Psychophysiology and Biofeedback* 40.2 (Jun. 2015): pp. 107-115.

Jerome. *The Perpetual Virginity of the Blessed Mary*. In *Nicene and Post-Nicene Fathers, Second Series*. Vol. 6. Edited by Philip Schaff and Henry Wace. Translated by W. H. Fremantle, et al. Buffalo, NY: Christian Literature Publishing Co., 1893. Revised and edited for New Advent by Kevin Knight. http://www.newadvent.org/fathers/3007.htm.

Jewish Encyclopedia: The unedited full-text of the 1906 Jewish Encyclopedia. 1901-1906. Available at http://www.jewishencyclopedia.com/.

John of the Cross. *John of the Cross: Selected Writings*. Edited by Kiernan Kavanaugh. New York: Paulist Press, 1987.

John of Damascus. *An Exposition of the Orthodox Faith*. In *Nicene and Post-Nicene Fathers, Second Series*. Vol. 9. Edited by Philip Schaff and Henry Wace. Translated by E.W. Watson and L. Pullan. Buffalo, NY: Christian Literature Publishing Co., 1899. Revised and edited for New Advent by Kevin Knight. http://www.newadvent.org/fathers/3304.htm.

Johnson, Christopher Jay and Marsha G. McGee, eds. *How Different Religions View Death and Afterlife*, 2nd ed. Philadelphia: The Charles Press, 1998.

Johnson, Maxwell E., ed. *Issues in Eucharistic Praying in East and West: Essays in Liturgical and Theological Analysis*. Collegeville, MN: Liturgical Press, 2010.

Josephus. *The Works of Flavius Josephus*. Translated by William Whiston. Grand Rapids, MI: Christian Classics Ethereal Library, n.d. http://www.ccel.org/ccel/josephus/works/files/works.html.

Julian of Norwich. *Revelations of Divine Love*. Translated by Elizabeth Spearing. London: Penguin, 1998.

Justin Martyr. *The First Apology*. In *Ante-Nicene Fathers*. Vol. 1. Edited by Alexander Roberts et al. Translated by Marcus Dods and George Reith. Buffalo, NY: Christian Literature Publishing Co., 1885. Revised and edited for New Advent by Kevin Knight. http://www.newadvent.org/fathers/0126.htm.

Kalomiros, Alexandre. *The River of Fire: A Reply to the Questions: Is God Really Good? Did God Create Hell?* Seattle, WA: St. Nectarios Press, 1980.

Kaltenbach, Caleb and Matthew Vines. "Debating Bible Verses on Homosexuality." *The New York Times*, 8 Jun. 2015, https://www.nytimes.com/

interactive/2015/06/05/us/samesex-scriptures.html (accessed 6 Jun. 2017).

Kamali, Mohammad Hashim. *A Textbook of Hadith Studies: Authenticity, Compilation, Classification and Criticism of Hadith*, 3rd impression. Leicestershire, UK: The Islamic Foundation, 2004.

———. *Shari'ah Law: An Introduction*. Oxford: Oneworld Publications, 2008.

Kaplan, Stephen. *The Beta Israel (Falasha) in Ethiopia: From Earliest Times to the Twentieth Century*. New York: New York Univ. Press, 1992. Kindle.

Katz, Birgit. "A Dracula Ant's Snapping Jaw Is the Fastest Known Appendage in the Animal Kingdom." *Smithsonian.com*, 18 Dec. 2018, https://www.smithsonianmag.com/smart-news/dracula-ants-snapping-jaws-are-fastest-known-appendage-any-animal-180971061/ (accessed 22 Dec. 2018).

Kaufmann, Walter, ed. *Existentialism from Dostoevsky to Sartre*. Rev. ed. New York: Meridian/NAL Penguin, 1975.

Keller, Timothy. *The Reason for God*. New York: Riverhead Books, 2008.

Keltner, Dacher and Jonathan Haidt. "Approaching Awe, a Moral, Spiritual, and Aesthetic Emotion." *Cognition and Emotion* 17.2 (2003): pp. 297–314.

Kelly, William E. "An Investigation of Worry and Sense of Humor." *The Journal of Psychology* 136.6 (Nov. 2002): pp. 657-66.

Kenner, Craig and William Heth. "Remarriage: Two Views." *Christianity Today*, 31 Aug. 2000, http://www.christianitytoday.com/ct/2000/augustweb-only/48.0c.html?start=1 (accessed 24 Jul. 2016).

King, Barbara J. and Michel Martin. "Discoveries Give New Clues to Possible Neanderthal Religious Practices." *NPR*, 11 Dec. 2016, http://www.npr.org/2016/12/11/505187953/discoveries-give-new-clues-to-possible-neanderthal-religious-practices (accessed 1 Jan. 2017).

King, Karen. *The Gospel of Mary of Magdala: Jesus and the First Woman Disciple*. Santa Rosa, CA: Polebridge Press, 2003.

King, Martin Luther, Jr. "Letter from a Birmingham Jail." *Univ. of Pennsylvania African Studies Center*, 16 Apr. 1963, http://www.africa.upenn.edu/Articles_Gen/Letter_Birmingham.html (accessed 21 Apr. 2016).

King, Robert H. *Thomas Merton and Thich Nhat Hanh: Engaged Spirituality in an Age of Globalization*. New York: Continuum, 2003.

Kirsch, Jonathan. *A History of the End of the World: How the Most Controversial Book of the Bible Changed the Course of Western Civilization*. San Francisco: HarperSanFrancisco, 2006.

Klaassen, Walter. "A Fire that Spread Anabaptist Beginnings." *Christian History*, 4.1, issue 5 (1985): pp. 7-9.

Knott, Kim. *Hinduism: A Very Short Introduction*. New York: Oxford Univ. Press, 1998.

Knox, John. *The First Blast of the Trumpet Against the Monstrous Regiment of Women*. Edited by Edward Arber. Grand Rapids, MI: Christian Classics Ethereal Library, orig. pub. 1558. https://www.ccel.org/ccel/knox/blast.pdf.

Kolbert, Elizabeth. "Why Facts Don't Change Our Minds: New Discoveries about the Human Mind Show the Limitations of Reason." *The New Yorker*, 27 Feb. 2017, http://www.newyorker.com/magazine/2017/02/27/why-facts-dont-change-our-minds (accessed 23 Feb. 2017).

The Koran. Translated by N. J. Dawood. New York: Penguin Books, 1974.

Krajick, Kevin. "Discoveries in the Dark." *National Geographic* (Sep. 2007): pp. 134-47.

Krause, Neal and Christopher G. Ellison. "Forgiveness by God, Forgiveness of Others, and Psychological Well-being in Late Life." *Journal for the Scientific Study of Religion*, 42.1 (Mar. 2003): pp. 77-94, https://www.ncbi.nlm.nih.gov/pmc/articles/PMC3046863/ (accessed 15 Dec. 2018).

Kreiser, B. Robert. "Religious Enthusiasm in Early Eighteenth-Century Paris: The Convulsionaries of Saint-Médard." *The Catholic Historical Review* 61.3 (Jul. 1975): pp. 353-385.

Krulwich, Robert. "Which Is Greater, the Number of Sand Grains on the Earth or Stars in the Sky?" *NPR*, 17 Sep. 2012, http://www.npr.org/sections/krulwich/2012/09/17/161096233/which-is-greater-the-number-of-sand-grains-on-earth-or-stars-in-the-sky (accessed 23 Oct. 2016).

Ku, Yu-hsiu. *History of Zen*. Singapore: Springer, 2016.

Kurzbahn, Robert. *Why Everyone (Else) Is a Hypocrite*. Princeton, NJ: Princeton Univ. Press, 2010.

Kushner, Harold S. *When Bad Things Happen to Good People*. New York, Avon Books, 1981.

Lactantius. *Divine Institutes*. In *Ante-Nicene Fathers*. Vol. 7. Edited by Alexander Roberts, et al. Translated by William Fletcher. Buffalo, NY: Christian Literature Publishing Co., 1886. Revised and edited for New Advent by Kevin Knight. http://www.newadvent.org/fathers/07015.htm.

Langley, Liz. "7 Gender-Altering Animals." *National Geographic*, 22 Sep. 2013, http://voices.nationalgeographic.com/2013/09/22/7-gender-bending-animals/ (accessed 24 Sep. 2016).

Lao Tzu. *Tao Te Ching*. Edited by Yi-Ping Ong. Translated by Charles Muller. New York: Barnes and Noble, 2005.

Lao Tzu. *Tao Te Ching: The Book of the Way and Its Power*. Translated by John R. Mabry. Berkeley, CA: The Apocryphile Press, 2017. Kindle.

Law, Timothy Michael. *When God Spoke Greek: The Septuagint and the Making of the Christian Bible*. Oxford Univ. Press, 2013. Kindle.

Lazar, Sara W. et al. "Meditation Experience Is Associated with Increased Cortical Thickness." *NeuroReport* 16.17 (2005): pp. 1893-7 https://www.ncbi.nlm.nih.gov/pmc/articles/PMC1361002/ (accessed 1 Nov. 2018).

Leith, John H., ed. *Creeds of the Churches: A Reader in Christian Doctrine from the Bible to the Present*. 3rd ed. Louisville: John Knox Press, 1982.

Leslau, Wolf. *Falasha Anthology: Translated from Ethiopic Sources*. New Haven: Yale Univ. Press, 1979.

Lewis, C. S. *The Great Divorce*. New York: MacMillian Publishing Co., 1946.

———. *The Joyful Christian: 127 Readings from C. S. Lewis*. New York: Collier Books, 1977.

———. *Mere Christianity*. Rev. ed. New York: Collier Books, 1952.

Liao, Yue, Eleanor T. Shonkoff, and Genevieve F. Dunton. "The Acute Relationships between Affect, Physical Feeling States, and Physical Activity in Daily Life: A Review of Current Evidence." *Frontiers in Psychology* 6.1975 (Dec. 2015): pp. 1-7, http://citeseerx.ist.psu.edu/viewdoc/download?doi=10.1.1.791.5099&rep=rep1&type=pdf (accessed 30 Oct. 2018).

Lim, Timothy H. *The Formation of the Jewish Canon*. New Haven: Yale Univ. Press, 2013.

"Litanies." *EWTN*, n.d., http://ewtn.com/Devotionals/Litanies/index.htm (accessed 8 May 2016).

"Litany of Humility." *EWTN*, n.d., http://www.ewtn.com/devotionals/prayers/humility.htm#ixzz20KnAgVOc (accessed 18 Jan. 2013).

The Little Flowers of Saint Francis. Translated by Raphael Brown. New York: Image Books, 1958.

Livingstone, E. A., ed. *The Concise Oxford Dictionary of the Christian Church.*, 3rd ed. Oxford: Oxford Univ. Press, 2013.

Loftus, Elizabeth. "How Reliable Is Your Memory?" *TED Global 2013*, Jun. 2013, https://www.ted.com/talks/elizabeth_loftus_the_fiction_of_memory#t-10018 (accessed 27 Sep. 2018).

Loftus, John. "The Outsider Test for Faith." *Debunking Christianity* (blog), 20 Mar. 2009, http://debunkingchristianity.blogspot.com/2009/03/outsider-test-for-faith_20.html.

———. *Why I Became an Atheist: A Former Preacher Rejects Christianity*. Amherst, NY: Prometheus, 2012. Kindle.

Loisy, Alfred. *My Duel with the Vatican: The Autobiography of a Catholic Modernist*. Translated by Richard Wilson Boynton. New York: Greenwood Press, 1968.

Lukefahr, Oscar. *"We Believe ... ": A Survey of the Catholic Faith*. Ligouri, MO: Ligouri, 1990.

Lundberg, Magnus. "Holy Apostolic Palmarian Catholic Church." *World Religions and Spirituality*, 28 Sep. 2015, https://wrldrels.org/2016/10/08/palmarian-catholic-church/ (accessed 16 Mar. 2018).

Luther, Martin. *The Bondage of the Will*. Translated by Henry Cole. Legacy Publications, 2011. Kindle.

———. *Commentary on Galatians*. Grand Rapids, MI: Fleming H. Revell, 1988.

———. *Lectures on Titus, Philemon, and Hebrews*. In *Luther's Works*. Vol. 29. Edited and translated by Jaroslav Pelikan. St. Louis: Concordia Publishing House, 1968. Kindle.

———. *On the Jews and Their Lies, 1543*. In *Internet Medieval Sourcebook*. Translated by Martin H. Bertram. Edited by Paul Halsall, Fordham University, 21 Feb. 2001, https://archive.org/details/MartinLuther-14831546OnTheJewsAndTheirLies (accessed 15 Nov. 2018).

———. *Sermons on the Gospel of St. John Chapters 1-4*. In *Luther's Works*. Vol. 22. Edited by Jaroslav Pelikan. Saint Louis: Concordia, 1957.

———. *Table Talk*. Translated by William Hazlitt. Grand Rapids, MI: Christian Classics Ethereal Library, n.d. http://www.ccel.org/ccel/luther/tabletalk.pdf.

———. *Works of Martin Luther—Prefaces to the Books of the Bible, 1522-1545*. Godrules.net, n.d. http://www.godrules.net/library/luther/NEW1luther_f8.htm (accessed 12 Aug. 2018).

Mabry, John R. *The Monster God: Coming to Terms with the Dark Side of Divinity*. Berkeley, CA: Apocryphile, 2015. Kindle.

———. *Salvation of the True Rock: The Sufi Poetry of Najat Ozkaya*. Berkeley, CA: Apocryphile, 2011.

MacKinnon, Matthew. "The Science of Slow Deep Breathing." *Psychology Today*, 7 Feb. 2016, https://www.psychologytoday.com/us/blog/neuraptitude/201602/the-science-slow-deep-breathing (accessed 1 Nov. 2018).

Mahaffy, John W. "Wine or Grape Juice: Theological and Pastoral Reflections on the Fruit of the Vine in Communion." *Ordained Servant Online*, Feb. 2011, https://opc.org/os.html?article_id=237&issue_id=62 (accessed 10 Jul. 2018).

Mahayana Lankavatara Sutra. Fodian.net (Buddhist Scriptures in Multiple Languages). Translated by Daisetz Teitaro Suzuki, n.d. http://www.fodian.net/world/0672.html.

Maiklem, Lara, ed. *Ultimate Visual Dictionary of Science*. New York: Barnes and Noble, 2005.

Maimonides. *The Guide of the Perplexed*. Abridged ed. Edited by Julius Guttman and Chaim Rabin. Indianapolis: Hackett Pub. Co., 1995.

Mann, Charles C. "The Birth of Religion." *National Geographic* (Jun. 2011) pp. 39-59.

Mapson, Knujon, ed. *Pandeism: An Anthology*. Winchester, UK: iff Books, 2017.

Marcellinus, Ammianus. *Roman History*. Translated by C. D. Yonge. London: Bohn, 1862. Available at https://archive.org/details/romanhistoryamm01marcgoog/page/n14.

Marshall, Howard. *Luke: Historian and Theologian*, 3rd ed. Downers Grove, IL: InterVarsity Press, 1998.

Marshall, John W. ed. *The Five Gospel Parallels.* Dept. for the Study of Religion, Univ. of Toronto, 1996-2001, http://sites.utoronto.ca/religion/synopsis/ (accessed 7 Mar. 2016).

Massey, Edmund. "A sermon against the dangerous and sinful practice of inoculation." Boston: Benjamin Indicott, 1730. Available at http://quod.lib.umich.edu/e/evans/n02782.0001.001?rgn=main;view=fulltext.

Masters, Kevin S. and Glen I. Spielmans. "Prayer and Health: Review, Meta-Analysis, and Research Agenda." *Journal of Behavioral Medicine* 30.4 (2007): pp. 329-38.

Mastrantonis, George. *A New-Style Catechism on the Eastern Orthodox Faith for Adults.* St. Louis: The OLOGOS Mission, 1969.

Matt, Daniel C. *The Essential Kabbalah: The Heart of Jewish Mysticism.* Edison, NJ: Castle Books, 1997.

Matthews, Victor H. and Don C. Benjamin. *Old Testament Parallels: Laws and Stories from the Ancient Near East.* New York: Paulist Press, 1991.

Matyszak, Philip. *The Enemies of Rome: From Hannibal to Attila the Hun.* London: Thames and Hudson, 2004.

Mawdsley, Roberta H., Elizabeth J. Verazin, Eric S. Bersch, et al. "The Relationship between Humor and Physical Therapist Students' Anxiety." *Journal of Physical Therapy Education*, 21.1 (Spring 2007): pp. 70-5.

Maxwell, James A., ed. *America's Fascinating Indian Heritage.* Pleasantville, NY: Reader's Digest Assn., 1978.

McBirnie, William Steuart. *The Search for the Twelve Apostles.* Wheaton: Living Books, 1973.

McBrien, Richard P. *Lives of the Popes: The Pontiffs from St. Peter to John Paul II.* New York: HarperCollins, 2000.

McDowell, Josh. *Evidence That Demands a Verdict: Historical Evidences for the Christian Faith.* Vol. 1. San Bernadino: Here's Life Publishers, 1979.

―――. *More Than a Carpenter*, 5th printing. Wheaton, IL: Living Books, 1982.

McDowell, Sean. "Did the Apostles really Die as Martyrs for Their Faith?" *Biola Magazine*, Fall 2013, http://magazine.biola.edu/article/13-fall/did-the-apostles-really-die-as-martyrs-for-their-f/ (accessed 21 Jul. 2018).

McGrath, Alister E., ed. *The Christian Theology Reader*, 2nd ed. Oxford: Blackwell Publishing, 2001.

———. *Iustitia Dei: A History of the Doctrine of Justification*, 3rd ed. New York: Cambridge Univ. Press, 2005.

———. *Justification by Faith*. Grand Rapids, MI: Zondervan, 1988.

———. *A Life of John Calvin: A Study in the Shaping of Western Culture*. Oxford:Basil Blackwell Ltd., 1990.

McGrath, William R. *The Anabaptists: Neither Catholics or Protestants*. Crossreach Publications: 2015. Kindle.

McLeod, Hew. *Sikhism*. London: Penguin, 1997.

McMinn, Bernard, John J. Collins, and Stephen J. Stein, eds. *The Continuum History of Apocalypticism*. New York: Continuum, 2003.

McMurphy, Kathleen B. "John Wesley and the End of the World." *Ministry*, Apr. 1960, https://www.ministrymagazine.org/archive/1960/04/john-wesley-and-the-end-of-the-world (accessed 1 May 2015).

Meacham, Jon. "Pastor Rob Bell: What if Hell Doesn't Exist?" *Time*, 14 Apr. 2011, http://content.time.com/time/magazine/article/0,9171,2065289-1,00.html (accessed 7 Feb. 2019).

Mead, Frank and Samuel Hill. *Handbook of Denominations in the United States*. Nashville: Abingdon Press, 1995.

Meltzer, Milton. *Slavery: A World History*. Updated ed. Vols. 1-2. New York: Da Capo Press, 1993.

Merck, Mandy, ed. *After Diana: Irreverent Elegies*. London: Verso, 1998.

Merrick, J. and Stephen M. Garrett, eds. *Five Views on Biblical Inerrancy*. Grand Rapids, MI: Zondervan, 2013.

Merton, Thomas. *The Seven Storey Mountain*. San Diego: Harvest/Harcourt Brace Jovanovich, 1978.

Mettaous, H. G. Bishop. *Sacramental Rites in the Coptic Orthodox Church*, 2nd ed. Coptic Orthodox Church Network, 1998-2014, http://www.copticchurch.net/topics/thecopticchurch/sacraments/3_repentance_confesstion.html.

Metzger, Bruce M. *The Canon of the New Testament: Its Origin, Development, and Significance*. Oxford: Clarendon Press, 1997.

———. *The Text of the New Testament: Its Transmission, Corruption, and Restoration*, 2nd ed. New York: Oxford Univ. Press, 1968.

Metzger, Bruce M. and Roland E. Murphy, eds. *The New Oxford Annotated Bible with the Apocrypha*. New York: Oxford Univ. Press, 1991.

Miles, Tom. "Irreverent Atheists Crowdsource Charitable Giving." *Reuters*, 11 Dec. 2011, https://www.reuters.com/article/us-atheists-donations-idUSTRE7B81SU20111209 (accessed 29 Mar. 2017).
Miller, James. *Daoism: A Short Introduction*. Oxford: Oneworld, 2003.
Miller, Kenneth R. *Finding Darwin's God: A Scientist's Search for Common Ground Between God and Evolution*. New York: Harper Perennial, 2002.
Milligan, Brantly. "A Protestant Defense of Mary's Perpetual Virginity." *Aleteia*, 10 Oct. 2013, http://aleteia.org/2013/10/10/a-protestant-defense-of-marys-perpetual-virginity/ (accessed 8 Sep. 2016).
Mitchell, Deborah. "Mother Teresa Less Than a Saint for the Sick." *EmaxHealth*, 3 Mar. 2013, http://www.emaxhealth.com/1275/mother-teresa-less-saint-sick (accessed 5 May 2013).
Mills, Watson E., ed. *Mercer Dictionary of the Bible*, 3rd corrected printing. Macon, GA: Mercer Univ. Press, 1992.
Modi, Jivanji Jamshedji. *A Catechism of the Zoroastrian Religion*. Bombay: J.N. Petit Parsi Orphange Captin Printing Works, 1911. Available at https://archive.org/details/catechismofzoroa00modirich.
Montley, Patricia. "A Humanist's Guide to Prayer." *UU World*, 25 Feb. 2013, www.uuworld.org/articles/humanist-guide-prayer (accessed 23 Sep. 2016).
More, Thomas. *The Apology of Sir Thomas More, Knight*. Edited by Mary Gottschalk. Center for Thomas Moore Studies, 2014. file:///E:/Sources%20and%20articles/Thomas%20More,%20Apology.pdf.
———. *Utopia*. Edited by Henry Morley. Project Gutenberg, 22 Apr. 2005, http://www.gutenberg.org/files/2130/2130-h/2130-h.htm.
Morgan, David. *The Mongols*. Malden, MA: Blackwell Publishers, 2000.
Morris, Charles G. *Psychology: An Introduction*. Englewood Cliffs, NJ: Prentice Hall, 1988.
Moss, Vladimir. "'The River of Fire' Revisited." *Orthodoxchrisitianbooks.com*, rev. 10 Feb. 2014, http://www.orthodoxchristianbooks.com/articles/837/-river-fire-revisited/ (accessed 13 Jul. 2018).
Mother Teresa. *Mother Teresa: Come Be My Light*. Edited by Brian Kolodiejchuk. New York: Doubleday, 2007.
———. *No Greater Love*. Edited by Becky Benenate and Joseph Durepos. Novato, CA: New World Library, 2001.

Movsesian, Vazken. *The Bible in the Armenian Church*. Burbank, CA: Western Diocese of the Armenian Church: Department of Youth Ministries, 2003. Available at http://armenianchurchlibrary.com/files/BibleintheArmenianChurchMovsesian.pdf.

Mujahid, Abdul Malik ed. and trans. *200 Golden Hadiths*. Darussalam Publishers, 2013. Kindle.

Müller, F. Max, ed. *Jaina Sutras: Part II*. Translated by Hermann Jacobi. Oxford: The Clarendon Press, 1895. Available at http://www.sacred-texts.com/jai/sbe45/index.htm.

Murdoch, Adrian. *The Last Pagan: Julian the Apostate and the Death of the Ancient World*. Rochester, VT: Inner Traditions, 2008.

Murray, William R. *Reason and Reverence: Religious Humanism for the 21st Century*. Boston: Skinner House Books, 2007.

Murrock, Carolyn J. and Abir K. Bekhet. "Concept Analysis: Music Therapy." *Research and Theory for Nursing Practice: An International Journal* 30.1 (2016); pp. 44-59.

"Myth 4: God Is a Trinity." *The Watchtower*, Nov. 2009, http://www.jw.org/en/publications/magazines/wp20091101/myth-god-is-a-trinity/ (accessed 18 Dec. 2014).

Nashmi, Tarmida Yuhana. "Contemporary Issues for the Mandaean Faith." *Mandaean Associations Union*, 28 Mar. 2013, http://www.mandaeanunion.com/culture/item/172-mandaean-faith (accessed 11 Sep. 2016).

Nassif, Bradley. "Kissers and Smashers: Why the Orthodox Killed One Another over Icons." *Christian History* 16.2, issue 54 (1997): p. 20.

Neill, Stephen and Tom Wright. *The Interpretation of the New Testament: 1861-1986*, 2nd ed. Oxford: Oxford Univ. Press, 1988.

Nemeroff, Adam. "Apocalypticism and the First Crusade." *Dartmouth University*, 24 Apr. 2016, https://sites.dartmouth.edu/crusadememory/2016/04/24/apocalypticism-and-the-first-crusade/ (accessed 23 Nov. 2017).

Netherton, Dana. "Taking the Long View." *Christian History* 18.1, issue 61 (1999): p. 11.

New American Bible. St. Joseph Medium Sized edition. New York: Catholic Book Publishing Co., 1992.

New American Standard Bible. Text edition. Anaheim, CA: Foundation Publications, 1997.

Newman, John Henry. *Apologia Pro Vita Sua: Being a History of His Religious Opinions*. London: Longmans, Green and Co., 1888. Available at https://archive.org/details/apologiaprovitas00newm_2/page/n5.

———. *An Essay on the Development of Christian Doctrine*. London: James Toovey, 1845. Available at https://archive.org/details/OnTheDevelopmentOfChristianDoctrine1845/page/n3.

Niebuhr, Gustav. "'The Family' and the Final Harvest." *The Washington Post*, 2 Jun. 1993, http://www.washingtonpost.com/wp-srv/national/longterm/cult/children_of_god/child1.htm, (accessed 23 Jan. 2016).

Nigosian, S. A. *The Zoroastrian Faith: Tradition and Modern Research*. Montreal: McGill-Queen's Univ. Press, 1993.

Nolt, Steven M. *A History of the Amish*, 3rd ed. New York: Good Books, 2015.

Noonan, John T., Jr. *A Church that Can and Cannot Change: The Development of Catholic Moral Teaching*. Notre Dame, IN: Univ. of Notre Dame Press, 2005.

Nouwen, Henri. *Ministry and Spirituality*. New York: Continuum, 1996.

Norwich, John Julius. *A Short History of Byzantium*. New York: Vintage Books, 1999.

The NRSV Notetaker's Bible: New Revised Standard Version with the Apocrypha. New York: Oxford Univ. Press, 2009.

Oberman, Heiko. *Luther: Man between God and the Devil*. New Haven: Yale Univ. Press, 2006.

Oden, Thomas. *The Justification Reader*. Grand Rapids: Wm. B. Eerdmans, 2002.

Odisho, Mar. *The Book of Marganitha (The Pearl) On the Truth of Christianity*. Nestorian.org, n.d. Available at http://www.nestorian.org/book_of_marganitha_part_i.html.

Ohnuma, Tohru and Heii Arai. "Genetic or Psychogenic? A Case Study of (Folie à Quatre) Including Twins." *Case Reports in Psychiatry* 2015: pp. 1-3.

Oremus Bible Browser. New Revised Standard Version. http://bible.oremus.org/.

Origen. *Against Celsus (Contra Celsum)*. In *Ante-Nicene Fathers*. Vol. 4. Edited by Alexander Roberts, et al. Translated by Frederick Crombie. Buffalo, NY: Christian Literature Publishing Co., 1885. Revised and edited for New Advent by Kevin Knight. http://www.newadvent.org/fathers/0416.htm.

———. *Commentary on the Gospel of Matthew*. In *Ante-Nicene* Fathers. Vol. 9. Edited by Allan Menzies. Translated by John Patrick. Buffalo, NY: Christian Literature Publishing Co., 1896. Revised and edited for New Advent by Kevin Knight. http://www.newadvent.org/fathers/1016.htm.

Ortberg, John. "Tithing: Law or Grace?" *Christianity Today*, Spring 2013, www.christianitytoday.com/pastors/2013/spring/tthing-law-or-grace.html (accessed 10 Feb. 2017).

Orth, Maureen. "The World's Most Powerful Woman." *National Geographic* (Dec. 2015): pp. 40-1.

OrthodoxWiki. https://orthodoxwiki.org/Main_Page.

O'Carroll, Eoin. "Judgment Day? Five Failed End-of-the World Predictions." *Christian Science Monitor*, 18 May 2011, http://www.csmonitor.com/Science/2011/0518/Judgment-Day-Five-failed-end-of-the-world-predictions/1806 (accessed 31 Aug. 2018).

O'Shea, Stephen. *The Perfect Heresy: The Revolutionary Life and Death of the Medieval Cathars*. New York: Walker and Co., 2000.

O'Toole, Garson. "Be Kind; Everyone You Meet is Fighting a Hard Battle." *Quote Investigator: Tracing Quotations*, 29 Jun. 2010, http://quoteinvestigator.com/2010/06/29/be-kind/ (accessed 9 Dec. 2016).

Oyer, John S. "Sticks and Stones Broke Their Bones, and Vicious Names Did Hurt Them!: 16th-Century Responses to the Anabaptists." *Christian History* 4.1 (1985): pp. 17-19.

Ozar, Alex. "Purim and the Exceptional Book of Esther." *First Things*, 9 Mar. 2012, http://www.firstthings.com/onthesquare/2012/03/purim-and-the-exceptional-book-of-esther (accessed 31 Jul. 2013).

Padover, Saul K. *Jefferson*. Abridged ver. New York: Mentor, 1970.

Pagels, Elaine. *The Gnostic Gospels*. New York: Vintage Books, 1989.

Paine, Thomas. *Works of Thomas Paine*. Coyote Canyon Press, 2010. Kindle.

Pak, Ung Kyu. *Millennialism in the Korean Protestant Church*. New York: Peter Lang Publishing, 2005.

Palmer, G. E. H. et al., ed. and trans. *The Philokalia: The Complete Text*. Vols. 1-2, 4. London: Faber and Faber, 1979-1995.

———. *The Philokalia: The Complete Text*. Vol. 3. New York: Farrar, Straus and Giroux, 1984.

Palmer, Jason. "Kepler telescope: Earth-sized planets 'number 17bn.'" *BBC News*, 8 Jan. 2013, http://www.bbc.com/news/science-environment-20942440 (accessed 8 Jan. 2017).

Palmer, R. R. and Joel Colton. *A History of the Modern World to 1815*, 6th ed. New York: Alfred A. Knopf, 1983.

Papal Encyclicals Online. http://www.papalencyclicals.net/.

Parekh, Bhikhu. *Gandhi: A Very Short Introduction*. Oxford: Oxford Univ. Press, 1997.

Pargament, Kenneth I. *The Psychology of Religion and Coping*. New York: Guilford Press, 1997.

Parrinder, Geoffrey, ed. *World Religions: From Ancient History to Present*. New York: Facts on File, 1985.

Pascal, Blaise. *Pensées*. Rev. ed. New York: Penguin, 1995.

Pathak, Sushmita. "Cow Dung Soap is Cleaning Up in India." *NPR*, 3 Oct. 2018, https://www.npr.org/sections/goatsandsoda/2018/10/03/653739760/cow-dung-soap-is-cleaning-up-in-india (accessed 3 Oct. 2013).

Pennington, Kenneth, ed. "The Council of Elvira, ca. 306." *Catholic University of America*, n.d., https://www.webcitation.org/6AS7rgB-7f?url=http://faculty.cua.edu/pennington/canon%20Law/ElviraCanons.htm (accessed 24 Aug. 2018).

Perciavalle, Valentina et al. "The Role of Deep Breathing on Stress." *Neurological Sciences* 38.3 (2017): pp. 451-8.

Pérez, Joseph. *The Spanish Inquisition: A History*. Translated by Janet Lloyd. New Haven: Yale Univ. Press, 2005.

Philaret (Drozdov) of Moscow. "The Longer Catechism of the Orthodox, Catholic, Eastern Church." In *The Creeds of Christendom with a History and Critical Notes*. Edited by Philip Schaff. Translated by R. W. Blackmore. Available at http://www.pravoslavieto.com/docs/eng/Orthodox_Catechism_of_Philaret.htm#gen0.

Phillips, Jonathan. *The Fourth Crusade and the Sack of Constantinople*. New York: Penguin, 2004.

Philo. *The Works of Philo Judaeus.* Vols. III-IV. Translated by C. D. Yonge. London: Henry G. Bohn, 1855. Vol. III available at https://archive.org/details/worksofphilojuda03phil/page/n5. Vol. IV available at https://archive.org/details/worksofphilojuda04phil/page/n3.

Plato. *Great Dialogues of Plato.* Edited by Eric H. Warmington and Philip G. Rouse. Translated by W. H. D. Rouse. New York: Mentor, 1956.

Plummer, John P. *The Many Paths of the Independent Sacramental Movement.* Berkeley, CA: Apocryphile Press, 2006.

The Poetic Edda. Translated by Henry Adams Bellows. New York: The American-Scandinavian Foundation, 1923. Available at https://archive.org/details/poeticedda00belluoft/page/n5.

Polo, Marco. *The Travels of Marco Polo.* Edited by Manuel Komroff. New York: Modern Library, 2001.

Polycarp. Epistle of Polycarp to the Philippians. In *Ante-Nicene Fathers.* Vol. 1. Edited by Alexander Roberts, et al. Translated by Alexander Roberts and James Donaldson. Buffalo, NY: Christian Literature Publishing Co., 1885. Revised and edited for New Advent by Kevin Knight. http://www.newadvent.org/fathers/0136.htm.

Prabhupada, A. C. Bhakivedanta Swami. *Bhagavad-gita As It Is.* Los Angeles: Bhaktivedanta Trust International, 1972-2004. Available at: http://www.bhagavatgita.ru/files/Bhagavad-gita_As_It_Is.pdf.

Price, Robert M. "Jesus' Burial in a Garden: The Strange Growth of the Tradition." *Religious Traditions* 12, (1989): http://www.robertmprice.mindvendor.com/burial.htm (accessed 4 Nov. 2015).

"Progressive Muscle Relaxation (PMR): A Positive Psychology Guide." *Positive Psychology Program,* 26 Jan. 2018, https://positivepsychologyprogram.com/progressive-muscle-relaxation-pmr/ (accessed 25 Mar. 2018).

Pullella, Philip. "Catholic Church Buries Limbo after Centuries." *Reuters,* 20 Apr. 2007, https://www.reuters.com/article/us-pope-limbo-idUSL2028721620070420 (accessed 1 Oct. 2018).

Quammen, David. "Forest Giant." *National Geographic* (Dec. 2012): pp. 34-7.

Rachels, James. *The Elements of Moral Philosophy,* 3rd ed. Boston: McGraw-Hill College, 1999.

Raffaele, Paul. *Among the Great Apes: Adventures on the Trail of Our Closest Relatives.* New York: HarperCollins, 2010.

———. "Keepers of the Lost Ark?" *Smithsonian.com*, Dec. 2007, https://www.smithsonianmag.com/travel/keepers-of-the-lost-ark-179998820/ (accessed 10 Mar. 2018).

———. "Sleeping with Cannibals." *Smithsonion.com*, Sep. 2006, https://www.smithsonianmag.com/travel/sleeping-with-cannibals-128958913/ (accessed 30 Nov. 2018).

Randi, James. "Another Baba Leaves the Scene." *James Randi Educational Foundation*, 24 Apr. 2011, archive.randi.org/site/index.php/swift-blog/1290-another-baba-leaves-the-scene.html (accessed 1 Feb. 2017).

Rao, Goparaju Ramchandra. *An Atheist with Gandhi*. Mkgandhi.org, orig. pub. 1951. Available at http://www.mkgandhi.org/ebks/an_atheist.pdf (accessed 13 Feb. 2017).

Redd, Nola Taylor. "What Is the Biggest Star?" *Space.com*, 25 Jul. 2018, https://www.space.com/41290-biggest-star.html (accessed 17 Sep. 2018);

Renard, John. *The Handy Religion Answer Book*, 2nd ed. Canton, MI: Visible Ink Press, 2012.

Reps, Paul and Nyogen Senzaki, ed. and trans. *Zen Flesh, Zen Bones: A Collection of Zen and Pre-Zen Writings*.

Rutland, VT: Tuttle, 1985. Kindle.

Reston, James, Jr. "Be Christian or Die." *Christian History* 18.3, issue 63 (1999): pp. 13-17.

———. *The Last Apocalypse: Europe at the Year 1000 A.D.* New York: Anchor, 1998.

Reynolds, Philip Lyndon. *Marriage in the Western Church: The Christianization of Marriage in the Patristic and Early Medieval Periods*. Boston: Brill Academic Publishers, 2001.

Richards, John. *The Mughal Empire*. Cambridge: Cambridge Univ. Press, 1995.

Richards, P. Scott and Allen E. Bergin. *A Spiritual Strategy for Counseling and Psychotherapy*. Washington, DC: American Psychological Association, 1997.

Ridderbos, Herman. *Redemptive History and the New Testament Canon of Scripture*. Phillipsburg, NJ: Presbyterian and Reformed, 1988.

Roach, John. "How 'Jesus Lizards' Walk on Water." *National Geographic*, 16 Nov. 2004, http://news.nationalgeographic.com/news/2004/11/1116_041116_jesus_lizard.html (accessed 20 Dec. 2016).

Roebuck, Carl. *The World of Ancient Times*. New York: Charles Scribner's Sons, 1966.

Romey, Kristin. "What Made This Ancient Society Sacrifice Its Own Children?" *National Geographic*, Feb. 2019, https://www.nationalgeographic.com/magazine/2019/02/chimu-people-sacrificed-children-llamas-peru-mystery/ (accessed 7 Feb. 2019).

Rose, Jenny. *Zoroastrianism: An Introduction*. London: I.B. Tauris, 2012.

Rolston, Dean. "Memento Mori: Notes on Buddhism and AIDS." *Tricycle: The Buddhist Review* (Fall 1991), https://tricycle.org/magazine/memento-mori-notes-buddhism-and-aids/ (accessed 17 Oct. 2018).

Roth, Cecil. *The Spanish Inquisition*. New York, W.W. Norton and Co., 1964.

Roussopoulos, Demetrios, ed. *Faith in Faithlessness: An Anthology of Atheism*. Montreal: Black Rose Books, 2008.

Routledge, Clay. "Science Reveals the Benefits of Prayer." *Psychology Today*, 21 Mar. 2016, https://www.psychologytoday.com/blog/more-mortal/201603/science-reveals-the-benefits-prayer (accessed 23 Sep. 2016).

———. "5 Scientifically Supported Benefits of Prayer." *Psychology Today*, 23 Jun. 2014, https://www.psychologytoday.com/blog/more-mortal/201406/5-scientifically-supported-benefits-prayer (accessed 23 Sep. 2016).

Rubinart, Marta, Albert Fornieles, and Joan Deus. "The Psychological Impact of the Jesus Prayer among Non-Conventional Catholics." *Pastoral Psychology* 66.4 (2017): pp. 487-504.

Ruffin, C. Bernard. *Padre Pio: The True Story*. Revised and expanded ed. Huntingdon, IN: Our Sunday Visitor, 1991.

Russell, Bertrand. *Why I Am Not a Christian and Other Essays on Religion and Related Subjects*. Edited by Paul Edwards. New York: Touchstone/Simon and Schuster, 1957.

Ruthven, Malise. *Islam: A Very Short Introduction*. Oxford: Oxford Univ. Press, 1997.

Rymer, Russ. "Vanishing Voices." *National Geographic* (Jul. 2012): pp. 60, 92-3.

Safi, Omid. *Memories of Muhammad: Why the Prophet Matters*. New York: HarperOne, 2009.

Sassoni, Shomron and Osher. *The Samaritan-Israelites and Their Religion: Educational Guide*. Vol. 1. Holon, Israel: 2004. Available at http://drshirley.org/rel402/samaritan-educationalguide.pdf.

Sawant, Neena and Chetan Vispute. "Delusional Parasitosis with Folie a Deux: A Case Series." *Industrial Psychiatry Journal* 24.1 (Jan.-Jun. 2015): pp. 97-8.

Shepherd, William. *Historical Atlas*, 4th ed. New York: Henry Holt and Co., 1924.

Szabo, Attila. "The Acute Effects of Humor and Exercise on Mood and Anxiety." *Journal of Leisure Research* 35.2 (2nd Q. 2003): pp. 152-62.

The Sayings of the Desert Fathers: The Alphabetical Collection. Rev. ed. Translated by Benedicta Ward. Kalamazoo, MI: Cistercian Publications, 1984.

Schaeffer, Francis A. *Escape from Reason*. Rev. ed. Downers Grove, IL: InterVarsity Press, 2006.

Schaff, Philip. *Creeds of Christendom*. Vol. 1. Grand Rapids, MI: Christian Classics Ethereal Library, orig. pub. 1876. http://www.ccel.org/ccel/schaff/creeds1.pdf.

———. *History of the Christian Church, Nicene and Post-Nicene Christianity A.D. 311-600*, revised 5th ed. Vol. III. Grand Rapids, MI: Christian Classics Ethereal Library, n.d. http://www.ccel.org/ccel/schaff/hcc3.pdf.

Schaff, Phillip and Henry Wace, eds. *The Seven Ecumenical Councils of the Undivided Church*, in *Nicene and Post-Nicene Fathers of the Christian Church*, Series 2. Vol. 14. Translated by Henry R. Percival. Oxford: Benediction Classics, 2011. Also available at Christian Classics Ethereal Library http://www.ccel.org/ccel/schaff/npnf214.

Schleitheim Confession of Faith, 1527. University of Washington. Translated by J. C. Wenger., n.d., http://courses.washington.edu/hist112/SCHLEITHEIM%20CONFESSION%20OF%20FAITH.htm (accessed 15 Feb. 2014). Orig. from *The Mennonite Quarterly Review*, 19.4 (Oct. 1945): pp. 247-53.

Schneider, Kirk J. "Rediscovering Awe: A New Front in Humanistic Psychology, Psychotherapy, and Society." *Canadian Journal of Counselling* 42.1 (Jan. 2008): pp. 67-74.

Schnepper, Rachel. "Yuletide's Outlaws." *The New York Times*, 14 Dec. 2012, http://www.nytimes.com/2012/12/15/opinion/the-puritan-war-on-christmas.html?_r=0 (accessed 22 Jan. 2016).

Schriner, Roger Christan. *Bridging the God Gap: Finding Common Ground Among Believers, Atheists and Agnostics*, 2nd ed. Fremont, CA: Living Arts Publications, 2011.

Schultz, Colin. "You Can't Throw a Rock in the Milky Way Without Hitting an Earth-Like Planet." *Smithsonian.com*, 8 Jan. 2013, http://www.smithsonianmag.com/smart-news/you-cant-throw-a-rock-in-the-milky-way-without-hitting-an-earth-like-planet-562384/ (accessed 8 Jan. 2017).

Schulz, Kathryn. *Being Wrong: Adventures in the Margin of Error*. New York: Ecco/HarperCollins, 2011.

"Scientists and Belief." *Pew Research Center*, 5 Nov. 2009, www.pewforum/org/2009/11/05/scientists-and-belief/ (accessed 29 Mar. 2017).

Scorgie, Glen G. *A Little Guide to Christian Spirituality: Three Dimensions of Life with God*. Grand Rapids, MI: Zondervan, 2007.

Scott, Michael. *Delphi: A History of the Center of the Ancient World*. Princeton: Princeton Univ. Press, 2014. Kindle.

Scruton, Roger. *Spinoza: A Very Short Introduction*. Oxford Press, 2002.

Second Clement. In *Ante-Nicene Fathers*. Vol. 9. Edited by Allan Menzies. Translated by John Keith. Buffalo, NY: Christian Literature Publishing Co., 1896. Revised and edited for New Advent by Kevin Knight. http://www.newadvent.org/fathers/1011.htm.

The Second Helvetic Confession. Grand Rapids, MI: Christian Classics Ethereal Library, orig. pub. 1566. http://www.ccel.org/creeds/helvetic.htm.

Seiling, Jonathan R. "Solae (Quae?) Scripturae: Anabaptists and the Apocrypha." *Mennonite Quarterly Review*, 80.1 (Jan. 2006): pp. 5-34.

Seven Taoist Masters: A Folk Novel of China. Translated by Eva Wong. Boston: Shambhala, 1990.

Shah, Idries. *Tales of the Dervishes*. New York: Penguin, 1993.

Shelley, Bruce. "The Great Disappointment." *Christian History* 18.1, issue 61 (1999): pp. 31-3.

Shenouda, H.H. Pope III. *Life of Faith*. Dar El Tebaa El Kawmia Press, 1989. Available at http://tasbeha.org/content/hh_books/faith/.

Shermer, Michael. *The Moral Arc: How Science Makes Us Better People*. New York: St. Martin's Griffin, 2015.

———. *Why People Believe Weird Things: Pseudoscience, Superstition, and Other Confusions of Our Time*. Revised and expanded ed. New York: Henry Holt & Co., 2002.

Shore, John. "Taking God at His Word: The Bible and Homosexuality." *Johnshore.com* (blog), 2 Apr. 2012, http://johnshore.com/2012/04/02/the-best-case-for-the-bible-not-condemning-homosexuality/ (accessed 2 Feb. 2013).

Shrady, Nicholas. *The Last Day: Wrath, Ruin and Reason in the Great Lisbon Earthquake of 1755*. New York: Penguin, 2008.

Siegel, Ethan. "Space is Full of Planets, and Most of Them Don't Even Have Stars." *Forbes*, 13 Mar. 2018, https://www.forbes.com/sites/startswithabang/2018/03/13/space-is-full-of-planets-and-most-of-them-dont-even-have-stars/#24440a733b2a (accessed 17 Oct. 2018).

"The Sigillion of the Pan-Orthodox Council of Constantinople, 1583." *Confessor*, no. 7 (14 Sep. 2018), http://www.omologitis.org/?p=1517 (accessed 8 Nov. 2017).

Simms, Luma. "Uncovering the Head Covering Debate." *Christianity Today*, Sep. 2013, www.christianitytoday.com/women/2013/septemeber/uncovering-head-covering-debate.html (accessed 24 Feb. 2017).

Simons, Menno. *The Complete Works of Menno Simons*. Edited by John Christian Wenger. Translated by Leonard Verduin. Scottsdale, PA: Herald, 1956.

Singer, Tovia. "Outreach Judaism Responds to Jews for Jesus: Why Did Jews for Jesus Criticize Rabbi Tovia Singer's Audio Series." *Outreach Judaism*, n.d., http://outreachjudaism.org/outreach-judaism-responds-to-jews-for-jesus/ (accessed 16 Nov. 2014).

———. "The Trinity." *Let's Get Biblical*, Outreach Judaism, n.d., https://outreachjudaism.org/the-trinity-audio/ (accessed 19 Mar. 2018).

———. "Who Is God's Suffering Servant? The Rabbinic Interpretation of Isaiah 53." *Outreach Judaism*, n.d., https://outreachjudaism.org/gods-suffering-servant-isaiah-53/ (accessed 11 Jan. 2019).

Slick, Matt. "Is It OK for Christians to Dance?" *Christian Apologetics and Research Ministry*, https://carm.org/christians-dancing (accessed 26 Aug. 2018).

———. "Testimonies from ex-Roman Catholic Priests." *Christian Apologetics and Research Ministry*, https://carm.org/testimonies-ex-roman-catholic-priests (accessed 8 Nov. 2017).

Soulen, Richard N. and R. Kendall Soulen. *Handbook of Biblical Criticism*, 3rd ed. Louisville, KY: Westminster John Knox Press, 2001.

Spinoza, Benedict de. *Theological-Political Treatise*. Edited by Jonathan Israel. Translated by Michael Silverstone and Jonathan Israel. Cambridge Univ. Press, 2007.

Spong, John Shelby. *The Easter Moment*. San Francisco: Harper and Row, 1980.

Sproul, R.C. "How Do You Know the Bible Is True?" *Ligonier Ministries*, 23 Jul. 2010, www.ligonier.org/blog/how-do-you-know-bible-true/ (accessed 31 Mar. 2017).

———. *Justified by Faith Alone*. Wheaton, IL: Crossway Books, 1999.

———. "What is the Rapture?" *Ligonier Ministries*, 16 Jul. 2012, http://www.ligonier.org/blog/what-is-the-rapture/ (accessed 20 Nov. 2016)

Stackhouse, Reginald. "Columbus' Millennial Voyage." *Christian History* 18.1, issue 61 (1999): p. 19.

Stanford Encyclopedia of Philosophy. The Metaphysics Research Lab, Center for the Study of Language and Information (CSLI), Stanford University. 2016. https://plato.stanford.edu/index.html.

Staples, Tim. "Is Purgatory in the Bible?" *Catholic Answers*, 17 Jan. 2014, http://www.catholic.com/blog/tim-staples/is-purgatory-in-the-bible (accessed 24 Aug. 2018).

———. "Mortal and Venial Sin?" *Catholic Answers*, 14 Mar. 2014, https://www.catholic.com/magazine/online-edition/mortal-and-venial-sin (accessed 23 Dec. 2017).

Stark, Rodney. *For the Glory of God: How Monotheism Led to Reformations, Science, Witch-hunts, and the End of Slavery*. Princeton, NJ: Princeton Univ. Press, 2003.

"Status of Global Mission, 2017, in the Context of AD 1900–2050." *Center for the Study of Global Christianity*, Gordon-Conwell Seminary, 2017, http://www.gordonconwell.edu/ockenga/research/documents/Statusof-GlobalChristianity2017.pdf (accessed 14 Oct. 2018).

Stetka, Bret. "Where's the Proof That Mindfulness Meditation Works?," *Scientific American*, 11 Oct. 2017, https://www.scientificamerican.com/article/wheres-the-proof-that-mindfulness-meditation-works1/ (accessed 27 Apr. 2018).

Stewart, Robert B., ed. *The Resurrection of Jesus: John Dominic Crossan and N.T. Wright in Dialogue*. Minneapolis: Fortress Press, 2006.

Strobel, Lee. *The Case for Christ: A Journalist's Personal Investigation into the Evidence for Jesus*. Updated and expanded ed. Grand Rapids, MI: Zondervan, 2016.

Strong, John S., ed. *The Experience of Buddhism: Sources and Interpretations*, 2nd ed. Belmont, CA: Wadsworth, 2002.

Sullivan, Francis A. *Salvation Outside the Church?: Tracing the History of the Catholic Response*. Eugene, OR: Wipf and Stock Publishers, 2002.

Swarup, Ram. *Understanding the Hadith: The Sacred Traditions of Islam*. Amherst, NY: Prometheus Books, 2002.

Syndicus, Eduard. *Early Christian Art*. Translated by J. R. Foster. New York: Hawthorn Books, 1962.

Synan, Vinson. "The 'Second Comers.'" *Christian History* 18.1, issue 61 (1999): pp. 38-9.

Synod of Dort. Grand Rapids, MI: Christian Classics Ethereal Library, n.d. http://www.ccel.org/ccel/anonymous/canonsofdort.pdf.

"The Syriac/Aramaic/Assyrian Language." *Nestorian.org*, n.d., http://www.nestorian.org/the_syriac-aramaic-assyrian_language.html (accessed 16 Aug. 2018).

Talbert, Charles H. *What Is a Gospel? The Genre of the Canonical Gospels*. Philadelphia: Fortress Press, 1977.

Tan, Chade-Meng. *Joy on Demand: The Art of Discovering the Happiness Within*. New York: HarperCollins, 2016.

Tarico, Valerie and Marlene Winell. "The Sad, Twisted Truth about Conservative Christianity's Effect on the Mind." *Salon*, 1 Nov. 2014, https://www.salon.com/2014/11/01/the_sad_twisted_truth_about_

conservative_christianitys_effect_on_the_mind_partner/ (accessed 7 Feb. 2019).

Taylor, Daniel. *The Myth of Certainty: The Reflective Christian and the Risk of Commitment.* Waco, TX: Word, 1986.

Tertullian. *On Idolatry.* In *Ante-Nicene Fathers.* Vol. 3. Edited by Alexander Roberts et al. Translated by S. Thelwall. Buffalo, NY: Christian Literature Publishing Co., 1885. Revised and edited for New Advent by Kevin Knight. http://www.newadvent.org/fathers/0302.htm.

———. *To Scapula,* in *Ante-Nicene Fathers.* Vol. 3. Edited by Alexander Roberts et al. Translated by S. Thelwall. Buffalo, NY: Christian Literature Publishing Co., 1885. Revised and edited for New Advent by Kevin Knight. http://www.newadvent.org/fathers/0305.htm.

———. *The Shows (De Spectaculis).* In *Ante-Nicene Fathers.* Vol. 3. Edited by Alexander Roberts, et al. Translated by S. Thelwall. Buffalo, NY: Christian Literature Publishing Co., 1885. Revised and edited for New Advent by Kevin Knight. http://www.newadvent.org/fathers/0303.htm.

Thomas à Kempis. *The Imitation of Christ.* Edited by Harold C. Gardiner. New York: Image Books, 1955.

Thompson, Damian. *Waiting for Antichrist: Charisma and Apocalypse in a Pentecostal Church.* New York: Oxford Univ. Press, 2005.

Tillich, Paul. *The Courage to Be,* 2nd ed. New Haven: Yale Nota Bene, 2000.

Tindall, George B. and David E. Shi. *America: A Narrative History,* brief 2nd ed. New York: W. W. Norton and Co., 1989.

Teicher, Jordan G. "Why Is Vatican II So Important?" *NPR,* 10 Oct. 2012, https://www.npr.org/2012/10/10/162573716/why-is-vatican-ii-so-important (accessed 25 Aug. 2018).

Tolstoi, Lyof N. (Leo Tolstoy). *What Is Religion? And Other New Articles and Letters.* Translated by V. Tchertkoff and A. C. Fifield. New York: Thomas Y. Crowell and Co., 1902. Available at https://archive.org/details/whatisreligionot00tols/page/n11.

———. *My Confession and The Spirit of Christ's Teaching.* New York: Thomas Y. Crowell and Co., 1887. Available at https://archive.org/details/myconfessionands00tolsrich/page/n9.

Tolstoy, Leo. *A Confession and Other Religious Writings*. Translated by Jane Kentish. New York: Penguin, 1987.

Torrance, Thomas F. *The Doctrine of Grace in the Apostolic Fathers*. Grand Rapids, MI: Wm. B. Eerdmans, 1959.

Torrey, Norman L., ed. *Les Philosophes: The Philosophers of the Enlightenment and Modern Democracy*. New York: Capricorn Books, 1960.

Tov, Emmanuel. *Textual Criticism of the Bible*, 3rd ed. Minneapolis: Fortress Press, 2012.

Townshend, George, ed. *The Glad Tidings of Bahá'u'lláh: Being Extracts from the Sacred Writings of the Bahá'ís*. Rev. ed. Oxford: George Ronald, 1975.

"Translation of the Mahayana Buddhist Canon: The BDK English Tripiṭaka Project." *BDK America*, 2018, http://www.bdkamerica.org/translation-mahayana-buddhist-canon (accessed 20 Jan 2018).

Tree, Isabella. "Living Goddesses of Nepal." *National Geographic* (Jun. 2015): pp. 86-8.

Troyat, Henri. *Ivan the Terrible*. Translated by Joan Pinkham. New York: Dorset Press, 1987.

Tryphon, Abbot. "The Heresy of Penal Substitution." *Ancient Faith Ministries (blog)*, 6 Jul. 2016, https://blogs.ancientfaith.com/morningoffering/2016/07/heresy-penal-substitution/ (accessed 22 Sep. 2018).

Turner, Alice K. *The History of Hell*. Orlando, FL: Harcourt, 1993.

Turner, Shannon M. "Conciliar Creeds of the Fourth Century." *Fourth Century Christianity*, Wisconsin Lutheran College, 17 Apr. 2011, http://www.fourthcentury.com/conciliar-creeds-of-the-fourth-century/ (accessed 2 Oct. 2018).

Twain, Mark. *Letters from the Earth*. Edited by Bernard DeVoto. New York: Harper and Row, 1974.

———. *The Wit and Wisdom of Mark Twain: A Book of Quotations*. Mineola, NY: Dover Publications, 1999.

"The Twelve Steps of Alcoholics Anonymous." *A. A. World Services*, 9 May 2002, http://www.aa.org/en_pdfs/smf-121_en.pdf (accessed 29 Oct. 2012).

Tyson, Neil DeGrasse. *Astrophysics for People in a Hurry*. New York: W. W. Norton & Co., 2017.

Ultimate Weird but True. Washington, DC: National Geographic, 2011.

Underwood, Grant. "'Saved or Damned': Tracing a Persistent Protestantism in Early Mormon Thought." *Brigham Young University Studies*, 25:3 (Summer 1985): pp. 85-103. Available at https://byustudies.byu.edu/PDFLibrary/25.3UnderwoodSaved-861c2b45-a4e1-4d0d-81af-e7d-7c15f9d8b.pdf (accessed 1 Nov. 2013).

The Upanishads. Translated by Juan Mascaró. New York: Penguin, 1965.

Van Braught, Thieleman J. *Martyrs Mirror*, 1660 ed. Translated by Joseph F. Sohm. Grand Rapids, MI: Christian Classics Ethereal Library, n.d. www.ccel.org/ccel/vanbraght/mirror.pdf.

Van Cappellen, Patty, Maria Toth-gauthier, Vassilis Saroglou, and Barbara L. Fredrickson. "Religion and Well-Being: The Mediating Role of Positive Emotions." *Journal of Happiness Studies* 17.2 (Apr. 2016): pp. 485-505.

Van Over, Raymond, ed. *Taoist Tales*. New York: Meridian, 1984.

Van Voorst, Robert E. *Anthology of World Scriptures*, 6th ed. Belmont, CA: Wadsworth Cengage Learning, 2008.

Vance, Erik. "Mind Over Matter." *National Geographic* (Dec. 2016): pp. 30-55.

Vidler, Alec R. *The Church in an Age of Revolution: 1789 to the Present Day*. New York: Penguin, 1990.

Viereck, George Sylvester. *Glimpses of the Great*. New York: The Macauley Co., 1930.

Vincent of Lerins. *The Comminitory*. In *Nicene and Post-Nicene Fathers, Second Series*. Vol. 11. Edited by Philip Schaff and Henry Wace. Translated by C. A. Heurtley. Buffalo, NY: Christian Literature Publishing Co., 1894. Revised and edited for New Advent by Kevin Knight. http://www.newadvent.org/fathers/3506.htm.

Voltaire. *Voltaire in His Letters: Being a Selection from His Correspondence*. Edited and translated by S.G. Tallentyre. New York: G.P. Putnam's Sons, 1919. Available online at https://archive.org/stream/cu31924026378335#page/n9/mode/2up (accessed 20 Jan 2018).

Vonnegut, Kurt. *Slaughterhouse-Five*. New York: RosettaBooks, 2010. Kindle.

Waddell, Helen, ed. and trans. *The Desert Fathers*. Ann Arbor, MI: Univ. of Michigan Press, 1957.

Wade, Nicholas. *Before the Dawn: Recovering the Lost History of Our Ancestors*. New York: Penguin, 2007.
Walsh, Michael, ed. *Butler's Lives of the Saints*. Concise and rev. ed. New York: HarperSanFrancisco, 1991.
Ware, Timothy. *The Orthodox Church*, new ed. New York: Pelican, 1997.
Warfield, B. B. *Calvin and Augustine*. Edited by Samuel Craig. Philadelphia: The Presbyterian and Reformed Publishing Co., 1956.
Warraq, Ibn. *Why I Am Not a Muslim*. Amherst, NY: Prometheus Books, 2003.
Washoltz, Amy B. and Kenneth I. Pargament. "Is Spirituality a Critical Ingredient of Meditation? Comparing the Effects of Spiritual Meditation, Secular Meditation, and Relaxation of Spiritual, Psychological, Cardiac, and Pain Outcomes." *Journal of Behavioral Medicine* 28.4 (Aug. 2005): pp. 369-84.
Watts, Alan W. *The Wisdom of Insecurity: A Message for an Age of Anxiety*. New York: Vintage Books, 2011.
The Way of a Pilgrim and The Pilgrim Continues His Way. Translated by Helev Bacovcin. New York: Image/Doubleday, 1978.
Weir, Kristen. "The Exercise Effect." *American Psychological Association*, 42.1 (Dec. 2011): p. 48. Available at https://www.apa.org/monitor/2011//12/exercise.aspx (accessed 28 Oct. 2018).
Wesley, John. "Thoughts Upon Slavery." *Global Ministries: The United Methodist Church*, n.d., http://www.umcmission.org/Find-Resources/John-Wesley-Sermons/The-Wesleys-and-Their-Times/Thoughts-Upon-Slavery (accessed 3 Jul. 2013).
Westminster Confession of Faith, 1646 ed. *Center for Reformed Theology and Apologetics*, https://reformed.org/documents/wcf_with_proofs/index.html (accessed 21 Dec. 2018).
"What Do Jehovah's Witnesses Believe?" *JW.org*, n.d., https://www.jw.org/en/jehovahs-witnesses/faq/jehovah-witness-beliefs/ (accessed 9 Oct. 2017).
"What Is Hell? Is It a Place of Eternal Torment?" *JW.org*, n.d., https://www.jw.org/en/bible-teachings/questions/what-is-hell/ (accessed 9 Oct. 2017).
White, Carolinne, ed. and trans. *Early Christian Lives*. London: Penguin Classics, 1998.

Whittenberger, Gary J. "On Visions and Resurrections." *eSkeptic*, 1 Feb. 2012, https://www.skeptic.com/eskeptic/12-02-01/ (accessed 14 Jan. 2019).

Wilkinson, Bruce and Kenneth Boa. *Talk Thru the Bible*. Nashville: Thomas Nelson, 1980.

Winch, Guy. "Study Shows Prayer Reduces Anger and Aggression: Benevolent Prayer as an Effective Form of Emotional Regulation." *Psychology Today*, 20 May 2013, https://www.psychologytoday.com/us/blog/the-squeaky-wheel/201305/study-shows-prayer-reduces-anger-and-aggression (accessed 28 Oct. 2018).

Winters, Michael Sean. "Save Us from Gloomy Saints." *National Catholic Reporter*, 16 Oct. 2013, https://www.ncronline.org/blogs/distinctly-catholic/save-us-gloomy-saints (accessed 30 Nov. 2018).

"Why the King James Version Bible is the Only Word of God." *Use KJV Only Ministries*, 2008, http://www.usekjvonly.com/tracts/Tracts-Web/kjvtractmain.html (accessed 13 Sep. 2013).

Wilken, Robert Louis. *The Christians As the Romans Saw Them*, 2nd ed. New Haven, CT: Yale Univ. Press, 2003.

Williams, Rowan. *Arius: Heresy and Tradition*. Rev. ed. Grand Rapids, MI: Wm. B. Eerdmans, 2001.

Winell, Marlene. *Leaving the Fold: A Guide for Former Fundamentalists and Others Leaving Their Religion*. Oakland, CA: New Harbinger Publications, 1993.

Wise, Robert L. "Munster's Monster." *Christian History* 18.1, issue 61 (1999): pp. 23-5.

Wolf, David B. and Neil Abell. "Examining the Effects of Meditation Techniques on Psychosocial Functioning." *Research on Social Work Practice* 13.1 (Jan. 2003): pp. 27-42.

Wood, Douglas C. *The Evangelical Doctor: John Wycliffe and the Lollards*. Welwyn, England: Evangelical Press, 1984.

Wood, Paul. "The Unbroken Chain: Tolstoy's Legacy of Nonviolence Influenced Many Great Leaders." *LAS News Magazine*, Spring 2009, www.las.illinois.edu/alumni/magazine/articles/2009/tolstoy/ (accessed 27 Oct. 2017).

Woods, Thomas E. *How the Catholic Church Built Western Civilization*. Washington, DC: Regnery Publishing, 2005.

Wolfe, Nathan. "Small, Small World." *National Geographic* (Jan. 2013): pp. 138, 145.

Wong, Eva. *Tales of the Taoist Immortals*. Boston: Shambhala Publications, 2001.

Wulff, David. *Psychology of Religion: Classic and Contemporary*. Hoboken, NJ: John Wiley and Sons, Inc., 1997.

Yao, Richard. *Fundamentalists Anonymous: There Is a Way Out*. 3rd ed. New York: Luce Publications, 1985.

Younan, Paul D. "History of the Peshitta." *Peshitta.org*, 1 Jun. 2000, http://www.peshitta.org/initial/peshitta.html (accessed 12 Aug. 2018).

Zerwick, Max and Mary Grosvenor. *A Grammatical Analysis of the Greek New Testament*, 5th ed. Rome: Editrice Pontificio Istituto Biblico, 1996.

Zielinski, Sarah. "Hypatia, Ancient Alexandria's Great Female Scholar." *Smithsonian.com*, 14 Mar. 2010, https://www.smithsonianmag.com/history/hypatia-ancient-alexandrias-great-female-scholar-10942888/ (accessed 5 Dec. 2018).

Zimmer, Carl. "Meet Nature's Mindsuckers." *National Geographic* (Nov. 2014): pp. 36-55.

Zuckerman, Catherine. "Living It Up." *National Geographic* (Jun. 2011): p. 33.

Printed in Great Britain
by Amazon

41538006R00324